HUMAN RIGHTS: AN AGENDA FOR THE 21st CENTURY

Cavendish
Publishing
Limited

London • Sydney

A HUMAN RIGHTS:
AN AGENDA FOR THE
21st CENTURY

Edited by

Angela Hegarty, LLB, LLM, Solicitor
University of Ulster

and

Siobhan Leonard, LLB, LLM, Solicitor
Manchester Metropolitan University

Cavendish
Publishing
Limited

London • Sydney

First published in 1999 by Cavendish Publishing Limited, The Glass House, Wharton Street, London, WC1X 9PX, United Kingdom
Telephone: +44 (0) 20 7278 8000   Facsimile: +44 (0) 20 7278 8080
E-mail: info@cavendishpublishing.com
Visit our Home Page on http://www.cavendishpublishing.com

Hegarty, Angela
Human rights: an agenda for the 21st century
1. Human rights
I. Title II. Leonard, Siobhan
341.4'81

ISBN 1 85941 393 5

Printed and bound in Great Britain

For my parents, Maurice and Etta
Angela Hegarty

For my parents, Pauline and Kevin
Siobhan Leonard

FOREWORD

Over 50 years ago, in 1948, the world community took a bold step with the proclamation of the Universal Declaration of Human Rights. Two years later, the Member States of the Council of Europe took a step unprecedented in international law. Henceforth, human rights could not be regarded as just a matter for one government to invoke against another, at the former's discretion, in its role of providing consular protection to its own nationals. Individuals would not be mere pawns in inter-State negotiations. They would be actors in their own right on the international stage, entitled, as victims, to bring their own and other governments before an international adjudicatory body. Initially, this right depended on governments' acceptance of certain optional clauses of the European Convention on Human Rights but, today, submission to jurisdiction is compulsory for States party to the Convention.

While the status of the individual in Europe has been enhanced considerably over the past 50 years, work has continued both within Europe and in the wider international community to supplement the core guarantees – such as the right to life, freedom from torture, freedom of expression, and the rights to liberty and a fair trial – with additional protections more finely tuned to the circumstances of, for example, women or children or detainees who might be at risk of ill treatment. Much has been accomplished and much remains to be accomplished.

From this perspective, a major appeal of this book is the extent to which it affirms that old values will hold good for new times. On one level, the studies are firmly rooted in the existing achievements of what one of the many distinguished contributors calls this 'buccaneering age of rights'. The texts give an impressive overview of the work of regional and international bodies to ensure that there be a measure of protection – primarily at national level but, if necessary, elsewhere – against attacks on the humanity and integrity of individuals. This presentation of the status quo is probing and not uncritical. Reflections range from – on the one hand – gloomy forebodings about the ability of the reporting mechanisms of the United Nations or the capacity of the new European Court of Human Rights to cope with logistical, political or unusually sensitive problems that may be anticipated in certain fields, to – on the other hand – celebrations of the continuing power of often tiny non-governmental organisations to bring about change and the sharing of practical information about how they do so.

On another level, the reader is presented with a remarkably even selection of pressing challenges for the future development of rights and associated jurisprudence. How meaningful are international agreements on economic, social and cultural rights when there are still 1.2 billion people without access to clean water? Is the proud record of the European Union concerning gender equality in welfare and labour matters in 'judicial retreat'? How effective will the existing fora and the new international criminal court be when faced with continuing incidents of torture and disappearances? How will fragile court systems in new democracies cope with competing power interests when it is known that the exercise of power in older democracies is not invariably transparent? Where do minorities' and indigenous peoples' claims fit into the overall scheme of public international law and how do the two concepts differ? At a time when the Council of Europe Member States have found it necessary to agree a new Protocol in response to the cloning of an animal, the issues of abortion, fertility treatment and euthanasia come to mind: what will be the spillover effects in all such fields of the freedom to engage in what one writer graphically labels 'bioethical tourism'? How can children be protected against risks of genetic experimentation at embryo stage or commercial exploitation on the internet?

These are some of the varied questions prompted, if not always deliberately raised, by the material in this book. Underlying all of the themes is a deep commitment towards people whose circumstances render them vulnerable to violence, inequalities and arbitrary exercise of power. The thread of the universality of human rights, as distinct from cultural relativism, is to be discerned frequently. Given that the search for balance is inherent in the protection of human rights, it is fitting that some are willing to confront, whether hesitantly or robustly, the concept of duties and responsibilties corresponding to or coexisting with the rights of an individual who interacts with others on however modest a scale. Also raised is the stimulating concept of allying human rights responsibilities to the weighty powers of multinational corporations. It may not be entirely out of place to recall the words of Aleksandr Solzhenitsyn, in his essay 'Reflections on the eve of the twenty-first century':

> Today, self-limitation appears to us as something wholly unacceptable, constraining, even repulsive, because we have over the centuries grown accustomed to what for our ancestors had been a habit born of necessity. They lived with far greater constraints, and had far fewer opportunities. The paramount importance of self-restraint has only in this century arisen in its pressing entirety before mankind. Yet taking into account even the various mutual links running through contemporary life, it is nonetheless only through self-restraint that we can, albeit with much difficulty, gradually cure both our economic and political life ... [Gardels, NP (ed), *At Century's End*, 1995, San Diego: ALTI; 1997, Dublin: Wolfhound.]

If somewhat similar considerations could prompt concern over a possible need in the future for what one contributor terms 'quality control' to protect the label of internationally protected human rights, who would doubt the continuing pressing need to protect the core meaning values that were recognised in the light of the Holocaust more than 50 years ago? At a time of tragic events in Kosovo and elsewhere, it is salutary to read that in 1993 it was forecast that the last decade of this century and the first decade of the next century would be '*the* age of migration' and to learn of the relatively welcoming attitude of developing countries towards displaced people and refugees.

Events in various parts of the world still underline how true to the core values of the United Nations and the Council of Europe are practical and legal measures to address the phenomenon of violence against women; to protect human rights activists, lawyers and medical practitioners against intimidations or worse; to help establish, even in states of emergency, effective and impartial investigations at domestic level, with proper forensic evidence gathering techniques, whenever there is an allegation of death, disappearance, ill treatment or racial/ethnic harassment; and to pursue vigorously, at international level, acts of genocide. Experience in the European Commission of Human Rights has impressed upon me the difficulties that may be encountered by an international fact finding body when assessing evidence – perhaps through interpreters and without familiarity of the local conditions, perhaps without power to compel a witness to attend, perhaps without any contemporaneous eye witness statements about an incident, perhaps without detention records or scene of crime reports or autopsy examinations. It may be that one of the major challenges of the coming years will be the establishment of high quality investigation standards even in relatively poor countries so that rulings of law, whether at domestic or international level, can be based on reliable findings of fact supported by evidence that has been gathered, insofar as possible, while still fresh. Laws written on paper can be of questionable value in the absence of effective official investigations. Given the importance of the work of non-governmental organisations in this connection, their insights into such matters are particularly timely.

In these days when so many are in need of constructive words and actions in the cause of their human rights, the reader of the pages that follow will be heartened and encouraged by this forceful gathering of – to use Emerson's words – 'voices in the land, speaking for thoughts and principles not marketable or perishable'.

Jane Liddy
Formerly President of the First Chamber
of the European Commission of Human Rights
May 1999

PREFACE

This book seeks to highlight some of the key issues in the sphere of international human rights at the beginning of a new century and a new millennium. Millennial concerns apart, we have focused upon those areas within which human rights advances are presently occurring, and are therefore theoretically achievable within the next few years.

We are conscious of the fact that it is only during the past 50 years that real advances have been made in entrenching human rights protection on the international stage. This is largely due to this particular nettle having at last been grasped on a global scale by the United Nations and, regionally, in exemplary fashion, by the Council of Europe. Further entrenchment at national level will also be effected in the UK by the Human Rights Act 1998 which will come into effect in the next few years.

However, we must not lose sight of the way in which this 'rights revolution' has come about.

The mass violations of fundamental human rights occasioned by the Second World War precipitated the development of our existing canon of protective human rights instruments, such as the Universal Declaration of Human Rights and the European Convention for the Protection of Human Rights and Fundamental Freedoms. Although they were developed in response to very particular humanitarian crises, these have worked well in building a foundation for basic civil, political and, later, social, cultural and other rights.

As is roundly evidenced by recent crises as in Kosovo and Rwanda, it is sometimes difficult to protect even the most fundamental of human rights. Nonetheless, the human rights chart has changed as perceptibly as national borders since 1945. The number of individuals receiving basic protection has increased with record numbers of ratifications of instruments, such as the European Convention. The scope of the rights protected has increased, as is shown by the chapters found here on transgender, minority and reproductive issues, for example, and the power and zeal of non-governmental bodies in continually lobbying for improved human rights protection cannot be over-emphasised. The enforcement of rights has also been upgraded through institutional reforms, such as the new court structure brought about by Protocol 11 of the European Convention. Human rights concerns are becoming more refined and we are now not just examining the scope of rights protected, but also the nature and suitability of the protection offered. As this book makes clear, the real challenge facing us in the coming years is to realise, in fact, these rights which are now part of international law.

In compiling this book, we have endeavoured to raise awareness of these and other issues which demand resolution within a manageable time frame. To that end, we have compiled:

... contributions from leading and emergent human rights scholars, practitioners and activists,

to produce a text which, we hope, will be of use or interest to anyone teaching human rights, or working in areas where such issues are raised, whether in the academic, voluntary or public sectors.

We would especially like to thank Jane Liddy, formerly President of the First Chamber of the European Commission of Human Rights, for her invaluable help and advice in putting this book together, and Cara Annett, of Cavendish Publishing, who has been a mine of practical information and moral support.

Angela Hegarty and Siobhan Leonard

June 1999

CONTRIBUTORS

Christine Bell is a lecturer in law and Director of the Centre for International and Comparative Human Rights Law, School of Law, Queen's University, Belfast.

Bill Bowring teaches human rights law in Russia and Eastern Europe at the University of Essex, where he is also Director of the Pan-European Institute. As Legal and Human Rights Adviser for Russia to the UK Department for International Development's Know How Fund, and adviser to the EU, UN and other international organisations, he frequently visits Eastern Europe, Russia and Central Asia, where he also conducts human rights training for law lecturers and NGO activists. His research interests include issues of the theory and practice of judicial reform, and the protection of human rights including minority and group rights, and he has published edited collections and many book chapters and articles on questions of human rights and law reform in Russia and Eastern Europe.

Peter Cumper is a lecturer in law at the University of Leicester. He previously taught at the University of Hull and at Nottingham Trent University and, in the past, was a Visiting Professor at both William Mitchell College of Law, Minnesota, and at Loyola University, Chicago. He is particularly interested in the areas of constitutional law and civil liberties, and is the joint editor of *Minority Rights in the 'New' Europe* (1999).

Brice Dickson is Professor at the University of Ulster, and, from 1999 onwards, is Chief Commissioner of the Northern Ireland Human Rights Commission. He formerly lectured at Queen's University, Belfast, and at the University of Leicester. He has written books on French law and on Northern Ireland's legal system, and has edited books on civil liberties in Northern Ireland, the European Convention on Human Rights and the House of Lords.

Barry Fitzpatrick is Jean Monnet Professor of European Law at the University of Ulster at Jordanstown, having previously been taught at the University of Newcastle-upon-Tyne, Leicester Polytechnic and Lancashire Polytechnic. He is European Editor of the Industrial Law Journal and European Editor of the Web Journal of Current Legal Issues. He is also part time Chairman of Industrial Tribunals and a member of the Fair Employment sub-group of the Committee on the Administration of Justice. His major areas of interest include European social law and comparative and British labour law. He has published in numerous journals including the Modern Law Review, Oxford Journal of Legal Studies, Industrial Law Journal and International Journal of Comparative Labour Law and Industrial Relations.

Deirdre Fottrell is a lecturer in international law and human rights and Programme Director at the Institute of Commonwealth Studies, University of London. A graduate of University College Galway and the London School of Economics, her recent publications include 'The potential of international law to combat discrimination against girls' (with Geraldine Van Bueren) in Howland (ed), *Women's Human Rights and Religious Fundamentalism* (1999), and *Minority and Group Rights in the New Millennium* (with Bill Bowring) (1999).

Oren Gross is a lecturer in law at Tel-Aviv University Faculty of Law, Tel-Aviv, Israel. He teaches in the fields of international law and international trade law. He previously taught at Brandeis University as a Guberman Fellow in 1993. Between 1986 and 1991, Dr Gross was Senior Legal Advisor in the Judge Advocate General's Corps of the Israeli Defence Forces. He received his LLM while a Fulbright Scholar at Harvard Law School (1992), and subsequently completed his PhD in 1997 at Harvard Law School. Dr Gross was an Associate at Sullivan and Cromwell, New York between 1995 and 1996. He has published with the Michigan Journal of International Law and the Yale Journal of International Law.

Angela Hegarty is a lecturer in law in the School of Public Policy, Economics and Law at the University of Ulster. Her research interests and publications range from equality law to policing and human rights in Northern Ireland. She is a member of the Editorial Board of the International Journal of Discrimination and the Law. She is a former Commissioner with the Equal Opportunities Commission for Northern Ireland, the Standing Advisory Committee on Human Rights and is active in a number of human rights NGOs. In March 1999, she was appointed by the Secretary of State for Northern Ireland to the Northern Ireland Human Rights Commission.

Siobhan Leonard is a lecturer at Manchester Metropolitan University. She teaches European Community and human rights law. She received her LLM in European law from University College Dublin and is currently writing on the Bioethics Convention. She is Course Director of the MA Programme in law at Manchester Metropolitan University.

Stephen Livingstone is Professor of Human Rights Law at Queen's University, Belfast. He has previously taught at Nottingham University and the University of Detroit School of Law. Among his publications are *Prison Law* (with Tim Owen, 1999), *Reshaping Public Power: Northern Ireland and the*

British Constitutional Crisis (with John Morison, 1995) and *Civil Liberties Law* (with Thérèse Murphy and Noel Whitty, 1999). He is a former Chairperson of the Committee on the Administration of Justice in Northern Ireland and has acted as a consultant on human rights issues for the British Council and European Union in a number of African countries.

Margaret Logue has over 20 years' experience working in a finance environment, community and economic initiatives and credit unions. She is presently employed at the Women's Centre, Derry, as Project and Finance Co-ordinator. This work also involves networking and representing the centre on various bodies and initiatives. Through these contacts, she has been able to take gender equality and equal representation issues to the wider community. Since December 1998, she has served as a Commissioner on the Equal Opportunities Commission (Northern Ireland) and is Chairperson of the Northern Ireland Women's European Platform. She has over 15 years' involvement in management and development of women's centres locally and works on equality issues locally, nationally and internationally. In 1995, she attended the United Nations Fourth World Conference of Women in Beijing.

Deirdre Madden is a lecturer in law at University College, Cork. Her research and publication interests are in the area of medical law with particular emphasis on assisted conception and related issues. She has written on topics such as *in vitro* fertilisation, artificial insemination, the status of embryos, surrogate motherhood and the legal and ethical difficulties pertaining to such medical treatments.

Fionnuala Ní Aoláin is a lecturer in law at the Hebrew University Law Faculty, Jerusalem, Israel and a Visiting Professor at the School of International and Public Affairs, Columbia University, New York. She teaches in the field of international law and international human rights law. Previously, she was an Associate-in-Law at Columbia Law School from 1994 to 1996. She received her LLB from the Queen's University, Belfast, her LLM from Columbia Law School, New York. She held the Civil Liberties Trust Studentship while completing her PhD at the Queen's University, Belfast (1997). She has been a Fulbright Scholar and a Visiting Fellow at Harvard Law School (1993–94). She is also a current recipient of the Alon Prize in Israel. She has published with the Columbia Human Rights Law Review, the Michigan Journal of International Law, the Albany Law Review and the Harvard Human Rights Journal.

Martin O'Brien is Director of the Belfast based Committee on the Administration of Justice. The Committee, which is a cross Community human rights group, recently won the prestigious Council of Europe Human Rights Prize for its work in Northern Ireland. Mr O'Brien himself received the Reebok Human Rights Award in 1992. He has publicly campaigned on a wide range of civil liberties issues and was particularly active in working to secure strong human rights commitments in the Good Friday Agreement. He has written and spoken widely on civil liberties issues and has brought concerns about the abuse of human rights in Northern Ireland to an international audience particularly at the United Nations.

Paul Okojie is Senior Lecturer in Law at the School of Law, Manchester Metropolitan University. He is Reviews Editor of the International Journal of Higher Education, Chair of the Iqbal Ulla Race Relations Archives and Chair of Liberty (NCCL) (Manchester group). His main research interests lie in the fields of police, immigration and social policy.

Mary O'Rawe is a barrister, mother of two and lecturer in law at the University of Ulster. Her main research interests are: human rights; policing and criminal justice. Her publications include *Human Rights on Duty: Principles for Better Policing – International Lessons for Northern Ireland* (with Linda Moore, 1997); and 'International lessons for the transformation of policing in Northern Ireland' (1998).

Peter Pack has been a member of Amnesty International UK for 20 years. He has held a variety of posts within the organisation, and has a particular interest in encouraging membership involvement in policy debates.

Liz Parratt is Campaigns Manager at Liberty. She has written on racial discrimination and criminal law, including 'The UK Government's 13th Periodic Report to the UN Committee for the Elimination of Racial Discrimination' (1996); and *Criminalising Diversity, Criminalising Dissent* (1994) (both with C Foley).

Andrew Puddephat attended Sidney Sussex College, Cambridge, from 1968 to 1971. He has worked as a researcher, teacher and computer programmer. In 1982, he was elected to the London Borough of Hackney and served as Deputy Leader from 1984 to 1985 before becoming Leader of the Council in 1986. He held this post until 1989, when he resigned in order to become General Secretary of Liberty, a post he held until September 1995. In

September 1995, he joined Charter 88 as its Director. Charter 88 exists to promote democratic change, specifically campaigning for a written constitution and a Bill of Rights. In January 1999, he was appointed the Executive Director of Article 19, which exists to promote freedom of expression worldwide. In December 1998, he was appointed to the Government's Task Force on implementing the Human Rights Act.

Patrick Thornberry is Professor at Keele University and a leading authority on international relations. An expert in the area of minority rights, his publications include *International Law and the Rights of Minorities* (1992). He has written extensively on human and minority rights, especially in the area of international law, for example: 'Images of autonomy and individual and collective rights in international instruments on the rights of minorities' (1998); and 'Self-determination, minorities, human rights: a review of international instruments' (1989).

Stephen Whittle is Senior Lecturer in Law at Manchester Metropolitan University. He has written extensively in the area of sexuality and law, in particular on 'trans' issues, and he is the author (with M McMullen) of 'Transvestites, Transsexuals and the Law', and he has recently edited (with Kate More) *Reclaiming Genders, Transsexual Grammars at the Fin de Siècle* (1999). He took his own claim to be recognised as the father of his partner's children to the European Courts (*X, Y and Z v UK Government* [1997] Reports 1997-11, Appl 21830/93, 22/04/97 ECHR) and continues to campaign for civil status recognition of the trans community in the UK; as such he is a member of the Parliamentary Forum on Transsexual Issues.

Jane Winter is the Director of British Irish Rights Watch, an NGO that monitors the human rights dimension of the conflict and peace process in Northern Ireland. After taking her degree in social anthropology, she worked for two London Social Services Departments, researching the needs of children, the mentally handicapped and the elderly. She then moved to Battersea Law Centre where she did welfare rights, employment and immigration casework. After that she ran Wandsworth Citizens Advice Bureau for five years, then became a welfare rights consultant for the CAB service in London. From 1990 until 1994, she was the Project Co-ordinator for the Public Law Project. Throughout her working life, she has taught and published practical guides on issues such as fuel rights, community care and human rights.

CONTENTS

THEME TWO
NEW DILEMMAS

Contents

THEME THREE
EMERGING TRENDS

THEME FOUR
NGOS: AN EVOLVING ROLE

Contents

TABLE OF CASES

TABLE OF STATUTES

TABLE OF INTERNATIONAL INSTRUMENTS

TABLE OF ABBREVIATIONS

Journals

AIUK	Amnesty International United Kingdom
AJCL	American Journal of Comparative Law
AJIL	American Journal of International Law
Am Rev Can Stud	American Review Canadian Studies
Am Soc Rev	American Sociological Review
Anglo-Am L Rev	Anglo-American Law Review
California Western ILJ	California Western International Law Journal
Canadian J Law Soc	Canadian Journal of Law and Society
Canadian J Pol Sci	Canadian Journal of Political Science
CLJ	Cambridge Law Journal
CML Rev	Commonwealth Market Law Review
CMLR	Commonwealth Market Law Reports
Colum HR L Rev	Columbian Human Rights Law Review
D & R	Decisions and Reports
EHRLR	European Human Rights Law Review
EJIL	European Journal of International Law
EL Rev	European Law Review
EPL	European Public Law
Fordham ILJ	Fordham International Law Journal
Fordham L Rev	Fordham Law Review
Harv HRJ	Harvard Human Rights Journal
Harv ILJ	Harvard International Law Journal
Harv L Rev	Harvard Law Review
Harv WLJ	Harvard Weekly Law Journal
HR	Human Rights
HRLJ	Human Rights Law Journal
HRQ	Human Rights Quarterly
ICJ Rev	International Court of Justice Review
ICLQ	International and Comparative Law Quarterly
ICTLEP	International Conference on Transgender Law and Employment Policy
IJDL	International Journal of Discrimination and the Law
ILJ	Industrial Law Journal
Int J Children's Rights	International Journal of Children's Rights
Int J Soc L	International Journal of Society and the Law
Iowa L Rev	Iowa Law Review
Isr L Rev	Israel Law Review

J Int Aff	Journal of International Affairs
Leiden JIL	Leiden Journal of International Law
Melb UL Rev	Melbourne University Law Review
Mich J Int L	Michigan Journal International Law
Minn J Global Trade	Minnesota Journal of Global Trade
Minn L Rev	Minnesota Law Review
MLR	Modern Law Review
Neth HRQ	Netherlands Human Rights Quarterly
Neth QHR	Netherlands Quarterly on Human Rights
NLJ	New Law Journal
OJLS	Oxford Journal of Legal Studies
PL	Public Law
Virginia JIL	Virginia Journal of International Law
Web JCLI	Web Journal of Current Legal Issues
Yale J Int L	Yale Journal of International Law
Yale LJ	Yale Law Journal

Other

ACLU	American Civil Liberties Union
ACP	Africa, Caribbean and Pacific
BIRW	British-Irish Rights Watch
CAJ	Committee on the Administration of Justice
CAT	Committee against Torture
CELSCU	Centre for European Legal Studies, Cambridge University
CERD	Committee on the Elimination of Racial Discrimination
CPT	European Committee for the Prevention of Torture and Inhuman or Degrading Treatment or Punishment
CRC	Convention on the Rights of the Child
CRE	Commission for Racial Equality
CSW	Commission on the Status of Women

Table of Abbreviations

ECOSOC	Economic and Social Council
ECPT	European Convention for the Prevention of Torture and Inhuman or Degrading Treatment or Punishment
EOCNI	Equal Opportunities Commission Northern Ireland
ESC	European Social Charter
FDI	Foreign Direct Investment
FIDH	International Federation for Human Rights
GATT	General Agreement on Tariffs and Trade
HRC	Human Rights Committee
ICCPR	International Covenant on Civil and Political Rights
ICEARD	International Convention on the Elimination of All Forms of Racial Discrimination
ICESCR	International Covenant on Economic, Social and Cultural Rights
ICJ	International Commission of Jurists
ICM	International Council Meeting
IFHR	International Federation for Human Rights
IGC	Intergovernmental Consultations on Asylum, Refugee and Migration Policies in Europe, North America and Australia
IGO	international governmental organisation
ILA	International Law Association
ILO	International Labour Organisation
IMF	International Monetary Fund
INGO	international non-governmental organisation
IPPR	Institute for Public Policy Research
IRO	International Refugee Organisation
MFN	most favoured nation
MNC	multinational corporation
NCCL	National Council for Civil Liberties (Liberty)
NGO	non-governmental organisation
OCHA	(United Nations) Office for the Co-ordination of Humanitarian Affairs
OECD	Organisation for Economic and Cultural Development
OSCE	Organisation for Security and Co-operation in Europe
RUC	Royal Ulster Constabulary
SCM	Standard Committee on the Mandate

UNCHR	United Nations Commission on Human Rights
UNHCR	United Nations High Commissioner for Refugees
WTO	World Trade Organisation

CHAPTER 1

HUMAN RIGHTS: HISTORY, DEVELOPMENT AND CLASSIFICATION

Peter Cumper

INTRODUCTION

If there is one thing on which world leaders are agreed it is that, in principle, human rights should be respected. Of course, in practice, many governments pay no more than mere lip service to their human rights obligations, but it is significant that even those regimes which are often accused of being harsh, oppressive and authoritarian, routinely claim to respect the rights of their citizens.

Regrettably, however, the unanimity between States in the area of human rights clearly ends when one seeks to define, clarify and prioritise *specific* human rights. There is even little agreement over the scope of what constitutes perhaps the most basic of all rights, the right to life. This right is guaranteed in a variety of universal and regional human rights documents,[1] but the international community is split over when life begins (for example, the debate about abortion), when it ends (for example, the debate about euthanasia), whether it can ever be taken lawfully (for example, by capital punishment) and whether the State is under a 'positive' duty to prolong life (for example, by providing health care for the sick) or merely under a 'negative' duty not to take life (for example, not to kill its citizens). Civilisation may have progressed by way of rapid scientific, technical and medical advances, but mankind continues to struggle to agree upon ways of controlling even the most primitive and destructive of its members' urges.

As the next millennium draws closer, it is easy to be downcast about this paradox that *homo sapiens* has, on the one hand, the expertise to send men into space yet, on the other, seems incapable of protecting even the most basic rights of all other members of the species. Whilst such pessimism is understandable, particularly when one studies the often gruesome reports of various non-governmental organisations in this area,[2] it must be balanced by

---

1   The right to life is guaranteed by: Universal Declaration of Human Rights 1948, Art 3; International Covenant on Civil and Political Rights (ICCPR) 1966, Art 6; European Convention on Human Rights 1950, Art 2; American Convention on Human Rights 1969, Art 4; and African Charter on Human Rights 1982, Art 4.

2   Eg, Amnesty International claims that there are serious human rights abuses in 151 countries: *Amnesty International Report*, 1997, London: AIUK, p 1.

the fact that the last half century has witnessed hitherto unknown legal developments in the field of human rights. This chapter will trace the development of international human rights and it will be shown that individuals today have remedies under international law which did not exist 50 years ago. Of course, this does not mean that human rights abuses have suddenly ceased – atrocities, such as the frequent massacres in Algeria, genocide in Rwanda, ethnic cleansing in the former Yugoslavia, and the persecution of the Kurds in Iraq (to name but a few), still continue. However, what is particularly significant is an acceptance, by the world community, that human rights abuses are not merely 'morally' wrong, but are also 'illegal'.

David Weissbrodt claims that the protection of international human rights is 'the world's first universal ideology'.[3] There is controversy in the extent to which human rights may be described as 'universal', for many international lawyers (particularly those from the third world) claim that human rights should, instead, be defined on a 'regional' basis, taking account of local cultures and traditions.[4] Nevertheless, the fact that some provisions of the United Nations Declaration of Human Rights 1948 are part of customary international law (so that they bind all States, including non-Members of the United Nations),[5] that it is rare to find a State which has not signed or ratified at least one human rights treaty, and that a nation's failure to comply with its human rights obligations can have serious economic and political implications,[6] is evidence of the 'universal' impact of the principles of international human rights law. Thus, as Professor Louis Henkin points out, 'Human rights are the idea of our time ... everywhere acknowledged as "good"'.[7]

THE HISTORY OF INTERNATIONAL HUMAN RIGHTS

The phrase 'human rights' is itself 'relatively new[8] and it certainly did not have the same meaning in the period up until the Second World War that it has today. In the 19th century, the influential theory of positivism meant that

---

3   Weissbrodt, D, 'Human rights: an historical perspective', in Davis, P (ed), *Human Rights*, 1988, London: Routledge, p 1.

4   On this, generally, see Teson, F, 'International human rights and cultural relativism' (1985) 25 Virginia JIL 869.

5   Lillich, R, 'Civil rights', in Meron, T (ed), *Human Rights in International Law: Legal and Policy Issues*, 1984, Oxford: Clarendon, pp 116–18.

6   Eg, one of the reasons why Turkey has so far been refused permission to join the EU would appear to be the concern of many of its Western neighbours about its poor human rights record. On this, generally, see 'Turkish dilemma exposes EU rift' (1988) *The Times*, 13 March, p 15.

7   Henkin, L, 'Introduction', in *The Rights of Man Today*, 1979, London: Stevens.

8   Weston, B, 'Human rights', in *New Encyclopaedia Britannica*, 15th edn, 1992, Vol 20, p 656.

only States had rights in the international arena, because of their legal status as 'subjects' of international law.[9] On the other hand, since individuals were merely 'objects' of international law, they were denied any international legal recognition of their rights, so that the way in which a nation treated its own citizens was regarded as being a matter which came exclusively within the State's domestic jurisdiction. In so far as a State had any international obligations to individuals, it was only required to treat its non-nationals in accordance with certain international minimum standards.[10] Nevertheless, even here, these were merely obligations which were owed to the States whose nationality the aliens possessed, rather than being obligations to the non-nationals themselves.[11]

Traditionally, there were only a few exceptions to this rule that international law did not concern itself with the rights of individuals. First, the prohibition of slavery was recognised as a rule of customary international law and was re-affirmed in a number of international conventions in the 19th century.[12] Secondly, similar rules were introduced to outlaw the international trafficking in women and children.[13] Thirdly, under the Geneva Convention 1864, there was a requirement that 'wounded and sick combatants, to whatever nation they may belong, shall be collected and cared for',[14] and this formed the basis of the contemporary rules of 'humanitarian law' which regulate warfare.[15] Fourthly, there was an acceptance by early international lawyers that, in extreme circumstances, a State could intervene to prevent another State persecuting its own nationals ('humanitarian intervention').[16] The exact limits of this principle were, however, unclear and, whilst invoked by Britain, Russia and France in the 18th and 19th centuries as the justification for intervening to 'protect' Christian minorities in the Ottoman Empire, claims have been made that the actual reasons for such interventions were often less than altruistic.[17] Finally, and perhaps most significantly, the League of Nations was set up in 1919.

---

9   See Jones, JW, 'The "pure" theory of international law' (1935) 16 BYIL 5.

10 *The Neer Claim* (1926) UNRIAA IV 60.

11 See Oppenheim, L, *International Law: A Treatise*, 2nd edn, 1912, London: Longmans, Green, Vol 1, p 362.

12 On this, generally, see O'Connell, DP, *International Law*, 2nd edn, 1970, London: Stevens, Vol 2, pp 753–55.

13 Eg, see the International Convention for the Suppression of Traffic in Women and Children, 60 UNTS 416; UKTS 26 (1923).

14 Hague Convention No III of 1899, Art 6(1), extended the rules of the 1864 Convention to naval warfare.

15 On these, generally, see Roberts, A and Guelff, R, *Documents on the Laws of War*, 1982, Oxford: Clarendon.

16 See Lillich, RB, 'Forcible self-help by States to protect human rights' (1967) 53 Iowa L Rev 325; Fonteyne, JP, 'The customary international law doctrine of humanitarian intervention' (1974) 4 California Western ILJ 203.

17 Brownlie, I, 'Humanitarian intervention', in Moore, JN (ed), *Law and Civil War in the Modern World*, 1974, Baltimore MD: John Hopkins UP, p 217.

The League of Nations lacked any provisions which expressly guaranteed human rights, but it is worth noting that it extended the jurisdiction of international law in two respects. First, it established a 'mandate' system for administering the former colonies of States that had been defeated in the First World War, with the victorious (mandated) powers charged with running these territories and under a duty to ensure the protection of rights, such as freedom of conscience and religion.[18] And, secondly, Art 23 of the Covenant of the League of Nations, which provided that the populations of the mandated territories should be treated fairly, was one reason why a number of Balkan and Eastern European States signed five special minorities treaties at the end of the First World War.[19] These treaties guaranteed the rights of those who belonged to a racial, religious and linguistic minority and, as the Council of the League of Nations had the power to ensure that States complied with their new obligations,[20] minorities were accorded limited (albeit unprecedented) recognition under international law.[21] However, as can be witnessed from history, optimism in the League of Nations was misplaced and its impotence, in the wake of events before 1945, explains the post-war emergence of the human rights movement.

DEVELOPMENT OF INTERNATIONAL HUMAN RIGHTS LAW

United Nations Charter 1945

It was the holocaust, and the fact that Germany had been able to commit atrocities against millions of its own people in the 1930s with little interference from other nations, which finally jolted the international community into codifying rules to protect human rights. The United Nations Charter[22] signified that the rights of human beings were a matter of international concern, since a stated purpose of the United Nations was 'to achieve international co-operation ... in promoting and encouraging respect for human rights and for fundamental freedoms for all without distinction as to race, sex, language or religion'.[23] Moreover, it required the United Nations to promote

---

18 Covenant of the League of Nations 1920, Art 22.

19 These were the Treaties of St Germain, Cmd 400, Arts 62–69; Trianon, Cmd 896, Arts 54–60; Neuilly, Cmd 522, Arts 49–57; Sèvres, the Treaties of Peace, 1919–23, Vol II, p 908, Arts 140–51; Lausanne, Cmd 1929, Arts 37–45.

20 On this, generally, see Thornberry, P, 'Is there a phoenix in the ashes? International law and minority rights' (1980) 15 Texas ILJ 433.

21 Britain vetoed proposals by the US and Japan to give minorities more protection under the League of Nations Covenant, because of its fears that such provisions might be relied upon by the colonial peoples of the British Empire: see Ott, D, *Public International Law in the Modern World*, 1988, London: Pitman, p 241.

22 The UN Charter came into force 24 October 1945.

23 UN Charter, Art 1(3).

'universal respect for and observance of, human rights and fundamental freedoms for all without distinction as to race, sex, language, or religion',[24] and provided that Member States should 'pledge themselves to take joint and separate action' to achieve these aims.[25]

At first glance, the United Nations Charter seems to offer little by way of human rights. The Charter's language is vague, as it fails to define 'human rights and fundamental freedoms'. Moreover, the scope of the words 'promote' (Art 55) and 'pledge' (Art 56) is unclear, and there has been disagreement between those who have suggested that these Articles may impose legal obligations on States,[26] and others who have rejected this claim.[27] The fact that the United Nations Charter's provisions are so lacking in detail, and that the States which drafted the Charter probably never intended it to be legally binding, in view of their own vested interests,[28] seems to add considerable weight to the second view. Nevertheless, despite its many defects, the United Nations Charter is significant for at least two reasons. First, it recognised, formally, that human rights have an international dimension and are no longer solely a matter falling within the exclusive jurisdiction of a State; and, secondly, it granted the United Nations the legal authority to embark upon a codification of human rights which led to the drafting of what was the world's first international human rights document, the Universal Declaration of Human Rights.

Universal Declaration of Human Rights 1948

The United Nations Declaration of Human Rights was adopted on 10 December 1948 in the form of a resolution passed by the United Nations General Assembly.[29] It consists of 30 Articles which can be divided into two parts. The first part (Arts 1–21)) guarantees civil and political rights, while the second (Arts 22–30) recognises various economic, social and cultural rights. Although the Universal Declaration lacks any organs of implementation and many of its provisions are drafted rather vaguely,[30] it is unique in that no

---

24 UN Charter, Art 55.

25 *Ibid*, Art 56.

26 See Wright, Q, 'National courts and human rights – the *Fujii* case' (1951) 45 AJIL 73.

27 See Hudson, M, 'Integrity of international instruments' (1948) 42 AJIL 105, pp 105–08.

28 Buergenthal makes the point that it was not in the political interests of the victorious powers at the end of the Second World War to 'draft a charter that established an effective system for the protection of human rights ... [as] ... the Soviet Union had its Gulag, the United States its *de jure* racial discrimination [and] France and Britain their colonial empires': Buergenthal, T, *International Human Rights*, 2nd edn, 1995, St Paul: West, p 22.

29 GA Res 2174 (III), UN Doc A/810, p 71, adopted 10 December 1948.

30 Eg, Art 24 provides that 'Everyone has the right to rest and leisure, including reasonable limitation of working hours and periodic holidays with pay'.

other human rights document has, as yet, been so influential. Humphrey suggests that the Universal Declaration has become 'the Magna Carta of the world',[31] while it has been described by Pope John Paul II as the 'cornerstone of the United Nations'.[32] Certainly, its influence is considerable and this can be seen in at least three ways.

First, the Universal Declaration has been referred to by national courts[33] and the International Court of Justice[34] as an aid to the interpretation of cases. Secondly, as was mentioned earlier, it has been 'argued persuasively that substantial parts of the Universal Declaration ... have become ... part of customary international law binding upon all States'.[35] Thirdly, the Universal Declaration has been commonly accepted as being 'the source of inspiration' and the 'basis for the United Nations in making advances in standard setting as contained in the existing international human rights instruments'.[36] In particular, these instruments include: the International Covenant on Civil and Political Rights (ICCPR);[37] the Optional Protocol to the ICCPR;[38] and the International Covenant on Economic, Social and Cultural Rights.[39]

CLASSIFICATION OF INTERNATIONAL HUMAN RIGHTS

For the past 50 years, international lawyers have had to grapple with the problem of agreeing how to balance conflicting definitions of and different regional approaches to human rights. The 'Cold War' polarised the international community, with Western nations prioritising what have been called 'first generation' rights (that is, the right to life, a fair trial, liberty, assembly, privacy, speech, religion), whilst Communist States and their allies tended to stress the importance of 'second generation' rights (that is, the right

31 See Humphrey, JP, 'The Magna Carta of mankind', in Davis, P (ed), *Human Rights*, 1988, London: Routledge, p 37.

32 *Ibid.*

33 Eg, see *Filartiga v Pena-Irala* (1980) 630 F 2nd 896.

34 Eg, see the *Corfu Channel* case (1949) ICJ Rep 4, pp 4, 22.

35 *Op cit*, Lillich, fn 5, p 116.

36 Vienna Declaration and Programme of Action, 25 June 1993; (1993) 32 ILM 1661, p 1663.

37 ICCPR, GA Res 2200 21 UN GAOR, Supp (No 16) 52 UN Doc A/6316 (1966). The ICCPR was adopted 16 December 1966, entered into force 23 March 1976, and there are now 136 contracting parties to it, including the UK.

38 Optional Protocol to the Covenant on Civil and Political Rights, 16 December 1966, GA Res 2200A (XXI) 21 UN GAOR Supp (No 16) 59 UN Doc A/6316 (1966). This entered into force 23 March 1976, and there are 89 parties to it, although it has not, as yet, been signed or ratified by the UK.

39 International Covenant on Economic, Social and Cultural Rights (ICESCR), 16 December 1966, GA Res 2200A (XXI), 21 UN GAOR Supp (No 16) 49 UN Doc A/6316 (1966), entered into force 3 January 1976, and there are 135 parties to it, including the UK, but not the US.

to work, shelter, food, social security, health care). Ideological and political differences meant that it was impossible to agree upon a single document to protect these various rights,[40] so the international community chose, in 1966, to create two International Covenants which would deal with these matters separately: the International Covenant on Civil and Political Rights and the International Covenant on Economic, Social and Cultural Rights.

At first glance, there seemed to be little in common between first and second generation rights. The former were embraced by Western nations, and the latter by socialist States. First generation rights stemmed principally from the Western liberal tradition,[41] while second generation rights were based mainly on Marxist theory.[42] Finally, as can be seen from studying the two 1966 Covenants, first generation rights appeared to be capable of immediate implementation by States, while second generation rights required only progressive compliance, as permitted by the strength of the State's economy.[43]

Despite these differences, the rigid classification between civil and political rights on the one hand, and social, economic and cultural rights on the other, was never easy to sustain in practice. There were always exceptions to the rule that the obligations imposed by civil and political rights were only negative (that is, the State was not to kill, torture, etc), while economic, social and cultural rights placed the State under a duty to take positive measures (that is, to provide its citizens with housing, education, employment, etc). After all, a civil and political right, such as the right to a fair trial,[44] ensures that the State must set up and finance a legal system by providing, among other things, court buildings, trained judges, legal aid for those who cannot afford a lawyer, and interpreters for those who do not understand the language being spoken in court. Similarly, some economic and social rights, such as an individual's freedom to join a trade union,[45] merely involve non-intervention by the State. Thus, contemporary international lawyers have accepted, at least to some extent, that 'the full realisation of civil and political rights without the

---

40 As was pointed out earlier in the main text, the Universal Declaration distinguished between civil and political rights (Arts 1–21) and economic, social and cultural rights (Arts 22–30), but even this compromise failed to satisfy a number of Eastern European countries which chose to abstain when the Declaration was passed in the General Assembly.

41 On these, generally, see Shestack, J, 'The jurisprudence of human rights', in *op cit*, Meron, fn 5, pp 75–80, 85–97.

42 For an analysis of the theories of human rights from a socialist perspective, see Szabo, A, 'Historical foundations of human rights', in Vasak, K and Alston, P (eds), *The International Dimensions of Human Rights*, 1982, Westport, CT: Greenwood, Vol II.

43 Eg, the obligation under Art 2(1) of the ICESCR, requiring States 'to take steps ... with a view to achieving progressively the full realisation of the rights recognised in the present covenant', can be contrasted with the more immediate requirement on States to comply with their obligations, under Art 2(1) of the ICCPR.

44 See ICCPR 1966, Art 14.

45 See ICESCR 1966, Art 8.

enjoyment of economic, social and cultural rights is impossible',[46] and that all human rights are 'indivisible and interdependent'.[47]

This is particularly the case now that the cold war is over, so, today, it is unwise to make generalisations about the attitude of contemporary States to first and second generation rights. As we approach the new millennium, it is a fallacy that western governments fail to recognise economic and social rights, or that socialist nations are not committed to civil and political rights. On the contrary, most Western European nations are parties to the European Social Charter[48] and, even the US, which traditionally has been the nation most reluctant to recognise economic and social rights,[49] provides (at least in global terms) a relatively extensive welfare system for its citizens. Similarly, civil and political rights are no longer the sole preserve of western powers. A number of socialist and third world countries, including, most recently, China[50] have signed the International Covenant on Civil and Political Rights, and one prominent international lawyer has claimed that there is nothing inherently 'western' in the acceptance, by many non-western States, of 'a civilisation of tolerance, freedom and personal self-determination'.[51]

Finally, traditional distinctions between first and second generation rights seem outmoded in view of the increasing recognition accorded to what are sometimes called 'third' generation rights. These are collective or group rights, which include the right to self-determination,[52] the right to development,[53] the rights of indigenous peoples[54] and the right to a protected environment.[55] The extent to which these third generation rights impose positive legal obligations on States is debatable,[56] but they are of considerable symbolic

---

46 Proclamation of Teheran 1968, UN Doc A/CONF 32/41 (1968), p 3, para 13.

47 Vienna Declaration and Programme of Action 1993, UN Doc A/49/668 (1993), Pt 1, para 5.

48 However, it must be conceded that the European Social Charter has considerably less power and prestige than its equivalent in the area of civil and political rights, the ECHR. On the European Social Charter generally, see Harris, D, *The European Social Charter*, 1984, Charlottesville, VA: Virginia UP.

49 For an explanation of the US position, see UN Doc A/40/C 3/36 (1985), p 5.

50 (1998) *The Times*, 16 March, p 13.

51 Franck, T, 'Is personal freedom a Western value?' (1997) 91 AJIL 593, p 624.

52 See Koskenniemi, M, 'National self-determination today – problems of legal theory and practice' (1994) 43 ICLQ 241.

53 See Declaration on the Right to Development, GA Res 41/128 (1986); Alston, P, 'Revitalising United Nations work on human rights and development' (1991) 18 Melb UL Rev 216.

54 See Barsh, RL, 'Indigenous peoples: an emerging object of international law' (1986) 80 AJIL 369.

55 See Boyle, A and Anderson, M (eds), *Human Rights Approaches to Environmental Protection*, 1996, Oxford: Clarendon.

56 One third generation right which is legally binding is the right of self-determination. In relation to colonial territories, this is a rule of customary international law: the *Namibia* case (1971) ICJ Rep 16.

value and reflect the growing importance of many African and Asian nations which, as victims of colonisation, had been unable to influence the way in which the Universal Declaration and the 1966 International Covenants were drafted.

The enthusiasm of many Asian and African nations for third generation rights has contrasted sharply with the indifference and apathy of many Western nations to these newly claimed rights. In an effort to find some common ground, the Vienna World Conference on Human Rights was held in June 1993. Representatives of the world's nations accepted that human rights are 'interrelated' and that 'the international community must treat human rights globally in a fair and equal manner, on the same footing, and with the same emphasis'.[57] Thus, economic, social and cultural rights should be taken as seriously as civil and political rights and, whilst rejecting a proposal supported by a number of third world countries that, without economic development, 'human rights are completely out of the question',[58] the World Conference accepted that the right to development is a 'universal and inalienable right and an integral part of fundamental human rights'.[59]

The agreed text of the Vienna Declaration also covers a wide range of issues such as minorities rights,[60] women's rights,[61] human rights education[62] and ways of implementing and monitoring human rights.[63] While some are pessimistic, seeing the conference as a 'predictable diplomatic compromise ... that settled very few things',[64] others are more optimistic,[65] and perhaps only time will tell whether the Vienna Declaration turns out to be the 21st century's equivalent of the Universal Declaration.

CONCLUSION

Tony Blair's Labour Government has pledged to put human rights at the heart of British foreign policy.[66] The Foreign Secretary, Robin Cook, has justified

---

57 Vienna Declaration and Programme of Action UN Doc A/49/668 (1993), Pt 1, para 5, adopted 25 June 1993. See, also, (1993) 32 ILM 1661.
58 Liu Huaqiu, Chinese Vice Minister of Foreign Affairs, 15 June 1993, UN Press Release HR/VIE/10, 13.
59 Vienna Declaration 1993, Pt 1, para 10.
60 Ibid, Pt 2, paras 25–27.
61 Ibid, Pt 2, paras 36–44.
62 Ibid, Pt 2, paras 78–82.
63 Ibid, Pt 2, paras 83–98.
64 Kausikan, B, 'Asia's different standard' (1993) 92 Foreign Policy 24.
65 Marks, S, 'Nightmare and noble dream: the 1993 World Conference on Human Rights' (1994) 53 CLJ 54.
66 'Cook takes on global "evil"' (1997) The Guardian, 18 July, p 5.

this on the ground that 'we are an instant witness in our sitting rooms, through the medium of television, to human tragedy in distant lands [and are therefore] obliged to accept moral responsibility for our response'.[67]

However, the moral ambiguities of this were illustrated by the fact that, shortly after the launch of Britain's new ethical foreign policy, in a decision taken under the British presidency of the European Union, EU governments agreed not to sponsor any United Nations Resolutions critical of China.[68] Moreover, having announced a 'fresh start' with the Government in Beijing,[69] Robin Cook only agreed to meet Wei Jingsheng, a leading Chinese dissident, in private,[70] having refused to see him three months earlier, allegedly because of an imminent visit by Mr Cook to China.[71] The Foreign Secretary insists that there will be 'no question of us picking on the little guys and letting the big guys go',[72] but it is difficult to avoid the suspicion that many Western governments which are strong on human rights rhetoric are noticeably reluctant to take action against those States which have rapidly growing economies that may offer them fresh markets and new trading opportunities.[73]

Therefore, the unprecedented development of human rights jurisprudence in the second half of the 20th century, must not allow scholars to become complacent. Whilst the 'humanisation of international law ... [has] produced a world movement of profound political significance',[74] the positive realisation of some of even the most basic human rights has yet to be achieved. For example, although there are a plethora of international conventions relating to economic, social and cultural rights, there are still 1.2 billion people without access to clean water and 1.3 billion people living below the United Nations income poverty line.[75] In addition, notwithstanding the fact that there is an

---

67 (1997) *The Times*, 14 May, p 24.

68 (1998) *The Times*, 13 March.

69 'West hails China's olive branches' (1998) *The Guardian*, 20 January, p 12.

70 See 'China exile attacks "gambler" Cook' (1998) *The Daily Telegraph*, 11 March, p 12; and 'Cock-up or Cook-up?' (1998) *The Daily Telegraph*, 12 March, p 25.

71 'Chinese dissident censures Europe's inaction' (1998) *The Times*, 11 March, p 12.

72 (1997) *The Independent*, 18 July, p 13.

73 Perhaps the US is the best example of this in terms of its relations with China. The key principle of US foreign policy has changed from the prioritisation of human rights (see 'Bottom line for US and China: no kowtows on human rights' (1994) *The New York Times*, 27 March) to one of encouraging co-operation and trade (see 'Clinton U-turn as he defends links with China' (1997) *The Daily Telegraph*, 25 October, p 11; 'Clinton steers clear of human rights in talks with Jiang' (1997) *The Times*, 5 November, p 9; 'America retreats from human rights motion against China' (1998) *The Times*, 16 March, p 13).

74 Buergenthal, T, 'The normative and institutional evolution of international human rights' (1997) 19 HRQ 722.

75 Human Development Report 1997, as cited in (1998) *New Internationalist*, January–February, p 33.

almost universal recognition of the rights of the child,[76] millions of children remain illiterate,[77] malnourished[78] and abused globally.[79] Finally, in spite of the international community's legal response to recent events in the former Yugoslavia[80] and Rwanda,[81] and the fact that genocide is prohibited under international law,[82] many States still refuse to countenance the creation of a full time international criminal court.[83]

The failure of international law to deal with these issues often itself creates tension which further leads to strife. Therefore, perhaps a salutary lesson for the statesmen and politicians of the 21st century is that, in the words of one of the Universal Declaration's original drafters, 'the world has no future unless the rule of law, including the recognition of human rights, is embedded at the supranational level'.[84]

---

76 The UN Convention on the Rights of the Child 1989 has been ratified by 190 States.

77 It is thought that 23% of children under 11 in developing countries are deprived of a formal education. See *op cit*, Human Development Report, fn 75.

78 It has been estimated that there are 158 million malnourished children under the age of five: *ibid*.

79 A common form of abuse is the use of children as soldiers in armed conflicts. On this, generally, see Van Bueren, G, 'The international legal protection of children in armed conflicts' (1994) 43 ICLQ 809.

80 See Shraga, D and Zacklin, R, 'The international criminal tribunal for the former Yugoslavia' (1994) 5 EJIL 360.

81 See Sunga, L, 'The commission of experts on Rwanda and the creation of the International Criminal Tribunal for Rwanda' (1995) 16 HRLJ 121.

82 Genocide Convention 1948.

83 International Law Commission in 1994 adopted a draft statute for an international criminal court. However, States such as Russia, China, the US and the UK have traditionally opposed the creation of such an international criminal court. On this, generally, see Crawford, J, 'The ILC adopts a statute for an international criminal court' (1995) 89 AJIL 404; 'US tries to limit war crimes court' (1998) *The Times*, 30 March.

84 *Op cit*, Humphrey, fn 31, Chap 3, p 38.

THEME ONE

EXISTING STANDARDS

THE UNITED NATIONS: STRUCTURE VERSUS SUBSTANCE (LESSONS FROM THE PRINCIPAL TREATIES AND COVENANTS)[1]

Mary O'Rawe

INTRODUCTION

This chapter deals with the principal human rights treaties of the United Nations, through an analysis of the content and implementation potential of the International Bill of Rights. It pays particular attention to the initial stages of 'visioning' the human rights concept into positive international law and considers whether the dilution of the vision to serve the interests of national governments, and their different ideological ends, has resulted in a fundamentally flawed system for the protection of human rights.

Prior to 1945, international law regulated transactions between States only to the extent that certain inter-State dealings had come to be governed by custom[2] or had been made the subject of treaties.[3] Treaties bound only contracting parties and custom could largely be dispensed with if, and when, individual States considered it necessary. A national or colonial government thus did not need to fear unwanted external scrutiny or adjudication of its activities within what were deemed to be its own territorial boundaries. Coupled with this was the fact that State representatives were not considered legally liable for actions undertaken in their official capacity. In essence, the twin principles of State sovereignty and territorial integrity were sacrosanct. Governments were generally well pleased by such arrangements and, by and large, pleased themselves.

In the twilight zone following the Second World War, people reeled from the horror of atrocities committed behind these veils and recognised some of the flaws in a world order entrenched too stolidly on such principles. A need was felt, on many levels, to create a new world order that would save

---

1   This chapter deals only with the framework set up by the UN for human rights protection and, thus, does not touch upon all aspects within the UN's remit. However, as will be seen, many of the problems faced in other areas of its work have been played out in the debates, drafting and dilution of measures for increased human rights protection.

2   Eg, the customary rule granting States the right to diplomatic protection of their nationals vis à vis a foreign country.

3   Relating mainly to trading interests (including the slave trade) or post-conflict settlements between States.

humanity from the ravages of war. The world stage was changing in respect of a move away from colonialism and the emergence of many newly independent States with the potential to become international players. In a sense, it was a time when many lines were being redrawn and anything might have been possible.

Before 1945, there had been a number of piecemeal attempts to rein in actions likely to jeopardise friendly relations between States,[4] but these had failed to keep war at bay or prevent major human rights abuses. By dint of such arrangements, individuals were rarely considered as subjects of international law in their own right,[5] but still very much as State appendices.[6] This fuelled the potential for unchallenged abuse within, and sometimes beyond, territorial boundaries.

In 1945, fundamental to the setting up of a new international system for the protection of humanity, was an idea that world peace was fundamentally linked to ensuring respect for individuals and groups at all levels, irrespective of political and geographic boundaries. However, attitudes between States differed as to how this could best be achieved.

Many (essentially Western) governments had begun to recognise a concept of indivisible, inalienable, individual human rights as necessary to prevent the abuse of human beings by their political leaders. Those governments with a more socialist bent, or those newly emerging from the legacies of colonialism, saw self-determination and the rights of communities and peoples as key to ending oppression. All wished to see these objectives writ large in a normative spelling out of rights by the international community and, drawing lessons from the past, many realised that fundamental human rights protection needed to transcend both borders and political diplomacy. However, most were only concerned with setting standards, leaving it to national governments to comply as best they might, rather than engaging in a fundamental rethink as to how the world might be ordered differently to ensure the implementation of basic minimum standards in a meaningful way.

There lay the rub. To ensure that human rights truly came to be protected would have involved such radical changes in State power and policy, that States eventually balked at the enormity of the challenge. Instead, the human

---

4   Eg, through inter-State conventions or under the auspices of the League of Nations after the First World War.
5   An initial move away from viewing individuals merely as State pawns occurred after the First World War with the International Labour Organisation (ILO) granting a limited right to workers to demand compliance with ILO conventions by Member States.
6   Antonio Cassese has described individuals 'as puny young Davids confronted by overpowering Goliaths holding all the instruments of power': see *International Law in a Divided World*, 1986, Oxford: Clarendon, p 9.

rights vision was, and has constantly been, tempered to be acceptable to political will and present power structures.[7]

On one level, the governments involved in ushering in the new order knew that they themselves would have to cede some sovereign power, and to ensure that others did so, in order to better serve their people. However, the same governments also jealously guarded their own national sovereignty. They, therefore, faced the dilemma of how to create and maintain a new international structure that would work to prevent the horrors of the Second World War occurring in the future, but which would also make individual perpetrators and aberrant governments accountable to the wider community for crimes against humanity, while keeping national sovereignty more or less intact.

DRAFTING THE BASIS OF A NEW WORLD ORDER?

The United Nations Charter[8] was drafted on the basis of this dichotomy and resulted in many compromises to power politics. While attempting to protect people from abuse by executive power, the United Nations repeated many of the same patterns of dominance within its own systems and structures. By enshrining the supremacy of the Nation State (and, indeed, some Nation States in particular) at the heart of the organisation, the United Nations was in many ways a fudge where human rights were concerned. It was an international body charged with performing the necessary balancing act between often unstated competing interests of territorial integrity and effective human rights protection. At the same time, it was run by and dependent on the very political structures which had previously diluted the potential of international law as a vehicle for ensuring a legally binding social contract of respect for the governed.

The United Nations was hailed as opening a door to a new era and, in a sense, it did begin a process in respect of placing human rights protection at the centre of international law. However, this new champion of human rights also served to underscore the political dominance of a small number of countries by giving them a disproportionate say in how the new organisation would develop and act. This ensured that the organisation would continue to be dogged by many of the unresolved difficulties which had beset its predecessors. The United Nations failed to jettison past difficulties, but,

---

7   For one of the most recent examples of this phenomenon, see various government attitudes towards the setting up of an international criminal court which resulted in the US and China failing to sign up to the relevant UN Statute in Rome in July 1998.

8   The Charter was signed 26 June 1945, and came into force 24 October 1945, thus establishing the United Nations Organisation.

instead, (unwittingly or otherwise) sought to ensure them a permanent home within the new era.

The primary aim of the United Nations was to prevent war and human rights abuse[9] yet, six weeks after the Charter was signed in 1945, atomic bombs were dropped on Hiroshima and later Nagasaki. The main objective of the United Nations was to bring nations together in solidarity, yet, before the ink was dry on the Universal Universal Declaration of Human Rights 1948, a Cold War had begun which set major powers within the organisation against each other as enemies. The new organisation's stated intention was to prize supranational values over domestic politics. Many 'Third World' countries, newly formed with the break-up of colonial empires after the Second World War, found themselves at the beginning of a new era of 'sovereign equality' among States, with a seat at the United Nations and formal independence. However, international political will to change conditions of poverty, unfair trade and unjust regimes did not extend to globalising domestic interests to meet the very practical and basic needs of the people of these countries.

The General Assembly, which was intended to allocate equal power and say to the smallest of nations in formulating United Nations policy through Resolutions, managed to do so only on the basis of maintaining an uneven playing field. Calls to concrete action in the worst cases of abuse would ultimately lie with the smaller overarching body of the Security Council,[10] which took pains to enshrine the dominant political hegemony of five countries[11] over all the others. This lay the groundwork for narrow politicking to continue either as the cause or effect of armed conflicts and the violation of human rights the world over.

Today, the United Nations is a sprawling bureaucracy consisting of the Security Council, General Assembly and a range of bodies which deal with fundamental human rights, development and peacekeeping concerns. Normative standards have been distilled and refined through a range of regional and international treaties and conventions on everything from the elimination of racism and torture, to the prevention of discrimination against women and the securing of the rights of the child. Nation States are

---

9   This was highlighted from the outset in the recognition by the Universal Declaration of Human Rights 'of the inherent dignity and ... the equal and inalienable rights of all members of the human family [as] the foundation of freedom, justice and peace in the world' (Preamble, Universal Declaration of Human Rights 1948). Peace and respect for human rights became inextricably intertwined from this moment on.

10   Even naming the supreme body a 'Security' Council was indicative of a narrow, Statist and militaristic interpretation of peacebuilding which has, arguably, reduced the ability of the UN to act in a visionary and insightful way to make global peace more achievable.

11   Britain, China, France, the US and the USSR (as was) were appointed to be permanent members of the UN's overarching body – the Security Council. Article 27(3) of the Charter gives these States a veto, preventing the adoption of any deliberation on matters of substance without their agreement.

answerable to a plethora of committees and commissions as to how well they implement their obligations under this spiralling number of treaties and conventions.

The world has also changed dramatically since 1945. In terms of access to information, through developments in international communications and the information superhighway, we now know much more and have the potential to quickly access information about what is happening around the globe. Through the influence of multinational organisations, our daily lives are linked to those of countless thousands of other people through trade and consumerism. Non-governmental organisations have sprung up in numerous places, willing, and occasionally able, to engage with human rights issues at national and international levels. In many ways, the world has become a much smaller place. In theory, such developments should have eased the job of the United Nations, and regional organs such as the Council of Europe, in identifying and remedying abuse wherever it occurs in the world. However, in terms of ending human rights abuse, or ensuring respect for human dignity, progress has been somewhat slower than anticipated or, on occasion, claimed.

Although having limited success in a number of areas, the United Nations has failed in its major mission: to prevent widespread crimes against humanity. On the one hand, human rights law is still in its infancy, so a harsh judgment of inadequacy might be premature. However, this chapter posits the contention that there may be something in the genesis and make-up of the current system for human rights protection that will actually prevent the United Nations from growing to the maturity necessary to either reach its potential or deliver on its promises. This is not just by reason of excessive bureaucracy or the failure of governments to meet their financial commitments[12] in respect of the organisation, though these play their part. Rather, the pre-eminence of the Nation State within the organisation, and its machinations in defining and diluting the human rights concept to allow for 'acceptable levels' of abuse, would appear to doom the United Nations to continued failure in its primary purpose, in the absence of substantial rethinking and reform.

---

12 In 1997, the approved regular budget of the UN system amounted to something in excess of US$3,000 million. The main sources of funding for this are the contributions of the Member States, assessed on a sliding scale, which is supposed to reflect real capacity to pay. As of 31 December 1994, Member States' unpaid contributions amounted to almost US$1.8 billion (source: UN Department of Public Information). Presently, the greatest debtor in respect of its financial obligations is the US, despite its increasingly visible control of the organisation on many levels, and the fact that, since it began to develop the atomic bomb in 1940, it has spent US$3.5 trillion on nuclear arms and $19 trillion on defence (source: Brookings Institution Report, published July 1998, US).

DRAFT DODGING

Lessons from the principal treaties

The seeds of difficulty in ensuring global respect for human rights are, perhaps, most obviously found in the drafting process of the Universal Declaration of Human Rights 1948 and the subsequent International Bill of Rights 1966, which gave rise to the International Covenant on Civil and Political Rights and the International Covenant on Economic, Social and Cultural Rights (documents which remain fundamental to the ability of the United Nations to promote and protect human rights). A study of these principal treaties is useful, therefore, not just to ascertain those minimum human rights standards States are obliged to nurture, but also to identify the gaps and question the 'newness' of the world order ushered in by the United Nations. These lacunae in many ways hold the key to the effectiveness or otherwise of the 'human rights revolution' in international law.

Lessons from the Universal Declaration of Human Rights

It was the UN Charter which established the United Nations, but the philosophy of the organisation is most clearly spelt out in the Universal Declaration of Human Rights 1948. The General Assembly had moved quickly to the drafting of general principles which were to be non-binding, but which would pave the way for a more specific and enforceable International Bill of Rights.[13] The result was a document of commitment which included a preamble and 30 articles, proclaiming such recognised standards as non-discrimination,[14] with 'all human beings ... born free and equal in dignity'[15] to enjoy 'the right to life, freedom and security of the person'.[16] The Universal Declaration continues in this vein, declaiming a range of civil and political rights, from the right to be free from slavery[17] to the right to freedom of thought, conscience and religion[18] and the right to take part in the

---

13 In practice, the Universal Declaration has become a norm of customary international law, through constant reference, and may now be considered binding.
14 Universal Declaration of Human Rights 1948, Art 2.
15 *Ibid*, Art 1.
16 *Ibid*, Art 3.
17 *Ibid*, Art 4.
18 *Ibid*, Art 18.

government of one's own country.[19] Article 22 contains the first mention of a 'new generation'[20] of rights with reference to the right to social security and other economic, social and cultural rights 'through national effort and international co-operation and in accordance with the organisation and resources of each State'. The Universal Declaration then spends a total of six further articles dealing with the right to work,[21] leisure,[22] a decent standard of living,[23] education,[24] protection of cultural life[25] and entitlement to 'a social and international order in which the rights and freedoms set forth in this Universal Declaration can be fully realised'.[26]

Much of what inspired the Universal Declaration came from 18th century 'Western' political thought,[27] even to the point of using similar language in the idea of 'inalienable rights' and 'inherent dignity'. The Universal Declaration demonstrated an acceptance of the idea that rights are part of the human condition, not favours granted by States. On the contrary, the protection and promotion of such rights was deemed to be 'the only mode in which governments have a right to arise and the only principle on which they have a right to exist'.[28] Article 29 of the Universal Declaration further recognises that the protection of an individual's human rights corresponds to duties owed to 'the community in which alone the free and full development of ... personality is possible'.[29] The Universal Declaration, therefore, enshrines the rights of individual human beings, while rejecting individualistic or opportunistic interpretations by the State.

However, not too far beneath the surface, lurk political and ideological differences between States. The final text of the Universal Declaration is not just a product of compromise: the priority which appears to be given to some rights over others, reveals that certain States are in superior bargaining

---

19 Universal Declaration of Human Rights 1948, Art 21.

20 These rights are often known as second generation rights, in that those rights initially coming out of Western revolutionary tradition were deemed to deal with the civil and political rather than economic, social and cultural aspects of human dignity. This ranking of rights in generations is problematic in many respects, not least because it appears to relegate many basic and fundamental necessities, such as the right to food, work, rest and shelter as secondary to the concerns of more 'developed' countries.

21 Universal Declaration of Human Rights 1948, Art 23.

22 *Ibid*, Art 24.

23 *Ibid*, Art 25.

24 *Ibid*, Art 26.

25 *Ibid*, Art 27.

26 *Ibid*, Art 28.

27 In particular, the French Declaration on the Rights of Man and of the Citizen 1789, and the Amendments to the US Constitution (Bill of Rights) 1791.

28 Paine, T, *Rights of Man* (1791–92), 1915, Rhys, E (ed), pp 47 and 154.

29 Universal Declaration 1948, Art 29. This provision was passed by 23 votes to five with 14 abstentions, indicating a certain reticence to commit too fully to a non-individualistic interpretation of rights and their implications.

positions to others in the 'universal' scheme of things. Even the positioning of various rights within the text indicates very different understandings and expectations of human rights, depending on the political allegiances of the States involved in the drafting process.

The Universal Declaration is very much skewed in favour of Western ideologies and notions of rights. This is, perhaps, most clearly evidenced by the position of economic and social rights within the body of the text. These were new rights, different in character from those outlined in earlier universal declarations of rights, and all having 'in common the fact that 'national effort and international co-operation' were needed for their realisation'.[30] They represented a new departure, the beginnings of a recognition that economic, social and cultural rights must be ensured in any world order seeking stability in peace. Yet their place in the Universal Declaration was that of 'a 20th century graft on an 18th century tree'.[31] Although much argument ensued, especially from 'less developed' States to ensure that these rights were not ranked secondary to civil and political concerns, they finished by being relegated to seven articles tacked on after the others and qualified as dependent on the 'organisation and resources of each State'[32] in a way that civil and political rights were not.

This is indicative of the power struggles already happening at the core of the new organisation. States like Uruguay, Cuba, Lebanon and Mexico moved to amend Art 3[33] of the Universal Declaration to read thus: 'Everyone has the right to life, honour, liberty, physical integrity and to the legal, economic and social security which is necessary to the full development of the human personality', but such states were still too weak to make their voices sufficiently heard. The amendment would have had the effect, symbolic or otherwise, of 'pulling the concept of social and economic rights forward towards the very beginning of the Universal Declaration. It thus would have lessened the initial emphasis on civil and political rights and given the reader a more balanced view of the scope of human rights'.[34]

The vote, which went against the amendment by 21 to 20 with seven abstentions, revealed a complete lack of consensus as to the status of economic and social rights in the world order, and pointed clearly to the southern hemisphere as being responsible for the progressive nature of the Universal Declaration in this respect. The Universal Declaration is, therefore, very much

---

30 Cassin, 31 UN GAOR 183d plen mtg, p 49.
31 Morinsk, J, 'The philosophy of the Universal Declaration' (1984) 6 HRQ 309, p 326.
32 Universal Declaration of Human Rights 1948, Art 22.
33 Which finally read 'Everyone has the right to life, liberty and security of the person'.
34 *Op cit,* Morinsk, fn 31, p 327.

a Western construct.[35] It does not mention self-determination,[36] or the need for support for poorer countries, to ensure that human rights stand the best chance possible of becoming ingrained in the psyche of the world economic, as well as legal and political, order.

Despite all the far-sightedness apparently at work in certain measures drafted, and the nice warm feeling induced by the strength of the Universal Declaration's ringing endorsement of human rights as the 'foundation of freedom, justice and peace in the world',[37] what was left out of the final text is at least as significant as what was put in. It is these omissions which underscore the reluctance of representatives of national governments to go too far, and which are key to understanding the many subsequent failures of the United Nations to secure world peace and respect for human rights.

Essentially, the final document, flavoured by the variety of political allegiances and interests which continue to splinter the potential of the organisation, attests to a fear to risk too much. Despite the commitment to a naturalist theory of rights, an underlying tension regarding the need to protect State interest is evident just beneath the surface of the rhetoric. Thus, the right to petition, though deemed an 'essential human right' during the third Committee negotiations, was not included in the final Universal Declaration. Ostensibly, this was for practical reasons, such as the lack of possible implementation measures and the fact that there was not sufficient time. However, these are considerations which could equally have applied to the majority of principles in the final document. Furthermore, the non-binding nature of this statement of principles meant that the drafters did not need to concern themselves with implementation potential.

Another right which 'vanished' during the course of negotiations was the right to resist oppression, which had been considered fundamental by revolutionaries in the past. The concern here was that this could in no way be implemented by governments as other rights could be, also that to include it 'would be tantamount to encouraging sedition, for such a provision could be interpreted as conferring a legal character on uprisings against a government which was in no way tyrannical'.[38] The UK delegate, for example, felt that 'such a step would be inopportune and dangerous'[39] and 'not a right, but a last resort'.

---

35 A product of its time, it is also very much a male construct in calling for freedom from discrimination and then using the non-inclusive language of 'brotherhood' to bind all people together (Art 1).

36 The right to self-determination is used in this context merely as an example of a concept espoused chiefly by non-Western countries. In a number of ways, the right itself is problematic in terms of its potential to entrench 'Nation Statehood' still further at the heart of the world order.

37 Preamble, Universal Declaration of Human Rights 1948.

38 Roosevelt, E, US Delegate, 3rd Committee Records 3(1) UN GAOR C3 88–180 mtg (1948), p 749.

39 *Ibid*, p 751.

A number of commentators[40] see this as philosophical short-sightedness in a document supposed to usher in a truly people-oriented order. The fact that the committee felt unable to do other with these rights than to refer them back for further discussion and allow them subsequently to become lost, again is indicative of their unwillingness to abandon themselves fully to the social theory of government.

This *danse macabre* went on to seep into the more specific formulation of rights and their implementation, thus making the philosophy of human rights law, and its potential in reality, contingent on a 'statist' view of the world in which we live.

BEYOND THE UNIVERSAL DECLARATION OF HUMAN RIGHTS

The final Universal Declaration is deceiving, not least because it evinces an apparent consensus on the position of human rights and peace-building in a new world order which clearly did not exist. Instead, this 'consensus' thinly papered over a substantial lack of agreement and merely postponed, until after the adoption of the text, the settlement of all the problems, nuances and concerns that the Universal Declaration was intended to overcome. As soon as the question of implementing international decisions arose at United Nations level, the same differences were bound to and did re-emerge 'with all the attendant political problems'.[41]

Following adoption of the Universal Declaration of Human Rights, the General Assembly mandated the drafting of a legally binding international bill of rights, which would introduce rights into positive law and provide mechanisms for supervised implementation. The false consensus, and the competition and frustration between various ideologies which had been pivotal in the drafting of the Universal Declaration of Human Rights, returned to dog these subsequent human rights treaties.

Initially, it had been envisaged that a single international Bill of Rights could be drawn up to reflect the principles agreed and enunciated in the Universal Declaration of Human Rights. In the event, political disagreements between North and South resulted in a delay of nearly two decades before a final Bill was agreed. During negotiations, the 'Group of 77' socialist and developing countries, used their new found power at United Nations level to ensure that the needs of poorer countries were taken into account. But still, in the final formulation of a mutually agreeable Bill, economic, social and

---

40   Eg, for an excellent exposé, see *op cit*, Morinsk, fn 31, pp 309–33.
41   *Op cit*, Cassese, fn 6, p 197.

cultural rights had to occupy a separate covenant from the more traditional rights.[42]

The content of these two covenants does indicate that, by this stage, socialist and 'developing countries' were becoming stronger, or at least forming alliances among themselves that were able to stave off Western domination to some degree. For example, both covenants recognise the right to self determination and neither includes the right to own property.[43] There appeared to be some movement away from the hypocrisy of formal equality to a recognition of the need to address fundamental practical inequalities between States, if not between people in different countries.

However, even within these documents, the use of language is often all that was shared by the various governments involved. States, in agreeing to accept human rights standards, still had very different motivations and ideas as to what they were committing to, and how their commitments should be policed. This led to weak implementation mechanisms, which served to exacerbate the enormous difficulties in ensuring respect for the spirit of human rights conventions in practice.

IMAGINING IMPLEMENTATION

As States have been cast as the key subjects of international law, one consequence is that the current system of human rights protection is not self-sufficient, but must rely heavily on the good will and obeisance of national governments. Cassese has argued that:

> ... since national implementation of international rules is of crucial importance, one would expect there to be some form of international regulation of the matter or at least a certain uniformity in the ways in which domestic legal systems implement international law.[44]

He concludes that, instead, 'national self-interest stands in the way of a sensible regulation of this crucial area'. As States had no wish to surrender this aspect of their sovereignty to international control, each country has retained complete freedom to translate its international duties into domestic standards.

Such international structures as have been set up to ensure some degree of implementation of human rights obligations, are predicated on this notion. They, once again, are the result of the appeasement of narrow self-interest

---

42 Although both these Covenants were opened for signature in 1966, they only entered into force 10 years later.

43 As the Universal Declaration and Regional European Convention on Human Rights had done.

44 See *op cit*, Cassese, fn 6, p 15.

rather than a consistent and creative attempt to put an end to the abuse of human dignity.

Disagreements did emerge along political lines as to just what scope the United Nations should have to ensure human rights protection. During the San Francisco Conference which followed the 1944 Dumbarton Oaks Conference, a number of Latin American countries, aligned essentially with Norway, Australia and India, had pushed for an obligation to respect human rights within the body of the Charter. However, the major Western powers, though espousing the rhetoric of human rights protection, were chiefly concerned to limit the United Nations sphere of intervention in this regard.[45]

On this basis, the Charter itself fudged the issue of human rights protection, viewing it as merely a means of safeguarding peace, all countries appearing to agree that international legal adjudication was not appropriate. From the outset, therefore, implementation mechanisms essentially arose from either the treaties themselves or from specific resolutions dealing with gross and consistent patterns of violation. These shared a lack of judicial teeth that might have ensured some degree of compliance from aberrant States.[46]

Although international legal adjudication on its own may not have proven particularly useful in countering many major abuses, it is arguable whether the main, essentially low key, monitoring and reporting mechanisms which have been instituted for the implementation of human rights protection, from the inception of the United Nations, have been any more useful in dealing with widespread violations.

The Convention on the Elimination of Racial Discrimination, which first saw the light of day in 1965, and the International Covenant on Civil and Political Rights with its Optional Protocol in 1966, contained their own mechanisms for examination of State practice. Essentially, these revolve around the examination of periodic reports by States to designated committees[47] Provision was also made for inter-State applications if the State in question, as well as ratifying the Convention, had accepted a special clause permitting this to happen. It was probably anticipated, and has subsequently proved to be the case, that inter-State applications would be rare, resulting as they often do from political differences between countries in conflict rather than from altruistic concern for broader human rights principles. Finally, the

---

45   Countries such as the USSR and Czechoslovakia (as were), while committed to ensuring self-determination, were also anxious not to give the UN too much power in respect of other rights.

46   This is not to say that an international court of human rights would be a panacea for all ills. While potentially providing remedies for individuals, or classes of people in a position to finance and prepare a viable case, the move to establish a permanent international criminal court and the operation of war crimes tribunals for Bosnia and Rwanda at The Hague, Holland, have thrown up the same old difficulties as to the practicalities of rendering such international jurisdiction operational.

47   Eg, the Human Rights Committee under the International Covenant on Civil and Political Rights (ICCPR), Art 40.

right to individual petition was also accorded, but again only if the State concerned chose to accept this as an option.

Otherwise, Resolution 1235 of the Economic and Social Council (ECOSOC) in 1967, and Resolution 1503 in 1970, made provision for 'communications' by individuals and certain groups to a number of human rights bodies, where there is evidence of 'a consistent pattern of gross violations' of human rights. The 1235 procedure has the advantage of being public. The 1503 procedure soon 'remedied' this, as it is intended to be confidential, and thus provides more protection for State sovereignty with only its final outcome being made public. Both procedures involve a range of bodies, from the Sub-Commission on the Prevention of Discrimination and Protection of Minorities to the Commission on Human Rights and the Economic and Social Council. Unlike the treaty provisions, these two procedures are not optional. The first has had limited success in that it has identified a select number of pariah States and requested them to put an end to the gross violations of which they have been accused. The selection of States which fall to be treated in this way has, however, tended to be based more on political allegiances than respect for human rights.[48] At the same time, despite the potential for appointment of special *rapporteurs* (either thematically or by country), and visitations, resolutions, etc, the 1503 procedure continues to provide a shield behind which countries accused by the Sub-Commission can hide.

Much of the lack of concrete commitment to eradicating human rights abuse can be seen especially clearly in the area of implementation of economic, social and cultural rights. These are still accorded that lesser place witnessed in the Universal Declaration, and qualified into hopeful aspirations rather than rights. The International Covenant on Economic, Social and Cultural Rights recognises that:

> ... the ideal of free human beings enjoying freedom from fear and want, can be achieved only if conditions are created whereby everyone may enjoy his [*sic*] economic, social and cultural rights as well as his civil and political rights.[49]

On the other hand, Art 2 obliges States merely:

> ... to take steps individually and through international assistance and co-operation ... to the maximum of its available resources, with a view to achieving progressively the full realisation of the rights recognised in the present Covenant by all appropriate means, including particularly the adoption of legislative measures.

Again, as regards these rights, a number of governments have argued against any judicial body being set up on an international level to monitor observance of the progressive steps of those States choosing to ratify the International

---

48 For a good analysis of this phenomenon, see Donnelly, P, 'Human rights at the UN 1955–85: the question of bias' (1988) 33 ISQ 275, pp 275–303.
49 Preamble, International Covenant on Economic, Social and Cultural Rights (ICESR) 1966.

Covenant on Economic, Social and Cultural Rights, and it was only in 1986 that the United Nations inaugurated an expert committee to deal with all the ramifications of the implementation of these rights. Both because of the nature of their formulation, and the mechanisms set up to ensure implementation, it becomes increasingly difficult to defend the view that the United Nations takes economic, social and cultural rights just as seriously as civil and political rights, 'when the institutional arrangements for implementing the former were clearly inferior to those relating to the latter'.[50]

In part, the fault undoubtedly lies with the unwieldy nature of the United Nations bureaucracy, but again, there is more to it than red tape. Here, also, false consensus has played a role leading either to States doing little or nothing, owing to the progressive nature of the obligations in the International Covenant on Economic, Social and Cultural Rights, or to States using the desirable goal of economic, social and cultural development to justify the curtailing of other rights. The necessity of international co-ordination in this area, attested to in the Covenant itself, has been rendered obsolete by a 'when it suits' agenda, and the difficulty of defining 'available resources'. Obviously, in an unequal world, poor, exploited, war waging, interest paying States can never hope to achieve an adequate standard of living for their people, but arms sales to these countries, and self-interested intervention in their economies, and the exploitation of their natural resources, etc, cannot be in keeping with either the spirit or the letter of the International Covenant on Economic, Social and Cultural Rights. The devotion of vast resources to military projects continues dramatically to diminish our ability to provide shelter, food, clean water and health for the world's people.

An international dimension is clearly needed to solve the problems of the world in this respect, but this must be based on justice and the needs of all people (not the dictates of one monetary system or an economic growth-oriented view of development). It is this idea which rocked the United Nations to its foundations in the 1960s and 1970s, when 'developing' countries began to reject the Western models extrapolated to apply to them, and demanded the institution of a new international economic order encompassing a fresh basis for international relations, also a new and vital view of development preconditions through which peace and human rights might realistically be achieved.

---

50   Alston, P, 'Out of the abyss' (1987) 9 HRQ 347.

Though mooted as early as 1947,[51] it was only in the late 1970s that the United Nations began to move towards the idea of embracing solidarity or 'third generation' rights within the human rights framework. This break with the traditional concept of rights (as defined in relation to individuals and guaranteed by States) derived from a more holistic legal philosophy which sought to depict our shared needs and dreams as dependent upon a concept of mutual interconnectedness, entailing recognition of our common humanity and our need to work together to achieve our goals. These new rights writ large the ideals of a healthy and clean environment, sustainable and dynamic development, the cultural heritage of humankind and peace as the ultimate, all embracing goals of human existence. The thinking behind them augured an era of real revolution, of a need once again to break out of narrow confines that too often seemed to place States and financial gain before people. These ideals demanded that human rights should not be interpreted legalistically, technically or narrowly, as this would deny the factors which shaped and moulded them. Human rights had too long rested within the domain of State definition and distortion. There was still room for new ideas and directions. We all had a need to be educated as to our responsibilities towards others in our global community and to be empowered by both the realisation and challenge that:

> For the first time in history, responsibilities of individuals vis à vis peoples in other nations were arising ... the first cornerstones of a new international social order were being laid down.[52]

The United Nations, however, still has a long way to go to ensure that these rights are guaranteed by a necessarily new and different world order.

DEROGATION FROM 'NORMALITY'

So far, we have considered some of the problems generated by the language encasing rights standards within the treaties themselves, and the weaknesses of implementation mechanisms instituted to ensure that rights are protected by States. Just as problematic has been the margin of appreciation allowed to

---

51 In the late 1940s, a number of proposals were made to incorporate variations on the theme of a Right to Peace into a Universal Declaration on the Rights and Duties of States. Eg, a draft Universal Declaration submitted to the General Assembly by Ecuador in 1947 included an article stating that 'the maintenance of peace based on justice and on law is a fundamental rule of conduct in relations between States, and these have the right to peaceful and secure development', cited in Alston, P, 'The right to peace, colloquium on the new human rights: the rights of solidarity', Mexico 1980, UNESCO DOC SS – 80/CONF 806/7.

52 Klingenthal Symposium on Peoples and Human Rights [1986] HRLQ 413.

national governments, which has enabled them to dictate additional limits to basic human rights as they adjudge to be 'necessary in a democratic society'.[53]

In drafting limitation and reservation clauses, the genuine potential for conflict of rights was used as a foil to permit all manner of limitations on inherent and inviolable rights, purely on a government's say so. However, the potential for reserving acceptance of particular provisions, or limiting others, are not the only exceptions. It is also open to States to derogate completely from their obligations in relation to the vast majority of human rights, in 'time of war or other public emergency threatening the life of the nation'.[54]

It is perhaps the presence of these derogation provisions in human rights conventions which is most disturbing. These are included with all manner of safeguards, both substantive and procedural, but, in effect, they stand as stark testimony to the fact that a world order, supposedly committed to the achievement of peace through the protection of human rights, still recognises the right of the executive to override basic principles and minimum standards, which are thereby rendered neither basic nor minimum. A short list of rights are considered non-derogable[55] in any circumstances.

In one way, this might be seen as a further safeguard to those rights touching most deeply on human life and dignity. On the other hand, the need for such a list is, in itself, an admission that doctrines of necessity and proportionality tend to be forgotten in emergency situations. Derogation clauses mark an attempt to curtail the rule that necessity knows no bounds, by introducing a non-collapsible legal framework which could still be tailored to any given situation. Instead, once the executive arm of a national government is given rein to encroach on the rights which would ordinarily be the measure of its legitimacy, it is only a short step towards believing that it has free rein to trample over rights in the pursuit of a self-styled higher goal.

This phenomenon is borne out by empirical evidence. The International Commission of Jurists has noted 'the understandable link between states of emergency and situations of grave violations of human rights'.[56] Time and again, measures derogating from obligations under human rights conventions have remained unchallenged by the international community, even though manifestly unjustified by 'the exigencies of the situation'.[57] The tendency has, instead, been for so called 'emergency' measures to become entrenched and

---

53 This begs the question as to the supposed political neutrality of human rights documents when it comes to advocating any particular ideology.

54 Derogation Clauses are found in the main treaties: cf ICCPR, Art 4; ECHR, Art 15; and AMCHR, Art 27. However, in ICESR, and the most recent regional treaty, the African Charter on Human and People's Rights, there is no provision for derogation in any circumstances.

55 Eg, the right to be free from torture.

56 'Preface', in International Commission of Jurists, *States of Emergency: Their Impact on Human Rights*, 1983, Geneva: International Commission of Jurists.

57 ICCPR 1966–76, Art 4.

thereby normalised. States the world over (including non-constitutional dictatorships, often themselves responsible for the existence of the emergency in the first place), have continually used and abused the power to derogate. Its existence in treaties is not intended to give *carte blanche* to governments, but, as with the exceptions to the use of force in the United Nations Charter,[58] the very potential to derogate in this way constantly widens the field of play and is itself widened thereby. Here again, the exception has become the rule, and where emergencies are perceived to exist, despite national, constitutional safeguards or international treaties, often *de facto* (if not *de jure*) derogation measures have acted as a cover for *incommunicado* detention, torture,[59] disappearance,[60] extra-judicial killings[61] and suspension of the laws of due process, to the point where Amnesty International gives the number of political prisoners held without charge or trial as 294,000 spread through 60 countries.[62]

Robertson and Merrills have commented that 'there are more countries in the world today where fundamental rights and civil liberties are regularly violated than countries where they are effectively protected'.[63] Experts at Siracusa,[64] Paris[65] and Turku-Abo[66] have sought to have the list of non-derogable rights extended, even with the risk of this diluting the effectiveness

---

58 A radical and sweeping ban on the use or threat of military force is contained in Art 2(4) of the UN Charter which states:

> All Members shall refrain in their international relations from the threat or use of force against the territorial integrity or political independence of any state, or in any other manner inconsistent with the purposes of the United Nations.

Article 2(4) has, however, been interpreted to allow force not directed at the territorial integrity or political independence of States if its motives are in conformity with the purposes of the UN. This interpretation has justified, for many States, the recourse to 'humanitarian military intervention', ostensibly to counter human rights abuses or to protect nationals abroad but, all too often, for mixed or purely self-interested motives, as, for example, in the actions of the US in the Dominican Republic 1965, Chile 1970–73, Panama 1989; the intervention of the former USSR in Afghanistan, Hungary and Czechoslovakia; the US and UK in the Persian Gulf, to name but a few manifestations of this tendency. Invariably strong States have acted against weaker States.

59 According to Amnesty International, detainees were tortured or ill treated in prisons, police stations and secret detention centres in 104 countries throughout 1991 (*Annual Report 1992*).

60 At least 1,270 people were reported to have 'disappeared' after arrest by security forces in some 20 countries, and many remained missing in at least 26 countries from previous years (*Amnesty International Annual Report 1992*, London: AIUK).

61 Suspected government opponents, members of targeted ethnic groups or people living in opposition strongholds were apparently victims of extra-judicial executions in 45 countries (*ibid*).

62 *Ibid.*

63 Robertson, AH and Merrills, JG, *Human Rights in the World*, 3rd edn, 1989, Manchester: Manchester UP, p 2.

64 Siracusa Principles 1984.

65 Paris Minimum Standards 1984.

66 Turku-Abo Universal Declaration 1991.

of the concept, as adding to the list of sacrosanct rights seems the only way of ensuring any form of protection in an emergency. Even then, the protection is only relative.

The doctrines of necessity and proportionality embedded in the derogation principle do seek to introduce a concept of acceptable behaviour under pressure and herald a return to normality as soon as possible. Here too, even without the documented occurrence of phenomenal and systematic abuse of rights under emergency regimes, there is an inherent and fundamental flaw in the philosophy behind derogation, for our normality is violent and disrespectful of rights and, therefore, cannot act as a standard by which to measure abuse.

Again, voluntary self-regulation by States has proved ineffective, and we have not ushered in the human rights era which is so fundamental to worldwide peace. United Nations bodies, through reporting procedures, visits by special *rapporteurs*, inter-States complaints systems and a limited provision for individual application under the Optional Protocol to the Covenant on Civil and Political Rights, have gone some way toward spotlighting both gross and persistent rights violations, and those where a victim is identifiable and able to come forward. However, international embarrassment can only have limited effects in a world where 'normality' permits lesser, more ignored human rights abuses, in which all States participate to some degree.

CONCLUSION

There is something within the body of human rights law generally, and an organisation such as the United Nations in particular, which flinches at the mention of a new international order, being based itself on a particular way of looking at the world from within particular structures. There is also within the human spirit, a need for credibility that pushes beyond predefined boundaries and strives for the achievement of a world in which human rights and peace are indivisible, neither being sacrificed for the supposed protection of the other.

The United Nations human rights machinery has been hampered by narrow politics. The concept of human rights has been contained and constrained by Statist definitions of what human rights are and how they should be achieved. A re-visioning is required that might well break apart both the organisation and our notions of the Nation State as best suited to meet the needs of the world's people. This re-visioning might also require a redefinition of human rights, stressing the centrality of respect, dignity, integrity and solidarity in our highly interconnected world. This is not to say that the notion of human rights holds all the answers. The concept may not prove strong enough on its own to contain all the changes necessary to restructure our various ways of life. However, what can be said is that: human rights will only realise their revolutionary potential if more inclusive dialogue and definition enable human beings to reflect more deeply on how we can best order our world to live in real solidarity and respect with one another.

CHAPTER 3

THE EUROPEAN CONVENTION ON HUMAN RIGHTS: A NEW ERA FOR HUMAN RIGHTS PROTECTION IN EUROPE?

Siobhan Leonard

INTRODUCTION

The aims of this chapter are to describe and analyse the system of human rights protection afforded by the European Convention on Human Rights in the context of recent institutional changes. From this examination, it is hoped that conclusions may be drawn as to whether the Convention is sufficiently equipped to deal with applications which are increasing in number and intricacy.

PROTECTING HUMAN RIGHTS IN EUROPE

The development of internationally binding, codified systems for human rights protection has only happened relatively recently. On a global scale, such co-operation was realised in the aftermath of the Second World War, initially through the formation of the United Nations. One of the principal aims of the United Nations was to prevent the recurrence of wartime atrocities through the evolution of commonly accepted standards in human rights preservation.[1] The first fruits of this hitherto unparalleled co-operation, was the Universal Declaration of Human Rights,[2] which, although merely 'declaratory', nonetheless provided the motor for developing binding standards in a European context.[3]

The need to set up a specific pan-European system for human rights protection, in keeping with the aims and objectives of the Universal Declaration, was recognised by the Council of Europe. This renowned Strasbourg based international organisation has as its primary objective the

---

1   The UN, through the adoption of such instruments as the Convention against torture (adopted 1 February 1989), has continued to improve the standard of basic human rights protection in Europe, particularly through the work of the European Committee for the Prevention of Torture and Inhuman and Degrading Treatment (CPT) in its recent dealings with Turkey. See the public statement on Turkey, 15 December 1992 (1993) 14(1) HRLJ 49.

2   Adopted 10 December 1948.

3   See Steiner, HJ and Alston P, *International Human Rights in Context*, 1996, Oxford: OUP, pp 571–82.

achievement of 'a greater unity between its members for the purpose of safeguarding and realising the ideals and principles which are their common heritage and facilitating their economic and social progress'.[4]

Coming together in this way, States[5] could simultaneously defuse the political time bomb which was post-war Germany and rebuild relationships between Western European nations. As the conditions for membership of the Council are 'the existence of a genuine pluralistic democracy, the rule of law and enjoyment by all persons within its jurisdiction of human rights and fundamental freedoms',[6] the formation of the Council also effectively created a political buffer zone against ongoing Communist agitation in Eastern Europe.

The twin concepts of political co-operation and unity central to this new intergovernmental organisation provided both a backdrop for, and stimulus to, the development of supranational bodies, such as the European Union,[7] and other international organisations, such as the Organisation for Security and Co-operation in Europe (OSCE).[8] Both of these, to a greater or lesser extent, have subsequently taken an interest in the promotion of human rights. Neither has succeeded, however, in matching either the scale of operation of the Convention, or its impact on the administrative practices and legal systems of the high Contracting Parties.

The reason for this lies in the fact that the Council of Europe laid down a political and philosophical framework for the adoption of instruments, thereby entrenching human rights protection within the European psyche. The European Convention for the Protection of Human Rights and Fundamental Freedoms (ECHR),[9] and the European Social Charter (ESC),[10] were the results of that endeavour. The European Social Charter effectively complements the protection afforded by the Convention, but falls outside the

---

4 Statute of Europe, Art 1a.

5 Originally comprising 10 States, the Council now has 40 members.

6 Statute of Europe, Art 3.

7 The EU has evolved a system of human rights protection through the endeavours of its institutions, primarily the ECJ, based on the constitutional traditions common to Member States and international treaties such as the ECHR. See Case C4/73, *Nold v Commission* [1974] ECR 491. Moves toward accession to the Convention have been halted by an advisory opinion of the ECJ, Opinion 2/94, in which the Court said that, at present, the EEC Treaty does not provide the necessary power to do so. See Centre for European Legal Studies, 'The Human Rights Opinion of the ECJ and its constitutional implications' in *CELS Occasional Paper No 1*, 1996, Cambridge: CELSCU; Toth, AG, 'The European Union and human rights: the way forward' [1997] 34 CMLR 491.

8 The OSCE is a trans-European institution whose membership comprises, *inter alia*, all the European States, and which was set up with the primary purpose of monitoring conflict within and between European States. It operates solely at a diplomatic level and its primary instrument, the Helsinki Accord, is non-binding. There is some overlap between its work and that of the Convention organs. See Schlager, EB, 'The procedural framework of the CSCE: from the Helsinki consultation to the Paris Charter; 1972–90' (1991) 12(1) HRLJ 22.

9 In force 3 September 1953.

10 In force 26 February 1965, the scope of which lies outside the ambit of this discussion.

scope of the present discussion as it advocates respect for basic social, cultural and economic rights.

The protection accorded human rights within the system set up by the Convention has been described as 'the best known and most effective'[11] in the world, providing a template for the construction of subsequent instruments. It also represents the first time that a human rights code, developed at international level, was backed up by a fully sanctioned enforcement system. At the time of writing, it has been ratified by all 40 States of the Council of Europe, Russia being the last State to do so, the Convention entering into force there on 5 May 1998.[12]

The list of rights and freedoms protected by the Convention, and set out in Arts 2 and 12, are principally of a civil and political nature, reflecting the humanitarian concerns of the Contracting States after the Second World War. These include, for example, the right to life,[13] freedom from torture, inhuman or degrading treatment,[14] the right to a fair trial,[15] privacy[16] and freedom of expression.[17] This list has been added to as the years have progressed via additional Protocols 1, 4, 6 and 7,[18] illustrating a common acceptance by Contracting Parties that the Convention is, in the words of the Court, 'a living instrument',[19] capable of responding to evolving societal needs.

However, the Convention did more than simply set out a list of rights and freedoms to which the high Contracting Parties could pay lip service. In an unprecedented move, it also stipulated the mechanisms whereby these basic standards could be properly enforced. In keeping with the Council's aim of ensuring 'observance of the engagements undertaken by the high Contracting Parties', the Convention itself initially provided for the creation of two institutions charged with just such a task, namely, the Commission and Court of Human Rights.[20] In addition, the Council reserved to its own Committee of

---

11 Dankwa, EVO, 'Conference on regional protection systems of human rights protection in Africa, the Americas and Europe' (1992) 13(7–8) HRLJ 314.

12 White, RCA, 'State of ratification of human rights instruments' (1998) 23 EL Rev Checklist No 1 HR, p 91.

13 *Ibid*, Art 2.

14 *Ibid*, Art 3.

15 *Ibid*, Art 6.

16 *Ibid*, Art 8.

17 *Ibid*, Art 10.

18 Which deal respectively with such diverse matters as educational and property rights, freedom from imprisonment for certain types of offences, the abolition of the death penalty and referral of individual complaints to the Court.

19 Extract from the judgment in *Tyrer v UK*, Judgment of 25 April 1978, Series A.31 Vol 26.

20 See ECHR, Art 19, pre-amendment.

Ministers a residual judicial power to deal with cases which were not brought before the Court[21] and to supervise the execution of judgments.[22]

Two aspects of Convention protection, namely, limitations on the rights secured and provision for their enforcement, warrant further scrutiny.

RIGHTS, FREEDOMS AND THEIR LIMITATIONS

Inherently, the Convention is subject to a number of limitations. The only rights protected are those set out in the main text of the Convention itself and in the supplementary protocols. In addition, official recognition of the right of individuals to petition the Commission[23] was initially made optional for States. Theoretically, if an individual had previously complained of a violation by a State which had not formally recognised the jurisdiction of this institution, that individual was effectively bereft of a remedy. In practice, however, all high Contracting Parties accepted the jurisdiction of Commission and Court. Now, all Contracting States are compelled to accept the 'new' Court's jurisdiction,[24] (see below),[25] thus removing a potential deterrent to individuals wishing to complain of violation.

The exercise of convention rights is also subject to qualifications of both a temporal and territorial nature. Violations predating State ratification of the Convention, or the coming into operation of the protocols, cannot form the subject matter of an action.[26] Another restriction is that it only applies in those territories to which a contracting party has specifically extended Convention protection.[27] There are a number of miscellaneous rules in relation to the admissibility of applications under Art 35, relating *inter alia* to the prior exhaustion of domestic remedies, time limits for initiating actions, anonymous actions and matters which have been dealt with before.[28]

As stated earlier,[29] the main rights and freedoms secured appear in Arts 2–12, but additional rights are entrenched in Arts 13 and 14. The former states that Contracting Parties have an obligation to provide a remedy for

---

21 ECHR, Art 32(1), pre-amendment.
22 *Ibid*, Art 54, pre-amendment.
23 The Commission dealt with individual complaints under ECHR, Art 25, pre-amendment.
24 *Ibid*, Art 32. See, also, ECHR, Art 46(1): 'The high Contracting Parties undertake to abide by the final judgment of the Court in any case where they are parties.'
25 At p 49.
26 See *ibid*, Art 59(3). A similar provision appears within the text of each protocol.
27 *Ibid*, Art 56(1).
28 See *ibid*, Art 35, paras 1–3.
29 See p 37.

Convention breach at national level, failing which they themselves are in breach of the Convention.[30] Article 14 stipulates that the rights outlined must be secured without discrimination, although it fails to secure for individuals an independent right not to be discriminated against.[31]

Of all the rights protected, only Art 3, which prohibits torture, inhuman or degrading treatment, contains an absolute guarantee. Indeed, Arts 8–11, which protect, *inter alia*, privacy and freedom of expression, contain express limitations permitting State interference where the interests of democracy deem it necessary on common grounds, such as: 'national security,'[32] 'public safety ... the protection of health or morals ... or the rights of others.'[33] Elsewhere, as, for example, under Art 6, which deals with a person's right to liberty and security, restrictions are implied by the narrow phrasing of the Convention text, which precludes specified types of State interference from scrutiny by the Convention organs.[34] Derogation is also explicitly permitted elsewhere, under Art 15 of the Treaty, 'in time of war or other public emergency'.[35]

These limitations aside, the substantive rights contained in the Convention are not subject to other lawful qualification. Indeed, the Convention has been amended by protocol on a number of occasions, both to expand the protection extended and to improve the efficiency of the enforcement system. The Convention organs have also shown themselves willing to interpret the text 'in the light of present day conditions',[36] as opposed to viewing them simply as fixed historical documents.

ENFORCEMENT

As of 1 November 1998, under Protocol 11, the new Court of Human Rights took over the function of enforcement, previously discharged on a joint basis

---

30 See Jacobs, FG and White, RCA, *The European Convention on Human Rights*, 1996, Oxford: Clarendon, pp 335–39.

31 The need for an effective anti-discrimination provision within the text of the Convention has frequently been criticised. See Partsch, KJ, 'Discrimination', in MacDonald, RStJ (ed), *The European System for the Protection of Human Rights*, 1993, Dordrecht: Martinus Nijhoff, p 571.

32 ECHR, Arts 8, 10 and 11.

33 *Ibid*, Arts 8, 9, 10 and 11.

34 Cases in point being '(a) the lawful detention of a person after conviction by a competent court' and '(e) the lawful detention of persons for the prevention of the spreading of infectious diseases of persons of unsound mind, alcoholics or drug addicts or vagrants'.

35 Except ECHR, Arts 3 and 7. Article 3 prohibits torture, inhuman or degrading treatment. Article 7 proscribes punishment without law.

36 See *Tyrer v UK*, Judgment of 25 April 1978, Series A.31 Vol 26.

by the Commission and Court,[37] as assisted by the Committee of Ministers.[38] As this marks a radical change in the supervisory mechanisms which have been in place for four decades, the present inquiry scrutinises the reasons predicating change, the reformed procedure for bringing a complaint and the consequences thereof for the Convention as a whole.

REASONS FOR CHANGE

Protocol 11 is designed to make the Convention's system of enforcement more efficient. It represents the first major change to the fabric of a procedure widely deemed to be 'obsolete' since the Convention's inception.[39] The adoption of the new system at this point was necessitated by a number of factors, the most significant of which are as follows:

(a) the unremitting upsurge in the number of applications made,[40] due not only to the number of High Contracting Parties, but also to the growth in public perception of the Convention.[41] This situation, it was believed, could lead to the institutions being 'overwhelmed by their own success'[42] and unable to 'cope with the need for rapid changes';[43]

(b) the increasing sophistication of the applications made;[44]

(c) the ongoing absorption of the former Communist countries of Central and Eastern Europe into the Council of Europe.

Other factors taken into account in reaching the conclusion that some form of structural re-adjustment was required, include the fact that, under the pre-existing system, neither the Court nor the Commission sat on a full time basis. Applications were processed at a seemingly snail like pace, a fact which is in

---

37 Under ECHR, Art 19, pre-amendment.

38 Especially under ECHR, Arts 32 and 54, pre-amendment, which outlined its judicial and supervisory roles.

39 Schermers, H, 'The Eleventh Protocol to the ECHR' (1994) 19 EL Rev 369.

40 Eg, the number of provisional files opened in 1997 was 12,469 as compared with 12,143 in 1996, and 10,201 in 1995. Source: Council of Europe, Survey of Activities and Statistics, 1995–97, quoted in White, RCA, 'State of ratifications of human rights instruments' (1998) 23 EL Rev; Checklist No 1, HR/89, HR/102, p 102.

41 See Mowbray, A, 'Procedural developments and the ECHR' [1991] PL 353, p 354.

42 Warbrick, C, 'Rights, the ECHR and English law' (1994) 19 EL Rev 34, p 34.

43 Schermers, H, 'Factual merger of the European Court and the Court of Human Rights' (1986) 11 EL Rev 350, p 351.

44 See Drzemczewski, A and Meyer-Ledwig, J, 'Principal characteristics of the new ECHR control mechanism, as established by Protocol 11, signed 11 May 1994' (1994) 15(3) HRLJ 81, p 83.

part explicable by reference to the quantity of applications and the relatively low numbers of staff available to deal with them.[45]

'The need for radical overhaul',[46] pinpointed as far back as the late 1980s, was acted upon in May 1993, when the Committee of Ministers agreed that a new protocol be drafted with a view to replacing the then two-tiered structure with a new, streamlined Court, operating out of Strasbourg on a permanent basis. Both the Commission and Court agreed that the need for reform was pressing.

Two thirds of the Commission endorsed the institution of a bipartite judicial system, with a new Court of First Instance replacing the Commission and the existing Court being transformed into a Court of Appeal.[47] The Court, however, was somewhat divided as to the nature of the planned restructuring: a number of judges advocated maintenance of the status quo, with some upgrading of existing arrangements, while others favoured the adoption of the single court system, initially suggested by several of the Contracting States.[48]

In the event, the granting of the judicial mandate to a single court commanded most support, the deciding factor being that 'a single court would encourage greater unity between Member States'.[49] Protocol 11 was prepared on that basis. Signed on 11 May 1994, it did not come into force until 1 November 1998, although it had been anticipated that it would have come in earlier, given the general consensus as to the validity and urgency of the reforms.[50] However, objections to these modifications had been raised in many quarters on jurisprudential,[51] practical, financial and even humanitarian grounds.[52] As will become apparent below, Protocol 11 has effected substantive procedural changes in relation to the processing of complaints, as well as radically modifying the Convention's institutional structure.

---

45 See Rowe, N and Schlette, V, 'The protection of human rights in Europe after Protocol 11 to the ECHR' (1998) 23 EL Rev; Checklist No 1, HR/3, HR/8.

46 Drzemczewski, A, 'The need for radical overhaul' (1993) 143 NLJ 126.

47 See Mowbray, AR, 'The reform of the control system of the ECHR' [1993] PL 419, p 426; and 'The reform of the judicial control mechanism of the ECHR, Opinion of the Commission' (1993) 14(1–2) HRLJ 47.

48 Opinion of the European Court of Human Rights, p 48, paras II–IV.

49 *Ibid*, para 15.

50 See, eg, Drzemczewski, A, who anticipated that it would have been operational from the end of 1996: 'Principal characteristics of the new ECHR control mechanism, as established by Protocol 11, signed May 1994' (1994) 15(3) HRLJ 81, pp 81–86.

51 Eg, Schermers, H, has noted that 'The rule that two members of the first instance chamber (its president and the national member) shall sit again in appeal is difficult to accept ... the Court ... has held that a State infringes ECHR, Art 6, if a national court of appeal contains judges who also sat in first instance.' See *op cit*, Schermers, fn 39, p 374.

52 *Ibid*, pp 377–79.

BRINGING A COMPLAINT

Two types of application may be brought under the Convention, interstate and individual.

With the interstate complaint, under Art 33 of the Convention as amended, a high contracting party to the Convention has *locus standi* to seise the Court where 'an alleged breach of the provisions of the Convention and the protocols thereto by another high contracting party ...' has occurred. A State may invoke this procedure on its own behalf, or on behalf of an aggrieved national.

In accordance with convention under international law, each Contracting State is viewed as both the lawful subject of the Convention and, by implication, its principal guardian. However, in common with enforcement provisions in European Community law,[53] this method of complaint is rarely used, resolution of disputes between States being dealt with largely through diplomatic channels.[54] The procedure has survived recent reforms, despite the fact that its utility has been called into question in the past, on account of a noted tendency, particularly of the Committee of Ministers, to 'allow for exceptions on grounds of political expediency'.[55]

Individual complaint was originally provided for in the Convention under Art 25 (now Art 34), which enabled any 'person, non-governmental organisation or group of individuals' with requisite 'victim' status,[56] to bring a complaint of violation before the Commission, provided that the offending State had formally recognised its competence. The procedure was originally optional, due to the failure of the majority of States to agree otherwise. This was largely because of the Article's relative newness in international law at that time.[57] As has been noted, 'the original purpose of the Convention was not primarily to offer a remedy for particular individuals ... but to provide a collective interstate guarantee that would benefit individuals generally by

---

53   This provision enables one Member State to initiate enforcement proceedings against another for failure 'to fulfil an obligation' under the treaty. To date, only one case has been settled by the Court on this basis: Case 141/78, *France v UK* [1979] ECR 2923. For further information on this procedure, see Weatherill, S and Beaumont, P, *EC Law*, 2nd edn, 1995, London: Penguin, p 208.

54   The procedure has only been invoked on 20 occasions up to 31 December 1997, only one case, *Ireland v UK* being dealt with by the Court. Source: ECHR website, http://194.250.50.201(02.06.98)

55   Tomuschat, C, '"*Quo vadis argentoratum?*", the success story of the ECHR – and a few dark stains' (1992) 13(11–12) HRLJ 402.

56   For further discussion of this concept in the context of the ECHR, see Rogge, K, 'The victim requirement in Art 25 of the ECHR', in Matscher, F and Petzold, H (eds), 1988, *Protecting Human Rights: The European Dimension. Studies in Honour of Gerard J Wiarda*, Cologne: Carl Heymanns, pp 539 *et seq*.

57   See Robertson, AH and Merrills, JG, *Human Rights in the World*, 3rd edn, 1989, Manchester: Manchester UP, p 109, fn 52.

requiring the national law of the Contracting Parties to be kept within certain bounds.'[58]

The right of the individual to petition the 'new' Court has now been secured in the amended Convention under Art 34. This therefore rids the system of the anomaly whereby States, but not individuals, had an automatic right to circumvent the Commission and go directly to the Court. An individual, on the other hand, could only seise the Court via the procedures provided by Protocol 9.[59]

Although the protocol met with the approval of both the Commission and the Court,[60] the individual's application was still subject to in-depth scrutiny by the latter. The Court had two alternatives under this system – to refuse such requests, or simply to refer the matter on to the Committee of Ministers – if it did not 'raise a serious question' concerning the application or interpretation of the Convention, or other matters meriting deliberation by the Court.[61]

As Protocol 9 is a relatively new procedure, most individual complaints have been dealt with by the Commission,[62] providing it with the bulk of its work to date.[63]

PROCESSING THE COMPLAINT

There are many similarities between the procedure for bringing a complaint under Art 33 or 34. As the procedure under Art 34 is the one most frequently used, a simplified version of the newly modified procedure, appears below.

Making a formal application

Applications are now lodged with the new Court Registry instead of the Secretariat to the Commission, which formerly dealt with the initial stages of the application process.

---

58 Harris, DJ, O'Boyle, M and Warbrick, C, *Law of the European Convention on Human Rights*, 1995, London: Butterworths, p 33.
59 Which came into operation on 1 October 1994.
60 *Op cit*, Mowbray, fn 41, p 357.
61 ECHR, Art 5(2), sub-para 2.
62 Commission website http://www.dhcomm.hr.coe.fr.
63 A total of 39,047 individual applications had been received by the Commission up to 31 December 1997. Of these, 4,161 have been declared admissible and 903 were referred to the Court of Human Rights. Source: ECHR website http://194.250.50.201(02.06.98).

Preliminaries: legal aid/assignment to a chamber

The issue of legal aid continues to be dealt with in the usual way, once the application has been sanctioned. Once accepted, the case will be assigned to a chamber or, more usually, to a committee, of three judges,[64] a *rapporteur* appointed from among their number and the issue of admissibility considered.

Admissibility

The committee of three judges[65] can unanimously and finally declare an application inadmissible.[66] As such, the committee acts as a filter system, fulfilling the role previously assigned in the first instance to three Commissioners.[67] If not declared unanimously inadmissible, it will be referred to the Chamber seised of the application,[68] which will rule on the question of admissibility by majority vote and, later, on the substance of the case. Occasionally, both issues may be dealt with jointly.

Communication

If not inadmissible, the complaint will be communicated to the respondent government as before and the Court will begin to examine the case,[69] 'placing itself at the disposal of the parties concerned with a view to securing a friendly settlement'[70] of the dispute. The procedure involved in settling a complaint retains its conciliatory nature, unless the matter cannot be resolved through negotiation. If this happens, there may be a hearing on the merits of the case once the admissiblity issue has been decided, following which, the Court gives judgment by majority vote.

Judgment

Previously, at the end of the negotiation period, a report would be drawn up for publication, if negotiations had been successful.[71] If not, a confidential report to that effect would be sent to the Committee of Ministers,[72] the

---

64   ECHR, Art 27(1).
65   *Ibid*, Art 28.
66   *Ibid*.
67   *Ibid*, Art 20(3), pre-amendment.
68   *Ibid*, Art 29.
69   *Ibid*, Art 38(1)(a)
70   *Ibid*, Art 38(1)(b). Thus far, 369 friendly settlements have been achieved out of the 4,161 applications declared admissible by the Commission (up to 31 December 1997). Source: ECHR website http://194.250.50.201(02.06.98).
71   *Ibid*, Art 28(2), pre-amendment.
72   *Ibid*, Art 31, pre-amendment.

respondent government and the individual applicant (where Protocol 9 applied). This report would have included the established facts of the case, together with the Commission's opinion on the merits. The Commission and government concerned would have the case referred automatically to the Court.[73] However, in the case of individual applications, referral would have to be made to the Court within three months,[74] and a panel of three judges would then determine whether the case was appropriate for the Court's consideration.[75]

Where the new procedure does differ substantially, is that, when judgment is delivered now, State or individual parties may ask for the case to be referred to the Grand Chamber, but only where it 'raises a serious question concerning the interpretation or application of the Convention or its protocols, or if it raises an issue of general importance'.[76] Under the old system, the Chamber was only competent to deal with a case where it didn't raise such issues. The new provision not only mirrors the power of relinquishment formerly enjoyed by the chamber of nine judges under Rule 51 of the Rules of Court,[77] but expands upon it, upgrading the position of the individual applicant within the Court system. Nonetheless, as was the case under Rule 51, and having regard to the very specific wording of the provision,[78] this will probably be a rare occurrence. Where the chamber decides not to make a referral, its judgment shall be given by majority vote and will only become final and binding when this issue has been dealt with definitively.[79]

Under Art 46 of the modified Convention, all high Contracting Parties must 'undertake to abide by the final judgment of the Court in any case where they are parties', which is in line with the powers of the old Court under Art 53. Thus, acceptance of the Court's jurisdiction is now compulsory for all States which have ratified the Convention.[80] These new provisions serve to enhance the position of the individual applicant within the judicial process quite significantly, effectively removing many of the old distinctions between individual and State parties concerning *locus standi*.

The new Court has retained its power to 'afford just satisfaction to the injured party',[81] when a complaint is upheld, continuing to make the process attractive to prospective applicants.

---

73 ECHR, Art 48, pre-amendment, and Protocol 9, Art 3.

74 *Ibid*, Art 47.

75 If the panel was unanimous, the matter would be left to the Committee of Ministers to dispose of, otherwise the case would ordinarily be decided by a chamber of nine judges, including the president and vice president as well as the judge from the respondent State: see Art 43 of the Convention pre-amendment.

76 See ECHR, Art 43(2). The request is initially examined by a panel of five judges.

77 Rules of the ECHR, 1 February 1994 (revised) Rules of Court B.

78 For further comment, see *op cit*, Drzemczewski, fn 46, p 85; Harris, O'Boyle and Warbrick, fn 58, p 662.

79 See ECHR, Art 44(2).

80 In practice, this will make little difference to pre-existing high Contracting Parties, all of whom had accepted the Court's jurisdiction in this matter.

81 See ECHR, Art 41.

Enforcement

The only function still retained by the Committee of Ministers under the new system pertains to its supervisory role, as it loses its ability to decide cases with which the Court has not been seised,[82] its role in this capacity being reduced to ensure that States comply with Court judgments, but not eradicated entirely, as it has always played an important role in this process.[83] It can also seek advisory opinions on questions regarding interpretation of provisions of the Convention or its supplementary protocols.[84]

CONSEQUENCES OF TRANSFORMATION

In the recent shake-up, the Commission suffered the most radical cut of all. It will cease to exist upon the conclusion of the transitional arrangements for the commencement of business by the single Court.[85] As discussed above, the Committee of Ministers has also experienced a considerable diminution of its role in enforcement proceedings, which should satisfy critics who have denounced the overtly political character of this establishment.[86] Conversely, the profile and output of the new Court should now increase significantly, as a direct result of acquiring full time status.[87] The implications of these changes are considered below.

The Commission

Many have mourned the passing of the Commission as a classic example of an efficient institution deriving maximum output from minimum resources.[88] The primary function of the Commission was to work in tandem with the original Court 'to ensure the observation of engagements',[89] a role it discharged from a pivotal position in the admissibility process, most notably through vetting individual complaints and, in its attempts by conciliation, to effect a friendly settlement.[90]

Composed of one suitably qualified representative per contracting State,[91] acting independently of his or her State of origin, the Commission's principal

---

82 Which it formerly exercised under ECHR, Art 32, pre-amendment.

83 *Ibid*, Art 46(2).

84 *Ibid*, Art 47.

85 See Protocol 11, Art 5.

86 *Op cit*, Schermers, fn 39, p 368.

87 See *op cit*, Harris, O'Boyle and Warbrick, fn 58, pp 711–12.

88 Schermers, H, 'Has the ECHR got bogged down?' (1988) 9(2) HRLJ 175, p 176 and *op cit*, Schermers, fn 39, p 372.

89 ECHR, Art 19, pre-amendment.

90 *Ibid*, Art 28, pre-amendment.

task was to examine 'petitions submitted under Art 25 according to specific admissibility criteria ...'.[92] Although once condemned for the political flavour of its initial membership, it was later conceded that the Commission eventually developed into a 'purely legal organ',[93] its main achievements being the evolution of a formidable corpus of decisions on admissibility, and its moderately successful attempts to overcome its limitations in the administrative field.

It has also been noted that the Commission's determinations became more liberal during the course of its history and that it 'developed its role as a fact finder ... [and] in its decisions on admissibility ... [became] noticeably more willing to refer cases to the Court'.[94] Where a case was declared admissible, the Court accepted the facts of the case as determined by the Commission. In 1990, 151 applications were declared admissible compared with 624 in 1996 and 703 in 1997,[95] the principal grounds for refusal are that a complaint is manifestly ill founded or breaches essentially procedural rules, such as non-exhaustion of domestic remedies and the rule on bringing a complaint within six months of the final decision on the matter in the home State.[96] Whereas the Commission has been criticised for its overuse of exclusion on the basis of a complaint being manifestly ill founded, it has nevertheless shown foresight in dealing with other applications. For example, it has been responsible, *inter alia*, for admitting applications which, it had been alleged, fell outside the parameters of Convention competence *ratione personae*. In *Open Door and Well Woman v Ireland*,[97] the Commission accepted the litigants' contention that they satisfied the 'victim' requirement specified in relation to individual applicants, being members of a class of child bearing women directly affected by an injunction, issued by the Irish Supreme Court, banning, in Ireland, provision of information on the availability of foreign abortion. Similar decisions in which the Commission has advocated a wide interpretation of the term 'victim', are to be found in a series of applications involving Art 8 of the Convention, the 'privacy' provision, despite the fact that the legislation complained of did not, at the time of complaint, directly affect them. The fact that it could do so in the future, was considered sufficient.[98]

---

91 The original Convention, Art 21, stipulated the procedures for, and conditions of, appointment.

92 See ECHR, Arts 25–27 pre-amendment. Now, these criteria are found under Art 35.

93 *Op cit*, Schermers, fn 39, p 368.

94 *Op cit*, Jacobs and White, fn 30, p 407.

95 For a thorough analysis of the Commission's decisions with regard to both the admissibility and merits of a given application, see *op cit*, Harris, O'Boyle and Warbrick, fn 58, Chap 23.

96 ECHR, Art 35(1).

97 (1992) Series A.246, para 41.

98 Particularly see *Norris and Gay Federation of Ireland v Ireland* (Appl 10581/83), 16 May 1984; (1984) 44 D & R 132; *Dudgeon v UK*, Judgment of 22 October 1981, Series A.45; (1982) 14 EHRR 149, para 41, both of which deal with challenges to legislation proscribing male homosexual conduct. Reference provided is for the Court judgment only.

The Commission's opinions on the merits of cases dealing with other aspects of privacy have also been influential. It has advocated the extension of rights to minority groupings, such as homosexuals[99] and transsexuals[100] among others, some of which have subsequently been taken on board by the Court. Here, as elsewhere, it has consistently shown itself to be more willing to countenance change than the Court.

However, some would argue that it did not go quite far enough on other occasions, declaring itself hemmed in by concepts such as the margin of appreciation accorded to Member States in interpreting the Convention, which had inevitably caused some of its opinions to take on a more cautious tone.[101]

On the administrative side, widespread recognition has been given to the Commission's organisational skills in dealing with a heavy workload efficiently.[102] Some 12,469 complaints were received by the Commission up to 31 December 1997. While these statistics exemplify the increased efficiency of the Commission, they are also partly explicable by the fact that, during the last couple of years of its existence, applications had increased by 25%.[103] Approximately 9–10% of complaints were declared admissible by the Commission since its inception in 1954, these statistics indicating the full extent of the administrative burden borne by this institution.[104]

---

99 In both *Norris* and *Dudgeon* (cited in fn 98, above), the applicants were successful before the Court, which, by majority, confirmed that, because a person's sexuality is part of private life, as protected by Art 8, any interference can only be justified by reference to the inbuilt limitations of that provision as outlined at Art 8(2). However, as indicated by recent developments in cases such as *Laskey, Jaggard and Brown v UK* (1997) 24 EHRR 39, the margin of appreciation accorded to States by the Court and Commission in this area, in determining the level of State interference permissible in individual sexual activities, is extremely wide. See Moran, LJ, '*Laskey v UK*: learning the limits of privacy' (1998) 61 MLR 77.

100 Eg, in *Van Oosterwijck v Belgium*, Judgment of 6 November 1980, Series A.40; (1981) 9 EHRR 557; and *Rees v UK*, Judgment of 17 October 1986, Series A.106; (1987) 9 EHRR 56, the Commission was sympathetic to applicants wishing to alter a birth certificate/birth register to complement their new appearance, post surgery. However, on both occasions, the Court ruled against the applicant – in the first case on procedural grounds, but in the second, more significantly, on the grounds that the State had a wide margin of appreciation in this area, given the lack of a European consensus on alteration of documentation of this type.

101 One such example is again provided by Art 8, in particular, the recent unanimous decision of the Commission in *Roezheim v Germany* (Appl 31177/96), which denied an application by a male to female transsexual, who refused to have gender re-assignment surgery, when he sought to challenge a German statute under Art 8 for failing to enable him to change his civil status to female. The reasons cited include the 'remaining uncertainty as to the essential nature of transsexualism and the extremely complex legal situations which result therefrom'.

102 Discussed at length by Schermers, *op cit*, fnn 39 and 88.

103 In 1995, 10,201 provisional files were opened by the Commission. This figure reached 12,143 in 1996 and 12,469 in 1997. Source: Council of Europe, *Survey of Activities and Statistics*, 1997, Strasbourg: Council of Europe.

104 ECHR website http://194.250.50.201(02.06.98).

Various strategies were adopted to assist the Commission through the years. Its staff numbers were increased and some internal reorganisation took place through the operation of Protocol 8. This enabled the Commission to do the bulk of its work by sub-dividing into chambers, thus disposing of greater numbers of applications than previously.[105] In addition, the Secretariat of the Council of Europe was given power to act as primary filter for applications, registering complaints and advising complainants where grievances fell outside Convention parameters.

Despite this assistance, the burgeoning numbers of applications threatened to inundate the Commission, highlighting its insupportable administrative load and the necessity of providing some form of permanent institution to deal with the ever increasing numbers of applications. This task has now befallen the members of the 'new' Court and its administrative staff.

The 'new' Court

The new permanent Court replaces the original Court, which was originally established in 1959,[106] and existed in its original form until 1998. Its composition and functions are described below.

Composition

In its previous incarnation, all Member States of the Council of Europe were allocated one judge each. However, under Art 20 of the Convention as amended, only High Contracting Parties are entitled to judicial representation, an innovation criticised on account of the potentially restrictive effect that this will have on States seeking future inclusion, in particular those Eastern European States making the transition towards democracy, at a time when they require help, not hindrance.[107] Georgian and Russian judges have not been appointed yet.[107a]

Of the 39 judges appointed, 20 have first hand experience of the old system and the rest are newcomers. Article 21 stipulates the qualifications which candidates for the judiciary should possess in order to be considered for office, namely 'high moral character' and requisite judicial/specialist academic experience. Judges are elected from lists of three nominees *per* high contracting party,[108] and will hold office for six years now[109] instead of nine as was previously the case, with provision for re-election. In all probability,

---

105 *Op cit*, Schermers, fn 39, pp 370–71.

106 It came into operation on 21 January 1959.

107 *Op cit*, Schermers, fn 39, p 376.

107aSource: ECHR website http://www.dhcour.coe.fr.

108 The first choice of nominee used to be automatically chosen, so the new process is more democratic now, thus demonstrating the gradual decline in State influence over judicial decisions. See Krüger, HC, 'Selecting judges for the new ECHR' (1996) 17(11–12) HRLJ 401, p 403.

109 ECHR, Art 23.

this change has been effected because 'continuity and irremovability from office are important features in guaranteeing the independence of judges'.[110]

As in the European Court of Justice, whose rules on appointment these new provisions mirror considerably, there is provision in the modified Convention to appoint the judiciary on a staggered basis, half of the Court standing down every three years.[111] Again, the need for fluidity and efficiency in decision making seems the likely explanation for this. Retirement of judges at 70 years of age is also automatic now, in keeping with international convention.

There is little doubt that these changes have brought about an 'institutional revolution',[112] designed to enable the new Court to cope with what is effectively a double workload, given the demise of the Commission and the removal of the Committee of Ministers from judicial duties. What then is the function of this new institution?

Function

The primary function of the new Court remains the ensuring 'of the observance of the engagements undertaken by the high Contracting Parties'.[113] It discharges this duty in two ways: it can, at the suit of the Committee of Ministers, give advisory opinions on legal issues concerning how the Convention and its protocols are to be interpreted. Alternatively, it can render judgment based under Art 42. These two functions can be looked at individually.

The Court has had power to give advisory opinions since 1970, but this has been of limited use due to the fact that it continues to be unable to:

> ... deal with any question relating to the content or scope of the rights or freedoms defined in s 1 of the Convention and the protocols thereto, or with any other question which the Court or the Committee of Ministers might have to consider in consequence of any such proceedings as could be instituted in accordance with the Convention.[114]

Given that this provision effectively denies the Court jurisdiction regarding most of the Convention, it is practically redundant and has never been used. On the other hand, the number of cases referred to the Court is fast approaching 1,000.[115] It is anticipated that the new scheme should have the effect of enabling the Court, operating under a full time mandate, to increase

---

110 *Op cit*, Krüger, fn 108.
111 ECHR, Art 23.
112 Mowbray, A, 'A new ECHR' [1994] PL 540, p 540.
113 ECHR, Art 19.
114 *Ibid*, Art 47.
115 Source: ECHR website http://194.250.50.201(02.06.98).

the volume of cases dealt with, as well as reducing the turnaround time for processing them. It is a well documented fact that under the old system it took on average of four years and eight months for a case to proceed from initial registration to judgment, thus 'there is some irony in the fact that the Commission and the Court are sometimes asked to condemn a Member State for tolerating overlengthy legal proceedings, yet they themselves allow the judicial process at Strasbourg to be so protracted'.[116]

Institutional change aside, does the evolution of newly improved enforcement mechanisms signify alteration elsewhere? Will having an expanded full time Court impact upon the quality of judgments for which the original Court was renowned? The new procedures have already been examined and evaluated above, but what of their effect on the Court itself ?

To date, the greatest accomplishment of the Court must be the level of respect for human rights it has engendered across Europe. In the UK alone, its decisions have given rise to legislative and administrative change in reaction to adverse Court judgments, in matters as diverse as the decriminalisation of homosexual activity[117] in Northern Ireland, phonetapping,[118] and limitations on State interference with prisoners' correspondence, to name but a few.[119]

All of these are linked by the fact that, in each case, a violation of one Convention provision[120] was involved. However, by simply focusing on this one provision, it is possible to see the extent to which the Court has had an influence on domestic legal systems, over the years. An illustration in point is provided by the effect of Art 8 on Irish case law, for example, in *Johnston*[121] and *Airey*,[122] which respectively gave rise to changes in the Irish law pertaining to illegitimacy, and access to legal aid schemes.

Despite effecting sea changes in the law and the attitudes of State parties, the Court has also attracted its fair share of criticism respecting its temerity in other areas. Again Art 8 and its veritable mountain of case law, proves a fertile ground for further inquiry. In its decisions on both homosexual and transsexual issues, discussed above, the Court has a noted tendency to rely on the rather flexible parameters of a State's 'margin of appreciation' in

---

116 Dickson, B (ed), *Human Rights and the European Convention: The Effects of the Convention on the UK and Ireland*, 1997, London: Sweet & Maxwell, p 213.
117 See *Dudgeon v UK*, Judgment of 22 October 1981, Series A.45; (1982) 14 EHRR 149.
118 See *Malone v UK* (1985) 7 EHRR 14.
119 *Silver v UK*, Judgment of 25 March 1983, Series A.61; (1975) 5 EHRR 347; and *Golder v UK*, Judgment of 21 February 1975, Series A.18; (1979–80) 1 EHRR 524.
120 ECHR, Art 8.
121 *Johnston v Ireland*, Judgment of 18 December 1986, Series A.112; (1987) 9 EHRR 203.
122 *Airey v Ireland*, Judgment of 9 October 1979, Series A.32; (1979–80) 2 EHRR 305.

traditionally controversial or new areas of concern. It has also been widely criticised regarding its perceived capitulation to Member States using this doctrine where provisions, such as Art 10 (freedom of expression), are concerned. Whereas the Court has generally kept a tight check on both State intervention couched in moral terms,[123] and where political speech is concerned,[124] the same cannot be said where so called national security issues are raised. The UK has discovered this to its (albeit limited) advantage in the *Spycatcher*[125] case, or where the independence of the judiciary is impugned.[126] Over reliance on the doctrine has been widely criticised as being 'an abdication by the Court of its duty of adjudication',[127] especially where contentious issues are involved. However, others have viewed it as 'the natural product of that distribution of powers between the Convention institutions and the national authorities'.[128]

Whatever the truth of the matter, the decisions of the old Court have cut a swathe through Europe. It has been praised for its 'recent and almost revolutionary assertion of judicial power'[129] over most European States and their inhabitants, through the development of an extensive body of case law, which national courts tend to emulate.[130] It is widely hoped that, as the newly invigorated judicial system finds its feet, it will carry on and improve upon the work of the original institution, having the time, commitment and increased administrative backup, to do so.

The Committee of Ministers

It is not proposed to deal with the revised powers/duties of this institution at length, its remaining supervisory role in relation to judgments having previously been examined in the context of the complaints procedure. The Committee of Ministers is still obliged to monitor compliance by States which have violated the Convention.[131] As this may necessitate modifying State law, the Court does not specify time limits for remedying violations.

---

123 See *Handyside v UK*, Judgment of 7 December 1976, Series A.24; (1979–80) 1 EHRR 737.

124 As in *Lingens v Austria*, Judgment of 8 July 1986, Series A.103; (1986) 8 EHRR 103.

125 *The Observer and The Guardian v UK*, Judgment of 26 November 1991, Series A.216; (1992) 14 EHRR 153

126 *Barfod v Denmark*, Judgment of 22 February 1989, Series A.149; (1991) 13 EHRR 493.

127 Mahoney, P, 'Judicial activism and judicial self-restraint in the ECHR: two sides of the same coin' (1990) 11(2) HRLJ 80.

128 Lester (Lord), 'The European Convention in the new architecture of Europe' [1996] PL 6.

129 Gearty, CA, 'The ECHR and the protection of civil liberties: an overview' [1993] CLJ 91.

130 *Op cit*, Drzemczewski and Meyer-Ladewig, fn 44, p 83.

131 In accordance with its supervisory powers under Art 46.

One direct consequence of this is that individuals who have been successful in establishing violation, may have to wait years before the law giving rise to the breach is finally expunged from the statute books.[132] This is out of keeping with the spirit of the Convention, as reflected in the Preamble, which states that 'fundamental freedoms ... are best maintained ... by a common understanding and observance of the human rights upon which they depend'.

Another failure of the present system, which could never be wholly rectified for purely practical reasons, is that the efficacy of any new legislation brought in by a State to comply with any finding of the Court or Committee, cannot be tested by the Convention organs other than through the consideration of further applications alleging Convention breach.[133] Both defects in the system suggest that the procedures currently in place to deal with enforcement are in need of modification, the opportunity for which was clearly presented when Protocol 11 was under discussion. Given that this problem may be exacerbated by the recent influx of Eastern European States into the Council of Europe, reform in this area would seem pressing, especially since the threat of publication and/or withdrawal or expulsion from the Council are the only other sanctions that can be employed against defaulting States.[134]

Under the old system, the Committee had the power to take final decisions in cases not referred to Court within three months of the Commission's opinion being delivered.[135] The finding of a violation was determined by a two-thirds majority, but unlike the Court, the Committee did not have the power to order compensation or impose other sanctions against a State in default. However, in practice, the Commission has recommended to the Committee of Ministers a sum of money it should award after a finding of violation, although there is no explicit Convention basis for them doing so. The only weapon in its armoury was the power to publish ongoing violations where remedial measures had not been taken.[136]

Given the width of its powers, and the fact that it provided much needed backup to the Court, why then has the role of the Committee been reduced? One reason is the widespread censure of the Committee's performance of the dual function of arbiter and enforcer, given its composition: many derided the old system for 'giving to a political body ... a function which is judicial in character'.[137] However, on a more positive note, it has been credited with

---

132 As in *Norris v Ireland*, Judgment 26 October 1988, Series A.142; (1991) 13 EHRR 163, where it took five years for the Government to amend the law to conform with the Court's decision. *Op cit*, Tomuschat, fn 55, p 406.

133 For further information, see *op cit*, Jacobs and White, fn 30, p 398.

134 See Art 8 of the Statute of the Council of Europe. Greece is the only State against which this power of expulsion has been exercised. See *op cit*, Jacobs and White, fn 30, p 398.

135 ECHR, Art 32, pre-amendment.

136 *Ibid*, Art 32(3), pre-amendment.

137 Janis, MW, Kay, RS and Bradley, AW, *European Human Rights Law*, 1995, Oxford: Clarendon, p 95.

instigating legal reform for that very reason: '... its own authority as a political institution ... makes it well suited to perform such a role'.[138]

A NEW COURT FOR A NEW AGE ?

It would appear from the changes effected by Protocol 11, that from both a procedural and institutional perspective, the amended European Convention should be able to adapt to meet the physical challenge presented by a substantially increased number of high Contracting Parties and a consequent rise in applications to the Court.

Aside from this, some doubts persist in relation to the practicalities of the new system. Time is seen to be of the essence in preparing the new Court to fulfil its mandate. Doubts have been expressed as to how quickly it will match, or even exceed, the level of efficiency achieved by the old institutions, particularly the Commission.[139] If the transition is not made smoothly, this could have global repercussions for the Convention itself, the old Court having had an internationally prestigious reputation.

Several of the new procedural provisions adopted have also been roundly criticised, most notably for the fact that, theoretically, two judges can hear a case both at first instance and on appeal to the Grand Chamber, which runs contrary to the case law of the old Court and to commonly accepted international judicial standards.[140] As has also been suggested above, the reforms precipitated by Protocol 11 do not go far enough to remove some of the difficulties that continue to bedevil the enforcement procedure.

It may be concluded that adjudging the system a success or failure from an enforcement perspective will only be possible when the Court has been operating unassisted by the Commission for some time, as such novel arrangements will inevitably experience some teething problems at their commencement.[141]

From a purely judicial position, the question may be asked as to whether the new Court will add to the corpus of rights protected by the Convention. Equally known for its 'activism' as its 'self-restraint',[142] will the newly constituted Court tread the same judicial paths as its predecessor? It has been alleged that, under the old system, the Court's approach 'proved, on occasion, to be timid and conservative'.[143] This has been amply demonstrated by its

---

138 *Op cit* Harris, O'Boyle and Warbrick, fn 58, p 705.

139 *Op cit*, Schermers, fn 39, p 379.

140 See *op cit*, Rowe and Schlette, fn 45, HR/15.

141 The estimated workload of the new Court lies in the region of 3,000–4,000 applications a year. See *op cit*, Krüger, fn 108, p 404.

142 *Op cit*, Mahoney, fn 127.

143 Beddard, R, *Human Rights and Europe*, 1993, Cambridge: Grotius, p 238.

unwillingness to widen the boundaries of substantive provisions, such as Art 8, as discussed above.

Despite this, it is accepted that the timbre of applications commonly being made is also becoming increasingly complex and sophisticated. Witness, for example, the following applications which, while not concerning Court decisions, are nonetheless indicative of the types of issues under debate in Europe today: for example, the as yet unsuccessful claims being made by Eastern Europeans, under Art 1 of Protocol 1, to land expropriated by former Communist regimes, and the limitations imposed on the UK under Art 3 by a decision proscribing the removal to his home State of a drug trafficking illegal immigrant suffering from Aids.[144]

Members of the old Court brought, in some instances, many years of experience, if not political stamina, to their decision making. However, the new judicial appointees, although eminently qualified, have no first hand experience of operating either under the old or new systems. Consequently, decision making, even with the assistance of the Commission during the transition period, may well prove to be laborious. The relative youth and inexperience of the new Court could, however, operate to an applicant's advantage by negating the suggestion that there is a real danger of some hardening of Court attitudes in certain areas, which may curtail the Convention's inherent potential for growth.[145]

In conclusion, it can be stated, with some certainty, that the challenges facing the new Court, be they administrative, procedural, judicial or political in character, are indeed manifold. As former Vice President Rolf Bernhardt has said:

> We are standing at the threshold of a new era for human rights protection in Europe. We have felt, for a long time, the pressing need to overhaul the Convention system, so that it can meet the new challenges that lie ahead ... we are determined to make the reform succeed, because quite simply, it must succeed if we want the Convention to continue to serve the purpose its authors intended, that is to secure the effective protection of those 'fundamental freedoms which are the foundation of justice and peace in the world'.[146]

---

144 Both of which instances are discussed in Farran, S, 'Facing contemporary challenges' (1997) 22 EL Rev 18, HRC 17–31, pp 18 and 27.

145 *Ibid.* Farran analyses the attitude of the Strasbourg organs to the broadening spectrum of challenges to the parameters of substantive provisions such as Arts 3, 8, 9 and 10.

146 Excerpt from a speech delivered 29 January 1998 by Mr Rudolf Bernhardt, Vice President of the Court, on the first session of the year. See ECHR website http://www.dhcour.coe.fr/speeches.htm.

THEME TWO

NEW DILEMMAS

CHAPTER 4

THE HORIZONTAL APPLICATION
OF HUMAN RIGHTS LAW

Brice Dickson

INTRODUCTION

Up to now, the paradigm human rights dispute has involved, on the one hand, an individual (or an organisation), and on the other, a State. The nature of the complaint has typically taken one of two forms. First, an individual might be complaining that the State has *directly* violated his or her rights, because an agent of the State has personally done something illegal; a police officer, for example, might have deprived the individual of his or her liberty without proper justification, or a registrar of births might have refused to issue the individual with an altered birth certificate after the individual has had a sex change operation. When this type of direct complaint is dealt with by a court, the process can be described as the *vertical* application of human rights law, represented as such in Figure 1 below. For present purposes, it does not matter whether the court in question is a national court or an international court – the nature of the dispute remains the same whatever the forum.

Alternatively, an individual might be complaining that the State has *indirectly* violated his or her rights, because someone other than an agent of the State has, for example, invaded the individual's privacy or refused to offer the individual a job on account of his or her homosexuality. The complaint in such cases is not that the non-State agent has committed an illegal act, but that the State has not got a law in place which makes the act illegal or provides a remedy to anyone suffering as a result of it. When this type of complaint is dealt with by a court, the process can best be described as the *diagonal* application of human rights law, also illustrated in Figure 1. Again it does not matter whether the forum is national or international.

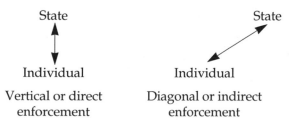

State   State

Individual   Individual

Vertical or direct   Diagonal or indirect
enforcement   enforcement

Figure 1: Conventional types of human rights disputes

What this chapter wishes to argue is that there should be a third variety of the paradigmatic human rights claim.[1] Rather than insisting that one of the parties to a human rights dispute must always be a State, human rights law should be allowed to play a part even in disputes where no State is involved, directly or indirectly. The disputants might both, or all, be individuals or organisations. In such cases the court process could be described as the *horizontal* application of human rights law, as represented in Figure 2 below.[2]

Individual ◄──────────► Individual

Figure 2: Proposed further type of human rights dispute

HOW THE NEW APPROACH WOULD WORK IN PRACTICE

What is being called for here is the infiltration of human rights norms into the private and public law of national States. Because human rights law is, generally speaking, about protecting victims, not about punishing offenders, it is more appropriate for this infiltration to take place at the level of civil rather than criminal law. (Whether a form of behaviour should be dealt with as being contrary to the criminal law is, to a great extent, a matter for the public policy of each State, and as yet international law dictates the content of that policy only rarely).[3] Civil law – more particularly, the law of obligations (referred to as tort, contract and trust law in common law countries) – should be based, first and foremost, on the principle that each individual in society has certain basic rights; these should be enforceable against all comers,

---

1   For an excellent development of the same line of thinking, see Clapham, A, *Human Rights in the Private Sphere*, 1993, Oxford: Clarendon, and his 'The privatisation of human rights' [1996] 1 EHRLR 20. For a more nuanced approach, see Hunt, M, 'The "horizontal" effect of the Human Rights Act' [1998] PL 433.

2   In some books, the effect of human rights norms on third parties (ie, not the State or the victim) is known by the German expression *Drittwirkung*. For an account of this concept in domestic German law, see Lewan, KM, 'The significance of constitutional rights for private law: theory and practice in West Germany' (1968) 17 ICLQ 571. In fact, the expression embraces both the diagonal and the horizontal application of human rights law. For an account of *Drittwirkung* and the ECHR, see van Dijk, P and van Hoof, GJH, *Theory and Practice of the European Convention on Human Rights*, 2nd edn, 1990, Deventer, Netherlands: Kluwer, pp 15–20; an excellent comparative account is provided in Forde, M, 'Non-governmental interferences with human rights' (1985) 66 BYIL 253.

3   See, eg, the Convention on the Prevention and Punishment of the Crime of Genocide 1948 and the Convention for the Suppression of the Traffic in Persons and of the Exploitation of the Prostitution of Others 1949. For a rare instance of where the European Court of Human Rights held that the most appropriate way in which to protect the right to a private life, under Art 8 of the European Convention, was by charging the infringer with a criminal offence: see *X and Y v Netherlands* (1986) 8 EHRR 235.

whether State agencies, private entities or individuals. In so far as the civil law of a country does not protect those rights, the judges should be empowered to fill the gaps by drawing on other parts of national law, or international law, and applying it to the facts of the case. If, for instance, a company makes it a condition of employment in its workforce that employees must not write articles for newspapers or give interviews to journalists, the State court could draw upon one or more of the human rights documents guaranteeing freedom of expression and hold that the company has violated a basic human right of people applying to, or already members of, the workforce. If, likewise, a person takes away another's right to vote in an election by impersonating that person at a polling booth, the former should have a means of vindicating his or her human right to vote.[4]

This is not to say, of course, that the whole of a country's law of obligations should be recategorised as part of human rights law. There are interests protected by tort and contract law which are not fundamental enough to be designated as human rights (a claim for lost profit springs to mind), although these are few and far between if the right to undisturbed enjoyment of property is included in the list of human rights, as it was in the French Declaration of 1789 and in Art 1 of Protocol 1 to the European Convention. In situations where a basic right has been breached (that is, a right which people can claim because they are human beings, not because they have earned or bought it), and where the existing national law of obligations fails to recognise this, judges should step in to plug the gap. Human rights law should thus form a kind of safety net, catching those claims which fall from the high wire on which the law of obligations otherwise operates. Rather than try to distort these new claims by artificially squeezing them into existing categories, as has happened in English law, with the new tort of harassment being portrayed as a species of nuisance,[5] they should be given an independent existence as free-standing 'constitutional' torts. This was recognised as a possibility when the House of Lords Select Committee looked at whether there should be a Bill of Rights in the UK as far back as 1978.[6]

Judges in common law countries, where there is considerable freedom for the judiciary to make law, should have little difficulty with this proposal. As Hunt has recently written: 'the weight of authority and opinion seems to

---

4   As conferred, eg, by Art 25(b) of the International Covenant on Civil and Political Rights 1966. In fact, English law does seem to recognise such a right: *Ashby v White* (1703) 2 Ld Raym 938. For a more general discussion of the extent to which the right to vote is protected in English law, see Klug, F, Starmer, K and Weir, S, *The Three Pillars of Liberty: Political Rights and Freedoms in the United Kingdom*, 1996, London: Democratic Audit/Routledge, Chap 14.

5   *Khorasandjian v Bush* [1993] QB 727 (CA).

6   HL Paper 176 (June 1978, para 4), p 37, cited in Zander, M, *A Bill of Rights?*, 4th edn, 1997, London: Sweet & Maxwell.

favour the view that rules of customary international law are automatically part of the common law, albeit that they are overridden by inconsistent statutes'.[7] Hunt even resurrects the formerly discredited thesis of Andrew Drzemczewski that some of the rights in the European Convention are automatically part of the common law by virtue of their status as customary international law.[8] To make the proposal attractive to judges in other countries, where judicial law making is, in theory at least, not acceptable,[9] an international convention should be agreed whereby States acknowledge the right of judges to use international standards on human rights in this way. By doing so, of course, they would be turning international human rights law, or an agreed part of it, into *ius cogens*. This would extend what is already a trend in relation to specific human rights standards, including anti-discrimination norms.

Once the national court has held that a private body or individual has violated a person's basic human right, it must then decide what remedy to provide for the victim. Here too, the requirement under international law that any such remedy must be effective should be adhered to.[10] This does not necessarily mean that compensation has to be paid: the courts may simply want to declare that a person or organisation has breached the human rights of another and demand an undertaking that no further breach will occur. But, if the national law is to be internally consistent, it should treat the victims of such human rights violations no less generously, from the remedial point of view, than it treats victims of other comparable breaches of the law of obligations. To ensure that the ruling is not merely a one-off occurrence (which should not be the case if the country adheres to the doctrine of binding precedent), an international convention should require future disputes of a comparable nature in that country to be dealt with in the same way. In this manner, the undertaking given by the respondent in one case can be generalised to bind other potential respondents as well.

THE SUPPORTING ARGUMENTS

Three main arguments can be used to support the horizontal application of human rights standards in national legal systems. The first, and most weighty,

---

7   Hunt, M, *Using Human Rights Law in English Courts*, 1997, Oxford: Hart, p 12. The majority judgments in the first House of Lords hearing of the *Pinochet* case can be read as supporting this view: see [1998] 3 WLR 1456. See, also, the text at fn 63, below.

8   *Op cit*, Hunt, fn 7, pp 29–35.

9   According to Art 5 of the French Code Civil: 'Il est défendu aux juges de prononcer par voie de disposition générale et réglementaire sur les causes qui leur sont soumises.'

10 See, eg, the ECHR, Art 13. Inexplicably, this Article has been omitted from the version of the Convention being incorporated into UK law by the Human Rights Act 1998.

is that existing national and international laws, whether applied vertically or diagonally, inadequately protect people against human rights violations committed by non-State bodies. Rather than wait for these laws to be corrected, claims should, in the meantime, lie directly against non-State bodies within each State. The second is that to maintain a distinction between, on the one hand, accountability for 'state' functions, which *are* to be measured against human rights standards, and, on the other, accountability for 'non-State' functions, which are *not*, is artificial in this day and age. The third is that the general public does not appreciate the difference between human rights violations committed by the State and similar acts committed by non-State players: unless comparable harms are tarred with the same brush, it will be difficult to develop respect for the very notion of human rights. These arguments will now be set out in more detail before a suggestion is made as to how the proposed reform could be realised in practice.

There are gaps in existing human rights protection

The most powerful argument in favour of extending the operation of human rights standards in the way indicated is that present laws, whether national or international, do not provide extensive enough protection against human rights violations by non-State bodies. If gaps exist, they should be filled, and the material used to fill them is entitled to be called human rights law, even if it is also categorised, in national terms, as something such as tort law or the law of obligations.

At the national level, and taking English law as an example, the fault clearly lies with the inadequacies of existing civil legal processes, processes which have been developing over many generations and not just in the last 50 years or so when 'human rights' has become the new coinage. Through its use of categories such as tort, breach of contract and breach of trust, English law has traditionally focused on the nature of the wrong committed rather than on the nature of the right violated. Civil law countries also speak of a law of obligations, rather than of a law of entitlements. While the philosophy underlying such an approach may originally have been laudable, in that it encouraged an entrepreneurial spirit and the efficient allocation of scarce resources, the fact that it has been applied incrementally and adventitiously over the centuries – dependent largely on the vagaries of litigation – means that today the law is full of inconsistencies and lacks a coherent base. Even in the 1990s, claims based around conduct, such as interference with television reception,[11] or failure to take steps to avoid the sexual abuse of children,[12] are dealt with by the courts more in terms of what the precedents say about the

---

11   *Hunter v Canary Wharf Ltd* [1997] AC 655 (HL).
12   *W v Essex County Council* [1998] 3 All ER 111 (CA).

meaning of land, or about the duties falling on public authorities, than in terms of the rights of those who have suffered. To revert to the examples used above, a person whose privacy has been breached has no right to sue in tort under English law (unless convolutedly, by invoking an action in 'malicious falsehood'),[13] and a person who is denied a job on account of his or her homosexuality cannot sue for discrimination.[14]

Instances of such omissions to protect rights in English law could be multiplied. Thus, a person who has been employed for less than two years has no right to bring an unfair dismissal claim against his or her employer, however outrageous the conduct of the employer might have been;[15] a woman living in Northern Ireland has no right to have an abortion performed in a local health clinic, even though she would have that right if she lived in England or Wales;[16] a person who has suffered sexual abuse as a child has no right to claim compensation for the injuries and anxiety caused if he or she waits until after the age of 24 before suing.[17] Indeed, there is a case for arguing that a great part of the law of tort in England, Wales and Northern Ireland[18] is contrary to human rights standards because it bases liability upon vague and uncertain tests. Success or failure in a claim for negligence (which may be for hundreds of thousands of pounds) can ride on whether the court happens to think that it is 'fair, just and reasonable' to impose a duty of care on the defendant.[19] An example is *X and Others v Bedfordshire County Council*,[20] where the House of Lords held, *inter alia*, that a local authority owed no duty of care to children who had not been placed on the Child Protection Register, even though, over a five year period, there had been reports from relatives, neighbours, the police, the family's doctor, a head teacher, a social worker, a health visitor and the NSPCC that the children were

---

13 *Kaye v Robertson* (1990) *The Times*, 21 March.

14 *R v Ministry of Defence ex p Smith* [1996] QB 517 (CA). Leave to appeal to the House of Lords was refused: [1996] 2 All ER xix.

15 Whether this rule is challengeable on the basis that it is indirectly discriminatory against women is currently the subject of a reference to the European Court of Justice by the House of Lords in *R v Secretary of State for Employment ex p Seymour-Smith* [1997] 1 WLR 473.

16 This is because the Abortion Act 1967 has never been extended to Northern Ireland.

17 *Stubbings v Webb* [1993] AC 498.

18 No comment is intended on the scope of delict law in Scotland.

19 *Murphy v Brentwood District Council* [1991] 1 AC 398; *Caparo Industries plc v Dickman* [1990] 2 AC 605.

20 [1995] 2 AC 633 (HL).

at risk of abuse. In the judgments, no reference at all is made to the human rights of the children involved.[21]

The reason why gaps such as these exist is that the principle underlying the protection of human rights in the UK, as has often been observed, is that all of us have the right to do anything we like provided it is not expressly prohibited by law. Although, on the face of it, this principle seems preferable to one which gives us the right to do anything which is expressly permitted by law, we have to remember that the principle also holds good for actions taken by the State itself, or by other large and powerful organisations within the State, whether they are officially connected to the State or not. These organisations include those in the newspaper and broadcasting industries, multinational pharmaceutical companies, automobile manufacturers, churches and supposedly independent financial houses such as banks, building societies and investment companies. In all of these sectors, the potential for vast numbers of people suffering very serious consequences as a result of incompetence, recklessness, fraud or simple greed is very large indeed.[22]

It might be supposed that, whatever failings there may be to protect human rights at the national level, or to engage in human rights discourse when dealing with wrongful acts, the picture is different at the international level. But this is not the case, certainly not as far as violations of human rights by non-State bodies are concerned. For one thing, the international human rights documents allow claims to be made only against States and, while they impose duties on States to put in place laws protecting certain basic rights (what is here designated as the diagonal application of human rights law), they tend not to identify specific situations where those rights are to be taken as having been breached. The documents usually confine themselves to saying that, as far as the right to sue for a civil wrong is concerned, everyone should be entitled to a fair trial.[23] Their approach is essentially a procedural one, leaving the substance of the civil law of obligations (in English law this is the

---

21 A similar, but more deliberate, blindness occurred in the US Supreme Court decision in *DeShaney v Winnebago County Department of Social Services*, 109 S Ct 998 (1989) (discussed in *op cit*, Clapham, fn 1, pp 160–62), where a child and his mother tried to rely upon the 14th Amendment to the US Constitution, the so called due process clause, to argue that the State of Wyoming, by failing to protect the child from his abusive father, had denied him the equal protection of the laws. The Supreme Court concluded that 'nothing in the language of the due process clause itself requires the State to protect the life, liberty, and property of its citizens against invasion by private actors'.

22 Names such as Rupert Murdoch, Robert Maxwell, Ernest Saunders and the Bank of Credit and Commerce International spring to mind in this context. On a global scale, it is well known that the turnover of some large multinationals is greater than the GDP of many small independent States.

23 A typical example is the start of Art 6(1) of the European Convention on Human Rights 1950: 'In the determination of his civil rights and obligations ... everyone is entitled to a fair and public hearing within a reasonable time by an independent and impartial tribunal established by law.'

law of tort, contract and trusts) to the discretion of each State. Then again, if a claim is brought against a State in an international court for not having in place a law which prevents or remedies a human rights violation committed by a private body, the State can often defeat the claim by arguing that its position is within the 'margin of appreciation' accorded to all States by international human rights documents or by the international courts themselves.[24]

Recent applications taken by dissatisfied litigants in England, point up the inadequacies of the European Convention on Human Rights in this context.[25] In *Stubbings and Webb v UK*, the European Court of Human Rights refused to interfere with the English law concerning the limitation period for claims to compensation following alleged sexual abuse.[26] In *Laskey, Jaggard and Brown v UK*, the Court refused to decriminalise private participation in consensual sado-masochism.[27] In *Fleming v UK*, the European Commission of Human Rights held inadmissible an application arising out of the dismissal from the armed forces of homosexuals.[28] There have, however, been some successes. In *Halford v UK*, the Court allowed the applicant's claim that her employers (the police) had illegally eavesdropped on her private telephone conversations at work.[29] In *Tinnelly & Sons Ltd and McElduff v UK*, the inability of a firm of demolition contractors and of a group of self-employed joiners to obtain a court hearing into the 'national security' reasons for depriving them of work with an electricity company and a government department, was held by the Court to breach Art 6(1) of the Convention.[30] In *I v UK*, the Commission held admissible an application based on the applicant's inability to have her sex change operation officially recognised.[31] In *KL and Others v UK* and *TP and KM v UK* – cases arising out of *X and Others v Bedfordshire County Council*, mentioned above – the Commission held admissible applications relating to the failure of local authorities to take proper steps to protect children against abuse.[32] The conclusion is that the Commission and Court will be able to assist applicants only if some State body has been involved in the violation of

---

24 For the position under the ECHR, see Harris, DJ, O'Boyle, M and Warbrick, C, *Law of the European Convention on Human Rights*, 1995, London: Butterworths, pp 12–15.

25 For an earlier review, see Alkema, EA, 'The third party applicability or "Drittwirkung" of the European Convention on Human Rights', in Matscher, F and Petzold, H, *Protecting Human Rights: The European Dimension. Essays in Honour of Gérard J Wiarda*, 1988, Cologne: Carl Heymanns, pp 33–45.

26 (1997) 23 EHRR 213.

27 (1997) 24 EHRR 39. The House of Lords had already refused to overturn the convictions: *R v Brown* [1994] 1 AC 212 (HL).

28 (1997) 23 EHRR CD 207 (20 May 1997).

29 (1997) 24 EHRR 523.

30 Judgment handed down 10 July 1998.

31 (1997) 23 EHRR CD 66.

32 Decisions of 26 May 1998 (1998) 26 EHRR CD113 and CD84 respectively.

rights or, where that is not the case, if the state of domestic law is clearly outside the margin of appreciation allowed to each country. In other words, only vertical and diagonal application of the Convention is permitted, even though the latter sometimes places a positive obligation on the State to protect one individual's rights against violation by another. There is no opportunity for an individual to sue another, whether in Strasbourg or elsewhere, and use the European Convention as an aid to winning the case.

State functions are now widely dispersed

A second argument in support of 'privatising' human rights law is that the concept of 'State action' is, these days, becoming more and more nebulous. Functions which were previously the preserve of agencies that were unambiguously arms of the State are today, in many countries and with increasing frequency, carried out by what are essentially private bodies. The third quarter of the 20th century may later be viewed as the apogee of State involvement in private lives: in the fourth quarter, the pendulum has swung away from State interference and back towards private initiative. In the United Kingdom, for example, Margaret Thatcher's proud boast was that, through initiatives such as the Next Steps reforms, she had rolled back the State.[33] Successor Prime Ministers, whether Conservative or Labour, have followed that lead.

So as not to have a situation where individuals, who formerly might have been able to claim that their human rights had been violated, can no longer do so just because the State has divested itself of its functions in respect of those persons, the non-State bodies which are performing those functions in place of the State should be accountable to those individuals instead. But this should not be because the non-State bodies are performing 'State action'. It should be because the harm suffered by the individuals is a breach of human rights, and thereby deserving of a remedy whatever or whoever the cause.

To adopt this line would be but to recognise the growing fluidity of legal categories in English law over the past few years. A good example occurs in the law on judicial review. Traditionally restricted to the review of acts performed by administrative bodies, this law has recently been applied to essentially private institutions which are considered to be undertaking public

---

33 In the first volume of her memoirs, *The Downing Street Years*, 1993, London: HarperCollins, p 687, Margaret Thatcher wrote:

> By the time I left office, the State owned sector of industry had been reduced by some 60%. Around one in four of the population owned shares. Over six hundred thousand jobs had passed from the public to the private sector. It constituted the greatest shift of ownership and power away from the State to individuals and their families in any country outside the former communist bloc.

functions.[34] The *locus standi* rules for judicial review have also been liberalised, to the extent that the procedure is no longer focused on the vindication of particular victims, but on the legitimate expectations of all who might, at some point, be affected by the act or decision in question.[35] At the same time, the legal rules on the tortious liability of public authorities have come into their own in the past 30 years or so. The tort of misfeasance in public office looks set to take off in the near future,[36] as does the availability of exemplary damages.[37] Restitutionary remedies against public and private authorities are now clearly recognised as part of English law.[38] Perhaps most importantly of all, damages for mental distress are now commonplace, especially in cases of discrimination in the employment field. Even employees affected by a company's fraudulent management can now sue for damage caused to their mental health.[39]

Section 6 of the Human Rights Act 1998 states that the incorporated European Convention on Human Rights is to apply to all 'public authorities' and that this term embraces 'any person certain of whose functions are functions of a public nature'. The term also includes courts and tribunals. As s 6 says that it is unlawful for a public authority to act in a way which is incompatible with a Convention right (defined in s 1 as Arts 2–12 and 14 of the Convention, Arts 1–3 of the First Protocol and Arts 1–2 of the Sixth Protocol, as read with Arts 16–18 of the Convention), it is clear that judges must henceforth develop the common law in a way which complies with the Convention.

It might be argued that 'a Convention right' means 'as interpreted by the European Court and Commission of Human Rights', but there is nothing in the Bill to compel that interpretation. Section 2 simply requires courts and tribunals to 'take into account' judgments, decisions and opinions of the Court, Commission and Committee of Ministers. It is just as possible to interpret the phrase as referring simply to the rights themselves, as set out in the specified articles. On that basis, it would be perfectly consistent to hold that the rights in those articles are binding on private bodies as well as on public authorities. Thus, if a person were to want to sue a newspaper for invasion of privacy, he or she could be allowed to rely upon the right to a

---

34 *R v Panel on Takeovers and Mergers ex p Datafin* [1987] QB 815.

35 *R v Secretary of State for the Environment ex p Greenpeace Ltd* [1994] 4 All ER 352, QB.

36 See Heuston, RFV and Buckley, RA, *Salmond and Heuston on the Law of Torts*, 21st edn, 1996, London: Sweet & Maxwell, pp 35–36, pointing out that the tort has twice been recognised in recent decisions of the House of Lords: *Jones v Swansea City Council* [1990] 1 WLR 54; and *Racz v Home Secretary* [1994] 2 AC 45.

37 See Law Commission, *Aggravated, Exemplary and Restitutionary Damages*, Report No 247, 1997, London: HMSO, where one of the recommendations is for a principled extension to the class of situation where 'punitive' damages may be awarded.

38 See Tettenborn, A, *Law of Restitution in England and Ireland*, 2nd edn, 1996, London: Cavendish Publishing, Chap 1.

39 *Malik v Bank of Credit and Commerce International SA (in liq)* [1997] 3 WLR 95 (HL).

private life conferred by Art 8 of the Convention (subject to the special protection afforded the right to free speech by s 12(4) of the 1998 Act). As pointed out in one of the leading English textbooks on the Convention, if Arts 2–18 of the Convention are incorporated into domestic law, a limited effect on third parties may be allowed, since these articles do not themselves confine liability to the State.[40]

Even the function of law making, which is *par excellence* the function traditionally allocated to the State, is today rightly viewed, in reality, as being more dispersed. There are organisations within States which, in effect, create a set of special laws for their 'members'. Universities, colleges and schools regulate the activities of their students; employers impose conditions on what their employees can or cannot do; professional organisations place constraints even on the private lives of their associates. In practice, these 'private' rules often impact on individuals more severely than public laws. It can, therefore, only be right that they too can be measured by the courts against human rights standards.

The view just expressed is shared by no less an authority than Sir William Wade QC, who feels that if the courts do their job private bodies will be just as much affected by the Human Rights Act as public authorities. Taking his cue from the Lord Chancellor, Lord Irvine, who stated during the committee stage of the Bill in the House of Lords that the government believed 'it is right as a matter of principle for the courts to have the duty of acting compatibly with the Convention, not only in cases involving other public authorities but also in developing the common law in deciding cases between individuals',[41] he added:

> It would be a poor sort of 'incorporation' which exempted private individuals and bodies from respecting the fundamental rights of their fellow citizens and drove them back to Strasbourg with all its cost in time and money (the very evil which 'incorporation' is supposed to remedy. It must surely be correct to read the Bill as requiring courts and tribunals to recognise and enforce the Convention rights, taking account of the ECHR materials catalogued in cl 2, and subject only to contrary primary legislation. This will be a statutory duty in all proceedings, whether the defendant is a public authority or a private person.[42]

---

40 Jacobs, FG and White, R, *The European Convention on Human Rights*, 2nd edn, 1996, Oxford: Clarendon, p 18.

41 HL Deb Vol 583 Col 783, 24 November 1987.

42 Wade, W (Sir), 'The United Kingdom's Bill of Rights', in *Constitutional Reform in the United Kingdom: Practice and Principles*, 1998, Oxford: Hart, pp 61–63. In the same collection, an opposing view is expressed by Sydney Kentridge QC. He did not see the inclusion of 'courts' in the definition of 'public authority' as implying that the Convention has horizontal application. He thought it meant only that 'the courts in their own sphere must give effect to such fundamental rights as the right to a fair trial ... [and] observe general prohibitions, such as the prohibition of discrimination to be found in Art 14 [of the Convention]': Kentridge, S, 'The incorporation of the European Convention on Human Rights', in Wade, p 70.

Sir William goes on to plead for the term 'public authority' to be dropped from the Act altogether:

> Since the repeal of the Public Authorities Protection Act 1893 in 1974, the law has been free of the problem of defining [public authorities], and our law of human rights will be much the better if it does not demand a definition. Perhaps, the intention of the Bill is that the meaning of 'public authority' shall coincide with the vague definition which limits the scope of judicial review to cases where there is a 'public element', or possibly with the definition in EU law which governs the 'vertical' effect of directives. In both cases, there is abundant room for doubt. The best scenario will be one where there is no need for definition at all and the endless difficulties of case by case elucidation are eliminated.[43]

Evidence for the unworkability of a distinction between State and non-State action can be gathered from the US. Since it was first created in the civil rights cases in 1883,[44] the doctrine of State action has dogged the American courts and led to many contrasting decisions which are very difficult to distinguish. Some of the decisions holding that no State action was involved seem highly questionable. In *Moose Lodge v Irvis*, for example, the Supreme Court held, by six votes to three, that there was insufficient involvement by the State of Pennsylvania in the racially discriminatory policies of a private club, even though the State had issued the club with a licence to sell alcohol.[45] Similarly, in *Jackson v Metropolitan Edison Co*, where a customer of a private utility had her electricity connection severed without proper notice or the chance of a hearing, the Supreme Court held that there was insufficient State involvement (again by Pennsylvania) to merit the application of the due process clause of the constitution.[46]

The public's perceptions are important

The general public, it is submitted, does not understand that human rights, if viewed in conventional terms, are a concept which can be applied only when a State body has committed a violation. In Northern Ireland, for example, most people would say that the paramilitary organisations denied others their

---

43 *Op cit*, Wade, fn 42, p 64. In a footnote, Wade refers to the *Datafin* case (note 34) and to *Foster v British Gas* [1991] 1 QB 405. In the same collection, Geoffrey Marshall says that the criteria used for the definition of 'public body' in these lines of decision 'are, to a degree, vacuous and circular, turning upon the empty notion of exercising a "public function"': Marshall, G, 'Patriating rights – with reservations', in *op cit*, Wade, fn 42, p 79. For confirmation of Sir William Wade's views, see his 'Human rights and the judiciary' [1998] EHRLR 520.

44 109 US 3 (1883).

45 407 US 163 (1972). The court's judgment was given by Rehnquist J. The three dissenters were Douglas, Brennan and Marshall JJ.

46 419 US 345 (1974). Again, Douglas, Brennan and Marshall JJ dissented.

human rights by shooting and maiming them, by intimidating them out of their homes, by destroying their property and by restricting their movements. The egregious nature of these breaches may, to some, make the undoubted breaches committed by members of the official security forces look comparatively insignificant, which, of course, they are not, certainly as far as the victims of those breaches are concerned. One or two non-governmental organisations, working in the field of human rights – notably Amnesty International – have recognised this truism by extending their remit to cover not just State-sponsored abuses, but also paramilitary abuses of human rights. On occasions, the judges in Northern Ireland have also said, referring to Art 17 of the Convention,[47] that people who deny others their rights cannot themselves claim the benefit of the rights conferred by the Convention:[48] this implicitly recognises that non-State bodies are themselves bound to adhere to the standards set by the Convention.[49]

To restrict use of what can be rather emotive language, such as 'guilty of a breach of fundamental human rights', to actions committed directly by the State, or actions tolerated by the State because it has not passed a law to prohibit them, does the cause of human rights in general no good. A justification for such a restriction can be concocted, perhaps along the lines that, as it is only States that sign up to international human rights documents, it is only they who should be considered bound by them. But this is too legalistic a point to be acceptable to the public. In their eyes, and quite rightly, if a person is unlawfully detained, or denied access to information, or discriminated against on unjustifiable grounds, it matters not a jot that the perpetrator of the violation was a private rather than a public body; the hurt suffered is just the same.

This is not to assert, however, that the full panoply of international human rights norms should be allowed to infiltrate into all private relationships at all levels. If human intercourse is to retain any spontaneity, if we are to avoid an Orwellian world where 'Big Brother' oversees everything we do, we must repudiate such a scenario. There must be some areas of purely private interpersonal relations where the language of human rights is deemed to be inappropriate.[50] The extent of these areas can be expected to change over

---

47 Nothing in this Convention may be interpreted as implying for any State, group or person any right to engage in any activity or perform any act aimed at the destruction of any of the rights and freedoms set forth herein or at their limitation to a greater extent than is provided for in the Convention.

48 *Curran and McCann's Application* [1985] NI 261.

49 The leading case in Strasbourg is an opinion of the European Commission of Human Rights in *Kommunistische Partei Deutschland v FRG* (1955–57) 1 YB 223. For a discussion of Art 17, see *op cit*, Harris, O'Boyle and Warbrick, fn 24, pp 510–13.

50 For a thoughtful piece critiquing the idea of a rights based society ('an immature stage in the development of a free and just society'), see Laws, J (Sir), 'The limitations of human rights' [1998] PL 254.

time. Until just a few years ago, for example, the prevailing legal view within the UK was that a woman could not complain to the police that she had been raped if her husband forced her to have sexual intercourse against her will; now, quite rightly, that thinking is regarded as antediluvian.[51] But, should a person be able to sue her partner for not doing his share of the housework? Should a person be able to claim a breach of human rights if he loses friends because he rarely washes? Should a football team be able to go to law if their opponents win the game by handling the ball as it goes into the goal but out of the sight of the referee? The answer in all these cases must be in the negative. Brutal as it sounds, there must be some no-go areas for human rights law. By all means, let us try to encourage good practice in all of these fields, let us try to be fairer and more honest in our dealings with relatives, friends and sports opponents, but let us not elevate all grievances to the level of human rights issues. To do so would be just as damaging to the cause of human rights as limiting the concept exclusively to public body functions.

HOW BEST TO FILL THE GAPS

What is lacking in the United Kingdom's legal systems is a *Grundnorm* which would permit people to vindicate their human rights against everyone else. Yet, the judicial power to expound and develop such a principle undoubtedly exists. It is even within the bounds of possibility that the judges could confer upon themselves the power to strike down legislation which is not in conformity with such a *Grundnorm*. For them to do so would be to go only one step further than the judges of the US Supreme Court went in 1803 when, in *Marbury v Madison*,[52] they decided that they had the power to strike down legislation not conforming with the US Constitution. There was nothing in the Constitution itself which conferred such a power. In that case, as in the two House of Lords' decisions to date where legislation has been struck down because of its inconsistency with European Community law,[53] the yardstick was itself a piece of legislation, admittedly of a higher order than 'ordinary' legislation, but, in theory, there is no reason why the yardstick could not be a fundamental principle of the judges' own creation. This is, after all, the model adopted in many other areas of law. In property law, the role of equity could well be described as a precursor to the modern notion of human rights. Did

---

51 *R v R* [1992] 1 AC 599; see, also, *CR v UK* (1996) 21 EHRR 363, where the European Court of Human Rights upheld R's conviction, even though it was for something which was not a crime when he carried out the act.
52 1 Cranch 137 (1803). See, on this case, Rehnquist, WH, *The Supreme Court: How It Is*, 1987, New York: Quill, Chap 4.
53 *Factortame Ltd v Secretary of State for Transport (No 2)* [1991] 1 AC 603; and *R v Secretary of State for Employment ex p Equal Opportunities Commission* [1995] 1 AC 1.

not the courts of equity devise the doctrine of part performance in order to ensure that the Statute of Frauds could not itself be used as an engine of fraud?[54] Equity's well established maxims demonstrate a distinct sympathy with basic fairness and justice: he or she who comes to equity must come with clean hands; he or she who seeks equity must do equity; no-one should be allowed to profit from his or her own wrong.[55] Judges can, therefore, and do, lay down fundamental principles. Even in civil law systems, this is now axiomatic.[56]

The Human Rights Act 1998 will not, unfortunately, supply the *Grundnorm* here referred to. The Act will simply allow people to claim their existing rights more locally and, hence, more speedily. It will require judges to interpret legislation 'so far as it is possible to do so' in a way which makes it compatible with the standards set by the European Convention on Human Rights,[57] and it will authorise judges to issue a declaration of incompatibility if they think that a legislative provision cannot be interpreted in that way.[58] The onus will then shift to the government to instigate remedial action.[59] Judges may, of course, use the new context provided by the 1998 Act to develop their own common law principles concerning human rights, including the one suggested in the previous paragraph, but the Act itself imposes no obligation on them to do so. If a judge were to refer to the Labour Party's paper, 'Bringing rights home', which was published before the 1997 general election, he or she would see that the party's intention was not to alter existing legal relationships between individuals,[60] even though, as Rabinder Singh has written, 'in principle, there is a powerful case for saying that human rights should be protected against everyone, not just against the State',[61] and even though the Lord Chancellor expressed himself differently during the debates on the Bill in Parliament.

If national judges and legislators do not take the initiative in this regard, then international human rights law should be altered so as to oblige the law makers within States to fill the gaps. Ideally, this gap filling should occur

---

54 *Maddison v Alderson* (1883) 8 App Cas 467.

55 *Ex turpi causa non oritur actio.*

56 Two well known examples from French law are the principles developed by the *Cour de cassation* on the basis of Art 1382 (liability for fault) and those developed by the *Conseil constitutionnel* on civil liberties. See Dickson, B, *Introduction to French Law*, 1994, London: Pitman, Chaps 5 and 9.

57 Human Rights Act 1998, s 3(1). For the potential difficulties arising out of this provision, see Marshall, G, 'Interpreting interpretation in the Human Rights Bill' [1998] PL 167; and Lester (Lord), 'The art of the possible – interpreting statutes under the Human Rights Act' [1998] EHRLR 665.

58 Human Rights Act 1998, s 4(2).

59 *Ibid*, s 10.

60 [1997] EHRLR 71, p 76.

61 Singh, R, *The Future of Human Rights in the United Kingdom*, 1997, Oxford: Hart, p 25.

before anyone feels the need to take his or her case to court. A committee of Parliament, for example, or a National Human Rights Commission, could be tasked with keeping the country's laws under review and recommending appropriate changes to existing or proposed laws.[62] At the moment, the international community is slowly moving towards requiring States to create such institutions, but so far the provisions have been exhortatory rather than mandatory. The Paris Principles of 1993 certainly do not lay down very exacting standards.[63] For situations where laws have to be interpreted by judges, or even made by them, the Bangalore Principles of 1988 already encourage judges 'to have regard to international obligations which a country undertakes – whether or not they have been incorporated into domestic law – for the purpose of removing ambiguity or uncertainty from national constitutions, legislation or common law'.[64] One or two countries have, in effect, incorporated these principles into their domestic constitutional law: South Africa seems to have been quite successful to date,[65] Hong Kong much less so.[66] Moreover, ever since international courts began applying human rights law, they have spawned a very sophisticated body of jurisprudence. There is now a wealth of case law enshrining a host of principles and values which are legally attractive, whatever the setting. It is a waste of judicial

---

62 For a discussion of these possibilities, see Blackburn, R, 'A Human Rights Committee for the UK Parliament – the options' [1998] EHRLR 534; and Spencer, S and Bynoe, I, *A Human Rights Commission: The Options for Britain and Northern Ireland*, 1998, London: IPPR.

63 These were agreed by the UN's General Assembly. The latest Resolution is that passed by the UN's Commission on Human Rights at its 52nd meeting on 17 April 1998 (Resolution 1998/55). This re-affirmed the importance of the development of effective, independent, pluralistic national institutions for the promotion and protection of human rights, and encouraged States to establish or, where they already exist, to strengthen such institutions.

64 Bangalore Principles 1988, para 7. The Bangalore Principles are conveniently reprinted in Appendix II of *op cit*, Hunt, fn 7, and discussed at pp 35–37. Paragraph 8 goes on to say that, in common law countries, where national law is clear and inconsistent with the international obligations of the State concerned, the judges should draw the inconsistency to the attention of the appropriate authorities.

65 Constitution of South Africa 1996, s 39(1):
    When interpreting the Bill of Rights, a court, tribunal or forum:
    (a) *must* promote the values that underlie an open and democratic society based on human dignity, equality and freedom;
    (b) *must* consider international law; and
    (c) *may* consider foreign law. [Emphasis added.]
    For a survey of the interpretations adopted by the South African Constitutional Court to date, see Dickson, B, 'Protecting human rights through a constitutional court: the case of South Africa' (1997) 66 Fordham L Rev 531. I point out, on p 549, that, although the 1996 Constitution is more explicit in its acceptance of the horizontal effects of rights than the 1994 Interim Constitution, the Constitutional Court has, nevertheless, reacted quite conservatively to calls for it to be applied horizontally (while not ruling it out in all eventualities).

66 Chan, J, 'Hong Kong's Bill of Rights: its reception of, and contribution to, international and comparative jurisprudence' (1998) 47 ICLQ 306.

ingenuity not to transpose these principles into the national sphere, the more so because their focus is the harm suffered by individuals, and that harm is experienced as the same phenomenon regardless of its source, State or non-State. What is required is an international convention which obliges States to apply this international jurisprudence nationally.

THE BASIS FOR APPLYING HUMAN RIGHTS NORMS TO PRIVATE RELATIONSHIPS

One of the concepts underpinning the protection of human rights in international law is the dignity of the individual. As stated in the first paragraph of the Preamble to the Universal Declaration of Human Rights 1948, and repeated in the Preambles to the two International Covenants of 1966, 'recognition of the inherent dignity and of the equal and inalienable rights of all members of the human family is the foundation of freedom, justice and peace in the world'. Some national Constitutions or Bills of Rights make reference to the same concept.[67]

The best known example of a country which has already developed its legal system in a way which allows values, such as dignity, to infuse the content of private law, is probably Germany, where as long ago as 1958, in the *Lüth* case, the Federal Constitutional Court overturned the decision of the Hamburg Court of Appeals that Mr Lüth could be restrained from urging people to boycott an anti-semitic film. In doing so, the Constitutional Court held that provisions of the Civil Code had to be read subject to the provisions in the country's Basic Law. Thus, para 826 of the Civil Code, which imposes a duty on whoever causes damage to another (intentionally and in a manner offensive to good morals) to compensate that other, had to take second place to Art 5(1)(1) of the Basic Law, which guarantees the right to free speech. The Court said:

> ... the Basic Law is not a value-neutral document. Its section on basic rights establishes an objective order of values, and this order strongly reinforces the effective power of basic rights. This value system, which centres upon dignity of the human personality developing freely within the social community, must be looked upon as a fundamental constitutional decision affecting all spheres of law [public and private]. It serves as a yardstick for measuring and assessing all actions in the areas of legislation, public administration, and adjudication. Thus, it is clear that basic rights also influence [the development] of private

---

67 Eg, Constitution of the Russian Federation 1993, Art 21(1) reads: 'The dignity of the individual is protected by the State. Nothing may be grounds for disparaging it.'

law. Every provision of private law must be compatible with this system of values, and every such provision must be interpreted in its spirit.[68]

Another instance is provided by a case in 1961, where a law professor sought compensation for non-pecuniary loss arising out of an article suggesting he was an expert on ginseng. Although para 253 of the German Civil Code states that non-pecuniary harm can lead to damages only if specifically provided for in the Code (which is not the case for defamation claims), the Federal Supreme Court, relying mainly on the right to dignity in Art 1 of the Basic Law,[69] set aside para 253.[70]

In Canada, debate has raged for years as to the extent to which the Charter of Rights and Freedoms of 1982 should be binding on private bodies. The dominant view is still that it should not,[71] but powerful arguments have been raised to the contrary.[72] The fact that 'the dignity and worth of the human person' were part of the Preamble to the earlier, and discredited, Canadian Bill of Rights of 1960, but not of the Preamble to the 1982 Charter, has not helped the cause for extension of the values into the private sector. In South Africa, on the other hand, restrictions on rights, more particularly on the right to equality, have been justified by the Constitutional Court on the basis that the alleged victim's dignity has not been affected by the restriction.[73] In Hong Kong, although the Bill of Rights Ordinance 1991 incorporated into domestic law the International Covenant on Civil and Political Rights, Art 7 specifically provides that the Ordinance is binding only on the government and public authorities; the Hong Kong Court of Appeal has confirmed this in a case

---

68 7 BVerfGE 198; this (not altogether satisfactory) translation is taken from Kommers, D, *The Constitutional Jurisprudence of the Federal Republic of Germany*, 1989, Durham, North Carolina and London: Duke UP, p 370. He cites, as 'an excellent critical analysis of *Lüth* in English', Quint, P, 'Free speech and private law in German constitutional theory' (1988) 48 Maryland L Rev 252.

69 Which reads:

> ... protection of human dignity: (1) The dignity of man is inviolable. To respect and protect it shall be the duty of all public authority. (2) The German people, therefore, uphold human rights as inviolable and inalienable and as the basis of every community, of peace and of justice in the world.

This is from the official translation supplied by the German Government in 1994 and reprinted as an appendix to Foster, N, *German Legal System and Laws*, 2nd edn, 1996, London: Blackstone.

70 BGHZ 35, 363 (included as Case 21 in Markesinis, B, *The German Law of Torts*, 2nd edn, 1990, Oxford: Clarendon, p 304).

71 In *Dolphin Delivery Ltd v Retail, Wholesale and Department Store Union Local 58* (1987) 33 DLR (4th) 174, the Canadian Supreme Court refused to apply the Charter's guarantee of free speech to a secondary picketing dispute. McIntyre J (for the court) explained that the Charter did apply to the common law, whether in public or private litigation, but 'only in so far as the common law is the basis of some governmental action which, it is alleged, infringes a guaranteed right or freedom'. In *McKinney v University of Guelph* (1991) 76 DLR (4th) 545, the Supreme Court would not apply the equality provision to a mandatory retirement policy in a university.

72 See, eg, Gibson, D, *The Law of the Charter: General Principles*, 1986, Toronto: Carswell, pp 110–19.

73 *Prinsloo v Van der Linde* (1997) (3) SA 1012.

where a debtor was challenging a creditor's efforts to obtain a court order stopping the debtor from leaving the territory.[74] In so deciding, the Court of Appeal had to admit that the Ordinance did not fully comply with the International Covenant in this regard.

In England, a rights based law is also seeping into nooks and crannies to which it was formerly a stranger. People are going to court with arguments which previously would have been deemed outlandish. Injuries and losses are being granted legal recognition when, in earlier years, they would have been staunchly ignored. A large part of this new civil law, like the old, is, in fact, based on principles which also underlie human rights law.[75] It is, therefore, possible to assert that, although the term human rights law can be appropriated, rather arbitrarily, to designate only those claims made by people against governments, in situations where agents of those governments have allegedly failed to adhere to the provisions of a document setting out people's rights, or where the governments as a whole have not taken steps to ensure a change in the law, it is better to look upon human rights law as but one part of the law in general. It is different not because of the values underpinning it, but because its content is influenced, more than that of other branches of the law, by international agreements.

Even this last point of difference, though, is not as valid as it once was, certainly not within the Member States of the European Union, because the influence of the law making organs in Brussels and of the European Court of Justice in Luxembourg is now such that very large areas of domestic law in all the Member States owe their content to standards set elsewhere. This is particularly true of company law, consumer law, employment law, environmental law and transport law.[76] Indeed, European Union law is encroaching ever more on the territory once occupied exclusively by international human rights norms, so much so that it is now possible for residents of the European Union to sue their own governments for not implementing a European Directive, when the Directive is one which unequivocally confers rights on individuals.[77] Still within a European context, Christopher Graber and Gunther Teubner have recently argued, noting the power of broadcasting authorities in particular, that constitutional rights need to be extended into the regimes of private governance.[78]

---

74 *Tam Hing Yee v Wu Tai-wai* [1991] 1 HKPLR 261, discussed in *op cit*, Chan, fn 65, pp 315-17.

75 See Hooper, A (Sir), 'The impact of the Human Rights Act on judicial decision-making' [1998] EHRLR 676.

76 See, in particular, O'Neill, A and Coppel, J, *EC Law for UK Lawyers*, 1994, London: Butterworths; and *R v Chief Constable of Sussex ex p International Trader's Ferry Ltd* [1999] 1 All ER 129 (HL).

77 Cases C-6/90 and C-9/90, *Francovich and Bonifaci v Italy* [1991] ECR I-5357.

78 Graber, C and Teubner, G, 'Art and money: constitutional rights in the private sphere' (1998) 18 OJLS 61.

CONCLUSION

Human rights have served a purpose as an organising concept within legal discourse. In a short space of time, the concept has highlighted the responsibilities of States to abide by international agreements to which they are signatories. The *raison d'être* of this legal development has been to prevent any future dictator, just because he or she was democratically elected, from ever being able to ride roughshod over the rights of individuals or groups within that society. But it is surely time to move on to the next great development, the use of human rights standards to govern not just inter-State or State-personal relationships, but also inter-personal relationships. The values and principles enshrined in human rights law deserve to be transplanted into private law, so that its future can be informed by them. All bodies concerned about human rights, including non-governmental organisations, need to take on board this reality.

CHAPTER 5

TO KNOW WHERE WE ARE GOING, WE NEED TO KNOW WHERE WE ARE: REVISITING STATES OF EMERGENCY

Oren Gross and Fionnuala Ní Aoláin

To beat off your enemy in a war, you have to suspend some of your civil liberties for a time. Yes, some of those measures do restrict freedom. But those who choose to live by the bomb and the gun, and those who support them, can't in all circumstances be accorded exactly the same rights as everyone else. We do sometimes have to sacrifice a little of the freedom we cherish in order to defend ourselves from those whose aim is to destroy that freedom altogether.

Margaret Thatcher[1]

The whole post-fascist period is one of clear and present danger ... I maintain that our society is in such an emergency situation, and that it has become the normal state of affairs.

Herbert Marcuse[2]

INTRODUCTION

Emergencies provoke the use of emergency powers by governments. The vast scope of such powers – their ability to interfere with fundamental individual rights and civil liberties and to allow governmental regulation of practically all aspects of human activity – as well as the possibility of their abuse by whoever exercises them – emphasise the pressing need for clearly defining the

---

1 Quoted in Fisher, D, 'Critics see nation switching roles with Soviets: own rights eroding, Britons say' (1989) *LA Times*, 6 April, p 6.
2 Marcuse, H, 'Repressive tolerance', in Connerton, P (ed), *Critical Sociology*, 1976, Harmondsworth: Penguin.

situations in which they may be invoked.[3] Yet, defining a 'state of emergency'[4] is no easy task.[5]

Traditionally, emergencies were thought of in terms of a dichotomised dialectic. The term 'emergency' connotes a sudden, urgent, usually unforeseen event or situation, which requires an immediate action, often, without having time for prior reflection and consideration.[6] The notion of 'emergency' is

---

3   'The absence of consensus as to when a public emergency occurs [makes it] by no means plain when exactly a State is allowed by international law to derogate from its obligations to respect and ensure human rights.' Dinstein, Y, 'The reform of the protection of human rights during armed conflicts and periods of emergency and crisis', in International Colloquium on Human Rights (ed), *The Reform of International Institutions for the Protection of Human Rights: First International Colloquium on Human Rights*, 1993, Bruxelles: Bruylant, pp 337, 349.

4   Domestic legal systems employ a wide variety of terms when dealing with the phenomenon of emergency. Frequently, one may encounter several terms used within the same legal system. Many constitutions establish a dual structure of emergency regimes, recognising two possible types of emergencies, such as a 'State of Emergency' and a 'State of Siege' or a 'State of War'. See, eg, the Dutch Constitution, Arts 96 and 103; the Portuguese Constitution, Arts 19 and 141; the Slovenian Constitution, Art 92. Some systems adopt multilevel legal and constitutional arrangements dealing with emergencies. Thus, eg, in German Basic Law, Art 91 tackles the issue of Internal Emergency (Innerer Notstand), Art 80a refers to the State of Tension (Spannungsfall) and Art 115a–i (Chap Xa) deal with the state of defence (*Verteidigungsfall*). See, generally, 'Recent emergency legislation in West Germany' (1969) 82 Harv L Rev 1704; Finn, JE, *Constitutions in Crisis – Political Violence and the Rule of Law*, 1991, New York: OUP, pp 197–99. Similarly, the Canadian Emergencies Act authorises the Governor in Council (the federal government) to declare four different types of emergencies: 'public welfare emergency' (s 5); 'public order emergency' (s 16); 'international emergency' (s 27); and 'war emergency' (s 37). See Rosenthal, P, 'The new Emergencies Act: four times the War Measures Act' (1991) 20 Manitoba LJ 563; Tenofsky, E, 'The War Measures and Emergency Acts: implications for Canadian civil rights and liberties' (1989) 19 Am Rev Can Stud 293, pp 296–97. Finally, no fewer than nine different states of exception can be found in the constitutions of Latin and South American countries, including, among others, the state of siege (*estado de sitio*); state of emergency (*estado de emergencia*); state of alarm (*estado de alarma*); state of prevention (*estado de prevención*); state of defence (*estado de defensa*); and state of war (*estado de guerra*). See, generally, Valdés, D, *La Dictadura Constitucional en América Latina*, 1974, Mexico: Instituto de Investigaciones Juridicas; Lugones, NJ, *Leyes de Emergencia: Decretos de necesidad y urgencia*, 1992, Buenos Aires: La Ley.

5   The term 'emergency' is, by its nature, an elastic concept. See Lee, HP, *Emergency Powers*, 1984, Sydney: Law Book Co; see, also, *Ningkan v Government of Malaysia* [1970] AC 379, p 390 ('The natural meaning of the word [emergency] itself is capable of covering a very wide range of situations and occurrences, including such diverse events as wars, famines, earthquakes, floods, epidemics and the collapse of civil government'); *Bhagat Singh and Others v The King Emperor* (1931) AIR 1931 PC 111, p 111 ('A state of emergency is something that does not permit of any exact definition. It connotes a state of matters calling for drastic action ...'). Moreover, as the International Law Association maintained:

     ... it is neither desirable nor possible to stipulate *in abstracto* what particular type or types of events will automatically constitute a public emergency within the meaning of the term; each case has to be judged on its own merits taking into account the overriding concern for the continuance of a democratic society.

     ILA Paris Report 59 (1984), quoted in Oraá, J, *Human Rights in States of Emergency in International Law*, 1992, New York: OUP.

6   See *New Shorter Oxford English Dictionary*, 5th edn, 1993, p 806.

inherently linked to the concept of 'normalcy', in the sense that the former is considered to be outside the ordinary course of events or of anticipated actions. To have an emergency we must, therefore, have the background of normalcy. Furthermore, in order to be able to talk about normalcy and emergency in any meaningful way, the concept of emergency must be informed by notions of temporariness and exception. For normalcy to be 'normal', it has to be the general rule, the ordinary state of affairs, whereas emergency is to constitute no more than an exception to that rule. In order for it to constitute that exception, emergency must be of a relatively short duration and not yield substantial permanent effects. Thus, traditional discourse concerning emergency powers is based on an assumption of the exception or the 'normalcy-rule, emergency-exception' paradigm.[7]

This essay examines the viability of the traditional discourse on emergency powers through the prism of the derogation regime established under three major international human rights conventions. The derogation regime is premised on and constructed around the basic assumption of exception. We assert that a critical analysis of that discourse is crucial to understanding the failure of international human rights law to oversee adequately and monitor the excessive recourse to crisis powers by States.

The first part challenges the paradigm upon which the traditional discourse concerning emergency regimes is constructed. The derogation regime demonstrates the weaknesses and inadequacies of the 'normalcy-rule, emergency-exception' paradigm in dealing with real world situations. It also explains why viewing reality through the prism of that paradigm is dangerous. It argues that the normative rules, established on the basis of the assumption of the exception, fail to safeguard the very interests that the human rights conventions are aimed at protecting when applied to situations diverging from the basic paradigm. Over-reliance on such rules leads to ignoring the phenomena of permanent, entrenched, or *de facto* emergencies.[8] This may lead, in turn, to attempts at solving questions at hand by applying the wrong medicine as a result of a faulty diagnosis of the malaise.

The second part demonstrates how the derogation regime is founded on the basic 'normalcy-rule, emergency-exception' paradigm and the twin components of temporariness and exceptional nature. The third part combines the discussion in the previous sections through a brief analysis of the jurisprudence of the European Court of Human Rights ('European Court') and the European Commission of Human Rights ('European Commission') – in two types of cases. First, cases arising in the context of the conflict in Northern Ireland and involving a situation of an entrenched emergency.

---

7   Gross, O, '"Once more unto the breach" – the systemic failure of applying the European Convention on Human Rights to entrenched emergencies' (1998) 23 Yale LJ 437.

8   See Fitzpatrick, J, *Human Rights in Crisis: the International System for Protecting Rights During States of Emergency*, 1994, Philadelphia: Pennsylvania UP.

Secondly, relatively recent cases coming out of Turkey in the context of that nation's campaign against the Kurds. These cases raise the issue of systematic practices of violation of human rights by Turkish forces. Their common denominator is the underlying factual negation of any claim to a reality of normalcy as the general way of things. In both categories of cases, it can be argued that the exception has overtaken the general rule. Entrenched emergency has become the ordinary state of affairs in Northern Ireland,[9] while violations of human rights in Turkey have become a matter of ongoing practice, rather than constituting a mere aberration. The argument is made here that the both the European Court and Commission have failed adequately to address the challenges raised by these two categories of cases. The main reason for that systemic failure is to be found in their attachment to the notion of 'normalcy-rule, emergency-exception'.

CONCEPTUALISING EMERGENCY REGIMES: THE TRADITIONAL DISCOURSE

Examination of current thinking on the phenomena of emergencies reveals a strong reliance on the notion of 'the ideal emergency' which, in turn, is constructed around the 'normalcy-rule, emergency-exception' paradigm. This is the core conceptual reference point for courts and academic commentators alike. However, the model rarely exists in practice.

Numerous examples of State practice demonstrate that the exception has, in fact, become the norm. Emergencies have become systematically entrenched in State legal and political systems and in culture. The conceptual model is significantly out of touch with the practical realities of emergency experience. As a result, the tools with which emergencies are confronted may be ineffectual.

The practice of States

Crisis and emergency are no longer sporadic and episodic in the lives of many nations; they are increasingly becoming a permanent fixture in the unfolding story of mankind. One need not necessarily ascribe to notions of a 'climacteric

---

9   Although there may be some diminution of this if the current peace process succeeds. The Good Friday Agreement signed in Belfast 10 April 1998 commits the UK Government to 'make progress towards the objective of as early return as possible to normal security arrangements in Northern Ireland consistent with level of threat and with a published overall strategy, dealing with ... (iii) the removal of emergency powers in Northern Ireland; ...', in 'Security', *Agreement Reached in the Multi-Party Negotiations*, Cmnd 3883, 1998, Belfast: Northern Ireland Office, para 2.

of crises'[10] to recognise that fact. For example, a study published in 1978 estimated that at least 30 of the then 150 countries existing were under a state of emergency.[11] Similarly, a substantial number of States have entered a formal derogation notice under Art 4(3) of the International Covenant on Civil and Political Rights (ICCPR).[12] It should be noted that this number did not take into account States which were not signatories to the ICCPR, or which experienced *de facto* emergencies that were not officially proclaimed and notified. Equally, this also does not take account of those States that have routinised and institutionalised emergency measures in their ordinary legal system.[13]

Other studies have also confirmed the persistent resort of a significant number of States to emergency powers. In 1983, the International Commission of Jurists (ICJ) undertook a comprehensive analysis of states of emergency throughout the world.[14] The study examined in-depth the practices of 14 States which had experienced states of emergency in the 1960s and 1970s.[15] In addition to the case studies, two questionnaires were circulated to 158 governments. Of these, replies were received from 34 countries of which 28 were not subjects of the in-depth studies. The Commission outlined from the outset the premise that there is a frequent link between states of emergency and situations of grave violations of human rights.[16] It also clearly enunciated the principle that many governments regard any challenge to their authority as a 'threat' facilitating the use of derogation provisions, allowing for the dismantling of existing legal machinery for the protection of the citizen.[17]

What is most notable about the ICJ study is the assessment by the authors that, of the 14 countries considered in the examination (excluding the Eastern European countries), nine fall into the category of the permanent emergency type.[18] Only two States, Canada and India, fit the exemplary emergency

---

10   Miller, AS, 'Reason of State and the emergent constitution of control' (1980) 64 Minn L Rev 585, p 613.

11   O'Donnell, D, 'States of exception' (1978) 21 ICJ Rev 52, pp 52–53.

12   International Covenant on Civil and Political Rights, 999 UNTS 171, 6 ILM 368 (1967), adopted by the General Assembly of the UN 16 December 1966, entered into force 23 March 1976 (CCPR). For a list of derogation notices so entered, see the UN Treaty Collection: International Covenant on Civil and Political Rights website http://www.un.org/Depts/Treaty/final/ts2/newfiles/part_boo/iv_boo/iv_4.html.

13   See *op cit*, Fitzpatrick, fn 8.

14   ICJ, *States of Emergency: Their Impact on Human Rights*, 1983, Geneva: ICJ.

15   The case studies examined are Argentina, Canada, Colombia, Ghana, Greece, India, Malaysia, Northern Ireland, Peru, Syria, Thailand, Turkey, Uruguay and Zaire. In addition, one chapter – devoted to Eastern European countries – examined the practice of the Soviet Union, Hungary, Czechoslovakia, Yugoslavia and Poland.

16   *Op cit*, ICJ, fn 14, p 1.

17   *Ibid*.

18   See Ní Aoláin, F, *An Investigation of the Right to Life in Situations of Emergency with Particular Reference to Northern Ireland*, 1997, Belfast: Queen's University (PhD dissertation).

model that is the working assumption of the major studies on emergency norms. The ICJ is only one of many major studies that ignore the prevalence of the permanent emergency and clings to the sanctity of the 'ideal' emergency as the means to examine and control the resort to crisis powers by States. We argue strongly that, if the control of emergencies is to be made meaningful in the approaching century, then rethinking the conceptual framework of crisis powers is essential. Moreover, not only has the phenomenon of emergencies expanded to an ever greater number of nations, but also, within the affected nations, it has extended its scope and strengthened its grip. Observations that 'emergency government has become the norm'[19] can, therefore, no longer be dismissed out of hand.

The reference model and deviations from it: the Questiaux Report

Research principally undertaken to assist in the monitoring, supervision and movement towards ending emergency regimes, has shed much light on the practices of States during emergency rule.[20] The Questiaux Report[21] was undertaken at the behest of the United Nations Sub-Commission on Prevention of Discrimination and Protection of Minorities,[22] and is concerned with the general risks to protection of rights during states of emergency.[23] Taking municipal practice as its starting point, the report offers a profile of patterns evidenced by national legislation concerning emergency powers, postulating a 'reference model'[24] with a high degree of formality.

Chapter 1 of the study opens with the premise that the fundamental precept on limiting governments in bringing states of emergency into effect is consistency between emergency legislation and democratic principles.[25] This

---

19 'A brief history of emergency powers in the United States', a working paper prepared for the Special Committee on National Emergencies and Delegated Emergency Powers, United States Senate, 93 Cong, 2nd session v. See, also, Miller, AS, 'Crisis government becomes the norm' (1978) 39 Ohio St LJ 736.

20 See ILA, *Report of the 64th conference held at Queensland*, 1990; Chowdhury, SR, *Rule of Law in a State of Emergency*, 1989, London: Pinter; UN Commission on Human Rights, 'Study on the implications for human rights of recent developments concerning situations known as states of siege or emergency', 35th session, agenda item 10, UN Doc E/CN 4/Sub 2/15 (1982) (Questiaux Report).

21 *Ibid.*

22 Resolution 10 (XXX) of 31 August 1977, UN Doc E/CN 4/1261, E/CN 4/Sub 2/399, H8 (1977).

23 Reports of the special *rapporteur* for the UN Sub-Commission on Prevention of Discrimination and Protection of Minorities should also be noted in this context. Despouy, 'First annual report and list of States which, since 1 January 1985, have proclaimed, extended or terminated state of emergency', UN Doc E/CN 4/Sub 2/1987/19 (18 August 1987).

24 Joan Fitzpatrick describes Questiaux's standards in this matter. See *op cit*, Fitzpatrick, fn 8, p 21.

25 *Ibid.*

is subject to three conditions: that the legislation (1) predates the occurrence of the crisis; (2) that it contains *a priori* or *a posteriori* control procedures; and (3) that it is to be applied as a provisional or, more correctly, a temporary measure.[26] Thus, 'states of emergency' are referred to in the report as a generic juridical term reflecting the use of emergency powers in exceptional circumstances. The exceptional character of the situation is measured by certain temporary factors as well as by the extremity and imminence of the danger facing the nation.[27]

In her report, Questiaux offers a typology of State acts that fall outside the norm pertaining to emergency regimes. Such acts are treated as 'deviations' from the reference model,[28] which, in turn, is taken as a consensual and generally applied starting point for States. Joan Fitzpatrick synopsises the five 'deviations' as follows:

(1) the formal emergency not notified to treaty implementation bodies;

(2) the *de facto* emergency, during which rights are suspended without proclamation or notification, or suspension of rights is continued after termination of a formal emergency;

(3) the permanent emergency arising out of continual and decreasingly valid formal extensions of the emergency;

(4) the complex emergency involving overlapping and confusing legal regimes, through partial suspension of constitutional norms and issuance of a large volume of far reaching decrees; and

(5) the institutionalised emergency under which an authoritarian government prolongs an extended transitional emergency regime with the purported, but questionable, aim of returning to democracy and the full reinstitution of constitutional guarantees.[29]

While the models outlined as 'deviations' are well defined within their own terms of reference, the choice of terminology is misleading. The emphasis on formalism and procedure fails to recognise that formal legal validity does not necessarily detract from legal recognition and political acceptance within a regime. Questiaux's opening remarks on the scope of the study underscore this formalistic mode of assessment, and thus the limitations of the study:

In theory, the *de facto* situation, which constitutes the exceptional circumstances, is thus without legal validity (a) in municipal law, as long as a state of emergency has not been proclaimed, and (b) to a lesser degree in international law, as long as the state of emergency has not been the subject of communication to the competent international bodies ...[30]

---

26 *Op cit*, Questiaux Report, fn 20, para 23.
27 *Ibid*, para 97.
28 *Ibid*, paras 40–63.
29 *Op cit*, Fitzpatrick, fn 8, pp 21–22.
30 *Op cit*, Questiaux Report, fn 20, para 24.

There is no subsequent recognition that the *de facto* situation may, in fact, endure and flourish without explicit legal validation, and that, as a result, the process of formally authenticating its existence requires critical assessment.

Questiaux's work concentrates on the procedural mechanisms that allow for such validation to occur. These include formal procedural guarantees, substantive guarantees and the actual implementation of such guarantees.[31] This emphasis on formal procedures incurs the following problems. First, it assumes that the existence of these formal requirements is *per se* sufficient to assure protection of human rights in situations of exigency.[32] What is missing is the possibility, within the parameters offered, of a critical assessment of their success in guaranteeing the rights whose fragility prompted the initiation of the study in the first instance. Secondly, the conceptual framework gives insufficient weight to the widespread proliferation of *de facto* emergencies. Finally, the analysis in this form distorts the discussion of the permanent emergency phenomenon, leaving it as part of a peripheral discussion about emergencies that are 'deviations', rather than as central to our understanding of how the various phenomena of emergency have developed, and their current place in the national and international arenas.

While the 'deviations' outlined are those most frequently encountered in practice, there is an unwillingness to acknowledge that the exceptions are far more likely to be encountered than the norm.[33] What is needed, therefore, is a theoretical re-evaluation of what the 'norm' of emergency regimes is. Existing positive legal norms, both on the national and international levels, have fixed such assessment into an inquiry of whether any given emergency regime 'fits' the procedural mechanisms which legally validate the existence of, and justification for, such a regime. The Questiaux Report falls into the trap of assuming that these positive norms reflect and shape the practice of emergencies, rather than examining whether the practice circumvents and subverts them. Questiaux does not completely ignore the permanent emergency problem. The study identifies three common features of such emergencies. These are the fact that, as the emergency progresses (over time),

---

31 *Op cit*, Questiaux Report, fn 20, paras 40–63.

32 Fitzpatrick is highly critical of Questiaux's methodology. She states:

> She [Questiaux] does little more than note the proliferation of permanent national security laws as a means of repression as potentially effective as one of her 'deviations' from the reference model. She fails to recognise that in a common law system a perceived crisis might be efficiently dealt with through the increased application of prior-enacted permanent national security legislation, or through the rapid passage of new security legislation by a compliant legislature, all without any formal declaration of an emergency, the suspension of constitutional provisions, or formal alteration in the separation of powers. (See *op cit*, Fitzpatrick, fn 8, p 22.)

33 ILA, *Second Interim Report of the Committee on the Enforcement of Human Rights Law*, 1988 (Warsaw Report), confirms this:

> ... an exclusive focus on formal states of emergency barely scratches the surface of the widespread phenomenon of human rights abuses associated with states of emergency.

less account is taken of the imminence of the danger facing the State, that the longer the emergency lasts the less important the principle of proportionality is considered to be, and that as the emergency persists, time limits are disregarded as meaningless or useless.[34]

Questiaux also identifies the particular problems associated with complex states of emergency. The dividing line between a permanent and a complex emergency may be difficult to draw. By definition, emergencies do not commence in a permanent form and States rarely (if ever) defend the choice of using emergency powers in terms of their permanent imposition. Permanent emergencies have an increasingly unhealthy cross-pollination with complex states of emergencies. The latter are defined by Questiaux's study as:

> ... [a] great number of parallel or simultaneous emergency rules whose complexity is increased by the 'piling up' of provisions designed to 'regularise' the immediately preceding situation and, therefore, embodying retroactive rules and transitional regimes.[35]

The 'piling up' effect is often one of the practices which facilitate the creation of a legal and political culture supportive of an extended emergency regime. The system becomes self-defined and reliant upon the legislative support structures created by the emergency; 'normal' supports are lost in the process, thus making the process of return to normality more difficult. Complex states of emergency also sustain the enactment of repressive laws assuming the features of ordinary law. Thus, the emergency is hidden. In this manner, its permanent creation is easily facilitated in political terms and more difficult to challenge in a legal manner. As we shall demonstrate later, it is international courts which have proven practically unwilling to initiate this challenge.

Dealing with aberrations: the Paris minimum standards

The Paris minimum standards of human rights norms in a state of emergency represent eight years of study by the International Law Association from 1976–84, during which the Association worked to develop minimum standards for a rule of law in states of emergency.[36] In this comprehensive study of the regulation and limits of governmental exercise of emergency powers, 'aberrations' from the reference model are stated to include the *de facto* state of emergency, the permanent state of emergency, institutionalisation of the emergency regime and complex states of emergency, following the pattern outlined in the Questiaux Report.[37] Once again, the

---

34 *Op cit*, Questiaux Report, fn 20, para 118.
35 *Ibid*.
36 The work was primarily conceived and undertaken for the ILA by Subrata Roy Chowdhury, a noted Indian human rights lawyer. See *op cit*, Chowdhury, fn 20.
37 *Ibid*, pp 45–55. See, also, Questiaux Report, *op cit*, fn 20, paras 103–45.

limited view of extended emergency as a *deviation* from the norm, and the existence of an 'ideal' emergency type, dominates the agenda. What is important to understand is that these influential studies have shaped, in a myriad of ways, the manner in which the international community of States, courts and observers view the practice of emergencies. The belief in the 'normalcy-rule, emergency-exception' paradigm also shapes the ways these institutions respond to the abuse of emergency powers, leading them to chase illusory solutions to an unreal problem.

The Siracusa Principles – an attempt at concrete rules to limit abuse of emergencies.

The Siracusa Principles[38] resulted from the work of international experts coming together to interpret and give meaning to the concept of limitations and derogations under the ICCPR. The Principles are further evidence that concern about emergencies has spawned a widespread response to the interpretative task. This has been taken up by the treaty bodies legally charged with that obligation and also by a variety of non-governmental and intergovernmental agencies.[39] The Siracusa Principles address both the substantive limits and procedural requirements of Art 4 of the ICCPR.[40] The emphasis on Art 4 may be ascribed to the paucity of jurisprudence that had emanated from the Human Rights Committee, particularly with respect to procedural requirements.[41]

The definition of 'public emergency' draws heavily on the terminology adopted by the European Court in the *Lawless* case.[42] A State is deemed to have the privilege of derogation only when faced with 'a situation of exceptional and imminent danger which threatens the life of the nation'.[43] Concrete steps are outlined to fulfil the proclamation, notification and termination requirements.[44] The emphasis on the formalist requirements may be explained by the lacuna in the positive standards. This only calls for the State to provide information about 'the provisions from which it has

---

38 Siracusa Principles on the Limitation and Derogation Provisions in the International Covenant on Civil and Political Rights (1984) 6 HRQ 3, reprinted 1985 (Siracusa Principles).

39 The conference of experts was organised by several non-governmental organisations in 1984.

40 For an outline of the work of the group of experts, see Hartman, JF, 'Working paper for the committee of experts on the article derogation provision' (1985) 7 HRQ 89, p 90.

41 The emphasis is described by Hartman as follows:

   The devotion of a week's labor by one-half of the experts attending the Siracusa Conference to the interpretation of a single Article (Art 4) reflects the central importance of states of exception to promote respect for human rights.

42 *Op cit* Questiaux Report, fn 20.

43 *Op cit*, Siracusa Principles, fn 38, Principle 39.

44 *Ibid*, Principles 42–50.

derogated and of the reasons by which it was actuated'.[45] In contrast, the European Convention for the Protection of Human Rights and Fundamental Freedoms ('ECHR')[46] requires a State party to provide full information on 'the measures which it has taken and the reasons therefore'.[47] The Principles recognise the inherent dangers in the perpetuation of the emergency state. This is revealed by the emphasis on the severity and scope of each individual emergency measure,[48] the unwillingness to accept national determinations of facts as the sole determinant of authenticity[49] and the stress laid on the short term and limited nature of derogation.[50] While the Principles are a useful guide to the augmentation of procedural matters for the Human Rights Committee, and offer practical guidelines to assist its confrontation with states of emergency, they do not come to terms with the consistent practice of States in abusing the emergency regime and the derogation process.

The Siracusa Principles and similar studies are partly responsible for perpetuating the distance that exists between the 'ought' and the 'is' of emergency practices by States. The experts recognise the deviations that exist from the model emergency.[51] There is an acknowledgment that such 'aberrations' have been documented and authenticated. Nonetheless, there is an unwillingness to question whether the widespread proliferation of such deviations ought to prompt a fundamental rethink about the viability of orthodox academic conceptualisations of the emergency phenomena. We conclude that this is precisely what is required to close the gap between the empirical experience of emergency and theoretical explorations of the problem. In short, there is an immediate need to reshape the primacy of the normalcy-emergency dichotomy.

Weaknesses of the 'aberration' discourse

The approach taken by both the Questiaux study and the International Law Association is premised on the conception that the 'model' emergency type is the archetypal emergency experience, and that flowing from this are the

---

45 ICCPR, Art 4(3).

46 ECHR, 213 UNTS 221, ETS 5, signed in Rome 4 November 1950, entered into force 3 September 1953 (ECHR).

47 *Ibid*, Art 15(3).

48 *Op cit*, Siracusa Principles, fn 38, Principles 51, 53, 54.

49 *Ibid*, Principle 57.

50 *Ibid*, Principle 64.

51 Hartman concedes that the Questiaux Report distinguishes categories of deviations from the model emergency that she accepts as valid, proof of the capacity of governmental abuse. Nonetheless, instead of following this practice through its direct implications on the relevance of the treaty standards, the response is simply to stress the importance of *bona fide* derogations.

'problem' emergencies which fail to conform to the norm. Questiaux and the International Law Association replicate one another's stated 'deviations' from the model emergency formula. Both list *de facto*, permanent, complex and institutionalised emergencies in this manner.[52] Questiaux adds one additional category, that of unnotified emergencies. However, empirical assessment shows that the stated aberrations come closer than the model type to being the norm of practice. This approach is understandable when one starts the evaluative assessment of emergencies from the treaty standards downwards, the criterion shaping one's view of the experience.[53] There is a tautological aspect to the inquiry, when the treaty standards shape the way in which one comes to examine the empirical examples of government practices preceding, during and after crisis. It is abundantly clear that State practices illustrate the fallacy of the 'ideal' emergency type. What may not be sufficiently understood are the limitations that are created in reigning in 'problem' emergencies by clinging to an inappropriate conceptual model. By perpetuating a myth that emergencies follow a static pattern, and failing to identify shifting patterns of crisis management (warranted or not), academic commentary, court jurisprudence and institutional international actors fail to come to terms with the emergency phenomena adequately. We argue that in re-examining the conceptual framework, albeit that no easy solutions offer themselves to resolving the problems associated with extended emergencies, we may at the very least have a starker and more realistic understanding of the problems that face the international community in protecting human rights.

THE DEROGATION REGIME AND THE RELATIONSHIP BETWEEN NORMALCY AND EMERGENCY

The law in the books

The vision of an 'ideal emergency' based on an assumption concerning the emergency's exceptional and temporary nature, underlies the derogation regime established under the ECHR, the ICCPR, and the American

---

52 *Op cit*, Chowdhury, fn 20, pp 45–55. See, also, Questiaux Report, *op cit*, fn 20, paras 99–147.

53 Legal realism has a significant jurisprudential value to this discussion. Karl Llewellyn's assessment of the failure of the legal system to reflect practices on the ground is as valid a critique of academic approaches to the emergency question as it is to judicial decision making and legal education. Llewellyn consistently emphasised the need to narrow the scope of legal concepts, using more specific, particularised categories in doctrinal classification which reflect actual distinctions patterned in judicial practice, but not necessarily recognised in paper rules and text book concepts. See Llewellyn, K, *The Bramble Bush: On Our Law and Its Study*, 2nd edn, 1951, New York: Oceana.

Convention on Human Rights.[54] The main purpose of the derogation clauses found in these international documents, is to allow governmental action infringing on recognised individual rights in a period of an extreme emergency, going beyond the authority granted governments in times of normalcy. The derogation regime may thus be said to 'embody an uneasy compromise between the protection of individual rights and the protection of national needs in times of crisis'.[55] Under special circumstances of 'public emergency threatening the life of the nation', governments may derogate from certain individual rights 'to the extent strictly required by the exigencies of the situation'.[56] Measures which, if employed in ordinary times, would have been considered violations of the international obligations undertaken by the State, may be legitimate if taken against the background of exceptional circumstances.[57]

The main requirement posed by the derogation regime, for there to be a legitimate derogation from otherwise protected rights, is that the circumstances in which the derogation has been effected constitute an exceptional threat.[58] A derogation justifying emergency cannot be just any crisis. It has to be a truly extraordinary exigency, a 'public emergency threatening the life of the nation'.[59] The vision adopted by the derogation system is one of crises which constitute episodic and sporadic events, albeit very serious in nature, that last for a relatively brief period of time before being terminated and normalcy is restored. Putting the emphasis on the exceptional nature of emergencies comports, therefore, with the basic paradigm regarding the relationship between normalcy and emergency – that of 'normalcy-rule, emergency-exception'.[60]

---

54 ACHR, OAS Official Records OEA/Ser K/XVI/1 1, Doc 65, Rev 1, Corr 1, 7 January 1970, 9 ILM 101, 673 (1970), signed in San José, Costa Rica 22 November 1969, entered into force 18 July 1978 (ACHR).

55 Hartman, JF, 'Derogation from human rights treaties in public emergencies' (1981) 22 Harv ILJ 1, p 2.

56 ECHR, Art 15(1); ICCPR, Art 4(1); ACHR, Art 27(1).

57 The question whether the right to derogate excuses a breach of the conventions or, alternatively, prevents a breach from taking place due to the fact that the derogation suspends the derogating State's obligations under the conventions, is an open one. See *op cit*, Hartman, fn 55, p 13, n 70.

58 Other relevant principles in this context are those pertaining to proclamation, notification, non-discrimination, and consistency with obligations of the derogating State under international law. See *op cit*, Gross, fn 7, pp 449–51.

59 See, eg, Buergenthal, T, 'To respect and ensure: State obligations and permissible derogations', Henkin, L (ed), *The International Bill of Rights: the Covenant on Civil and Political Rights*, 1981, New York: Columbia UP, p 79 ('a public emergency whose seriousness is beyond doubt').

60 Several factors are considered when giving specific content to the principle of exceptional danger: first, the particular crisis is actual or imminent. Derogation may not be used as a purely preventive mechanism unless an imminent danger exists. Secondly, normal measures available to the State are manifestly inadequate and insufficient to give an effective answer to the crisis. The panoply of 'normal measures' includes also those measures available to the State in accordance with the limitation clauses that (contd)

The overarching requirement of temporary duration and effect is being further strengthened by the principle of proportionality that forms another fundamental pillar of the derogation regime.[61] Even when an act of derogation may be justified under the human rights conventions, the State does not enjoy an unfettered discretion with respect to the derogation measures that it wishes to pursue.[62] Such measures can only be taken 'to the extent strictly required by the exigencies of the situation'.[63] This means that derogation measures employed by a government must be proportional to the particular threat, both with respect to *degree* and *duration*.[64]

The vision adopted by the derogation regime separates normalcy, which is considered to be the general rule, from emergency, which is the exception thereto. It is premised – as the name 'derogation' itself indicates – on the aberrational nature of emergencies. The derogation clause is dormant so long as the conditions are those of calm and tranquillity. It awakens only when certain circumstances of exceptional predicament are present, only to return to hibernate with the subsequent return to normalcy. The basic rationale underlying this regime is that human rights are susceptible to incursions and infringements, more so than any other time under the acute pressures of emergency and crisis. To protect these rights, and prevent their dilution and relegation to a meaningless verbiage, it is imperative to ensure that 'emergency' and 'crisis' are not used as an expedient governmental tool to facilitate transgression against individual rights. To that end, derogation from such rights is made possible only in the most extreme of circumstances. Derogation measures can only be of a temporary character and their ultimate purpose ought to be that of bringing about a rapid return to normalcy:[65]

> Above and beyond the rules [the general principles of the derogation system] ... one principle, namely, the principle of provisional status, dominates all the

---

60 (contd) apply in times of normalcy. Thirdly, the threat must endanger the whole population and either the whole of the territory of the State or certain parts thereof. Finally, the threat must be to the very existence of the nation, that is to the 'organised life of the community constituting the basis of the State'. See *op cit*, Gross, fn 7, pp 453–54.

61 For a discussion of the principle of proportionality in the context of derogation from the human rights conventions, see *op cit*, Oraá, fn 5, p 140–70; also, *op cit*, Chowdhury, fn 20, pp 101–19.

62 *Op cit*, Oraá, fn 5, p 146.

63 ECHR, Art 15 and ICCPR, Art 4. ACHR, Art 27 uses a somewhat different language by stating that the derogation measures may only be taken 'to the extent and for the period of time strictly required by the exigencies of the situation'. The textual difference does not reflect any substantive difference between the three articles.

64 See, eg, Hartman, *op cit*, fn 55, p 17. Eg, derogation measures may not be employed once the situation no longer constitutes a 'public emergency threatening the life of the nation'.

65 See, Rossiter, CL, *Constitutional Dictatorship – Crisis Government in the Modern Democracies*, 1948, Princeton, NJ: Princeton UP, pp 7, 306 (arguing that return to status quo ante is the only legitimate purpose of emergency measures). But see, also, *op cit*, Finn, fn 4, pp 40–43 (possibility of constitutional reconstruction).

others. The right of derogation can be justified solely by the concern to return to normalcy.[66]

The twin principles of temporal duration and exceptional nature have long been recognised by the European Court and Commission. In the *Lawless* case,[67] the nine members majority in the Commission defined a 'public emergency' for the purposes of Art 15 of the European Convention as 'a situation of exceptional and imminent danger or crisis affecting the general public, as distinct from particular groups, and constituting a threat to the organised life of the community which composes the State in question'.[68] The Court affirmed the decision of the Commission without attempting to give a definition of its own.[69]

---

66   See *op cit*, Questiaux Report, fn 20, para 69. Eg, derogation measures must be limited to the duration of the particular emergency. This is explicitly recognised by the ACHR, but is also implied by the derogation clauses included in the ECHR and the ICCPR. See, eg, the European Commission's Report in *De Becker* [1962] ECHR, Series A.4 and EHRR 43, where it concluded that the extension of the suspension of a Belgian national's rights under ECHR, Art 10 over a period of 15 years was not in conformity with the requirements of Art 15 as it was not a proportionate measure, and the derogating government did not claim that a situation of 'public emergency' had continued in Belgium. The European Court, in a terse reference, noted the Commission's position on this issue. See, also, Higgins, R, 'Derogations under human rights treaties' (1976–77) 48 BYIL 281, pp 293–95. A similar conclusion was reached by the UN Human Rights Committee in the *Landinelli Silva* case (*Jorge Landinelli Silva et al v Uruguay*, Communication No 34/1978, in Selected Decisions of the Human Rights Committee under the Optional Protocol (1985) 65–66.

67   *Lawless v Republic of Ireland* (Appl 332/57); (1960–61) 1 E Ct HR, Series B.56, para 82; (1960–61) 3 E Ct HR, Series A.3 (Court).

68   *Ibid*, p 56. Some of the five minority members of the Commission proposed an even more rigorous reading of the term 'public emergency' See, also, p 95 (dissenting opinion by Commission member Süsterhenn that 'public emergency' must be construed as 'tantamount to war' or as analogous to circumstances of war); also, p 101 (dissenting opinion by Commission member Ermacora 'a public emergency exists only when resulting in a complete breakdown of the constitutional order of the State).

69   The Court's theoretical treatment of this issue was as follows:

> ... in the general context of Art 15 of the Convention, the natural and customary meaning of the words 'other public emergency threatening the life of the nation' is sufficiently clear ... they refer to an exceptional situation of crisis or emergency which affects the whole population and constitutes a threat to the organised life of the community of which the State is composed ... [*Ibid*, p 56, para 28.]

It is interesting to note that there are two points of difference between the English text of the Court's judgment and the French text (designated as the authentic text) with regard to the excerpt above. Whereas the English text refers to 'an exceptional situation of crisis or emergency ...', the French text reads 'une situation de crise ou de danger exceptionnel et imminent ...'. Thus, the French text adds the notion of an 'imminent emergency', which does not appear in the English text. The qualification 'exceptional', which is attached in the English text to both crisis and emergency, applies, in the French version, only to the latter.

In his concurring individual opinion, Judge Maridakis, after identifying the principle of *salus rei publicae suprema lex est* as the rationale underlying Art 15 of the European Convention, went on to state that:

> ... by public emergency threatening the life of the nation, it is to be understood [as] a quite exceptional situation which imperils or might imperil the normal operation of public policy, established in accordance with the lawfully expressed will of the citizens, in respect alike of the situation inside the country and of relations with foreign Powers. [*Ibid*, p 64.]

Similarly, in the *Greek* case,[70] the majority of the members of the Commission identified four characteristics of a 'public emergency' in the context of Art 15:

- it must be actual or imminent;

- its effects must involve the whole nation;

- the continuance of the organised life of the community must be threatened;

- the crisis or danger must be exceptional, in that the normal measures or restrictions, permitted by the Convention for the maintenance of public safety, health and order, are plainly inadequate.[71]

Similar declarations have also been made by other international judicial or quasi-judicial bodies operating under the ICCPR and the ACHR.[72] As mentioned above, statements emphasising the temporal duration and the exceptional nature of 'public emergencies' can also be found in studies prepared by international and non-governmental organisations.

The law in action

As a matter of practice, the concept of 'public emergency' came to stand for something far less than truly exceptional, transitory circumstances threatening the life of the nation. It has also become clear that the derogation clauses only theoretically provided objective criteria against which any particular derogation might be compared and assessed. Experience has revealed, time and again, that the European Court and Commission give great deference to the particular decisions of national governments and to the manner in which those governments exercise their discretion with respect to the question of derogation and emergency. The rhetoric of the Court and Commission helps to mask and cloud that fact but cannot hide it.

---

70 The *Greek* case (1969) 12 YB ECHR 45.

71 *Ibid*, para 153. With regard to the actual or imminent character of the emergency, the Commission noted that this imposes a limitation in time, ie, the legitimacy of a derogation undertaken at a certain date depends 'upon there being a public emergency, actual or imminent, at that date' (para 157). In a dissenting opinion, Mr Delahaye sought to clarify that the qualification of an emergency as 'actual' was superfluous, and the operative qualification ought to be only 'imminent' (para 169).

Mr Eustathiades, relying on the French text of the European Court judgment in the *Lawless* case, stated in his dissenting opinion, that Art 15 recognises two situations which justify derogation from a State's obligations under the European Convention: first, a situation of exceptional and imminent danger which affects the whole population and constitutes a threat to the organised life of the community of which the State is composed; and, secondly, a situation of crisis which has the same effect as the former (para 182).

72 *Op cit*, Gross, fn 7, pp 458–59.

ANALYSIS OF THE JURISPRUDENCE

Exceptional circumstances, permanent emergency: Northern Ireland

The normalcy of emergency

A state of emergency has become the norm, the ordinary state of affairs, in Northern Ireland.[73] While the history of the prolonged violent conflict which has plagued this region (and, before 1922, the whole island of Ireland)[74] is well known and is reflective of the permanence of the crisis,[75] we wish here to discuss two additional aspects of the *legal* situation which support our claim that emergency has become the norm in Northern Ireland. One aspect concerns the role of emergency legislation in the jurisdiction and its relationship to ordinary legislation; The other concerns the UK's own perception of the situation as reflected in its derogation notices made under Art 15 of the ECHR.

Special emergency legislation has been applied to Ireland by the UK government since the 1820s.[76] In addition, a significant number of emergency powers were made part of the general, permanent legislative landscape of Ireland.[77] Interestingly enough, Townshend traces the impetus behind this second pattern to the UK Government's belief that 'normality would reassert itself'.[78]

---

73 See Boyle, K, 'Human rights and political resolution in Northern Ireland' (1982) 9 Yale J World Pub Order 156, p 175.

> The concept of an emergency gives rise to the expectation that such a state of affairs is temporary and that normal conditions will be restored. In Northern Ireland, however, there can be no such expectation ... Normal conditions will not be restored in Northern Ireland. Instead, normal conditions will have to be built from the ground up.

See, generally, Walsh, DPJ, *The Use and Abuse of Emergency Legislation in Northern Ireland*, 1983, London: Cobden Trust.

74 See, eg, Lyons, FSL, *Ireland Since the Famine*, 2nd edn, 1973, London: Fontana; and *Culture and Anarchy in Ireland 1890–1939*, 1979, Oxford: Clarendon.

75 See, generally, Townshend, C, *Political Violence in Ireland: Government and Resistance Since 1848*, 1983, New York: OUP; Bew, P and Gillespie, G, *Northern Ireland: A Chronology of the Troubles 1968–93*, 1993, Dublin: Gill & Macmillan.

76 Campbell, C, *Emergency Law in Ireland, 1918–25*, 1994, New York: OUP.

77 See, eg, the following statutes: Peace Preservation Act 1870 (empowering magistrates to compel witnesses to testify during an investigation of a crime before any trial); Protection of Life and Property (Ireland) Act 1871 (permitting arrest and detention without trial of persons reasonably suspected of membership in a secret society); Prevention of Crimes (Ireland) Act 1882 (allowing suspension of jury trial in certain cases); Criminal Law and Procedure (Ireland) Act 1887 (allowing the declaration of an association unlawful, permitting magistrates to interrogate witnesses in private and so forth).

78 *Op cit*, Townshend, fn 75, p 63.

As normality did not reassert itself, and security considerations remained prominent on the Northern Irish agenda,[79] numerous emergency legislative measures have been applied to the jurisdiction during the 20th century. As a result of violent clashes between Loyalists and Nationalists, resulting in the deaths of some 300 people within two years,[80] the Government introduced the Civil Authorities (Special Powers) Act (Northern Ireland) of 1922.[81] This Act was renewed annually between 1922 and 1928, when it was extended for a five year period. Upon the expiration of that period, the Act was made permanent.[82] Indicative of the state of affairs in the six counties constituting the Northern Irish territory, is the fact that, since the very creation of Northern Ireland emergency legislation, such as the Special Powers Act, has been normalised as part of State procedure.

In 1973, following the bloodiest year of the 'troubles' and the introduction of 'direct rule' over Northern Ireland in March 1972, the UK Parliament enacted the Northern Ireland (Emergency Provisions) Act 1973 (EPA) which repealed the Special Powers Act. Many of the repealed statute's provisions were re-enacted into the new legislation.[83] In addition, the EPA established the Diplock courts, where the trial of persons suspected of certain scheduled offences was to be conducted by one judge sitting without a jury.[84] The EPA also relaxed the rules of evidence to be applied by the courts.[85] The EPA was further amended in 1975, 1978 and 1987. In 1991, this prior legislation was replaced by the Northern Ireland (Emergency Provisions) Act (EPA 1991)

---

79 Ní Aoláin, F, 'Where hope and history rhyme – prospects for peace in Northern Ireland?' (1996) 50 J Int Aff 63, pp 67–68.

80 *Op cit*, Finn, fn 4, p 53.

81 The Special Powers Act created two categories of offences: those specified in the act itself and those included in regulations issued by the Minister of Home Affairs (who could delegate the power to issue regulations to his subordinates, including RUC officers) under the act. The result of the emergency regime under the Act was that 'the Government enjoyed powers similar to those current in time of martial law'. Palley, C, 'The evolution, disintegration and possible reconstruction of the Northern Irish Constitution' (1972) 1 Anglo-Am L Rev 368, p 400.

82 The radical nature of this piece of legislation was best reflected in s 2(4) which provided that:

> ... if any person does any act of such nature as to be calculated to be prejudicial to the preservation of the peace or maintenance of order in Northern Ireland and not specifically provided for in the regulations, he shall be guilty of an offence against those regulations.

The South African Minister of Justice was quoted to refer to s 2(4) when he said he 'would be willing to exchange all the [South African] legislation of that sort for one clause in the Northern Ireland Special Powers Act', quoted in Committee on the Administration of Justice, *No Emergency, No Emergency Law*, 1993, Belfast: CAJ, p 6.

83 See, generally, Boyle, K, Hadden, T and Hillyard, P, *Law and State: The Case of Northern Ireland*, 1975, London: Martin Robertson.

84 See, generally, Jackson, JD and Doran, S, *Judge Without Jury: Diplock Trials in the Adversary System*, 1995, New York: OUP.

85 See, eg, Lord Lowry, 'National security and the rule of law' (1992) 6 Isr L Rev 117.

which, among other things, created new offences and gave the authorities additional emergency powers.[86] Another layer of emergency legislation applying to Northern Ireland is the series of Prevention of Terrorism (Temporary Provisions) Acts (PTAs) starting as of 1974.

In 1974, the pattern of special emergency legislation for Northern Ireland was altered as emergency statutes were introduced in Great Britain. Just a few days after a 21 November bombing in a pub in Birmingham which killed 21 and injured more than 180 people, Parliament passed the Prevention of Terrorism (Temporary Provisions) Act.[87] While the EPA's sphere of applicability was limited to Northern Ireland, this has not been the case with respect to the series of the PTAs.[88] The PTA was thus enacted in the face of what was seen as the extension of the IRA's terrorist campaign to the UK itself. Once again, the story of temporary emergency legislation obtaining permanent status was repeated when, after being amended in 1975, 1983 and re-enacted in 1984, the PTA became a permanent statute with the passage of the PTA of 1989.[89]

Emergency legislation in Northern Ireland has an awesome scope in breadth and substance of regulation. It has facilitated the abrogation of jury trial, limitations on right of access to counsel, seven day detention in contravention of European Court of Human Rights standards, changes in standards of evidence, extensive search and seizure provisions, internal exile by exclusion within the UK, censorship and proscription of organisations to name but some of its provisions. It has been maintained as a permanent feature of the legal landscape of that jurisdiction. Indeed, with time, its hold on the Northern Irish legal system became ever more entrenched and broad based, as the issues regulated under it increased in breadth and scope. Furthermore, such expansive emergency legislation did not remain without substantial impact also on 'ordinary' non-emergency related legislation. The occurrence of spillovers from emergency to non-emergency legislation resulted in the claws of emergency digging even deeper.[90] Allied with the use of expressly defined emergency powers in Northern Ireland, came an

---

86 See, eg, Dickson, B, 'Northern Ireland's emergency legislation – the wrong medicine?' [1992] PL 592.

87 See, generally, Hillyard, P, *Suspect Community – People's Experience of the Prevention of Terrorism Acts in Britain*, 1993, London: Pluto.

88 The most recent in this series is the Prevention of Terrorism (Temporary Provisions) Act of 1989, which has been amended several times. It should be noted that this Act is permanently renewable. See Walker, C, *The Prevention of Terrorism in British Law*, 2nd edn, 1992, Manchester: Manchester UP; Bonner, D, 'Combating terrorism in the 1990s: the role of the Prevention of Terrorism (Temporary Provisions) Act 1989' [1989] PL 440; *op cit*, Finn, fn 4, pp 118-34.

89 *Op cit*, Walker, fn 88, pp 33–39; Wade, ECS and Bradley, AW, *Constitutional and Administrative Law*, 11th edn, 1993, Harlow: Longman.

90 The phenomenon of spillovers is the subject of Gross, O, 'On terrorists and criminals: states of emergency and the criminal legal system', in Lederman, E (ed), *New Trends in Criminal Law*, 1999.

increasing emphasis on using and modifying the ordinary law in order to cope with the civil strife. The prime example of this is the abrogation of the right to silence, first in Northern Ireland, now extended to the rest of the UK.[91] Hence, the story of the Northern Irish legislation is a story combining permanent, complex and *de facto* aspects of emergency regimes. Yet, to conceptualise the situation in terms of 'deviations' and 'aberrations' is, patently, missing the point. Emergency is the norm in Northern Ireland; it is not the exception.

The Northern Ireland exigency further illustrates the limit of the 'model' emergency type. While the UK Government has been, generally, exemplary in notification obligations,[92] the procedural correctness hides its substantive flaws. The existence of a permanent emergency has gone without substantive oversight or scrutiny because the mechanisms that exist for assessment are ill prepared to countenance the possibility of its existence. As the permanent emergency has evolved, it is also apparent that the emergency framework is limited in its application to the actual exigency of the situation on the ground. Extended civil strife is being subsumed in the emergency apparatus as a means of limiting both legal and political analysis of what the nature and extent of that conflict may be.

The UK practice with respect to making derogation notifications as required by Art 15 of the ECHR also attests to the entrenched nature of the conflict and the transformation of the emergency into the normal way of things. From August 1971 to date, Northern Ireland has been the subject of an almost unbreakable chain of derogation notices made by the UK Government.[93] In other words, since the introduction of the British army into Northern Ireland in 1969, a declared emergency has been the legal norm, as far as the UK's obligations under the ECHR were concerned. Once again, to speak of a 'reference model' of emergency regimes in circumstances such as these is, at best, meaningless.

Public emergency and derogations: three post-1969 cases

The dissonance between the theoretical premises underlying the derogation regime and a reality of continuous conflict is clearly evident in three cases coming before the European Court and Commission since 1969, in which the existence of a 'public emergency threatening the life of the nation' in Northern Ireland received some sort of judicial attention.

---

91 See Gross, O, *Theoretical Models of Emergency Powers*, 1997, Harvard: Harvard Law School (SJD dissertation).

92 Derogation of 20 August 1971 (1971) YB ECHR 32; Derogation of 23 January 1973 (1973) YB ECHR 24; Derogation of 16 August 1973 (1973) YB ECHR 26; Derogation of 18 December 1978 (1978) YB ECHR 22 (EC on HR); Derogation of 23 December 1988 (1988) YB ECHR 15.

93 *Ibid*.

Ireland v United Kingdom

In this case,[94] the existence of an emergency situation in Northern Ireland was not a matter of dispute between the parties. The specific events which invoked the application by the Republic of Ireland against the UK concerned the re-introduction into Northern Ireland on 9 August 1971, of such measures as detention and internment under the Special Powers Act and regulations issued thereunder.[95] At least some of the detainees were subject to the 'five techniques', during their interrogation. The five techniques consisted of hooding, standing against a wall, subjection to noise, deprivation of food and water and deprivation of sleep.[96]

We wish to highlight one difficulty with the European Court and Commission's treatment of the issues brought before them. Although the existence of a 'public emergency threatening the life of the nation' in Northern Ireland at the times relevant to the case at hand, was not contested by the Republic of Ireland, the Commission positively found that such an emergency did, in fact, exist.[97] An agreement between the parties to the effect that an emergency situation exists, cannot exempt the Commission and the Court from independently reviewing this question. The ECHR is directed at the protection of individual rights which States cannot waive or forego. In that respect, the Commission behaved correctly when arriving independently at its

---

94 *Ireland v UK* (1976) YB ECHR 512 (Commission); (1978) 2 EHRR 25 (Court). See, generally, O'Boyle, M, 'Torture and emergency powers under the European Convention on Human Rights: *Ireland v the United Kingdom*' (1977) 71 AJIL 674.

95 On 9 August 1971, the Government of Northern Ireland brought into operation various special powers involving the arrest, detention or internment without trial of large numbers of persons. The arrests took place under the Special Powers Act and Regulation 10 thereunder. By virtue of this regulation, a person could be arrested and held in custody for 48 hours for the purposes of interrogation. Under Regulation 11(1), a person could be arrested for the same purpose with no apparent time limitation. The detention operation was based on intelligence information gathered by the RUC. Much of the information was dated or inaccurate, resulting in the arrest of many persons wholly unconnected with the paramilitary activities; 354 people were arrested on August 9, suspected of connection with the terrorist activity of the IRA. By 10 November 1971, about 980 people were arrested; 770 detention orders were made; 525 internment orders were issued. See Lowry, DR, 'Internment: detention without trial in Northern Ireland' (1976) 5 HR 261, p 274; 1972, Ulster, *The Sunday Times* Insight Team; *Ireland v UK* (1976) YB ECHR 512 (Commission), pp 670–84; *op cit*, Finn, fn 4, pp 68–69.

96 *Op cit, Ireland v UK* (1976) YB ECHR 512 (Commission), p 513 (introduction).

97 *Ibid*, pp 584–86. ('The Commission is satisfied that there existed in Northern Ireland at all times material for the present case, a public emergency threatening the life of the nation within the meaning of Art 15. The degree of violence, with bombing, shooting and rioting was on a scale far beyond what could be called minor civil disorder. It is clear that the violence used was in many instances planned in advance, by factions of the community organised and acting on paramilitary lines. To a great extent the violence was directed against the security forces which were severely hampered in their function to keep or restore the public peace. The existence of an emergency within the meaning of Art 15 is not in dispute between the parties.')

conclusion that a state of emergency had existed in Northern Ireland.[98] It is the substance of its decision on this point that is troubling.

The circumstances of the Northern Irish conflict, so well depicted by the Commission in its report, strongly challenge the fundamental premises upon which the derogation system is based. The *continuous* crisis in that area stands in stark contradiction to the idea that a state of 'public emergency' ought to be an exceptional phenomenon, a temporary deviation from the normal state of affairs, and that the employment by a government of emergency measures is directed to restore normalcy in as speedy a manner as possible.

Emergency has not been the exception in Northern Ireland; it has been the norm. Despite having its ups and downs of intensity, emergency has been a constant feature in the day to day life of the jurisdiction. In setting the outline of the case before it, the Commission began its report by stating that:

> ... the *lasting* crisis in Northern Ireland gave rise to the present application ... The present emergency is not as such in dispute between the parties. *It began in 1966* with the first use of violence for political ends in Northern Ireland in recent years.[99]

It is difficult, indeed impossible, to reconcile this statement – appearing in the Commission's Report, which was handed down some 10 years after 'the first use of violence for political ends in Northern Ireland' – with the definitions put forward by the Commission and the Court concerning the constitutive elements of 'public emergency threatening the life of the nation'. It runs squarely contrary to the very foundation of the whole derogation regime, as expressed in the concept of 'normalcy-rule, emergency-exception'. Yet, neither the Commission nor the Court acknowledged the strain which such a 'prolonged crisis' puts on the derogation regime. Similarly, neither institution addressed itself to the fact that the UK has practically maintained an ongoing derogation notice with respect to Northern Ireland. That too ran against the theoretical underpinnings of the derogation system. Thus, the insistence on viewing issues pertaining to derogation under Art 15 through the false mirror of theoretical definitions, has worked in this case to prevent the Commission or the Court from realising that 'something completely different' was going on. It also led the two institutions to try and impose the straightjacket of the derogation regime on actual situations that called for a different treatment.

Brogan and Others v United Kingdom

Brought to Strasbourg in 1988, this case involved the applications of four persons arrested in Northern Ireland under the provisions of s 12 of the PTA

---

98 *Ireland v UK* (1976) YB ECHR 512 (Commission); (1978) 2 EHRR 25 (Court), pp 608, 630–702.

99 *Ibid*, p 512 (emphasis added).

1984, which provided for special powers of arrest without warrant.[100] The applicants were held in detention for periods ranging from four days and six hours (Mr McFadden) to six days and sixteen and a half hours (Mr Coyle), during which they were interrogated by the police concerning various offences, ranging from membership in the IRA to participation in deadly attacks on police and the army. None of the four applicants was brought before a judge, and none was charged after his subsequent release.[101]

While both the European Commission and the Court rejected most of the allegations that the UK Government had violated the ECHR with respect to the applicants,[102] the Court ruled, by a 12 to seven majority, that there occurred a violation of Art 5(3) of the Convention, according to which a person arrested or detained 'shall be brought *promptly* before a judge or other officer authorised by law to exercise judicial power ...'.[103] A majority of 13 judges also found a violation of Art 5(5) of the Convention concerning the availability of an enforceable right to compensation to anyone who was subject to an arrest or detention in contravention of that Article's provisions.[104]

Brogan was *not* a derogation case. On 22 August 1984, the UK Government notified the Secretary General of the Council of Europe that it was withdrawing a previously submitted notice of derogation.[105] No claim for derogation was made with respect to the factual or legal circumstances giving rise to the applications in this case.[106] However, both the Court and the Commission stated that 'proper account [ought to be] taken of the background circumstances of the case'. Thus:

---

100 See *Brogan and Others v UK* (1988) 145-B E Ct HR, Series A.16; (1988) 11 EHRR 117 (Court); (1987) 145-B E Ct HR, Series A.57 (Commission).

101 *Ibid* (Court), paras 11–21.

102 *Ibid* (Court), paras 53–54. (16 to three majority concerning Art 5(1) of the Convention); para 65 (unanimous decision concerning Art 5(4)). *Ibid* (Commission), para 98 (unanimous decision concerning Art 5(1)); paras 111–14 (10 to two majority concerning Art 5(4)).

103 *Ibid* (Court), para 62. The Court did not specify precise definition as to when ought a detainee or a person arrested be brought before a judge in order to comply with the 'promptness' requirement. The Commission's decision on this aspect of the case (by a majority of 10 to two) was that Art 5(3) had been violated with respect to two of the applicants who had been detained for periods of five days and 11 hours and six days and sixteen and a half hours, but had not been so violated with respect to the other two detainees held for periods of four days and six hours and four days and 11 hours (a decision supported by an eight to four majority). No clear guideline was given by the Commission as to how it reached that particular decision, nor as to where the dividing line between what was 'prompt' and what was not passed. *Ibid* (Commission), paras 107–08.

104 *Ibid* (Court), para 67; *ibid* (Commission), paras 118–19 (nine to three majority).

105 See Bonner, D, *Emergency Powers in Peacetime*, 1985, London: Sweet & Maxwell, p 88. British notices of derogation were given, prior to 1984, in 1971, 1973 and 1978. See Livingstone, S, 'A week is a long time in detention: *Brogan and Others v United Kingdom*' (1989) 40 NILQ 288.

106 *Brogan and Others v UK* (1988) 145-B E Ct HR, Series A.16 (Court), para 48.

... [i]t is against the background of a continuing terrorist threat in Northern Ireland and the particular problems confronting the security forces in bringing those responsible for terrorist acts to justice that the issues in the present case must be examined.[107]

The opinions written by the seven dissenting judges of the Court resonated even more of explicit derogation style utterances. In a joint dissenting opinion of six of the judges, the following language was used:

> The background to the instant case is a situation which no one would deny is *exceptional*. Terrorism in Northern Ireland has assumed alarming proportions ... It is, therefore, necessary to weigh carefully, on the one hand, the rights of detainees and, on the other, those of the population as a whole, which is *seriously threatened* by terrorist activity ... While considering, therefore, that there was no breach of Art 5 § 3 in the instant case, we are anxious to stress that this view can be maintained only in so far as such exceptional conditions prevail in the country, and that the authorities should monitor the situation closely in order to return to the practices of ordinary law as soon as more normal conditions are restored ...[108]

The opinion of the majority of the judges reveals that they too shared this sense of emergency and urgency. Referring to its decision in the *Klass* case,[109] the Court remarked that:

> ... having taken notice of the growth of terrorism in modern society, [the Court] has already recognised the need, inherent in the Convention system, for a proper balance between the defence of the institutions of democracy in the common interest and the protection of individual rights.[110]

Such language, stressing the exceptional nature of the situation and the need to return to ordinary legal practices as soon as normalcy is restored, could, without any need for further modification, be transplanted into any emergency-related judicial decision. But, if the situation had been so exceptional, posing a grave threat to the population, was not an official derogation of Art 5 adequate? Why would the UK Government choose to withdraw its former derogation notices at a time when such exceptional circumstances still existed in Northern Ireland? The position adopted in

---

107 *Brogan and Others v UK* (1987) 145-B E Ct HR, Series A.57 (Commission), paras 79–80. In its opinion, the Commission quoted from its report in the case of *McVeigh and Others v UK* (Commission's Report of 18 March 1981 (1981) 15 D & R 34, para 157) to the effect that: 'the existence of organised terrorism is a feature of modern life whose emergence since the Convention was drafted cannot be ignored any more than the changes in social conditions and moral opinion which have taken place in the same period ... It faces democratic Governments with a problem of serious organised crime which they must cope with in order to preserve the fundamental rights of their citizens ...' (*Brogan*, para 84).

108 *Brogan* (Court), paras 39–40 (*per* Vilhjálmsson JJ, Bindschedler-Robert, Gölcüklüi-Matscher and Valticos JJ, dissenting) (emphasis added).

109 See *Klass v Federal Republic of Germany* [1979] 28 ECHR, Series A.5.

110 *Brogan* (Court), para 48.

Brogan enabled the UK Government to enjoy the fruits of derogation without having to incur the legal and political costs involved in such a formal act.

Although no claim for the existence of a public emergency was made, the possibility of 'context justification' for governmental actions, in fact, derogating from otherwise protected rights, was recognised.[111] A derogation treatment was accorded in circumstances when none of the parties coming before the Court or the Commission had formally requested it. It is a far cry indeed from the paradigmatic principles of exceptionality and temporal duration.[112]

Brannigan and McBride v United Kingdom

Following the Court's decision in *Brogan*, the UK Government submitted a *Note Verbale* to the Secretary General of the Council of Europe notifying him of the Government's exercise of its right of derogation under the Convention.[113] In this Note, the UK Government mentioned, in a general language, the existence of a public emergency in the UK emanating from the 'campaigns of organised terrorism connected with the affairs of Northern Ireland'.[114] The government made a specific reference to three legislative provisions dealing with powers of detention and arrest, including s 12 of the PTA. Yet, the derogation notice did not include any mention of events or developments taking part after 22 August 1984 (the date on which the previous derogation notice was withdrawn), that might justify the conclusion that a state of emergency has

---

111 See Ní Aoláin, F, 'The emergence of diversity: differences in human rights jurisprudence' (1995) 19 Fordham Int LJ 101, pp 118–19, 121–22. On the other hand, with respect to the alleged violation of Art 5(1)(c) of the Convention, which permits an arrest or detention of a person when that procedure is 'effected for the purpose of bringing him before the competent legal authority on reasonable suspicion of having committed an offence ...', the Court adopted the position of the Commission (and the UK Government) that 'such an intention (to bring the person arrested before the competent legal authority) was present and that if sufficient and usable evidence had been obtained during the police investigation that followed the applicants' arrest, they would undoubtedly have been charged and brought to trial'. *Brogan and Others v UK* (1988) 145-B E Ct HR, Series A.16 (Court), para 52. Both the Court and the Commission chose to ignore substantial empirical indications that the reality was in fact different. See *op cit*, Walsh, fn 73, pp 33–34. Despite this body of evidence, both the Court and the Commission chose to accept the UK Government's claim that the arrest powers under Art 12 had been used with the intention of bringing the persons so arrested or detained to trial. While ready to examine the broad picture of terrorism in Northern Ireland, neither the Court nor the Commission were ready to apply a similar approach towards the exercise of governmental powers of arrest and detention by the UK Government under Art 12, focusing on the specific case and eliminating from review the general experience concerning these extraordinary powers of arrest.

112 The approach of the Court and the Commission concerning the consideration of background circumstances of terrorism in Northern Ireland is especially alarming in light of the fact that Art 5 of the European Convention is not subject to a limitation clause. Thus, Art 5 was limited by the European institutions beyond what had been envisioned by the Convention. *Op cit*, Ní Aoláin, fn 111, pp 121–22.

113 'Note Verbale' 31 (1988) YB ECHR 15.

114 *Ibid*.

developed in the UK since that date.[115] The only mention of any such development was a reference to the Court's adverse judgement in *Brogan*.[116]

Under these circumstances, one could question whether a 'public emergency threatening the life of the nation' did, in fact, exist in Northern Ireland in December 1988, compared with the situation prevailing in that area in August 1984, which, by the UK Government's own admission, did not constitute a public emergency. Was not the derogation of 1988 but a reaction to the previous adverse *Brogan* judgment rather than the result of a true necessity?[117]

This question came before the European Court in *Branningan and McBride*.[118] Peter Branningan and Patrick McBride were arrested by the Royal Ulster Constabulary (RUC) under s 12 of the PTA. Mr Branningan was held in detention for a period of six days, 14 hours and 30 minutes and was subsequently released without charge. Mr McBride was detained for four days, six hours and 25 minutes, subsequent to which he too was released without charge. The facts of this case were, therefore, substantially similar to those coming before the Court and Commission in *Brogan*. This time, however, the UK Government conceded that the requirement of 'promptness' under Art 5(3) was not met, but invoked as a defence the derogation notice submitted by it in December 1988, claiming that the violation of Art 5(3) was justified under Art 15.[119] The issue, then, was whether the derogation claimed by the UK Government was a valid one under the provisions of Art 15 or not. This was the very question that the Court did not need to answer and left open in *Brogan*.[120]

---

115 See van Dijk, P and van Hoof, GJH, *Theory and Practice of the European Convention on Human Rights*, 3rd edn, 1998, The Hague, Kluwer, pp 745–46.

116 'Note Verbale' 31 (1988) YB ECHR 15, p 16.

117 See Lustgarten, L and Leigh, I, *In From the Cold – National Security and Parliamentary Democracy*, 1994, Oxford: Clarendon, p 346:

> When faced with the Court's judgment [in *Brogan*], instead of reversing the policy and amending the legislation ... the government entered a derogation from Art 5(3). On the face of it this appeared as a blatant disregard of international law, not least because the government had earlier explained to the Court during the course of the case that it had not felt that a derogation was necessary ... the timing [of the derogation] indicated bad faith and an attempt to avoid compliance with the *Brogan* judgment, rather than a necessary response to an emergency.

See, also, *op cit*, Ní Aoláin, fn 111, p 122. A counter argument might have been that the withdrawal of the derogation notice in August 1984 was not due to a recognition that no state of emergency existed at the time, but rather was a result of a conviction that the domestic legislative scheme then in existence did not violate any of the provisions of the European Convention, and that therefore there was no need for a derogation notice. The Court's decision in *Brogan* drew the government's attention to its mistake, and required a derogation in order to maintain the Government's obligations under the Convention.

118 *Branningan and McBride v UK* (1993) 258 E Ct HR, Series A.34.

119 *Ibid*, paras 37–38.

120 In the *Brogan* case, the Court stated that, in the circumstances of that case there was 'no call ... to consider whether any derogation from the United Kingdom's obligations under the Convention might be permissible under Art 15 by reason of a terrorist campaign in Northern Ireland'. *Brogan*, para 48.

The Court, accepting the positions of the Government and the Commission on this matter, concluded that the 1988 derogation was a genuine response to a *persistent* emergency situation.[121] According to the Court's own words:

> ... in exercising its supervision the Court must give appropriate weight to such relevant factors as the nature of the rights affected by the derogation, the circumstances leading to, and the duration of, the emergency situation.[122]

Yet, the Court failed to apply its own set of criteria. There is no discussion of the circumstances leading to the particular emergency and, even more significantly, there is no consideration of the 'duration of the emergency'.

When the UK Government made its notice of derogation in 1988, the situation in Northern Ireland was not in any material way different from what it had been in August 1984.[123] Furthermore, under an unbreakable line of derogation notices, the United Kingdom derogated from its obligations under the European Convention, due to the situation in Northern Ireland, from 1971 to 1984. Hence, if a 'public emergency' did exist with respect to the troubles in Northern Ireland, it did so from 1971 until 1989, when Branningan and McBride were arrested. Thus, under these circumstances, there is no relevance to notions of temporariness and exceptionality. What point is there in theorising about the extraordinary nature of emergencies and the need to return to normalcy, when the two are not separable and have become one? Indeed, the 1988 notice of derogation has yet to be repealed, and so it may be concluded that a situation of emergency has, legally, existed in Northern Ireland for close to 30 years.

Branningan and *McBride* put the Commission and Court in a position to express their opinion on the phenomenon of permanent emergency and its problematic relationship with the purpose and language of Art 15. Neither institution rose to the challenge.

Patterns of violations: the Turkish cases

Systematic violations of human rights in the southeast

The breakdown of boundaries between normalcy and emergency, between the rule and the exception, and the systemic failure of the European Court and

---

121 *Branningan and McBride v UK* (1993) 258 E Ct HR, Series A.34, para 51. The Court stated that 'there [was] no indication that the derogation was other than a genuine response'. Did the Court mean by that to say that the applicants had to demonstrate that the derogation was not genuine? If that is the case, the Court had completely reversed its position with respect to the burden of proof concerning the existence of a 'public emergency threatening the life of the nation'. *Op cit*, Ní Aoláin, fn 111, p 123.

122 *Ibid*, para 51.

123 See *op cit*, Ní Aoláin, fn 111, p 123; van Dijk and van Hoof, fn 115, p 745 (the position taken by the UK Government in the *Note Verbale* of 1988 as demonstrating bad faith on the part of that Government).

Commission to address this phenomenon, are also evident in the developing jurisprudence concerning systematic violations of human rights.

For some time now, cases have been brought to the Court and the Commission in which allegations of ongoing practices concerning human rights violations by Turkish security forces have been made.[124] The complaints have been, for the most part, concentrated geographically – coming mostly from the southeastern provinces – and involving mostly victims of Kurdish origin or those suspected of supporting the Kurdish cause.[125]

Since 1984, the Turkish government has been entangled in a bloody armed struggle against the Kurdistan Workers Party (PKK).[126] According to government data, between 1984 and November 1997, some 26,532 PKK members, 185 security forces personnel, and 5,209 civilians have lost their lives in the conflict.[127] Allegations of extensive and systematic human rights abuses have been made concerning the conduct of the Turkish security forces fighting against Kurdish guerrillas, particularly in the southeastern region of the country. Among other things, the authorities are charged with such human rights violations as forcible displacement of civilian non-combatants,[128] and deaths in detention as a result of using excessive force, mystery killings[129] and killings by execution squads,[130] disappearances,[131] and torture during detention or interrogation.[132] Charges have also been frequently made against Turkey's transgressions against civil and political

---

124 See, eg, *Aksoy v Turkey* (1996) 23 EHRR 553 (Court) (discussing torture of alleged member of Kurdistan Workers Party (PKK) in south eastern Turkey); *Akdivar and Others v Turkey* (1996) 23 EHRR 143 (Court) (discussing alleged burning of houses by security forces in south eastern Turkey).

125 See, generally, Amnesty International publications on Turkey: Amnesty International, *A Policy of Denial*, February 1995, London: AIUK; also, *No Security without Human Rights*, October 1996, London: AIUK.

126 See, generally, Gunter, MM, *The Kurds and the Future of Turkey*, 1997, New York: St Martin's Press.

127 US Department of State, 'Country reports on human rights practices for 1997 – Turkey', s 1(g). See website http://www.state.gov/www/global/human_rights/1997_hrp_report/.

128 It is estimated that between 2,600 and 3,000 villages in the southeastern provinces of Turkey have been affected by that policy and that some 560,000 persons have been forcibly displaced since 1984. *Ibid*, s 1(g).

129 *Ibid*, s 1(a).

130 'Bit by bit, ugly facts come out' (1998) *The Economist*, 31 January, p 55 (execution squad rumoured to have been responsible for the 'mysterious killing' of anywhere between 2,500–5,000 Kurds between 1990 and 1996).

131 *Op cit*, US Department of State, fn 128, s 1(b). See, also, Kinzer, S, 'Rights abuses stain Turkey's democratic image' (1997) *NY Times*, 13 July, p 3.

132 *Ibid*, s 1(c). See, also, European Committee for the Prevention of Torture and Inhuman or Degrading Treatment or Punishment, Public Statement on Turkey, 15 December 1992, reprinted in (1993) 14 HRLJ 49.

rights, in general, and those of the Kurdish minority, in particular.[133] Turkey's 'human rights' record and treatment of its minorities were explicitly mentioned as reasons behind the European Union's recent decision, adopted in the Luxembourg summit, to, in all but name, accord a lower priority to Turkey's application to join the EU, as compared with the treatment of similar applications submitted by ten former Communist countries and Cyprus.[134]

The Turkish cases

The mechanism used in most instances to bring these cases before the European Court and Commission has been that of individual complaints submitted under Art 25 of the ECHR.[135] An individual seeking to employ the petition mechanism of this Article must demonstrate to the Commission and the Court that he or she was the victim of a violation of protected rights by any of the Contracting States.[136] However, it has been accepted in the European jurisprudence that such a complaint may also raise a claim of 'administrative practice in breach of the Convention'.[137] To show the existence of such a practice of repeated violations and official tolerance,[138] it is necessary to examine not only the particular case at hand but also the more general context. As the Commission said in the *Friendly Settlement* case:

> ... [t]here is *prima facie* evidence of an alleged administrative practice where the allegations concerning individual cases are sufficiently substantiated, considered as a whole and in the light of the submissions of the applicant and the respondent Party.[139]

A state of public emergency was not an unfamiliar phenomenon in recent Turkish history. Between June 1970 and July 1987, Turkey has invoked Art 15 of the European Convention for more than 77% of the time, including a

---

133 *Op cit*, US Department of State, fn 28, ss 2–3.

134 See Luxembourg European Council, 12 and 13 December 1997: Presidency conclusions, ss 31–36; website http://europa.eu.int/council/off/conclu/dec97.htm. See, also, Mather, I, 'Ankara faces the reality of exclusion' (1997) *The European*, 18 December, p 16. Turkey first applied for inclusion in the EEC in 1963. For a critical assessment of the EU's decision, see, eg, 'The Luxembourg rebuff' (1997) *The Economist*, 20 December, p 17; 'Turkish wrongs and rights' (1997) *NY Times*, 18 December, p 26.

135 See, generally, van Dijk and van Hoof, *op cit*, fn 115, pp 44–65.

136 *X v Norway* (1961) 4 YB ECHR 270, pp 270, 276; *X v Austria* (1977) 7 D & R 87; *Webster v UK* (1974) 12 D & R 168. It seems that the existence of a potential risk of violation of a person's rights may suffice to consider him or her a 'victim' for the purpose of Art 25(1); see, eg, *Klass v Federal Republic of Germany* [1979] ECHR, Series A.28, para 18; *Marckx v Belgium* [1979] ECHR, Series A.31, para 12. See, also, *op cit*, van Dijk and van Hoof, fn 115, pp 46–60.

137 See, eg, *Donnelly v UK* (1973) 16 YB E Conv HR 212, p 216.

138 The *Greek* case (1969) 12 YB ECHR 45, p 195.

139 *France, Norway, Denmark, Sweden and The Netherlands v Turkey* (1984) 35 E Com HR D & R 143, p 165.

continuous stretch of almost seven years from September 1980 to May 1987.[140] Derogations under Art 15 were re-invoked by the Turkish government in August 1990 and have been maintained to date.[141] In fact, since 1987, most of the provinces of the southeastern region of Turkey have continuously been subjected to an emergency regime.[142] Yet, this data did not move the Commission to an independent review of the existence of a state of public emergency in the cases coming before it. Much like the case in *Ireland v United Kingdom*, the Commission was content with the fact that the issue of whether a 'public emergency threatening the life of the nation' did or did not exist was not a point of contention between the parties. Thus, in its decision in *Aksoy*, the Commission ruled that:

> There is no serious dispute between the parties as to the existence of a public emergency in South-East Turkey threatening the life of the nation. In view of the grave threat posed by terrorism in this region, the Commission can only conclude that there is indeed a state of emergency in South-East Turkey that threatens the life of the nation.[143]

Similarly, the Court in its ruling on this matter made but a terse statement, ruling that:

> ... in the light of all the material before it ... the particular extent and impact of PKK terrorist activity in southeast Turkey has undoubtedly created, in the region concerned, a 'public emergency threatening the life of the nation'.[144]

Thus, the Court and the Commission have not investigated at all whether, in the circumstances brought before them, a 'public emergency' existed. Their decisions on this matter have been conclusory, taking the parties at their face value while completely ignoring the realities of continuous crisis and

---

140 Turkey invoked Art 15 from 16 June 1970 to 5 August 1975, from 26 December 1978 to 26 February 1980 and from 12 September 1980 to 25 May 1987. See (1970) 13 YB ECHR 18; (1975) 18 YB ECHR 16; (1978) 21 YB ECHR 18; (1979) 22 YB ECHR 26; (1980) 23 YB ECHR 10; (1987) 30 YB ECHR 19 (informing of the lifting of martial law in all Turkish provinces).

141 (1990) 33 YB ECHR 14 (derogation from Arts 5, 6, 8, 10, 11 and 13 of the European Convention. The derogation notice mentions the death of 136 civilians and 153 members of the security forces in 1989 as a result of terrorist attacks, and the deaths of 125 civilians and 96 members of the security forces since the beginning of 1990); (1992) 35 YB ECHR 16 (12 May 1992, limiting the scope of the existing derogation, so as to apply only with respect to Art 5 of the European Convention).

142 To date, a declared state of emergency persists in six provinces. Six other provinces are under an 'adjacent province' status which grants the provincial governors and the security forces certain special powers. See *op cit*, US Department of State, fn 28, s 1(f). Emergency rule was lifted in October 1997 from three provinces – Bingol, Batman and Bitlis – although the implications of this move on the extensive powers granted to the provincial governors have been quite minimal. 'Turkey and the Kurds. By the gun alone' (1997) *The Economist*, 11 October, p 57. See, also, Zwaak, L, 'The European Court of Human Rights has the Turkish security forces held responsible for violations of human rights: the case of *Akdivar and Others*' (1997) 10 Leiden JIL 99, p 100.

143 *Aksoy v Turkey* (1996) 23 EHRR 553 (Court), p 572.

144 *Ibid*, p 587.

derogation from rights.[145] This approach is all the more striking when it is contrasted against two other elements of the Court's decision. First, the Court made the strong statement that in exercising its supervision over States' actions, the Court 'must give appropriate weight to such relevant factors as the nature of the rights affected by the derogation and the circumstances leading to, *and the duration of*, the emergency situation'.[146] Secondly, with respect to the compliance of the Turkish Government with the requirements of Art 15(3), the notification requirements, the Court pointed out that '[n]one of those appearing before the Court contested that the Turkish Republic's notice of derogation complied with the formal requirements of Art 15(3) ...'.[147] However, it went on to state that '[t]he Court is competent to examine this issue of its own motion ...'.[148]

The decisions of the two European human rights judicial institutions in the various Turkish cases, like those concerning the conflict in Northern Ireland, have repeatedly demonstrated a systemic inability to come to terms and deal with a 'normal reality of emergency'. Whereas, in the jurisdiction of Northern Ireland, emergency has become somewhat the norm, in Turkey, or at least in its southeastern provinces, violations of protected rights of Kurdish persons have departed from their exceptional, aberrational status. However, in neither case has the Court nor the Commission openly recognised the inadequacy of thinking about the questions raised before them in particular incidents, in terms of exceptionality, temporal nature, singularity or particularity. The Northern Irish cases came before the European institutions against the background of a 'prolonged crisis'. The Turkish cases – if only by virtue of their sheer number – were each a reflection of a more general phenomenon. Neither of these backgrounds was given its rightful place among the various interests and considerations weighed by the two institutions.

The Turkish cases have, for the most part, been dealt with by the Court and the Commission on an individual, particular, case by case basis. The implications of the more general picture of systemic abuses and violations of

---

145 Whereas it may be argued that, in *Ireland v UK*, the Commission was right in independently examining whether a 'public emergency threatening the life of the nation' had existed (in spite of the parties' agreement to that effect), but was wrong in its substantive conclusion, in cases such as *Aksoy* neither institution has done as much as engaging in a meaningful independent review of the existence of such a state of emergency to start with.

146 *Aksoy v Turkey* (1996) 23 EHRR 553 (Court), p 587 (emphasis added).

147 *Ibid*, p 590.

148 *Ibid*.

rights were not taken into account in deciding the concrete case at hand.[149] Thus, for example, on the issue of domestic remedies, Reidy, Hampson and Boyle have concluded that:

> [I]n over 60 cases from South-East Turkey declared admissible, the Commission has found in each case that the applicants did not have an adequate remedy at their disposal to address their particular complaint. However, the Commission has also always held that as the individual applicants, on the particular facts of their complaints, had no remedy available to them, the question of a *systematic* failure to provide domestic remedies need not be addressed. The Commission's approach ... nevertheless prompts the question of how many cases are necessary in which applications, raising essentially similar complaints, are admitted by reason of lack of effective remedies, before the conclusion is reached that there is a practice of violation of the right to an effective domestic remedy?[150]

Furthermore, as their study shows, both the Commission and the Court have so far been reluctant in individual cases to take 'a more pro-active role in examining claims as to the existence of a governmental policy from which serious and large scale violation stems'.[151] In cases coming before them in which claims of systematic governmental practice of rights violations have been made, the Court and the Commission failed to address the issue. Their focus has been case specific, examining each case as a singularity without examining the overall picture. Yet, on the other hand, the more complete picture was available to the European organs had they chosen not to ignore it. First, it unfolded before them in dozens of cases coming from the same jurisdiction, each raising substantially similar allegations against the Turkish security forces.[152] Secondly, in certain cases, the complainants furnished the Court and the Commission with external evidence – accumulated by prestigious NGOs as well as by such organs as the UN Committee Against

---

149 See, eg, *Aslan v Turkey* (1995) 80-A E Com HR D & R 138, p 144; (Appl 221/97/93), where the Commission stated that it did not 'deem it necessary to determine whether there exists an administrative practice on the part of the Turkish authorities of tolerating abuses of human rights of the kind alleged by the applicant, because it agrees with the applicant that it has not been established that he had at his disposal adequate remedies to deal effectively with his complaints'. See, also, Tomuschat, C, '*Quo Vadis, Argentoratum*? The success story of the European Convention on Human Rights and a few dark stains' (1992) 13 HRLJ 401, p 406 (the European system as focused on individual applications).

150 Reidy, A *et al*, 'Gross violations of human rights: invoking the European Convention on Human Rights in the case of Turkey' (1997) 15(2) Neth Q HR 161, p 165 (emphasis in original).

151 *Ibid*, p 172.

152 Nine hundred and twenty seven applications were registered against Turkey in 1996 and 1997 (562 and 365, respectively). During the same period, 66 applications were declared admissible by the Commission (37 and 29, respectively), while 422 were referred to the Turkish government (78 and 344, respectively). See European Commission of Human Rights, *Survey of Activities and Statistics*, 1997, website http://www.dhcommhr.coe.fr/eng/97tables.bil.html.

Torture and the European Commission on the Prevention of Torture[153] – pointing to the systematic abuse and violation of rights. For the most part, neither the Court nor the Commission sought to use this information as a catalyst to determine whether an 'administrative practice' had, in fact, occurred.[154]

That this has been the judicial practice of the European human rights organs operating under the ECHR may not be that surprising. It is doubtful to what extent the Convention was meant to deal with allegations of systematic, large scale violations of individual rights. Such violations might be said to lie outside the vision of the Convention, perhaps because such practices were considered to be 'un-European'. As with the case of the derogation regime, which is premised on the twin assumptions of exceptionality and temporal duration, so too it may be said that the Convention as a whole was premised on the assumption that human rights violations in any given nation would be the exception. The Convention was meant, after all, to apply only to countries devoted to democratic ideals.[155] Surely, in countries such as these, respect for human rights and the rule of law is going to be the norm? Moreover, even if systematic violations of human rights had been contemplated by the drafters of the Convention, the subsequent practice under that human rights instrument relegated this function of the Convention to a secondary role.[156]

---

153 Reidy, A *et al* 'Gross violations of human rights: invoking the European Convention on Human Rights in the case of Turkey' (1997) 15(2) Neth Q HR 161, p 171.

154 *Ibid*, p 171–72.

155 Thus, the Preamble to the European Convention speaks of the European States as being 'likeminded and [having] a common heritage of political traditions, ideals, freedom and the rule of law'. It also includes a reaffirmation by the signatory States of 'their profound belief in those fundamental freedoms which are the foundation of justice and peace in the world and are best maintained on the one hand by an effective political democracy and on the other by a common understanding and observance of the human rights upon which they depend'.

156 See Harris, DJ, O'Boyle, M and Warbrick, C, *Law of the European Convention on Human Rights*, 1995, London: Butterworths, p 2:

> It was believed that the Convention would serve as an alarm that would bring such large scale violations of human rights to the attention of other Western European States in time for action to be taken to suppress them. In practice, this last function of the Convention has remained largely dormant, coming to life in just a small number of inter-State applications so far. The Convention has instead been used primarily to raise questions of isolated violations of human rights in legal systems that basically conform to its requirements and are representative of the 'common heritage of political traditions, ideals, freedoms and the rule of law' to which the Convention Preamble refers.

It may be argued that, paradoxically, the lack of experience in dealing with situations of systematic patterns of human rights violations within the European context has made more difficult the adjustment necessary to deal with such situations when they arise: see Brennan, WJ Jr, 'The quest to develop a jurisprudence of civil liberties in times of security crises' (1988) 18 Isr YB HR 11, p 18 ('Prolonged and sustained exposure to the asserted security claims may be the only way in which a country can gain both the discipline necessary to examine asserted security risks critically and the expertise necessary to distinguish the *bona fide* from the bogus').

Be that as it may, the Convention, as it stands today, is ill equipped to deal with such systematic infringements of human rights.[157]

CONCLUSION

The analysis offered in this essay of a predominantly academic discourse in tandem with the jurisprudence of the European Human Rights system, in cases involving states of emergency, reveals the consistent failure of both institutions to come to terms with the inadequacy of traditional paradigms in dealing with actual reality. Our fundamental assertion is that this failure to negotiate the actuality of emergencies results in a deficiency of control over, and monitoring of, crisis powers by international courts.

International human rights law, in theory and practice, has regarded emergency as a temporary and exceptional occurrence. As we have demonstrated above, the reality of State practices does not support this view. Thus, we believe that an overhaul of traditional thinking on states of emergency is required.

The jurisprudence of the European Court and Commission shows the difficulties arising when one attempts to apply the derogation regime without examining the applicability of its underlying assumptions to the real world. Having to treat emergencies as exceptional in order to maintain the paradigmatic regime, the Court and Commission have consistently ignored the entrenched nature of emergency in cases coming before them, with respect to the conflicts in Northern Ireland and the southeastern provinces of Turkey. They have preferred to zoom in on one pixel, rather than move back and view the whole screen in front of them. Their review of the relevant circumstances treats the pertinent facts as a series of pictures rather than as an ongoing, continuous motion picture. Thus, *Ireland v United Kingdom*, *Brogan* and *Brannigan* and *McBride* are considered as three distinct scenarios, rather than constituting complementary parts of a greater whole in which the relationship between normalcy and emergency is reversed; it is emergency which constitutes the virtual norm with normalcy forming a somewhat theoretical exception. Neither Court nor Commission has stopped to consider the implications of having this series of cases coming before them. Both institutions have so far managed to avoid taking the fact that the United Kingdom has maintained an almost permanent derogation notice with respect to Northern Ireland, and that the situation there constitutes a 'lasting crisis', heading for a logically required conclusion.[158] Both institutions have also

---

157 Kamminga, MT, 'Is the European Convention on Human Rights sufficiently equipped to cope with gross and systematic violations?' (1994) 12(2) Neth HRQ 153, p 154.

158 *Op cit*, Ní Aoláin, fn 111, p 124–26.

disregarded the prolonged state of emergency applying in the southeastern regions of Turkey. A reality in which emergency is routinised, is ignored in favour of hanging on to legal myths of normalcy and regularity.

If, as we contend, 'emergency government [may have] become the norm', some serious rethinking is required. As a starting point, we submit that there is a need for academic commentary to acknowledge, on both the theoretical and practical level, that permanent, entrenched and *de facto* emergencies play a growing role in the experience of emergency in many countries. They also constitute the majority of cases (both adversarial and review oriented) that appear before international supervisory authorities when they deal with the issue of 'public emergency'.

What does this mean for international human rights law? On the one hand, international supervisory organs such as the European Court and Commission can continue to operate on a 'business as usual' basis. This means shutting one's eyes against the reality of emergencies coming before the judicial bodies, with resulting and inevitably misplaced legal assessment of what occurs within the State. Human rights are inevitably less well protected when international legal oversight chooses to operate behind a self-imposed veil of ignorance.

Acknowledging that emergencies are tenacious requires entry into a different kind of dialogue with States which permanently resort to the legal device of a state of exception. It means that courts must be politically as well as legally honest in their factual evaluations of the situations that come before them, in an emergency context. There can be no crystal balling of what such a change in the legal discourse might mean for the control and monitoring of states of emergency. Nonetheless, we envisage the following potential results. First, a sense from the multiple actors in the human rights drama (non-governmental organisations, victims, other concerned parties) that the Courts are intellectually honest in defining the nature of the human rights problem they face. Secondly, rogue States that have relied on the existing legal double standard as a means to avoid meaningful scrutiny of the nature and extent of their internal problems, will no longer be afforded this zone of comfort. Thirdly, States will be more cautious about extended reliance on derogation provisions, as they are forewarned that there will be strict international scrutiny of those who invoke these clauses. Finally, the ultimate hope is that, where treaty standards facilitating emergency powers are given meaningful and strict interpretation, with a primary emphasis on the protection of rights, existing patterns of correlation between gross and systematic human rights violations and states of emergency, will be undercut and restrained. The long term and material protection of rights in situations of emergency is significantly dependent on a new starting point. That point can only be reached by a willingness to look anew at traditional ways of thinking about crisis powers in international law, and to recognise their limitations in the current world order.

THEME THREE

EMERGING TRENDS

CHAPTER 6

GENDER FOR EQUALITY: A MOVE TOWARDS AN 'EQUALITY ETHOS' MODEL?

Barry Fitzpatrick

INTRODUCTION

The purpose of this essay is to consider the recent and possible future development of employment equality principles at the level of the European Community. First, a brief review will be made of the range of equality principles and some overriding policy themes will be addressed. In particular, the possibilities of an 'equality ethos' model will be explored. Each of the major equality principles will then be examined from a European perspective and conclusions will be made upon the challenges ahead for the Community gender equality law regime.

LEGAL AND POLICY PERSPECTIVES

Equality principles can be viewed from both legal and policy perspectives. From a legal perspective, it is typical to compartmentalise the principles into categories, such as direct discrimination, indirect discrimination, equal pay and positive action.[1] Such precision is necessary in order to establish whether specific legal provisions have been breached, but also because it is possible to place these principles on a continuum, on the basis of which, most equality law regimes have evolved. Hence, in this chapter, the future development of equality principles will be considered by examining first the principle of direct discrimination, which is the most 'traditional' and least controversial of equality principles. Nevertheless, as we shall see, efforts within the European Community to extend the principle of direct discrimination, for example, in

---

1   See Fitzpatrick, B, Hegarty, A and Maxwell, P, 'A comparative review of the law on equality of opportunity', in Magill, D and Rose, S (eds), *Fair Employment Law in Northern Ireland: Debates and Issues*, 1996, Belfast: Standing Advisory Commission on Human Rights, pp 151–71; Fitzpatrick, B, Hegarty, A and Maxwell, P, 'Trends in employment equality law: a comparative review', in Clark, R and McMahon, J (eds), *Contemporary Issues in Irish Law and Politics, No 1*, Dublin: Round Hall/Sweet & Maxwell, pp 1–43. For a general review of Community social policy, see Barnard, C, *EC Employment Law*, 1997 (rev edn), Chichester: Wiley; Bercusson, B, *European Labour Law*, 1996, London: Butterworths; Burrows, N and Mair, J, *European Social Law*, 1996, Chichester: Wiley.

relation to pregnancy and sexual orientation, have placed significant strains upon the vitality of the principle.

Since the development of the principle of 'disparate impact' by the US Supreme Court,[2] equality regimes have also come to incorporate what is now known in Europe as the principle of indirect discrimination, whereby apparently neutral policies and practices can be open to challenge, on the basis of their disproportionate effect on one sex. The battle surrounding the scope of indirect discrimination is a vital one for the development of equality objectives, as it is a more intrusive principle than direct discrimination. But, indirect discrimination is also a more opaque principle, requiring high levels of expertise on the part of those utilising it. It is therefore hardly surprising that there has been little litigation in the Member States of the European Community on indirect discrimination questions.[3]

In the same way, the principle of equal pay is one which presupposes significant appreciation of its nuances. The relative opacity of the equal pay principle also explains why its utilisation appears to be relatively low.

Inevitably, from a public policy perspective, emphasis may well be upon the achievement of 'measurable' advances in the situation of those seen to be most disadvantaged within (or without) the labour market. In earlier work, Fitzpatrick, Hegarty and Maxwell have identified such an approach as being based upon a 'redistributive' or 'differential reduction' model towards particular groups, for example, in Northern Ireland, between Catholic and Protestant rates of employment, or, within the European Union, between promotion rates of females and males. In relation to this policy objective, one might expect an emphasis upon anti-direct discrimination measures. What might be viewed as a more sophisticated and comprehensive approach to equality objectives, which we describe as an 'equality ethos' model, would involve the giving of significant, although not necessarily equal, weight to all aspects of disadvantage and, similarly, of giving equal priority to other aspects of payment systems and working conditions than that of recruitment. Here, the emphasis is more upon identifying structural discrimination and hence, we would expect a focus upon anti-indirect discrimination and equal pay measures.

While direct discrimination requires a full review of recruitment, promotion and dismissal procedures and the training of those involved with regard to potential stereotyping, both indirect discrimination and equal pay principles require a more general auditing of working conditions and payment systems. Indeed, the potential expansion of the direct discrimination

---

2   *Griggs v Duke Power Co* 401 US 424 (1971). On the principle of indirect discrimination, see, generally, McCrudden, C, 'Institutional discrimination' (1982) 2 OJLS 303, pp 303–62.

3   Blom, J, Fitzpatrick, B, Gregory, J, Knegt, R and O'Hare, U, *The Utilisation of Sex Equality Litigation Procedures in the Member States of the European Community*, 1996, Brussels: European Commission.

principle into wider areas of scrutiny is also consistent with an 'equality ethos' approach.

Once a move is made into the area of positive action, fresh problems of definition arise. In one sense, the more traditional principles already outlined require some form of 'affirmative action' in response. In this chapter, 'positive action' is taken to mean something more than expected responses to the traditional aspects of equality law regimes. More obviously, positive action can involve the converse of direct discrimination, namely, using the otherwise prohibited factor as the basis for an employment decision, for example, operating a quota whereby a given percentage of women, members of ethnic minorities or Catholics must be achieved through preferential hiring of those disadvantaged classes. For the purposes of this chapter, this will be described as 'positive direct discrimination'. Less controversially, an employer may decide to favour a disadvantaged group by focusing upon a structural factor which, in practice, would otherwise work to the disadvantage of that group, for example, preferring to employ part time workers in anticipation of them being female, recruiting from particular geographical areas where ethnic minorities predominate or, in Northern Ireland, giving preference in recruitment to the long term unemployed, on the basis that the ratio of Catholic long term unemployed to Protestant stands at two to one. For the purposes of this chapter, this strategy will be described as 'positive indirect discrimination'. Both of these approaches distance themselves from a symmetrical approach to equality. However, where symmetry reigns, any attempts to compensate the predominantly disadvantaged group are fraught with contention. In the European Community, it has been only after great controversy that the Court of Justice of the European Communities (ECJ) has acknowledged a substantial basis for positive direct discrimination on grounds of sex.

In relation to our two models, the 'disparity reduction' model is more consistent with an abrupt shift from emphasis upon anti-direct discrimination measures to positive direct discrimination measures. The 'equality ethos' model presupposes, first, that efforts to remove discrimination have been exhausted before even positive indirect discrimination measures are invoked, which are, in turn, focused upon perceived areas of particularly potent disadvantage. Positive direct discrimination might, therefore, be seen as a strategy of 'last resort' when inequalities persist despite best efforts to eradicate them.

From a labour market perspective, priorities may be seen differently. On a day to day basis within the workplace, simple and less intrusive solutions will be sought to the extent that legal requirements permit. Hence, the answer to a rigorous approach to 'differential reduction' may well result in bureaucratic systems of recruitment to counter potential allegations of direct discrimination. So, also, a 'quick fix' preference for positive direct discrimination may preclude efforts to counter indirect discrimination, to explore a strategy of positive indirect discrimination. In short, labour market pressures may lead towards an emphasis on pursuit of a 'disparity reduction' model rather than an 'equality ethos' one.

DIRECT DISCRIMINATION

Article 119 of the Treaty of Rome provides:

> Each Member State shall, during the first stage, ensure and subsequently maintain the application of the principle that men and women should receive equal pay for equal work.

Directive 76/207 on Equal Treatment in Working Conditions[4] sets out a more detailed definition of discrimination :

> For the purposes of the following provisions, the principle of equal treatment shall mean that there shall be no discrimination whatsoever on grounds of sex either directly or indirectly by reference in particular to marital or family status.

The legal principles underlying 'straightforward' cases of direct discrimination are rarely problematic, based largely on questions of causation rather than motive or intent. Hence, controversies surrounding direct discrimination are largely evidential. Was the decision made on grounds of sex or some other factor? In this regard, the European Community has moved to ease the burden of proof on claimants in sex equality cases through the Burden of Proof Directive 1997.[5] Nevertheless, the greatest controversies in Community sex equality law have revolved around issues of direct discrimination in occupational pension schemes. More recently, the focus in Community law has been upon attempts to broaden the direct discrimination principle in relation to two 'sex plus' categories, the first concerning pregnancy and, the second, sexual identity/orientation.

OCCUPATIONAL PENSION SCHEMES

It is beyond the scope of this chapter to give an extensive review of a series of cases triggered by Case C-262/88, *Barber v Guardian Royal Exchange Assurance*

---

4   Directive 76/207/EEC (OJ L24, 14 February 1976, p 40).
5   Directive 97/80/EC (OJ L14, 20 January 1998, p 6).

Group,[6] in which the ECJ concluded that UK occupational pension benefits were 'pay' within the meaning of Art 119, even though the scheme was closely linked to the State pension scheme. The Court also concluded that the conditions attached to receipt of pension entitlement, in this case, the pension age, were also pay questions. Although *Barber* was anticipated to some extent by the earlier ruling in Case 170/84, *Bilka-Kaufhaus*,[7] in which a purely contractual German scheme was at issue, there were statutory derogations in both the Equal Treatment in Social Security Directive 1979[8] and, indeed, in the Equal Treatment in Occupational Social Security Directive 1986,[9] most notably on the *Barber* question of retiring ages and also on questions of survivors' benefits and actuarial reductions.

The crux of *Barber* was a prospective effect ruling by the Court which sought to restrict the availability of the *Barber* ruling largely to those who became entitled to a pension from the date of the ruling. The consternation, much of it misplaced, which was triggered by *Barber*, rocked the ECJ, for the first time, buffeted by intense political pressures, orchestrated largely by a hostile UK Government. This pressure culminated in an effective rewriting of the prospective ruling in the '*Barber* Protocol' annexed to the Treaty of Rome by the Treaty on European Union 1992.

While many commentators had concluded that the *Barber* ruling meant that equal pension ages applied to those who *retired* after May 1990, the Protocol intimated that it should only apply to *service* after May 1990. Many saw the *Barber* Protocol as a political 'shot across the bows' of the Court and there can be little doubt, in what some have described as 'post-*Barber* trauma', that the ECJ is today a much more cautious, indeed conservative, Court than it was in the 1980s and very early 1990s. For example, within the *Barber* saga of cases, the Court concluded in Case C-109/91, *Ten Oever*[10] that the Protocol represented what it had meant to say in *Barber*. Having bestowed fundamental status on the equal pay principle since 1976,[11] the Court allowed Art 119 and, hence, both the equal pay and the direct discrimination principles, to be devalued in a hectic rush to limit the 'damage' caused by

---

6   [1991] ECR I-1889. See Curtin, D, 'Scalping the community legislator: occupational pensions and *Barber*' (1990) 27 CML Rev 475. For a general review of Community law on occupational pensions, see Whiteford, E, *Adapting to Change: Occupational Pension Schemes, Women and Migrant Workers*, 1996, The Hague: Kluwer.

7   [1986] ECR 1607.

8   Directive 79/7/EEC (OJ L16, 10 January 1979, p 24).

9   Directive 86/378/EEC (OJ L225, 12 August 1986, p 40), enacted shortly after the *Bilka-Kaufhaus* litigation.

10   [1993] ECR I-4879.

11   Case 43/75, *Defrenne v Sabena* [1976] ECR 455. See Docksey, C, 'The principle of equality between men and women as a fundamental right under Community law' (1991) 20 ILJ 258, pp 258–80.

Barber.[12] We can see the effects of this post-*Barber* trauma, in particular, a sensitivity to the concerns of the Member States, throughout the case law which are about to examine.

PREGNANCY

The ECJ was confronted with the relationship between sex equality and pregnancy in Case 177/88, *Dekker v Stichting Vormingscentrum voor Jonge Volwassen (VJV-Centrum) Plus*.[13] Mrs Dekker was about to be employed by a youth centre when it discovered that she was pregnant. Hence, due to vagaries of Dutch welfare law, it could not recover payments from the Dutch welfare authorities during her absence, because it was already aware of her condition at the time of recruitment. As is well known, there are three broad approaches in relation to such situations. One is to say that, because only women can be pregnant, and men never can, there is no comparison to be made and that the issues have nothing to do with sex equality at all. A second approach is to construct a comparison with a man who would ask the employer for an equivalent period of leave, most obviously, but also most unfortunately in the circumstances, a man who requires a period of time off in relation to a relatively serious illness. The third approach, and that favoured by the ECJ in *Dekker*, was to apply a causation approach. If only women could be pregnant, then discrimination against pregnant workers was *per se* discrimination on grounds of sex.

The underlying problem with 'sex plus' cases lies in determining the limits to be placed upon them. The added complication in direct discrimination cases is that it is a 'sacrosanct' rule, that derogations from the principle of direct discrimination can only be by way of express enactment. However, in enacting the Equal Treatment Directive in 1976, the Community legislator provided no exceptions to, or potential justifications for, discrimination on grounds of pregnancy, as this judicial extension of the principle was not contemplated. The underlying rationale of *Dekker* was that *any* employment decision on grounds of pregnancy was also on grounds of sex and, hence, unlawful. The Court was not prepared to countenance such an open ended commitment to pregnancy protection and, hence, in a case decided on the

---

12 See Fitzpatrick, B, 'Equality in occupational pension schemes: still waiting for *Colorol*' (1994) 23 ILJ 155, pp 155–63 and 204; Hervey, T, 'Legal issues of the *Barber* Protocol', in O'Keefe, D and Twomey, P (eds), *Legal Issues of the Maastricht Treaty*, 1995, Chichester: Wiley, pp 329–37; and Whiteford, E, 'Occupational pensions and European law: clarity at last?', in Hervey, T and O'Keefe, D (eds), *Sex Equality Law in the European Union*, 1996, Chichester: Wiley, pp 21–34.

13 [1990] ECR I-3941. See More, G, 'Reflections on pregnancy discrimination under European Community law' (1992) 5 JSWL 48.

same day as *Dekker*, Case C-179/88, *HK (acting for Hertz) v DA (acting for Aldi Marked K/S)*,[14] the Court concluded that this absolute protection for pregnant workers ended at the completion of the *national* period of maternity leave. Even though Ms Hertz's illness was pregnancy related, now that her maternity leave period was over, her point of comparison was a similarly placed male worker.

Indeed, in Case C-400/95, *HK (acting for Larsson) v Dansk Handel & Service (acting on behalf of Føtex Supermarked A/S)*,[15] the Court confirmed that there was no distinction between pregnancy related illnesses which originated during or after the worker's maternity leave. In each case, each must be treated like any other illness once the maternity leave period was over. The Court went so far as to say that, under the 1976 Directive, absences *during* the national maternity period could not be taken into account in calculating total absences for the purposes of later dismissal, but absences *up to* the date of maternity leave could be. Here, the Court is effectively caught by the logic of relying exclusively on the maternity leave period to delineate the scope of the 'pregnancy = direct discrimination' equation. Given that there are no legislative limitations in the 1976 Directive upon which to limit the scope of this 'sex plus' extension of the direct discrimination principle, we end up with a situation whereby a pregnant women could quite easily be dismissed for frequent pregnancy related absences well before she reaches her maternity leave period, an outcome inconsistent with the very essence of the *Dekker* judgment. Happily for pregnant workers, Art 10 of the Pregnant Workers Directive 1992[16] provides dismissal protection from the date of pregnancy up to end of maternity leave.

A second attempt to extend *Dekker* into the realms of pay, at the instigation of the Equal Opportunities Commission for Northern Ireland (EOCNI), floundered on this desire in the Court to limit the effect of 'sex plus' cases. In Case C-342/93, *Gillespie v Northern Health and Social Services Board*,[17] the Court rejected the logic that a pregnant worker should be entitled to maternity pay over the full period of maternity leave, admitting only that the level of maternity pay must not be 'such as to undermine the purpose of maternity leave'.

In the context of extrapolating the development of Community equality law into the next century, this *Dekker* saga already provides some useful pointers. *Dekker* was decided in the last days of the Court's more progressive era, before a more cautious ethos took hold in Luxembourg. Even in 1990, the

---

14 [1990] ECR I-3979.

15 [1997] ECR I-2757.

16 Directive 92/85 (OJ L348, 28 November 1992, p 1), Art 10. See, now, Case C-394/96, *Brown v Rentokil Ltd* [1998] IRLR 445.

17 [1996] ECR I-1475. See Conaghan, J, 'Pregnancy, Equality and the European Court of Justice: interrogating *Gillespie*' (1998) 3 IJDL 115, pp 115–33.

Court found a rather artificial limit to the 'golden circle' of equality protection through the use of the national maternity leave period. Refusing to follow the logic of the *Dekker* equation for fear of opening up unlimited rights for pregnant workers, the Court has instead followed the logic of *Hertz* and ended up with a highly circumscribed and barely defensible position. On this occasion, the Community legislator stepped in shortly after *Dekker* (although the Commission proposal predated *Dekker* by a substantial period) and produced what is in many ways a limited measure, premised on a 'health and safety' treaty base in order to ensure its passage through the Council of Ministers by qualified majority voting. The Pregnant Workers Directive 1992 does provide 14 weeks' maternity leave but only at a rate of pay equivalent to national statutory sick pay levels.[18] Hence, a picture emerges initially of a Court prepared to stretch Community equality principles quite widely, but then retreating from the full scope of what it has achieved and laterally of a legislator willing only to produce minimalist measures within the confines of its labyrinthine procedures. As such, a move towards an 'equality ethos' model has been marginally advanced in that such 'sex plus' cases broaden the focus of equality law into wider issues of working conditions and the actual position of women in the labour market.

SEXUAL IDENTITY/ORIENTATION

A similar pattern of judicial behaviour can be perceived in relation to recent case law on sexual identity/orientation, although this is an area in which there are no prospects of legislative action. In Case C-13/94, *P v S and Cornwall County Council*,[19] P was dismissed from her position as a cook in a police station after she had undergone a sex change operation. The Court held that discrimination against transsexuals was within the principle of equality irrespective of sex, since the sex of the applicant was central to the case. Although the Court proceeded to compare P with a man who had not undergone a sex change, rather than a woman who had become a man, it is arguable that no comparison was needed at all, given that fewer actions fall more within the definition 'on grounds of sex' than a dismissal for changing it. Nevertheless, it is significant that the Court chose not to avoid the 'sex plus' aspect of P's case, simply by comparing the Council's treatment of her to that which it would have applied to a woman who changed her sex to that of a man.

Accordingly, there was some anticipation that the Court might move on to bring same sex relationships within the scope of Art 119 in Case C-249/96,

---

18 Directive 92/85 (OJ L348, 28 November 1992), Arts 8 and 11.

19 [1996] ECR I-2143. See Skidmore, P, 'Sex, gender and comparators in employment discrimination' (1997) 26 ILJ 51, pp 51–61.

Grant v South-West Trains Ltd.[20] Here, South-West Trains operated a system whereby both spouses and common law partners of the opposite sex were entitled to free travel facilities. Advocate General Elmer gave his opinion that the sex of the applicant was, once again, central to the case as, if Grant had been a male, having a female partner would not have disqualified her from free travel facilities for her partner. However, the Court concluded that partnerships between gay men and lesbian partnerships were treated equally, and that neither Community nor national law were sufficiently advanced *at this time* to bring gay relationships within the sex equality principles of Community law. Clearly, there are conceptual distinctions between *P v S* and *Grant*. Although the Court chose to make a comparison in *P v S*, the sex of the applicant was the essence of the case. On the other hand, unless an extended 'sex plus' approach was taken in *Grant* to include sexual orientation within the principle of 'sex' itself, some form of comparison would be needed, albeit the superficially attractive one involving treatment of a male worker with a female partner.

The Court, on a more political level of analysis, can be seen in *P v S* to have discovered a spark of its old radicalism, albeit one which was quickly extinguished when the more contentious issue of gay rights was brought before it. It must be said that any other finding would have immersed the Court once again in all the pregnancy related issues attached to finding a limit to the scope of the direct discrimination principle, in circumstances in which the original legislator could not possibly have imagined such an extension to the legal principle. The answer in *Grant* was to close the door entirely, at least for the present, on such a development, leaving the more manageable question of transsexuals within the ambit of the sex equality principle.[21]

Parallels can be drawn with the experience of extending the direct discrimination principle to govern pregnancy related decisions. Initially, the approach is adventurous, adding a 'sex plus' category to the relatively non-controversial principle. Unfortunately, this is followed by retrenchment. It might be said that the *Grant* reference was five to ten years too early in terms of social attitudes, but five to ten years too late in terms of judicial activism. However, in this case, there is now a possible treaty base for Community legislation upon sexual orientation, in that the Treaty of Rome, if the Treaty of Amsterdam is ratified, will include in Art 13 a non-discrimination clause

---

20 [1998] IRLR 206.
21 It might be suggested that the later reference of *R v Secretary of State for Defence ex p Perkins* [1997] IRLR 297 (HC), dealing with the dismissal from the armed forces of servicemen and women discovered to be gay and/or lesbian, would have made a better test case on such a sensitive issue. Sadly, for those hoping that the possibilities of exploiting Community law were not exhausted after *Grant*, the ECJ has asked the High Court whether it wishes to proceed with its reference in *Perkins* and the reluctant conclusion has been reached that such a course would be pointless (1998) *The Times*, 16 July.

which merely permits the Council of Ministers to enact measures to combat a range of inequalities, including sexual orientation.[22] Therefore, although the Court did pay lip service to Art 13 in its judgment in *Grant*, it is hardly likely that any legislation on sexual orientation will emerge from it.

From the perspective of developing 'equality ethos', any widening of the equality principles is to be welcomed. Hence, these possible exploitations of the direct discrimination principle reflect efforts to move the equality agenda beyond concerns with employment ratios and recruitment patterns. Ultimately, these attempts have only encountered limited success before the ECJ, so an 'equality ethos' model has not been significantly advanced as a result.

INDIRECT DISCRIMINATION

As we have seen, Art 119 is silent on questions of indirect discrimination, while an undefined reference is made to the principle in the 1976 Directive. Nevertheless, the ECJ has constructed, again in its 'progressive era', a powerful definition of indirect discrimination, thus generating potential for an 'equality ethos', assault upon structural discrimination in both employment and welfare systems. In Case 170/84, *Bilka-Kaufhaus v von Hartz*,[23] Mrs von Hartz was excluded from a private sector occupational pension scheme allegedly contrary to Art 119, on grounds of her part time status, the issue around which nearly all European litigation on indirect discrimination hinges. A classic definition of indirect discrimination emerged from *Bilka-Kaufhaus* (para 29):

> If ... it should be found that a much lower proportion of women than men work full time, the exclusion of part time workers from the occupational pension scheme would be contrary to Art 119 of the Treaty where, taking into account the difficulties encountered by women workers in working full time, that measure cannot be explained by factors which exclude any discrimination on grounds of sex.

Unlike cases of direct discrimination, in which only specific statutory exceptions are permissible, cases of alleged indirect discrimination involve a test for objective justification. In *Bilka*, the Court provided a strenuous standard of objectively justifiable factors, namely (para 30):

---

22 See Bell, M and Waddington, L, 'The 1996 intergovernmental conference and the prospects of a non-discrimination Treaty article' (1996) 25 ILJ 320, pp 320–36. Indeed, it is Art 13 which may raise most expectations in relation to Community equality principles in the next century. Nevertheless, it is a very limited measure. Experience suggests that little if anything will emerge from a treaty base which is dependent upon unanimity in the Council, certainly since the number of Member States has expanded from six to 15.

23 [1986] ECR 1607.

measures ... [which] correspond to a real need on the part of the undertaking, are appropriate with a view to achieving the objectives pursued and are necessary to that end.

Remarkably, the Court carried this approach further into the contentious area of justification for State action. In Case 171/88, *Rinner-Kühn v FWW Spezial-Gebäudereinigung GmbH and Co KG*,[24] a challenge was made to an employer's adherence to the provisions in a statutory sick pay scheme and a consequent refusal to pay statutory sick pay to a part-time worker. The Court was happy to apply a *Bilka* type test of objective justification based on necessity to the employer's statutory obligation, even concluding that it was up to the German Government to persuade the national labour court that there was a real need in social policy for the exclusion of part time workers from the statutory scheme.

The ECJ has never shown the same enthusiasm for a rigorous test of objective justification in cases of welfare equality, particularly where the issues lie at the heart of welfare policy.[25] Nevertheless, a new suspicion of the indirect discrimination principle is exhibited in recent judgments, most notably Case C-444/93, *Megner and Scheffel v Innungskrankenkasse Rheinhessen-Pfalz*,[26] in which a challenge was made to minimum qualifications (15 hours a week employment and a minimum payment record) for entitlement to unemployment benefit (paras 29–30):

> In the current state of Community law, social policy is a matter for the Member States. Consequently, it is for the Member States to choose the measures capable of achieving the aim of their social and employment policy. In exercising that competence, the Member States have a broad margin of discretion.
>
> It should be noted that the social and employment policy aim relied on by the German government is objectively unrelated to any discrimination on grounds of sex and that, in exercising its competence, the national legislature was reasonably entitled to consider that the legislation in question was necessary in order to achieve that aim.

This is a remarkable judgment. Students of the growth of European social policy over the last twenty five years can only marvel at the audacity of the assertion that social policy is 'a matter for the Member States'. Art 5 of the Equal Treatment in Social Security Directive 1979 states simply that:

---

24 [1989] ECR 2743.

25 See Case 30/85, *Teuling-Worms* [1987] ECR 2497 and Case 229/89, *Commission v Belgium* [1991] ECR I-2205. See Bieback, KJ, *Indirect Discrimination within the Meaning of Directive (CE) 79/7 in the Social Security Law of the EC Member States*, 1996, Brussels: European Commission; Banks, K, 'Social security – objective justification in the context of indirect discrimination' (1991) 20 ILJ 22, pp 22–23.

26 [1995] ECR I-4741. See Brett, A, 'Indirect discrimination in social security schemes' [1997] 4 Web JCLI.

Member States shall take the measures necessary to ensure that any laws, regulations and administrative provisions contrary to the principle of equal treatment are abolished.

This principle of equal treatment is acknowledged by the Court to be a fundamental principle of Community law.[27] Hence, it is difficult to accept that the required abolition of laws and regulations which contravene it can be anywhere but at the heart of Community social law obligations upon the Member States. And, yet, the Court proceeded to devalue the principle of indirect discrimination by declaring that the measures at issue were not directly discriminatory and devalued it further by invoking what amounts to little more than a test of legislative subjective justification, that the legislature was reasonably entitled to consider that the measure was necessary. The effect of *Megner* is to neutralise the principle of indirect discrimination in relation to welfare equality, in this case concerning qualifications based not, as in earlier cases, on welfare policy but rather on labour market policy, an area much closer to the heart of the Community's social policy.[28]

Given the Court's reluctance to intrude into welfare policy at all, the most worrying implications of *Megner* lie in its potential effect on employment equality cases, most obviously concerning statutory employment schemes where, once again, the purported 'sovereignty' of the Member States over social policy is most obviously at issue, but where the Court appeared to apply a *Bilka* type approach in *Rinner-Kühn*. Here, we find the Court driven by the logic of *Megner* rather than *Rinner-Kühn*, but being more circumspect in its application of the indirect discrimination principle. In Case C-457/93, *Kuratorium für Dialyse und Nierentransplantation eV v Lewark*,[29] the Court was dealing with the aftermath of an earlier controversial indirect discrimination ruling on a German statutory scheme for time off for works councillors.[30] Here, indirect discrimination was established where the statutory scheme allowed for continuation of payment during attendance at works council duties during, but not outside, working hours. This had the effect of favouring full time workers over part time workers. This latter decision, *Bötel*, has caused consternation in Germany, inflicting Community equality law principles upon the sacrosanct world of German works councils. Therefore, the return of the *Bötel* questions in *Lewark* was always going to be a sensitive question. The formulation in *Lewark* was more measured than in *Megner*, but

---

27 This is also the case for the principle of equal treatment in social security schemes (Case C-343/92, *De Weerd* [1994] ECR I-571).

28 See Fitzpatrick, B, 'Summary of the conference', in 'Beyond equal treatment: social security in a changing Europe – *Report of the Conference of the Irish Presidency of the European Union, Dublin, 10–12 October 1996*, Dublin: Department of Social Welfare, pp 12–19.

29 [1996] ECR I-243.

30 Case 360/90, *Arbeiterwohlfahrt der Stadt Berlin EV v Bötel* [1992] ECR I-3589.

still showed a significant deviation from the 'purity' of the *Bilka* ruling. The Court concluded:

If a Member State is able to show that the measures chosen reflect a legitimate aim of its social policy are appropriate to achieve that aim and are necessary in order to do so, the mere fact that the legislative provision affects far more women workers than men cannot be regarded as a breach of Art 119.

On the one hand, *Lewark* does not go down the path of invoking a minimalist 'subjective' test of justification. On the other hand, the vital ingredient in *Bilka*, the demonstration of a 'real need' on the part of an undertaking, is substituted by a 'legitimate social objective' of the Member State in a purely employment-related case, albeit concerning a statutory scheme. Once that devaluation of the justification for *objectives* is in place, the continuing invocation of tests of appropriateness and necessity of *means* is much less rigorous than in *Bilka*.

Indeed, this partial influence of *Megner* is carried into the realms of general public employment in Case C-1/95, *Gerster v Freistaat Bayern*,[31] concerning statutory arrangements for the promotion of Bavarian civil servants. On the positive front, the Court indicated strongly in *Gerster* that it is impermissible for any employer merely to treat part time employees on the basis of proportionate periods of employment for promotion purposes, eg, ten half time years' employment is equivalent to five full time years, unless it could be shown that 'part time employees are generally slower than full time employees in acquiring job related abilities and skills' (para 40). Such an incisive conclusion clearly promotes an 'equality ethos' approach towards promotion questions. But, then, the *Lewark* formula is applied, even though the statutory scheme provided merely the standard conditions of employment for public sector workers. In effect, *Bilka* is overtaken by the weaker 'legitimate social policy' test in all statute controlled public employment, and a significant distinction is thereby made between public and private employment.

What we see, therefore, is a slippery slope towards statutory schemes down which the Court has travelled from purely welfare equality cases, through employment-related welfare cases, to purely employment cases. In each situation, the 'sovereignty' exercised by Member States over social policy seems to take precedence over a rigorous 'equality ethos' approach to the indirect discrimination principle. An interesting test of the extent of the Court's adherence to this revised approach will be the much awaited ruling in C-167/97, *R v Secretary of State for Employment ex p Seymour-Smith*, in which the English House of Lords has referred to the ECJ, questions concerning the indirectly discriminatory effect of the two year qualification period in UK unfair dismissal protection.[32] The House had previously concluded, without

---

31 [1997] ECR I-5253. For some comments on *Gerster*, see Schiek, D, 'More positive action in Community law' (1998) 27 ILJ 155, pp 155-61.

32 [1997] IRLR 315 (HL(E)). See, also, earlier rulings at [1994] IRLR 448 (Div Ct); [1995] IRLR 464 (CA). See, now, Case C-167/97 [1999] All ER (EC) 97.

reference to the Court, that another qualification requiring at least 16 hours' employment a week to enjoy this two year qualification period was indirectly discriminatory and not objectively justified.[33] It may well have been that an application of the *Lewark* test might have resulted in a different outcome even in *ex parte EOC*. Hopefully, we will at least be spared a resuscitation of the *Megner* test in *Seymour-Smith*.

This detailed analysis has been necessary in order to appreciate the extent to which the principle of indirect discrimination, vital to an 'equality ethos' model, has undergone a significant reappraisal by the ECJ in a widening range of contexts. As indicated earlier, the pursuit of indirect discrimination claims is a central impetus towards the auditing of employment practices as part of an 'equality ethos' approach. A vigorous approach towards objective justification is an essential ingredient in the intrusiveness of the principle but it is this very intrusiveness which brings with it the critical scrutiny of a Court increasingly cautious of equality law principles and wary of antagonising the interests of the Member States. Hence we see the gradual erosion of a 'necessity' standard for objective justification, initially in those areas of welfare policy furthest from the heart of Community social policy, and indeed closest to the heart of national social policy. Rather than sustaining the universal logic of *Bilka* as the issues have moved closer to the labour market sphere within which Community policy holds significantly greater legitimacy, the Court has been prepared to pursue its modified version in *Lewark* of its *Megner* formula, a scenario not dissimilar to the tussle observed earlier between *Dekker* and *Hertz* in relation to pregnancy protection. Once again, we cannot pretend that these developments augur well for Community equality law. While the extensions of the principle of direct discrimination in relation to pregnancy and sexual orientation can be seen as rather adventurous exercises reined back by pragmatic considerations, the conclusions to be drawn in relation to the recent indirect discrimination cases before the Court are somewhat more bleak. It might be thought that the greatest duty to promote 'equality ethos' in employment lies upon the Member States but it is in response to national governmental pressures that the Court has weakened the test of 'objective justification' in statutory schemes and hence obstructed the pursuit of 'equality ethos' where it might be expected to be most effective.[34]

It remains to be seen whether a statutory definition of indirect discrimination, to be introduced through the Burden of Proof Directive 1998,[35]

---

33 *R v Secretary of State for Employment ex p EOC* [1995] AC 1 (HL(E)). See Deakin, S, 'Part time employment, qualifying thresholds and economic justification' (1994) 23 ILJ 151, pp 151–55.

34 Ironically, this retreat from a rigorous approach to indirect discrimination in State action coincides with a Commission led campaign to promote the 'mainstreaming' of gender questions in all aspects of policy making; see Commission Communication on 'Incorporating equal opportunities for women and men into all Community policies and activities', COM(96) 67 final of 21 February 1996.

35 Council Directive 97/80/EC of 15 December 1997 (OJ L14, 20 January 1998, p 6).

redresses this growing imbalance between public and private sector employment. Article 2(2) of the Directive provides that:

> ... indirect discrimination shall exist where an apparently neutral provision, criterion or practice disadvantages a substantially higher proportion of the members of one sex unless that provision, criterion or practice is appropriate and necessary and can be justified by objective factors unrelated to sex.

This appears to herald a return to a 'necessity' test as far as objectives as well as means are concerned. One can therefore only speculate whether the *Leward* test will survive the implementation of the Directive and hence whether the 'legitimate social policy' objectives approach will re-emerge in relation to statutory schemes.

POSITIVE ACTION

Article 2(4) of the Equal Treatment Directive 1976 states:

> This Directive shall be without prejudice to measures to promote equal opportunity for men and women, in particular by removing existing inequalities which affect women's opportunities in the areas referred to in Art 1(1) ...

This formulation was understood in many Member States to permit a wide range of positive action measures, not merely what has been described as 'positive indirect discrimination' but also 'positive direct discrimination'. These presumptions were rebutted in Case C-450/93, *Kalanke v Freie Hansestadt Bremen*.[36] Mr Kalanke was the 'victim' of a 'tie break' system whereby a female applicant would be promoted ahead of a male applicant if both were equally qualified, in situations where there was less than 50/50 representation of women in that department. The Court concluded that Art 2(4) was a derogation from the principle of equal treatment in Art 2(1) of the Directive and therefore had to be strictly construed. It did not protect:

> ... national rules which guarantee women absolute and unconditional priority for appointments and which seek to achieve equality of outcome rather than equality of opportunity [para 22].

It was intimated that only 'starting line' measures, which allowed women to improve their position in the labour market, might be permitted under Art 2(4), although various paragraphs of the judgment indicated that the Court

---

36 [1995] ECR I-3051. See O'Hare, U, 'Positive action before the European Court of Justice' [1996] 2 Web JCLI (http://webjcli.ncl.ac.uk); Prechal, S, 'Note on *Kalanke*' (1996) 33 CML Rev 1245; and Schiek, D, 'Positive action in community law' (1996) 25 ILJ 239, pp 239–46. For an earlier analysis of German 'positive action' programmes, see Shaw, J, 'Positive action for women in Germany: the use of legally binding quotas', in Hepple, B and Szyszczak, E (eds), *Discrimination: The Limits of Law*, 1993, London: Mansell, pp 386–411.

might be divided on the scope for positive discrimination. In response to the furore which surrounded *Kalanke*, the Commission issued a communication seeking to clarify *Kalanke*, in order to preserve the legitimacy of positive action measures which fell short of rigid quotas.[37] There was also the possibility of amending Art 2(4) in order to counteract the effect of *Kalanke*, although the prospect of 'tinkering' with the 1976 Directive filled many with trepidation.

Much of the anxiety surrounding *Kalanke* was dispelled by the later judgment in Case C-409/95, *Hellmut Marschall v Land Nordrhein-Westfalen*.[38] What was only obliquely apparent to those without intimate knowledge of German positive action programmes, was that there was a vital distinction between the Bremen 'tie break' system and those in other Länder and cities, namely the 'automatic' nature of the preferential treatment of the equally qualified female applicant. Other systems allowed a countervailing process to be instigated, whereby consideration had to be given to any possible 'unbearable individual hardship' to the male applicant. Hence, in *Marschall*, the ECJ was able to accept that, due to prejudices and presumptions, men are still promoted ahead of women, even if both are equally qualified:

> It follows that a national rule in terms of which, subject to the application of the saving clause, female candidates for promotion who are equally as qualified as the male candidates are to be treated preferentially in sectors where they are under-represented may fall within the scope of Art 2(4) if such a rule may counteract the prejudicial effects on female candidates of the attitudes and behaviour described above and thus reduce actual instances of inequality which may exist in the real world [para 31].

> Unlike the rules at issue in *Kalanke*, a national rule which, as in the case in point in the main proceedings, contains a saving clause does not exceed those limits if, in each individual case, it provides for male candidates who are equally as qualified as the female candidates a guarantee that the candidatures will be the subject of an objective assessment which will take account of all criteria specific to the individual candidates where one or more of those criteria tilts the balance in favour of the male candidate. In this respect, however, it should be remembered that those criteria must not be such as to discriminate against female candidates [para 33].

The Court was therefore giving *carte blanche* to a wide range of positive action measures, including those involving positive direct discrimination. Indeed, a significant restraint was placed upon the 'unbearable hardship' exception by the Court's insistence that the operation of the 'saving clause' could not result in indirectly discriminatory consequences, which might often be the case when, for example, seniority or the 'breadwinner' status of the male applicant is taken into account.

---

37 COM(95) 381 final.

38 [1997] ECR I-6363. See Schiek, D, 'More positive action in Community law' (1998) 27 ILJ 155, pp 155-61.

There has been, after all, some legislative activity concerning positive action but in relation to Art 119 of the Treaty of Rome on equal pay rather than Art 2(4) of the Equal Treatment Directive 1976, which has been left undisturbed. Initially, a revised version of Art 119 was included in the Social Policy Agreement annexed to the Treaty of Rome via the Social Policy Protocol of the Treaty on European Union and, hence, applies at present to the 14 Member States, excluding the UK. The Treaty of Amsterdam, once ratified, will amend (and renumber the provisions of) the Treaty of Rome, so that what will thereafter be Art 141(4) of the Treaty, will state:

> With a view to ensuring full equality in practice between men and women in working life, the principle of equal treatment shall not prevent any Member State from maintaining or adopting measures providing for specific advantages in order to make it easier for the under-represented sex to pursue a vocational activity or to prevent or compensate for disadvantages in professional careers.

While *Kalanke* reflected a strongly symmetrical approach to equality between men and women, *Marschall* acknowledges a more asymmetrical approach. There was an emphasis in *Kalanke* on the fundamental importance of 'parity of esteem' between men and women, but it was accepted in *Marschall* that women in general suffer significantly greater disadvantage than men, particularly in recruitment. What was ironic about *Kalanke* was that the Court suddenly rediscovered the fundamental nature of the equality principles, in much the same way it did in *P v S*, while pointedly ignoring this context in a range of restrictive judgments, as we have seen, in relation to pregnancy, sexual orientation and indirect discrimination, and also in the long saga of post-*Barber* cases on equality in occupational pension schemes.

Given the level of national uproar caused by *Kalanke*, the *Marschall* judgment is in fact consistent with a view of the Court as being more receptive, if not subservient, to national considerations in the field of social policy. It augurs well for the increased scope of positive discrimination measures in those Member States, unlike the UK, where a wide range of such measures is permissible. However, it would be more reassuring if the Court had found a way of rationalising an asymmetrical approach within the context of the fundamental nature of the equality principles.

Nonetheless, the outcome of *Marschall* ought to be treated with some caution. It has been suggested earlier that there are dangers in resorting to positive direct discrimination at the expense of thorough equality auditing of working conditions. The pursuit of equality ought to pervade all aspects of the employment relationship in an 'equality ethos' approach. Public policy objectives can drive the emphasis of an equality regime towards the reduction of disparities between disadvantaged and advantaged groups. This 'disparity reduction' approach can degenerate into a 'body counting' approach to labour market composition, on grounds of religion, race, sex, etc. Under such pressures, it is tempting to move swiftly across the spectrum of equality principles from anti-direct discrimination measures, which may fail to provide the short term results required, to positive direct discrimination without some serious exploration on the way of the possibilities of anti-indirect discrimination, and positive indirect discrimination measures. The outcome may well be that such positive direct discrimination measures end up advantaging the least disadvantaged of the disadvantaged class, for example, middle class Catholics (in a Northern Irish context) and childless women, rather than providing opportunities for those who need them most. For example, an organisation which makes no effort to reconcile working life and domestic life, or to provide child care facilities, need not be surprised if women with domestic responsibilities fail to find their way into the 'tie break' with an equally qualified man. Nor are they likely to be of assistance to those suffering a double discrimination, for example, Catholic or black women. It is only if rigorous auditing of working practices is instigated that true equality of opportunity for most elements of the disadvantaged class can be hoped for. There was an indication in *Kalanke* that the Court was aware of this. In para 23, of its judgment, the Court proceeded to state:

> Furthermore, in so far as it seeks to achieve equal representation of men and women in all grades and levels within a department, such a system substitutes for equality of opportunity as envisaged in Art 2(4), the result of which is only to be arrived at by providing such equal opportunities.

It is arguable that para 23 goes too far, closing off any prospect of positive measures to achieve equality of outcome. Where the germ of truth lies is in the proposition that undertakings should not be allowed to opt out of rigorous equality monitoring through the crude device of positive direct discrimination. What ought to be permissible is a rolling programme, whereby an organisation first seeks to redress any perceived inequalities in its payment systems and working practices through traditional anti-direct and anti-indirect discrimination measures. Advocate General Jacobs in his opinion in *Marschall* gives an example. The European Commission operates an ageist policy whereby candidates for most Commission positions must be under an age limit set at 35. However, the age limit is extended for 'candidates who for at least one year have not pursued an occupational activity in order to look after a young child living in their home' (para 43 of his opinion). The Advocate General categorises this as an exercise to which Art 2(4) might apply (para 44). This is, in fact, a doubtful proposition. An age limit of 35 is indirectly discriminatory against women because of their predominant child care responsibilities. This extension is merely a sensible reaction to that reality. To the extent that it is indirectly discriminatory against men, it is easily justifiable as being necessary to combat indirect discrimination against women.

Nevertheless, it is possible to concur with the Advocate General that gender neutral measures – described here as positive indirect discrimination – which seek to alleviate disadvantage, are preferable to positive direct discrimination measures. Indeed, it seems clear from his observations that he envisages many examples of positive indirect discrimination coming within the scope of a *Kalanke* analysis of Art 2(4). What might be envisaged would be a programme, in keeping with an 'equality ethos' approach, whereby special allowance was made for social responsibilities, for example, the care of children or ageing relatives, in the process of evaluating the merits of candidates for recruitment or promotion. It might well go beyond what could be described as an anti-indirect discrimination measure and might be more difficult to justify under a strict 'necessity' test in an indirect discrimination action by a disappointed male applicant. Indeed, if it can be contended that intentional indirect discrimination is in reality 'on grounds of sex', etc, and, hence, a form of direct discrimination, no objective justification would be permissible. Hence, some form of protection of immunity along the lines of Art 2(4) of the 1976 Directive would be required.

A programme of positive indirect discrimination flows naturally from a programme of anti-indirect discrimination measures. Both are directed at the particular structural disadvantage which members of the disadvantaged class suffer rather than mere membership of that class. Where the Court may have gone too far in *Marschall,* was in allowing itself to be totally focused on the question of the 'saving clause' without considering the extent to which the organisation seeking to invoke positive direct discrimination had done everything possible to achieve equality of outcome, without resorting to positive direct discrimination measures. Where an organisation can show that there is still inequality in aspects of its working practices which resists all efforts at eradication, the threshold for positive direct discrimination measures has been reached. But, there remain dangers of 'quick fix' solutions to inequalities through a 'disparity reduction' approach rather than the 'equality ethos' approach which is more likely to bring medium and long term results.

CONCLUSIONS

Prediction of the future development of equality principles within the European Community is dependent upon the extent to which patterns can be discerned in their development. There is a consistent pattern whereby adventurous interpretations of sex equality principles in the 1980s and into the early 1990s have been revised by a more cautious Court of Justice, since its authority was obliquely attacked in the aftermath of the *Barber* saga. That saga involved the diminution of the direct discrimination principle through restrictive judgments upon examples of direct discrimination in occupational pension schemes. Potential extensions of the direct discrimination principle into areas of 'sex-plus' criteria have been curtailed, in the case of pregnancy, or thwarted, in the case of sexual orientation. So too, a major retreat has occurred in relation to the indirect discrimination principle, one which is naturally intrusive in the rare circumstances in which it is possible to invoke it. In a tussle between purported national 'sovereignty' over social policy and a fundamental principle of Community law, the former has triumphed, not just where Community legitimacy is at its weakest, in relation to welfare policy but also now at the heart of labour market policy, concerning public sector employment. In relation to positive action, the Court's view can be seen as the adoption of an asymmetrical approach, encompassing positive direct discrimination for disadvantaged groups within the scope of equality principles. More realistically, *Marschall* can be seen as another case of national priorities taking preference over Community ones. It is, therefore, difficult to see Community law being the powerhouse for the development of equality principles into the next century. Certainly, once ratified, Art 13 of the Treaty will allow for a possible legislative agenda encompassing a wide range of inequalities[39] but, given the requirement of unanimity within Art 13, it is difficult to imagine any significant developments beyond perhaps a race relations directive.[40] If an 'equality ethos' objective is sought from adherence to equality principles, Community law made great strides in that direction through the development of a coherent principle of indirect discrimination but it would appear to be that this potential of motivating significant changes in welfare and labour market systems has brought on the judicial retreat from its full implications. Certainly, national systems are free to permit positive indirect discrimination but the Court has missed an opportunity in *Marschall* to insist on the pursuit of coherent equal opportunities policies prior to resorting to positive direct discrimination.

Although the Court certainly had filled in the detail of Community sex equality law up until its post-*Barber* trauma, it is today particularly sensitive to the fact that Community law is a quasi-federal system. As such, it can do little more than set a framework within which it is permissible for the Member States to decide upon the extent of any innovation in both principles and procedures. One can only imagine that the Court's more conservative phase is set to continue into the next century. Future changes in personnel and ethos may alter this assessment but it sometimes appears inevitable that, once the rather insulated existence of the Court was shattered, the progressive approach to equality principles would be lost and would be difficult to

---

39 The ratified treaty will also provide two specific treaty bases for legislation on gender equality, in each case by qualified majority voting, namely, Arts 137(1) and 141(3).

40 See Bell, M, *EU Anti-Discrimination Policy: From Equal Opportunities between Women and Men to Combating Racism*, LIBE 102 EN, 1998, Brussels: European Parliament.

restore. Whatever momentum might have been created through European law for an 'equality ethos' approach has now been largely dissipated and a relaxed attitude towards positive direct discrimination may reinforce the attractiveness of 'disparity reduction' at the expense of 'equality ethos'.

As indicated in the Introduction, labour market pressures may favour the 'simplicities' of 'disparity reduction' over 'equality ethos'. So, also within the judicial process sphere, still further perspectives come into play. Courts are more used to individual justice issues than collective justice ones. Lawyers prefer transparent principles to opaque ones. Access to the system of judicial process is problematic and its capacity to deliver public policy objectives may be limited by the nature of judicial process in employment law litigation. Out of such imponderables emerges an initial perception that, what may be seen as measures directed towards a valid public policy objective, once put into practice in the labour market and then litigated upon in the tribunals and courts, may result at the other end of the process in effects which are disappointing, if not, counter-productive. Given the relative transparency of direct and positive direct discrimination principles, and a greater willingness of applicants to invoke them within the judicial process, it may be that use of judicial process actually favours a 'disparity reduction' approach at the expense of an 'equality ethos' one. Concepts at the heart of an 'equality ethos' approach, namely, indirect and positive indirect discrimination, therefore, need sensitive handling within the judicial process in order to maximise their effectiveness. So also, as well as an expansive approach to the direct discrimination principle, a cautious approach to positive direct discrimination might be anticipated. On all these counts, the picture in Community law is less encouraging than it might have been had the Court not prioritised national sensitivities in social law cases. In consequence, the momentum towards an 'equality ethos' model of gender equality law has suffered a series of significant, but not terminal, setbacks as the 21st century approaches.

CHAPTER 7

WOMEN'S RIGHTS AS HUMAN RIGHTS: OLD AGENDAS IN NEW GUISES

Christine Bell

Equality on the basis of sex would seem to be at the heart of the United Nations mission. Article 1 of the Charter sets out three main purposes of the United Nations, the last of which includes, 'to define and protect the rights and freedoms of every individual regardless of race, sex, language or religion'. The United Nations Universal Declaration on Human Rights of 1948 included the proclamation that all human rights and freedoms are to be enjoyed equally by women and men without distinction of any kind. Article 2, for example, states that:

> Everyone is entitled to all the rights and freedoms set forth in this Declaration, without distinction of any kind, such as race, colour, sex, language, religion, political or other opinion, national or social origin, property, birth or other status.[1]

All the general human rights conventions at regional and international level have provision for equality and non-discrimination on the basis of sex.[2] This international commitment to equality stands in contrast to the economic, political, and social marginalisation of women in most countries of the world. It also stands in contrast to the under-representation of women and women's rights in human rights machinery, from international institutions to non governmental organisations (apart, of course, from those focusing explicitly on women's rights).

Over the last decade or so, the phrase 'women's rights as human rights' has been used to explore, assert and redress the gap between the stated international commitment to equality for women and the actual experience of women. The ambiguity of the phrase captures the essence of the feminist claim: an assertion for inclusion in the project of human rights and a radical redefinition of what that project entails. This chapter reviews feminist theory of human rights suggesting that, at the turn of the century, it stands in uneasy harmony with agendas which seek to deny the universality (and therefore

---

1   See, also, Universal Declaration on Human Rights 1948, Art 1 ('all human beings are born free and equal in dignity and rights ...'); Art 7 (equal protection of the law and against discrimination); Art 16 (equal rights in marriage and after dissolution; Art 23 (right to equal pay for equal work).

2   See ICESCR 1966, Arts 2(2) and 3; ICCPR 1966, Arts 2(1), 24(1) and 26; ECHR 1950, Art 14; Preamble, European Social Charter 1961; African [Banjul] Charter on Human and Peoples' Rights 1981, Arts 2, 3 and 5; American Convention on Human Rights 1969, Arts 1(1) and 24.

enforceability) of human rights. On entering the new century, the path which human rights take through these challenges will shape and scope new agendas, not just in relation to women's rights, but more broadly.

WOMEN'S RIGHTS AND INTERNATIONAL HUMAN RIGHTS LAW

In addition to the equality and non-discrimination provisions of general conventions, there is a wealth of international instruments, declarations and initiatives on human rights and women's rights. The gap between reality and practice is not due to international inaction in the area of women's rights; rather, it is due to the precise nature of the international response, which has been criticised as inadequate and serving to marginalise rather than mainstream women's rights.[3] To fully document and analyse international instruments on women's rights is beyond the scope of this chapter, but a few milestones can be noted.[4]

In a pattern similar to that of women's rights in Western States, women's approach to international law can be analysed as a two stage process: first a strategy of addressing the legal status of women and, secondly, scepticism as to the gains of this strategy and a more ambivalent critical response to law, with an increasingly theoretical approach.[5] The period of codification of women's legal status lasted from 1945 until the 1960s. In addition to the general equality provisions of post-Second World War conventions, specific initiatives directed at women soon proliferated.[6] In 1946, the Economic and Social Council, one of the six main organs of the United Nations established by the Charter, itself established the Commission on Human Rights, with a sub-commission on the status of women,[7] which was later elevated to a

---

3   See, eg, Byrnes, A, 'Women, feminism and international human rights law: methodological myopic, fundamental flaws or meaningful marginalisations?' [1992] AYIL 205, pp 205–40; Gallagher, A, 'Ending the marginalisation: strategies for incorporating women into the United Nations human rights system' (1997) 19 HRQ 283, pp 283–333.

4   For a detailed account, see *The United Nations and the Advancement of Women: 1945–95*, 1995, UN Blue Books Series, New York: Department of Public Information, United Nations, Vol VI.

5   Cf Smart, C, 'Feminist jurisprudence', in Fitzpatrick, P (ed), *Dangerous Supplements*: *Resistance and Renewal in Jurisprudence*, 1991, London: Pluto, pp 133–58; Smart, C, *The Power of Law*, 1989, London: Routledge, Chap 4, pp 66–89.

6   Indeed, these had pre-Second World War precursors, eg, Montivideo Convention on the Nationality of Married Women 1933.

7   Economic and Social Council (ECOSOC) resolution establishing the Commission on Human Rights and the Sub-commission on the Status of Women E/RES/5 (I), 16 February 1946.

Commission on the Status of Women.[8] In 1946, a section on the status of women was established within the Human Rights Division of the United Nations Secretariat's Department of Social Affairs. During the next two decades, a number of General Assembly resolutions, regional and international conventions were promulgated which dealt with the equality and status of women.[9] However, 'it became clear during the 1960s that the legal status of women was only one element of a larger theme: the advancement of women within a broader social and economic context', so addressing equality for women meant addressing the broader context.[10] This entailed a reworking of the ambit of human rights law. In 1967, the General Assembly unanimously approved the Declaration on the Elimination of Discrimination against Women, which was an attempt to consolidate in one document all of the standards on women's rights developed since 1945.[11] The Declaration recognised that non-discrimination involved not just a negative obligation on States, but a positive obligation to take action against discrimination by individuals. Thus, Art 2 provided that:

> All appropriate measures shall be taken to abolish existing laws, customs, regulation and practices which are discriminatory against women, and to establish adequate legal protection for equal rights of men and women ...

This declaration formed the precursor for the Convention on the Elimination of All Forms of Discrimination against Women, which itself was one of the

---

8   ECOSOC resolution establishing the Commission on the Status of Women (CSW) E/RES/2/11, 21 June 1946. See, generally, Reanda, L, 'The Commission on the Status of Women', in Alston, P (ed), *The United Nations and Human Rights: A Critical Appraisal*, 1992, Oxford: Clarendon, pp 265–303; Galey, ME, 'Promoting non-discrimination against women: the UN Commission on the Status of Women' (1979) 23 ISQ 273, pp 273–302.

9   General Assembly resolution calling on Member States to adopt measures necessary to fulfil the aims of the UN Charter in granting women the same political rights as men A/RES/56 (I), 11 December 1946; Convention for the Suppression of the Traffic in Persons and of the Exploitation of the Prostitution of Others, adopted by the General Assembly 2 December 1949, UNTS 1342, Vol 96, p 271; Convention on the Political Rights of Women, adopted by the General Assembly 20 December 1952, UNTS 2613, Vol 193, p 135; Convention on the Nationality of Married Women, adopted by the General Assembly 29 January 1957, UNTS 4468, Vol 309, p 65; Convention on Consent to Marriage, Minimum Age for Marriage and Registration of Marriages, adopted by the General Assembly 7 November 1962, UNTS 7525, Vol 521, p 231; General Assembly resolution adopting the Recommendation on Consent to Marriage, Minimum Age for Marriage and Registration of Marriages A/RES/2018 (XX), 1 November 1965; General Assembly resolution calling on Member States to eliminate customs, ancient laws and practices affecting the human dignity of women A/RES/843 (IX), 17 December 1954. In this period, women's rights were also recognised in international humanitarian law applicable in times of international and internal armed conflict, see, eg, Convention Relative to the Protection of Civilian Persons in Time of War, Art 27, 12 August 1949, 75 UNTS 287, Geneva; see, also, Protocol Additional to the Geneva Conventions of 12 August 1949 and Relating to the Protection of Victims of International Armed Conflicts (Protocol I), Art 768, June 1977, 1125 UNTS 17512.

10 *Op cit*, Fitzpatrick, fn 5, p 26.

11 General Assembly Resolution adopting the Declaration on the Elimination of Discrimination against Women A/RES/2263 (XXII), 7 November 1967.

most significant steps in the assertion of women's rights.[12] CEDAW emerged during a decade proclaimed by the United Nations as the 'United Nations Decade for Women: Equality, Development and Peace' during 1976–85. CEDAW was significant in providing the first international instrument to define discrimination[13] and in extending State responsibility clearly into the realm of private action. Thus, it commits States not just to refrain from 'engaging in any act or practice of discrimination against women',[14] but to 'take all appropriate measures to eliminate discrimination against women by any person, organisation or enterprise',[15] and to 'modify or abolish existing laws, regulations, customs and practices which constitute discrimination against women'.[16] CEDAW explicitly excludes affirmative action measures from its definition of discrimination.[17] Its provisions are broad ranging, covering public and political life (Art 7(8)); nationality (Art 9); education (Art 10); employment (Art 11); health care (Art 12); other aspects of social and economic life (Art 13); specific provision for rural women (Art 14); and a list of specific rights for women (Art 16). The Convention has an enforcement mechanism whereby governments report to a Committee on the Elimination of Discrimination against Women (Arts 17–22).

One striking omission from the Convention was the issue of violence against women, which was not specifically categorised as a human rights abuse. In recent times, the issue of State, and indeed non-State violence against women, has become a main focus of NGOs working on women's rights, domestically and internationally. While the Declaration and Convention had marked a breaking down of the State/non-State dichotomy in human rights law, the extension of non-discrimination to include gender violence marked a more clearly analytical critical approach to human rights law. In 1992, the Committee on the Elimination of All Forms of Discrimination against Women adopted General Recommendation 19 on Violence against Women, stating that the issue of violence against women was covered by most of the articles of CEDAW as a matter of discrimination.[18]

> [The] definition of discrimination includes gender-based violence, that is, violence which is directed against a woman because she is a woman or which affects women disproportionately. It includes acts which inflict physical, mental or sexual harm or suffering, threats of such acts, coercion and other deprivations of liberty. Gender based violence may breach specific provisions

---

12 Convention on the Elimination of All Forms of Discrimination against Women, adopted by the General Assembly 18 December 1979, UNTS 20378, Vol 1249, p 13.

13 *Ibid*, Art 1.

14 *Ibid*, Art 2(d).

15 *Ibid*, Art 2(e).

16 *Ibid*, Art 2(f).

17 *Ibid*, Art 4.

18 See Official Records of the General Assembly, 47th session, Sup 38 (A/47/38), Chap I.

of the Convention, regardless of whether those provisions expressly mention violence.[19]

In 1993, the General Assembly adopted the Declaration on the Elimination of Violence against Women, which defined 'violence against women' as 'any act of gender based violence that results in, or is likely to result in, physical, sexual or psychological harm or suffering to women, including threats of such acts, coercion or arbitrary deprivation of liberty, whether occurring in public or in private life'.[20]

In March 1994, the United Nations Commission on Human Rights appointed a special rapporteur, Radhika Coomeraswamy, to collect information on acts of gender based violence and to recommend measures at the national, regional and international levels for its elimination.[21] In November 1994, the special rapporteur presented her first report on 'Violence against women, its causes and consequences',[22] setting out the major themes she wished to explore. These included themes which were fully analysed in her reports to the Human Rights Commission in following years. These were: violence in the family (reported on 1996,[23] including model legislation on domestic violence);[24] violence in the community (reported on 1997);[25] violence by the State (reported on 1998).[26]

The special rapporteur has also produced reports correlating with these general themes, based on field visits to Korea and Japan (dealing with the so called 'comfort women' issues),[27] to Poland (dealing with trafficking and forced prostitution),[28] to Brazil (dealing with domestic violence),[29] to South Africa (dealing with rape in the community)[30] and to Rwanda, dealing with genocide and war).[31] The reports are striking for their criticism of

---

19 Report of the Secretary General to the General Assembly on the improvement of the status of women in the Secretariat, November 1994 (A/49/587), Chap 1, para 466.
20 General Assembly Resolution adopting the Declaration on the Elimination of Violence against Women, Art 1, A/RES/48/104, 20 December 1993.
21 Commission on Human Rights resolution appointing a special rapporteur on violence against women, Commission on Human Rights resolution 1994/45, ESCOR, March 1994, Sup 4, p 140.
22 Special rapporteur on violence against women, Preliminary Report, Commission on Human Rights, E/CN 4/1995/42, issued 22 November 1994.
23 E/CN 4/1996/53, issued 5 February 1996.
24 E/CN4/1996/53/Add 2, issued 2 February 1996.
25 E/CN 4/1997/47, issued 12 February 1997.
26 E/CN 4/1998/54, issued 26 January 1998.
27 E/CN 4/1996/53/Add 1, issued 4 January 1996.
28 E/CN 4/1997/47/Add 1, issued 10 December 1996.
29 E/CN 4/1997/Add 2, issued 21 January 1997.
30 E/CN 4/1997/47/Add 3, issued 24 February 1997.
31 E/CN 4/1998/54/Add 1, issued 4 February 1998.

international human rights law as 'failing to be concerned with the "women question"', a criticism which is worked through analytically and theoretically to address the complex interrelationship between international and domestic law. They are also striking for their breadth. Although there is a specific mandate and focus – violence against women, its causes and consequences – the reports deal with the totality of women's social and economic marginalisation. Violence is linked to dress codes, traditional practices, health care, police action, pornography and sexual harassment, to name a few. These are connected through a theoretical framework whereby violence against women is linked to 'historically unequal power relations between men and women'. Thus, the avenue to address the totality of those power relations is opened up. The reports are also broad in the areas of law addressed: human rights law generally, refugee law and law of war.

In 1995, the push for 'women's rights as human rights' culminated in the Fourth UN Conference on Women, which took place in Beijing with a parallel Forum for Non-Governmental Organisations taking place in Huairou, China. The Beijing *Declaration* and *Global Platform for Action*, adopted at the conclusion of the Fourth UN Conference, and building on the Vienna Declaration and Programme of action,[32] can be described as a Bill of Rights for Women. The 150 page document identifies poverty as the principal area requiring priority action and the platform acknowledges that sustainable development and economic growth are only possible through improving the economic, social, political, legal and cultural status of women.[33] Other areas of priority include education and training, health, violence against women, armed conflict, economic structures, power sharing and decision making, human rights, the environment, the media and the girl child.

---

32 Vienna Declaration and Programme of Action, adopted by the World Conference on Human Rights, held in Vienna, 14–25 June 1993, s II A3: 'The equal status and human rights of women', paras 36–44.

33 Report of the Fourth World Conference on Women (Beijing, 4–15 September 1995) A CONF 177/20, 17 October 1995.

WOMEN'S RIGHTS AND THEORY

The theoretical approach to women's rights as human rights has consisted of an exposition of international human rights law's androcentric bias through a series of increasingly profound challenges.[34]

Theoretical challenges

International human rights law, it is claimed, fails to recognise women even when they suffer the same human rights abuses as men. Neither the 1951 Convention Relating to the status of refugees, nor the 1969 Organisation of African Unity Convention on the specific aspects of refugee problems in Africa, for example, recognise gender based persecution as a grounds for granting refugee status. International human rights law further fails to recognise the specific gender dimension of abuse that characterises the denial of rights to women. Thus, international law has had difficulty recognising the gender dynamics of the often sexual violence which characterises torture visited on women, or rape as a war crime within the context of international humanitarian law, although this is changing.[35] More problematically, international human rights law is challenged as excluding many women's rights from human rights discourse altogether through a series of related processes.

The public/private construction of international human rights law, whereby State action is required before there is a 'human rights' violation, and

---

34 A growing and already large literature. See, generally, Cook, R, (ed), *Human Rights of Women: National and International Perspectives*, 1994, Philadelphia: Pennsylvania UP (Pennsylvania Studies in Human Rights); Peters and Wolper (eds), *Women's Rights, Human Rights: International Feminist Perspectives*, 1995, New York: Routledge; Centre for Women's Global Leadership, *Gender Violence and Women's Human Rights in Africa*, 1994, New Jersey: Plowshares; Binion, G, 'Human rights: a feminist perspective' (1995) 17 HRQ 509, pp 509–26; Bunch, C, 'Women's rights as human rights: towards a re-vision of human rights' (1990) 12 HRQ 486, pp 486–98; *op cit*, Byrnes, fn 3; Charlesworth, H, Chinkin, C and Wright, S, 'Feminist approaches to international law' (1991) 85 AJIL 613; Cook, R, 'International human rights law concerning women: case notes and comments' (1990) 23 Vand J Trans L 779, pp 779–818; Cook, R, 'Women's international human rights law: the way forward' (1993) 15 HRQ 230, pp 230–61; Eilser, R, 'Human rights: toward an integrated theory for action' (1987) 9 HRQ 287, pp 287–308; *op cit*, Gallagher, fn 3; Oloka-Onyango, J and Tamale, S, '"The personal is political" or "Why women's rights are indeed human rights: an African perspective on international feminism"' (1995) 17 HRQ 691, pp 691–731.

35 See, eg, *Aydin v Turkey* ECHR judgment of 25 September 1997, Appl 57/1996/676/866, reported in [1998] HRLJ 59 (the Court held that, *inter alia*, the applicant had been subjected to torture through being raped and otherwise ill treated, contrary to Art 3 of the Convention); cf Case 10.970, *Meija v Peru* Report No 5/96 of 1 March 1997, Inter-American Commission.

whereby private actors are beyond its scope, has been critiqued as gendered.[36] Research has exposed the exclusionary nature of the public/private divide with regard to domestic violence, violence of war, and dowry deaths, to name a few.[37] A second critique has focused on the hierarchy of rights, where civil and political rights are enforceable and enjoy a central position as 'violations' within the human rights system.[38] In contrast, social, economic and cultural rights, and groups rights are more difficult to enforce and less accepted as judiciable minimum standards. Given that women's advancement is clearly linked to social, economic and cultural status, the lesser status of such rights diminishes women's rights. A third critique has been the denial of rights to women on the grounds that they will attack 'cultural', 'personal' or 'religious' views. The charge of 'cultural relativism' has been levelled in an attempt to diminish State accountability.[39] Theocratic States, some developing States, and Asian States, for example, have challenged the human rights order as implicitly Western. They have challenged the universality of human rights, asserting that rights must be seen as culturally relative and secondary to local, customary or traditional standards. This challenge seeks to decrease the scope of normative standards generally, and is particularly undermining of women's rights, which so often conflict with patriarchal religious structures, as is reflected in many of the reservations to CEDAW.[40]

Structural deficit

Compounding these problems is a structural deficit in enforcement of women's rights, which is both a product of the international marginalisation of women, and, in turn, contributes to the ongoing processes of that marginalisation.[41]

The structural deficit includes lack of participation of women at the international and non-governmental level. It includes flawed methodologies

36 See, eg, generally, *op cit*, Cook, 1994, fn 34; Peters and Wolper, fn 34; and Centre for Women's Global Leadership, fn 34; see, also, Romany, C, 'Women as *aliens*: a feminist critique of the public/private distinction in international human rights law' (1993) 6 Harv HRJ 87, pp 87–125.
37 See, eg, MacKinnon, CA, 'On torture: a feminist perspective on human rights', in Mahoney, K and Mahoney, P (eds), *Human Rights in the Twenty First Century*, p 21; MacKinnon, CA, 'Rape, genocide and women's Human rights' [1994] HW L Rev 5, pp 5–16; Copelon, R, 'Recognising egregious in the everyday: domestic violence as torture' (1994) 25 Colum HR L Rev 291, pp 291–305.
38 For an overview of inter-relationship, see Steiner, H and Alston, P, *International Human Rights in Context: Law, Politics and Morals*, 1996, Oxford: Clarendon.
39 *Ibid*, pp 166–255.
40 See Cook, R, 'Reservations to the Convention on the elimination of all forms of discrimination against women' (1990) 30 Va J Int L 643. See, generally, Higgins, T, 'Anti-essentialism, relativism and human rights' (1996) Harv WLJ 89, pp 89–126.
41 See *op cit*, Byrnes, fn 3; Gallagher, fn 3.

in investigating and documenting human rights violations, which leave out the question of women. Byrnes, for example, notes how the questions asked of refugees, and the methods of asking them, determines the information elicited, particularly on sexual violence.[42] Sadasivam has critiqued structural adjustment policies, arguing that standard methods of policy evaluation render women invisible, and cites feminist research which, in contrast, provides empirical evidence of heavy transitional costs to women.[43] Gallagher provides a critique of the methodologies of the United Nations mechanisms, which often fail women by failing to specifically address them.[44] She argues, for example:

> ... it is only in the past few years that Member States and the policy making organs of the United Nations have adopted the position that integration of a gender perspective into the work of the treaty bodies is both desirable and necessary ...

and provides the striking example of the Committee on the Elimination of Racial Discrimination (CERD). CERD has not only failed to address gender in its general recommendations, and in its concluding comments on States' parties reports, but in 1996 its chairman publicly stated that directives regarding amendment of reporting guidelines to encourage the integration of gender into States' parties reports were 'fundamentally misconceived'.[45]

Perhaps most crucially, feminist critique has focused on the inadequacies of women specific mechanisms. It was not until the mid 1980s that the Commission on the Status of Women was granted authority by ECOSOC to receive and respond to communications revealing a consistent pattern of reliably attested to injustice and discriminatory practices against women.[46] Further criticism attached to enforcement of the main women specific mechanism CEDAW.[47] Two main criticisms are, first, its enforcement mechanism is weak, there is no individual complaints procedure (although steps have been underway for some time to add an optional protocol providing for such a procedure), reporting is late and has taken some years to refine. Secondly, although CEDAW is widely ratified and broad in scope, this has been bought at the price of reservations. CEDAW contains more State

---

42 See *op cit*, Byrnes, fn 3; Gallagher, fn 3.
43 Sadasivam, B, 'The impact of structural adjustment on women: a governance and human rights agenda' (1997) 19 HRQ 630, pp 630–65.
44 *Op cit*, Gallagher, fn 3.
45 *Ibid*, p 304.
46 See Stamatopoulou, E, 'Women's rights and the UN', in *op cit*, Peters and Wolper (eds), fn 34, p 36.
47 See, generally, Zearfoss, S, 'Note, the Convention for the elimination of all forms of discrimination against women: radical, reasonable, or reactionary?' (1991) 12 Mich J Int L 903, pp 903–42; Welch, CE, 'Human rights and African women: a comparison of protection under two major treaties' (1993) 15 HRQ 549, pp 549–74; Byrnes, A, 'The "other" human rights treaty body: the work of the Committee on the Elimination of Discrimination Against Women' (1989) 14 Yale J Int L 1.

reservations than any other human rights convention, many of which are notoriously broad in scope and would seem to violate the Vienna Convention on the Law of Treaties.[48]

Theory and practice: an inter-relationship

As with feminist legal theory at domestic level, theorisation of women's rights as human rights has emerged not as a free-floating abstraction, but as an attempt to understand and address the problems with law, in this case international human rights law, as a tool for women.[49] Many of the significant developments in the international arena would not have been possible without a degree of theorisation. Violence against women within their homes may 'feel' like a human rights violation to women, but giving it a basis as an international law claim required at least some theorising about the distinctions international law draws between State and non-State action. The notion of positive non-discrimination obligations, which are strongly affirmed in CEDAW, blurred the public/private distinction of international law by providing for a more extensive notion of State responsibility. The subsequent extension of discrimination to include violence against women had clear theoretical underpinnings through work such as that of Catherine MacKinnon and others.[50] The work of the special rapporteur on violence against women in particular, illustrates a high degree of feminist analysis. She uses the theoretical debates in analysing gendered violence as a discrimination matter (including analysis of pornography and sexual harassment), and shows full awareness of the theory of the public/private dichotomy and cultural relativism, also the general complexities of designing effective strategies for women around violence.[51] Perhaps most significant for women's rights is the fact that she does this not as an academic, but as part of the United Nations human rights machinery.

48 *Op cit*, Cook, fn 40.

49 See, also, *op cit*, Smart, 1991 and 1989, fn 5. Feminist theorisation, no doubt, can be given mundane empirical explanations, such as transition of women from activists outside the academy, to academic insiders.

50 See, eg, MacKinnon, CA, *Toward a Feminist Theory of the State*,1989, Cambridge, Mass: Harvard UP.

51 See, also, Coomaraswamy, R, UN special rapporteur on violence against women, *Reinventing International Law: Women's Rights as Human Rights in the International Community*, 1997, Harvard Rights Program, Harvard Law School, for an indication of the overlap between theory and practice for the special rapporteur.

FROM THEORY TO STRATEGIES

The link between theory and practice is a cyclical one: as practice generates theory, then theory informs practice. Crucially, strategies for future action differ according to analysis of the nature of the problem. Where women are excluded merely because human rights violations against them are not taken as seriously as those against men, then processes and structures can be designed to overcome this, provided that political will exists. Thus, CEDAW has developed its reporting mechanism so as to elicit the information it needs, and other non-specific mechanisms have also on occasion taken steps to make sure that they elicit information on women.[52] Non-governmental organisations such as Amnesty International have also increased their emphasis on women's rights, focusing on gendered aspects of torture.[53]

If, however, addressing women's rights can only be achieved by a fundamental redrawing of the boundaries of human rights law, then this raises other strategic difficulties. Feminist writers have suggested different (overlapping) strategies, such as recharacterising non-discrimination, civil and political rights to involve positive duties, or asserting a more positive status for economic, social and cultural rights, or even by just asserting that women's rights, as defined by women experientially, are human rights.[54] While giving creative energy to the women's rights as human rights project, the strategies have practical and conceptual problems.

Practically, it can be difficult to convince grassroots women's groups that international mechanisms have a powerful and universal language, and so should be used as part of a strategy, when attempts to use human rights language and mechanisms quickly reveal increasingly subtle exclusions and marginalisation, which themselves need reform. Women must be persuaded to use international mechanisms not just to achieve their goals, but to reshape the legal world at international level. For many women, underfunded and unsupported in domestic systems, and perhaps artificially locked into single issue work, this holds out little prospect of any concrete gain and must be low in any list of priorities.

Even if women are persuaded to undertake this project, success may come at a price. As women break down the barriers between public (State) and private (non-State) spheres, they blur the line between legitimate international interference and internal state responsibility, increasing the former and decreasing the latter. As international human rights law expands its remit, it faces increased challenge to its legitimacy and authority. This crisis is fuelled

---

52   *Op cit*, Gallagher, fn 3.

53   See, eg, Amnesty International's *Rape and Sexual Abuse: Torture and Ill Treatment of Women in Detention*, 1991 (Act 77/11/91), London: AIUK.

54   See literature cited at fn 34.

at any particular time by the political nature of institutions such as the United Nations and imbalances of State power within them. For all its faults, the public/private distinction and correlative requirement of State action for international intervention, contains the promise of State accountability by making it more difficult for States to challenge the entire project of human rights as political, or deflect attention to policing non-State groups. The drawing of a line between law and politics – between international and national spheres – may be artificial, but it, at least, provides some response to the challenges of cultural relativism. It is easy to surmise that feminism, in seeking to expand the label of human rights, may undermine the effect of that label. Exposing law as politics enables States to play more explicit political games with human rights law. In other words, it kills the goose which lays the golden egg.[55]

Such a charge is not entirely fair. It can easily be responded that the public/private dichotomy did not, in practice, provide the protection to human rights that is suggested, and that the price paid was the exclusion of women. It can also be argued that it was precisely this coincidence between enlightenment ideas and international human rights order (so unsatisfactory to women) which also triggered the cultural relativism/communitarian backlash, with women's rights merely caught in the crossfire.

Further, the women's rights agenda is not the only one to push for expansion of human rights discourse. Proliferating instruments on minority rights also blur the public/private, law/politics dichotomies. Other groups, such as indigenous peoples, have both asserted rights and changed the shape of those rights in stating their claims. The power of the 'human rights' label not only tempts new constituencies, but continually prompts the formulation of new rights, such as with the right to development or a bio-ethics and human rights agenda. These, in turn, prompt concern over quality control, which would protect the meaning of the label.[56] When should a right become an internationally protected 'human right;' what type of thresholds should apply; and who should be the guardian of the threshold, the United Nations General Assembly, international consensus or some other group? These contexts all illustrate a tension in human rights discourse between expansion and core meaning, a tension raised with a backward glance to the cultural relativism challenge.

---

55 Cf, critique of feminist critique of public/private division: Engle, K, 'After the collapse of the public/private distinction: strategising women's rights', in Dallmeyer, D (ed), *Reconceiving Reality: Women and International Law*, 1993, Washington: American Society of International Law, p 143.

56 See, eg, Alston, P, 'Conjuring up new human rights: a proposal for quality control' (1984) 78 AJIL 607.

WHO NEEDS THEORY?

At the turn of the century, it could be argued that a theoretical project is one of the most important new agendas for human rights. The challenge from both left and right to international human rights law has exposed the lack of a coherent grand theory, which would justify human rights law.[57] This makes it susceptible to challenge, both from those who would seek to undermine it and from those who would seek to make it more inclusive.[58] The analogy between international human rights order and the liberal State is a tempting one and useful to some extent: it is, however, an imperfect analogy. The liberal State is concerned with policing the division between State and individual, between group needs and individual choice. The international order is a more complicated three way relationship between State, individual and supranational structure (or other States). The dynamics in the three way relationship are more self-evidently politically contingent. Natural law accounts are similarly difficult to sustain, and sociological accounts of international law and the symbolic importance of human rights, fail to address its normative source. This would seem to point to a need to find a theoretical justification for human rights law that would enable it to retain its power.

It can optimistically be suggested that feminist theory can form the basis of the rescue operation by evading both 'homogenising universalism or the paralysis of cultural relativism'[59] and rebutting the expansion/meaning challenge more generally. Feminism is, if nothing more, comfortable with the idea that grand theories are unobtainable. Indeed, it often views them as undesirable.[60] Feminists themselves have faced a charge of cultural relativism from within their own ranks. During the last decade particularly, white Western feminists have been charged with 'colonialism': that they have assumed that a feminist agenda containing a core number of issues (as defined by them) could unite women across class, ethnic and national boundaries. As women of different backgrounds – women of colour, women from developing countries, working class women, lesbian women, disabled women – have struggled for a public voice, they have questioned both the relevance of this feminist agenda to their concerns and the exclusionary processes by which this agenda is achieved.[61] Indeed, as Higgins writes, 'the claim that Western

---

57 See Howard, R, 'Cultural absolutism and the nostalgia for community' (1993) 15 HRQ 315, pp 315–38, where she notes the twofold attack on human rights – from both the right and the left.

58 For a useful review of the legal theory and human rights, see Shestack, JJ, 'The philosophic foundations of human rights' (1998) 20 HRQ 202, pp 202–34.

59 *Op cit*, Cook, 1993, fn 34, p 235.

60 *Op cit*, Smart, 1989, fn 5.

61 Loude, A, *Sister Outsider*, 1984, California: Crossing Press/Freedom, pp 110–13; *op cit*, Oloka-Onyango and Tamale, fn 34.

concepts of women's equality are exclusionary or imperialist strikes at the heart of one of feminism's central commitments – respect for difference'.[62] Yet, while cultural relativists seek to deny universality to evade responsibility for human rights, feminists deny universality to expand the scope and protection human rights offer. Feminism has sought to retain clear political goals and to move forward with agendas for equality, while taking account of the multiplicity of women's identities and perspectives. It locates the answers in 'cross cultural dialogue' and notions of positionality.[63] A detailed examination of this approach is beyond the scope of this chapter: however, the issue of female circumcision as a human rights issues provides a good working illustration. While clear arguments can be made that the practice violates rights of children and rights of women, addressing it as a human rights violation has often proved counter-productive in threatening cultural community norms, and in failing to address the context in which women consent to the practice. Taking the cultural relativism charge seriously means acknowledging that if human rights norms are to become effective against mainly private action, they need to be based on shared values. In her article on the issue, Gunning suggests:

> ... it is not that there are 'universals' out there waiting to be discovered. But through shared dialogue, shared values can become universal and be safeguarded. The process by which these universal standards are created is important. A dialogue, with a tone that respects cultural diversity, is essential. From that dialogue a consensus may be reached, understanding that as people and cultures interact they do change and learn from each other.[64]

Thus, standpoint and perspective affect how we deal with human rights.

It remains to be seen whether such an approach carves out a clear conceptual space between universalism and relativism, or is merely a sensitive/'politically correct' approach to restating the universalist claims which seem so vital to human rights[65] (although that, of course, may be still be useful). In either case, the approach seems to free human rights law for the activist to work in an ongoing cycle, connecting the plight of human beings with international human rights mechanisms, so as to change both human condition and mechanism in a constant evolutionary process. It is precisely this dialectical relationship between activist and instrument that gives human rights the dynamism which has led to their development thus far. While this

---

62 *Op cit*, Higgins, fn 40, p 91.

63 *Ibid*. It is interesting that others who accept the relativist position also seek to provide some justification of human rights. Cf, also, the work of Na'im, A, 'Human rights in the Muslim world' (1990) 3 Harv HRJ 13.

64 Gunning, S, 'Arrogant perception, world travelling and multicultural feminism: the case of female genital surgeries' (1991–92) 23 Colum HR L Rev 189, p 238.

65 See, eg, Annan, K, 'Strengthening United Nations action in the field of human rights: prospects and priorities' (1997) 19 Harv HRJ 1, pp 1–9.

approach may not have the clear defences of liberalism, in acknowledging the political nature of the battle, it trains resources on that battle. As Sandel writes:

> Liberalism teaches respect for the distance of self and ends, and when this distance is lost, we are submerged in a circumstance that ceases to be ours. But by seeking to secure this distance too completely, liberalism undermines its own insight. By putting the self beyond the reach of politics, it makes human agency an article of faith rather than an object of continuing attention and concern, a premise of politics rather than its precarious achievement.[66]

Paradoxically, feminist engagement with international law indicates that emerging theoretical agendas may prove a detour which brings us out the other side to affirm a 'just do it' approach to human rights law, which concentrates on inclusive methodologies. This imperative is particularly important for women. Given that 'globalisation' is the watchword of the millennium and human rights one of the few global values with a clear ethical and potentially radical content, women have little choice other than to use international human rights law to frame their claims.

---

66   Sandel, M, 'Justice and the good', in Sandel, M (ed), *Liberalism and its Critics*, 1984, New York: New York UP, pp 159–76.

CHAPTER 8

THE PRACTICE OF EQUALITY

Margaret Logue

INTRODUCTION

The challenge of the implementation of equality is a major issue locally, nationally and internationally. It is a tall order to translate legislation and policy into action and develop models of good practice, which will move forward a process to guarantee respect for the human dignity of women and access to full participation of women in economic and social life

As we move into the 21st century, there is still a major gap between the principle of gender equality and its practice. The challenge ahead is to develop our capacity to implement policies and laws to make the practice of equality second nature. Some countries have legislated and moved on, while others have made hardly any progress.

This chapter examines some of the women's equality issues identified at the 4th World Conference of Women held in Beijing in 1995. At this United Nations conference, 186 governments throughout the world signed up to a *Global Platform For Action*, a document with strategic objectives to be implemented by governments over the next 10 years. It is written primarily from the perspective of an activist: I attended the Beijing conference as part of an NGO delegation. There are many ideas and dilemmas around the areas of resistance to the implementation of effective equality practices, and this chapter examines some of those. It outlines some aspects of positive action and the debate and controversy about its acceptance as an instrument of effective change. It also examines the effect of ambivalence, which might well be a key factor in explaining the stubborn resistance to change that exists when it comes to the practice of equality. The final part focuses on the traditional, predominantly male leadership culture, present in hierarchical structures (most organisations in society), and how this contributes to the maintenance of the status quo. Does the influence of this prevailing culture go some way to explain the ambivalence of many influential individuals and leaders? These are people who, on the one hand, articulate the principles of gender equality, but remain passive and silent when it comes to supporting effective action and equality practice. By identifying and discussing all of these barriers to equality practice, we will be better able to move on and identify strategies to influence and bring about real change in practice.

THE CONTEXT

The tide has turned almost full circle. We used to hear that the education of women would be the vital factor in achieving equality. I now hear it said increasingly, that the greatest need is to educate men to understand women's rights issues.[1] Another major challenge for society and individuals is to create a culture and environment in which women and men equally share the work within families.

The emphasis is changing for women. Formerly, we looked for answers inside ourselves, as in the early consciousness raising groups of the 1960s and 1970s. Now, we also take a more outward approach, which looks at the world outside ourselves, to develop thinking about counteracting oppression in a much broader framework. Moving towards the millennium, we are beginning to open our eyes and to articulate the world from a gender perspective.

All over the world, women are identifying and organising on issues of equality and human rights. By and large, we still organise in women only groups or groups dominated by women. This is not to underestimate or ignore the very important and positive contribution made by men in the struggle for women's liberation. However, women are now central in the movements, and we insist on articulating our own oppression and developing our strategies for action.

BEIJING

Improved, accessible travel and high technology communication systems have meant close connections developing among women locally, nationally and internationally. This global networking could be seen clearly in practice at the Fourth World Conference of Women in Beijing, China, in August 1995. Thirty thousand women from non-governmental organisations (NGOs) were there, the biggest United Nations NGO conference in history. The international women's movement was visible and vibrant. The conference contributed to raising awareness about the varied interpretations of equality in diverse cultures, and the different priorities identified in different parts of the world. The stark gaps in the distribution of material resources between the North and the South were articulated and obvious. It also became clearer that women and children bear the burdens of poverty the world over, in whatever way it manifests itself. The issues around poverty now include the fact that women and children feel its effects to a far greater extent. This can be seen

---

1   See Hinds, B, Hope, A and Whitaker, R, *From the Margins to the Mainstream – Working Towards Equality*, Development and Peace, Northern Ireland/Beijing NGO Report, 1997, Belfast: Northern Ireland Women's European Platform, p 24.

from figures, such as the proportion of lone parents (70%) in Northern Ireland who are dependent on State benefits.[2]

THE ISSUES: PUBLIC LIFE AND POLITICS

Under Strategic Objective G1 from the *Global Platform for Action*, governments have agreed to take measures to ensure women's equal access to and full participation in power structures and decision making.

One effective way governments can implement this is by gender balancing public appointments. Attempts are being made here to make this happen, but the leadership of public bodies remains male dominated. Yet, equal numbers alone do not resolve the problem. Key leadership positions on public bodies remain male dominated, as well as whole sectors, for example, agriculture and economics.[3]

There is a growing recognition within political parties that major change is needed on the issue of women's equality and representation. This is vital if politics is to become more democratic and participatory. The starkest example of the democratic deficit is the small number of women holding political positions, especially at leadership level. Family friendly structures and environments need to be created inside traditionally male dominated politics. Electoral systems that result in a more equal representation of women and men are ways forward. Models of these systems are being developed in the discussions to set up the new Scottish Parliament.[4] Elsewhere in the UK, parties like the Northern Ireland Women's Coalition are also pressing for an electoral system which will have a better chance of advancing the equal participation of women in political life here.[5]

The cornerstone of a democratic society is the principle of the full and equal participation of citizens in political and economic life. The equal participation and responsibility sharing of women and men in decision making is a crucial foundation for equality between the sexes and the creation of a better society.[6]

---

2   *Ibid*, p 31.

3   Northern Ireland Office, *Report of the Central Appointments Unit,* 1996, Belfast: HMSO. See, also, EOCNI, *Where Do Women Figure?*, 1996, Belfast: EOCNI.

4   The Scottish Labour Party and the Liberal Democrats in Scotland have agreed an electoral pact, which obliges them to nominate equal numbers of women and men for winnable seats.

5   See *In Pursuit of Equality – a National Agenda for Action,* Policy Paper 2, UK: COI for the Women's National Commission.

6   *Ibid,* Policy Paper 3.

THE ISSUES: CHILDCARE

The *Global Platform for Action* calls for the harmonisation of work and family responsibility between women and men, and identifies affordable, flexible and high quality childcare as one major factor in bringing this about.

The provision of quality childcare is recognised as a vital factor in establishing women's equal access to economic independence and well paid work. Current levels of childcare provision in the UK are abysmal when compared to other European countries. In France, 10 times more children are in publicly funded day care than in the UK.[7] The situation in Northern Ireland in relation to publicly funded childcare places is significantly worse than in other parts of the UK.

However, strategies to implement widespread childcare provision are being developed, and women are proactive and united in the campaigns on this issue. Action is also needed to create a culture of equal responsibility between women and men. A key element in this will be the provision of statutory paternity, parental and family leave. Education, training and awareness raising among men and women will be necessary to support these radical changes. Stereotypes still prevail on the roles and directives women and men should take in their lives.[8]

A shift in the distribution of resources to support publicly funded quality childcare provision and preschool education would require a radical shift in values and would be a great step forward for the well being of society's human resources, people. This would be a very worthwhile investment as we move into the next millennium.

THE ISSUES: VIOLENCE AGAINST WOMEN

Strategic Objective D in the *Global Platform for Action* required that measures to prevent and eliminate violence against women should be a major focus point for governments all over the world.

The organisation, Women's Aid, has developed a powerful and well organised strategy to deal with domestic violence issues here. With growing recognition from the government, Women's Aid is slowly being better resourced[9] – recognition at statutory level that this organisation plays a key

---

7   See Waddington, S, *Women and Europe: A Statistical Portrait*, 1997, Leicester: Rural.
8   *Op cit*, COI for the Women's National Commission, fn 5.
9   See *Tackling Domestic Violence – A Policy For Northern Ireland*, 1995, Belfast: Department of Health and Social Services and Northern Ireland Office/HMSO; *Northern Ireland Women's Aid Federation Annual Report 1997–98: Recent Landmarks in Development of Northern Ireland Women's Aid Federation*, 1998, Belfast: Northern Ireland, Women's Aid Federation. There are now 14 Women's Aid refuges operating in Northern Ireland.

role in counteracting this major social problem. At Beijing, the issue of violence against women was recognised as one of the most obstructive to the liberation of women. The evidence of its prevalence on a global scale was astonishing. In every country represented at the Beijing Conference there were women organising to offer practical support and refuge to victims of domestic and sex related violence.[10]

Over 13,000 women sought help from Women's Aid in 1997/1998. Nine hundred and twenty three women and 1,467 children were housed in temporary accommodation. Another 541 women and 1,067 children were referred by Women's Aid to other agencies.[11] Over 600 calls each month are handled by the Women's Aid Helpline which operates a 24 hour a day, seven days a week telephone response.[12]

The Northern Ireland Women's Aid Federation and the 14 women's aid refuges working in the region, are an outstanding example of an effective grass roots response to an endemic social problem. In this field, in the last quarter of this century, women have developed courage, leadership and managerial skills. Women's Aid organisations directly challenge behaviour and cultural attitudes that reinforce the social acceptance of domestic violence perpetrated by men on women. They also facilitate safe environments with a strong self-help ethos to offer substantial practical support. This firmly feminist and self-help approach is the hallmark of this successful movement for change.

The Beijing *Global Platform for Action* calls for the strengthening of national machinery and governmental bodies for the advancement of women. Mainstreaming and monitoring are recommended as vehicles for implementing the strategic objectives of the platform, so that all policy development at government level builds in a gender equality dimension. Monitoring and evaluation would follow to identify the progress on gender equality that the mainstreaming process is designed to deliver.

The *Global Platform for Action* calls for governments to enact and enforce laws to prohibit direct and indirect discrimination. There is growing recognition in Northern Ireland that current sex discrimination legislation requires replacement. The Equal Opportunities Commission here is also calling for easier and more open access to information on the impact of all national legislation on women. Gender equality training for judges and job protected parental leave are just two methods suggested as ways to move

---

10 See Courtney, A, *Domestic Violence – A Political Issue*, May 1998, p 47; and *Sharing Shifting Shaping – Women on the Move*, May 1998, Northern Ireland Report, Women's National Commission in association with women's organisations in Northern Ireland.

11 *Op cit*, fn 9.

12 *Op cit*, fn 10.

forward in the practice of equality. The Northern Ireland Women's Aid Federation is currently training the local judiciary on domestic violence issues. This is an example of influential work at policy level translating to grass roots practice.[13] The inter-agency work being undertaken in Northern Ireland, for example, is proving successful and effective. This approach involves close co-operation between women's aid, the police, judiciary, social services and housing agencies. Much of this work is being pioneered in the north west of the region, good practice models are developed and translated to other agencies and areas.[14]

POSITIVE ACTION

The argument about equal opportunities has broadened to include the issue of positive action. Positive action means a focus on the promotion of equality backed up by proactive programmes leading to measurable results. Inequality between the sexes is endemic in our culture and society, but it can be effectively tackled by a determined focus on developing measures that will place the *practice* of equality high on the agenda. Effective positive action programmes need to be proactive. Results have to be measurable, stating specified targets and timetables with constant monitoring, evaluation and changes to improve positive action measures and outcomes.

The European Union recognises that it is not enough to practice equal treatment and ensure that a climate of equal opportunities exists for women and men. Effective equality practice also entails being proactive in implementing measures which will reduce the endemic structural differences in the position of women and men in public, economic and social life.[15]

There is growing recognition that legislation and policy changes are not delivering the equality agenda in practice. There is overt and subtle resistance to the practice of gender equality within organisations and in society generally.

It is important to be aware of the structures, both formal and informal, which contribute to and often strengthen the segregation and discrimination between women and men. The concept of 'gender neutral' decisions, for example, will promote gender inequality. This sort of thinking is a good example of the resistance that exists to the concept of using positive action as a means to combat the existing situation of endemic gender inequality. Where there has been prior discrimination, disadvantage and existing prejudice, the

---

13 *Op cit*, fn 9.
14 *Op cit*, fn 10.
15 See *Equal Opportunities for Women and Men in the European Union: 1997 Annual Report*, 1998, Luxembourg: Office for Official Publications of the European Communities.

vehicle of a positive action programme is one that can work effectively and in a reasonable time period. Women will no longer accept the excuse that it will take a 'very long' time to bring about equality in practice. We demand change now to create a fair society for our daughters and ourselves.

In Northern Ireland, the Policy Approval and Fair Treatment (PAFT) guidelines have been in existence for some time. These are a set of written guidelines and policies, intended to ensure that all issues of equality condition policy making decisions by government at every level. They have not, however, been very effective as instruments to deliver equality in practice. There are no effective positive action measures or mechanisms to bring about real change in practice.[16] Recent proposals to amalgamate the various equality agencies under a single Equality Commission have not had a favourable response from the Northern Ireland Equal Opportunities Commission, or from most organisations working on women's equality in the region. Only 15% of the people who responded to the Government White Paper 'Partnership for Equality' came out in favour of the proposed merger.[17] Despite this negative response at consultation stage, the Government still included the proposals in the Northern Ireland Bill. Both British and Northern Irish EOCs do sterling work on gender equality with very limited resources, and this specific focus on gender equality issues is vital if laws and policies are to be effectively implemented and practised widely. Progress on women's equality may be slowed down considerably if these changes go ahead in their present form.

Among the EOCNI recommendations for equality implementation in the next few years are:

(a) a recommendation that positive action measures should be obligatory for employers to promote equal opportunity;

(b) a recommendation that the Sex Discrimination legislation and the Equal Pay legislation be brought together;

(c) a recommendation that European Rights should be written in to domestic law.[18]

In all sectors of society, there is still a huge gap between the principle of equality and its application. There are many inconsistencies about equal opportunities. Some organisations have begun to develop policies and principles, while others have made hardly any progress. Even where comprehensive written policies exist, there is little evidence that this has been translated into real changes for women, whether in workplaces, public sector

---

16 See McCrudden, C, *Benchmarks for Change: Mainstreaming Fairness in the Governance of Northern Ireland – A Proposal*, 1998, Belfast: CAJ.

17 See EOC Briefing, 'Northern Ireland Bill fails women', August 1998, Belfast: EOCNI.

18 EOCNI, *Twenty-First Report*, March 1997, Belfast: EOCNI, p 34.

agencies, business, economic or political life. There is a need to encourage more comprehensive 'gender equality audits' to ascertain and measure what stage organisations are at in relation to women's equality. This would be a starting point, and a valuable exercise to build a base of information about leadership and management within organisations. Gender equality audits would lay the groundwork to enable the development of effective strategies so that the practice of equality follows swiftly the recognition of the principle of equality.

In social, economic, public and political life, the typical traditional patterns of women and men's employment and representation are reproduced. A strong tendency still prevails for women to be located towards the less influential, lower paid, bottom of the hierarchies, while the top echelons are almost exclusively male.[19]

Effective measures and means are required to translate equality policies into results. There is still a lot of work to be done before we can claim to have reached the goal of equal outcomes, which is one real measure of success for equality policies and legislation. One of the big debates at the moment is about the use of 'positive action' as an instrument to counter endemic discrimination and make progress towards equality. Proposals include targeted proportions of representation: leadership positions, management, jobs, training places and services backed up by constant monitoring and evaluation.[20] Positive action is an effective way to establish the goal of equal outcomes and goes some way towards dealing with situations of prior discrimination, disadvantage and existing prejudice. However, it is also controversial. Disturbing the status quo, and creating shifts in the traditional structure and hierarchical order of organisations, will not be brought about without strong resistance emerging from those who benefit from the current system. Equal opportunities training, awareness raising and other special support measures are needed to encourage level playing fields in areas where there has been and still is prejudice and discrimination. It is easy for most of us to agree on the definition of discrimination as 'treating similar situations differently'. It is a bit more difficult to accept the definition of discrimination as 'treating different situations identically'.[21]

However, if we can accept that treating different situations identically can perpetuate and reinforce discrimination, then the idea of 'positive action' begins to make more sense. This is so particularly when pursuing the goal of

19 See Pincus, I, *Between Insight and Action – Gender Equality, Men and Ambivalence in Municipal Organisations*, 1996, Sweden: Statskunskapens, p 26. See, also, *op cit*, EOCNI, fn 4.

20 See Logue, M and Whitaker, R, 'The future of EU social policy: *Report of the Northern Ireland Committee, des Sages Consultation Seminar'*, in *Equal Opportunities: Creating an Anti-Discrimination Framework and Culture*, 1997, Belfast: Northern Ireland Council for Voluntary Action, p 24.

21 See Bell, C, Hegarty, A and Livingstone, S, 'The enduring controversy: developments in affirmative action law in North America' (1996) 3 IJDL 253.

equal outcomes, and seeking to challenge inequality where there has been prior discrimination, disadvantage and existing prejudice.

There is now widespread recognition that there are particular deep rooted problems of participation for significant numbers of women. Why then is it proving so difficult to implement effective action and see results? Why is there resistance, subtle and overt, to turning words into practice? Ambivalent attitudes to action on inequality are widespread among many in key leadership positions, even when these same people articulate support for the principles of equality. Discrimination, disadvantage, exclusion and marginalisation will not go away because there is agreement that they are wrong. Words are meaningless unless they are translated into real practice with measurable results. Positive action programmes are required with real commitment to implementation, including targets and timetables. Marginalised groups require encouragement and financial support to create their own spaces. The women's movement and women's organisations have been effective and instrumental in bringing about major shifts in consciousness and in practice. However, support resources and positive action measures are required if we are to influence the culture and structures of organisations and groups from which we are still largely absent.

AMBIVALENCE

Within society there is a broad range of organisations, groups and individuals that have different and often opposing views and interests. However, there has developed a consensus among many that counteracting discrimination and increasing equality are positive values to be nurtured and supported. Added to this, funding bodies are often insistent that the 'equality agenda' is included in the work of organisations. Evidence of implementation of this agenda is frequently required in order for funding applications to succeed. This has been evident in Northern Ireland for those seeking support under the European Support Programme for the Peace and Reconciliation (EUSSPPR) programme, and has been a successful tool in persuading groups to look at the composition of their organisations from an equality perspective.

Despite this, obstacles remain in the process of moving from theory to practice. In the case of women's equality, in most organisations there is still powerful resistance to change. For example, although women are active and involved in community groups, the leadership and decision making, as well as the executive and higher paid professional positions, remain dominated by men. This domination has reproduced to a large extent the hierarchical values and structures of our male dominated culture.

In my experience, it is almost exclusively women, collectively and individually, who work towards bringing about gender equality in organisations. In just one recent example, at a recent community sector consultation seminar I attended, the workshop on equality was the only one facilitated by two women and was attended by only one courageous man. This experience is not an uncommon one across the UK. Although most men will have no problem agreeing with the principle of women's equality, there are different forms of resistance, which contribute to a less than enthusiastic approach when it comes to effective action.

Leadership in our society is still predominantly male and leadership indifference, even resistance, to the implementation of equality practice is an obstacle that needs exposure and discussion. Are there any identifiable clues as to why this gap exists between the words and the action? Silence and inaction are very subtle, commonly used obstacles, worthy of some attention. For example, why do many men, who say they support equality, remain silent and passive when it comes to implementation? Why do they stand by when colleagues resist and obstruct moves towards equality practice, which will lead to change in their organisations? There have to be ways to explain the gap between what many men say and what they do. It is not enough to say that ambivalence, when faced with the opportunity to change, is only about prejudice or ignorance.

There are many organisations that 'in principle' say they are positive to equality initiatives. However, when it comes to translating this into practice, there are many individuals within these organisations who do not engage in or do not support those who work for change. The hierarchical structures and culture of many organisations are factors in the environment of persistent resistance to gender equality. This makes it difficult for many men and women to actively, openly support moves towards the practice of equality, which will bring about real results and shifts in the traditional structures within their organisations.

Even when positive action measures are agreed and articulated, often there is still subtle resistance from individuals and organisations' leaders when it comes to implementation. There has only been very slow progress towards real results and equality of outcomes. Some studies have identified that the ambivalence of influential individuals within organisations is an important factor in ongoing resistance to effective change.[22] There is a real need for discussion; dialogue is needed, addressing the dilemmas facing male leadership (or, indeed, some females in leadership) working within established groups, organised around hierarchical management models. Many individuals will be likely to put up subtle resistance to effective action on equality.

---

22 *Op cit*, Pincus, fn 19, p 5.

ORGANISATIONAL HIERARCHIES

Hierarchical forms of management and leadership, where power and prestige are limited to a small number of top positions, are the least amenable to change and inclusion. Most organisations adopt these 'top down' forms of management based on hierarchical structures with little chance of creating an environment to encourage and invite interaction from the excluded and disadvantaged. Within these systems it is very difficult for women to make their voices heard. It is also difficult for men to articulate different values, or to support a culture of equality within these very tight, traditional, hierarchical environments. These powerful structures shape the culture of organisations and the relations between the individual people who work in them.

The 'top down' approach to managing groups is regarded by many people as right and proper, and there is a great lack of awareness about alternative, more accountable and creative methods of organising. Hierarchical systems will experience effective equality initiatives as intrusions, which threaten the status quo and cause anxiety at the very least. It is not surprising or unexpected that initiatives for change will meet with ambivalence and thereby resistance.

Hierarchical organisations impede the development of equality. They perpetuate the traditional structures of power and leadership. It is difficult for individuals working within these hierarchies, who are positive to equality, to act on their convictions.

As the growth of the NGO sector continues unabated, the ability of community organisations to move forward on equality will be of major importance if community development is to continue to gain recognition in society as a player at the front line in progressive thinking and effective action. There is an important role for community associations in social and civil development, articulating the position of marginalised groups. It is still the case that women remain marginalised, treated differently in economic, political and social life. This discrimination, disadvantage and prejudice is reproduced in the NGO sector. The remarkable vigour of women in 'civil society' is recognised widely. In Northern Ireland alone, over 1,000 groups, from mother and toddler to lobbying and campaigning organisations, are run specifically for and by women.[23] This plethora and diversity of women-led organisations would suggest that autonomy is valued. The challenge for society generally is to build on this movement which is growing and is a vital element in the putting into practice of equality rights.

Women are not yet represented in sufficient numbers to achieve the 'critical mass' necessary to even begin to argue for major change in their status

---

23   See Fearon, K, *Power Politics and Positioning*, 1996, Belfast: Democratic Dialogue.

and ensure their issues and values are influential in the policy agenda. Even when the 50/50 representation in numbers is achieved, there often remains the problem of exclusion from leadership positions, management and decision making. Inequality in access to power and status, lack of resources, education, training and childcare are just some of the factors in the gross under representation of many women in key decision making bodies. There is plenty of effective work in spheres on the margins of life, but women, as well as other groups, are still kept out of many arenas where important decisions are made. It is essential to have equality of representation in key policy areas, so that particular perspectives and experience of people previously excluded can influence decisions and practice.

If any organisation is to have legitimacy in calling itself representative, it is not enough to write the principles of equality into its policy and constitution. The practice of equality needs to be central to its day to day activities and structures. Success on equality will be measured by results. Many women's organisations seek new ways of managing, with networking, effective and efficient systems of carrying out their work in a way which compliments family and community life. This demonstrates new and creative thinking in a world, which demands openness, transparency, accountability and equality.

We will continue to develop models of good practice and encourage others to develop policies and effective positive action measures leading to equal outcomes. By doing so in Northern Ireland, as elsewhere in the world, women already make a significant contribution to equality in our communities, thereby leading the way on one of the major debates of the moment.

CHAPTER 9

CHILDREN'S RIGHTS

Deirdre Fottrell

INTRODUCTION

Since 1989, when the United Nations General Assembly adopted the Convention on the Rights of the Child, there has been an unprecedented growth in the commitment to children's rights internationally.[1] This is reflected by both the proliferation of universal and regional standard setting instruments,[2] and, also, the almost universal ratification of the Children's Convention itself.[3]

The United Nations Convention is the culmination of a 60 year campaign to achieve recognition of the child as an independent rights holder. The significance of the Children's Convention lies not just in the achievement of this goal, but also in its holistic and all encompassing approach to the rights of the child, evidenced by the inclusion of an unparalleled range of rights in a single binding treaty.

Van Bueren argues that children's rights can be distilled down to four core elements identified as protection, prevention, provision and participation, which she calls 'the four Ps'.[4] The initial focus for children's rights activists was on the first three Ps, reflecting a conceptualisation of the child as essentially weak and dependent, which dominated relevant international instruments from the early part of this century up to the late 1970s. Recently,

---

1   UN Convention on the Rights of the Child (CRC), adopted 20 November 1989, GA Res 44/25 (1989) 28 ILM 1448. The Convention entered into force on 2 September 1990 having received the 20 signatures required by Art 49(1).

2   Among the international conventions and declarations concerning children which have come into being since 1989 are the European Convention for the Exercise of Children's Rights (Council of Europe) 1996; the African Charter on the Rights and Welfare of the Child (Organisation for African Unity) 1990; the Jomtien Declaration on Education for All (UN) 1990. See, further, Van Bueren, G, *International Documents on Children*, 2nd edn, 1998, Dordrecht: Kluwer.

3   As of May 1998, 191 States have ratified the Convention; only two States have not yet done so – Somalia and the US. President Clinton signed the Convention in February 1995, but it is likely to be some years before it is through the US Senate ratification procedure.

4   See Van Bueren, G, 'The struggle for empowerment: the emerging civil and political rights of children', in *Selected Essays on International Children's Rights*, 1993, Geneva: Defence for Children International, Vol 1, p 49. See, also, Van Bueren, G, *The International Law on the Rights of the Child*, 1995, Dordrecht: Kluwer, Chap 1.

however, a consensus emerged that in addition to enjoying certain rights associated with their status and their particular needs, children are autonomous beings. The child has been reconceptualised as a participant in the wider society, independent of the family unit and, consequently, as a holder of participatory rights not traditionally associated with childhood, including, for example, freedom of association, expression and religion.

This latter approach is central to the Children's Convention, but it does not obliterate the fact that, in some societies, the autonomous child is an anathema and a perceived threat to the family, with the latter prioritised as both the foundation of the society and a rights holder whose interests may trump those of its individual members.

This translates into resistance to the more radical Convention provisions on the participatory rights of the child, evidenced by a worryingly large number of very wide reservations. In the long term, this raises questions about commitment to children's rights in many States and, of course, ultimately requires a reassessment of the universal ratification, since the effect of some reservations will be to render much of the domestic law beyond the reach of the Convention. States then have the moral benefits of ratification, but wide reservations limit the legal consequences and obligations.

This chapter will explore the process by which children's rights came to occupy such a prominent position on the current human rights agenda, by focusing on the Children's Convention.

EARLY DEVELOPMENT OF THE RIGHTS OF THE CHILD

Although children's rights were an early concern of international law, the history of the rights of the child at an international level has been inconsistent, and progress has essentially taken place at two levels. First, the development of child centred instruments over 60 years which led to the 1989 Children's Convention. The second level of activity was a gradual strengthening of children's rights through general human rights treaties, either through case law or, less frequently, through the inclusion of child specific articles. We will review these two levels of activity separately.

Child centred instruments

The first effort to address the rights of the child on an international level was the 1924 League of Nations Declaration on the Rights of the Child. This is a five point aspirational document which was inspired by the experiences of Save the Children founder, Eglantyne Jebb, in the First World War, and its tone is best captured by the rather syrupy assertion in the preamble that 'mankind owes to the child the best that it has to give'.[5] The tone of the Declaration is paternalistic, and it is firmly rooted in the dominant conceptualisation of the child as vulnerable, powerless and thus in need of special care.[6] Its significance is largely symbolic, but Van Bueren observes that, as it predates the Universal Declaration on Human Rights by 24 years, it debunks the myth that children's rights are a recent phenomenon for international law.[7]

The position was not much altered by the 1959 Declaration on the Rights of the Child, passed by the United Nations General Assembly to commemorate the thirty-fifth anniversary of the 1924 Declaration. The entrenched view of the child as best protected within the family dominates this later Declaration and it does not advance the rights of children under international law.[8] Children's rights were not at that time conceived as human rights, as any rights the child enjoyed were limited particularly by the sanctity of the child-parent relationship. In fact, the 1959 Declaration is very much about the relationship between the parent and the State, the child being a passive beneficiary who played no active role. Both of these declarations reflect very much the political and historical context in which they were conceived.[9]

Children's rights under general treaties

In addition to the development and expansion of their rights under child specific treaties, children have benefited from and had access to general human rights instruments, since neither the universal nor the regional treaties place any lower age limit on the rights which are guaranteed. Theoretically then the rights in these treaties apply to both adults and children.

General human rights treaties in the pre-Convention era also included a number of child specific provisions, most notably Art 24 of the International Covenant on Civil and Political Rights 1966 and Art 16 of the American Convention on Human Rights 1969. Interestingly, these provisions generated no case law and made little impact in advancing children's rights through the reporting system.[10]

---

5   For the text of the 1924 Declaration, see, further, Van Bueren, G, *International Documents on Children*, 1993, Dordrecht: Kluwer, p 3. See, also, *op cit*, Van Bueren, 1993, fn 4, pp 6–12.
6   *Op cit*, Van Bueren, 1995, fn 4, p 6, where Van Bueren describes the 1924 Declaration as being essentially concerned with children as 'recipients of treatment rather than as the holders of specific rights'.
7   *Op cit*, Van Bueren, 1995, fn 4, p 9.
8   For the text of the declaration see, further, *ibid*, pp 4–6.
9   *Ibid*.
10 Children's rights were included in certain humanitarian documents, particularly the Geneva Conventions of 1949. See, further, Hamilton, C and El-Haj, A, 'Armed conflict; the protection of children under international law' (1997) 5 IJCR 1, pp 1–46.

Far more significant were the provisions of universal and regional treaties which had particular resonance for children, most notably on the question of education, which is guaranteed in the Universal Declaration,[11] the International Covenants[12] and in European Convention,[13] and has generated a significant jurisprudence, particularly before the judicial forums of the latter. The right to education illustrates well how the rights of children have been advanced by the Children's Convention, the focus of the right under these earlier instruments being on the right to have the child educated in accordance with a parent's religious or philosophical convictions. This dominates both the treaty text and the relevant decisions. For example, in *Busk, Madsen and Pedersen v Denmark*, parental objections to sex education were weighed against State duties not to indoctrinate children.[14] The rights and needs of the child were presumed to be best represented by parents or the State, and the child's wishes are not separately considered in the judgment of the court. Were a similar case to come before the European Court of Human Rights in the post-Convention era, greater attention would be paid to the rights of the child.

This is not to say that children were prevented from accessing the Convention mechanisms in the pre-Convention period; on the contrary, before the European Court on Human Rights was created, children have enjoyed considerable success.[15] They have won cases with their parents: in *Marckx v Belgium*, a process of maternal affiliation for single mothers to achieve the legal status of guardian was found by the court to violate the rights of both the mother and the child to respect for their family life under Art 8.[16] Furthermore, children have sometimes succeeded where their parents failed. In *Johnston v Ireland*, the European Court of Human Rights upheld a violation of a child's rights under Art 8 while rejecting that there had been any violation of the parents' rights.[17] Finally, a limited number of cases have concerned

---

11 Universal Declaration, Art 26.

12 See ICCPR 1966, Art 18(4); and ICESCR 1966, Art 13. For the full text, see Brownlie, I, *Basic Documents on Human Rights*, 3rd edn, 1992, Oxford: OUP.

13 European Convention 1952, First Protocol, Art 2. See, further, *ibid*, Brownlie.

14 [1976] Series A.23.

15 For an excellent account of children before the European Court of Human Rights in the pre- and post-Children's Convention era, see, further, Van Bueren, G, 'Protecting children's rights in Europe' (1996) 2 EHRLR 171, pp 171–80.

16 [1979] Series A.31.

17 [1986] Series A.112. The case involved a claim by a man and a woman, the former of whom was prevented from marrying the latter by the fact that he was still married to someone else and unable to obtain a divorce in Ireland, and their child. Their claim was that the absence of divorce violated their rights under Art 8 to have their family life respected, a claim which the Court rejected. The Court did, however, uphold the claim of their daughter that the continued existence of the concept of illegitimacy in Irish law, which would placed her in an unfavourable position if her father died intestate, violated her rights under Art 8. See, further, Jacobs, F and White, R, *The European Convention on Human Rights*, 2nd edn, 1996, Oxford: OUP, pp 172–210.

children's rights alone. For example, in *Tyrer v UK*, the European Court of Human Rights found that judicial corporal punishment violated the right of a 15 year old boy under Art 3 to be protected from degrading punishment.[18]

These cases illustrate that international forums have a record, albeit quite limited, of protecting children's rights which predates the Children's Convention. The dearth of cases can be explained by two factors: first, many children do not have access to either the information or advice which may lead them to challenge rights violations and, secondly, many violations of children's rights occur in the so called private sphere and are thus considered to be outside the mainstream of human rights protection.

THE CHILDREN'S CONVENTION

As we noted at the outset, the Children's Convention was the climax of a long international campaign. The Convention was proposed in 1979, the International Year of the Child, and 10 years later, after an arduous drafting process, it was passed by the General Assembly.[19]

The explicit dual aim of the Children's Convention is to bring together in a single binding instrument the full canon of human rights applicable to children, and to assert the right of children to full equality in the enjoyment of these rights. The range of rights guaranteed by the Convention is sufficiently broad to cover all aspects of children's lives and the different stages of a child's development.

The Children's Convention is an ambitious document. There are 54 Articles in all, 40 of which concern substantive provisions under which States agree to guarantee the rights of the child in economic, social, political, cultural and civil areas.

The central ethos of the Convention is that children are equal in worth to adults, and this theme runs through each of the articles. The importance of this ethos cannot be overemphasised. In many States and societies, children's rights and those of their parents are always viewed as coinciding, despite the fact that some of the worst violations of children's rights take place within the family, and the interests of the family and the child may well be at variance. By asserting the equality of the child as a rights holder, the Convention deconstructs normative structures which have presented the interests of the child and the family as coterminous.

Furthermore, the Convention can be distinguished from earlier global efforts in that children's rights are couched in the language of human rights.

---

18 [1978] Series A.26. See, further, Harris, DJ, O'Boyle, M and Warbrick, C, *The Law of the European Convention on Human Rights*, 1995, London: Butterworths, p 84.

19 See *op cit*, Van Bueren, 1995, fn 4, Chap 1.

This is largely due to the highly successfully and constructive input from non-governmental organisations (NGOs) during the drafting of the Convention.[20]

THE RIGHTS PROTECTED

The Convention applies to all children, defined in Art 1 as persons under 18, although the age of majority may be attained earlier under domestic law.[21]

The rights covered by the Convention include many which appear in other human rights treaties, but were rewritten to inject the child's perspective. These include the right to life (Art 6), which traditionally concerns the right not to be killed, but is expanded here and linked to the right to the survival and development of the child. Similarly, the prohibition on torture, cruel, inhuman and degrading treatment and punishment (Art 37(a)) incorporates a prohibition on the imposition of life imprisonment or capital punishment on persons under 18.

In addition, there are many articles protecting rights which are essentially child specific, including protection from abuse (Art 19); prohibition on child trafficking (Art 35); special protection for disabled children (Art 23); protection from economic exploitation (Article 32); right to education (Arts 28 and 29); protection for children separated from their families (Art 9); protection from illicit use of narcotic drugs (Art 37).

The most controversial section governs the so called participatory rights, found in Arts 12–16, which provide for freedom of expression, freedom of religion, freedom of association and assembly and the right to privacy.

There are two new rights in the Convention: first, the right to identity (Art 8), which reflected the concerns of the Argentinian delegation that the removal of children from their 'disappeared' parents during that country's 'dirty war' be prevented through the promotion of the child's right to an identity. The second new right in the Convention concerns adoption (Art 21), the provisions of which were enormously controversial because of the non-existence of this concept in Islamic law.[22]

Despite these innovative and exciting new developments which do enhance the protection of children's rights, the Convention is not without its disappointments. For example, the provision on recruitment of children to the

---

20 See, further, Price-Cohen, C, 'The role of non-governmental organisations in the drafting of the Convention on the Rights of the Child' (1990) 12 HRQ 136.

21 There was a concerted effort by some States, led by the Holy See, at the drafting stage to extend protection to life *in utero*, but this did not succeed. See, further, Alston, P, 'The unborn child and abortion under the draft Convention on the Rights of the Child' (1990) 12 HRQ 157.

22 Islam has developed the concept of *Kafalah* to allow for a child who cannot be with the parents to be placed with another family: *op cit*, Van Bueren, 1995, fn 4, p 95.

armed forces (Art 38) failed to raise existing international standards, and the minimum age of recruitment was set at 15.[23] Similarly, the Convention is silent on the particular circumstances of the girl child; there is no mention of her needs, and consensus could not even be achieved on the abolition of female genital mutilation. Instead, States are required under Art 24(3) to take measures to abolish 'traditional practices prejudicial to the health of children', a diluted and genderless provision. This must be viewed as a lost opportunity, given the precarious and disadvantaged position of the girl child in many societies.[24]

In assessing the nature of their obligations, States are guided by the four central principles which underpin the Convention. First, Art 3 requires that the 'best interests of the child' be a primary consideration in all matters and decisions affecting the child. Implicit in this provision is the fact that the best interests of the child is a concept in transition throughout childhood. Decisions motivated by best interests can mean at one stage special protection, and at another involve respect for the individual's autonomy.[25]

The second principle underpinning the Convention is the duty of States to ensure that the views of the child are given due weight in all decisions which affect them (Art 12). Thirdly, account must be taken of the evolving capacities of the child (Art 5), introducing once again the notion that childhood is not fixed and the ability of children will increase with age.

The fourth pillar of the Convention is the anti-discrimination provision in Art 2, which requires the State to guarantee all of the rights to all children without discrimination. These four principles are to be read into all other Convention articles and form a backdrop against which all legislative and administrative actions by the State are to be judged.[26]

---

23 The Committee on the Rights of the Child established a working group in 1994 to draft an optional protocol to the Convention on the issue of children and armed conflict, one of its aims being to raise the age of recruitment into the armed forces to 18. See, further, E/CN 4/1996/102.

24 See, further, Olsen, F, 'Children's rights: some feminist approaches to the United Nations Convention on the Rights of the Child', in Alston, P, Parker, S and Seymour, J (eds), *Children, Rights and the Law*, 1992, Oxford: Clarendon, p 193.

25 See, further, Wolfson, C, 'Children's rights: theoretical underpinning of the best interests of the child', in Freeman, M and Veerman, P (eds), *The Ideologies of Children's Rights*, 1992, Dordrecht: Kluwer. See, also, An-na'im, A, 'Cultural transformation and normative consensus on the best interests of the child', in Alston, P (ed), *The Best Interests of the Child*, 1994, Oxford: OUP, p 62.

26 See Hammarberg, T, 'Children', in Eide, A, Krause, K and Rosas, A (eds), *Economic, Social and Cultural Rights: A Textbook*, 1995, Dordrecht: Kluwer.

IMPLEMENTATION OF THE CONVENTION

When ratifying the Convention, States agree to guarantee the rights contained in its articles by updating and amending relevant legislative and administrative practices.

The Convention is implemented by way of State reports to the Committee on the Rights of the Child, established under Art 43. This method of implementation is the weakest possible under an international human rights treaty, and although not unique to the Children's Convention, settling on this mode of supervision indicates a desire on the part of States to avoid the possibility of individual petitions and inter-State claims. There is, of course, the consideration that had the Convention included a stronger implementation system, it may not have attracted so many ratifications, nor would States have agreed to the inclusion of such a range of rights if the possibility existed of those rights being directly challenged by children before an international forum.

The Committee is made up of 10 experts who serve in their individual capacity. The main function of the Committee is to receive and consider initial reports within two years of ratification, and periodic State reports every five years thereafter. The Committee meets three times a year to carry out its functions.

The surprisingly rapid ratification of the Convention has had the effect of creating a huge backlog and, despite the frequency of its meetings as of January 1998, the Committee has received 113 initial State reports, of which it has examined 82; it is, thus, running two to three years behind. This situation is likely to get worse, because the Committee is due to examine periodic reports from September 1998.

The breadth of rights covered by the Convention also creates its own problems for the Committee: different standards of implementation apply to the economic, social and cultural rights compared with civil and political rights. To assist States and also to minimise any difficulties which may arise in its own functioning, the Committee has grouped rights together in its examination of State reports. For example, under the heading of 'Basic health and welfare', the Committee considers State performance on the right to life, survival and development (Art 6); the right to health (Art 24); social security rights (Art 26); and adequate standard of living (Art 27).[27] This grouping system also helps to overcome the fact that some rights do not clearly fall into

---

27 The Committee has grouped together the rights of the Convention under eight headings: General Measures of Implementation; Definition of the Child; General Principles; Civil Rights and Freedoms; Family Environment and Alternative Care; Basic Health and Welfare; Education, Leisure and Cultural Activities; and Special Protection Measures. See, further, Mower, G, *The Convention on the Rights of the Child*, 1997, Westport, Connecticut: Greenwood, pp 100–08.

traditional categories, and it is considered a suitable system by both the Member States and the Committee.[28]

In its reporting guidelines to the Convention, the Committee placed considerable emphasis on the general measures of implementation, which are to be found in Arts 4, 42 and 44.[29] The latter two refer to the duty of the State to make both the Convention and its own State report widely known to the public. The former provision lays down the appropriate standard of conduct for States to implement the economic, social and cultural provisions of the Convention.[30]

The difficulties of implementing the economic and social provisions of the Convention were addressed by the World Summit for Children in 1990 and the consequent World Declaration on the Survival, Protection and Development of Children.[31] The purpose of this summit was to flesh out some of the Convention provisions and devise practical mechanisms for ensuring their achievement: the agreed means of doing so was to encourage the formulation of National Programmes of Action (NPA). The NPA set specific targets and goals to be achieved over five and ten years on such issues as the reduction of child mortality, access to safe drinking water, universal access to education and protection of children in difficult circumstances. Although UNICEF reported in 1994 that, by the half way point, 'more than 100 of the developing nations, with over 90% of the developing world's children were making significant progress',[32] the realities of resource allocation are such that the majority of NPA are well behind in their achievement of their goals, and many were hampered by the absence of costing and strategic planning from the outset.

The Committee has attempted to overcome the inherent weaknesses in the supervisory system, by engaging in a robust and informed examination of State reports. The NGO Working Group, which proved so influential in the drafting process, continues to function now that the Convention is operational and its input has been central to the work of the Committee on the Rights of

---

28 See, further, *op cit*, Hammarberg, fn 26, pp 294–96.

29 Reporting Guidelines to the Convention on the Rights of the Child, UN Doc CRC/Add 5 (1991).

30 See, further, Parker, S, 'Resources and child rights: an economic perspective', in Himes, J (ed), *Implementing the Convention on the Rights of the Child, Resource Mobilization in Low-Income Countries*, 1995, Dordrecht: Kluwer. See, also, Leary, V, 'The social and economic rights of the child', in *op cit*, Van Bueren, 1993, fn 4, Vol 1, pp 15–43.

31 See, further, Ledogar, R, 'Implementing the Convention on the Rights of the Child through national programmes of action for children' (1993) 1 IJCR, 371, pp 371–91. For the text of the Declaration, see *op cit*, Van Bueren, fn 5, p 326. See, also, UN 'Plan of action for implementing the World Declaration on the Survival, Protection and Development of Children', in *op cit*, Van Bueren, 1993, fn 4, p 330.

32 See UNICEF, *The State of the World's Children*, 1995, Oxford: OUP. See, further, Black, M, *Children First: The Story of UNICEF, Past and Present*, 1996, Oxford: OUP, pp 275–305.

the Child. Following the practice of other treaty bodies, the Committee issues Concluding Observations on State reports.

The Committee has demonstrated a willingness to address sensitive issues which the State may prefer to avoid. For example, in 1994, in its Concluding Observations on the initial report of Pakistan, the Committee expressed its concern about child labour, inadequate attention to the needs of the girl child and the harshness of the juvenile justice regime, all issues of some sensitivity to the State.[33]

The Committee has also set a high standard for reports and indicated the seriousness with which States were to view their obligations by criticising the poor quality of information provided in the reports of, *inter alia*, Argentina and the UK.[34] It has also made extensive use of its powers under Art 44(4) to request additional information on particular issues, including further details about juvenile justice in Vietnam, minority children in Sweden and the effect of law reform on children's rights in Indonesia.[35]

Perhaps realising the inherent shortcomings of the reporting system as a method of implementation, the Committee has creatively interpreted its role and has developed other methods of promoting and protecting children's rights.

The most influential of these methods is the holding of discussion days on children's rights issues: thus far, these have included such topics as children and armed conflict and the economic exploitation of children. This process has fed into the Committee's powers under Art 45(c) to make recommendations to the Secretary General. One such discussion led to the appointment of a special *rapporteur* on the sale, prostitution and trafficking of children by the Commission on Human Rights in 1994. The discussion eventually resulted in a General Assembly resolution to appoint Special Representative Graca Machel to study the impact of armed conflict on children.[36] The Machel Report, which was presented to the General Assembly in 1996,[37] is comprehensive and authoritative: a second special representative was appointed in December 1997 for three years, with a mandate to follow up on

33 See Bi-Annual General Assembly Report of the Committee on the Rights of the Child, 18/06/96, Doc A/51/41, paras 19–31.

34 See *op cit*, Mower, fn 27, p 110.

35 See *ibid*, p 111.

36 See GA Res 48/157 of 20 December 1993, in which the General Assembly requested of the Secretary General that an expert be appointed to study the 'means of improving the protection of children in armed conflicts'.

37 Machel, G, *Report on the Impact of Armed Conflict on Children*, GA Doc A/51/306. For analysis of the Machel Report, see *op cit*, Hamilton, fn 10; see, also, UNICEF and Minority Rights Group Report, *War: The Impact on Minority and Indigenous Children*, 1997, London: UNICEF.

many of issues raised by the Machel Report.[38] The Committee has also held discussion days on the girl child, for the benefit of the Fourth World Conference on Women in 1995, and on children and the environment for the Habitat II Conference in 1996.[39]

Despite the obvious and considerable achievements which can be directly traced to the Children's Convention, there are doubts about the commitment of States to realising children's rights, as envisaged under the Convention regime. Resistance to the participatory rights in Arts 12–16, which was so in evidence during the drafting of the Convention, did not prevent States from signing up to the treaty, but it does find full voice in the sweeping and wide reservations which have been entered by no fewer than 56 States.[40] Reservations are, of course, permissible, and many relating to the Children's Convention are in accordance with the requirements of international treaty law under the Vienna Convention on the Law of Treaties 1969, in that they are narrow in scope and not clearly defined.[41]

However, there is cause for particular concern if we examine the reservations from mainly Islamic States, which seek to give primacy to domestic law. The practical effect of such reservations is to place substantial tracts of municipal law beyond the reach of the Convention. For example, Pakistan has attached a reservation which states that 'the provisions of the Convention shall be interpreted in the light of principles of Islamic laws and values'. Similarly, Djibouti ratified with the following reservation: 'The Government of Djibouti shall not consider itself bound by provisions that are incompatible with its religion and its traditional values.' Both of these are so far reaching that it is not inconceivable that the States concerned are seeking to limit the application of every single provision in the treaty.[42]

This trend is evidence of a reprehensible duplicity on the part of these States. No country wants to be seen as unsupportive of an international treaty

---

38 The Special Representative for Children in Armed Conflict, Olara Ottunu, was appointed by the General Assembly in October 1997. See Thalif, D, 'United Nations cracks down on the use of child soldiers' (1997) International Press Service, 12 October.

39 *Op cit*, UNICEF, fn 32.

40 In addition to reservations, a number of States have entered interpretative declarations, which have a similar effect in that the intention is to limit the application of the treaty. See, further, Schabas, W, 'Reservations to the Convention on the Rights of the Child' (1996) 18 HRQ 472, pp 472–91; see, also, Le Blanc, L, 'Reservations to the Convention on the Rights of the Child' (1996) 4 Int J Children's Rights 351, pp 357–81.

41 On reservations and human rights treaties, generally, see Higgins, R, 'The United Nations: still a force for peace?' (1989) 52 MLR 1, pp 1–21; Lowe, V, 'Reservations to treaties and human rights, Committee General Comment No 24(52)' (1997) 46 ICLQ 391, pp 391–411.

42 See, also, the reservations and interpretative declarations of Algeria, Bangladesh, Brunei, Dar-es-salam, Egypt, the Holy See, Indonesia, Iran, Jordan, Kiribati, Malaysia, Oman, Pakistan and Qatar, which, to varying degrees, seek to limit severely the application of the Convention. Many of these have been the subject of objections from other States. See, further, CRC/C/2/Rev 5 07/03/96.

which promotes children's rights, yet, on the other hand, these States intend to proceed with impunity to violate children's rights in a way which is incompatible with the letter, not to mention the spirit of the Children's Convention. If we revisit the universal ratification in the light of such disingenuous behaviour from State parties, it seems less impressive.

A challenge lies ahead for the Committee, in responding appropriately to the reservation problem. Under Art 51, reservations which are contrary to the object and purposes of the Convention are not permitted, but the Convention does not provide guidance on the effect of incompatible reservations and it is also silent on whether the Committee is itself to adjudicate on this matter.

Faced with a similar dilemma, the human rights Committee reserved for itself the right to decide on incompatible reservations following the 1994 General Comment on Reservations. However, this only added to the confusion surrounding reservations to human rights treaties, when, in the same year, the Committee noted in its concluding comments on the US initial report that one of that country's reservations ran counter to the letter of the Covenant. The effect of that observation is unclear; the US has not withdrawn the reservation and the Committee itself, having bared its teeth, has shown no desire to bite. Despite a clear finding of incompatability in the reservation by the Committee, the US has defiantly ignored theses findings, thereby undermining the authority of the Committee and the treaty itself. A possible way for the children's Committee to confront the threat posed to the Convention by reservations, would be to refer the matter to the Secretary General suggesting that he seek an advisory opinion from the International Court of Justice. Any judgment by the International Court would have a knock on benefit for other human rights treaties and may clarify one of the most difficult current issues in human rights law, namely the effect or status of incompatible reservations on a State's ratification of a human rights treaty.

CONCLUSION

As the Convention on the Rights of the Child approaches its 10th birthday, the position of Children under international law has changed beyond recognition over the past decade. Advances in the international legal protection of children have been supplemented by the increasing acceptance of the standards of the Children's Convention as the authoritative statement on children's rights. There has been a marked shift in the attitude of international forums to children, in the post-Convention era, and its principles have trickled down into the judgments of the European Court of Human Rights, whose judges have turned to the Convention for guidance and relied on its provisions to resolve ambiguities.[43] The Convention has inspired a range of initiatives and instruments, including regional treaties in Africa, Europe and the Americas.

However, children's rights and the Convention are not without their detractors and there is a very real danger that children may become the focus of the ideological battles and culture wars which question the very universality of human rights. The vehement opposition with which the presidential signing of the Children's Convention was greeted in the US is mirrored in the cynical and limiting reservations which have been made by many States to the Convention.[44] Until and unless the Committee on the Rights of the Child finds a way of confronting and coping with this challenge, many of the persistent and harmful violations of children's rights will continue, and may not even be perceived as human rights problems.

---

43 See *Keegan v Ireland* [1994] Series A.290.
44 See, further, Thalif, D, 'Right wingers block UN Children's Treaty' (1995) International Press Service, 15 February.

CHAPTER 10

ECONOMIC STRATEGIES FOR THE ENFORCEMENT OF HUMAN RIGHTS[1]

Stephen Livingstone

INTRODUCTION

The period since 1945 has witnessed a remarkable growth in international human rights instruments at both the global and regional levels. Many human rights lawyers have commented adversely on the 18 years it took the United Nations to move from the Universal Declaration of Human Rights to the more detailed Covenants on Civil and Political Rights and on Economic and Social Rights. However, compared with the failure to produce any detailed human rights treaties in the first half of the century, it seems a swift and dramatic achievement. Since 1966, the United Nations has continued to produce landmark charters on Racial Discrimination (1966), Discrimination Against Women (1979), Torture (1984) and the Rights of Children (1989). This treaty making activity has been supplemented by the extensive creation of 'soft law' declarations, bodies of principles or codes of conduct. In addition, regional human rights commitments have been institutionalised in Africa, Europe and the Americas.

Although advocates of 'second' or 'third' generation rights may argue that the international legal regime fails adequately to reflect their concerns, it can be strongly argued, that as regards its normative framework, international human rights law is now in a very healthy state. Much of what could only be said to be disputed ethical imperatives in 1945, has now become a matter of international legal obligation. Moreover, international human rights institutions, such as the Human Rights Committee or the European Court of Human Rights, are increasingly refining the content of these obligations, not just establishing that everyone has a right to be free from torture, inhuman or degrading treatment, but also defining what amounts to torture, etc. While international lawyers may continue to proffer new candidates for recognition as rights, there is clearly now a rich normative framework covering many areas of the activities of States and their peoples.

However, it is far from clear that this normative explosion in what is recognised as a right at the international level has corresponded with greater

---

1   A version of this paper was given to the Law and Society Association Conference at Aspen, Colorado, June 1998. I would like to thank those present for their comments.

respect of such rights. The recent experiences of Rwanda and former Yugoslavia would tend to suggest very much the opposite. The annual reports of organisations, such as Amnesty International or Human Rights Watch, continue to display extensive violations of even the most fundamental human rights throughout the world. There seems little immediate chance of either organisation folding up for lack of work. In this climate, international lawyers have begun to look increasingly at what mechanisms might better ensure the effective protection of the rights guaranteed in all these treaties.

The primary method of enforcement of international human rights guarantees, is and always has been through national legal systems. Parties to the International Covenant on Civil and Political Rights undertake to 'respect and ensure to all individuals within its territory and subject to its jurisdiction the rights recognised in the present Covenant'.[2] This remains the most effective way of guaranteeing that international human rights are respected and, in many parts of the world, national legal and political systems are organised to ensure that, by and large, they give effect to international human rights commitments.[3] However, even in these systems, there remain points where national law arguably fails to give effect to international standards, while in many other parts of the world it remains regrettably true that the national legal system is either unable or unwilling to offer protection against even the most gross human rights violations. In these circumstances, international human rights law needs to find a way of impacting directly on those responsible for committing human rights violations, or at least those whose international responsibility it is to prevent them occurring.

To date, four broad mechanisms of enforcement of international human rights law can be identified. The first, perhaps the most beloved of international human rights lawyers, is to have an international court of human rights capable of considering claims of human rights violations and rendering binding judgments on defendant States in respect of them. This has reached its highest form of development in the European and American regional systems, with both the European Court of Human Rights and the Inter-American Court of Human Rights being capable of considering individual applications, rendering binding judgments, awarding compensation and even, in the case of the San José Court, being empowered to issue interim injunctions. The second approach is reporting requirements. This has become the standard enforcement procedure in the United Nations treaty mechanisms and imposes an obligation on governments to submit their laws and policies in respect of a defined area of human rights obligations to scrutiny, normally

---

2   ICCPR, Art 2(1).

3   For a recent example of how international human rights commitments have been incorporated into a domestic legal system, see Drzemczewski, A and Nowicki, M, 'The Impact of the ECHR in Poland: a stock taking after three years' [1996] EHRLR 261.

by an independent committee of international experts. Those experts may make comments at various levels of detail on these reports.[4] The third approach may be referred to as periodic inspection. This is the approach adopted by most of the United Nations Charter bodies, where resolutions may be passed condemning countries for human rights violations, and also by the various mechanisms set up by these bodies such as the country special *rapporteurs* or those on Torture or on Summary and Arbitrary Executions.[5] Where sufficient reports of human rights violations arise, or sufficient political pressure is generated, these bodies may seek to examine the human rights situation in a particular country and perhaps issue resolutions condemning the State in question and calling for change. The fourth, perhaps the most recent approach, is continual inspection. The European Committee for the Prevention of Torture and Inhuman or Degrading Treatment or Punishment (CPT), established under the 1987 European Convention for the Prevention of Torture, is perhaps the best example of this approach, though the International Committee of the Red Cross pioneered it. While limited to places of detention, the CPT is empowered to carry out unimpeded inspections of exactly those places where the most serious human rights violations are likely to occur and, with the consent of the States involved, to publish their findings on whether such violations have occurred and what needs to be done to prevent them occurring.[6]

These various mechanisms clearly take us beyond the realm of moral persuasion and into that of international legal obligation. They compel international institutions and the States which are members of them to exert pressure on those States which are found to have violated treaty or customary international human rights obligations. However, it is clear that they have not proved entirely effective in ensuring that human rights are protected. There are a number of reasons for this. Perhaps the most effective mechanisms, human rights courts and regular inspection mechanisms, only apply to a limited number of countries that have signed the treaties establishing such institutions. Many of the countries with the most serious human rights problems in the world, notably in Africa, the Middle East and Asia, are largely outside the remit of such bodies.[7] Even where States are subject to their jurisdiction, human rights courts have been criticised for being slow to reach decisions, reluctant to find patterns as opposed to individual instances of human rights abuse and unable, ultimately, to do more than request that a

---

4   For an analysis of some of these mechanisms, see Alston, P (ed), *The United Nations and Human Rights: A Critical Appraisal*, 1992, Oxford, OUP.

5   See Weissbrodt, D, 'The three "theme" special rapporteurs of the UN Commission on Human Rights' (1986) 80 AJIL 685.

6   For a discussion of the CPT's work, see Kelly, M, 'Preventing ill treatment: the work of the CPT' [1996] EHRLR 287.

7   While many African countries are subject to the African Charter of Human and Peoples Rights, its enforcement lies in the hands of a Commission which does not have the power to issue binding rulings.

state take action and award a limited amount of compensation. To date, the European and Inter-American courts have fortunately found that States will largely respect their judgments and take appropriate remedial action,[8] although the European system may be about to be sorely tested in respect of cases concerning torture in Turkey.[9] The United Nations treaties reporting mechanisms may expose a State to temporary embarrassment, but can do little more than this. In any case, it is increasingly coming under pressure, as States claim they are unable to keep up with the sheer number of reports required by the various treaty bodies.[10] Often those most tardy to report are those with the most to be concerned about. The various *rapporteur* mechanisms are often overworked and under resourced. Further, while the censure of the United Nations Commission or Sub-Commission on Human Rights may be what States, or at least their foreign ministries fear most (judging by the amount of work they put into avoiding such resolutions), this is a form of enforcement which is notoriously open to political manipulation.[11]

In view of these limitations, human rights lawyers and activists have begun to look more deeply at other approaches to the enforcement of human rights, especially with regard to those countries where the most fundamental human rights seem to be violated with impunity. One of these is to move the focus from the civil liability of States to the criminal liability of individuals. Whereas States can seek to resort to diplomatic means to avoid responsibility or, if this fails, blame it on a previous regime, individuals must bear personal responsibility. Making individuals personally responsible for their human rights violations may, it is argued, decrease the number of people willing to violate human rights in the service of a State. Hence the increased interest in using national criminal or civil law to punish foreign human rights violators,[12] as well as in the establishment of Truth Commissions around the world[13] and in the creation of an international criminal court.

A second approach, and one which I wish to explore more in this chapter, is to make more explicit the link between money and human rights. It has often been felt that some of the world's greatest human rights violators have

---

8   In respect of the UK, see Churchill, R and Young, J, 'Compliance with judgments of the European Court of Human Rights and decisions of the Committee of Ministers: the experience of the United Kingdom 1975–87' (1991) 62 BYIL 283.

9   See Boyle, K, Hampson, F and Reidy, A, 'Enforcing fundamental human rights: the European Court of Human Rights and Turkey' (1997) 15 Neth QHR 161.

10 See Bayefsky, A, 'United Nations human rights treaties: facing the implementation crisis' (1996) 15 Windsor Yearbook of Access to Justice 189.

11 See Guest, I, *Behind the Disappearances: Argentina's Dirty War Against Human Rights and the United Nations*, 1990, Philadelphia: Pennsylvania UP, for a discussion of one country's efforts to avoid UN censure.

12 Perhaps the best known example being the suing of torturers under the US Alien Tort Statute, as in *Filartiga v Pena-Irala* (1980) 630 F 2d 876.

13 See the discussion in Steiner, H and Alston, P, *International Human Rights in Context*, 1996, Oxford: OUP, pp 1084–1109.

escaped punishment, either because they had sufficient economic resources to buy their critics off or because they were in some way economically useful to those who might otherwise have been critical. This approach accepts that money talks, but seeks to make it speak in favour of rather than against human rights. It argues that States have considerable economic leverage, notably through aid and trade provisions, to influence each other either to respect human rights or ignore them. It also suggests, that in a world which has seen the shrinkage of the State and the extension of private corporate power in the past two decades, that such power brings with it responsibilities. It is arguable that multinational corporations, many of which are considerably richer and more influential than many States, should also play a role in the advancement of human rights concerns.

THE GLOBAL ECONOMY AND HUMAN RIGHTS

The development of a truly global economy, through a dramatic increase in the volume of international trade and investment over the past two decades, is clearly of significance for human rights.[14] However, exactly what that significance is remains a matter of some controversy. To some, globalisation poses a significant threat to human rights, especially the rights of people in developing countries. They fear that, as footloose capital roams the world in search of profits, labour rights in particular will be diminished as governments around the world seek to reduce labour costs to attract foreign investors. This in turn may lead to social unrest and a subsequent reduction in political rights as governments crack down on dissidents in order to create a peaceful, investor friendly social environment. The perceived need to reduce the costs of investment may also lead to the creation of low tax environments and a consequent decline in health and education services available to the population, while the end of import restrictions may see the destruction of a market for locally produced goods and hence widespread unemployment. The rights of indigenous peoples may also come under increasing threat as capital sees new opportunities to exploit their land for industry, agriculture or tourism.

In contrast to this vision of doom, others see globalisation as having a more positive impact on human rights. They suggest that the protectionist barriers governments have invoked to protect indigenous industry, have often served more to keep out new ideas and new ways of doing things which

---

14 According to the WTO, the volume of world trade has tripled since 1950 and has grown especially quickly since 1990. See *International Trade Trends and Statistics*, 1996, Geneva: WTO. However, some argue that, while the world economy is more integrated now than in 1945, it is less so than in 1914, see Hirst, P and Thompson, G, *Globalisation in Question*, 1996, Cambridge: Polity, Chap 1.

might be unwelcome to those in power. They have also been the foundation of a network of corruption whereby those in power have enriched themselves at the expense of the majority of the population. In turn, the existence of such corruption has poisoned the political system and necessitated widespread official secrecy and suppression of civil rights to prevent the truth becoming widely known. The most optimistic supporters of liberalised capital and trade markets argue that, in the long run, these will bring greater economic growth around the world and create the conditions in which rights to employment, health and education stand a better chance of being realised. Those less confident argue that the greater international communication and connection this process leads to will at least help civil and political rights to flourish, as people become less willing to be dictated to by local masters and the international community is more rapidly sensitised to serious human rights violations occurring anywhere in the world.

It is far from clear as yet which of these two views is the more plausible. Central and Eastern Europe perhaps presents the clearest example of an economy and society, which was closed for decades and which then, rapidly, opened to the outside world. Clearly the civil and political rights of people in this part of the world have considerably improved, but the position is less optimistic when one comes to economic and social rights, especially the further east one goes. Much of South East Asia became open to outside investment and dramatically increased its level of trade without this leading to a significant change in the human rights situation, though this view may shortly be open to correction after the recent economic downturn and its link to transparency problems.[15] In Central and Latin America, political change largely preceded economic liberalisation, while much of sub-Saharan Africa has yet to really feel the effects of economic globalisation. Countries such as India and China, where the process has only recently got under way, may prove perhaps the most interesting case studies. The former has a strong and largely distinguished tradition of civil and political rights, but has struggled to live up to its commitments to respect the economic and social rights of its people. The latter claims to give effective recognition to economic rights, but has long fought shy of according the same respect to civil and political rights. Whether economic globalisation will lead to a greater indivisibility of rights protection in each, or a general decline in the actual, as opposed to the paper, protection of human rights in these countries is a fascinating question for the future.

What is beyond dispute is that globalisation creates a greater opportunity for people in one part of the world to influence the state of human rights in another. As trade and inward investment become more important to a country's economy, it becomes more important how it is perceived abroad.

---

15 Such problems include the need for greater political accountability as a protection against cronyism and corruption, as well as a need for a more free press which might bring such problems to light earlier, and more effective separation of powers.

Political repression to create a low wage, low tax economy may seem more attractive to foreign investors and trading partners, but it may also create pressure on the governments and corporations of that trading partner not to do business with what is seen as a repressive State. Moreover, greater economic intercourse creates greater formal opportunities for people in one country to condition their economic relations with another on respect for human rights. The remainder of this chapter examines three types of economic 'leverage' which can be used to advance the cause of human rights. They are conditionality in aid policy, the use of trade sanctions and the adoption by corporations of human rights codes in respect of trading and investment activity. The focus will be on developments in the US and European Union countries, both for reasons of economy and because this is where the most significant developments thus far have taken place.

CONDITIONING FOREIGN AID ON RESPECT FOR HUMAN RIGHTS COMMITMENTS

Both the US and the European Union, the world's largest aid donor, have legal provisions in respect of foreign aid which require them to take human rights considerations into account. In the US, this is achieved through ss 116 and 502B of the Foreign Assistance Act of 1961. Section 116 prohibits the provision of aid to a government 'which engages in a consistent pattern of gross violations of internationally recognized human rights', unless 'such assistance will directly benefit the needy people in such country'. The phrase 'Patterns of gross violations' refers to non-derogable international human rights, such as torture and the right not to be arbitrarily killed, but also extends to disappearances and prolonged detention without trial. House and Senate Committees on Foreign Affairs are empowered to seek information from the executive, both on the extent to which the human rights situation in a country amounts to a pattern of gross violations and whether any assistance will benefit the needy people in a country. Section 502B prohibits the provision of any security assistance to a country where its government is engaged in a pattern of gross violations (defined as in s 116), unless the President 'certifies in writing that extraordinary circumstances exist warranting the provision of such assistance'.

These amendments were introduced into the Foreign Assistance Act in 1974, at the height of concerns as to the presidential conduct of foreign affairs in the later stages of the Nixon administration, and also of rising concern regarding human rights violations in the Soviet Union.[16] The same legislative

---

16 The Jackson-Vanik Amendments to the Trade Act, to be discussed further in the next section, also originated in 1974 and were particularly targeted at the Soviet Union's restrictions on Jewish emigration.

initiatives also introduced the requirement for the State Department to make a report to Congress each year on the human rights situation both in countries which receive foreign assistance and on all other countries which are members of the United Nations.[17] While these State Department country reports have gone on to be of significant assistance to people working on human rights around the world, it is less clear that the foreign assistance provisions have been. Even the Carter administration, which made the protection of human rights a prominent aspect of its foreign policy, generally avoided making formal decisions that a country was involved in gross violations and decided to refuse security assistance to only a very small number of countries.[18] The Lawyers Committee for Human Rights has observed that s 502B has never been formally applied (in most cases where this appeared likely presidential 'exceptions' have been certified) but argues that its presence may well have influenced the executive in deciding whether to supply aid or security assistance.[19] Perhaps more directly effective have been a variety of country specific pieces of legislation, which condition the further appropriation of funds for a country on compliance with certain human rights conditions. These have been used more extensively, but are perhaps even more vulnerable to charges of political partisanship.

The European Union came later to the linking of economic assistance to human rights. Under Art 238 (Art 310 in the post-Amsterdam version) of the Treaty of Rome the Community (now Union) can enter into association agreements with other States or international organisations. With regard to development aid, perhaps the most significant of these have been the four Lome Conventions with what the European Union terms the ACP (Africa, Caribbean and Pacific) group of nations, concluded between 1975 and 1989. Under these agreements, about US$4 billion of aid flows from the EU to ACP countries every year and ACP counties are granted preferential access to EU markets. The first three Lome agreements contained no reference to human rights but Clause 5 of the Fourth, which came into force in 1991, indicated that:

> Co-operation operations shall thus be conceived in accordance with the positive approach, where respect for human rights is recognized as a basic factor of real development and where co-operation is conceived as a contribution to the promotion of those rights.[20]

This commitment to human rights as a relevant consideration in development policy was reinforced by the Community's Resolution of 28 November 1991

---

17 Foreign Assistance Act of 1961, ss 116(d) and 502B, as amended.

18 For a fuller discussion, see Cohen, S, 'Conditioning US security assistance on human rights practices' (1982) 76 AJIL 246.

19 Lawyers Committee for Human Rights, *Linking Security Assistance and Human Rights*, 1989, New York: Lawyers Committee for Human Rights.

20 For the background to Cl 5 of Lome IV, see Marantis, D, 'Human rights, democracy and development: the European Community model' (1994) 7 Harv HRJ 1.

on Human Rights Democracy and Development, which also explicitly linked human rights with democracy,[21] and by Art J.1(2) (Art 11 in the post-Amsterdam version) of the Treaty of European Union. This includes a commitment to 'develop and consolidate democracy and the rule of law, and respect for human rights and fundamental freedoms' among the objectives of the common foreign and security policy. Following the 1991 resolution, many association agreements have included human rights clauses of varying levels of strength.[22] These extend the European Union's linkage of development assistance and human rights beyond countries which are part of the Lome Conventions.

The European Union has been anxious to pursue an 'incentives' approach to linkage rather than a 'sanctions' approach. Its 1991 resolution envisages a range of positive measures, which may be offered to States to assist with the better protection of human rights and democratic governance. These include support for electoral processes, for the judiciary and for access to law programmes. As Marantis observes, this positive approach is seen as more beneficial as it directly targets immediately perceived needs in the human rights field, helps to develop a dialogue between the European Union and the donee State with regard to human rights issues, and can often be delivered through NGOs rather than government.[23] However, a gradually rising level of sanctions is also envisaged, moving from confidential or public statements of concern up to postponement of new projects or even suspension of co-operation. The regime for sanctions was strengthened by the introduction into the Treaty of Rome of Art 228a (now Art 301 in the post-Amsterdam version) by the Treaty of European Union. This provides for urgent measures suspending economic co-operation to be taken by the Council where a common position or joint action has been taken on a matter relating to common foreign and security policy.

Any measures taken which affect economic co-operation must be consistent with the European Union's international legal commitments. As Cremona has observed, this has given rise to difficulties where sanctions are envisaged in respect of ACP countries.[24] Such countries argue that cl 5 of the Lome Convention does not provide a legal basis for the suspension of co-operation where human rights violations have occurred in the ACP Member State, and that consequently the imposition of economic sanctions is in violation of the treaty. The argument is even greater where trade sanctions as

---

21 Resolution of the Council and Member States meeting in Council on human rights, democracy and development 28 November 1991 (1991) 11 Bulletin of the EC, p 122.

22 For a discussion of these, see Cremona, M, 'Human rights and democracy clauses in the EC's trade agreements', in Emiliou, N and O'Keefe, D (eds), *The European Union and World Trade Law*, 1996, Chichester: Wiley, pp 62–77.

23 See *op cit*, Marantis, fn 20.

24 *Ibid*, p 71.

opposed to the suspension of development assistance is contemplated. Perhaps, as a result of this, the Union has been very reluctant to suspend co-operation with such countries on the grounds that human rights and democracy clauses have been violated in the absence of United Nations Security Council Resolutions. Sanctions imposed on Haiti in 1993 expressly referred to such a United Nations Resolution, and the fact that it stated it would apply notwithstanding any previous agreements between States. In negotiations on the Fifth Lome Convention, which will come into force in 2000, the European Union has sought to strengthen the human rights and democracy clause in order to provide a better legal basis for action taken in respect of human rights violations.

As with the US, critics of the European Union's linkage of human rights and development assistance argue that it has tended only to target weak States where the European Union has few significant financial or political interests. Supporters would tend to point to the positive impact of the incentives approach and the fact that the European Union has channelled substantial funds to programmes aimed at assisting the protection of human rights. Much of this has gone to NGOs, which have continued to receive funding on humanitarian grounds, even when co-operation with the State they are located in has been suspended.

The UK does not have the same legal basis for the linkage of human rights and development assistance that exists in the US or the European Union. Instead, decisions as to whether aid given by the Department for International Development (formerly the Overseas Development Administration) is purely an executive matter. A White Paper issued by the department in November 1997 included respect for human rights among the objectives of aid policy, and indicated that where a country was ruled by a government which had no commitment to allowing the poor to realise their human rights, then the Government would seek to provide aid through alternative channels.[25] The White Paper also held out the possibility of a new International Development Act, without indicating explicitly whether human rights concerns might be given effect to in this. Overall, it seems likely that Britain will continue to seek to follow an incentives approach, seeking to provide support for programmes which are likely to advance the effective protection of human rights, rather than resorting to sanctions to penalise States for human rights violations.

The vexed question remains as to whether the conditioning of aid on compliance with human rights standards does actually ensure the better protection of human rights in donee States. Some commentators have argued that precisely targeted withdrawals of aid (for example, until a promised

---

25 *Eliminating World Poverty: A Challenge for the 21st Century*, Cm 3789, 1997, London: HMSO, para 2.24.

election is held) may have a beneficial approach.[26] Others have suggested that the overall record of the use of aid conditionality is negative.[27] The World Bank, which has in the past pursued strict conditionality requirements in relation to financial performance, has increasingly moved towards making aid dependent on measures which encourage 'good governance'.[28] Governance is perceived as a rather more broad term which encompasses good administration, transparency and anti corruption measures, as well as respect for basic civil and political rights.

THE LINKAGE OF HUMAN RIGHTS AND TRADE

Significant though development aid is to the States receiving it, the total amount of aid provided is minuscule compared to the volume of world trade. Development assistance, in both its bilateral and multilateral forms, is currently estimated by the United Nations as amounting to about US$55 billion per year. This compares to a volume of world trade which currently exceeds US$5.2 trillion. While most of this occurs between States which are not engaged in practices of gross human rights violations, a significant amount of it concerns States which are. While aid has been declining around the world (the United Nations now only seeks for States to devote 0.7% of national wealth to aid), trade has been substantially increasing and therefore provides a greater potential for impact on human rights violations. However, the recent trends on the world stage have, if anything, been in a direction away from using trade as a leverage against human rights violations.[29]

In the US, the most significant legal measure regarding the relationship of human rights to trade can be found in s 402 of the Trade Act 1974, the so-called Jackson-Vanik Amendment. This indicates that products from a 'non market economy' will not be entitled to receive most favoured nation (MFN) treatment where the President determines that the country is imposing a range of restrictions on the emigration of its citizens. Although originally motivated by concerns as to the plight of Soviet Jews, this provision has been employed to deny MFN status to a range of countries, including Afghanistan, Albania, Cambodia and North Korea. Recently, its application has been most

26 See, eg, Kumado, K, 'Conditionality: an analysis of the policy of linking development aid to the implementation of human rights standards' (1993) 50 ICJ Rev 23.

27 See, eg, Crawford, G, *Promoting Democracy, Human Rights and Good Governance through Development Aid: A Comparative Study of Four Northern Donors*, 1995, Leeds: University of Leeds Centre for Democratisation Studies (Working Paper), arguing that such measures are often limited and inconsistently applied. See, also, Muller, N, 'The World Bank, human rights, democracy and governance' (1997) 15 Neth QHR 21.

28 See World Bank, *Governance: The World Bank's Experience*, 1994, Washington DC: World Bank.

29 See Hart, M, 'The WTO and the political economy of globalisation' (1997) 31 J World Trade 75, p 79.

hotly contested in relation to China. US presidents have consistently favoured granting MFN status to China, formerly for political reasons, but more recently for economic ones. Some in Congress have attempted to strengthen the human rights preconditions for granting MFN status to China, for example, by passing the United States China Act of 1992. This provided that the President would not recommend continuation of the MFN waiver for China after 1993, unless he reported that China had taken appropriate steps to adhere to the Universal Declaration of Human Rights in respect of Tibet. President Bush vetoed this Act and the veto was sustained after the Act's supporters were unable to obtain the necessary two-thirds majority in the Senate to overturn the veto.[30] President Clinton's administration initially showed much more interest in using MFN as a means of securing human rights reforms. However, by May 1994, the president's team adopted the line that imposing trade sanctions would simply hurt the US economy without producing significant change in the human rights situation in China. Although trade sanctions were renounced as a means of influencing change on human rights, the same administration continued to see them as being of value in respect of trade policy. In 1995, the US introduced the largest trade sanctions in its history in respect of China in an attempt to stop piracy of American music, movies and software.[31] Many human rights observers commented that this indicated that the Government took the view that trade sanctions were a useful tool of influence, but was prepared to use them only when it felt US economic or political interests were in danger.

The US Trade Act provisions were always somewhat ideologically conditioned. Providing for the denial to MFN status only in respect of non-market economies, seems to ignore the fact that many governments in market based economies may be guilty of human rights violations, and immediately invites charges of inconsistency. The European Union regime is at least formally free of such restrictions. Much of it has already been alluded to when considering the EU's position on development assistance. Under Art 228a of the Treaty of Rome, urgent action may be taken to suspend economic co-operation with any State, pursuant to a common foreign policy position having been reached. The reference to economic co-operation includes actions such as suspending transport links or freezing assets of the foreign State within the jurisdiction, but excludes activities such as arms embargoes or sporting boycotts.[32] These remain within the exclusive competence of the Member States. However, as was noted already with regard to development assistance, the European Union has been reluctant to resort to such measures without the backing of a United Nations Security Council resolution.

---

30 See, also, Drinan, R and Kuo, T, 'The 1991 battle for human rights in China' (1992) 14 HRQ 21.

31 See (1995) *New York Times*, 5 February.

32 For a discussion, see McLeod, I, Hendry, I and Hyatt, S, *The External Relations of the European Community*, 1996, Oxford: Clarendon, pp 354–56.

Sanctions in relation to travel imposed on Nigeria following the execution of environmental activist Ken Saro-Wiwa in 1995, are one example of an exception to this. The scope for the use of such sanctions has been decreased as a result of developments in the Uruguay Round of GATT. Article XX of GATT provides that, with regard to trading partners who are also members of GATT, only preferential conditions granted in a specific trading agreement may be suspended, not underlying GATT based free trade provisions.

The UK lacks any general legal provisions which limit trade on human rights grounds. Sanctions may, however, be imposed on specific forms of trading pursuant to United Nations or European Union resolutions. One particular form of trade with major human rights obligations is subject to legal regulation, namely the arms trade. Here the Foreign Secretary has powers to decide whether licences will be granted for the export of weapons, and has indicated that he will refuse these where he believes that the weapons will be used to repress human rights. This is of no little significance given that the UK's sales currently reach about US$20 billion a year, making it the world's second largest arms dealer with about 22% of the world market.[33] However, there remain considerable doubts as to how consistently this policy will be followed. In September 1997, Foreign Secretary Robin Cook did refuse licences for the export of about £1 million worth of armoured personnel carriers and rifles, which were to be sent to Indonesia, on the grounds that these might be used for internal repression. The British Government has also pushed successfully for a stronger EU code on the arms trade. However, Cook had earlier approved a £160 million contact to send Hawk jets to Indonesia on the grounds that this had already been agreed by the previous administration. Britain's largest arms contract, a US$2.5 billion a year deal with Saudi Arabia first signed in 1985, is untouched by these restrictions, despite Saudi Arabia's deplorable human rights record on the grounds that these weapons are used purely for external defence.

CORPORATE CODES OF CONDUCT

Linking development assistance to human rights conditions, or imposing trade sanctions to discourage human rights violations, still involves a focus on States as the main actors in this field. However, one of the main themes of observers on globalisation is the growing role of corporations, particularly multi-national corporations (MNCs), as key actors on the world stage.[34] A

---

33 See Black, I and Fairhall, D, 'The profits of doom' (1997) *The Guardian*, 16 October.

34 UN study in 1993 estimated that there were 37,000 MNCs, controlling 170,000 affiliated organisations. UN, *World Investment Report 1993: Transnational Corporations and Integrated International Production*, 1993, New York: UN. In the early 1970s, it was estimated that there were about 7,000 MNCs.

1996 Policy Studies report indicated that of the top 100 economies in the world, 51 were multinational corporations and 49 nation States.[35] The fact that several of the larger MNCs now have economies substantially larger than most countries, arguably puts them in a position to dictate terms to government rather than the other way round.[36] MNCs have arguably been both the chief movers and chief beneficiaries in the liberalisation of world trade, which is central to globalisation and, especially through the growth of Foreign Direct Investment (FDI), are in a strong position to influence what happens in the countries which they invest in.

This was not always the case. From the 1970s to the early 1990s, attempts were made at the United Nations to limit the influence of the multinationals, which were widely perceived as harmful to the interests of people in developing countries. Inconclusive discussions took place on the drafting of a United Nations Code of Conduct on Transnational Corporations, whose sponsors sought mainly to subject MNCs to increased regulation by States in the developing world. By the time these negotiations ground to a halt in 1992, the global environment was already changing and many developing countries were actively seeking an increase in such investment.[37] However, although MNCs thus became more free of international pressure to take ethical questions seriously in their investment and trading policies, at the same time there was a growth in domestic pressure, manifested through shareholder resolutions and consumer boycotts, to pay greater attention to such issues. Much of this pressure has been targeted at a corporation's environmental responsibilities. However, an increasing amount of it is raising questions about how far a corporation should take into account the human rights situation of a country in which it invests.[38]

The idea that corporations should take account of the human rights situation in a country they chose to invest in is not entirely new. In the US, sponsors of the Sullivan Principles in relation to South Africa and the MacBride Principles[39] in relation to Northern Ireland, sought to link continued investment to specific improvements in the human rights situation.

---

35 An *Economist* survey on multinationals estimated that the 300 largest multinationals now control about one third of the world's productive assets. See (1993) *The Economist*, 27 March, pp 5–6.

36 See, eg, Eyal, J, 'Conspiracy of silence' (1996) *The Guardian*, 11 December, arguing that the 'real rulers of the world today are the chairman of MNCs, not politicians'.

37 For a discussion of the negotiations and ultimate fate of this UN Code, see Frey, B, 'The legal and ethical responsibilities of transnational corporations in the protection of international human rights' (1997) 6 Minn J Global Trade 153, pp 165-67.

38 For a good source of information on such issues, see the Ethical Trading Initiative website http://www.ethicaltrade.org.

39 See Bertsch, K, *The MacBride Principles and US Companies in Northern Ireland*, 1991, Washington DC: Investor Responsibility Research Centre. The Principles sought to commit corporations to non-discrimination and affirmative action measures in respect of their operations in the relevant countries. They were also employed by a number of public authorities in making investment decisions.

What is new is that corporations, under a variety of pressures, are seeking themselves to initiate statements of corporate responsibility, and are making these general to all their investments, rather than specific to particular countries where concerns have arisen. Many of these are corporations whose profitability depends heavily on the successful marketing of a brand name, something which may render them especially susceptible to public criticism. Often such statements only arise after criticism and through dialogue. The Starbuck's Coffee Code is a good example of this development. Challenged initially by a US activist labour coalition on the conditions for workers at its Guatemalan suppliers' plantations, Starbucks initially responded defensively and pointed to its generous support for CARE as an expression of its social responsibility. However, the labour coalition persisted in its campaign, providing information to Starbuck's customers and urging them to write to the company asking for further action, but stopping short of a consumer boycott. Within a year, Starbucks agreed to design its own code on labour practices, the first in respect of the agricultural commodities sector.[40] In the UK, Shell responded to similar pressure with regard to its activities in Nigeria, by including support for the United Nations Declaration of Human Rights in its Statement of Business Principles.[41]

About 10% of US corporations are now reckoned to have initiated or signed up to some form of social responsibility statement.[42] This development has perhaps gone furthest in the footwear and apparel industries, where widespread concerns have existed as to the use of cheap labour and child labour by US corporations or their suppliers.[43] Although some attempts have been made to produce standards codes, for example, President Clinton's Apparel Industry Partnership Code in 1997, the content of these codes and their methods of enforcement continue to vary widely. As befits the origin of codes in concerns as to the use of cheap labour, notably prison labour, in the manufacturing of clothes, the main focus tends to be on labour rights. Most codes tend to include a commitment to a safe system of work and the absence of forced or child labour. Some, such as those adopted by Timberland or Wal-Mart, also prohibit discrimination based on a range of criteria including race, sex, disability or sexual orientation. Less agreement exists on the issue of wages and union organisation. Some codes make no reference to wages,

---

40 On the origins of the Starbucks Code, see Compa, L and Hinchcliffe-Darricarrere, T, 'Enforcing international labor rights through corporate codes of conduct' (1995) 33 Col J Trans'ntl L 637, pp 683–86.

41 Beavis, S and Brown, P, 'Shell has human rights rethink' (1996) *The Guardian*, 6 November.

42 See IRRC, *Social Issues Service: 1997 Background Report J: International Labor Standards*, 1997, Washington: IRRC, p 6.

43 See Cassel, D, 'Corporate initiatives: a second human rights revolution?' (1996) 19 Fordham ILJ 1963, p 1973, noting that firms representing 90% of sales in the athletic footwear sector signed up to an industry code.

others make only very general references[44] or require that the legal minimum wage be paid, even though no legal minimum may exist in that country. The President's Code indicates that workers should be paid the legal minimum or 'the prevailing industry wage, whichever is the higher'. Critics argue that requiring at least the provision of a 'living wage' would be a more progressive step. On union organisation one again finds that, while companies such as Reebok require union recognition, other codes, such as that of Levi-Strauss, are silent on the issue. In respect of labour rights, a further matter of divergence is the extent to which firms monitor not just their direct suppliers, but also the companies to whom they 'outsource' aspects of the production process.

The next level of divergence is the extent to which the company sees its responsibility as being limited to the conditions of its own workers, or whether it also takes account of the general human rights situation in the country. Human rights groups have argued that, in many countries, MNCs are directly implicated in the government's repression, for example, where it has supplied resources to the government or has benefited from repressive government action to remove opposition to the companies' activities. This, they argue, clearly creates a responsibility for the government's actions. Even where not directly implicated, they argue that companies, by reason of their position of influence, may be well placed to bring pressure to bear on a government involved in human rights violations. Thus, Amnesty International, for example, in its statement of Human Rights Guidelines for Companies calls on companies to 'use their influence to mitigate the violation of human rights by governments, the forces of law and order or opposition groups in the countries which they operate'. Some corporations have taken this on in their codes of conduct. Shell, for example, indicates that it has a right to make its position known to countries in which it operates, but stops short of explicitly indicating the conditions on which it may withdraw from a country. Timberland goes further and includes in its codes a set of 'country standards' which it considers in deciding to do business in a country. These include the commitment that it will not favour a partnership in countries where 'human rights are pervasively violated'.[45] On the basis of this consideration, Timberland, for a time, withdrew involvement in China while other companies, such as Levi-Strauss, withdrew from Burma on similar grounds.

Perhaps the most difficult issue has been monitoring and enforcement of these codes. Most codes provide only for internal company monitoring, raising fears that the whole exercise may be little more than a whitewash.

---

44 Shell's 1997 Statement of General Business Principles 2(c) states only that employees should be provided with 'good and competitive terms and conditions of service'.

45 For further discussion of the Timberland code, see the contribution of their counsel, Bruce Landay, to a symposium on 'Human rights, multinational business and international financial institutions' (1994) 88 Proc ASIL 271, p 282.

Human Rights and labour organisations have urged companies to move towards independent monitoring by local or international groups. They have sought to argue that just as companies now recognise the need for financial audits by independent accountants so they should accept the need for social or human rights audits by similarly qualified independent agencies. Some organisations have accepted this, though usually under pressure. The Gap, for example, agreed to independent monitoring at a Salvadorian factory in 1995, after it was exposed that its code had never been translated into Spanish or seen by any of its workers. However, even it has resisted independent monitoring at its other factories, and most other corporations have displayed a similar reluctance.[46] The President's Apparel Code goes no further than urging the development of training for company monitors and consultation with 'Labor, human rights, religious or other local institutions'.

Most of these codes are of recent vintage and the effect they have had on human rights is difficult to assess at this stage. China, Burma and Nigeria, three countries that have featured prominently in debates about corporate policy and human rights, remain countries where serious human rights concerns exist. Perhaps the least that can be said is that debates around the actions of major corporations from the developed world in these States have broadened the debate and kept the human rights issues in the public domain, at a time when politicians appeared to be losing interest.

CONCLUSIONS

The use of economic pressure to secure human rights improvements remains very limited. This chapter does not aim to argue that the presence of such pressures could replace the present and developing institutions of international human rights law. However, it does suggest that the use of economic pressure is worth considering as a supplement to such strategies. The use of trade pressures and aid conditionality is perhaps of particularly limited value. For a start, most trade continues to take place between rich countries, where many other mechanisms for human rights protection exist.[47] Such countries seem particularly unlikely to utilise these economic pressures against each other to secure human rights improvements. Where they do use such pressures, notably conditioning foreign aid on compliance with human rights standards, in respect of developing countries they remain very vulnerable to charges of partiality. As we have seen, these charges are not

---

46 On the Gap situation, see, further, Jeffcott, B and Yanz, L, 'Code breaking' (1998) 302 New Internationalist 23.

47 *Op cit*, Hirst and Thompson, fn 14, p 69. They estimate that nearly 70% of world trade takes place between the US, Canada, Japan and Europe.

without some merit and their force is increased by the failure to link debt relief (which, arguably, has a much more significant impact than aid for many developing countries) with human rights concerns. In any case, the trend in world trade negotiations, as envisaged by GATT and the OECD's developing Multilateral Agreement on Investment, appears to be away from removing any restrictions on trade and investment, including human rights based restrictions. In time, issues concerning labour rights and, perhaps other human rights matters, may become part of the new international rules governing trade and investment, but that seems unlikely in the short term.[48]

More opportunities in the immediate future may therefore lie with the development of the regime of corporate codes. Once again, one must counsel caution. The commitment of many corporations to human rights issues may be only skin deep and end where they are sure that their brand name is not at risk of being compromised. Just as international trade is limited, although developing, so is the extension of the sphere of influence of MNCs beyond their 'home bases' in the developed world. In addition, active engagement with multinationals poses risks for the unity of the human rights community itself. There are many human rights activists in the developing world who see the greater penetration of MNCs into their countries as something to be resisted as only adverse to human rights. Helping MNCs to refine their codes of conduct, and the means of monitoring and enforcing them, may only be seen as providing comfort to the enemy. However, overall it seems unlikely that protectionism is likely to be a viable political or economic strategy for the developing world. If trade and investment are likely to continue to increase, then multinationals are likely to continue to be a part of it. In this scenario it seems important that human rights activists continue to engage with these companies in a debate about the extent of their responsibilities, and the best means to give effect to these. Such an involvement may also help energise the human rights movement in the developed world too. Companies have grown rich through promoting associations of quality, reliability and a desirable lifestyle with their brand name – witness the growth of supermarket 'loyalty cards'. International brand names increasingly trade on ideas of global competence and imply that you continue to have faith in them, even if you no longer believe in the State. Yet such faith is a fragile thing and vulnerable to information that a corporation is acting in ways governments have often been criticised for. People who show little interest in what their State does abroad may nevertheless care that their favourite shop or petrol station is one they

---

48 For a discussion to develop labour rights through GATT, see Ehrenberf, D, 'From intention to action: an ILO-GATT/WTO enforcement regime for international labor rights', in Compa, L and Diamond, S (eds), *Human Rights, Labor Rights and International Trade*, 1996, Philadelphia: Pennsylvania UP, p 163. However, for indications that the WTO has been reluctant to develop this, see 'GATT at 50' (1998) *The Economist*, 16 May.

can believe in.[49] Involving money in the protection of human rights may not be a strategy for the purists, but strategies that bring change have rarely been without risk.

---

49 Christian Aid has recently published an 'ethical league table' for British supermarkets, many of which participated in its compiling, see (1997) *The Guardian*, 27 October.

CHAPTER 11

TRANSGENDER RIGHTS:
THE EUROPEAN COURT OF HUMAN RIGHTS
AND NEW IDENTITY POLITICS FOR A NEW AGE

Stephen Whittle

INTRODUCTION

In 1995, I wrote that:

> ... though transsexuals are seeking a unique set of freedoms that are related to the process of undergoing gender reassignment or assertion, they are not seeking a new set of rights. Transsexuals are seeking for the law to acknowledge that they have rights, not as transsexuals, but as men and women who have finally become appropriately recognisable through medical intervention.[1]

Three years later, I would not change my view that transsexuals are seeking a set of freedoms related to gender assertion, but would now argue that the identity politics of transsexuals, as a sub-group of the larger transgender community, has shifted considerably. They are no longer asking the law to recognise them simply as men and women, but rather they are seeking for the law to recognise them as transmen and transwomen – a status that goes beyond the dichotomous structures of sex and gender roles recognised within and by the law. This will be evident in the following analysis, which aims to explain and analyse the early cases dealt with under the ECHR, to contextualise them and finally to explain how human rights issues in this field have evolved beyond the traditionally stereotypical, to encompass basic questions concerning recognition of the civil status of members of the trans community.

CLAIMING A LEGAL STATUS

It would be facile to say that, by virtue of this new claim, the trans community wishes to be recognised as having a unique position, a third gender or rainbow gendered approach to their legal status. The massive ideological shift within the trans community of the last few years may have seen a move from claims to rights within gender roles, to claims to needs regarding the

---

1   Whittle, S, 'Legislating for transsexual rights: a prescriptive form', in Bullough, B, Bullough, V and Elias J, *Gender Blending*, 1997, New York: Prometheus, pp 430–46, 433.

expression of gender roles, but there is a pragmatic acceptance that gender roles, as defined by those outside of the community, still exist. Most importantly, though, as we move toward the new millenium, members no longer see as a privilege, 'passing' – the ability to hide a transsexual identity in a new gender role. Passing has been, for over 50 years, the defining political movement in transsexual identity politics. This could be seen in the demands for birth certificate and identity card amendment along with the right to marry in the 'transsexual' cases before the European Court of Human Rights in the 1970s and 1980s.[2]

To date, all of the applications in the transsexual cases have claimed a violation of Art 8 of the European Convention on Human Rights (ECHR), and all have in essence sought an identical solution: the legal recognition of their true gender identity (after gender reassignment) in all civil status documents, whether birth certificate or identity card. Article 8 of the Convention States:

> (1) Everyone has the right to respect for his private and family life, his home and his correspondence.
>
> (2) There shall be no interference by a public authority with the exercise of this right except such as is in accordance with the law and is necessary in a democratic society in the interests of national security, public safety or the economic well being of the country, for the prevention of disorder or crime, for the protection of health or morals, or for the protection of the rights and freedoms of others.

Until very recently (in *X, Y and Z v UK* and *Roetzheim v Germany*),[3] applicants have demanded that transsexual men and women are issued with new civil documentation that recognises them as non-transsexual men and women. This relies upon the State accepting a positive obligation to appear to recognise as a fact, something that many have argued is a fiction or, if not a fiction, then at the very least an assertion based on scant scientific evidence.

This call for a response to a positive obligation arises out of para 1 of Art 8 of the ECHR. Paragraph 2 of Art 8 appears to imply that public authorities simply have a duty not to interfere with private and family life, home and correspondence. However, para 1, which stipulates the right to 'respect for private and family life ...', has been interpreted by the Court and the Commission 'as a basis for expanding the duties in Art 8(1)', thus giving rise to a State's possible positive obligations to fulfil its duty under Art 8.[4] The Court itself has stated:

---

2   *Van Oosterwijk v Belgium* [1980] ECHR, Series A.40; (Appl 7654/76), 6 November 1980 (Court); *Rees v UK* [1986] ECHR, Series A.106; (Appl 9532/81), 17 October 1986 (Court); *Cossey v UK* [1990] ECHR, Series A.184; (Appl 10843/84), 27 September 1990 (Court); *B v France* [1992] ECHR, Series A.232; (Appl 13343/87), 25 March 1992 (Court), all of which are discussed below.

3   *Roetzheim v Germany* (1997) (Appl 31177/96), 23 October 1997 (Court).

4   *Kroon and Others v Netherlands* [1994] ECHR, Series A.297; (Appl 18535/91), 27 October 1994 (Court).

[Article 8] does not merely compel the State to abstain from ... interference: in addition to this primarily negative undertaking, there may be positive obligations inherent in the effective respect for private and family life ...[5]

The extent of the State's possible positive obligations under Art 8 in the 'transsexual' cases by the European Court of Human Rights has proved to be a moot point. In *Van Oosterwijk v Belgium*,[6] the Court upheld by 13 to four, the Belgium Government's position of 'non-exhaustion of domestic remedies', despite the fact that there was no indication that domestic remedies could in anyway resolve the problems faced by the transsexual applicant, as was pointed out by the dissenting judges. In *Rees v UK*,[7] the Court held, by 12 votes to three, that an amendment of the applicant's birth certificate would impose new duties on the State and the rest of the population, by insisting that they recognise current civil status rather than historical record, and that the Court could not impose duties of such magnitude.

In *Cossey v UK*,[8] the Court refused to distinguish this case from *Rees*, preferring instead to consider whether there were persuasive reasons for departing from its previous decision. By 10 to eight, the Court reiterated that the refusal to amend the applicant's birth certificate, or to allow her to marry a member of the opposite gender, did not constitute an interference with her private life. The Court said that the applicant was invoking a positive obligation, and that this obligation was subject to the wide margin of appreciation afforded to the differing practices of Member States, that is, the striking of a fair balance between the general interests of the community and the interests of the applicant. In this case, it was held that, although social change had taken place, the State had not contravened its obligations under the ECHR.

All of these cases have concerned the 'traditional' transsexual person and what might be considered the traditional issues: privacy and marriage. However, the next UK case posed the questions differently. *X, Y and Z v UK* presented an alternative way for the Court to look at the civil status of the transsexual. It cited Art 8 and also Art 14, which reads as follows:

The enjoyment of the rights and freedoms set forth in the ECHR shall be secured without discrimination on any ground such as sex, race, colour, language, religion, political or other opinion, national or social origin, association with a national minority, property, birth or other status.

The case concerned a transsexual man, X, his partner, Y, and her birth child, Z, who had been conceived using donor insemination. The family had

---

5   *X and Y v Netherlands* [1985] ECHR, Series A.91; (Appl 8978/80), 26 March 1985 (Court), para 23.
6   *Van Oosterwijk v Belgium* [1980] ECHR, Series A.40; (Appl 7654/76), 6 November 1980 (Court).
7   *Rees v UK* [1986] ECHR, Series A.106; (Appl 9532/81), 17 October 1986 (Court).
8   *Cossey v UK* [1990] ECHR, Series A.184; (Appl 10843/84), 27 September 1990 (Court).

been refused permission to register X as the father of Z on her birth certificate, on the basis that only a biological male could register as the father of a donor inseminated child, albeit not biologically related. The family invoked Art 8, arguing that it had been contravened in relation to family privacy. They did not request that X be recognised as a man, nor that he be allowed to marry a woman. They were hoping that if he could be recognised as the father of Z, then the UK Government would be obliged to consider the other issues raised.

The Court unanimously decided that Art 8 was applicable in this case as they considered that *de facto* family ties did exist between the three applicants, despite arguments to the contrary advanced by the UK Government. However, did this mean that the State had a positive obligation to recognise the *de facto* family through civil registration procedures? The Court, unfortunately, went on to say that there is little common ground among the Member States of the Council of Europe as to whether any non-biological father should be recorded on donor inseminated children's birth certificates. Accordingly, if there is no common European standard with regard to the granting of parental rights to transsexuals, the law here is in a transitional stage and States must be allowed a wide margin of appreciation in dealing with this question.

On the point as to whether a fair balance had been struck between the interests of the applicants and the interests of the State, the Court then held that, because transsexuality raises complex scientific, moral and social issues, Art 8 cannot, in this context, be taken to imply an obligation for the State to recognise as the father of a child a person who is not a biological father. That being so, the failure of UK law to recognise the relationship between X and Y does not amount to a failure to respect family life. The Court further held that the complaint made under Art 14 was tantamount to a restatement of the complaint under Art 8, and consequently raised no separate issue. In view of their findings, there was no need to examine the matter again in the context of Art 14.

The case raises many issues and its failure tends to say more about the current State of the European Court of Human Rights, rather than the State of transsexual rights in the UK. In this, as in other recent decisions, the width of the margin of appreciation that the Court is currently according to Member States in this area, could be said equally to be increasing in many areas of the Court's jurisdiction and this does not bode well for the future of human rights in Europe. However, the case itself makes some progress, not least as the Court held that Art 8 was applicable because there was a recognisable *de facto* family relationship in existence. Nonetheless, the decision fails to recognise, that in this area, there are, or should be, limits imposed on the respect for fundamental rights guaranteed by the Convention. In the *Cossey*[9] case, Judge Martens held, in his dissenting opinion, that the refusal of a new identity in

---

9   *Cossey v UK* [1990] ECHR, Series A.184; (Appl 10843/84), 27 September 1990 (Court).

law for those who had undergone gender reassignment treatment 'can only be qualified as cruel'.[10]

In *X, Y and Z*, if we look to the dissenting opinions, Judges Casadevall, Russo and Makarczyk argue that the Government should accept the consequences of allowing X to have gender reassignment, and of allowing Y to have fertility treatment during which X was obligated to acknowledge paternity. This, they consider, to positively bind the Government to take all measures needed, without discrimination, to allow the applicants to live a normal life.

Judge Thor Vilhjalmsson, also dissenting, argues that, as other non-biological fathers are allowed to be registered on the birth certificates of donor inseminated children, to refuse to allow X to do so constitutes discrimination on the grounds of sex under Art 14. Further, this also leads him to conclude that the family ties between X, Y and Z were not being respected under Art 8. The fact that the male partner is a transsexual should be irrelevant. Judge Foighal, who also dissents, argues that, in *Cossey*, the Court held that, even though the law was in a transitional state, legal measures should be kept under review to take account of medical, social and moral developments. He maintains that the majority decision in the case does not reflect the changes that have taken place in recent years, although the Court was given ample evidence of those changes. He also states that it is part of our common European heritage that governments are under a duty to take special care of individuals who are disadvantaged in any way. The Government did not advance any convincing arguments with regard to competing interests, nor had they made any attempt to justify their failure to help X further by ensuring that his change of sex receives legal recognition, even though this would help him and harm no one. These reasons lead him to conclude that, in his opinion, a violation of Art 8 had occurred. Following the dissenting judgment of Thor Vilhjalmsson, he similarly finds a contravention of Art 14.

Judge Gotchev also argues that a contravention of both articles has occurred, but from the standpoint of the 'welfare of the child', which should, in his opinion, be the prevailing consideration. He states that this obliges a State to allow what had been unanimously agreed upon as being de facto family ties to be legally safeguarded so as to render possible from the moment of birth, or as soon as practicable thereafter, the child's integration into the family. This would include recognising X as Z's father.

States appear to have been afforded a wider margin of appreciation than would seem to be required as a result of recent social and legal developments within the membership of the Council of Europe and the rest of the world. Indeed, the margin appears wider than appears to be indicated by the

---

10 *Cossey v UK* [1990] ECHR, Series A.184; (Appl 10843/84), 27 September 1990 (Court), dissenting judgment, para 64.

balancing test supposedly applied by the court to its decisions. Doerfal has argued that, the reason for this, is that these decisions are a reflection of 'the apprehension and prejudices' of the majority of the Court's judges.[11] Is it that the Court's judges cannot imagine recognising the transsexual person as being of equal worth to others? It is perhaps in response to this, and to the theoretical and social changes that transsexuals have achieved over the last decade, that the applicants in X, Y and Z did not ask for X's right to marry or to have his birth certificate changed. Rather, the demand being made was that the transsexual man be recognised for what he is, namely a transsexual man, but that that should not exclude him from recognition as a social and legal father. By considering these social changes and the more recent case of *Roetzheim v Germany*,[12] decided by the Commission and discussed below, it is possible to see both how transsexual and transgender people are claiming a new class of civil status and the implications for sex and gender categories as we know them. The dissenting opinions in X, Y and Z offer some hope in that they indicate possible ways forward for the future. However, they also acknowledge that identity documentation is not the same as status recognition, nor will it necessarily provide privacy, personal safety, employment or relationship protection. The trans community is now arguing that it is only status acknowledgment as transsexual men and women which will afford true protection on these levels. In order to understand the change in the community's calls for status recognition we need to consider how 'passing' has no longer become the pre-eminent consideration for the trans community.

DECONSTRUCTING PASSING

Throughout the 1990s, many 'pre-existent' community members, who had transitioned into their new gender roles in the 1970s and early 1980s, and who initially identified as transsexual, were to re-address their personal sense of self and place. This was to result in profound changes in the trans politics of the community and its members. The reasons for this are manifold and space does not permit their exploration, but Sandy Stone's 'The empire strikes back: a post transsexual manifesto'[13] is a striking example of the new self analysis taking place within the Community itself during the early 1990 s. In this examination, Stone called for 'A deeper analytical language for transsexual theory, one which allows for the sorts of ambiguities and polyvocalities which

---

11 Doerfal, J, 'Transsexuality and the European Convention on Human Rights', 1998, unpublished essay.

12 See *Kroon and Others v Netherlands* [1994] ECHR, Series C.297.

13 Stone, S, 'The empire strikes back: a post transsexual manifesto', in Epstein, J and Straub, K (eds), *Body Guards: the Cultural Politics of Gender Ambiguity*, 1991, London: Routledge, pp 280–304.

have already so productively informed and enriched feminist theory'.[14] and she suggested 'constituting transsexuals not as a class or problematic "third gender", but rather as a *genre,* a set of embodied texts whose potential for *productive* disruption of structured sexualities and spectra of desire has yet to be explored'.[15]

For many, in what was to become the trans community, Stone articulated the limitations of the medical 'mental disorder' model of transsexuality that had arisen historically. Medicine had singularly failed to afford many the ability to 'pass', and even when it did, it had often been at too great a cost: a loss of personal history, sexual sensation and ability, and a lack of any form of legal protection in the workplace or on the streets. Stone's work was to become a rallying call for a 're-visioning of our lives', not only to the old guard – who, in their positions as community leaders and spokespeople, were to be very influential on new and younger community members – but also to a new school of trans academics whose work with feminist praxis, postmodernist theory and 'Queer' identity have gelled into a new framework of identity politics and a new school of theory, 'trans'.

As such, the trans community is approaching the next century with the tools to develop a diverse and embracing acknowledgment of the many voices and lifestyles which exist as gender (or body) variant, which are oppressed because of that gender (or body) variance, and which are, in Stone's words, potentially disruptive of structured sexualities. There can be no denial of the effect that trans theorists are having, but as Riki Anne Wilchins of 'Transsexual Menace' says:

> Trans identity is not a natural fact. Rather, it is a political category we are forced to occupy when we do certain things with our bodies ... The regime of gender is an intentional, systematic oppression. As such, it cannot be fought through personal action, but only through an organized systematic response.[16]

Trans theory provides the background, trans people provide the victims but organisation has provided some (albeit few) victories in the struggle for gender freedoms – or should that be freedom from gender?

THE TRANS MOVEMENT

The organisational movements within the trans community that have taken place over the last 10 years have seen an astonishing growth in a variety of

---

14 *Op cit*, Stone, fn 13, p 297.

15 *Ibid*, p 296 (italics in the original).

16 Wilchins, R, *Read My Lips: Sexual Subversion and the End of Gender*, 1997, New York: Firebrand, p 25.

organisations catering for the different political forms and processes in which members of this diverse community are able to feel comfortable and participate. These are not just Western, Euro-American groups, though these do currently dominate the world of gender politics, but interaction with political and community diversity has enabled a wide ranging set of common sites of oppression to be identified and to be acted or campaigned upon.[17]

The three types of groups – the self-help, the direct action and the political lobbying groups – have developed a 'working together' model based on the fact that many of their 'leaders' were drawn initially from a small core of individuals who had transitioned gender roles in the 1970s and early 1980s. They were to be at the forefront of the mail and telephone help support systems that developed through the 1980s. From the numerous stories they were to hear and collect, many were then to go on to become involved in writing and theorising about the oppression that community members faced. They were to be among the first to develop a trans theory in which the actual sense of gender that previously was theoretically tied to trans bodies, whether through performativity or biological essentialism, was successfully recodified outside limiting paradigms.

As such, these models still exist for the trans community, but they have been successfully deconstructed by community leaders and theorists as being irrelevant to transgender lives, other than as external mechanisms of power and oppression. This theorisation was to lead to the resultant changes in activism which were to found the direct action groups and, ultimately, the political lobby groups and their agendas. It is also important to understand how, as Kate Bornstein has put it, 'gender defenders ... bang their heads against a gender system which is real and natural and ... then use gender to terrorise the rest of us'.[18] The 'rest of us' are trans people for whom gender is

---

17   Self-help groups were the earliest types of trans groups often divided into specific 'camps' such as heterosexual transvestite, male to female transsexual, female to male transsexual, etc. In these groups, excellent knowledge and expertise of particular issues and problems faced by members was developed. These groups still participate in the main educational thrusts of trans and other people. They were also to be instrumental in the development of the direct action groups and the political lobbying groups. Direct action groups such as 'Transsexual Menace' are instrumental in trans people and their loved ones getting over one very clear message: we are your neighbours, your friends, your co-workers and keeping trans matters alive and in the public domain, using quick response mechanisms to ensure that immediate direct, and public action is taken in response to specific events.

The political lobbying groups are the politically wise face of the community. They are at the forefront of organising and co-ordinating political lobbying, such as the 'Days on the Hill' which GenderPac and ITA have organised in Washington, and the Downing Street lobby in London organised by Press For Change in October 1997. They also co-ordinate legal challenges at every level, and both in the UK and the US have positively promoted transgender and transsexual claims through the courts.

18   Bornstein, K, *Gender Outlaw: On Men, Women and the Rest of Us*, 1994, London: Routledge, p 72.

'real and natural' (neither merely biologically determined nor mere performativity), a concept at the heart of the newly developed transgender activism. The self with its trans identity can now be experienced as an authentic self rather than as the medicalised paraphilia, currently imposed by physicians, attached to the body and regarded as the trans sense of identity by the rest of society.

Through its organisational processes, the transgender community itself is being redefined, and is reordering its priorities. The personal recognition of the actual self; internally defined, as opposed to the medical self, which had been externally dictated, has meant that transgender politics has already undergone a huge ideological shift: the body or its performativity is no longer the dictator of gender. Gender has become who or what you experience through your experience of oppression, as well as through a celebration of diversity of experience and lifestyles. The basis of the self-help, activist and political lobbying groups has quickened the decline of the legitimacy of the politics of 'passing' for the trans community, and has provided both the catalyst and the mechanism for that decline. Previously, as Stone put it, it was 'difficult to generate a counter discourse if one [was] programmed to disappear'.[19]

One example of the frequently condemned features of a transgender life is that it abounds in stereotypes which reinforce oppressive gender roles. As Raymond puts it:

> ... transgenderism [has] reduce[d] gender resistance to wardrobes, hormones, surgery and posturing – anything but real sexual equality. A real sexual politics says yes to a view and reality of transgender that transforms, instead of conforming to, gender.[20]

If the transgender movement were as Raymond suggests, it would indeed have little to offer, other than being a self-help network in which people are 'taught' how to reinforce the values of a white, heterosexist patriarchy. Trans women would endeavour to 'pass' as the oppressor, leaving others behind to bear the brunt of struggle and discrimination. Such a view singularly fails according to trans theory, because if it is right that there are far more transsexual women than vice versa, they are, in fact, struggling to become the oppressed, and to leave behind a position of privilege. It also assumes that a move to 'female genre' is the same as disappearance into femaleness, an experience that is very infrequent for transsexual women who rarely experience an easy transition or future acceptance as 'women born women'. The reality of an oppressed experience based on gender representation is, in fact, all too true for the majority of the transgender community. It is that

---

19 *Op cit*, Stone, fn 13, p 295.
20 Janice Raymond, quoted in Ekins, R and King, D, *Blending Genders: Social Aspects of Cross-dressing and Sex-changing*, 1996, London: Routledge, p 223.

oppressed experience the community ultimately wishes to address. If there is to be a fundamental change in understanding the nature of this oppression, doors have to be opened to those who were previously unable to have a voice in the politics surrounding transgender (or as it was then, transsexualism) because of their social position, both within and outside of the trans community.

RECREATING THE SELF

Most members of the trans community would accept that there had been, in the 'real world', a *de facto* hierarchy that was very much concerned with 'passing'. 'Passing' – some notion of feminine or masculine 'realness' – would provide for many a physically safe, although restricted, and unauthentic, way of living. Furthermore, 'the principle of passing, denying the destabilising power of being "read" [means that] relationships begin as lies'.[21] The truth of the matter, though, was that even the most 'passable' transsexual woman could find herself vulnerable. This is what happened to Caroline Cossey (Tula) when her privacy disappeared after the *News of the World* published an exposé of her transsexual status in September 1982.

The hierarchy based on 'passing' was such that those who were the most 'non-transsexual' looking were awarded status and privilege, whilst those who were most obviously transsexual or transgender were often the butt of private jokes and exclusionary behaviour.[22] By default, they were also to be the front line of any political or social movement that existed. By not 'passing', they daily faced the street battles which often resulted in emotional, financial and even physical scars. The privileged few would, however, get to dictate what were to constitute the important and significant issues. If you 'pass', then the issues are bound to be based around matters such as further privacy rights, for example, the right to have birth certificates reissued and further relationship rights, such as the right to marry in one's new gender role. Feinberg, in particular, asserted that the community could no longer afford to use this assimilationist approach to activism, seeing it as one consequence of early minority rights activism, and as far too limiting:

> When a young movement forms, it gets a great deal of pressure to put forward only its best dressed and most articulate – which is usually a code word for white ... These 'representatives' are seduced into thinking the best way to win is to not rock the boat and ask for only minimal demands. A more potent strategy relies upon unified numbers ... We need everyone and cannot afford

21 *Op cit*, Stone, fn 13, p 298.
22 Green, J and Wilchins, R, 'New men on the horizon' (1996) 33 FTM Newsletter, January, San Francisco: FTM International, p 1.

to throw anyone overboard. After all, we could never get rid of enough people to please our enemies and make ourselves 'acceptable'.[23]

The plain fact is that the majority of transgender or transsexual women[24] cannot and will never 'pass', and so assimilationist politics are consequently inadequate in such situations. For these women, their issues are not necessarily going to be those of the select few who could seek integration. For them, such rights are meaningless in the context of their lives – if you cannot pass beyond the most casual of inspections, then any reissued birth certificate will certainly not prevent your discovery as a transsexual woman, whether by prospective employers or by observers on the street, and you are very unlikely to find a relationship which is so conventional that marriage matters. It would only be by providing a proper forum for these people that a unified group could form which could address fully the legal issues that caused real and universal oppression. However, as Stone puts it:

> For a transsexual, as a transsexual, to generate a true, effective and representational counter discourse is to speak from outside the boundaries of gender, beyond the constructed oppositional nodes which have been pre-defined as the only positions from which discourse is possible.[25]

As enunciated by gays, lesbians and people of colour in their articulation of arguments for solidarity, deconstructing the demands of passing implies that all transsexuals must take charge of the history of all of their community. The only way to do that is by sidestepping the notion of 'passing', preferring to speak instead from outside the boundaries of gender. Ironically, however, many of the community leaders were and are people who could have chosen to pass, and who fall victim to the politics of passing. That they have chosen not to, not only results from their experiences at the forefront of the self-help groups where the oppression that others faced was made all too clear, but the mechanisms chosen to run and co-ordinate those groups have been instrumental in informing both the theoretical and, ultimately, the political stance they have adopted.

For trans men, the internet and cyberspace have provided a much needed space in which the (invariably housebound) victims of poor surgical procedures,[26] could talk freely about their experiences, without presenting

---

23 Leshko, I, 'Determine, define, modify gender' (1996) website http://planetq.com/pages/lfeinberglnt.html.

24 These are trans people whose sense of actual gender means that they self-identify as belonging in that place in the gendered framework that most natally designated women automatically occupy.

25 *Op cit*, Stone, fn 13, p 295.

26 Phalloplasty (the surgery to create an artificial phallus) has always been extremely problematic, with a very low rate of success in terms of providing an aesthetic phallus, which could be used for voiding and sexual intercourse. Further, many such attempts at these surgical procedures have resulted in ongoing long term disability for the recipients, ranging from incontinence, excessive abdominal scarring, long term catheterisation to loss of mobility in the lower limbs. See *op cit*, Green and Wilchins, fn 22.

their failed body image. For others who had not yet undergone the procedures, an opportunity was provided whereby they could assess whether they wanted to take such great risks in an attempt to fully pass. This opened a discussion around what makes a 'real' man, and the body was able to be dismissed as a socially controlling mechanism that dictated power roles, but which for the transsexual man was shown to be an inadequate, inauthentic device. Many transsexual men started to view the body differently as a faltering 'vision' of 'passing', reclaiming their identities as trans men. This combination of 'representing the body image' and the privacy afforded by a public display of the personal alongside the new spatial dynamics of the internet, has contributed greatly over the last five years, to the immense change in trans politics. Many trans/gender/sexual women and men have discovered a way of possessing for themselves, entirely subjectively, an actual identity as trans people.

As a result, the trans organisations have presented a safe area where body image and presentation are not fundamentally important to the issues of personal judgment and social hierarchy within the transgender community, so extending the range of potential community members and voices and thus reformulating the community's understanding of gender oppression.

A NEW COMMUNITY

The denotation of the community has been re-ordered through community politics. This means that we no longer see the definitions provided by the medical profession being adopted by the community as boundary identifiers. In 1990, the Gender Trust, a UK self-help membership group for transsexuals defined its members as having:

> ... a profound form of gender dysphoria, and persons thus affected have the conviction of being 'trapped in the wrong body' and feel compelled to express themselves in the gender to which they feel they belong.[27]

By 1996, however, the online Trans Male Task Force defined itself as:

> ... a grassroots organisation of transsexual and transgender men who are committed to creating action on major issues affecting our community. Our membership is open to all those who identify as male but were born with female anatomy. Some of us have or are seeking medical treatment to change our bodies – others are not. Many of us live full time as male, while others are either just beginning their process or are still considering it. We are a diverse group, comprised of all ages, races, sexual orientations, professions, and lifestyles.[28]

---

27 Gender Trust, *Gender Trust Handbook*, 1990, London: Gender Trust.
28 TMTF, *Mission Statement*, 1996, San Francisco: Trans Male Task Force.

The mission statement then goes further:

> The usage of the term 'transgender' has undergone a tremendous amount of change over the past decade, and is currently used in a number of different ways. Some political action and educational groups are promoting its use as an umbrella term to include transsexuals, transgenderists, cross dressers (transvestites), and other groups of 'gender variant' people, such as drag queens and kings, butch lesbians and 'mannish' or 'passing' women. However, it must be realised that many people belonging to the aforementioned groups do not wish to be included under this umbrella, and prefer to retain their distinct identities ... Some transgender people consider themselves a third sex, neither male or female but combining characteristics of both (also called an epicene or 'third'). Most commonly, transgender people live as, identify as, and prefer to be treated as, belonging to the 'opposite' sex, but do not wish to change their bodies through surgery.[29]

In the six years between these statements, we see a series of changing emphases. First, there is a move from a medical naive paradigm which excludes most people, to a complex paradigm which is inclusive rather than exclusive. The defining process is no longer medical, and the community boundaries are neither based on surgical procedures, nor even controlled in any way by physicians. Instead, the boundaries are flexible, encompassing rather than proscribing. Thus the definitional limits are experientially informed by the self who chooses inclusion, rather than being medically informed. Accordingly, inclusion is not forced upon the individual through specific medical intervention.

It is perhaps this aspect of 'choice' which is most interesting, because it is a reflection of the process of re-embodying the self which has taken place, particularly within cyberspace. Because inclusion in the cyber trans community is a matter of individual choice, it removes the need (as felt by many in the past) to aim for the status of being a 'non-trans/gender/sexual person'. Historically, the authors of 'transsexual' autobiographies have often sought hard to distinguish themselves from the rest of the trans/gender/sexual community by claiming some sort of intersex disorder such as Kleinfelter's syndrome.[30] Whether or not this is a true reflection of their situation, there are certainly many reasons why such people should wish to portray an identity 'in effect' in the real world.

The resulting recreation of the community, both in terms of its hierarchical structure and the prioritisation of basic issues of concern has resulted in a re-evaluation of the legal questions which are important: the reality was that, for most women, the debate did not concern individual privacy but personal

---

29 Op cit, TMTF, fn 28.
30 See Allen, R, But For The Grace: The True Story of a Dual Existence, 1954, London: Allen; Cossey, C, My Story, 1991, London: Faber and Faber; Langley Simmons, D, Dawn: A Charleston Legend, 1995, Charleston: Wyrick.

safety regardless of trans visibility, and for most men it was to do with expressing the actual masculinity of the self through a failed body site, which would never in itself afford them legal status as men. New forms of legal activism have come about through the new consciousness evident in community politics.

A NEW AGENDA

Legal activism in this area has tended to concentrate on 'quality of life' issues such as the transsexual's right to birth certificate change, the right to marry and the medico-legal issues of treatment and surgery. Of recent years, the issues of concern have changed within the new community, the emphasis on birth certificates and marriage (which are to do with the further privacy of 'passing') giving way to concerns about the right to personal physical safety, about the right to keep a job regardless of a transgendered status and resultant lifestyle, about the right to be treated equally before the law, particularly in the area of relationship rights, and the right to medical treatment (including reassignment), in relation to all of which 'passing' should be irrelevant.

The 1990s cases before the European Courts have clearly illustrated some of these trends, with cases concerning employment rights,[31] parenting,[32] the right to face arbitrary discrimination in areas such as cross border immigration, marriage status, employment regulation, and the right not to have to disclose medical treatment except where absolutely necessary.[33] However, one particular application to the European Commission on Human Rights sums up the essence of the new campaign issues surrounding gender identity rights.

Roetzheim v Germany[34] concerned the application by Dora (formally Theodor) Roetzheim to the Commission alleging that the German Government had failed in its obligations, in that its refusal to recognise her new gender for civil status purposes violated Art 8 of the ECHR. German law provides two remedies for transsexuals: first a change of forenames which does not require there to have been any surgical intervention and, secondly, an amendment of public registries following surgical reassignment treatment. Particular features of the application were that Roetzheim, although living as a woman and taking female hormones, had not undergone any gender reassignment surgery and further, that she had given up a well paid job in order to work as a woman. Accordingly, she argued that her maintenance

---

31 *P v S and Cornwall County Council* [1996] IRLR 347.

32 *X, Y and Z v UK Government* (1997) (Appl No 21830/93), 22 April 1997 (Court).

33 *Sheffield and Horsham v UK Government* (1997) (Appl No 22985/93–23390/94), 30 July 1997 (Court).

34 *Roetzheim v Germany* (1997) (Appl No 31177/96), 23 October 1997 (Court).

obligations to the children of a former marriage should be reduced. The local courts had held that, without genital surgery, there was no obligation to amend her public status and that, because of the lack of surgery, there was no reason why she should not resume her male role and take up her former profession, hence retaining the value of her maintenance obligations.

Section 8 of Germany's Transsexuals Act (*Transsexuellengesetz*) 1980 indicates that, for a change of civil status to be effected, a person must be unmarried, permanently unable to procreate and have undergone gender reassingnment surgery with the consequence that the outer appearance resembles closely the phenotype of the opposite sex. Roetzheim argued that this was a violation of her right to respect for her private life under Art 8 of the Convention. Fundamental to Roetzheim's argument was that her gender identity should be recognised regardless of her body morpholgy. The Commission went on to unanimously declare Roetzheim's application ill founded and inadmissible.

Roetzheim's claims before the Commission closely mirror those made in the International Bill of Gender Rights[35] wherein fundamental human and civil rights are articulated from a gender perspective. The rights claimed are not be viewed as special rights applicable to a particular interest group, but are to be regarded as universal rights both claimable and exerciseable by any and every human being. These range from the right to define and have free expression of gender identity for one's self, to the right to conceive, bear or adopt children, to nurture and have custody of them regardless of a self-defined gender identity or the expression of such identity. These rights are both transformative and embedded in notions of personal liberty and free expression. They provide a framework for the claims of the new trans community and as such are increasingly being seen as the paradigms that inform the legal battles the community is undertaking. As yet, they may be seen as being too revolutionary for justice systems, yet they are simple truisms with which it is hard to argue. For example, 'the right to train and to pursue an occupation ... nor to be denied ... employment ... or just compensation by virtue of chromosomal sex, genitalia, assigned birth sex, or initial gender role' reflects what we might see as essential interpretations of the Equal Treatment Directive[36] of the European Community, or the Sex Discrimination Act 1986. Yet, for trans people, those rights have to be fought for and clearly articulated, as was to happen in *P v S and Cornwall County Council* [37] in the European Court of Justice.

---

35 ICTLEP, *Proceedings from the Fourth International Conference on Transgender Law and Employment Policy*, 1995, Houston: ICTLEP, pp viii–xi

36 Council Directive 76/207 EEC on the implementation of the principle of equal treatment for men and women as regards access to employment, vocational training and promotion and working conditions .

37 *P v S and Cornwall County Council* [1996] IRLR 347.

It can only be a matter of time before arbitrary and unfounded discrimination of any kind on the grounds of gender identity and gender expression is outlawed. This is the agenda for the new millennium which the re-organised, newly informed and highly politicised trans community is determined to make happen. They have not flinched as yet from battle as they are extremely determined to win the war against gender identity discrimination, Increasingly, we will be seeing them use the courts and the tools of the political lobby to ensure that their issues and claims are heard and heeded.

CHAPTER 12

REPRODUCTIVE RIGHTS AND ASSISTED CONCEPTION

Deirdre Madden

INTRODUCTION

This chapter examines the concept of reproductive rights in the context of assisted reproductive technologies used in the treatment of human infertility. It considers whether a legal right to reproduce may exist and, if so, whether it may be used by a childless couple to insist on treatments being made available to them in their own State. It also analyses the contribution which international human rights instruments may make to this discussion and whether the wording of those documents is conducive to such an extension. It concludes by questioning whether consensus will ever be achieved on an international level in relation to human reproduction and bioethics in the coming years.

WHAT IS INFERTILITY?

Infertility can be defined as the inability to conceive a child after at least one year of regular unprotected sexual intercourse, or the inability of a woman to carry a pregnancy to live birth.[1] The statistics for infertility are that at least one in six couples[2] need specialist help to conceive at some stage in their lives. However, it must also be noted that these statistics do not accurately reflect the extent of the problem as they do not account for those who remain childless voluntarily, those who do not seek specialist help, or those who remain unmarried.[3] In any event, the treatment of infertility has become a

---

1   Ellis, GB, *Infertility: Medical and Social Choices*, 1988, US Congress, Office of Technology Assessment: Biological Applications Program, p 35.

2   Behrman, SJ and Kistner, RW, 'A rational approach to the evaluation of infertility', in Newill R, *Infertility in Marriage*, 1974, Harmondsworth: Penguin, p 13; Departmental Committee on Human Artificial Insemination, *Report of the Departmental Committee on Human Artificial Insemination*, Cmnd 1105, 1960, London: HMSO, para 239 (Feversham Report).

3   This difficulty was addressed by the Warnock Report in the UK in recognising the difficulty of providing reliable statistics on infertility: Committee of Inquiry into Human Fertilisation and Embryology, *Report of the Committee of Inquiry into Human Fertilisation and Embryology*, Cmnd 9314, 1984, London: HMSO.

multi-million pound industry worldwide[4] with couples in almost every country in the world seeking and receiving treatment to enable them to have a child of their own.[5]

The effects of infertility may be described as an emotional trauma for many who do not wish to remain childless.[6]They may suffer a range of emotions from anger, isolation, grief and desperation to loss of self-esteem and sexual identity. The social context in which infertility takes place is also important in that infertile couples often feel isolated from friends and family who have expectations of them reproducing a new family member/ grandchild.

The treatments for infertility commonly range from artificial insemination to *in vitro* fertilisation, gamete (egg or sperm) donation and surrogate motherhood. With the decrease in the number of children available for adoption, and the strong wish on the part of many couples to have a biological link to their child, reproductive technology has become the light at the end of the tunnel for many couples who want to have a family. However, the ethical and religious objections to these treatments make them controversial and often inaccessible to couples in many countries, and the high emotional, physical and financial costs involved may also be prohibitive for many. It therefore becomes relevant to question whether childless couples have a *right* to reproduce such that they may be enabled to force their government to provide the means by which they might conceive a child, or at least to enable them to prevent interference by the State in decision making in procreational matters.

IS THERE A LEGAL OR CONSTITUTIONAL RIGHT TO REPRODUCE?

Is there a right to reproduce and, if so, is there a correlative duty on the State to enable individuals to reproduce by the provision of treatment to those who may be unable to reproduce without medical assistance? Is such a right negative or positive? What is the practical effect of such a distinction? These are questions which remain unanswered as yet, for they have not been squarely dealt with by judicial decision, legislation or international

---

4   Rinehart, LA, 'Infertility: the market, the law and the impact' (1994) 35 Jurimetrics J pp 77–106.

5   Holmes, S and Tymstra,T, '*In vitro* fertilisation in the Netherlands: experience and opinions of Dutch women' (1987) 4 J In Vitro Fertilisation and Embryo Transfer 116, p 120.

6   For further description of the effects of infertility, see Lauritzen, P, *What Price Parenthood?*, March/April 1990, Hastings Center Report, p 38; Leiblum, SR *et al*, 'Unsuccessful *in vitro* fertilisation: a follow-up study' (1987) 4 J In Vitro Fertilisation and Embryo Transfer 46.

convention. Nonetheless, they will surely become topical issues in the 21st century, as the advances in medical technology, which have enabled thousands of children to be born thus far, continue to be perfected.

First, is there a 'right' to reproduce? John A Robertson argues convincingly in favour of procreative liberty, that is, the freedom to decide whether or not to have children and to control the use of one's reproductive capacity.[7] He notes that while this value is widely acknowledged when reproduction occurs naturally, 'it should be equally honoured' when reproduction requires technological assistance'.[8] The argument is that if there is a moral right to reproduce for the coitally fertile, then the same right should apply to the coitally infertile as they have the same needs, desires and biological urges. This is a logical proposition as it is premised upon basic principles of anti-discrimination that are presumed to guide our law makers and policy drafters. It points out the simple truth that whether one is born with reproductive potential or not, or whether one loses the potential in the course of one's life, the same principles should apply to its fulfilment.[9]

Robertson is of the opinion that procreative liberty should be given presumptive priority in all conflicts due to its central importance to individual meaning, dignity and identity, and that there should be a burden on opponents of any particular technique to show that harmful effects from its use justify limiting procreative choice. He seems to place reproduction in the same category as liberty and freedom of expression which, though of fundamental importance to each individual in society, are not guaranteed absolute protection.

However, he also admits that procreative liberty is a *negative* right, which means that other persons have a duty not to interfere with the exercise of a procreative choice, albeit that this does not extend to the imposition of a duty on others to provide the resources necessary to exercise that choice, 'despite plausible moral arguments for governmental assistance'.[10] This, he admits, is more a question of social justice than law. It is also a question relating to the proper allocation of resources in any given society. Many would feel that the world is over-populated already and money should not be spent on bringing

---

7   Robertson, JA, *Children of Choice, Freedom and the New Reproductive Technologies*, 1996, Princeton, NJ: Princeton UP, p 16.

8   *Ibid*, p 4.

9   There are, however, those who would argue that such a principle, if it were to become enshrined as a matter of constitutional law, would be too broad and would not necessarily be in the interests of the child. See, eg, Bartholet, E, *Family Bonds: Adoption and the Politics of Parenting*, 1993, Boston: Houghton Mifflin, p 229:

> If we really care about children, we should question why there is so much talk of the adult's right to procreate, right to control his or her body and right to parent, but so little talk of the child's right to anything.

On this point, see, also, MacLean, MA, 'Regulating choice: a constitutional law response to Professor John A Robertson's children of choice' (1995) 52 Wash and Lee L Rev 133.

10   *Op cit*, Robertson, fn 7, p 23.

more children into existence when their education and employment prospects may be low. Others may feel that the ethical implications of these techniques for society sufficiently outweigh any one individual's need to have a child as compared to the funding of treatment for cancer sufferers, for example. Such issues concern societal priorities and offer no easy answers. Nonetheless, the allocation of resources in health care should not be simply reduced to a balancing exercise whereby the needs of those suffering from infertility and those suffering from other ailments compete against one another. It must be remembered that these techniques are, it is hoped, going to result in the creation of new members of society, whose interests must also be taken into account in the equation.

Robertson admits that the use of a rights based approach to reproduction may be open to criticism from feminists among others, who may see the use of reproductive technology as another way of enforcing male dominance over women by emphasising the traditional roles of women as child bearers and rearers. However, he is of the view that technology offers so many new options to women who would otherwise have remained childless, that, in fact, technology advances the interests of women.[11] Even if, through the availability of technology, some women are pressurised into embarking on treatments for infertility, this does not necessarily mean that women thereby end up with less reproductive freedom. It is more a question of social policy to ensure that coercion does not take place and to support women's procreative autonomy. This is an argument which has divided the feminist movement for some years, particularly in relation to gestational surrogacy which may be viewed as exploitative or liberating of women, depending on the importance placed on both the woman's ability and right to choose her own path.

The principle of procreative liberty does not take account of differences in class and wealth which, for some, may make the exercise of procreative choices impossible. This is evident in many countries, including the Republic of Ireland where the lack of funding or assistance by the State makes the availability of *in vitro* fertilisation limited to those who can afford it. Robertson's view of reproduction as a negative right which does not impose any duty on the State to provide financial assistance for these treatments, means that no positive assistance is given to someone who lacks the resources essential to exercise the right. He admits that the distribution of wealth acts as a prime determinant as to who exercises reproductive rights, particularly in relation to access to reproductive technology. Nonetheless, he does add that 'it does not follow that society's failure to assure access to reproductive

---

11 Robertson's principle of procreative liberty has been criticised as rendering invisible the experiences of women, particularly those in minority groups, despite its seeming empowerment of women generally. See, further, 'The invisible woman', anon book review of Robertson's 'Children of choice' (1996) 108 Harv L Rev 953.

technologies for all who would benefit justifies denying access to those who have the means to pay'.[12]

At the end of the day, questions of social justice are not compelling reasons for limiting the procreative choice of those who can pay for treatment. Issues relating to unequal distribution of wealth and State allocation of resources cannot determine whether the treatments are made available as curtailing the availability of these opportunities would effectively discriminate against those who can afford the treatment. Although some might perhaps argue in favour of a systematic prohibition of services that only a small percentage of the population can afford, this does not accord with the concept of a modern democratic society in which financial and lifestyle incentives exist to encourage productivity and enthusiasm for one's work. These issues are rightly regarded as social justice issues which should not impinge on the availability of health care treatments and technologies *per se*.

The use of the language of rights in this context emanates from the history of the debate on reproductive freedom which began in the late 19th century. At that time, the feminist movement viewed the twin demands of voluntary motherhood and the right to birth control as validating the procreational right of women to choose whether and when to reproduce. This was more of a right *not* to reproduce or to control reproduction, rather than a right to reproduce in itself, but it did prove to be a starting point in the debate on procreational autonomy.

Concern was expressed about the ability of another party such as the State to intervene in an individual's right to bodily integrity and self-determination. This was also evidenced by the condemnation of the eugenics movement, voiced in the US in 1927 in the case of *Buck v Bell*,[13] in which a statute providing for compulsory sterilisation of inmates in a mental hospital was upheld. Eugenics was seen as a means of protecting society from the burden of having to cope with individuals who were considered to be unfit. It was argued that compulsory reproductive control was essential if societies were not to be swamped by the unfit, the disabled, the poor and the shiftless. This argument found favour in America by drawing on the fears at that time that America would become black and that certain immigrant races were inferior. These theories which were incorporated into legislation in most American States were '... surely the clearest example of the non-recognition at that time of a universal right to reproduce'.[14]

Reproduction was seen as a duty for those deemed to be biologically superior, and a capacity which could be controlled by State interference for those who did not fall within that elite group. The *dicta* of Justice Holmes in

---

12 *Op cit*, Robertson, fn 7, p 226.

13 274 US 200 (1927).

14 McLean, S, 'The right to reproduce', in Campbell, T (ed), *Human Rights: From Rhetoric to Reality*, 1986, Oxford: Blackwell, p 105.

Buck v Bell demonstrates the thinking at that time, when he said that 'The right to reproduce was not perceived to be a right and it was more of a privilege'.[15]

Although such a policy seems anathema to our tradition of human and constitutional rights, our anti-discrimination policies and our morality, the statement nonetheless reflected the concerns and fears of American society during that era. If nothing else, it demonstrates how issues concerning public morality and policy statements are clear indicators of the era in which they are made, and should not automatically be presumed to be applicable to every other time and place in the future.

Other cases in the US have gone on to broaden the concept of reproductive freedom, but these have been largely in the context of sterilisation, contraception and abortion. Such cases deal with a person's right or freedom to choose not to procreate or the right to resist interference with the exercise of reproductive potential rather than a positive right to be facilitated in the fulfilment of that potential. One such example is provided by *Skinner v Oklahoma*,[16] where the United States Supreme Court held unconstitutional a statute which provided for the involuntary sterilisation of certain classes of offenders. The court stressed the importance of marriage and procreation as among 'the basic civil rights of man' and noted that 'marriage and procreation are fundamental to the very existence and survival of the race'. However, the right to reproduce was not seen so much as a positive right deserving of protection, but rather a means of resisting unwarranted State interference in decisions involving procreational choices. It is doubtful, therefore, that this case could be used to found a case against the State, to compel the provision of infertility treatments, given that it concerned State interference with a civil right to reproduce naturally, and not the application by a citizen to enforce his/her procreational choices against the State through insistence upon provision of artificial methods of reproduction.

The substantive content of the right to reproduce was not clarified by the court in terms of determining who can invoke the right or, whether it applied to social as well as biological parenting – does the right apply to those who intend to bring up the child after a surrogate birth, for example? These issues were not directly relevant to the facts of the aforementioned cases as the concepts of surrogate motherhood and egg donation had not been brought to judicial attention at that stage. The issue may turn on whether the right to reproduce is simply a biological right, or whether it also encompasses the right to rear a child. In most instances, the right to reproduce would include both aspects of parenting but this will not always be the case. It may be, for example, that a woman has the right to conceive and give birth to a child without ever having the intention to raise it, as is the case in surrogacy.

---

15   274 US 200 (1927), p 207.
16   316 US 535 (1942).

In re Baby M[17] is an example of a case in which the two aspects discussed above were seen as separate issues. This infamous American case involved a surrogacy arrangement in which a couple, the Sterns, commissioned a surrogate, Mary Beth Whitehead, to be artificially inseminated with Mr Stern's sperm and carry the child to term. Upon delivery, it was to be given to the Sterns. When the child was born, Mary Beth Whitehead changed her mind and attempted to retain custody of the child. In examining the right to procreation, the New Jersey Supreme Court said:

> The right to procreate very simply is the right to have natural children, whether through sexual intercourse or artificial insemination. It is no more than that ... The custody, care, companionship, and nurturing that follow birth are not parts of the right to procreation.[18]

Thus, in this case, the court held that the biological and social aspects of parenting are divisible, and that the right to procreate only encompasses the former out of necessity. In the event, Mrs Stern's situation was given some recognition in law and she acquired visitation but not custodial rights. The biological contributors to Baby M's life, Mr Stern and Mrs Whitehead, were both recognised as the child's parents but, due to the circumstances and the conflict involved in the custody dispute, only Mr Stern was given the right to social parenthood, that is, the right to rear the child.

The right to reproduce, as such, has not been significantly judicially developed on its own account. Therefore, it is necessary to consider whether and to what extent protection may be given under other constitutional provisions. The right to privacy has been seen as a means of including procreation in the realms of constitutional protection. However, this extension has most commonly been seen in relation to the availability of contraceptives, which again reflects the distinction between the enforcement of a negative right and a positive right. In relation to contraception, the right in question would probably be seen as a negative right to privacy, in that it legitimately resists State interference with reproductive choices. However, it does not easily extend to the enforcement of a positive right to insist upon the State making provision for assisted reproduction unless, perhaps, it could preclude State interference in a surrogacy arrangement entered into between a married couple and a freely consenting surrogate.

The case law in the US and elsewhere generally indicates that for a married couple, and probably an unmarried individual too, a constitutional right to resist State interference with coital reproduction may be inferred, unless the State can show that great harm would result from the reproduction in question. The law has not yet dealt with the legal claim of a married infertile couple to procreate although, as has been stated earlier in connection with the presumption in favour of procreative liberty, the same underlying principles should apply. If this is so, they would have a constitutional right to access to a wide variety of non-coital reproductive technologies. This right, by analogy with the right to procreate given to fertile couples, should only be interfered with if justified by the State on the same standard as that applicable to fertile couples. However, the only cases that directly consider the extension of married couples' procreational rights into the realm of non-coital reproduction, involve surrogacy contracts, for example, *Doe v Kelley*,[19] where this extension seems to have been rejected without much analysis.

The English position as regards the right to privacy is not even as favourable as the position in the US where the right to privacy is a recognised right, albeit that it is not absolute. In relation to the right to procreate, however, it may be that the UK is more forthright in its avowed support for freedom of choice in reproductive matters. Again, this has not been developed judicially except insofar as it relates to abortion, contraception and sterilisation. It would seem to be the case that a woman, married or unmarried, can choose whether to have children and consequently may take whatever action she thinks appropriate to further implement her choice. The autonomy of the individual and her right to self-determination is regarded as being of fundamental importance and worthy of protection, subject to what is stated below in relation to those with a mental handicap who may be sterilised in their own best interests.

Athena Liu[20] points out that the decisions in relation to sterilisation do not really have any bearing on the establishment of a general right to reproduce. The ability of the court to override the freedom to reproduce in the case of a mentally handicapped girl, does not mean that the right to reproduce *per se* cannot be used to found a claim in other circumstances. In relation to most fundamental rights, there is a provision whereby the court can intervene, whether through protection of the individual concerned, as in this instance, or through protection of the common good, such as the deprivation of liberty of someone who has committed a criminal offence. Such provisions do not, therefore, have any relevance for the consideration of the extent and applicability of the wider rights concerned. None of these cases relates directly to the right of the infertile to procreate, rather they relate to the right of the fertile to choose whether and when to exercise their freedom to have a child. This reinforces the distinction discussed earlier in the chapter between negative and positive rights.

19   106 Mich App 169; 307 NW 2d (1981).
20   Liu, A, *Artificial Reproduction and Reproductive Rights*, 1991, Aldershot: Dartmouth, pp 37–39.

AN INTERNATIONAL RIGHT TO REPRODUCE?

Is there a recognisable right to reproduce in international human rights instruments which may be relied on to insist on the provision of assisted reproductive technologies by a State? Some of the human rights instruments and bodies have drawn very wide principles which may be relevant here. For example, Art 16(3) of the Universal Declaration on Human Rights of 1948 provided that the family was 'the natural and fundamental group unit of society' and was therefore entitled to State protection. Article 12 of the European Convention on Human Rights provides that men and women have 'the right to marry and to found a family' according to the national laws governing the exercise of that right.

In 1996, the Secretary General of the United Nations Commission on Human Rights recommended that governments develop reproductive health in a climate of respect for human dignity and protection of fundamental human rights. That report also recognised that governments have a special responsibility to realise that reproductive health is so central to personal wellbeing and human dignity as to be an important social good. Governments should make the necessary investments in health care to ensure that reproductive health is not treated as a commodity. 'Leaving the provision of reproductive health services to market forces will mean that not everyone may have access to reproductive health.'[21]

While the ideas behind these provisions and recommendations are laudable, the scope of the provisions themselves is uncertain. For instance, does the reference in the ECHR to the right being subject to national laws mean that the State could legitimately deprive its citizens of the rights contained in Art 12 without thereby infringing the Convention? It is thought that the limitations meant by the expression used in the Convention must relate to legitimate purposes, such as to prevent incest or bigamy, and do not sanction a complete and arbitrary deprivation of rights by national laws. If this were not the case, the Convention would be meaningless as it would entitle national governments to ignore its provisions without legitimate justification.[22]

Another difficulty perceived in the wording of the ECHR provision is that it appears to link the right to found a family with marriage, which implies that unmarried people may not avail themselves of the right. In the *Van Oosterwijck* case,[23] the complainant argued that the Belgian authorities were

---

21 Report of the Secretary General of the Commission on Human Rights, Human Rights and Scientific and Technological Developments, E/CN 4/1997/66.

22 *Op cit*, Liu, fn 20, pp 27–31; Harris, DJ, O'Boyle, M and Warbrick, C, *Law of the European Convention on Human Rights*, 1995, London: Butterworths, p 435.

23 Report of 1 March 1979, B 36 Com Rep (1983), pp 28–29.

violating his right to marry and found a family, by not permitting him to change his birth certificate to reflect the fact that he had undergone a sex change operation. The Commission agreed with this contention, but the Court did not consider the point, holding that there had been a failure to exhaust domestic remedies.

The Commission said that the right to found a family was attached indissolubly to the right to marry in Art 12. The Commission gave the view that a marriage could be valid despite the absence of an intention or capacity to procreate, as the latter is not a prerequisite for marriage, but it did not mention the other side of the argument, namely, whether marriage was a prerequisite for procreation.

Although marriage and the family are in fact associated in the Convention and in domestic legal systems, there is nothing to support the conclusion that the capacity to procreate is an essential condition of marriage, or even that procreation is an essential purpose of marriage.[24]

This inextricable link between the two rights contained in Art 12 was also reverted to in another case concerning the right to adopt,[25] where the Commission said that:

> ... the provision [Art 12] does not guarantee the right to have children born out of wedlock. Article 12, in fact, foresees the right to marry and to found a family as one simple right.

It further said that even if it may be assumed that the right to found a family may be considered irrespective of marriage, Art 12 recognises that the existence of a couple is fundamental to the exercise of this right. Therefore, as is also pointed out by Liu,[26] it is doubtful whether a single individual right to reproduce can be found under Art 12 of the Convention. She says that, even within the marital relationship, there is no right to adopt or found a family by alternative means. The possibility of artificial reproductive techniques being used to create a family was certainly not in the minds of those who drafted the Convention. Accordingly, while State interference in relation to the family unit must clearly be justified, this appears only to relate to an existing family unit, and would not be of benefit to an individual or married couple who are seeking State provision of infertility treatment in order to create such a family unit.

Harris, O'Boyle and Warbrick are of a similar opinion in relation to whether a State could be forced to provide a couple, married or unmarried, with the means by which they might have a family.[27] They say that a State may be implicated under the Convention by either an action in relation to the

---

24   Report of 1 March 1979, B 36 Com Rep (1983), p 28.
25   Dec Adm Com Appl 6482/74, 10 July 1975; (1977) 7 D & R 55.
26   *Op cit*, Liu, fn 20, p 30.
27   *Op cit*, Harris, O'Boyle and Warbrick, fn 22, p 441.

availability generally of reproductive technologies, or an action to explain why the techniques are not made available to married couples. They are of the view that:

> It does not seem likely that the Convention imposes any limits on what choices a State may make and it is probably premature to decide that the Convention imposes a positive obligation on a State to legislate to allow any particular technique. However, as the acceptability of those measures which are closest to natural reproduction (for example, IVF) increases, States may find themselves having an increasingly heavy burden to explain why married persons may not avail themselves of them. It is much less likely that a positive duty will be placed on the State to provide the appropriate treatment.[28]

Although, on a global level, the United Nations recognises the importance of reproductive health in which respect for human dignity is paramount, and women are not treated as a means of reaching a reproductive goal, and on a regional basis, the ECHR provides for the right to marry and found a family, it is improbable that these instruments could be used in an individual case to establish a legal right to reproduce. Although political and social pressure may be brought to bear on governments, both nationally and internationally, to introduce and legislate for reproductive technologies in order to promote the reproductive health of their citizens, it is doubtful that a *positive* right to reproduce may be gleaned from international instruments for the protection of human rights.

ACHIEVING CONSENSUS FOR THE FUTURE

Many difficulties arise in attempting to conclude trying to find whether there is any consensus between European States on issues relating to reproductive technology. One of the most controversial questions here, which may be used to illustrate the level of difficulty involved, is to attempt to define what the legal and moral status of the embryo is for purposes of storage, disposal and experimentation. Some States, such as the UK and Denmark, have regulated *in vitro* fertilisation, embryo creation, storage of embryos and embryo research. Others, such as Italy and Ireland, have no legislative provisions in place to deal with these issues, and prefer to rely for the time being on ethical principles promulgated by medical professional bodies. The question thus arises as to whether it will ever be possible to achieve consensus on these emotive issues, approaches to which may differ regionally as well as globally, according to cultural diversity.

It appears that, in the context of legislating for reproductive technologies, 'there is a broad choice between aiming, on the one hand, at a uniform

---

28 *Op cit*, Harris, O'Boyle and Warbrick, fn 22, p 441.

minimum threshold of law and regulation – thus emphasising individual freedom of choice – and on the other hand, at a uniform maximum coverage of law and regulation, thus emphasising societal protection of embryonic life and future generations'.[29] In the European context, the differences between States on bioethical issues is reflected in the fact that in drafting the recent European Convention for the Protection of Human Rights and the Dignity of the Human Being with regard to the Application of Biology and Medicine (April 1997),[30] the first declaration in this field worldwide, there is no consensus as to the status of the embryo in principle. There is a provision dealing with embryo research (Art 18) but this merely states that if such research is permissible under national law, the embryo must have adequate protection. Some States, such as the Republic of Ireland, are not signatories to this convention due to perceived national constitutional difficulties relating to the protection of the unborn. In consequence, they are also unable to ratify the recent protocol to the convention, Prohibition of Cloning Human Beings (January 1998).[31] This ironically may leave the way open, in theory at least, for cloning to take place in Ireland due to the absence of any legislative provisions or international conventions dictating a prohibition on the use of such techniques. Although ethical guidelines of the Medical Council in Ireland would prohibit such a procedure, these principles do not have any binding effect in law.

Nielsen, in her analysis of the European regulation of this area, categorises the different approaches as ranging from prohibition, through to cautious regulation, liberal regulation, and even *laissez faire* approaches.[32] This diversity of viewpoints is illustrative of the difference in tradition, culture, legal systems and professional regulation between the States. Those which have not yet dealt with the issues thrown up by reproductive technologies, and which rely on professional ethical guidelines include those States such as Italy and Ireland which have traditionally been regarded as having a strong religious influence in their political and legal systems. Ironically, the absence of legal regulation in these jurisdictions may make it easier to practice these techniques in circumstances which may be ethically questionable.

There *are*, however, a number of common features which may be averted to briefly here, such as the apparent discomfort generally expressed, in relation to any payment for the donation of gametes and embryos, the

---

29   Nielsen, L, 'Legal consensus and divergence in Europe in the area of human embryology – room for harmonisation?', in *Conceiving the Embryo: Ethics, Law and Practice in Human Embryology*, 1996, The Hague: Martinus Nijhoff, pp 325–38.

30   Convention for the Protection of Human Rights and Dignity of the Human Being with regard to the Application of Biology and Medicine (4 April 1997), ETS Protocol 164.

31   Convention on Prohibition of Cloning Human Beings (12 January 1998), ETS Protocol 168.

32   *Op cit*, Nielsen, fn 29, p 334.

generally universal prohibition of surrogate motherhood, (apart from in the UK, which prohibits only commercial surrogacy), the acceptance of *in vitro* fertilisation as an accepted technique for the alleviation of infertility and the practice of storage of surplus embryos (for between one and five years), the supervision of research on human embryos (up to seven or 14 days after fertilisation) by ethics committees often on a voluntary non-statutory basis, and the condemnation of projects involving cloning, parthenogenesis, gestation *in vitro*, and the creation of hybrids.

It is evident from the diversity of approaches taken to fertility and treatments offered for infertility that national influences tend to play an important role in determining both the way in which the issue is dealt with by the State, and, also, the resolution of the problems encountered. However, it can be argued that basic human values are generally agreed between the Member States, such as respect for human life and dignity, autonomy, prohibition of eugenics. Does this provide a solid basis for drafting a European convention on bioethics? Nielsen argues that, due to the difficulties involved in taking local cultural factors into account, 'it is probably not feasible to produce a detailed set of guidelines to which all nations within Europe could subscribe'.[33] Perhaps the assortment of controls and ethical principles evident in this context is, in itself, a characterisation of a community of States, but the danger of such contrasts is that it could lead to what may be described as bioethical tourism. Certainly for citizens of more restrictive regimes the benefits to be obtained by visiting another jurisdiction for treatment services must be sometimes too tempting to resist, although the disadvantages of financial costs, absence of familial support and distance from familiar surroundings must make the whole process more traumatic than it already is.

The advantages of seeking consensus in Europe as to broad issues, such as the prohibition of the commercialisation of reproduction, the prohibition of cloning, the setting of limits as to storage periods, and other general principles would be to provide protections for couples who are desperate enough to seize any chance offered to them, to safeguard the dignity of the unborn children who have no voice in this debate, and to set boundaries to the development of embryo research on an international level. The changes in human reproduction seen in the 20th century provide a basis for future development of fundamental rights in society as the issues raised by reproductive technology necessitate an examination and reappraisal of the social criteria for parenthood, the meaning of legal parentage, the rights of children, and the dignity to be accorded to the human person in the earliest stages of its development.

---

33   See *op cit*, Nielsen, fn 29.

THEME FOUR

NGOs: AN EVOLVING ROLE

CHAPTER 13

AMNESTY INTERNATIONAL: AN EVOLVING MANDATE IN A CHANGING WORLD

Peter Pack

INTRODUCTION

In November 1960, the British lawyer Peter Benenson read a newspaper report about two Portuguese students who had been arrested and sentenced to seven years' imprisonment for raising their glasses in a public toast to freedom in a Lisbon restaurant. Benenson wondered how pressure could be brought on the Portuguese authorities to release these victims of oppression, and how public attention could be drawn to the fate of political and religious prisoners throughout the world. His friend, David Astor, then editor of *The Observer* newspaper, agreed to help and, on 28 May 1961, Trinity Sunday, the paper carried a full page, 'Appeal for amnesty', seeking freedom for prisoners of conscience throughout the world.

The response to the newspaper article (and a simultaneous translation in *Le Monde* in France) was immediate and widespread, and the article was summarised in numerous other newspapers across the world. What was intended as a one year campaign quickly became an international movement. By July 1961, local Amnesty groups – each 'adopting' and working for the release of Prisoners of Conscience in the East, the West, and the non-aligned countries – were established in six countries, and the first international meeting of Amnesty delegates took place in a Luxembourg cafe. On 10 December 1961, the candle in the barbed wire, the now well known logo, was unveiled, and, later that month, the first national section outside the UK was established in West Germany.

Soon, the organisation was known as Amnesty International, and a small group of volunteers and staff were recruited to scan newspapers, monitor radio and TV broadcasts, and establish a rudimentary library and research facility in London. With the support of newspaper funding, research missions to Czechoslovakia, East Germany, Ghana and Portugal were undertaken in the first year. Within another two years, an International Secretariat had been created, more than 350 local groups had been formed around the world, and the organisation was active on behalf of around 1,300 Prisoners of Conscience.[1]

---

1   A good account of Amnesty International's early years can be found in Power, J, *Amnesty International: The Human Rights Story*, 1981, London: Pergamon.

From these modest beginnings, Amnesty International has grown into the global human rights organisation it is today. It now has around one million members and subscribers in over 160 countries and territories. There are over 4,200 local Amnesty International groups worldwide, and several thousand more school, university, professional and youth groups in more than 80 countries. In more than 50 countries, there is sufficient Amnesty International presence for a national section to be established to co-ordinate the work of Amnesty International groups, networks and members.

In a typical year, Amnesty International members will now work on 4,000–5,000 individual cases of victims of human rights violations, as well as numerous other actions, some dealing with thematic concerns (torture, women's rights, the rights of refugees), others with a range of violations within a particular country. As the movement has grown, so has the need for accurate research and information about human rights violations. The International Secretariat of Amnesty International in London – which is responsible for research and the overall running of the organisation – now employs over 300 full time staff and has an annual budget of about £18 million.[2]

AN EXPANDING MANDATE

As the movement has grown, so has its mandate (that is, the brief it takes upon itself and the rules stating which human rights violations it will concern itself with). When it started, AI had a very precise, prisoner orientated focus and dealt almost exclusively with the political abuse of power by governments. Its aim was to work impartially for the release of those imprisoned for their opinions, to seek fair trials for them, to enlarge the right to asylum, to help political refugees to find work, and to urge the creation of effective international machinery to guarantee freedom of opinion. In the early years, the vast majority of Amnesty International's efforts went into realising the first two aims. Initial successes, such as the release of 152 detainees by Kwame Nkrumah following an Amnesty International mission in 1962, and subsequent releases of Prisoners of Conscience in Burma, Egypt, Eire, Greece and Romania in 1964, ensured that the organisation became strongly identified in the public mind with Prisoners of Conscience.

Today, the mandate of Amnesty International is considerably wider than it was in the 1960s. It has moved from being a prisoner orientated organisation to one dealing with a wide range of violations of physical integrity. It is as concerned with long term preventative measures as with offering immediate

---

2   The last page of the annual Amnesty International report always contains summary statistics for the past year. A useful overview of some historical trends can be found in Amnesty International, *Report on the State of the AI Movement*, November 1997 (AI Index: ORG 53/05/97), London: AIUK.

assistance to the victims of human rights violations. The Statute of Amnesty International now states that the organisation aims to promote all of the rights set out in the United Nations Universal Declaration of Human Rights (as approved by the General Assembly in 1948). It states that, in particular, Amnesty opposes grave violations of these rights by working for the release of Prisoners of Conscience. It also seeks fair and prompt trials for all political prisoners; the abolition of torture, other forms of cruel treatment, and the death penalty; and an end to 'disappearances' and extra-judicial executions.

The highest policy making forum within Amnesty International is the International Council Meeting (ICM). This forum has successively amplified the mandate by stating that Amnesty International opposes a range of violations, including solitary confinement in prisons, forcible exile of political activists, indiscriminate and arbitrary killings in wartime, house destruction as a political punishment, adverse discrimination in legal systems, female genital mutilation, and hostage taking by armed opposition groups.[3]

This expansion of Amnesty International's mandate has occurred in several distinct (although partly overlapping) stages. Over the first 15 years of its existence, Amnesty International gradually moved from an almost exclusive concern for Prisoners of Conscience (defined as political prisoners who have neither used nor advocated violence), to including concerns for political prisoners, and then concerns for all prisoners within its mandate. During the mid 1960s, it started to collect information and report on the conditions in which political prisoners were detained; it then started to press for minimum international standards for their treatment, and to oppose their execution. Eventually, in 1974, it started to demand fair and prompt trials for all political prisoners.

Early on, Amnesty International also started to expand its mandate to cover the torture and ill treatment of all prisoners. In 1966, it decided to oppose the torture of all prisoners, and as early as 1968 stated its support for the total abolition of capital punishment. These decisions led to the steady development of Amnesty's work in these two areas, to the extent that, by the late 1970s, it was probably as well known for its opposition to torture and the death penalty as for its work on behalf of Prisoners of Conscience.

In parallel with these developments, Amnesty International gradually expanded its usage of the term Prisoner of Conscience, first recognising some conscientious objectors as Prisoners of Conscience; then including those imprisoned for advocating equality for homosexuals (1979);[4] and – after much debate – including those imprisoned for homosexuality (1991).[5] Over the

---

3   See, respectively, Decision 14 of the 1970 ICM; Decision 16 of the 1991 ICM; Decision 12 of the 1995 ICM and Decision 9 of the 1997 ICM; Decision 23 of the 1991 ICM; Decision 8 of the 1995 ICM; Decision 6 of the 1995 ICM and Decision 6 of the 1997 ICM; Decision 5 of the 1991 ICM.

4   Decision 7 of the 1979 ICM.

5   Decision 13 of the 1991 ICM.

years, there have also been decisions relating to when civil disobedience, or those disclosing State secrets, among others, can be classified as Prisoners of Conscience.[6]

Apart from widening its concerns relating to prisoners, Amnesty International has gradually included within its mandate many practices closely related to imprisonment. For example, during the 1970s, it started to oppose the political abuse of psychiatry (predominantly in the USSR), to oppose banning orders (predominantly in South Africa), to oppose internal (and later external) exile of political activists and to oppose forms of harassment, such as the requirement for political activists to report unreasonably frequently to police stations.[7]

Another related development has been the expansion of AI's work against forms of harassment that, although not analogous to imprisonment, are clearly motivated by the same grounds and have effects of equivalent severity. For example, in 1991, Amnesty International decided to oppose the destruction or sealing of houses when carried out by governments to punish their political opponents.[8]

A separate area of mandate growth relates to AI's opposition to killings by governments and others. Amnesty International has moved from opposing the death penalty in political cases, to opposing the death penalty in all cases, to opposing extra-judicial executions and, most recently, opposing killings in armed conflicts caused by either disproportionate or indiscriminate attacks. Amnesty International has also, since the early 1980s, opposed 'disappearances,' that is, detention without acknowledgement, often leading to torture and death.[9]

Until 1991, Amnesty International focused exclusively on human rights violations carried out by governments or by others acting on their behalf (most notably, the 'death squads' prevalent in Central and Latin America in the 1970s and 1980s). In 1991, however, Amnesty International decided to widen its concerns to cover equivalent violations by Non-Governmental Entities (more simply described as armed opposition groups). Another expansion occurred in 1997, when Amnesty International decided that it would hold governments responsible for their failure to act with due diligence against some human rights violations carried out by non-State actors.[10]

6   Decision 9 of the 1991 ICM.
7   This policy developed largely without explicit ICM Decisions. See, however, referred Resolution 3 of the 1979 ICM for an early reference to concerns about harassment falling short of imprisonment.
8   Decision 23 of the 1991 ICM.
9   This work started before it was mentioned in the Amnesty International statute. *Disappearances: A Workbook*, 1981, New York: AIUS, was the first practical workbook for those opposing the practice, but the first statute reference to 'disappearances' did not appear until 1987 (Decision 8 of the 1987 ICM), and 'disappearances' were not mentioned in the mandate until 1991 (Decision 1 of the 1991 ICM).
10   Decision 5 of the 1997 ICM.

Although the scope of this decision has yet to be worked out, it is clear that AI has taken a significant step in taking violations by private citizens (which could include actions such as trafficking in children, or enforced prostitution) into its mandate.

Finally, Amnesty International has, over the years, expanded its mandate by moving from work directed to assisting individual victims of human rights violations to more general preventative work. In this connection, significant developments have been the 1979 decision to oppose military, security and police transfers that could contribute to human rights violations (and the steady expansion of this work in recent years); the 1991 decision to make promotional and human rights educational work an obligatory part of all Amnesty International sections' workplans; and the work, during much of the 1990s, to campaign against impunity, opposing 'amnesty' laws under successor governments, pressing for international action against human rights violators, and putting a great deal of effort into lobbying for the creation of a permanent international criminal court.[11] Most recently, Amnesty International has started to lobby international economic organisations, such as the IMF and World Bank, to ensure that their activities do not contribute to human rights violations.[12]

It is worth noting how difficult it is to construct a precise chronology of Amnesty International's mandate development because, until very recently, AI's practice has expanded ahead of its rulebook. For example, although Amnesty International started to work against 'disappearances' in the mid-1970s, the first ICM decision referring to the phenomenon was not made until 1979. Opposition to 'disappearances' was then added to the Amnesty International statute as a working method in 1987, and only in 1991 was opposition to 'disappearances' written into the statute as an explicit part of Amnesty International's mandate.

MANAGING THE PROCESS OF CHANGE

The policy of Amnesty International is made by its biennial International Council Meeting (ICM), at which representatives from all parts of the movement vote on resolutions. Changes to the mandate are made by ICMs in two ways – they either vote to change the statute of Amnesty International (as occurred most significantly in 1972 and 1991), or they vote to expand Amnesty International's concerns by passing a resolution on a specific issue (for

---

11 A good summary of much of this work in contained in Amnesty International, *Amnesty International Annual Report*, 1996, London: AIUK, pp 35–64.

12 See, eg, the statement by Amnesty International on the occasion of the World Bank/IMF annual meetings, Hong Kong, September 1997 (AI Index: IOR 30/04/97).

example, the 1993 decision to oppose the detention of Prisoners of Conscience by armed opposition groups). Traditionally, respect for the wide social and cultural diversity of the organisation has resulted in mandate changes almost always proceeding by consensus.

Although a Borderline Committee was established in the late 1960s to decide whether borderline cases fell within the mandate of Amnesty International, there was no Mandate Committee until its creation for a one year fixed term in 1978.[13] Before then, individual issues were discussed on their merits at ICMs, without there being any overall framework for mandate development.

The role of the Mandate Committee was to clarify issues such as Amnesty International's standards for fair trials and, more importantly, to consider the merits of expanding Amnesty International's mandate with regard to human rights violations by opposition groups and violations in areas of armed conflict. The creation of this committee, which reported to the following year's ICM in Leuven, Belgium, marked the start of a systematic management of mandate development. However, there was still a culture of deciding individual issues in isolation (for example, expanding the concept of 'cruel, inhuman or degrading treatment or punishment'; making particular efforts to protect women and children from human rights violations; expanding work on behalf of refugees). Only in 1987 did the organisation create a Mandate Review Committee charged with a comprehensive revision of the mandate.[14]

The Mandate Review Committee report to the 1991 ICM not only led to the changes described below, but also – finally – led to the creation of a permanent, seven person Standing Committee on the Mandate (SCM). The SCM now meets twice each year and is charged with considering possible mandate changes, carrying out relevant studies and circulating proposals to the Amnesty International membership. Today, the SCM is the hub of mandate development within Amnesty International. The 1990s have seen Amnesty International adopt a three step procedure for mandate expansions: first, the ICM requests the SCM to produce a study (for example, on violations by non-State actors); then the study is circulated among the membership and meetings are held to discuss it further; finally, a later ICM decides to what extent the mandate should be altered.

Furthermore, the 1995 ICM drew up a set of criteria against which future proposals for mandate changes should be judged. These criteria are as follows:

- *focus* on defending basic rights against governments and armed opposition groups;
- *credibility* by reference to international standards;

---

13 Decision 7 of the 1978 ICM.
14 Decision 1 of the 1987 ICM.

- *relevance* to the changing nature of human rights abuses;
- *coherence* and consistency of the Mandate;
- *clarity* and ease of understanding of the Mandate;
- *resources* – the Mandate should be consistent with available resources within Amnesty International;
- *activism* – the Mandate should be oriented towards membership activism.

These developments have all led to a much more widespread debate within Amnesty International before new changes to the Mandate are agreed. At the most recent ICM (in Cape Town in December 1997), changes were only made on issues that had been widely discussed at many different levels within Amnesty International – ranging from Section Boards to local groups – for at least two years.

CAUSES OF THE CHANGING MANDATE

Amnesty International has always stated that it draws its mandate from three main sources: international human rights law; humanitarian law (the laws of war); and the collective moral convictions of its membership.[15] However, the very selective nature of its mandate, focusing mainly on violations of physical integrity, and the large number of changes that have taken place over the years inevitably raise the question, why has the mandate developed in the way that it has, rather than in other directions?

The best answer to this question is to look at five factors that have shaped the evolving mandate of Amnesty International. Most of these factors have contributed to most of the changes, but as the commentary below illustrates, some have been clearly dominant on particular issues.

The changing external environment

When Amnesty International started, prisoners of conscience were held by military dictatorships throughout much of Latin America; in the British, French, and Portuguese colonies across Africa; and throughout the Warsaw Pact countries, among others. Today, there are few or no prisoners of conscience in many of these countries, but there has been an increase in other human rights abuses, such as torture, extra-judicial executions, and 'disappearances'. Amnesty International has needed to respond to this changing pattern of violations.

---

15   See, eg, Mandate workshop (AI Index: POL 21/01/96), London: AIUK, p 65.

Secondly, the political map of the world has changed greatly over the last decade or so. The end of the Cold War has led to an upsurge in instability in much of Africa and Asia, leading to armed conflicts within States, a marked decrease in the power and authority of central governments in many countries and in the influence of outside powers on one-time client States. These changes have obliged Amnesty International to take more interest in violations occurring in armed conflicts. A key issue is how best to defend human rights in circumstances where the human rights monitor's traditional target – the strong, central government – is weak or ineffective. More positively, these changes have given Amnesty International opportunities to engage in much more strategic action, such as capacity building (working with other NGOs to build up indigenous human rights movements) rather than simply reacting to events.

The size of the Amnesty International movement

As Amnesty International has grown, its capacity to undertake research and campaigning has also grown. In 1971, Amnesty International had just eight full time and four part time paid researchers.[16] Today, although it still has fewer researchers than there are Member States of the United Nations, it has greatly increased its capacity to report on individual countries and on thematic abuses. Its ability to make detailed recommendations to governments and intergovernmental bodies, and to mount effective media campaigns, have also grown. These developments have enabled Amnesty International to expand into areas of work (such as lobbying for the creation of an international criminal court), which it previously lacked the resources to do. Furthermore, the greater size of the movement has led to much greater specialisation among the membership enabling, for example, groups of members to work on single countries or issues (such as arms transfers) for long periods. This has provided Amnesty International with the expertise to tackle new areas of work.

The influence of other non-governmental organisations

The perceived success of Amnesty International in its core areas of work has sometimes led members and outsiders to press for Amnesty International to

---

16 An historical overview of the growth of Amnesty International's research department can be found in Amnesty International, *Review of Amnesty International's Research*, June 1992 (AI Index: POL 40/01/92), London: AIUK.

take up concerns that are already being dealt with by other, usually smaller and less well known organisations. For example, the 'Free Vanunu' campaign specifically asked its supporters to lobby Amnesty International to seek the release of Mordechai Vanunu during 1994–95.[17] During the 1990s, there has been pressure on Amnesty International to take more action on anti-personnel landmines, and to oppose female genital mutilation, largely as a result of other NGOs drawing these issues to the attention of the wider public as well as Amnesty International's membership. Earlier on, Amnesty International took up the issues of extra-judicial executions and 'disappearances', in part because of the information provided by country solidarity groups in Latin America, and the cumulative effect of this information on Amnesty International members.

The wishes of the membership

Amnesty International's membership has consistently believed that a relatively narrow focus in the organisation's work is essential if it is to attract wide support and use very limited resources effectively. It has also been consistent in upholding the founding principles of impartiality, balance and accuracy. However, within these constraints, there has been continuous pressure to take on new areas of work.

For example, when Terry Waite and others were being held hostage in Lebanon in the early 1990s, many members felt that Amnesty International should be taking action on their behalf. This was one of the main reasons for the 1991 decision to oppose human rights violations by armed opposition groups.[18] On other issues, the wishes of the membership have made themselves felt over a much longer time scale as a minority have sought to persuade an initially reluctant majority to expand the scope of Amnesty International's mandate. Good examples of this are the 1991 decision to regard those imprisoned for being homosexual as prisoners of conscience (which was the culmination of a debate going back two decades), and the 1997 decision to selectively – and only as a last resort – call for the release of political prisoners who have been denied a fair trial but may have used violence.[19]

---

17 The 'Free Vanunu' campaign issued a circular asking supporters, among other actions, to write to the chair of Amnesty International's Standing Committee on the Mandate, asking that Amnesty International adopt Vanunu as a prisoner of conscience.

18 Decision 5 of the 1991 ICM. Whilst hostages were being held in Lebanon, Amnesty International members expressed repeated dissatisfaction at internal meetings that the organisation was doing too little on behalf of the hostages.

19 Decision 15 of the 1997 ICM.

RECONCEPTUALISING AMNESTY INTERNATIONAL'S ROLE

From being a straightforward, reactive, prisoner orientated organisation, Amnesty International has developed into a much more multi-faceted human rights movement. Aside from decisions to expand Amnesty International's mandate in specific areas, there has been, throughout most of the 1990s, a great deal of debate within Amnesty International about the role and nature of the organisation.

There have been debates about how far Amnesty International should be involved in preventative as opposed to ameliorative work, and to what extent it should focus on individual cases as opposed to mass violations.[20] A key debate has been the extent to which it should devote resources to building up human rights constituencies in newly independent countries, and how much it should co-operate with other NGOs – in the past if has often been accused of being rather aloof. Other concerns have included how effective Amnesty International can be in situations of armed conflict, and how far it should develop crisis response and field presence operations. The need to be involved in setting international standards has prompted a debate about the degree to which resources should be devoted to working with intergovernmental organisations and developing new international norms and enforcement mechanisms, and about how Amnesty International can best promote thematic concerns, such as the rights of women, the rights of children and the universality and indivisibility of human rights.[21]

Many of these debates have directly impacted on Amnesty International's mandate. For example, the 1991 decision to identify the promotion of all human rights as a core responsibility of all Amnesty International sections, and one which can best be carried out in co-operation with other NGOs, arose from the strong feeling within the movement that longer term preventative measures should be an increasing feature of Amnesty International's work. Similarly, the 1997 decision to begin holding governments accountable for their negligence in preventing violations by non-State actors (be they individuals or organised groups within society) arose from a long debate within Amnesty International about the extent to which governments should be held responsible for ensuring the rights of their citizens.

---

20 The 1995 Integrated Strategic Plan for Amnesty International was titled 'Responding to massive human rights abuses', reflecting the organisation's move away from a primary focus on individual prisoners.

21 For summaries of the debates mentioned in this paragraph, see Amnesty International, *International Issues 1995–96*, December 1996; and Amnesty International, *International Issues 1997–98*, April 1998, London: AIUK.

AN ASSESSMENT OF THE PRESENT POSITION

Amnesty International is the best known and largest human rights organisation in the world today. Its membership and budget have grown tenfold in the last two decades. It is now establishing a significant presence in many countries outside those areas of the world (principally Western Europe, North America and Australasia) in which it has traditionally been well established, and it is now also developing strong links with many other human rights NGOs. All of this is largely due to the organisation's ability to adapt to changing circumstances and the changing wishes of its membership, whilst continuing to focus most of its work on grave violations of the right to physical integrity that arise from the political abuse of power by governments.

Furthermore, although it always avoids claiming the credit for any reductions in human rights violations, there is a strong body of evidence – not least from former Prisoners of Conscience and other ex-victims of human rights violations – that its work has achieved a great deal. It has contributed to the release of many prisoners; mass interventions by its members have often led to the cessation of torture, to governments acknowledging that their security forces are holding 'disappeared' people, and to detainees being given access to medical and legal assistance.[22] It has also made a substantial contribution to the creation of new international standards (such as the 1984 United Nations Convention against Torture), and the creation of new international enforcement mechanisms (such as the United Nations Tribunals on Rwanda and Yugoslavia).

As well as these external achievements, Amnesty International has also achieved a great deal in terms of its own organisation. It has developed a wider mandate and a great increase in the range of its activities, whilst expanding its international presence and membership, and avoiding any significant divisions within its membership. It has also remained relevant and attractive to supporters and members across a vast range of cultures and societies.

Set against these achievements is a cluster of related difficulties with the present mandate. First, there is its conspicuous complexity. It has developed to such an extent, and in so many specialised areas, that there is no longer any straightforward mandate guide for members, and there is increasing concern within the organisation that understanding the mandate is becoming the province of only a few experts.

Secondly, the increasing complexity of the mandate has led to ever greater delays in implementing new policies. Amnesty International has developed

---

22   Examples of releases and other improvements in the conditions of the victims of human rights abuses are frequently reported in AI newsletters. For a recent set of examples, see Amnesty International, *Amnesty International News*, January 1998 (AI Index: NWS 21/01/98), London: AIUK.

new guidelines on issues as diverse as when Amnesty International should call on armed opposition groups to hold trials of prisoners they hold; on how to distinguish extrajudicial killings from acts of war; on how to interpret 'cruel, inhuman or degrading treatment' in relation to children. Yet, these policies have often taken years to appear, causing some frustration amongst the membership. And, when such guidelines do appear, they are often intimidatingly complex, dauntingly long, and only understandable by those with considerably above average levels of literacy. Similarly, the great and understandable value that Amnesty International places on developing its mandate by consensus increasingly leads to decisions that are verbose and hedged about with qualifications that only the most diligent members can understand.[23]

Thirdly, and perhaps most keenly felt by longer standing members, there is a perceived loss of personal contact in Amnesty International's work.[24] Whereas, in the early days, working for Amnesty International usually meant corresponding on behalf of (and sometimes with) a clearly identified individual, much of today's work is more impersonal, dealing with themes, whole country situations, and longer term preventative work. In due course, this may make it more difficult for Amnesty International to retain the involvement of members over many years.

Lastly, it is not clear whether the measures taken in recent years to improve the quality of decision making in relation to the mandate, will be successful. The criteria for mandate expansion described above are a useful first step, but contain their own tensions. For example, relevance and coherence are often at odds, since what is relevant in one country (for example, a focus on the death penalty) may be quite irrelevant in another one. Clarity and credibility also pull in different directions, since the credibility that comes from sticking to international standards (for example, the 1990 United Nations Basic Principles on the Use of Force and Firearms by law enforcement officials) may be difficult to state in clear, simple language that non-experts can understand and use in campaigning activities.

AMNESTY INTERNATIONAL IN THE 21ST CENTURY

Amnesty International has developed from being a simple organisation with a straightforward mandate into a complex organisation with a much more diffuse mandate. This trend is unlikely to be reversed. Indeed, it may well

---

23 See, eg, the six page Decision 16 of the 1993 ICM on improving Amnesty International's action techniques, or Decision 6 of the 1995 ICM, which stated that Amnesty International worked for the eradication of female genital mutilation without opposing the practice. (The later decision has been superseded by Decision 6 of the 1997 ICM.)

24 This point has been made at internal Amnesty International meetings by those members who have been involved with Amnesty International since its early days.

accelerate as a more international membership expects the organisation to become more flexible in its responses to different sorts of human rights violations in very different social and political contexts.

However, it may well be that the advantages of a gradually expanding mandate continue to outweigh the disadvantages. After all, throughout the world people join and work for political parties without understanding the details of all of their policies. In any case, it is likely that changes in working methods and in the emphasis given to different parts of the mandate – rather than changes in the scope of the mandate itself – that will have the most impact on Amnesty International's role in the coming years.

One of the strongest challenges to respect for human rights in the early part of the next century is likely to be the continuing strength of ethnic particularism and fundamentalist religious and nationalist beliefs. Amnesty International will need to combat these head on by finding effective ways of making the message of universal human rights plausible in many different and unpromising situations. It will also need to become more genuinely international in its organisation, thus undermining the accusation that it simply represents another wave of Western ideological imperialism. In this respect, the recent opening of an African regional office in Kampala, the strengthening of the Hong Kong office, and the newly created sections in Taiwan and Costa Rica are important developments. Within no more than a decade, there should be at least one substantial regional Amnesty International office in each world region, and this itself should help to galvanise local human rights and NGO communities. Furthermore, these should be the first step towards stronger links with local NGOs; today's joint press statements should be the precursors to tomorrow's joint publications and campaigns.

However, whilst Amnesty International will almost certainly be strengthened over the next decade or so by developing a stronger international presence, forging alliances with likeminded organisations, continuing to make use of new technologies to speed its response times and disseminate its concerns to wider audiences, and attracting young members, it will also face several acute dilemmas.

First, Amnesty International's limited resources simply do not allow it to do everything within its present mandate effectively. Eventually, it may have to do what it has not done to date and drop some areas of work to concentrate on others. For example, over the last five years, Amnesty International has decided to devote more resources to both crisis response activities and long term human rights education and training projects; it has also decided to give a higher priority than in the past to thematic concerns, such as women's human rights, the need to deny impunity to violators of human rights, and the plight of refugees. Whilst the reasoning behind the broadening of its approach is clear and convincing, it is still an open question whether the organisation can maintain its effectiveness on so many different fronts.

Secondly, there is a tension between the belief in Amnesty International as an organisation based on international solidarity (the 'Join Amnesty International and help people in other countries' sentiment) and the development of closer ties to domestic human rights NGOs. While such ties can be mutually beneficial, leading to information sharing, co-ordination of campaigning activities, and learning from each others' experiences, they may ultimately lead Amnesty International members to want to do more about human rights in their own countries. This would conflict with the long standing Amnesty International principle that, with a few exceptions, members do not work on the human rights situation in their own country.

Thirdly, there is also a tension between the relatively narrow focus of Amnesty International's work on behalf of the victims of selected human rights violations, and the much broader focus of its long term preventative work. At the September 1997 annual meeting of the World Bank and IMF, Amnesty International spoke out against a world 'in which the rights of people are frequently given less weight in public policy than the interests of capital'.[25] While it is easy to see what underlies such statements, and why Amnesty International feels it important to put 'disappearances', torture, and political killings in their social and economic context, it is also easy to see that such rhetoric is open to misinterpretation, and that Amnesty International could mistakenly be perceived as an unfocused but broadly anti-capitalist organisation.

Lastly, Amnesty International faces some awkward choices in relating its campaigning activities to the needs and motivation of its membership. There are some signs that membership figures are stagnating worldwide (with the exception of the growth of youth and student groups),[26] and this may be because the demands Amnesty International makes of its local groups are no longer as attractive to their members as in the past. The loss of long term personal contact with prisoners of conscience and their families is just one such factor. Other concerns are that members are simply being asked to act on too many different actions, that they receive insufficient positive feedback about the results of their efforts, and that Amnesty International is losing something of its special status as an organisation of activist volunteers because, increasingly, its day to day agenda is set by paid employees (now numbering just under 1,000 world wide).

The extent to which Amnesty International can address these dilemmas and develop in ways that are sensitive to both the needs of the victims of human rights violations and the practicalities of mobilising a diverse membership using very limited resources, will determine how effective it will be over the coming decades.

---

25 Statement by Amnesty International on the occasion of the World Bank/IMF annual meetings, Hong Kong, September 1997 (AI Index: IOR 30/04/97), London: AIUK.
26 *Ibid.*

CHAPTER 14

NON-GOVERNMENTAL ORGANISATIONS AND THE UNITED NATIONS

Martin O'Brien

INTRODUCTION

Non-governmental organisations (NGOs)[1] are very much at the heart and soul of work to promote and protect human rights. They come in all shapes and sizes ranging from groups like Amnesty International and Human Rights Watch, which deal with human rights on a worldwide scale, right through to small groups working on a plethora of local issues. NGOs have in particular been central to the development of the United Nations work on human rights, both in relation to the development of new human rights standards and in ensuring that the facts surrounding human rights problems are brought to light. They are, of course, more able to make this kind of contribution given that they are not bound by the same strictures that can encumber large bureaucracies and intergovernmental action.

Since the early days of the United Nations, there has been a massive growth in the number of NGOs participating, and their activities have made a profoundly important contribution, acting as a leaven in this vitally important work. It is very clear that the advances which have been made in relation to the protection and promotion of human rights, could not have been made without the work of NGOs. NGOs have themselves realised the potential to advance their own work to promote and protect human rights through involvement at the United Nations level.

What follows is, essentially, a case study which presents the experiences of the Belfast based Committee on the Administration of Justice (CAJ),[2] a non-governmental organisation committed to securing the highest possible standards in the administration of justice in Northern Ireland. In 1991, CAJ took a decision to step up its work with the various United Nations bodies which have developed over the years to protect human rights.

The CAJ is a small human rights NGO working to secure a just and peaceful society in Northern Ireland where the human rights of all are fully protected. It was felt that the UK Government would be more amenable to

---

1   For a general discussion on the work and role of NGOs, see Steiner, H and Alston, P, *International Human Rights in Context*, 1996, Oxford: Clarendon.

2   See Whelan, L, 'The challenge of lobbying for civil rights in Northern Ireland: the Committee on the Administration of Justice' (1992) 14 HRQ 149, pp 149–70.

international rather than simply domestic pressure. The Committee had been working for some time seeking to influence the domestic legislative and decision making process within the UK, but felt that its impact had been too limited. The CAJ's efforts and experience provide some useful examples for other NGOs interested in working at the United Nations. The chapter that follows is essentially in two parts. The first is a review of the various United Nations mechanisms that are likely to be of most use to human rights NGOs. In the second part, some useful lessons are drawn for other NGOs interested in exploring the potential which the United Nations system can offer.

THE UNITED NATIONS SYSTEM

The United Nations committees

There are six committees that oversee the implementation of the various United Nations treaties.[3] Each of these conducts periodic examinations of the countries that have signed the treaties, in order to monitor how well the treaty obligations are being complied with. The committees consist of independent experts who receive reports from governments on implementation of their responsibilities. Following receipt of the country reports, the committees in Geneva or New York publicly question government representatives. Any non-governmental organisation can prepare its own alternative information to brief the committee, and it is also able to attend the meeting to lobby. Generally, governments should be able to supply their domestic NGOs with a schedule of forthcoming examinations and reports.

Issues of human rights breaches in Northern Ireland have been raised extensively at five of these bodies: the Human Rights Committee; the Committee on the Elimination of Racial Discrimination; the Committee against Torture; the Committee on the Rights of the Child; and the Committee on Economic, Social and Cultural Rights. The sixth – which is not being dealt with in detail here – is the Committee on the Elimination of Discrimination against Women. This Committee will consider the UK's next report in 1999.[4]

---

3   Committee on the Rights of the Child; Committee on Economic, Social and Cultural Rights; Committee against Torture; Committee on the Elimination of Racial Discrimination; Human Rights Committee; Committee on the Elimination of Discrimination against Women; Convention on the Rights of the Child; International Covenant on Economic, Social and Cultural Rights; Convention against Torture and other Cruel, Inhuman or Degrading Treatment or Punishment; International Convention on the Elimination of all Forms of Racial Discrimination; International Covenant on Civil and Political Rights; Convention on the Elimination of Discrimination against Women.

4   CAJ and other NGOs in the UK are preparing material for consideration by this Committee. At the time of writing, the author has no first hand knowledge of the operation of this committee.

The Human Rights Committee

It is the Human Rights Committee (HRC) which has dealt with issues concerning Northern Ireland in the most comprehensive and sustained way. Under the International Covenant on Civil and Political Rights (ICCPR), countries are examined periodically on their implementation of the Covenant. The mechanism was established in 1976 and, since then, the UK has been examined on four separate occasions.[5] Over the years, increased attention on Northern Ireland has been encouraged by both international and domestic NGOs, most particularly Amnesty International and the Committee on the Administration of Justice.

The examination in 1995 was the most extensive and wideranging carried out. In addition to making submissions to the Committee and attending the hearing, representatives from CAJ and Amnesty also attended the preliminary meeting where the HRC developed a list of questions for the Government. The subsequent formal examination of the Government by the Committee initially focuses on the Government's response to these questions. Participation in the preliminary meeting, therefore, provided an important opportunity to influence the range of issues raised by the Committee. NGOs anxious to influence the outcome of the hearings, should, in addition to submitting their own information and attending the hearings, consider attending this preliminary session as well. In some respects, this is the most important pressure point for groups.

For the first time in 1995, the Human Rights Committee moved beyond a general discussion to adopt a number of final comments.[6] Such a development provides an agenda for action by government and by human rights groups monitoring government compliance with the international standards. Initially, this move towards more specific recommendations did not appear to have had any great impact on the UK Government. When questioned in the House of Lords in October 1995 on its response to the HRC recommendations, an interesting exchange took place between Baroness Blatch, a Minister of State at the Home Office and Lord Peter Archer for the (then) opposition.

Blatch: The government have noted the observations of the Human Rights Committee ... We do not plan any specific changes in our arrangements for the protection of human rights in the United Kingdom in light of the committee's views.

Archer: Does this mean that the Government have no proposals for action other than telling the Committee that it is wrong in every respect? In particular, do they see the need for any action on the right to silence; the provision of legal representation for asylum seeker ... and

---

5   1978, 1985, 1991 and 1995.
6   CCPR/C/79/Add 55.

249

> assessing the continuing need in Northern Ireland for the Prevention of Terrorism Act? Do the Government not consider it possible that they may be wrong? Or do they take the view that it is the committee which is out of step with them?

Blatch: The Government explained very carefully their position on all those issues during the oral hearing. The Government regret that the Committee does not appear to have taken into account our long standing cultural traditions and other particular circumstances which determine the way in which human rights are protected in this country, nor the fact that the protection provided in the United Kingdom in relation to human rights is among the best in the world.[7]

Ideally, the Human Rights Committee will begin future country examinations by asking governments to account for progress on each of the issues identified in a final comments document prepared at the end of the previous examination. Human rights groups will have to await the next examination of the UK, which is due to take place in the year 2000 to see how the HRC responds to many of its recommendations being dismissed in such a cavalier way by the Government.

Committee on the Elimination of Racial Discrimination (CERD)

Northern Ireland, unlike the rest of the UK, has until very recently not had any legislation to protect minority ethnic groups against racial discrimination. The Race Relations Act 1976, which applies in England, Scotland and Wales, was not extended to Northern Ireland. The CAJ and other Northern Irish NGOs have used the Committee on the Elimination of Racial Discrimination as part of an ongoing campaign to secure race relations legislation for Northern Ireland.[8] This was ultimately successful in August 1997 with the enactment of the Race Relations (Northern Ireland) Order 1997.

In 1993, this Committee received, for the first time, substantial submissions from NGOs in Northern Ireland[9] and was subject to fairly intense lobbying by these groups. As a result, the Committee urged the Government to act quickly to introduce Race Relations legislation in Northern Ireland.[10] However, by the time of the next appearance before the Committee in 1996, no legislation was in place, although the Government had now committed itself to introduce

---

7   *Hansard*, House of Lords, 26 October 1995, Cols 1189–92.

8   See Committee on the Administration of Justice, *Racism in Northern Ireland*, 1992, Belfast: CAJ, and CAJ submission to the UN Committee on the Elimination of Racial Discrimination in Northern Ireland, 1993.

9   These included the Chinese Welfare Association, the Northern Ireland Council for Travelling People and the Committee on the Administration of Justice.

10 See CERD/C/SR 997, paras 13, 43, 68, 81.

legislation.[11] The Committee described the commitment as 'welcome, although much belated'.[12] It made clear that legislation should be introduced as a matter of urgency.

Campaigning groups agree that the statements from the CERD were of particular benefit in securing the introduction of the legislation.[13] The Government was clearly uneasy as a result of the considerable media coverage, which accompanied the 1993, and 1995 hearings. While it is impossible to isolate the impact that such hearings made, given that they took place in the context of a wider campaign, it is clear that they exerted considerable moral pressure on the Government. The Government eventually decided that it was easier to introduce the legislation, than continue to justify its non-existence.

Committee against Torture

The UK was examined in 1991, 1995 and 1998 by the Committee against Torture (CAT); Northern Ireland has been a major focus of concern.[14] At the 1991 hearings, in addition to the Government's report, this Committee had submissions from the CAJ, Amnesty International and a firm of Northern Ireland solicitors to consider. These presented detailed information on a large volume of complaints from the summer of 1991, set in the context of the legal regime for detention. All three groups sent representatives to Geneva to lobby the Committee members. Their work succeeded and the Committee against Torture delivered a strong criticism of the UK's record in Northern Ireland.[15] This was covered extensively in the local and national press and was a major source of embarrassment to the Government.[16]

Serious allegations of ill treatment and abuse virtually disappeared as a direct result of the hearings and the subsequent negative publicity that they produced. The official statistics show a marked decline in the number of complaints of physical ill treatment of detainees.[17] In spite of this, the Committee continued to express concern about the detention regime when the Government were examined again in 1995. By 1995, CAT had also adopted

---

11 See Government Statement at Advisory Committee on Travellers Conference, Belfast, 14 March 1995. The Race Relations (NI) Order 1997 came into effect August 1997.

12 CERD/C/304/Add 9, para 9.

13 See Northern Ireland Council for Ethnic Minorities, minutes of Advisory Committee Meeting, 22 January 1997.

14 See CAT/C/9/Add 6; CAT/C/SR 91, 92; and CAT/C/25/Add 6; CAT/C/SR 234, 235.

15 See CAT/C/SR 91, paras 18, 20, 29–40.

16 See, eg, (1991) *The Irish Times*, 22 November; (1991) *The Guardian*, 29 October.

17 See Northern Ireland Independent Commission for Police Complaints, *Annual Reports*, 1990–95, London: HMSO.

the practice of issuing a set of conclusions and recommendations.[18] Among its main recommendations were calls for the abolition of detention centres and the repeal of emergency legislation.[19] While this has not yet taken place, objective evidence, such as the decrease in complaints to non-governmental organisations, indicates that their interventions at the CAT have resulted in concrete improvements for detainees in Northern Ireland. At the 1998 hearings, the Committee restated its concerns about the maintenance of emergency legislation, identifying it as the sole factor impeding compliance with the Convention. The Committee also called for restructuring of the police in Northern Ireland.[20]

Committee on the Rights of the Child

The UK was examined for the first time by the Committee on the Rights of the Child in January 1995. Just as with the Human Rights Committee, the Committee members hold a pre-sessional meeting, in advance of Committee hearings proper, to prepare the questions which they will present to governments. The CAJ and other domestic NGOs from the UK, and Human Rights Watch (New York), were invited to address the pre-sessional meeting for the United Kingdom, and this provided an important opportunity to brief Committee members. In this respect, the Committee on the Rights of the Child is almost unique in terms of the direct access which it provides to non-governmental organisations. NGOs anxious to have an impact on the final outcome of any hearings should write to the Committee, asking that they be allowed to make an oral presentation to this pre-sessional meeting. In the instance quoted above, the NGOs had also prepared detailed written submissions, which were sent some time in advance to the Committee members.[21]

In advance of the actual hearings, Thomas Hammarberg, the country *rapporteur* for the UK report, made a short visit to Northern Ireland where he met a number of young people and NGOs working on children's rights. The Committee appoints a *rapporteur* for each country, and it is his or her responsibility to take the lead role in the questioning of government officials during the formal examination. It is, therefore, important to ensure that this person in particular is well briefed.

NGOs should therefore find out who the country *rapporteur* is, and they should consider inviting him or her to make a visit. Committee members who

---

18 Committee against Torture, *Conclusions and Recommendations of UNCAT*, November 1995, Geneva: UN.

19 *Ibid.*

20 See CAT/C/SR, 354, 355 and 360.

21 Committee on the Administration of Justice, *CAJ Submission to the United Nations Committee on the Rights of the Child*, 1 August 1994, Belfast: CAJ.

have first hand knowledge are in a much better position to challenge and question the government representatives, and this proved to be the case with the UK's report. For example, when efforts were made by Government representatives to suggest that problems with policing were not so extensive, Mr Hammarberg was able to cite the accounts of young people he had met while in Belfast.

This advance preparation and lobbying at the actual hearings by NGO representatives contributed to considerable attention being paid by the Committee on the Rights of the Child to the situation of children in Northern Ireland when considering the UK's report. About 20% of the summary record directly addresses issues about Northern Ireland, whereas Scotland, which was not represented by NGOs at the hearings, was considered in some 2% of the paragraphs.

In the concluding observations of the Committee[22] under the heading 'Principal subjects of concern', Northern Ireland features prominently. The recommendations section called for 'race relations legislation to be introduced in Northern Ireland as a matter of urgency', and for proactive measures to ensure the rights of traveller and Gypsy children in relation to education and accommodation. The Government was also urged to provide further support for the teaching of the Irish language and for integrated education. The Committee recommended that the Government review the system of emergency legislation and the juvenile justice system, to ensure its compliance with the principles and provisions of the Convention on the Rights of the Child.

In the wake of the hearings, the Government announced its intention to introduce race relations legislation[23] and increased funding for Irish language education. As with other issues, however, it is difficult to assess the exact role which the Committee's comments played in these decisions, given that both issues are ones on which there have been ongoing local campaigns. Child care experts, however, are of the view that the Committee hearings provoked voluntary and statutory groups to look for the first time at the impact of the conflict on children in Northern Ireland.[24] This resulted in a major conference on this theme, which was organised by Save the Children. The hearings also stimulated a considerable level of activism in the field of children's rights in Northern Ireland.[25]

---

22 CRC/C/15/Add 34, pp 6–8.

23 See Government Statement at Advisory Committee on Travellers Conference, Belfast, 14 March 1995. The Race Relations (Northern Ireland) Order 1997 came into effect August 1997.

24 Interview with Anne McKeown, Convenor, CAJ subgroup on children's rights, 31 August 1996.

25 Evidenced by the conference on children's rights, We All Fall Down, organised by Save the Children, in Belfast, February 1996, and the subsequent establishment of the Children's Law Centre in October 1997.

The Committee on Economic, Social and Cultural Rights

This Committee has, until very recently, looked at the records of governments under various sections of the Covenant on Economic Social and Cultural Rights, rather than carrying out a complete examination. The UK was first examined under the new comprehensive system in November 1997. As with the Committee on the Rights of the Child, there is an opportunity for NGOs to make oral presentations to the Committee in advance of their formal examination of the government. CAJ, in addition to making its own submission, addressing a preparatory meeting of the Committee and attending the examination itself in Geneva, worked to brief other NGOs about the Committee process and the possibility of making submission. This resulted in a large number of submissions from organisations in Northern Ireland.

The Committee in its concluding comments highlighted concerns about discrimination and levels of disadvantage in Northern Ireland.[26] It also called for a human rights assessment to be made an integral part of every proposed legislative or policy initiative, a recommendation which added considerable weight to the ongoing campaign in Northern Ireland for equality impact assessments on government policy initiatives.[27]

The Sub-commission on the Prevention of Discrimination and the Protection of Minorities and the Commission on Human Rights

It is also possible for NGOs to raise concerns at the Sub-commission on the Prevention of Discrimination and the Protection of Minorities and at the Commission on Human Rights. This, however, only applies to organisations with what is known as 'consultative status'. This is a group of organisations specifically recognised by the United Nations.[28] Groups in this category can make both written and oral contributions to both of these bodies, and can also attend their meetings to lobby on behalf of a particular cause. CAJ, through its affiliation with the International Federation for Human Rights, an international NGO with consultative status, has been able to avail itself of these opportunities.

---

26 E/C 12/1/Add 19, paras 18, 20, 22, 24, 29, 32, 33.
27 For further information on the issue of equality impact assessments, see McCrudden, C, *Mainstreaming Fairness*, 1996 and *Benchmarks for Change*, 1998, Belfast: CAJ.
28 See Economic and Social Council resolutions 1996/31 of 26 July 1996 and 1296 of 23 May 1968.

Since 1992, the International Federation for Human Rights (IFHR) and its Northern Irish affiliate, CAJ, have submitted written statements[29] and made oral interventions at the Sub-commission.[30] These have all focused on the rights of detainees, states of emergency and the independence of judges and lawyers.

The impact of these statements has been variable, with the high point of their influence being in 1992. Mrs Claire Palley, who was then the member from the UK on the Sub-commission, called for an independent inquiry into the death of defence lawyer Patrick Finucane.[31] In addition to receiving the written statement, representatives of CAJ and the IFHR had spoken personally to Mrs Palley in advance of her intervention. This personal contact is the most effective method of lobbying. There is really no substitute for direct conversations with as many of the 26 individual experts who make up the Sub-commission, and are likely to be helpful to your cause.

Inevitably, Mrs Palley's comments attracted considerable media attention. An article in *The Guardian*[32] under the heading 'British voice at UN lambasts Ulster justice' carried her comments extensively. This provoked the Minister of State at the Northern Ireland Office, Michael Mates, to write to the newspaper about Mrs Palley's comments[33] and make it clear that the Government had no intention of acting on her comments because, in their view, there was no problem to address. In her response, Mrs Palley demolished the Minister's arguments one by one. In particular, she observed:

His letter exemplifies reflex governmental defensiveness ... Regrettably, substantiated allegations, reasonable criticisms and proposals, whether within the UK or at international fora exercising jurisdiction, are too often met by blanket ministerial rejection. Only when scandal becomes overwhelming is remedial action taken.[34]

Further letters followed[35] highlighting the Government's sensitivity to these kind of comments, but, also, their unwillingness to remedy the concerns.

NGO statements can also force a response from governments which draws further attention to the issue. The IFHR written statement in 1993, together with an oral intervention by the International Commission of Jurists,[36] resulted for the first time in the UK Government exercising its right to reply.

---

29 See E/CN 4/Sub 2/1992/NGO/11; E/CN 4/Sub 2/1993/NGO/15; E/CN 4/Sub 2/1994/NGO/10; E/CN 4/Sub 2/1995/NGO/54; E/CN 4/Sub 2/1996/NGO/30.
30 See Summary Records for Sub-commission, item 10, 1993, 1994, 1995 and 1996.
31 E/CN 4/Sub 2/1992/SR 23, para 62.
32 (1992) *The Guardian*, 21 August.
33 (1992) *The Guardian*, 29 August.
34 (1992) *The Guardian*, 5 September.
35 (1992) *The Guardian*, 29 September and 9 October.
36 E/CN 4/Sub 2/1993/SR 18.

The Commission on Human Rights is an even more political forum than the Sub-commission, in that the delegations are official government representatives. The NGO experience in relation to Northern Ireland has been that it is much harder to achieve results at the Commission. This may well be true of other jurisdictions.

The working methods and practices of those human rights mechanisms that report to the Commission are currently under review.[37] The outcome of the review is not expected to become clear until the next Commission meeting in March 1999, although it is expected that the major focus of change will be on the work of the Sub-commission. There may also be some changes to the opportunities for NGOs to participate in the system.

The special rapporteurs

These are a group of individuals appointed by the United Nations to report to the Commission or Sub-commission on a particular issue, theme or country. The rapporteurs are usually drawn from human rights experts around the world; they each prepare an annual report that is tabled at the meeting of their parent body. The post holders change from time to time; the particular personality and approach of the individual rapporteur is an important factor in the success or otherwise of this mechanism. NGOs can send information to rapporteurs about particular issues or cases that fall within their remit. The rapporteur will, if he or she is satisfied with the information, forward it to the relevant government for a reply. The mechanism is very under resourced and, as a result, there can be a considerable time lag between sending the information and some action being taken. Generally speaking, all that normally happens is that the rapporteur includes the information provided and any response in his or her annual report.

Northern Ireland concerns have been raised by NGOs with three of the rapporteurs, namely, the special rapporteur on torture, the special rapporteur on summary and arbitrary executions and the special rapporteur on the independence of judges and lawyers.

With the first of these two, the pattern has generally been for the rapporteur to mention the concerns raised and any governmental response he or she has received. The rapporteur does not appear to follow up on answers that fail to reply fully to queries. NGOs can, in particularly serious cases, request that rapporteurs intervene on a more urgent basis, and the rapporteur then contacts the government more quickly and seeks a speedy response.[38]

---

37 See (1998) 5(1–2) Human Rights Tribune 7, pp 7–8.
38 See reference to case of *Brian Austin*, E/CN 4/1995/61.

Regardless of the outcome of this procedure, it must be a matter of some embarrassment to the UK to feature on a recurring basis in the reports of these two rapporteurs. The rapporteur mechanism is not a particularly labour intensive one, in that NGOs are probably already preparing information on cases or issues of concern to them, and it is a relatively easy matter to add the rapporteurs to the circulation list, obviously tailoring material into the form of a submission.

The approach taken by the rapporteur on the Independence of Judges and Lawyers has, however, been particularly significant in relation to Northern Ireland. The first reference to Northern Ireland is in the 1992 report:[39] Mr Louis Joinet observes that 'Many sources agree that pressure is put on the lawyers of persons arrested in connection with the anti-terrorist campaign'.[40] The inclusion of Northern Ireland in his reports was directly attributable to submissions made to him by British Irish Rights Watch[41] and the CAJ.[42]

In 1996,[43] there was a change in rapporteur when Dató Param Cumaraswamy took over from Louis Joinet. In his 1996 report, Mr Cumaraswamy records that he made an informal visit to Northern Ireland in July 1995. The purpose of this visit was to carry out preliminary investigations into allegations of executive interference in the administration of justice. He notes that he met non-governmental organisations, in particular, the CAJ.[44] This was the first visit by a special rapporteur to Northern Ireland.

In October 1997, the rapporteur followed this up with an official visit to Northern Ireland and Britain. His visit was the first of its kind and was extremely significant. The rapporteur met a wide range of practitioners and government officials; aspects of his itinerary were arranged by CAJ. His report, which was tabled before the Commission in April 1998, was highly critical of the UK Government and its failure to address adequately the ongoing complaints about police threats and abuse of lawyers in Northern Ireland.[45] NGOs attended the Commission hearings in Geneva, and also organised a public briefing session, which was addressed by the rapporteur. A

---

39 E/CN 4/Sub 2/1992/25.
40 *Ibid*, para 110.
41 A small London based NGO working on human rights issues relating to Northern Ireland. See Chapter 17.
42 See *Intimidation of Defence Lawyers in Northern Ireland*, December 1991; *Further Submission on Intimidation of Defence Lawyers in Northern Ireland*, May 1992; *Defending the Defenders*, March 1993; *In Defence of the Defence*, March 1994; *Without Fear or Favour*, April 1995; *Supplementary Report to the UN special rapporteur on the Independence of Judges and Lawyers*, December 1995, all produced by BIRW, and correspondence from CAJ to the *rapporteur*, December 1991 and June 1992.
43 E/CN 4/1996/37.
44 *Ibid*.
45 E/CN 4/1998/39/Add 4.

broad consortium of NGOs made oral and written statements to the Commission supporting the concerns raised by the rapporteur. Both the Irish and UK Governments responded to the report and the NGOs worked to sustain a press story that ran for a full week with national television, radio and newspaper coverage.[46]

The Government's reaction to the report was to welcome it, but immediately to dismiss the detailed recommendations for action.[47] It seems likely, however, that the publicity surrounding the report will result in an improved environment for lawyers and a substantial decrease in threats against them.

GENERAL LESSONS FOR NGOS

Having looked at the main mechanisms likely to be of most use to NGOs, what lessons can be drawn from the CAJ's experience of using these mechanisms to advance its overall concerns, namely, to ensure greater protection of human rights in Northern Ireland?

Finding your way around

Sometimes, there is a strong sense that the United Nations is a massive and largely irrelevant bureaucracy. It is undoubtedly very large and bureaucratic, · but with careful planning, using the United Nations can become a powerful tool in NGO strategies to promote change. Fortunately, others have gone before in trying to work out the best way to use the United Nations, and there are two particularly useful books which any NGO interested in exploring a UN dimension to its work should consult. The first is the *Orientation Manual: The UN Commission on Human Rights, its Sub-commission, and Related Procedures*.[48] Although this book is now somewhat dated, it still provides a wealth of practical information on such things as how to get into the United Nations building on your first day, where to find photocopiers, how NGOs get to speak, what happens when and where. The second is a more recent publication: *Human Rights Human Wrongs: A Guide to the Human Rights*

---

46 See, eg, McKittrick, D, 'UN damns Ulster police intimidation' (1998) *The Independent*, 31 March.

47 'Response to the conclusions and recommendations to the UN special rapporteur's report' (1998) Northern Ireland Information Service, 1 April.

48 Weissbrodt, D and Parker, P, *Orientation Manual: The UN Commission on Human Rights, its Sub-commission and Related Procedures*, 1992, Minneapolis: Minnesota Advocates for Human Rights and the International Service for Human Rights.

Machinery of the United Nations.[49] This invaluable publication will help you work out which United Nations mechanisms might provide suitable opportunities for your NGO to pursue different aspects of its agenda. The guide clearly explains each aspect of the United Nations human rights system and outlines the ways in which NGOs can access these. Both of these books should provide the starting point for any NGO interested in exploring the United Nations, and the potential that it offers to advance NGO effectiveness.

ENHANCED CREDIBILITY FOR NGOS

Given the fact that governments often seek to undermine and dismiss the concerns of NGOs, comments by United Nations bodies can represent an important endorsement and legitimisation of the NGO concerns. In practical terms, in the context of Northern Ireland, it is no longer just the local NGOs or even international NGOs, such as Amnesty International, that are troubled by the human rights situation in Northern Ireland. As a result of several years of NGOs working on the issue at the United Nations, it is now the case that bodies such as the Human Rights Committee, the Committee against Torture, or the special rapporteur on the independence of judges and lawyers are lined up alongside the NGO community with the government on the opposing side seeking to justify the unjustifiable.

In the context of a campaign to secure both public support and the political will to bring about change, these alliances with heavyweight partners are particularly important. This has been a key element in the NGO strategy in Northern Ireland, and it has clearly paid off. Moreover, the longer it goes on the more success it has and the easier it is to recruit other partners to the cause. This is particularly important in dealing with a country like the UK where other countries and groups may have difficulty in believing that serious human rights violations take place.

Concrete manifestations of this are, for example, the more critical reports from the US State Department[50] and the report by the European Committee for the Prevention of Torture.[51] Criticism by the United Nations encourages and indeed to some extent requires criticism of the UK by other bodies, if they are to have any credibility.

---

49 Winter, J, *Human Rights Human Wrongs: A Guide to the Human Rights Machinery of the United Nations*, 1996, London: BIRW.

50 See, eg, *1997 US Department of State United Kingdom Report on Human Rights Practices*, released by the Bureau of Democracy, Human Rights and Labor.

51 *Report to the Government of the United Kingdom on the visit to Northern Ireland carried out by the ECPT from 20 to 29 July 1993*, CPT/Inf (94) 17, Strasbourg: Council of Europe.

PUBLICISING THE RESULTS

Obtaining supportive pronouncements from the United Nations bodies, while important, is not of itself enough to bring about change. A key factor in achieving this goal is the degree to which publicity can be obtained for the comments that are made. It has been pointed out that NGOs frequently devote a great deal of effort to compiling information, but fail to develop an effective dissemination strategy.[52] If the findings of the various United Nations bodies remain within the confines of a committee room in Geneva or New York, their impact is considerably lessened. For example, the 1991 comments by the Committee against Torture on ill treatment of detainees in Northern Ireland secured extensive media coverage both locally and nationally. The presence of a reporter from *The Guardian* newspaper at the hearings was particularly important in achieving this. It is clear that NGOs must develop effective strategies to secure publicity for their successes at the United Nations.

At another level, too, the NGOs can work to ensure that the outcome of the various hearings is widely known within the relevant sectors of society. For example, a major conference on racism[53] was held in Belfast to coincide with the 1996 CERD hearings on the UK in Geneva. The concluding comments from the Committee were relayed directly to the meeting and, aside from the dramatic effect, this placed extra pressure on the government officials in attendance. Those active on the issue were all appraised of the Committee's comments and could utilise them in their ongoing work.

Similar efforts could and should be made to ensure that the relevant constituencies are informed of the outcomes of interventions and of the content of the interventions themselves. It is clear that governments are rarely going to be active in publicising or circulating the criticisms that are made of them. The task must then fall to the NGOs. Thus, for example, the CAJ and a consortium of NGOs obtained multiple copies of the most recent report by the United Nations special rapporteur on the Independence of Judges and Lawyers. They also prepared a summary of its conclusions and are circulating both to a substantial mailing list, domestically and internationally. A cover letter has been prepared asking recipients to contact the relevant UK authorities to express their concern, and to request action on the recommendations. A campaign is now being organised around the United Nations findings. Additionally, NGOs have encouraged the US Congress to hold hearings on the report and to invite the special rapporteur to testify at

---

52 See Cohen, S, 'Government responses to human rights reports: claims, denials and counterclaims' (1996) 18 HRQ 518.

53 Tackling Racism Conference, Northern Ireland Council on Ethnic Minorities Conference, March 1996.

these. The House Sub-committee on International Operations and Human Rights held hearings on the the Cumaraswamy Report in September 1998. Mr Cumaraswamy briefed members of the Sub-committee on his findings, while two local defence lawyers and a staff member from CAJ gave evidence on the record.

UNITED NATIONS FINDINGS AND COURT ACTION

It is also important that the judiciary and the legal profession are appraised of United Nations deliberations and conclusions. Judges may think twice about supporting a particular practice if it has been clearly condemned at an international level. It is important that those involved in the administration of justice at an international level are themselves aware of the comments and observations of those charged with adjudicating on the protection of human rights.

Where this can be particularly effective is in the preparation of cases for legal argument. Frequently the comments made by United Nations bodies provide supportive arguments for domestic litigation. Indeed, an example of this is the summary records of the 1995 examination of the UK by the Committee against Torture which provided important information for a judicial review on access to legal advice.[54]

Greater efforts should be made to ensure that the results of attempts to raise human rights concerns at the United Nations are widely disseminated among those who can put them to good use. Another NGO, British Irish Rights Watch, points out that, increasingly, lawyers in Northern Ireland are citing United Nations principles and instruments, whereas several years previously they were largely unaware of their existence.[55]

ENHANCED CAMPAIGNS

Related to this issue is the integration of these interventions into ongoing campaigns. It is unlikely that comments by the United Nations alone will have an effect, but when coupled with an effective campaign they can prove very influential. Examples of this are the CAJ campaigns to secure race relations legislation and an end to the abuse of detainees. Interventions at the United Nations formed an important part of these campaigns, legitimating their goals, encouraging the campaigners, recruiting others to the campaign,

---

54 In the matter of applications by Michael Russell and others for judicial review.
55 Note from BIRW to Martin O'Brien, 6 August 1996.

providing opportunities for media coverage and adding to the pressure on the Government. Jane Winter of British Irish Rights Watch describes the situation as follows:

> A major lesson we have learned from our work at the United Nations, not only in relation to intimidation of lawyers but on other questions, such as, ill treatment in custody and abuse of lethal force, is that it is not so much what one does at the UN itself, although this is very important, but what one does afterwards with whatever pronouncements one has gained from the various mechanisms that determines how much impact such work has. We are still learning how to maximise the effect of our UN work.[56]

This highlights the importance of ensuring that those campaigning on particular issues are aware of the comments by United Nations bodies and are able to integrate them into their own campaigns. In Northern Ireland, there are numerous examples of the effectiveness of this (those involved in working to secure funding for the Irish language; in seeking improvements in the provision of services to the Chinese or Traveller communities; in campaigning for an end to the use of plastic bullets; for improvements in the juvenile justice system). The comments by various United Nations bodies provide useful information, which can be incorporated into their campaign and promotional literature.

MAXIMISING NGO IMPACT

Using the United Nations as part of an overall campaign, however, makes it difficult to determine the exact impact of specific interventions. This is especially so when work is being done on similar issues through the domestic courts, through the European Court or at a political level with the British, Irish or US Governments. In such situations, it is difficult to isolate the exact cause and effect of different actions.

The impact of interventions at the United Nations is clearly increased when a variety of different actors have raised concerns about Northern Ireland. The input from Amnesty International, the CAJ and a local Belfast lawyer seem to have particularly influenced the Committee against Torture in 1991. Similarly, the special rapporteur on the independence of judges and lawyers appears to have been mobilised by the reports of intimidation of defence lawyers, which were presented to him by a variety of sources.

It would appear that the Government has also felt obliged to respond to criticism on Northern Ireland when it has come from a variety of different non-governmental organisations, such as the Lawyers Committee, the

---

56 *Op cit*, BIRW, fn 55.

International Commission for Jurists and the International Federation for Human Rights. With this in mind, the CAJ has convened and participated in a number of co-ordination meetings, which have brought together representatives from these organisations. Amnesty International has also played a key role in this approach. The aim of these meetings has been to co-ordinate the efforts of the various groups with a view to maximising their collective impact at an international level. Arising out of the meetings, there have been a number of joint initiatives and the groups are committed to working together in the future to highlight their concerns about the human rights situation in Northern Ireland. This co-ordination has meant that organisations have been able to avoid duplication of effort, but also to co-operate to ensure that attention gets focused on a particular issue at a particular time. This is particularly important if the issue in question does not already enjoy some attention. Co-ordinated interventions by a variety of organisations help to create an awareness that this is an issue deserving attention.

MOST PRODUCTIVE UNITED NATIONS MECHANISMS?

From 1991 on, the NGO community has been working to ensure increasing international scrutiny of the UK Government's human rights record in Northern Ireland. Experience suggests that the greatest impact has been at the various committees that meet at periodic intervals to discuss the UK's record. Northern Ireland, particularly in recent years, has dominated these discussions. The Government's response has frequently been to promise new measures or to assure a committee that progress is in hand. A weakness, however, of the approach of these committees is that they do not appear to follow up on their previous comments and suggestions. The adoption of final comments and conclusions would certainly make such an approach feasible in the future.

It might also be helpful if a government were required to submit a short follow up[57] report on the action taken to respond to or to implement the points made by a committee. This would begin to establish some basis for rendering governments accountable for their failure to respond to a committee's comments. Such an approach might go some way towards eliminating the kind of comments made by the UK Government in Parliament in the wake of the 1995 HRC hearings.[58]

---

57 A similar approach is taken by the European Committee for the Prevention of Torture, which requires governments to respond to its reports.
58 *Hansard*, House of Lords, 26 October 1995, Cols 1189–92.

NGO interventions on Northern Ireland are a relatively recent phenomenon, and it is really only in the last five years that concerted efforts have been made to use the United Nations mechanisms. It is also the case however that many of the mechanisms are relatively new. They themselves are manifestations of the growing United Nations system, particularly in relation to human rights. The efforts made by the CAJ in respect of Northern Ireland have, however, led to increased interest in these mechanisms not just from other NGOs with an interest in Northern Ireland, but also among the NGO community in Britain. The CAJ's work has provided a model for training offered by Liberty, British Irish Rights Watch and the Immigration Law Practitioners Group. These training sessions have succeeded in ensuring that a much larger network of NGOs are both aware of and using the various committees.

Work at the Sub-commission and the Commission has been very much more difficult. Here, the non-governmental organisations are effectively competing with the rest of the world, and with more egregious violations of human rights. At the Commission, in particular, and to a lesser extent at the Sub-commission, narrow political considerations also dominate. Thus far, it has been extremely difficult to get countries to raise concerns about the UK; those involved in lobbying report that country representatives are extremely reluctant to embarrass a powerful ally and a key country at the United Nations. There has also been an unwillingness to believe that the UK could be guilty of serious violations of human rights. These considerations, however, do not apply to States such as China, Nigeria or Cuba which would be only too keen to criticise the UK, but whose interventions would do little to embarrass the Government or assist the cause of the NGOs. It is to be hoped, however, that over the years of lobbying, and with the growing volume of criticism from the various United Nations bodies, that this reluctance to criticise or question the UK will break down. Perhaps, the most likely candidates for this would be the Scandinavian countries. It is notable that the US, which has played an active part in the peace process in Northern Ireland, has remained silent on this issue at the United Nations.

CONCLUSION

There is a considerable overlap in the issues raised at the various bodies and mechanisms. A particular example of this relates to the emergency law regime and the situation of defence lawyers. British Irish Rights Watch has been monitoring the issue of intimidation of defence lawyers since 1992, and confirms that there has been a marked decrease in the reports of abuse of solicitors by police officers at Castlereagh Holding Centre.[59] Similarly, there has been a decrease in complaints of the physical abuse of detainees. At the same time, the official statistics on deferral of access to legal advice, show a dramatic reduction in the exercise of the deferral power. The statistics on *incommunicado* detention show a similar trend.[60] An independent commissioner has been appointed, codes of practice governing detention have been introduced and the Government has finally agreed to introduce electronic recording of interviews. Of course, it is not possible to attribute all of this to the work at the United Nations. Alongside this, there has been media attention, parliamentary lobbying, political interventions by the Irish and US governments and legal activism at a local and European Court level. There have also been changes in the wider political situation in the wake of the cease fires, and these have been particularly important.

It seems clear, however, that the pronouncements by the various United Nations bodies have played their part in bringing about these changes. What all of this illustrates is how difficult it can be to get the UK Government to moderate its practices and procedures, in order to bring them into line with its international obligations and responsibilities. Commentators have observed that:

> Despite the increasing influence of human rights discourse in the international arena, no human rights organisation has the power to undermine the standard lines of defense mounted by sovereign States and their patrons.[61]

In this context, it is especially important that non-governmental organisations use every avenue at their disposal, and that they develop coherent strategies to maximise the impact of their work. The United Nations provides one such avenue, and a particularly important one.

---

59 BIRW submission to the UN Committee against Torture, September 1998.
60 EPA Statistics for the years 1990–95, *Statistical Bulletins*, Belfast: Northern Ireland Information Service.
61 *Op cit*, Cohen, fn 52, p 538.

CHAPTER 15

NON-GOVERNMENTAL ORGANISATIONS: THE KEY TO CHANGE

Angela Hegarty

INTRODUCTION

During the past 25 years, there has been a steady evolution in non-governmental human rights advocacy by Amnesty International and other internationally focussed NGOs [non-governmental organisations]. There has also been a dramatic increase in non-governmental rights advocacy at a national level. In the last 20 years, non-governmental human rights groups have formed in every region of the world. In many United Nation countries, the existence of such groups was United Nations precedented.[1]

Much of the fact finding and reporting of human rights violations in the world is done by NGOs.[2]

Perhaps the most striking feature of the human rights field in the latter half of the 20th century has been the growth of the number of non-governmental organisations, their range of activities and their influence with governments and international bodies. The role of NGOs in investigating, monitoring and highlighting human rights abuses is now a familiar one, but it is a role which they have only really assumed in the past quarter century.

There are a variety of factors which have brought about this change. There has been an increased world focus on human rights generally,[3] a product of the various international and regional human rights treaties which have come into being since the ending of the Second World War. The plethora of bodies established under these United Nations treaties, for the purposes of monitoring their implementation, have naturally increased the numbers of interventions which NGOs can make on the world stage, although access to that stage has frequently proved tricky, especially for those smaller and more local NGOs.

Another factor has been the increase in interest in 'single issue' campaigns – such as the environment, poverty, peace, which has resulted in the emergence of 'civil society' – the churches, women's groups, welfare

---

1   Posner, M, 'Human rights and non-governmental organisations; foreword' (1997) 66 Fordham L Rev 627, pp 627–28.
2   Weissbrodt, D and McCarthy, J, 'Fact finding by international non-governmental human rights organisations' (1981) 22 Virginia J Int L 1.
3   See Davison, S, *Human Rights*, 1993, Buckingham: OU Press, pp 20–21, 163–78.

organisations, trade unions, and so on. This 'growth of citizen organisations at all levels of society'[4] has, consequently, been reflected in the human rights field, where human rights NGOs have frequently been at the forefront of social change.[5]

The nature of the work done by NGOs has naturally evolved in the last 50 years or so – the reach of human rights NGOs is both deeper and broader than ever. Many modern NGOs are 'sectional', specialising in particular areas of work, such as children's rights, refugees, women's rights and prisoners rights. Others are focused in a particular geographical area or region. Some are genuinely global NGOs – known as international or transnational NGOs. There are many NGOs concerned with human rights work within the boundaries of one particular State, and there has been a large growth in these sorts of organisation, often in newly democratic countries or those emerging from conflict.[6]

However, the increasing world political consciousness of rights has also been brought about by the NGO community, which carries out education work with a view to heightening the awareness of the international standards among the general public. The stream of reports, policy statements and press releases on a range of rights concerns emanating from the NGO community has also helped to raise the attention paid to human rights generally.[7] But what are the trends of the past few decades, and what signposts do they provide for the work by NGOs in the 21st century? How important will the work of NGOs become and what are the difficulties faced by such organisations?

DEFINITIONS

A human rights non-governmental organisation (NGO) is a private association which devotes significant resources to the promotion and protection of human rights, which is independent of both government and political groups that seek direct political power, and which does not itself seek such power ...[8]

---

4   Rice, AE and Ritchie, C, 'Relationships between international non-governmental organisations and the United Nations' (1995) 47 Transnational Assoc 254.

5   The primary example being South Africa. See Singh, M, 'The role of civil society in promoting democratic development: some aspects of the South African debate', in *The Role of Voluntary Organisations in Emerging Democracies: Experience and Strategies in Eastern and Central Europe and in South Africa*, 1993, Denmark: Danish Centre for Human Rights/Institute of International Education.

6   See Boli, J and Thomas, GM, 'World culture in the world polity: a century of international non-governmental organisation' (1997) 62 Am Soc Rev 171.

7   See Weissbrodt, D, 'The contribution of international non-governmental organisations to the protection of human rights', in Meron, T (ed), *Human Rights in International Law: Legal and Policy Issues*, 1989, Oxford: Clarendon.

8   Wiseberg, L, 'Protecting human rights activists and NGOs' (1991) 13 HRQ 525, p 529.

NGOs are voluntary organisations, made up of individuals who subscribe to similar principles and ideas. But NGOs are not political parties – indeed, a distance from party politics is essential if an NGO is to have credibility. Many NGOs take pride in that distance from party politics, not least because part of the *raison d'être* of an NGO is to campaign for the implementation of universal human rights standards. It is all the more difficult to do so if clearly aligned with a factional position. As Wiseberg observes:

> The foundation of human rights monitoring is political non-partisanship. The legitimacy and credibility of a human rights organisation rest in large part on the objectivity of its fact finding and the integrity with which impartially applies international human rights standards.[9]

Some NGOs may arise out of the concerns of one particular community or group, but such an NGO does not argue for specialist treatment for that group, but, rather, for the application of human rights standards to that group or community as well as to others in society. Thus, women's human rights groups, for example, do not argue for preferential treatment for their client group, but work as a result of their client group having been denied the benefit of the universal standards.

As well as the domestic or sectional NGOs, there are organisations which carry out activities in many countries:

> INGOs [international non-governmental organisations] are more or less authoritative transnational bodies employing limited resources to make rules, set standards, propagate principles and broadly represent 'humanity' vis à vis States and other actors. Unlike States, INGOs can neither make nor enforce law.[10]

The influence of these organisations is great: they frequently have good access to governments and international bodies such as the United Nations. In 1988, 6.3% of all INGOs were 'rights or welfare orientated',[11] with such as Amnesty International probably the most significant. They tend to be reasonably well resourced, especially in comparison with the smaller or sectional NGOs. Their capacity to produce reports or institute fact finding missions is, therefore, much greater and their status is substantial:

> Fifty years after the founding of the United Nations, transnational associations – commonly referred to as international non-governmental organisations or INGOs – have become major players on the international scene. The emergence during the past two decades of these organisations is one of the most striking global phenomena of the late 20th century ... [they] have become a significant third force in international systems, parallelling, although not yet equalling, the expanding role of inter-governmental organisations in the political sphere ...[12]

---

9   *Op cit*, Wiseburg, fn 8.
10 *Op cit*, Boli and Thomas, fn 6, p 172.
11 *Ibid*, p 183.
12 *Op cit*, Rice and Ritchie, fn 4, p 245.

The status and the legitimacy enjoyed by INGOs tend to be greater than those of the smaller, domestic NGOs. These larger INGOs frequently have greater political muscle, with their findings and reports often cited approvingly by governments. However, the scale of the global work encompassed by these INGOs sometimes means that it is the local NGOs which uncover first hand evidence of human rights abuses, and it is this work which the INGOs often rely upon.

NGO ACTIVITIES

Working at the international and national levels ... [NGOs] ... function as unofficial ombudsmen safeguarding human rights against governmental infringement, using such techniques as diplomatic initiatives, reports, public statements, efforts to influence the deliberations of intergovernmental human rights bodies, campaigns to mobilise public opinion and attempts to affect the foreign policy of some countries with respect to their relations with other countries that regularly commit human rights violations.[13]

The work done by human rights NGOs is various and diverse. Most of them carry out some form of information gathering and fact finding activities.[14]

The purpose of this kind of action is to record and present allegations of human rights abuses and it takes a number of forms – monitoring the activities of the State, statement taking, observing at a wide range of places and events – for example, at trials, in prisons, on the street and at demonstrations. It also involves the increasingly utilised 'Mission', which involves sending a team of trained representatives, often volunteers, to gather information and testimony in relation to human rights abuses. This is a technique that tends to be employed, although not exclusively, by regional or transnational NGOs investigating human rights concerns in particular countries. Whatever the method by which information is gathered, most NGOs seek to do so in an objective, methodical fashion. As Weissbrodt and McCarthy note:

NGOs employ a variety of techniques to determine the accuracy of information supplied to them, such as looking for circumstances which might cause the informant to be biased and testing for inconsistencies by careful questioning. In many cases, NGOs will attempt to corroborate the information acquired

13 *Op cit*, Weissbrodt and McCarthy, fn 2, pp 1–9.
14 See, eg, Dicker, R, 'Monitoring human rights in Africa' (1991) 29(3) J Mod African Studies 503; Beirne, M, *The Misrule of Law: A Report on the Policing of Events During the Summer of 1996 in Northern Ireland*, 1996, Belfast: CAJ; Winter, J, *Conditions in Detention in Castlereagh*, 1995, London: BIRW; Asia Watch, *Silencing All Critics: Human Rights Violations in Singapore*, 1989, New York: Asia Watch; Amnesty International, *Mexico 'Disappearances': A Black Hole in the Protection of Human Rights* (AMR 41/05/98), 1998, London: AIUK.

through their fact finding efforts...Corroboration is also facilitated by exchanges of information among NGOS with different sources of information and areas of expertise.[15]

The purpose of this work is not simply fact finding; the information obtained is used by the organisation to produce policy statements, reports, press and lobbying material. The information is given to governments and international bodies and used in campaigns and shared with other NGOs. The incidence of this kind of activity is indicated by 'human rights reporting' having increased immensely in the past quarter of a century.[16]

The information gathered and the networks engendered by such an exercise can also constitute early warning systems, formal or informal. Such systems alert other governments, international organisations, the media and other NGOs to possible future human rights abuses. Increasingly, the information gathered by NGOs in this fashion is being seen as essential if the international human rights bodies are to function properly. Furthermore, the trend is towards NGOs working in partnership with each other to bring human rights concerns to international attention. Such partnerships can be formal, by way of affiliation,[17] or informal, through casual contacts and unofficial networks. Many NGOs encourage individuals to act upon the concerns they raise by writing or e-mailing governments, heads of State, international bodies and the media.[18]

Different relationships

Non-governmental organisations of all types face different sets of relationships with policy formers, the media, government and international bodies, all requiring different approaches. Whilst issuing a press release may be a routine task, it can be difficult to get such a press release carried in the national press, or the issue it highlights raised on the broadcast media. Similarly, sending a report to a government minister is something regularly done by NGOs, but meeting with the minister and persuading him or her of the need to address the issues raised in it is much more arduous.

Many of these difficulties are made more acute by problems with funding and status. NGOs have fewer resources and less influence than the

---

15 *Op cit*, Weissbrodt and McCarthy, fn 2, p10.

16 See *op cit*, Posner, fn 1.

17 Such as through the International Federation of Human Rights (often known by its French acronym, FIDH) It was founded in 1922 by a number of European human rights NGOs and 'was the first international organisation created to defend human rights': International Federation of Human Rights, *About FIDH*, 1997, Paris: FIDH.

18 Eg, the Lawyers Committee's 'Lawyer to Lawyer Network', which alerts a network of judges, advocates and other legal professionals around the world to human rights violations against lawyers.

international bodies. NGO funding is often cyclical – a perennial problem in most voluntary organisations – and this has a detrimental effect on planning and goal setting. There are advantages, however, not least that NGOs, particularly those which are local and domestic, are less trammelled by the ties of diplomacy and protocol. Domestic NGOs are effectively freer to voice their criticisms than many IGOs or, indeed, some of the larger international NGOs. That, of course, brings the risk that the government under scrutiny will respond by harassing or even abusing human rights monitors and activists, a particular problem in many parts of the world. This risk is more acute when the status or the awareness of the domestic NGO is low – it is much easier to victimise or dismiss an NGO if it does not have consultative status at the United Nations:

> Consultative status is important to NGOs. It is what allows them to participate by making oral or written statements in the Commission and its Sub-Commission. It also entitles them to have some statements circulated as official United Nations documents, to receive United Nations documentation, and to be invited to United Nations meetings in their area of competence. And, finally, it conveys a degree of legitimacy and prestige in a place where such things are extremely important.[19]

There has been a recognition at international level of the difficulties faced by many NGOs in monitoring and reporting human rights – some governments are openly hostile to NGOs and engage in harassment and abuse of activists. The long awaited United Nations Human Rights Defenders Declaration was finally adopted in March 1998 by the 13th session of the working group of the United Nations Commission on Human Rights in Geneva.[20] It now must be adopted by ECOSOC and the General Assembly before it becomes a final United Nations Declaration. The draft declaration guarantees a number of rights, among them, the right to belong to NGOs, to gather information and to lobby 'to participate in peaceful activities against violations of human rights and fundamental freedoms'.[21] Significantly, it recognises the right to complain of human rights violations and to have an effective remedy, requiring that: 'The State shall conduct a prompt and impartial investigation or ensure that an inquiry takes place whenever there is reasonable ground to believe that a violation of human rights and fundamental freedoms has occurred in any territory under its jurisdiction.'[22]

---

19 Wiseberg, L, 'NGO self-examination is the missing link in ECOSOC Review' (1994) 2(3) Human Rights Tribune 11.
20 Draft Declaration adopted by consensus, E/CN 4/1998/WG 6/CRP 1/Rev I, 4 March 1998.
21 United Nations Human Rights Defenders Declaration, Arts 5(b), 6(1), 12(1) and 8(2), respectively.
22 *Ibid*, Art 9(5).

Many governments refrain from harassing human rights activists and tolerate the existence of the NGOs, but are openly critical of their actions. Some of these governments employ covert tactics in monitoring the activities of human rights NGOs. Others pay lip service to the notion of a thriving NGO community, but rarely take on board the criticisms and suggestions proffered by them. Fewer still work in partnership with the NGO community. Many governments display a number of these reactions to domestic NGOs.

There are, however, encouraging signs that some governments are beginning to recognise the worth of the role played by NGOs. In some countries, this is fuelled by the influx of some former NGO activists into government.[23] In other instances, it is the result of a conscious policy shift. For example, in the UK, the change of administration in May 1997 prompted such a policy change, when Robin Cook, the new Foreign Secretary said:

> Our foreign policy must have an ethical dimension and must support the demands of other peoples for the democratic rights on which we insist for ourselves. We will put human rights at the heart of our foreign policy.[24]

The UK Government's first annual human rights report refers in detail to the role of NGOs and others in civil society in promoting human rights and helping to shape government policy.[25] It remains to be seen, however, whether such a commitment will be delivered in full in practice.

This can manifest itself in a number of ways, such as government ministers signing up to an NGO campaign.[26] It may encompass a government contribution towards the cost of NGOs attending international events.[27] Some

23 Most obviously in South Africa, where many members of government are former NGO activists. There are other examples. The US Assistant Secretary of State for Democracy, Human Rights and Labor, John Shattuck, was formerly executive director of the American Civil Liberties Union and vice chair of the US section of Amnesty International. One former UK cabinet minister, Harriet Harman, was previously Legal Officer with the National Council for Civil Liberties (Liberty).

24 (1997) *The Times*, 13 May.

25 'Civil society', in Foreign and Commonwealth Office/Department for International Development, *Annual Report On Human Rights*, 1998, London: HMSO, Chap 4.

26 As Secretary of State for Northern Ireland, Dr Mo Mowlam, did recently, when signing up for Amnesty International's Charter (see Judge, T, 'Agreement in talks can be resolved, says Mitchell' (1998) *Irish News*, 31 March). The irony of this move, given the findings of many Amnesty International reports on the UK Government's record in Northern Ireland, was underlined when, some days later, the United Nations' special rapporteur on the independence of lawyers and the judiciary published a scathing report attacking the behaviour of members of the police and judiciary in Northern Ireland. See *Report of the special rapporteur on the independence of judges and lawyers, Mr Param Cumaraswamy, submitted pursuant to Commission on Human Rights Resolution 1997/23, Addendum: Report on the mission of the Special Rapporteur to the United Kingdom of Great Britain and Northern Ireland*, E/CN 4/1998/39/Add 4 1997.

27 Eg, the Irish Government assisted a delegation from domestic NGOs attend the NGO Forum at the UN World Conference on Human Rights in Vienna. *Challenges and Opportunities Abroad: The White Paper on Foreign Policy*, 1996, Dublin: Government of Ireland, Chap 8, para 8.74.

governments have even formalised the contact – the Irish Government recently set up a Joint Standing Committee between the relevant government department, NGOs and human rights experts 'for a regular exchange of views'.[28] In the UK, the recent experience at the Beijing conference on women suggests that, even before the change from Conservative to Labour administrations, there was an awareness of the need to work with NGOs. The UK Government delegation seemed keen to acknowledge the British NGOs present, arranging briefings and a reception, as well as taking account of drafting suggestions. As Julia Hausermann remarked:

> ... the commitment to NGO contact was particularly strong ... The three ministers who participated in Beijing constantly stressed the importance they attached to NGOs, and called on them to monitor implementation of the Platform for Action. The opportunity that I was given to play an active role in the negotiations was much welcomed by the human rights NGOs, whose views I was able to draw on in negotiating the parental rights paragraphs and contributing to the negotiations on sexual and reproductive rights.[29]

Undoubtedly, the work of human rights NGOs has contributed significantly towards such policy changes, creating an atmosphere where governments are keen to be seen as supportive of human rights standards.

Not all policy shifts are specific to the human rights community, but many impact upon it. In the UK, for example, there has been a trend towards partnership between government and the voluntary sector in many areas other than human rights – such as welfare work and community development. In many respects, this shift has been driven by economics rather than idealism – it is more cost effective in many instances for the State to fund activities by NGOs than to do them itself. But, for many human rights NGOs, this is not an option. Many refuse to take money from government, arguing that it would undermine their independence. In other cases, much of the work done by human rights NGOs – that of monitoring the activities of the State – is not something the State regards as worth investing money in. But the move towards partnership in human rights education may be a precursor of future trends.

There are many benefits in an improved relationship with government, but there are dangers too. In South Africa, there has been a transformation in NGO relations with the State since the advent of democracy. In many cases, people who had been actively involved in NGO work became members of the government or senior civil servants, and the advantages of this kind of awareness and experience in government is obviously helpful. But this brings its own difficulties: according to many observers this has precipitated a crisis

---

28 *Challenges and Opportunities Abroad: The White Paper on Foreign Policy*, 1996, Dublin: Government of Ireland, Chap 8, para 8.75.

29 Hausermann, J, 'Note on NGO participation in the UK delegation', in Sex and Race Equality Division, Department for Education and Employment, *Report of the UK Delegation on the UN Fourth World Conference on Women*, 1996, London: HMSO, Annex 5.

in the South African NGO community, as funding, which previously went to NGOs, goes directly to the new South African government. As one group of observers noted: '... a swathe of NGOs – and particularly those in the field of educational reform and human rights – face a far less certain future.'[30]

The South African government has attempted to address this by setting up a central National Development Agency to help fund NGOs, but there has been some reservation expressed about the amount of money available though the agency.[31] The loss of talented, experienced and able personnel has also wrought an unwelcome effect. There has been a real effort to work in partnership with NGOS, but for some in the human rights sector it has not always been an edifying experience.[32] Nonetheless, the experience of the transition to democracy and participation in it has shifted the style of NGOs from accusation and protest towards partnership.

The role of NGOs, and human rights experts associated with them, was crucial in South Africa in the drafting of the new constitution, and there are indicators from other parts of the world that this is not a unique experience. In Canada, human rights NGOs have been exercising influence over policy and legislation, with varying degrees of effectiveness for quite some time. 'In the history of Canadian human rights legislation, interest groups have either been a leading ... or a contributing force in the development of the legislation'.[33] In Northern Ireland, contributions from domestic human rights NGOs influenced sections of the North Commission's Report on Parades and Marches[34] and reframed the debate generally in terms of rights.[35] This tendency towards partnership between NGOs and governments is an emerging and important one. As UNICEF records in respect of the Convention on the Rights of the Child:

> ... [NGOs] are one of the main engines by which the treaty can be translated into action. In several countries, NGOs are working with government to help draft legislation and to disseminate the basic messages of the Convention.[36]

---

30 Interfund is a consortium of European NGOs formed to contribute to development through education and training. For programmes and background, see website http://www.pcb.co.za/interfund/frames.html.

31 The National Development Agency is expected to begin operating in mid-1999. (Eveleth, A, 'Too little, too late for NGOs' (1998) *South Africa Mail & Guardian*, 18 September.

32 Interview with Ntombi Mosikare, co-ordinator of the Khulamani Project, Johannesburg, South Africa, 16 March 1998.

33 Howe, RB and Andrade, MJ, 'The reputations of human rights commissions in Canada' (1994) 9 Canadian J Law Soc 1, p 4. See, also, Howe, RB, 'The evolution of human rights policy in Ontario' (1994) 24 Canadian J Pol Sci 787.

34 North Commission, *The Report of the Independent Review of Parades and Marches*, 1997, London: HMSO. See, in particular, Chap 6.

35 See Hegarty, A, 'Observing the rule of law: experiences from Northern Ireland' (1997) 66 Fordham L Rev 647, pp 675–76.

36 UNICEF, *The Progress of Nations 1996*, New York: UNICEF.

It is clear, therefore, that the altering nature of the sets of relationships engaged in by NGOs have prompted changes in the work they carry out. Further, the work has itself evolved, moving from purely information and research based activities to campaigning, lobbying and engaging policy makers at every level.

DEVELOPING STRATEGIES

The dynamic contribution of the NGO community has heightened the profile of human rights issues ...[37]

If the escalation in the visibility and the concerns of domestic and international human rights NGOs has been a striking feature of the past quarter century, what has been perhaps less obvious has been the increasing coherence of the work carried out by NGOs. Whilst, at times, it can seem that there is a bewildering array of human rights organisations, clamouring in different voices for different ends,[38] underneath the din, there is a strong trend towards incisive and politic planning.

Increasingly, the work is both upwardly and downwardly strategic. The legitimisation of the NGO, as an increasingly valid mechanism for reporting human rights abuses and policy concerns to INGOs, is certainly the product of the actual work carried out by NGOs. But, it is also a result of NGO's thinking and working in a much more strategic fashion with opinion formers and policy makers.[39] The better use of international contacts, the improved interventions at the United Nations, the growing influence with certain governments, the popularisation of the rights discourse are all indications of just how far NGOs have travelled towards the goal of setting the agenda.

In the human rights field, there is widespread acknowledgment that NGOs all but drive the United Nations human rights bodies. Without NGO information, the Commission on Human Rights and its Sub-Commission on the Prevention of Discrimination and Protection of Minorities, and the United Nations special mechanisms and treaty-monitoring bodies, would all but grind to a halt.[40]

This has partly been achieved by NGOs becoming better at programming and managing their work than before: there has been a general trend in NGOs towards a more professional managerial culture. Many organisations engage

---

37 *Challenges and Opportunities Abroad: The White Paper on Foreign Policy*, 1996, Dublin: Government of Ireland, Chap 8, para 8.

38 Nowhere was this more obvious than at the NGO forum at the Vienna World Conference on Human Rights, which frequently appeared chaotic and disorganised. Author's own record and notes, June 1993.

39 See O'Brien, in this volume, Chap 14.

40 *Op cit*, Wiseberg, fn 19, pp 11–13.

in formal forward planning activities,[41] a process which allows space for more strategic thinking about activities and their purpose.

Human rights and capacity building

At the same time, there has been an upsurge in the incidence of work on the ground, partly as a result of the recognition that a strong and vibrant human rights NGO community contributes greatly towards 'capacity building' in countries emerging from conflict. Human rights NGOs with their value systems of respect, democracy and support for international norms, are crucially important in transitional and post conflict societies. This has meant that the boom in NGO activity globally has been paralleled in the last decade by a deliberately stimulated growth in NGOs in regions such as Southern Africa, Eastern Europe, the Balkans and Central America. It has been cogently argued that one of the best ways of protecting and advancing respect for human rights is in the strengthening of NGOs and civil society.[42]

Capacity building, defined as 'systematic action on building and enhancing the critical capacities needed to sustain growth and development'[43] is usually twin tracked: providing domestic NGOs with the skills and resources necessary to construct a dynamic and vibrant civil society, as well as assisting with their aims on a macro level. Sometimes, this takes the form of influencing domestic NGOs in setting their goals,[44] but it clearly also involves supporting organisations on the ground.

In Afghanistan, for example, the United Nations deliberately focused some effort on the promotion of domestic NGOs, aware that government and foreign NGOs, whilst contributing to emergency relief, were not assisting with local development. The United Nations Office of the Co-ordination of Humanitarian Affairs (UNOCHA) 'adopted a policy of actively encouraging and facilitating the development of Afghan NGOs'. It also registered and provided some funds for the NGOs. However, there were problems, and the

---

41 Edwards, M, 'Organisational learning in non-governmental organisations: what have we learned?' (1997) 17 Public Administration and Development 235, pp 241–42.

42 Welch, CE, *Protecting Human Rights in Africa: Roles and Strategies of Non-Governmental Organisations*, 1995, Philadelphia: Pennsylvania UP, pp 34, 40–47.

43 UN Economic Commission for Africa, *Progress Report on the Elaboration of a Framework Agenda for Building and Utilizing Critical Capacities in Africa, Addis Ababa, Ethiopia 24–28 April 1995/1–4 May 1995*, 1995, E/ECA/CM 21/5, p 1.

44 Brysk, A, 'Social movements in Argentina' (1993) Comparative Political Studies 259, pp 259–85, 278–79 and 281–82 (reflecting upon the role of international actors during the transition to democracy in Argentina).

process was criticised by existing domestic NGOs for failing to adequately vet the *bona fides* of organisations seeking registration and funding.[45]

The importance of NGOs in the democratisation process is clear elsewhere. The recent Northern Ireland Agreement contains a proposal to establish a 'Civic Forum' to perform a consultative role on economic, social and cultural matters with the devolved Assembly, and will 'comprise representatives of the business, trade union and voluntary sectors'.[46] In South Africa, the vitality of the NGO sector was crucial during transition. Many of the NGOs had been in existence for years, but the need to maintain civil society beyond transition was clear:

> ... the survival of the NGO sector will enhance the future of South Africa's fledgling democracy. NGOs and the civil society of which they form the core have a crucial opposition and watchdog role over government. If South Africa is to avoid the fate of so many other developing countries ... where fragile democracies have been subsumed by state corruption and renewed authoritarian practices, and in which the needs of the poor and marginalised are again ignored, the project of sustaining NGOs is a critical one.[47]

A bridge between policy and experience

One way in which NGOs contribute to such a process is by providing a link between communities and policy formers. NGOs are increasingly being seen as 'bridging organisations'.[48] They provide the necessary links between experience and theory, raising the concerns and the abuses of individuals and communities and channelling them into policies.

Most human rights NGOs record human rights abuses, and raise both the specific abuses themselves and the policy issues they provoke with INGOs, governments and others. This process of recording abuses, reporting them at national and international level and synthesising them into policy concerns affords a mechanism by which a detailed critique can be offered of State behaviour. Such a detailed analysis often controverts the official story presented by national governments and may offer the only serious alternative

---

45 'Afghanization: the promotion and registration of Afghan NGOs', in UNOCHA Lessons Learned Unit, 1998, *Afghanistan Report: Co-ordination in a Fragmented State*, OCHA Online, Afghanistan website http://www.reliefwebint./dha_ol/programs/United nationsocha/afgrpt/lessons.html.

46 *Agreement Reached in the Multi-Party Negotiations*, Cmnd 3883, 1998, Belfast: Northern Ireland Office (Good Friday Agreement), 10 April 1998, para 34.

47 Interfund website http://www.pcb.co.za/interfund/ frames.htm.

48 See, generally, Brown, LD, *Creating Social Capital: Non-governmental Developmental Organisations and Intersectional Problem Solving*, 1994, Boston: Institute for Development Research.

version available to INGOs.[49] This process also legitimises the experiences of those reporting abuses, who are often dismissed by governments as partisan or political. The intervention of the human rights NGO, particularly if it is by a domestic NGO that has better access to the reports, supported by a larger transnational NGO, is crucial.[50] It also importantly validates the work of the NGOs and enhances their credibility.[51] This in turn bolsters the work they are doing and protects the organisation and its members from harassment.

Whilst it is clear that NGOs have become more effective in their dealings with international bodies, there are still many difficulties. The official bureaucracy that is such a feature of the United Nations often collides with the energy and activism of the NGO community.[52] This is, perhaps, typified by the uproar caused when NGO representatives were ejected from the drafting committee during the Vienna World Conference. Earlier in the conference, the programme for the NGO Panel and Parallel Activities had been confiscated by the United Nations authorities.[53]

In some respects, the appointment of Mary Robinson as United Nations High Commissioner for Human Rights may begin to defuse some of this tension. Robinson, a former president of Ireland, is a highly regarded human rights lawyer with a background in commitment to NGOs.[54] Furthermore, there are signs that the United Nations is beginning to take on board some of the criticisms of its process vis à vis NGOs.

The Vienna Declaration and Programme of Action, agreed at the United Nations World Conference on Human Rights in June 1993, specifically recognised the important role of NGOs in the promotion and protection of human rights. Despite the chaotic nature of many of the negotiations and parallel activities, a number of important developments have arisen directly from the Vienna conference. It is arguable that ECOSOC's recently improved arrangements for consulting with NGOs would not have occurred without the

---

49   As Stephen Ryan has observed:

> ... some non-governmental organisations can bring specific cases to the attention of the international community. Aid and charity bodies, human rights organisations and church groups may investigate and publicise abuses during inter-communal conflict. Some of these bodies may also have consultative status at the UN, where they can take up the cause of communal groups that may not otherwise have an international voice.

Ryan, S, 'Nationalism and ethnic conflict', in White, B, Little, R and Smith, M (eds), *Issues in World Politics*, 1997, Basingstoke: Macmillan, pp 154–78.

50   See *op cit*, Hegarty, fn 35, pp 673–75 for an illustration of this.

51   See Boli, J and Thomas, GM, 'World culture in the world polity: a century of international non-governmental organisation' (1997) 62 Am Soc Rev 171, pp 179–80.

52   See, generally, Weiss, TG and Gordenker, L (eds), *NGOs, the United Nations and Global Governance*, 1996, Colorado: Reinner.

53   Dias, C, 'Five not 25 should be our post-Vienna motto' (1993) 2(2) Human Rights Tribune 31, pp 31–32.

54   See Horgan, J, *Mary Robinson: An Independent Voice*, 1997, Dublin: O'Brien.

Vienna Declaration. The revised Resolution 1296 permits domestic NGOs to apply for consultative status at ECOSOC and its subsidiary bodies, among them the Commission on Human Rights. Whilst there are many criticisms of the new procedure,[55] it is an improvement on the previous status quo. It allows for the possibility of the opening up of many United Nations processes to domestic NGOs, provided, of course, that they have the resources to follow up on consultative status, once achieved.

The newly amended procedure still bars formal negotiation, but as Rice and Ritchie note:

> The current limit to NGO involvement is customarily identified as prohibiting a direct NGO role in negotiations among the United Nations member governments to reach policy consensus. But in practice this limit is quite evidently eroding. This is true not only in an indirect sense – that is, through the growing practice of including NGO representatives on the national delegations of Member States – but directly through the actual participation of NGO leaders in the corridor discussions and 'non-meeting' meetings which characterise much of the United Nations negotiating process ... NGO's roles have been so vital in so many such instances that it is difficult to see how governments can sensibly cut themselves off from such critical intellectual and specialist input.[56]

This growing, if perhaps slightly grudging, acknowledgment of the contribution made by NGOs through the increasing formalisation of that contribution represents a significant shift towards incorporating the work done by NGOs into the activities of the international organisations, such as the United Nations.

Partnerships and networking

An increasingly common feature of the work done by NGOs is their capacity for networking. Human rights activists have learned, from the internal conflicts in Africa, in Central and Southern America and, indeed, in Western Europe, that domestic monitoring of human rights needs to be supplemented by networking outside of, and beyond, the State – and not just at the United Nations level. As Brysk notes:

> Transitional human rights networks can rarely stop State repression, but human rights movements can use transnational networks to survive, save lives, delegitimise the State and foster new mechanisms and institutions during a transition.[57]

---

55 *Op cit*, Wiseberg, fn 19, pp 7–11.
56 *Op cit*, Rice and Ritchie, fn 4, p 258.
57 *Op cit*, Brysk, fn 44, p 261.

Networking can also pool limited resources and focus on particular concerns. This was the route taken by a coalition of women's groups during the Vienna United Nations World Conference on Human Rights, when they organised a day long tribunal on human rights abuses suffered by women around the globe. The tribunal heard testimony from many women, including those who had suffered domestic violence, rape victims from Bosnia and victims of forced prostitution in Japan.[58]

Many of the networks, formal and informal, have involved larger NGOs in sponsoring and promoting the concerns of smaller NGOs in other parts of the less industrialised world. Hence, many of the concerns articulated about US foreign policy in Central America, were raised firstly in the US by domestic NGOs or church groups, who frequently assisted Central American human rights activists in visiting the US and raising their concerns there. In Africa, especially during the anti-apartheid struggle prior to democracy, many non-African NGOs provided help and support, mainly through affiliation to the global anti-apartheid campaign.[59] The advice and support provided by larger NGOs extends beyond simple support for the aims and objectives of the domestic NGO – it involves training, technical support, skills transfer and help in planning.[60] Such activities and the campaigns of the domestic NGOs employ 'the new social movement logic of persuasion to deflate the State's power capabilities by undermining its mandate in the eyes of domestic and international supporters'.[61]

The partnership between the domestic NGO, which has the local contacts, the resources and the 'grassroots' credibility to gather the information on the ground and the larger or transnational NGO, with the international contacts, presence and credibility is a useful model. In Ireland and the UK, domestic human rights organisations work together as part of the British-Irish Rights panel of the FIDH.[62] Formed in 1994, the British-Irish panel comprises Liberty, the Scottish Council for Civil Liberties, the Irish Council for Civil Liberties (based in Dublin) and the Committee on the Administration of Justice (based in Belfast). It meets a number of times each year and agrees areas and avenues of common interest. It works closely as a group with the FIDH, with Amnesty International and two of the major US based human rights NGOs, The Lawyers' Committee on Human Rights and Human Rights Watch. This allows for shared goal setting in common areas and a pooling of resources and

---

58 Comeau, P, 'Women succeed in Vienna where others fail' (1993) 2(2) Human Rights Tribune 22, pp 22–24.

59 See Minty, AS, 'The anti-apartheid movement and racism in South Africa', in Wiletts, P (ed), *Pressure Groups in the Global System*, 1982, London: Frances Pinter, pp 28–45.

60 *Op cit*, Brysk, fn 44, p 277 (noting that the US based Lawyers Committee for Human Rights 'shaped the goals and methods of the legal arm of the Argentine human rights movement'.)

61 *Ibid*, p 275.

62 See *op cit*, International Federation of Human Rights, fn 17.

activities on certain issues – from the co-sponsoring and organisation of seminars and conferences to common submissions to IGOs.[63] Because the panel and the constituent organisations have good links with larger international NGOs, it allows for better access to the international bodies, especially the United Nations and to the international debate in general.

Nonetheless, there are tensions between NGOs, fuelled in part by the global north-south divide. Commenting on the Vienna conference, Wiseberg observes that:

> ... the 'have not' NGOs challenged what are termed the Geneva or New York NGO 'mafias', those with deep roots in the United Nations machinery. Having headquarters in Europe and America translates into a lack of interest/and or understanding of developing world issues, they argued, and an elitist attitude when it came to the workings of the United Nations. As well, southern NGOs were tired of having decisions made 'in their best interests' by northern based groups.[64]

The pattern of increasing internationalisation of domestic human rights concerns does present a number of problems, particularly for NGOs with very limited resources, principally outside Western Europe and North America. Nonetheless, the greater effort being devoted to human rights reporting at the United Nations and elsewhere does provide a sharper focus through which to view the state of human rights protection throughout the world. A clear challenge for the NGO community is to find ways in which the expertise that has been developed in some regions can be shared and transferred elsewhere. In certain regions, the effect of skills and knowledge transfer is emerging: as domestic NGOs learn from larger and more intentional organisations, the pattern of activities engaged in changes. The ways in which NGOs monitor the State become more creative and the use to which information is being put evolves.

NEW CHALLENGES

There has been a clear shift towards lobbying and engaging policy makers on the domestic level. For some organisations it has meant a move towards employing professional staff and away from membership based activities. After the surge in consciousness raising activities during the 1970s and 1980s, there has been an evolution towards the better and more strategic use of the international human rights machinery. This, in itself, has triggered a more effective networking operation: by pooling resources to access the United

---

63 See Committee on the Administration of Justice, 'Working with others', in *Annual Report*, 1995, Belfast: CAJ, p 3.
64 *Op cit*, Wiseberg, fn 19, pp 11–13.

Nations and the other international bodies, smaller NGOs exchange information and transfer skills.

But, increased human rights reporting at an international level is not an end in itself: its purpose is to bring to an end the abuses themselves. A major challenge facing NGOs in the next 20 years or more will be how to begin to use their expertise to prevent human rights abuses. There is some evidence that overt monitoring by NGOs deters States from committing abuses.[65] But, there are many places in the world where overt monitoring is not possible, and there are many governments which seem able to dismiss easily United Nations criticism of their human rights records.[66] There are immense problems with the United Nations machinery itself, highlighted perhaps best by the conflict in Rwanda.[67] Despite the fact that human rights monitors and others warned of a developing conflict with potential for violence, the international response was deeply flawed:

> The issue is not better quantitative data or formal modelling. More simply, the United Nations lacks a system for drawing on existing information sources, in the region and outside, from specialists in state agencies, academic institutions, rights monitoring agencies, and the various agencies of the United Nations itself. The United Nations lacks a specialised unit without operational responsibilities, for analysing such information and translating that analysis into evolving strategic options that can be channelled directly to the Secretary General. Both the United Nations and NGOs failed to relate human rights monitoring to analysis of the development of social conflict and, hence, to assess the direction of events.[68]

It is clear that the status and the influence of NGOs have been increasing since the 1960s. This is due, in some measure, to the increase in the number and range of activities of NGOs during that period, but it is also a product of the increasingly effective and strategic work carried out by human rights NGOs, especially, but not exclusively, at the United Nations. This growing authority is remarkable given that NGOs have no legal power even to set standards, let alone exercise sanctions. They are voluntary organisations, largely self-regulating, with no formal external source of legitimacy. Yet, as Boli and Thomas remark, 'they act as if they were authorised in the strongest possible terms ... [their] authority is thus informal – cultural, not organisational'.[69]

---

65 See Beirne, M, 'Observations about observing' (1996) *JustNews*, September, p 1.

66 See *op cit*, Cumaraswamy, fn 26.

67 See *Rwanda: Death, Despair and Defiance*, 1995, London: African Rights. An excellent journalistic account is found in Keane, F, *Season of Blood*, 1995, London: Penguin.

68 Eriksson, J, *The International Response to Conflict and Genocide: Lessons from the Rwanda Experience*, Synthesis Report, 1996, Copenhagen: Steering Committee of the Joint Evaluation of Emergency Assistance to Rwanda. The report recommends, among other things, a more effective early warning system and the establishment of a unit for strategic analysis of conflicts.

69 *Op cit*, Boli and Thomas, fn 6, p 181.

However, this growing status cannot be confused with very great influence. In many ways, human rights monitoring and reporting still only marginally affect governments. What is necessary is for NGOs to find ways in which they can begin to fundamentally alter government policy and practice. In some respects this will only happen when governments themselves recognise the value of involving NGOs in designing and implementing policies. There are some indications that this is beginning to happen, but it is only the glimmer of a trend: there is still a vast gap between what NGOs want and what governments do. There is still an immense sense of frustration throughout the NGO community at the behaviour and attitude of governments – even those which profess to support the cause of human rights.

CONCLUSION

> ... the initial and most widespread battle for many human rights occurs in individual psychology. [70]

Perhaps the single greatest challenge facing NGOs in the next century will be to translate the immense growth in their expertise and access into the actual redress of wrongs and the prevention of human rights abuses. It is still the case that the experience of human rights abuses – often appalling atrocities – on the ground does not frequently translate into a finding of wrongdoing by the international machinery set up to protect universal standards.[71] This is despite the exhortations of many guidelines and 'soft law'.

The Queensland Guidelines for Bodies Monitoring Respect for Human Rights During States of Emergency, for example, require treaty bodies such as the United Nations Human Rights Committee to 'actively seek out' information provided by NGOs.[72] The Guidelines specifically recognise the role played by NGOs, stating that:

> NGOs tend to specialise by region or by the types of human rights abuse they seek to expose and prevent, and this specialisation has the advantage of enhancing the depth of information they are able to develop ... [and]... promotes long term work against particular abuses ...[73]

---

70 Welch, CE, *Protecting Human Rights in Africa: Roles and Strategies of Non-Governmental Organisations*, 1995, Philadelphia: Pennsylvania UP, p 291.

71 Although the UN's recent decision to set up an International Criminal Court may begin to alter this. See Willan, P, 'War crimes court vote goes against Washington' (1998) *Irish Times*, July 18.

72 ILA, *Report of the 64th Conference held at Queensland*, 1990, Principle 3, pp 12–13, 232–36.

73 *Ibid*, p 19.

The contribution of NGOs to the global and domestic protection and defence of human rights has grown greatly in the past 25 years, partly because of an increased consciousness generally of the importance of the universal standards. This consciousness is itself a product both of the existence of those standards themselves and the work done by the treaty bodies. Increasingly, it is also the result of the activities of NGOs in investigating, reporting and insisting upon recognition of the continuing tragedies engendered by those abuses. Whether it is the mass murder of Rwanda, the oppression of the old South Africa, or the assault of a teenager in a holding centre on the outskirts of Belfast, those experiences have been made the concern of the world largely, though not entirely, because of the work of NGOs. The next century will no doubt see a deepening of that work and the challenge for NGOs will be to oblige governments, the treaty bodies and all other international actors to address each of those experiences and acknowledge every one of them as transgressions against the standards first agreed more than 50 years ago in the wake of the human rights atrocity of the holocaust. We are now at the stage where most governments accept on paper the need to honour those standards: the next step is to get governments to actually honour them in practice. That is still quite a distance away.

CHAPTER 16

UNFINISHED BUSINESS?
LIBERTY'S CAMPAIGN FOR A BILL OF RIGHTS[1]

Liz Parratt

INTRODUCTION

The Human Rights Act 1998 represents a significant shift in our constitutional arrangements, by incorporating the European Convention on Human Rights into UK law. For the first time ever, we will be able to look to our own domestic courts to enforce the civil and political rights which lie at the very core of human rights philosophy, ending the reliance on common law freedoms which sets us apart from nearly all modern democracies.

As a Bill of Rights, the European Convention is far from perfect: the limitations it places on rights are too broad, and the anti-discrimination provisions too narrow. It was drafted half a century ago, and thus some rights are missing altogether[2] Nevertheless, incorporation represents a new departure for our common law tradition. Most human rights NGOs seek to identify this as the beginning of a process, rather than an end. In an ideal world, it would be a prelude to widespread consultation on a second stage, modern, indigenous Bill of Rights. But this will not be achieved overnight and there is a range of opinion among campaigners, lawyers, academics and others about what it will take. 1999 is, therefore, a uniquely appropriate time to try to 'take stock'.

Liberty's current position as one of the leading organisations in the incorporation project is relatively recent. Although the organisation had adopted a policy supporting incorporation back in 1977,[3] this lay dormant

---

1   According to Ira Glasser, Executive Director of the American Civil Liberties Union (ACLU) in a speech to the ACLU Conference in June 1995, 'Liberty will always be unfinished business' – a definition which seems equally appropriate to the human rights movement in this country, as it does to campaigns for rights and freedoms in the US.

   The author would like to thank John Wadham, Director of Liberty, Andrew Puddephat, Director of Charter 88, and Francesca Klug, Research Fellow at Kings College London for their assistance with this chapter. All three were instrumental in the campaign to incorporate the ECHR from the beginning, and this chapter draws very substantially on interviews with each of them held in early 1998. Thanks, also, to Zoe Gillard for assistance with research.

2   For an account of the Convention's limitations, see Wadham, J, 'Why incorporation of the European Convention on Human Rights is not enough', in Gordon, R and Wilmot, R (eds), *Human Rights in the UK*, 1996, London: OUP.

3   Klug, F, 'Introduction', in *A People's Charter*, 1991, London: Civil Liberties Trust.

throughout the 1980s – indeed, some staff and members of the governing body were even quite hostile to it.[4] It has only been at the centre of Liberty's thinking for around eight years and, during that time, the idea gained sufficient momentum to become one of the first initiatives introduced by the new Labour Government, with the Human Rights Act published within months of their election. This is quite a swift success. Was it just a case of being in the right place at the right time with the right idea?

Campaigning for changes in government policy is at best an inexact science, for a number of reasons. First and most obviously, governments in general are reluctant to acknowledge publicly the influence of what they call 'special interest groups'. The current Labour administration is no exception. Secondly, the political and cultural environment in which NGOs operate is necessarily complex. The combination of Westminster, Whitehall, 'the Left', in all its mainstream and minority groupings, the many strands of 'public opinion' and their relationship with print and broadcast media, grass roots activism, and other phenomena, create an environment in which tracing cause and effect is not always straightforward. Finally, those of us who spend our working lives trying to change government policy will inevitably draw on a diversity of perspectives – whether personal, political, or methodological – in our retrospective reflections on how changes have been secured. In all the impassioned internal debate that drives NGOs through crises and victories alike, the organisation that can delineate a clear, objective, critical and consensual evaluation of its own history and its agency in the world is a genuine rarity.

Thus, this chapter seeks neither to provide a case study of 'how to do it', nor a definitive account of cause and effect. Instead, I have tried to explore the background to Liberty's campaign for the incorporation of the ECHR and some of the factors which may have helped the Government reach the starting line on domestically enforceable rights. This is done in the hope that it might shed some light on the often underestimated, little understood and rarely scrutinised role of NGOs in the political scene.

This chapter concentrates almost exclusively on the work of Liberty, the National Council for Civil Liberties.[5] Although Liberty has been one of the leading organisations in the campaign to incorporate the ECHR since the early 1990s, the Human Rights Act 1998 is not the result of Liberty's work alone, and the necessarily narrow scope of this chapter should not be taken to suggest this. It is vitally important to stress that the Institute of Public Policy Research (IPPR), Charter 88, Justice, and the Human Rights Incorporation project at Kings College London have also been closely involved in

---

4   Andrew Puddephat, interviewed 4 March 1998, and Francesca Klug, interviewed 24 February 1998.

5   The National Council for Civil Liberties was founded in 1934. In 1989, it shortened its name to Liberty. Thus, this chapter refers to NCCL up to 1989 and to Liberty subsequently.

influencing the current Government's plans. This has been the case both during the past year and whilst Labour was still in opposition: a more detailed exploration of the role of NGOs would encompass this. And, of course, Lord Anthony Lester of Herne Hill QC has been pressing successive governments to incorporate the ECHR for longer than most of us can remember.

BACKGROUND

The National Council for Civil Liberties was founded in 1934 by Ronald Kidd, a journalist who had been shocked to see the police using *agents provocateurs* during a hunger march. It has consistently had greater impact on the law and on public opinion than its numerical strength would suggest, and at the time of writing has around 7,000 members and 10 staff.

From early on, the three main forums used by NCCL to expose injustice and campaign to protect civil liberties have been Parliament, the courts and the media. It has challenged law and procedure in a range of areas on behalf of a disparate collection of individuals and groups: the unifying factor has been a threat to civil and/or political rights. In the 1930s, its main concern was the protection of freedom of speech and assembly, defending civil liberties against the fascists and monitoring the police's application of their new powers under the Public Order Act 1936. During the 1940s, it worked at protecting freedom within the context of extreme wartime emergency powers. In the 1950s, it focused on reforming mental health laws, resulting in the Mental Health Act 1959. In the 1960s, race and immigration became increasingly important, and by the 1970s, it had shifted its efforts to the repressive new measures adopted in Northern Ireland to counteract terrorism, and into new initiatives in the areas of gay equality and women's rights. And at the beginning of the 1980s, high profile campaigning and extraordinarily detailed and thorough lobbying resulted in significant improvements to the Police and Criminal Evidence Act 1984 (PACE).[6]

THE DARK AGES

The 1980s, however, swiftly became a political era which few campaigners and reformers remember with any degree of nostalgia or affection. Characterised by aggressive monetarism, widespread unemployment, a rapidly widening gulf of economic and social inequalities, the steady erosion

---

6   For a brief history of NCCL's first 60 years, see Dyson, B, *Liberty in Britain: A Diamond Jubilee History of NCCL*, 1994, London: Civil Liberties Trust.

of rights and freedoms, and perhaps most unforgivably, the deliberate, conscious and carefully planned creation of an underclass, the 1980s were the 'dark ages' of our recent political history.[7]

By 1985, legislation on police powers, nationality and trade union rights was already on the statute book. Restrictions soon followed on rights to demonstrate and picket, the rights of the press, of suspects, employees, local government staff, gay people and travellers. As Sarah Spencer, General Secretary of NCCL in the late 1980s, has remarked, 'My overwhelming impression of those years is just the sheer volume of work'.[8] The rare examples of progress – on data protection or equal pay, for example – were almost without exception due to pressure from Europe.[9]

As early as the miners' strike of 1983, the Government elected under Margaret Thatcher's leadership in 1979 had already accumulated the political forces necessary to take on the organised trade union movement. It proceeded to do so with considerable success: certainly by the second miners' strike, in 1988, it was virtually impossible to organise an effective industrial dispute and stay within the law.[10]

The relentless assaults on individual and collective rights affected NCCL itself. The organisation had always had strong connections with the independent left since its birth in 1934 – when it was founded by journalist Ronald Kidd, in response to the infiltration of hunger marches by police *agents provocateurs*. This overlap between a civil libertarian and left agenda has been a recurring theme throughout NCCL's existence until fairly recently – not least, of course, because historically the machinery of the State is in the hands of the right. By the early 1980s, a significant minority of the Executive Committee were still either leading trade union officials, Communist Party members, or both. The independent left influence within NCCL was quite strong, and separating this from the distinctive voice of an organisation whose aim was to promote *individual* rights was not always straightforward.[11]

---

7   Two of the best accounts of the erosion of individual rights and freedoms are Ewing, KD and Gearty, C, *Freedom Under Thatcher: Civil Liberties in Modern Britain*, 1990, London: Clarendon; and Thornton, P, *Decade of Decline: Civil Liberties in the Thatcher Years*, 1989, London: NCCL. For a broader critical account of Thatcherism, see Gamble, A and Wells, C (eds), *Thatcher's Law*, 1989, Cardiff: Cardiff UP.

8   Interview, in *Civil Liberty Agenda*, February 1994, 60th anniversary edn.

9   The Data Protection Act 1984 resulted from a Council of Europe Convention on Data Protection, and the Sex Discrimination Act 1986 was enacted to implement an EC Directive.

10 See Ewing, KD and Gearty, CA, *Democracy or a Bill of Rights?*, 1991, London: Society of Labour Lawyers, for a brief but useful account of industrial disputes and public order law in the 1980s, particularly the (then) new preventive powers in the Public Order Act 1986, as well as the use of Breach of the Peace powers by the police and restrictive bail conditions by magistrates to prevent individuals attending protests. For a more detailed account, see Alderson, J, Gostin, L, Martin, I, McCabe, S, Mason, C and Wallington, P, *Civil Liberties and the Miners Dispute*, 1984, London: NCCL.

11 Andrew Puddephat, interviewed 4 March 1998, and Francesca Klug, interviewed 24 February 1998.

Consequently, the miners' strike of 1984 had produced a dilemma for NCCL. In civil libertarian or human rights terms, it is difficult to defend physical intimidation on picket lines, and the issue of whether a closed shop is the only effective way to protect individual rights is debatable. Because Liberty had never challenged such practices in a more benign left wing climate, such as that prevailing in the 1970s, it found itself in a hopelessly difficult position. It is easy to observe in retrospect that the only proper approach would have been a principled neutrality. But, in the polarised climate of the times, this would have been an almost implausibly courageous position to take. NCCL could easily have lost significant political allies, supporters and members.[12]

Despite the recommendations made by the members of the independent inquiry set up by NCCL, and thoughtful and robust arguments mounted by the General Secretary Larry Gostin,[13] the organisation did not take that position. Instead, it opted to support trade union practices which many people believed to be incompatible with human rights thinking. While the organisation avoided the total collapse it had feared, it suffered its worst internal and political crisis ever. The liberals, the carefully cultivated conservative supporters, and the principal funders, all withdrew, leaving behind them an organisation seriously weakened and strained by internal disagreement.[14] By the late 1980s, years of relentless Government hostility to rights left NCCL's influence on the public and political agenda fairly low. It was in this climate – suffering the corrosive effect of internal problems and external threats – that NCCL realised it needed to change or die.

FROM LIBERTIES TO RIGHTS

For its first 50 years or so, NCCL was a straightforward civil libertarian organisation. As a mirror to our common law system in which rights are held to exist 'in the silence of the law' – unlike other continental jurisdictions – a civil libertarian tradition makes absolute sense. Although NCCL's Legal Department was increasingly using the European Convention in its litigation, as a way of pushing back the boundaries of rights, the organisation's campaigning and other work remained somewhat out of touch with international human rights thinking. It was isolated from any kind of

---

12 Andrew Puddephat, interviewed 4 March 1998, and Francesca Klug, interviewed 24 February 1998.
13 See *op cit*, Alderson *et al*, fn 10 and *Civil Liberty Agenda*, Newsletter of the NCCL, February 1985.
14 Andrew Puddephat, interviewed 4 March 1998, and Francesca Klug, interviewed 24 February 1998.

European perspective, in a way which Francesca Klug describes as 'Very English, but unself-consciously so'.[15]

But, the influence of Europe was increasingly difficult to ignore. In addition to the handful of gains brought by EC legislation, the European Convention on Human Rights had been the source of some improved safeguards to rights and freedoms in the 1980s. Because of proceedings under the Convention, the Government had agreed not to re-introduce interrogation techniques such as sleep deprivation, which had been used in Northern Ireland (*Ireland v UK*).[16] Mental patients under compulsory confinement had more rights and a fairer review procedure (*X v UK*).[17] Corporal punishment in State schools had been abolished (*Campbell and Cosans v UK*).[18] Other judgments meant that prisoners' rights had been extended, including the right of access to a lawyer (*Silver v UK*).[19] The laws of contempt, under which a ban was imposed on the *Sunday Times* thalidomide article, were held to be in violation of the Convention and were amended (*Sunday Times v UK*).[20] A judge's order imposing reporting restrictions about a case or restricting the public's access to court, was made subject to review by a higher court (*Hodgson v UK, Channel 4 v UK*).[21] By 1988, numerous UK laws or regulations had been repealed or amended as a result of proceedings under the Convention.[22] In Andrew Puddephat's words:

> It became clear that merely expressing concerns about civil liberties would no longer be enough: simply to be passive or content to respond to events would be a recipe for disaster. Liberty needed a positive vision as to how fundamental rights and freedoms should be guaranteed – something people could support. We needed a broader vision of how society should develop, and one which would extend our appeal beyond our traditional constituencies.[23]

The shift from civil liberties to human rights was catalysed by a number of changes. To observe that any government too secure in its exercise of power is likely to grow careless with the rights of its people is a cliché. But, in the 1980s,

---

15 Francesca Klug, interviewed 24 February 1998.

16 (1978) 2 EHRR 25.

17 (1981) 4 EHRR 188.

18 (1982) 4 EHRR 293.

19 (1983) 3 EHRR 475.

20 (1991) 14 EHRR 229.

21 (1987) 10 EHRR 503.

22 Of course, some of the decisions in Strasbourg had disappointed civil libertarians. For example, the trade union ban at GCHQ was upheld by the Commission (*Council of Civil Service Unions and Others v UK* (1987) 50 D & R 228), and the conviction of the publisher of the Little Red Schoolbook for obscenity was held not to violate the Convention (*Handyside v UK* (1971) 1 EHRR 737). See Hunt, P, *The European Convention on Human Rights*, NCCL Policy Paper 21/88, 1988, London: NCCL, which acknowledges this, while also drawing attention to the Convention's strengths.

23 Andrew Puddephat, interviewed 4 March 1998.

it was one that had an increasing resonance. It would have been difficult to find better evidence of the need for constitutional reform than the prospect of indefinite Conservative hegemony – which, by the early 1990s, had started to look like a real possibility. Furthermore, the argument that rights existed 'in the silence of the law' had never looked more unconvincing. It was increasingly easy to refute this merely by pointing to the evidence of the previous 10 years.

The Strasbourg human rights institutions, however, provided lawyers with a way of establishing rights, regardless of statute or Parliament – and this in turn influenced the rest of the organisation. According to John Wadham, who was then its Legal Officer:

> We had a whole variety of different concerns to get across to members of the public, journalists and policy makers, and we needed some kind of vehicle by which we could promote our views in a more philosophically coherent way. International jurisprudence was clearly a more reliable ideological tool against the abuse of rights than a manual of Liberty's own internal policy decisions.[24]

The newly established constitutional reform organisation Charter 88 had begun to succeed in springing constitutional issues onto the political agenda.[25] The appearance of a new 'competitor' (for want of a better word) spurred the organisation to a clearer definition of its own agenda, and of its own niche in the political ecosystem. Francesca Klug took over as Director of the Civil Liberties Trust in June 1989, and Andrew Puddephat took over as General Secretary in October of the same year: it would be difficult to overstate either the significance of a change in management in a small NGO, or the opportunities which such a change presents.

Francesca Klug had the opportunity to start thinking about international human rights instruments, and was surprised that human rights had not been more central to NCCL's approach:

> Human rights language is a whole philosophy – and, of course, it embraces civil liberties. But, civil liberties language on its own is a negative language, it doesn't have a whole narrative in such a complex way. Liberty wasn't really acting within a recognisable narrative except to say 'keep your tanks off my lawn'. We had to ask ourselves whether we wanted to be part of the international human rights movement, and if not, why not?[26]

In retrospect, this might seem surprising, as civil liberties are so clearly embraced by human rights, and even a relatively unsophisticated analysis

---

24 John Wadham, interviewed 25 May 1998.

25 Charter 88, a citizen's movement for democracy, was founded in 1988. Its wide ranging aims included a Bill of Rights, Freedom of Information, accountable government, fair votes, the reform of the House of Commons, a democratically elected second chamber, judicial and legal reform, redress for all State abuse, devolution of power, independence for local government, Parliaments for Scotland and Wales, and a written constitution.

26 Francesca Klug, interviewed 24 February 1998.

would allow that the State is not the only – nor, for many, the main – source of tyranny. But, given its history, it was not surprising that the organisation was prone to the traditional left anxieties about Bills of Rights. Many on the left have voiced fears about giving powers to the judiciary – seen by many as unelected, unaccountable representatives of a socially homogenous, privileged and politically conservative legal establishment. Similarly, there has been a resistance on the left to limiting the powers of government, thus arguably rendering it less effective and less able to carry out its own social and economic agenda.[27] So, first of all, Liberty had to set out to convince itself.

LIBERTY'S BILL OF RIGHTS: THE METHODOLOGY

The discussion of a Bill of Rights in the late 1980s had tended to regard it as just one element of a new constitutional settlement: together with electoral reform, a written constitution and a reformed upper house, it would automatically strengthen the rights of individuals.[28] Liberty, by contrast, set out to draft a Bill of Rights which would aim to strengthen rights as a first objective and could stand alone, and to identify which civil rights should be protected, who would benefit, and how.

This was always seen as a two stage process. It was particularly clear to Liberty's lawyers that the Convention would be a good start, but would not by any means be sufficient.[29] But, at least it already existed, and pressing for it to be incorporated into domestic law might, with a change of government, be a realistic proposition. A more modern, indigenous, up to date Bill of Rights would clearly be needed, but would always be a much longer term goal. And, of course, it would need to be consulted on widely in civil society during the process of drafting. Liberty decided that the best approach was to campaign for a two stage process. And to give the project real depth and conviction, set out to draft – and consult on – its own model Bill of Rights.[30]

Liberty's approach was similar to that already adopted by IPPR in their Bill of Rights: to draw on existing international sources such as the ECHR and

---

27 It is also worth noting that the long philosophical dispute between those who see rights and liberties as most successfully secured through 'the silence of the law' (on both the left and right of the political spectrum) is not necessarily replicated in the pro- and anti-camp on a Bill of Rights. See Ryan, A, 'The British, the American and rights', in Lacey, M and Haakonssen, K (eds), *A Culture of Rights: The Bill of Rights in Philosophy, Politics and Law, 1791 and 1991*, 1991, London: CUP; Klug, F, 'The role of a Bill of Rights in a democratic constitution' (1992) Liberty internal briefing, 3 July.

28 See Charter 88, 'The Charter', first published in (1988) *The Guardian*, 30 November.

29 *Op cit*, Wadham, fn 2.

30 Klug, F, *A People's Charter*, 1991, London: Civil Liberties Trust. A revised version has since been published: Klug, F, *A Bill of Rights*, 1991, London: Liberty.

the ICCPR and use what was best.[31] But, because Liberty had a more open mandate than IPPR, it was able to draw on a wider range of international treaties, as well as Bills of Rights in other jurisdictions, and then fill in the gaps from its own policy.[32]

Catch-all phrases such as 'national security' and 'protection of morals' – frequent grounds for limitation in the Convention – were removed, and replaced by tightly drawn exceptions, in every case based on the protections of the rights and freedoms of others. Significantly, in line with international jurisprudence, the Bill of Rights was drafted to apply to everyone, whether a citizen or not, who comes under UK jurisdiction. As the proposals in Liberty's Bill of Rights also involved somewhat increased judicial powers, it included plans for judicial reform.

Careful attention was paid to the process of drafting as well. Those involved were well aware that they were drafting a document which went to the very heart of what Liberty was all about. Thus, both the principle and detail of policy were comprehensively debated in a series of internal seminars which, over the course of a year, left no stone unturned. A range of other relevant NGOs was consulted, including the Joint Council for the Welfare of Immigrants, the Runnymede Trust, and the mental health group MIND. Liberty also took the critics of Bills of Rights very seriously. Far from dismissing opponents, staff acknowledged the potency of the arguments *against* enforceable rights, even inviting eminent critics such as Conor Gearty[33] to participate in the process by giving presentations to the staff on why their proposed solution would be wrong.

The greatest obstacle to securing political momentum behind a Bill of Rights was the issue of judicial entrenchment, which is the bedrock of left

---

31 This was a path which its sister organisation, the Committee for the Administration of Justice in Northern Ireland, had already taken. See Committee for the Administration of Justice in Northern Ireland, *Making Rights Count*, 1990, Belfast: CAJ. A revised version has since been issued.

32 In addition to the ECHR, sources for a People's Charter include the UN ICCPR; the UN Standard Minimum Rules for the Treatment of Prisoners; the Convention on the Rights of the Child; the Geneva Convention on the Status of Refugees; the International Labour Organisation Convention on the Right to Organise and Collective Bargaining; the Council of Europe's European Social Charter; the American Convention on Human Rights; the American Bill of Rights, and the Canadian Charter of Rights and Freedoms. Where such documents are weaker than UK law or are inappropriately drawn for our legal system, domestic legislation has also been utilised. Examples include sections from the Police and Criminal Evidence Act 1984; the Mental Health Act 1983; the Race Relations Act 1976; and the Sex Discrimination Act 1975. A *People's Charter* also draws on Liberty's own policies where no other alternative seems acceptable – eg, the inadmissibility of uncorroborated evidence in any criminal trial, and the right of all deportees to appeal against deportation according to the principles of natural justice.

33 Now Professor of Public Law at Kings College London.

anxiety.[34] The unique feature of Liberty's Bill of Rights was its solution to this problem that cut straight through the debate about the judiciary. As a result of listening to the Bill of Rights sceptics, a mechanism was devised which would involve both the courts and Parliament: 'democratic entrenchment,' as Liberty called it. This sought to ensure that controversial decisions about rights involved the full democratic process rather than being taken, in secret, by an unaccountable executive. It had a mixed reception. Some – particularly lawyers – were sceptical. But, as Andrew Puddephat says, 'in other – left wing – circles this might arguably have been an advantage'.[35]

Liberty's unique solution to the entrenchment issue demonstrated that a Bill of Rights didn't necessarily have to reflect the American approach, and that creative solutions to the entrenchment problem were possible. This was, says Francesca Klug 'absolutely crucial' in alleviating the traditional fears of the left – both old and new – and subsequently securing Labour support:

> The difficulties of entrenchment kept coming up: in every public meeting, every letter from civil servants, every private meeting with politicians. It was always the central issue. Everywhere we went we had to keep repeating our solution like a mantra. We demonstrated that the argument didn't have to take place on those terms. Without it we would never have got past first base.[36]

Within a couple of years, an eccentric, eclectic organisation whose priorities were drawn from a range of concerns on the left, had embraced international human rights standards. It had made the first coherent and systematic attempt to apply them to our domestic law, instead of regarding them as an irrelevance. Liberty had gradually come to realise the legitimacy of constraints on freedom, not just as a necessity to reach a compromise with the government, but to promote and protect the rights of others.

Thus, the Bill of Rights became an ambitious programme for reform, building on the best of Liberty, which was its casework, while providing a policy solution which could be campaigned for. It distilled the hard won wisdom of 50 years of the organisation's history, while providing a unifying theme and a set of guiding principles for the future. Liberty had decisively taken on, says Francesca Klug 'a set of values, rather than just a set of statements about freedom'.[37] Everyone involved with the intense debate and argument which drove the drafting of the Bill of Rights still speaks of that time with great warmth and affection – even though many of them now differ in their views about political priorities and tactics (and probably did then). In

---

34 *Op cit*, Ewing and Gearty, fn 10. See, also, Zander, M, *A Bill of Rights*, 4th edn, 1996, London: Sweet & Maxwell, Chap 3, for an outline and comprehensive refutation of the traditional arguments against a Bill of Rights, including anxieties about judicial entrenchment.

35 Andrew Puddephat, interviewed 4 March 1998.

36 Francesca Klug, personal communication, 15 June 1998.

37 Francesca Klug, interviewed 24 February 1998.

the words of Andrew Puddephat, 'We had this tremendous sense of discovery: our Bill of Rights was this enormously exciting land which had been there all along but which nobody had bothered to go to'.[38]

Liberty's Bill of Rights was finally launched on 30 October 1991. The press conference highlighted the UK's record in Strasbourg – it was then top of the league with 27 violations having been established against it, way ahead of countries such as Austria (15) or France (five).[39] An ambitious challenge was set out: 'Liberty's aim is to make the 90s a decade of rights: public awareness of human rights is the best defence against the abuse of power.'[40]

INFLUENCING THE OPPOSITION

Judicial entrenchment was not the only potential obstacle to widespread support for a Bill of Rights on the left. Historically, Bills of Rights are not part of the natural territory of the left at all. One of the greatest obstacles was what Andrew Puddephat calls 'the parochialism and narrowness of British culture'. This, he says, nurtured the commonly held view that constitutional issues were strictly for the chattering classes, unlike 'real' social and economic issues, and that individual rights were 'a bourgeois affectation'[41] – a depressing legacy which the trade unions had carried since the 19th century. Indeed, issues of democracy and rights had attracted relatively little interest in the left since the days of the Chartists.

Nevertheless, the Labour Party was clearly where Liberty had to take its ideas. The Liberal Democrats had already adopted their Bill of Rights policy well before the early 1990s, but their electoral chances would remain remote for the foreseeable future. The Conservatives had toyed with the idea in the past, but, as John Wadham says, were 'unlikely to be convinced of the merits of the idea while in government'.[42] Aware that policy arises from a number of sources, over the years, Liberty found a way into Labour via a number of different routes. Initially, direct approaches were made to Neil Kinnock and Roy Hattersley, Leader and Deputy Leader, in 1991. Later, following Labour's defeat in the 1992 election, key influential people approached included John Smith (then Leader of the Opposition), Tony Blair (who was then Shadow Secretary of State for Home Affairs) and Derry Irvine (then Shadow Lord Chancellor). Subsequently, after John Smith's death and the new appointment

---

38 Francesca Klug, interviewed 24 February 1998.
39 A more up to date summary of the UK Government's record in Strasbourg is in Klug, F, Starmer, K and Weir, S, *The Three Pillars of Liberty*, 1996, London: Democratic Audit/Routledge.
40 Liberty press release, 31 October 1991.
41 Andrew Puddephat, interviewed 4 March 1998.
42 John Wadham, interviewed 25 May 1998.

of Tony Blair to the leadership, Jack Straw was brought into the debate as well. Francesca Klug was invited to address the Constitutional Sub-committee of the NEC, a body with which Liberty subsequently developed useful working links, influencing the thinking which generated the papers which were subsequently adopted by the NEC.[43]

Though clearly most people who became actively engaged with a Bill of Rights did so for ideological reasons, there was also a discernible 'snowball' effect. Once Liberty was known to be having discussions with Labour directly, this started to give the organisation influence and status in other people's view, which in turn attracted further support – and so on. Although Labour's 1992 Election Manifesto included a Charter of Rights, the issue was barely visible at all during the run up to the election. There were 'vague noises about citizens' charters and the right to get your money back from British Rail, but not much about people's charters and the right to justice.'[44] This was despite a MORI poll showing 70% support for the idea, and a thoughtful and thorough attempt by Liberty to persuade the party of the main reasons why it would be tactically beneficial to flaunt it as one of the central features of their general election campaign.[45]

Following the shock of their unexpected electoral defeat in 1992, Labour became more open to new ideas. Neil Kinnock resigned and John Smith became the new party leader. A great supporter of constitutional reform since

---

43 Allen, G (MP), *Labour Participation Paper on Labour and the Constitution No 6: A British Bill of Rights*, 1993, London: HMSO.

44 Andrew Puddephat, General Secretary's speech to Liberty Annual Conference, 1992.

45 These were:

   (a) that support for a Bill of Rights could cement the link between democratic socialism and the enhancement of individual rights, restating the fundamental values which the party stands for and challenging the ancient order defended by the Conservatives;

   (b) committing Labour to supporting a Bill of Rights would not necessarily involve supporting judicial entrenchment: Labour could either support Liberty's model of democratic entrenchment or (perhaps more strategically sound), could commit itself to the principle of a Bill of Rights only;

   (c) that a Bill of Rights could be presented as modernising as well as liberating, and bringing the UK into line with the rest of Europe, thus addressing the need for Labour to present policies which sounded fresh but which were also in line with party policy;

   (d) it would be the only adequate reply to the Citizens' Charter, and could put the Conservatives on the defensive with the accusation that they had distorted the tradition of citizens' rights which had its roots in the French and American Bills of Rights and the British Campaign for universal franchise, and transformed it to one confined to consumer rights operated in the market place;

   (e) that support for a Bill of Rights could attract the wavering Liberal Democrat voter. Together with the party's support for a Freedom of Information Act, specific rights legislation, a Scottish Assembly, regional government and a revised second chamber this would amount to a decisive package for democratic and constitutional reform.

   From *A Bill of Rights: Liberty's Proposals for Democratic Entrenchment, a Briefing for the Labour Party*, 1992, London: Liberty.

his youth, Smith committed the party to a radical programme, unambiguously outlined in a speech in March 1993 as:

> ... a new deal between the people and the State that puts the citizen centre stage ... our crumbling constitution is at the heart of what's wrong with the country ... and our present arrangements are both anachronistic and inadequate ... the role of government is to be instrumental and subordinate ... subordinate above all to the democratic will.[46]

This was the discernible point at which Liberty realised that the momentum had swung. It would be easier from there on. In July 1993, a working conference on incorporation was organised by Liberty and Graham Allen MP, to review a draft of a Bill to incorporate the European Convention on Human Rights into domestic law.[47] In September, proposals were published in the Labour policy document 'A New Agenda for Democracy'.

Meanwhile, the Labour Rights Campaign had been encouraging Labour party members in constituency parties to support rights.[48] Motions to the annual party conference were submitted every year, until by 1993 there were fifteen, which resulted in a composite.[49] This, claims Andrew Puddephat, was significant: 'We knew that once that resolution was carried we were OK, because by then it was easier for people to go along with it than to argue against it.'[50] At last, Liberty could claim to have changed the policy of the second largest political party in the country. By November of the same year, Labour was consulting its constituency parties about a two stage process, and in January, Graham Allen introduced the fifth draft of the incorporation Bill to the House of Commons.[51] In addition to incorporating the Convention, it also sought to establish a Bill of Rights Commission whose task would be to prepare a 'draft Bill of Rights relating to all civil, political, economic and social rights in the United Kingdom'. [52]

Tragically, John Smith died in May 1994 – believed by many to be 'the best Prime Minister we never had'. His proposals for constitutional reform were taken up by his successor Tony Blair, elected leader of the party in July 1994.

---

46 Speech to Charter 88 Conference, Church House, Westminster, March 1 1993.

47 Unlike Liberty's own Bill of Rights with its unique 'democratic entrenchment' mechanism, this Bill to incorporate the European Convention was based on the Canadian Charter of Rights and Freedoms, allowing the courts to disapply primary legislation unless there was a specific 'notwithstanding' clause in the legislation.

48 The Labour Rights Campaign was a grouping within the Labour Party which was set up with the aim of promoting both civil and political and socio-economic rights.

49 Resolution Composite 39, 1993 Labour Party Annual Conference.

50 John Wadham, interviewed 25 May 1998.

51 Drafted by John Wadham, then of Liberty's Legal Department, now its Director.

52 Graham Allen MP had introduced a Human Rights Bill on five previous occasions, to keep the issue alive, but without any hope of seeing it debated. The prevailing view among the human rights lobby at that stage was that it would be tactically preferable to wait for a change of government, then ensure that the issue was addressed more thoroughly.

In a speech to the 1994 Labour Party Conference, Blair outlined a package of reform, including a Scottish Parliament and Welsh assembly. The package included a Freedom of Information Act, an increase in the number of women MPs, the abolition of voting by hereditary peers, a tightening of the rules of finance of political parties, and – most significantly for Liberty – a Bill of Rights.[53]

KEEPING UP THE PRESSURE: POPULIST INITIATIVES AND LITIGATION

Launching a Bill of Rights onto the agenda of the main opposition party was an impressive achievement. The next challenge facing Liberty and the other organisations involved was to maintain Labour's commitment to a Bill of Rights until a change of government. Liberty did this in three ways.

First, the Rights Convention Project laid the foundations of a more populist human rights movement by developing an interest in using a human rights approach among other, mainly 'single issue' NGOs. Secondly, Liberty seized an unexpected opportunity to turn the Government's drive to erode rights to its advantage, in the campaign against the highly controversial Criminal Justice and Public Order Bill (now Act). Finally, Liberty's ECHR test case litigation was decisive, not only in securing improvements to rights, but in repeatedly embarrassing the Government to the point where there was little to gain by leaving things as they were.

THE RIGHTS CONVENTION

In the early 1990s, Liberty's public and media profile had steadily increased. The Criminal Justice Campaign, launched in November 1991, submitted evidence to the Royal Commission on Criminal Justice calling for a range of reforms to the criminal justice system, and campaigned for the convictions of the Tottenham Three, the Bridgewater Four and others to be reviewed. Liberty's Northern Ireland Human Rights Assembly – the most comprehensive of its kind ever organised – examined the UK's observance of

---

53 Tony Blair, leader's speech to Labour Party Conference, 3 October 1994. Conference carried Composite 29 which said:

> Conference calls for a commitment to a Bill of rights to be included in Labour's manifesto as part of what John Smith called a new constitution for a new century which will include (1) the incorporation into UK law of the civil and political rights of the European Convention on Human Rights; (2) a commission to deliver to Parliament within two years of establishment an implementable package of civil, political, social and economic rights for all; (3) reform of the judiciary; (4) a Freedom of Information Act.

international human rights standards and its record in Northern Ireland, with over 254 submissions received and evidence from 150 witnesses, addressing difficult and unpalatable issues. By June 1993, the organisation had the confidence to initiate a two year project to secure a 'critical mass' of support for a Bill of Rights: The Rights Convention.

On 8 June 1993, Liberty and a coalition of more than 20 NGOs launched a major challenge to the British Government's human rights record.[54] Over the next two years, Liberty published a series of reports, highlighting human rights abuses by the British Government. These reports were written jointly with other specialist NGOs, highlighting breaches of international law codified in the UN ICCPR, and paying particular attention to the erosion of rights over the previous decade. This initiative culminated in two events: one domestic, one international. A three day event organised by Liberty in the heart of Westminster in June 1995, brought together over 3,000 people in a 100 different lectures, debates and cultural events. These ranged from a seminar for commercial lawyers on the effects on the right to silence of the case of Ernest Saunders in the European Commission of Human Rights, to 200 schoolchildren discussing children's rights for the first time. As the first major conference on domestic human rights in this country, it stimulated a deeper understanding of the principles and practices of human rights and the role of international treaty bodies, and brought together diverse strands of human rights thinking from over 100 different NGOs.

The second event was a month later: the lobby of the United Nations Human Rights Committee (HRC) when it met to review the UK Government's compliance with the International Covenant on Civil and Political Rights over the preceding four years. Liberty and other human rights NGOs had encouraged organisations in the UK to make written submissions to the Committee, and over 12 NGOs were represented at the hearing. The United Nations HRC criticised the UK's record yet again, noting that 'the legal system of the UK does not ensure fully that an effective remedy is provided for all violations of the rights contained in the Covenant'.[55] It criticised the UK's failure to adopt the first Optional Protocol that would allow individuals to petition the committee, and the absence of a Bill of Rights.[56] Other serious

---

54 Partner organisations in the Human Rights Convention Project were: Anti-Racist Alliance; Article 19; British Council of Organisations of Disabled People; Campaign for Press and Broadcasting Freedom; Change; Charter 88; Fawcett Society; Institute of Employment Rights; Joint Council for the Welfare of Immigrants; Law Centres Federation; MIND; Prison Reform Trust; Refugee Council; Scottish Council for Civil Liberties (now renamed the Scottish Human Rights Centre); Society of Black Lawyers; Southall Black Sisters; Stonewall; UK Forum on AIDS, HIV and Human Rights.

55 Consideration of reports submitted by States Parties under Art 40 of the Covenant: Comments of the Human Rights Committee on the Fourth Periodic Report of the United Kingdom of Great Britain and Northern Ireland, CCPR/C/798/Add 55, 1442nd mtg, 54th session, 27 July 1995.

56 Ibid, para 9.

criticisms included: the abolition of the right to silence in criminal trials; the continuing use of emergency laws in Northern Ireland; strip searching of prisoners; prison suicides; the disproportionate numbers of black people stopped and searched by the police; the treatment, detention and deportation of immigrants and asylum seekers, and the lack of effective action to tackle racial harassment.[57] United Nations committees have no powers of enforcement, but their findings can add moral and political authority to the campaigning efforts of NGOs, provide embarrassing publicity for a government, and of course can also be used in court cases.[58]

An invaluable direct consequence of the lobbying of the United Nations HRC was the subsequent lobby of the United Nations Committee for the Elimination of Racial Discrimination, co-ordinated by Liberty on a similar basis over the following months, culminating in a highly successful lobby of the Committee when it met in March 1996 to review the UK Government's compliance with the International Covenant on the Elimination of Racial Discrimination.[59] Here, the Committee's criticisms of the UK Government were even stronger. Despite the Government's extraordinary claim that 'the vast majority of racially motivated incidents are at a very low level of seriousness',[60] the Committee concluded that racism in the UK was institutionalised, widespread and routine, with unjust asylum and immigration laws, inadequate policing where racist attacks and deaths of black people in custody were not satisfactorily investigated. Finally, they noted, the legal framework for preventing racial discrimination was hopelessly inadequate, not least because of the absence of a Bill of Rights.[61]

---

57 Consideration of reports submitted by States Parties under Art 40 of the Covenant: Comments of the Human Rights Committee on the Fourth Periodic Report of the United Kingdom of Great Britain and Northern Ireland, CCPR/C/798/Add 55, 1442nd mtg, 54th session, 27 July 1995, paras 17, 4, 11, 12 , 14, 15 and 18.

58 For an account of the Government's claims and the Committee's findings, see Parratt, L and Foley, C, 'The UK Government's 13th Periodic Report to the UN Committee for the Elimination of Racial Discrimination' [1996] EHRLR 4.

59 Participating organisations included the Association of Black Probation Officers; Britain and Ireland Human Rights Centre; Charter 88; Newham Monitoring Project; the Refugee Council; the 1990 Trust; and the National Black Alliance (Asian Chamber of Commerce, Asian Congress on Local Affairs, Cardinal Hume Committee for the Caribbean, Croydon Asian and African Association, Indian Workers Association (Great Britain), Mangrove Community Association (Notting Hill), National Assembly Against Racism, National Black Caucus, Pakistani Human Rights Society (UK Branch), Society of Black Lawyers; South Islington Bangladeshi Association, Student Coalition Against Racism, Tower Hamlets Anti Racist Committee).

60 UK Government representative Stephen Wells, Police Department, Home Office, questioned by Professor Theo van Boven, UK Country Rapporteur, CERD, 48th session, 26 February–15 March 1996. Contemporaneous note by author. For a fuller account of the Government's claims and the Committee's findings, see op cit, Parratt and Foley, fn 58.

61 UN, Concluding Observations of the Committee for the Elimination of Racial Discrimination: United Kingdom of Great Britain and Northern Ireland, 26 February–15 March 1996.

RIGHTS, PUBLIC ORDER AND POPULAR CULTURE

In December 1993, not long after even the Royal Commission on Criminal Justice had recommended additional safeguards to the criminal justice system (see above), the Government started to dismantle them even further. It now proposed to remove the defendant's right of silence, both in the police station and in court, which appeared as one of a range of measures in the new Criminal Justice and Public Order Bill. The Bill proposed a wide ranging assault on individual rights, including further limitations on bail; increased police stop and search powers; police powers to take DNA samples. It contained a range of public order measures designed to curb the activities of people engaged in non-violent direct action protests; organisers of unlicensed 'raves', and people squatting or leading a travelling life, either through choice, tradition or necessity.

It is easy to see why a Conservative government would want Home Counties voters to believe that they were getting tough on those living on the margins of the cultural mainstream. But, the Bill turned out to be a serious error of political judgment. That it would become law was inevitable – but, in doing so, it became the most widely criticised piece of legislation since the poll tax. A large and loose constituency of predominantly young people had little in common but a feeling that mainstream politics was of no relevance to them, and a refusal to accept that inequality and discrimination and injustice are the natural order of things. They objected to being targeted as the new 'enemy within'. Even more sober and mainstream political commentators could see the bias and injustice in the Bill: reducing legal provision of travellers' sites while increasing the penalties for illegal camping would clearly help no one.[62] The Bill outlawed one minority leisure pursuit – unlicensed outdoor raves and festivals – while providing increased protection from opposition for another – hunting.[63]

In contrast to the late 1980s, where legislative assaults on rights had eventually resulted in stress and internal damage, this time, Liberty turned a hostile Government initiative into an advantage. Liberty could hardly claim credit for the mass opposition to the proposals, or blame for the passage of the Bill into law – both would have occurred regardless of any action it had taken. Where Liberty did succeed, in retrospect, was in transforming a loose alliance of the disaffected into an embryonic human rights movement. The organisation ensured that an incoherent basket of measures designed to crack down on the unpopular and disenfranchised became widely regarded as a set of systematic human rights abuses – primarily by young people who had only limited prior involvement in politics. Suddenly the concept of human rights

---

62 See, eg, (1994) *The Economist*, 30 July, p 28; 26 November, p 40.
63 Parratt, L and Foley, C, *Criminalising Diversity, Criminalising Dissent*, 1994, London: Liberty.

became a live focus for a generation which had never really thought about it. Ironically, the legislation seemed to stimulate more of the very protests it aimed to deter,[64] and alerted a new and important constituency to other, broader human rights issues. Liberty's hope at the time was that it would provide a timely warning to any potential future government that human rights breaches can bring incredibly unwelcome publicity – though whether this was heeded in any way is not known.

LITIGATION

Perhaps the most compelling strand – and, arguably, even the most influential one – was Liberty's litigation. Liberty was not by any means the first to use the European Convention: Anthony Lester QC, for example, had made a point of drawing attention to the Convention over and over again in the courts.[65] However, Liberty's legal team was possibly the first fully to exploit the potential for using Convention litigation to illustrate human rights issues, and to embarrass the Government in public. This did not apply solely to the cases which were won. Cases which the Government won could still be very effectively promoted through the media, to raise the profile of an issue or the quality of public debate and to develop a wider understanding of human rights. Such cases, whether taken in Strasbourg or in the domestic courts, were often transformed into political gains for the emerging human rights lobby.

One of the most striking features of Liberty's litigation is the sheer diversity of issues which it encompasses.[66] One early and well known success was *Harman and Hewitt v UK*,[67] in which the surveillance of two employees of Liberty (then NCCL) in the 1970s was revealed over a decade later by former MI5 agent Cathy Massiter. This resulted in MI5 being placed on a statutory footing by the Security Services Act 1989.

Hodgson v UK, Channel 4 v UK[68] concerned the TV reporting of the trial of Ministry of Defence whistleblower Clive Ponting, banned by the judge under

---

64 The author's favourite was a small, good natured party held – without permission – outside Home Secretary Michael Howard's country residence shortly after Royal Assent. A group of anti-roads protesters and others who proceeded to climb onto the roof of the house, waving copies of the European Convention on Human Rights and shouting 'Guilty! Guilty! Guilty!'. I remember listening to this on the Radio 4 midnight news, and thinking: we've been trying to create a popular culture of rights for over two years – this must be some kind of sign that it's started to emerge.

65 See, eg, *AG v Guardian Newspapers* [1987] WLR 1248; *R v Brind* [1991] 1 AC 696; *Airedale NHS Trust v Bland* [1993] 1 All ER 821; *Derbyshire County Council v Times Newspapers* [1993] AC 534.

66 For an account of Liberty's approach to test case litigation in the 1970s and early 1980s, see Cohen, B and Staunton, M, 'In pursuit of a legal strategy: The National Council for Civil Liberties', in Cooper, J and Dhavan, R, *Public Interest Law*, 1986, Oxford: Blackwell.

67 [1991] 14 EHRR 657.

68 [1987] 10 EHRR 503.

the Contempt of Court Act. The successful Strasbourg challenge resulted in the imposition of reporting restrictions about a case, or the restriction of the public's access to court, being made subject to review by a higher court.

In *Thynne, Wilson and Gunnell v UK*,[69] the lawfulness of detaining individuals following release on licence was challenged under Art 5. It resulted in the Criminal Justice Act 1991 amendment which placed control over discretionary life prisoners with a special panel chaired by a judge. As John Wadham has commented, 'one additional effect of such a case, of course, is that it shows other lawyers that if they do these kinds of cases – and succeed – they can have a real effect on the legal system itself'.

Similarly, in *Benham v UK*,[70] the Government was found to be in breach of Art 5. Stephen Benham was imprisoned for failing to pay his poll tax (community charge), could not afford a lawyer, and was not eligible for legal aid. This resulted in changes to the system, to ensure that, in future, legal aid would be available for all fine defaulters in the magistrates' courts.

There are several influential cases in which Liberty has submitted an *amicus* brief. In *Murray v UK*,[71] for example, the first UK 'right to silence' case to be heard by the European Court, an individual was convicted in a Diplock court in Northern Ireland, partly as a result of the judge assuming he was guilty because he kept silent. The defendant was also refused proper access to his lawyers when he was being questioned in the police station, something emergency legislation allows. The court found no violation in relation to his right of silence, but held that the denial of his access to a solicitor for 48 hours breached Art 6 (the right to a fair trial).[72] In *Chahal v UK*,[73] a Sikh activist was detained for five years pending deportation on the grounds that his presence was 'not conducive to the public good' resulted in the Special Immigration Appeals Commission Act. Other successful cases where Liberty submitted an *amicus* include *Halford v UK*[74] and *Saunders v UK*.[75]

Some Liberty cases have also been influential in securing rights and freedoms without the need for a long haul to Strasbourg. In *R v London Borough of Barnet ex p Johnson*,[76] for example, a council which had awarded itself the power to ban political organisations from organising stalls at local festivals was defeated in the domestic courts. In a scenario which would

---

69 Series A.190; (1990) 13 EHRR 666.

70 (1996) 22 EHRR 293.

71 (1996) 22 EHRR 29.

72 The Government is now bringing UK law into line with the judgment in *Murray*. Inferences can no longer be drawn from silence at interview if the suspect has not had prior access to legal advice.

73 (1996) 23 EHRR 413.

74 (1997) 24 EHRR 523.

75 (1997) 23 EHRR 313.

76 3 ALR 149.

almost be comical were it not such a grave infringement of privacy, Liberty's client, Mr Govell, came home one day and moved his sofa, only to find a hole in the wall containing a listening device planted by the police.[77] At the time, the only regulation was a code of practice from 1984 requiring the authorisation of a Chief Constable: in other words, the police had to seek permission from themselves. Within months of the case being declared admissible, the Government had brought forward the Police Bill (now the Police Act 1997) to regulate the use of such devices. John Wadham's view is that this and *R v Khan*,[78] in which Liberty became the first NGO given permission to intervene in a case in the House of Lords, pushed the Government into legislating.[79]

Liberty's European litigation has occasionally drawn on EU law as well. Gerry Adams, president of Sinn Fein, was banned from coming to England as a result of exclusion order powers in the Prevention of Terrorism Act (*Adams and Benn v UK*).[80] Liberty's legal team took the view that although this was not a direct breach of the ECHR because the Government had not ratified the fourth protocol (which includes freedom of movement), it could be challenged under amendments to the Maastricht Treaty. Ultimately, the case 'ran into the sand', but for very welcome reasons, when the exclusion order was lifted at the start of the peace process.

Perhaps the most unlikely political success was *Laskey, Jaggard and Brown v UK*,[81] in which several gay men were prosecuted for consensual and private sadomasochistic sexual activities. More popularly known as the '*Spanner* case', this had an extraordinarily positive impact on public opinion. Arguing that, where the 'victim' had consented or even requested the 'assault', there could be no crime, Liberty lost spectacularly. However, as John Wadham says, 'the greatest irony is that it was the long delays in the Strasbourg process which enabled the campaign in support of the men to gain momentum, and enhance public understanding of what S/M was all about. You didn't need to be a practising sadomasochist to see that the State has no role in dictating what consenting adults do in private'. The general view – which was not exclusively confined to pre- existing liberal opinion – was that the men should never have been prosecuted in the first place. Apart from one case involving branding, in which a conviction was overturned on appeal (*R v Wilson*)[82] there have been no S/M prosecutions since.

---

77 *Govell v UK* (1997) 23 EHRR 10.

78 (1996) *The Times*, 2 July.

79 The icing on the legislative cake here is that the prior judicial authorisation now required results from a successful amendment which Liberty helped shadow Home Secretary Jack Straw to draft – a rare occurrence indeed under the previous administration.

80 [1997] EHRLR 293.

81 [1997] 24 EHRR 39.

82 [1996] 3 WLR 125.

Thus, the Government was forced to wash some of its political dirty linen in the all too public human rights institutions of Strasbourg. At the same time, the ground was prepared for a more populist rights movement, including the development of a significant new constituency which absolutely no one had predicted, but who proved to be among the most vocal and energetic supporters of human rights. Subsequently, the attention given to human rights issues in the press steadily increased – a trend stimulated further by a Government whose disregard for individual rights and freedoms showed no signs of abating. Towards the end of 1996 and in early 1997, in the parliamentary term immediately before the general election, Liberty was actively opposing seven Bills. Throughout this period, direct lobbying of key opposition members and senior civil servants had continued. The pressure never dwindled – either from Liberty or from the other individuals and organisations engaged in the incorporation debate.[83] In 1996–97, Liberty organised a series of parliamentary seminars for members of the Labour front bench: Incorporating the Convention (June 1996); A Bill of Rights for Northern Ireland (November 1996); The Convention and Law and Order (January 1997).

Labour's consultation paper, *Bringing Rights Home,* was published in February 1997. Following the general election in May 1997, Liberty and others continued to meet with ministers and civil servants during the summer and early autumn. Although the Canadian entrenchment model, which would give the courts the power to strike down primary legislation where it breached the Convention, had enjoyed support from key figures such as Tony Blair[84] and Lord Irvine of Lairg,[85] it was not clearly set out in *Bringing Rights Home*. This precipitated considerable debate among the key NGOs about whether this indicated a change in party policy or merely a lack of clarity, and about what should be done.

Once the new Government had been elected, and the Bill to incorporate the Convention had been included in the Queen's Speech, Liberty seized the opportunity to press for a stronger entrenchment model. The political virtues of this were debated in the press over the course of the summer. Meanwhile, the tactical wisdom of this position was hotly debated within the Bill of Rights Consortium.[86] Some were critical, arguing that fighting for strong entrenchment of the Convention might delay the introduction of a domestic Bill of Rights, that years of work could be unravelled and the Bill pushed back

---

83 Francesca Klug, who by then had left Liberty to pursue academic work, continued to be centrally involved on behalf of and as an advisor both to Liberty and to Charter 88.

84 Speech by Tony Blair, City Hall, Cardiff, 15 July 1996.

85 Irvine (Lord), 'The legal system and law reform under Labour', in Bean, D, *Law Reform for All*, 1996, London: Blackstone.

86 The Bill of Rights Consortium at that time was a grouping of the key organisations and individuals involved in campaigning for incorporation: Liberty, Charter 88, IPPR, Justice, the Human Rights Incorporation Project at Kings College, the Constitution Unit at University College London, and the office of Anthony Lester QC.

down the political agenda by a Government unwilling to risk the critical controversy which they would inevitably attract if they gave the judiciary such power. Liberty argued that fears of jeopardising the whole project were groundless. According to John Wadham, 'The Government had gone too far along the road, and its commitment to an incorporated ECHR was too strong to be dropped at such a late stage'.[87] This is, of course, precisely the kind of internal political history which can never be clearly evaluated. All those involved would agree that what matters is that we do now have the Human Rights Act 1998 and look forward to it coming into effect in 2000.

CONCLUSION

When I agreed to write this chapter and began researching it, it was partly with an ulterior motive: I wanted to be made to consider whether there is anything specific to be learned from Liberty's experiences in securing a Bill of Rights – for us or for others. I still do not know the answer – perhaps because intelligent organisations generally learn more from failure, which by its very nature forces a degree of self-critical reflection, than from success, which can be attributed to pretty much anything. The only wisdom I can distil from Liberty's seven year campaign to incorporate the ECHR is largely conventional. Generate a 'Big Idea' and stick with it. Repeat and develop your policy in a way which is palatable to those you wish to influence. Seize every opportunity you are given, however unexpected. Use both sticks and carrots: make the Government understand that there is a critical mass of support for an idea, while making it increasingly clear that there is nothing to gain from leaving things as they are. Few NGOs would disagree with these principles; most would add that there is also an element of being in the right place at the right time.

The one element which may be surprising to readers outside the NGO world, is how much can be achieved by so few. On a recent visit to England, the Quebecois Human Rights Commissioner managed to meet all the key people in the domestic human rights movement in only three lunches. Should this be a cause for alarm or for optimism? I would opt for the latter. As Andrew Puddephat says, with a trace of self-effacing irony, 'at least it's evidence that we're not just at the mercy of grand sweeping historical forces, and that there is a point to individual human virtue'.[88]

---

87 Though supported by a number of key lawyers, Liberty was unable to convince the other NGOs. The Consortium's compromise, which all agreed on, was to argue for a model in which all primary legislation in existence at the time of incorporation would be set aside by the courts if it did not comply. Legislation enacted subsequently would be subject to a declaration of incompatibility, as in the New Zealand Bill of Rights.

88 Andrew Puddephat, interviewed 4 March 1998.

Finally, I asked the three people who have featured strongly in the campaign for incorporation of the European Convention throughout its history where they thought the human rights movement should focus its attention in the immediate future. All agree that two things are absolutely clear. Incorporation is a starting point for enforceable rights rather than a conclusion, a first step towards meeting the UK's full range of international human rights obligations, including social, cultural and economic rights. And the 'second stage' of a more modern, indigenous Bill of Rights is a long term project – perhaps longer than was once thought. But so, once, was incorporation. All three also agree that over the next few years it is vital to be evangelical about the Human Rights Act 1998, partly to show the Government that, as Andrew says, 'people like rights and want more of them', and partly to demonstrate its limitations and weaknesses and the need to go further. The need for a Human Rights Commission is pressing: no NGO has the resources to undertake the preventative work, education and consultation which would be at the heart of a Commission's role. At the time of writing, hopes for a Commission in the near future are slim,[89] but we will continue to lobby for one in the hope that the government will eventually realise that it is cheaper than litigation. Meanwhile, Charter 88 is campaigning for the consultation on a second stage Bill to begin as soon as possible, and raising the debate about how protection for social and economic rights can most effectively be introduced. Liberty is concentrating primarily on test case litigation, and on educating and engaging other NGOs and lawyers whose use of the Human Rights Act will be crucial over the next few years.[90] For the foreseeable future, liberty will indeed continue to be unfinished business.

89 A human rights commission is, however, part of the package contained in the Northern Ireland Good Friday Agreement ('New Institutions', in *Agreement Reached in the Multi-Party Negotiations*, Cmnd 3883, 1998, Belfast: Northern Ireland Office, para 5). But, there are fears that the powers which the government propose to give this Commission will be severely limited. (See 'Bill on NI accord criticised as flawed' (1998) *The Irish Times*, 17 July.)

90 Liberty, Charter 88, IPPR, Justice and the 1990 Trust are the principal organisations in the Task Force which is advising the Government on the implementation of the Human Rights Act.

CHAPTER 17

SMALL NGOS AND STRATEGIC MANAGEMENT

Jane Winter

This chapter examines how NGOs can maximise their effect. It is based on the author's experience of setting up, managing, and working for a variety of NGOs. It contains many counsels of perfection, the majority of them arrived at over a period of years by a process of trial and, more often than not, error.

IDENTIFYING THE ORGANISATION'S OBJECTIVES

Of prime importance for an NGO is a clear statement of the organisation's objectives, or 'mission statement'. This is a sentence or, more likely, a short paragraph, which explains the purpose of the organisation. It needs to be both precise and concise. It will become the signature tune for the organisation, the first paragraph in many of its documents and reports, and the benchmark against which to measure the organisation's success or failure. If it is unclear, other people, such as potential funders and those whom the organisation seeks to influence, are less likely to be persuaded to lend their support.

By way of example, British Irish Rights Watch's mission statement is as follows:

> British Irish Rights Watch is an independent non-governmental organisation that has been monitoring the human rights dimension of the conflict, and latterly the peace process, in Northern Ireland since 1990. Our services are available free of charge to anyone whose human rights have been violated because of the conflict, regardless of religious, political or community affiliations. We take no position on the eventual constitutional outcome of the conflict.[1]

Such a statement serves a number of purposes. It informs people of the work of the organisation. It explains that its services are free. It describes who is eligible for its services and, by implication, reserves to the organisation the right to refuse its services to anyone who is ineligible. It guarantees its services free from discrimination, and it declares itself to be apolitical. Thus, a number of key messages are delivered in a few words.

---

1   BIRW, *British Irish Rights Watch 1992–97*, 1997, London: BIRW.

Make sure that an existing NGO does not already exist for the same purposes. It is unhelpful to be competing for the same resources, and NGOs that replicate each other tend to dilute each other's work rather than enhance it. If a proposed new organisation has aims that appear similar to that of an existing organisation, it is important to identify where the differences lie and whether those differences are valuable. If in doubt, discussion with the existing body may help to clarify respective roles. Close liaison may be necessary to ensure that similar organisations enhance each other's effectiveness rather than diminishing it.

DRAWING UP A STRATEGY

Having worked out what the organisation wants to do, the next step is to identify how to achieve it.

First, identify what is required to make it happen – for instance, a change in the law, a change in public opinion, international pressure, and so on. In most cases, the answer will be a combination of factors.

Secondly, determine whether the organisation by itself can bring about the desired result. In all likelihood, it will not be able to do so, in which case it is necessary to identify who can, whether it is the government, those who make policy, the public, or someone else. Again, more than one person or group may be identified.

Thirdly, devise a strategy for influencing those people. Here, it is important to be hard-headed. Recognise any barriers that are in the way – for example, an NGO seeking to promote the welfare of immigrants must acknowledge that not everyone welcomes immigration. Do not expect people to agree with the organisation's aims; rather, be prepared to explain and persuade. Above all, avoid the common mistake of relying on friends who support the organisation but cannot help it to achieve its aims. If only the US President can bring about the objective, concentrate on how to recruit his or her support, however impossible such an approach may appear at the beginning.

MAINTAINING A FOCUS

When drawing up a strategy, always keep the organisation's mission statement in mind. Everything that is done should be measured against the primary objective and analysed to see whether it has contributed towards achieving it or not.

Try to avoid wasting time on things that eat into the organisation's resources but do not pay off in the long run. For example, while an NGO that relies on public participation will want to organise a membership scheme, even though it takes time and money to service it, a different sort of NGO may not need to do so, but can simply keep a mailing list of interested people.

Conversely, do pay attention to detail and recognise the value of long term investments of resources. For instance, a letter thanking someone for a donation takes time to write and costs something, but it makes further donations likely, whereas failing to thank a donor probably means he or she will not give again. It costs a lot of money to send someone to the United Nations, but it may be money well spent if the United Nations adopts a resolution that supports the organisation's aims. A good example of this is the report on the UK by the special rapporteur on the independence of judges and lawyers in 1988,[2] which vindicated eight written submissions and several visits to Geneva in which British Irish Rights Watch raised attempts to intimidate lawyers in Northern Ireland. Not only did the special rapporteur take up all the issues that had been raised by him, but he publicly thanked British Irish Rights Watch and another NGO, the Committee on the Administration of Justice, for their assistance.

BE PROFESSIONAL

Even if an NGO is made up entirely of unpaid volunteers and is operating on a shoestring, it should always be as professional as possible. Everything it does should be done as well as possible, and everything it promises should be delivered. Common mistakes made by NGOs with few resources include putting out publicity containing typing errors, advertising well known speakers at meetings who have not in fact agreed to participate, and failing to deal promptly and courteously with enquiries about their work. All such errors are counterproductive, and are completely avoidable.

If there is money to employ staff, they should be chosen carefully and properly managed. The same is true of volunteers. No contract should be entered into, whether paid or not, that allows any individual to hijack the organisation, and mechanisms should always be in place for parting company with those whose actions, intentionally or otherwise, are sabotaging the organisation's aims. If employees are paid, it is important to remember that being an employer brings with it legal responsibilities, and people must be

---

2   *Report of the special rapporteur on the independence of judges and lawyers, Mr Param Cumaraswamy, submitted pursuant to Commission on Human Rights Resolution 1997/23. Addendum: Report on the mission of the Special Rapporteur to the United Kingdom of Great Britain and Northern Ireland*, E/CN 4/1998/39/Add 4, 1997.

found who understand those responsibilities and can make sure they are fulfilled.

It is vitally important to get the finances of the organisation right. Proper accounts must be kept, and no one person should ever be allowed to control the finances. Regular financial reports should be produced and should be available, within reason, to anyone within the organisation who wants to look at them. Control should also be kept of budgets to ensure that they do not become overspent. Most funders expect some form of financial accountability in return for their support, and it never does any harm for an organisation to remember that the money it receives is given to further the aims of the organisation and to be ready to account for how it has used its money.

NGOs should also keep their own house in order. They should meet regularly, keep a record of their meetings, check the minutes at the next meeting to see that decisions have been implemented, and produce regular reports on their work, such as an annual report.

In other words, NGOs should take pride in their work. It is always worthwhile keeping a record of the organisation's successes – press cuttings, letters of praise, etc – to use when compiling reports, applying for funds, or publicising the organisation's work.

FUNDING

Although money is not everything, no NGO can do completely without it. Attention to raising money and to using it are both vital to an NGO's effectiveness.

So far as fundraising is concerned, it has to be done continuously. It is never a good idea to let the money run out and then try to raise another sum in a hurry. If such a strategy fails, the NGO may cease to exist, and even when it works it means that all the NGO's resources have to be diverted to crisis fundraising, stopping it from doing its real job. Furthermore, people who have given money in a crisis do not respond well to a series of crisis appeals, which give the impression of incompetence. It is far better to build fundraising into the day to day work of the organisation, and to develop a proper fundraising strategy that will avoid the pitfall of becoming funding led. An NGO with its fundraising under control will be able to raise money it needs to do what it wants, rather than running the risk of its aims becoming distorted by having to dance to a funder's tune.

There are many potential sources of funding: grants from foundations; gifts from individuals; responses to appeals; public collections; corporate sponsorship; wealthy benefactors; mail shots; sale of publications; course fees;

sale of products or services; and so on.[3] Most NGOs rely on a patchwork of funding from several different sources. If funding is given for a specific purpose, it should only be used for that purpose, or, if the NGO wants to use it differently, it should seek the donor's permission to do so. All NGOs need some flexibility in their finances in order to be able to respond to unforeseen developments, so it is always important to raise some money that comes with no strings attached.

Whenever money comes in the form of a donation, whether from an individual or a wealthy foundation, always acknowledge it, both by way of a letter of thanks and publicly, unless the donor wishes to remain anonymous. Always, also, give the donor feedback on how the money was used. A donor who feels that his, her or its money has been put to good use will give again. A donor who hears nothing until the next appeal for money will be less likely to repeat the donation.

Find out about tax efficient ways of giving money. People are often delighted if, when they give a certain sum, it can be enhanced by the NGO claiming any tax that has been paid on it. For example, in England, registered charities can claim back income tax paid by donors provided they covenant a regular sum for at least four years or give more than a certain amount as a lump sum.[4]

Consider whether the NGO can apply for charitable status.[5] Some tax efficient schemes are dependent upon charitable status, and many foundations can only give to other charities. However, charitable status restricts the ability of some organisations to campaign as vigorously as they might wish. It is worth talking to a registered charity about the ins and outs and pros and cons.

It is also worth considering registering the NGO as a company limited by guarantee. Although there are costs attached, such a step protects the board or management committee from financial liability should the NGO go broke, so long as they have acted properly and responsibly.

When it comes to spending money, NGOs can be among the most and the least of cost effective organisations, sometimes at one and the same time. It is certainly cheaper to buy envelopes that need sticking down rather than ones that are self-sealing, but if large mailings are a regular feature of the organisation's work, hours of person time can be spent sealing envelopes that might be better employed. Old computers may be cheaper, but they are also

---

3   The Directory for Social Change produces an invaluable series of guides to fundraising, A list of publications and fundraising courses is available from them at Radius Works, Back Lane, London NW3 1HL, UK. Telephone: + 44 (0) 207 435 8171.

4   This scheme is known as Gift Aid. For more information, contact the Inland Revenue.

5   In England, the Charity Commission produces many useful booklets for those who wish to set up a charity. Their address is Woodfield House, Tangier, Taunton, Somerset TA1 4BL, UK. Telephone: + 44 (0) 1823 345000. Fax: + 44 (0) 1823 345003.

slower and more prone to break down. So called new technology may be costly, but it can save a great deal of time and frustration, and can help to produce a more professional product. It is important not to under cost such items when fundraising.

Lastly, so far as money is concerned, money spent having the accounts done professionally, especially if there are wages to be paid, is always money well spent. It ensures that the organisation's finances are put under professional scrutiny, relieves those running the organisation of anxiety, and inspires confidence in potential funders – many of whom insist on seeing audited accounts or their equivalent – that everything is in order financially.

ESTABLISHING A TRACK RECORD

First and foremost, an NGO ought to be judged by the work that it does. Charismatic personalities, who tend to abound among NGOs, can be a great asset, but they can also become a liability. They can also come and go. What endures is the organisation's body of work and its list of achievements. Keep a copy of every report the organisation produces, and a running list of all its activities – it is surprising how easy it is to forget what has been done, especially if several people are involved.

Make sure that any work done is done well, whether it is organising a conference, putting out a press release, or researching a social problem. Excellence speaks for itself, wins friends, and gains influence. Shoddy work does the opposite.

NETWORKING

Make and nurture good alliances with other NGOs and with individuals or groups that can assist the organisation to achieve its aims. Working together with others can produce useful synergy.

However, it is necessary to understand the remit of other organisations, and the limits that remit may impose on their ability to co-operate with others. For example, an NGO set up to support the Asian community may not be able to sponsor a wholly Afro-Caribbean festival. Nevertheless, both groups may be able to work together to promote the interest of black people generally.

Nothing is more irritating to a poorly resourced NGO than to go into partnership with another group, only to find that it is doing all the work and bearing all the cost, while the other group shares in the credit. NGOs should neither 'freeload' themselves nor permit others to 'freeload' on them. Working together should always be to each other's mutual benefit, although stronger, well resourced NGOs should expect to make a greater contribution than poorer groups.

An effective NGO will soon become a useful resource or source of information to those whose support or influence it needs in order to achieve its aims. This is true even when an NGO's clients are relatively powerless. For instance, an NGO promoting services for the deaf can still become a resource to politicians debating legislation for people with disabilities, telephone companies wishing to improve their services, those who design road safety systems, and so on. At the same time, such people can themselves become a resource to the NGO.

Successful networking also involves an awareness of the role an NGO plays in the wider world and of how others' roles relate to that of the NGO. A good networker sees points of mutual interest between apparently disparate bodies, knows how to forge and maintain links, and if he or she does not know anyone who can help with a particular problem, knows someone else who does. Good networkers carry business cards and exchange them with others all the time. They keep other people's cards, or make a note of contacts they have made, and take whatever opportunities arise to reinforce mutually beneficial relationships.

Good networking includes keeping in touch with the organisation's own constituency, whether it consists of the membership, people who use the organisation's services, funders, or people on a mailing list. Keeping such people informed and involved always pays dividends. Some form of newsletter, regular meetings, or a website can all be useful mechanisms for keeping in touch. Remember that each individual involved in an NGO has his or her own networks that may be helpful in achieving the organisation's aims, especially if, in order to do so, it is necessary to reach out to people who might not naturally become involved with the NGO's work. Everyone knows someone who knows someone who knows someone else who knows a bishop, or a politician, or a millionaire.

BECOMING INFLUENTIAL

NGOs very rarely have much power, but the good ones rapidly gain influence. Many of the matters mentioned above – being focused on the main objective, acting professionally, establishing a track record, effective networking – should themselves contribute to an NGO's ability to be influential. However, attention should also be paid to acquiring influence in its own right.

First, establish who has the power to bring about a situation in which the organisation's objectives can be achieved. Once that person or institution – of whom, of course, there may be more than one – has been identified, work out how they can be influenced. This usually means working out who can influence them. Then, it is a matter of finding out how to reach those people and influence them. This is where networking comes into its own.

Being influential is largely a matter on putting oneself in someone else's shoes. If people one wants to influence are already sympathetic, that obviously helps, but if they will need persuasion, it is important to identify what will persuade them. It may be a question of finding someone they already trust who will help to persuade them. It may be a matter of finding ways to persuade people on whom they depend, such as voters or customers, to make them change their minds. Another avenue may be mobilising international pressure.

Never underestimate the power of the media. Skillful recruitment of journalists to an NGO's cause can greatly enhance its influence. They have access to all kinds of people, and it is their job to ask questions and get answers. The media can also cause problems for under-resourced NGOs. Researchers who know nothing about a subject can waste hours of an NGO's time, while the NGO teaches the researcher from scratch. This is rarely a worthwhile exercise, as the researcher moves on to a different assignment. It is more useful to cultivate regular correspondents who already know their subject, and to create a mutually beneficial relationship. Making the NGO's cause into the headline story on the national news can bring very powerful pressure indeed to bear on those whom an NGO wants to influence. The media, especially the tabloid press, also have tremendous influence on public opinion.

'BLOODY SUNDAY' – A CASE STUDY

It may be helpful to describe British Irish Rights Watch's experience of working on a very significant human rights issue, in order to show how some of the principles outlined above work – and fail to work – in practice.

On Sunday 30 January 1972, which has come to be known as 'Bloody Sunday', 13 people were killed by British soldiers and 14 others were injured in the city of Derry. One of the injured died prematurely young, not long after Bloody Sunday. The victims were taking part in a demonstration against internment without trial, in contravention of a six months' ban imposed on all demonstrations. The 1st Battalion Parachute Regiment (known as the Paras) was ostensibly deployed to mount an arrest operation within the Bogside area of the city, which had been a nationalist 'no go area' for British troops for the previous two years. Soldiers opened fire on the demonstrators, a small number of whom had previously been engaged in low level rioting, such as stoning soldiers. Accounts differ as to whether the soldiers were fired upon before opening fire or whether they fired without provocation, but it is undisputed that army statements issued after the incident claiming that the deceased were gunmen and bombers were untrue. There is no evidence that any of the deceased were engaged in attacking soldiers at the time of their deaths; on the contrary, most of them were fleeing from the soldiers. No soldier was prosecuted for any of the killings. The Government established an immediate Tribunal of Inquiry into the incident, undertaken by the then Lord Chief Justice, Lord Widgery. His report, published in April 1972, less than three months after the event, has been criticised and discredited in a number of important respects. Significant fresh evidence that has come to light since the Widgery Report[6] was published shows that the inquiry itself and the report were seriously flawed.

British Irish Rights Watch became involved in the Bloody Sunday case not long after the 20th anniversary in 1992. The relatives of those who died, who had been campaigning for a new public inquiry without success, put out a plea to NGOs to help them to achieve their aim. British Irish Rights Watch responded to this call and met the relatives to discuss ways in which human rights mechanisms might be used. Although the difficulty in re-opening such an old case was obvious, two tactics seemed worth trying. The first was a complaint to the United Nations special rapporteur on extra-judicial, summary or arbitrary executions, who looks into complaints of killings by members of the security forces. The second was an application to the European Commission on Human Rights claiming that the deceased had been deprived of their right to life under Art 2 of the European Convention on Human Rights.

Of the two, the United Nations route seemed less problematic than the European road. The special rapporteur had no time limit on dealing with complaints, whereas a complaint to the Commission ought to have been made within six months of the incident. It was decided, therefore, to try the United Nations first, and if that did not work, to go to Europe. At that point, it was not expected that either approach had much chance of success, but they both provided an opportunity to keep up the pressure for a new inquiry and to gain fresh publicity for what the media viewed as a tired issue.

In the event, neither tactic succeeded. The special rapporteur simply refused to look at such an ancient complaint when he had fresh problems on the scale of those in Bosnia and Rwanda arriving on his desk all the time. The Commission on Human Rights also refused to entertain the case because it was out of time, notwithstanding sophisticated legal arguments as to why they could and should look into the case. However, both approaches served their purpose. In order to complain to the United Nations, British Irish Rights

6   Widgery Report, *Report of the Tribunal Appointed to Inquire into Events on Sunday 30 January 1972*, 18 April 1972, London: HMSO.

Watch drew up a comprehensive report,[7] outlining all the facts as they were then known, and containing a detailed critique of the Widgery Report. When this was sent to the United Nations, the relatives put out a press release which attracted some publicity, and they also sent a delegation to London to deliver a copy to the prime minister, together with a letter seeking a new inquiry. The same report was used as the basis for the European application, and when this was submitted further publicity was received.

Perhaps British Irish Rights Watch's greatest contribution towards helping the Bloody Sunday relatives was its ability to persuade committed and competent lawyers in Northern Ireland to take on the case without payment. These lawyers put in many hours of unpaid work of a very high standard, and in the course of pursuing the European application they asked British Irish Rights Watch to visit the Public Records Office in London on their behalf to see what documents were lodged there concerning Bloody Sunday. Here, as is often the way, luck played a part, in that a copy of a minute of a meeting was discovered that showed that the Widgery Inquiry was flawed from the outset. This discovery led to more publicity. The visit to the Public Records Office also revealed that many of the documents lodged there had been closed to public scrutiny for as long as 75 years. The lawyers acting for the relatives pressed the government to open these files, and eventually they did release most of the documents.

The lawyers then asked Professor Dermot Walsh of the University of Limerick to examine the newly released papers. He produced a detailed report,[8] which showed that statements made by soldiers immediately after Bloody Sunday were significantly at variance with those they made on oath to the Widgery Tribunal. Judicial review proceedings were commenced to quash the findings of the Widgery Tribunal, and all the new evidence was presented to the British Government, which promised to study it. However, the very next day, the then Secretary of State for Northern Ireland, Sir Patrick Mayhew, said during a radio interview that there could be no question of an apology for Bloody Sunday. The relatives then presented their evidence to the Irish Government, which decided to make their own assessment of the case. They presented their report[9] to the British Government, which had recently changed its political complexion after a general election, in June 1997. In January 1998, on the eve of the 26th anniversary, the British Government announced a new public inquiry on Bloody Sunday.[10]

---

7   BIRW, *'Bloody Sunday': Submission to the United Nations Special Rapporteur on Summary and Arbitrary Executions – the Murder of 13 Civilians by Soldiers of the British Army on 'Bloody Sunday', 30 January 1972*, 1994, London: BIRW.

8   Walsh, D, *The Bloody Sunday Tribunal of Inquiry: A Resounding Defeat for Truth, Justice and the Rule of Law*, 1996, Derry: Bloody Sunday Trust.

9   Government of Ireland, *Bloody Sunday and the Report of the Widgery Tribunal: The Irish Government's Assessment of the New Material*, June 1997, Dublin: Government of Ireland.

10 Statement by the Prime Minister to the House of Commons, HC Deb Cols 501–03, 29 January 1978.

Two other factors played an important role in realising the relatives' aim of a new inquiry. In 1996, a book was published[11] of eyewitness accounts of Bloody Sunday that had been discounted by Lord Widgery, and which suggested that not only the Paras but other regiments might also have been responsible for some of the deaths and injuries. British Irish Rights Watch provided a detailed preface for the book. The book reached best seller status in Ireland[12] and generated considerable publicity.

British Irish Rights Watch also used its contacts with Channel Four News, a major UK television news company, to obtain national news coverage of the growing pressure for a new inquiry. They conducted their own research and interviewed eyewitnesses, experts and some of the key actors in the events of Bloody Sunday, including the former commanding officer of the Paras, Derek Wilford, and the prime minister of the day, Edward Heath. Their coverage, which made the issue headline news, undoubtedly helped to create a climate in which a new inquiry became inevitable.

British Irish Rights Watch would not for a moment suggest that it was the only organisation involved in bringing about a new inquiry into Bloody Sunday; indeed, it has always insisted that the relatives deserve the credit for keeping the flame of justice alive for so many years and involving those who could help to achieve their ends. Nevertheless, as the above description shows, the NGO did play a key role at several points. When it began work on the case in 1992, there was no certainty that six years later a new inquiry would be announced – if anything, the organisation would have predicted failure. However, by a combination of tactics – using human rights law and mechanisms, networking with lawyers and others, publicity, and mobilising political pressure – the seemingly impossible was eventually achieved.

CONCLUSION

There is no rule book for how to be an effective NGO. Every NGO makes mistakes, many learn the hard way, and some never learn. However, it is possible to learn to be effective, even when money and other resources are lacking. Belief in a just cause, coupled with common sense, can take an NGO a remarkably long way.

When NGOs are ineffective, it is usually because they do not have sufficient belief in their own abilities. Too often they stick to the people they know and the methods they know, with the result that they preach to the converted. The most effective NGOs learn all the time, trying new strategies,

---

11 Mullan, D (ed), *Eyewitness Bloody Sunday*, 1996, Dublin: Wolfhound.
12 An American edition has also sold very well.

adopting the successful tactics of others, and avoiding making the same mistakes.

Many NGOs are very lacking in self-confidence, thinking that they could never take on powerful vested interests, but they are wrong. NGOs can and do change the world. When they do so though, it is rarely a matter of accident or good luck. It is more usually the result of years of painstaking work, often undertaken with great dedication and courage, and the development of a clear and effective strategy.

THEME FIVE

FUTURE CHALLENGES

CHAPTER 18

INCORPORATING THE EUROPEAN CONVENTION ON HUMAN RIGHTS

Andrew Puddephat

INTRODUCTION

On 23 October 1997, the Lord Chancellor, Derry Irvine, stood up in the gilt splendour of the House of Lords and introduced the Human Rights Bill.[1] This Bill made provision to incorporate the European Convention for the Protection of Human Rights and Fundamental Freedoms (the ECHR) into the law of the UK. It formed a crucial part of a significant programme of constitutional reform enacted by the new Labour Government, which also included devolution, reform of the Commons and the Lords itself, and changes to the voting system. After successive attempts through private members to incorporate the Convention,[2] it finally received the backing of the government of the day. But, what difference will it make in reality – just how big a change to the culture of the UK will result?

The European Convention for the Protection of Human Rights and Fundamental Freedoms (ECHR), a treaty of the Council of Europe, came into force on 3 September 1953, having been ratified by the UK Government in March 1951. It was drafted principally by British lawyers, including Lord Kilmuir, later Lord Chancellor in the Conservative Government from 1954 to 1962. It reflected many of the common law rights and freedoms found in Britain. However, the inspiration undoubtedly came from the values that inspired the establishment of the United Nations and its Declaration of Human Rights.[3] In the aftermath of the Second World War and the stunned international reaction to the holocaust, a new determination gripped many States. There was a recognition that the development of a body of international human rights law was an essential part of ensuring that such horrors never happened again. Over time, signatory countries agreed to establish an international court at Strasbourg to enforce the Convention and to allow their citizens to petition the Court if they believed that government had abused their rights. This form of international redress is unique to Europe – nowhere else can a citizen seek legal redress against government in an

---

1 Human Rights Bill, HL Bill 382.
2 The most recent attempt was by Lord Lester of Herne Hill in 1996. See *Rights Brought Home: The Human Rights Bill*, Home Office: Cmnd 3782, para 1.15.
3 *Universal Declaration of the Rights of Man*, adopted as a resolution of the UN General Assembly, 10 December 1948, Res 217 A (III).

international court. Over the last 50 years, a substantial body of jurisprudence has built up.

THE DEVELOPMENT OF THE DEBATE IN THE UK

Most British politicians, including Labour politicians, were content to accept the developing role of the European Court and its judgments. Few opponents of incorporation have ever argued for withdrawal from the Convention. The traditional Diceyan view that freedom in Britain was best protected negatively, by the absence of laws constraining behaviour, held sway.[4] This was, of course, consistent with the uncodified constitution of the UK and the importance accorded to parliamentary sovereignty. The Strasbourg Court existed as a backstop to the common law structures protecting freedom.

This system began to come under strain at the end of the 1960s. The expulsion of people of Asian origin from countries in East Africa, particularly Uganda, led to those who were UK passport holders seeking entry to Britain. An ugly racist backlash followed, led by the maverick MP Enoch Powell, to which the then Labour Government capitulated, passing the Commonwealth Immigrants Act 1968 which – effectively – denied entry into the UK to these UK passport holders, solely because they were non-white.[5] The European Commission on Human Rights complained and condemned but was powerless to change the decision.[6] The lack of an effective domestic remedy to human rights abuses by the State was exposed.

The eruption of the conflict in Northern Ireland began to add to the pressure for change. The UK Government was found guilty of breaching the provisions of the Convention preventing inhuman and degrading treatment in a case that exposed controversial interrogation techniques in Castlereagh Barracks.[7] Further challenges followed – dealing with issues as sensitive as homosexuality in Northern Ireland, a *Sunday Times* exposure of thalidomide, to the provisions of the Prevention of Terrorism (Temporary Provisions) Act 1974.[8] Britain, which had prided itself on its human rights record, which had seen itself as the standard setter, now found itself in the painful position of appearing at the European Court at Strasbourg more than most other countries, and losing.

These judgments awakened the interest of non-government organisations, campaign groups and lawyers throughout the UK. They began to see the

---

4   See, eg, Dicey, AV, *Introduction to the Study of the Law of the Constitution*, 10th edn, 1959, London: Macmillan.
5   Commonwealth Immigrants Act 1968, Cmnd 3566.
6   *East African Asians v UK* (1973) 3 EHRR 76.
7   *Ireland v UK* (1978) 2 EHRR 25.
8   Respectively: *Dudgeon v UK* (1982) 3 EHRR 149; *Sunday Times v UK* (1979) 2 EHRR 245; *Brogan and Others v UK* (1988) 11 EHRR 117.

advantages of having positive rights, enforceable in law. They noticed that where the rights of unpopular groups were concerned – such as prisoners – no effective pressure could be brought to bear upon Parliament to effect a change. Arguing from human rights principles, however, at the European Court was quite a different matter. The outlines of domestic human rights movement in Britain and Northern Ireland began to take shape. Instead of rights being seen as a problem for other countries, it became part of domestic UK politics.

Politicians had different motives. At least part of their desire to incorporate the ECHR came from a desire to avoid continual embarrassment overseas in the European Court. Some, particularly from the right, became indignant that foreign Commissioners could pass judgment on UK law and practice.[9] Withdrawing from the Convention, after so long as a signatory, was not a realistic option but bringing the Convention into the remit of the British courts was – with the likely result of intercepting most cases before they reached Strasbourg. Indeed, the Government White Paper which set out the thinking behind incorporating the ECHR was called *Rights Brought Home* and said, 'The time has come to enable people to enforce their Convention rights against the State in the British courts ...'.[10]

Ministers have consistently talked of repatriating human rights implying that it is a patriotic act.[11] However, the move to incorporate the Convention represented more than a desire to avoid embarrassment. The Labour Party, in opposition, had become converted to supporting incorporation.[12] Previously, the Labour Party had opposed this policy – largely out of fear and distrust of the judges. Indeed, when Labour was last in government, it was Conservative opposition politicians who called for incorporation against the will of the Wilson and Callaghan governments.[13] Roy Hattersley, when shadow Home Secretary, fiercely opposed incorporation. He did so, as did outspoken Labour politicians, such as Clare Short, because of hostility to the extension of judicial power such a move could represent.

Judges are not regarded as popular in Britain. Widely seen as out of touch and often ridiculed for their public school backgrounds and ignorance of

9   *Farrell and Others v UK* No 9013/80; 30 DR (1982); 38 DR 44 (1984).

10   *Rights Brought Home: The Human Rights Bill*, Cmnd 3782, London: Home Office, para 1.18.

11   Eg, Tony Wright MP at Charter 88's Constitutional Convention, 12 July 1997 and Mike O'Brien MP at IPPR fringe meeting 1997 Labour Party Conference.

12   Labour's commitment to two stage implementation of a Bill of Rights was endorsed at the 1993 Conference. Stage one was to be the passing of a Bill to incorporate those civil and political rights found in the ECHR. Stage two proposed an all party commission to deliver to Parliament, within two years, a British Bill of Rights, updating the civil and political rights found in the ECHR and including social and economic rights. The latter stage was dropped in the 1997 manifesto.

13   In 1969, Lord Lambton sought to introduce a Bill of Rights under the Ten Minute Rule Bill and Conservative MP Quentin Hogg published a pamphlet in favour of a Bill of Rights (Conservative Political Centre Pamphlet No 430).

popular cultural heroes, judges did not seem in the 1980s to be a likely source of protection for human rights.[14] Campaign groups were hostile because of the perceived judicial collusion with police and prosecutors in many miscarriage of justice cases. Politicians of both left and right feared judicial encroachment upon deeply felt moral and political issues, if the judges came to wield the powers they might be granted by a Bill of Rights. The spectacle of the US, where issues, such as abortion, were fought out in the Supreme Court, which, at the same time, allowed the increasing judicial execution of prisoners, horrified politicians brought up in the British parliamentary tradition.

However, years of Conservative dominance began to change the outlook of many. The absence of constitutional checks on the power of the executive was emphasised by the often divisive policies of Mrs Thatcher.[15] With parliamentary opposition weak, the judges themselves became bolder in challenging government power, extending the scope of judicial review. A new reforming Lord Chancellor, Lord Mackay, had succeeded the sclerotic Lord Hailsham. A series of radical appointments to the bench followed and the High Court even took on – by British standards – a 'liberal' outlook. Meanwhile, in the background, intense lobbying by a small number of organisations and individuals had secured a change in Labour policy to support for a 'democratically entrenched' Bill of Rights by the time of the 1992 General Election.[16] The suspicion of the judiciary remained, but Labour was willing to contemplate introducing enforceable rights in certain circumstances. Further lobbying followed and, by 1997, Labour was committed to incorporating the ECHR as the first step towards a British Bill of Rights.

THE HUMAN RIGHTS BILL: OTHER COMMONWEALTH MODELS

Despite the explicit nature of the commitment in opposition, many observers were pleased that a commitment to human rights appeared in Labour's first Queen's Speech upon winning the 1997 General Election. The Home Secretary, Jack Straw MP, was known to be a keen supporter, and the influence of the new Lord Chancellor, Derry Irvine (who was personally close to UK Prime Minister, Tony Blair) must also have helped. With the prospect of

---

14 The argument is set out in Griffiths, J, *The Politics of the Judiciary*, 1985, London: Fontana.

15 See, generally, Thornton, P, *Decade of Decline: Civil Liberties in the Thatcher Years*, 1987, London: National Council for Civil Liberties.

16 Liberty and Charter 88 established a small lobby group, the Labour Rights Campaign, with financial support from the Joseph Rowntree Reform Trust. This organised mailings to Labour Party branches, drafted model resolutions, etc. Meetings were organised between myself and Francesca Klug with Labour Party researchers and key politicians, such as Clare Short, who were vocal opponents of a Bill of Rights.

incorporation, lobbying began in earnest with attention focusing on the model of entrenchment that the Government might adopt. Very rapidly, lawyers and legal based campaign groups began to pose the options as a choice between the Canadian model of entrenchment and that of New Zealand, a refrain that was then taken up by journalists.[17] Both countries had common law traditions and both had introduced Bills of Rights in recent times. Despite the Government's insistence that it was looking for a 'British' model of entrenchment, there was an attempt to portray it as leaning towards the 'weak' New Zealand model rather than the 'strong' Canadian model.

In essence, the difference between the two was as follows. The Canadian Charter of Rights and Freedoms was part of Canada's constitution, amendable only by means of a special majority. The Charter takes precedence over any law that is 'inconsistent' with it, thus allowing judges to strike down laws if, in their opinion, they conflicted with the Charter. However, Parliament or a provincial legislature can pass laws in breach of the Charter provided that they do so explicitly, by declaring that the law is passed 'notwithstanding' the Charter.[18] In practice, this power has been little used by the Federal Parliament, presumably because of the likely public outcry, although it has been extensively used at the provincial level.[19] In New Zealand, by contrast, the Bill of Rights is an ordinary Act of Parliament, not entrenched by means of a special majority. Nor can the courts invalidate laws that breach the Act, whether those laws were passed before or after the Bill. However, the Attorney General has to tell Parliament if a proposed law is in breach of the Bill. Both Canadian and New Zealand models allow the courts to strike down the common law, subordinate legislation and the discretionary acts of ministers and public officials.

From a lawyer's point of view, it is perhaps understandable that the Canadian model was preferable – the greater scope for judges to strike down laws would have many more opportunities for lawyers to make their mark. However, the strong parliamentary tradition in Britain, made the introduction of such a model very unlikely. It is worth noting that the New Zealand Government originally proposed introducing a Bill along Canadian lines, but the adverse public reaction persuaded them otherwise.

Furthermore, it is unwise to characterise the New Zealand model as 'weak'; rather it is interpretative.[20] Section 6 of the Bill states that:

17 See John Wadham, Director of Liberty (1997) *The Guardian*, 1 July, and the reply from Andrew Puddephat (1997) *New Statesman*, 18 July.
18 See, generally, Driedger, EA, 'The Canadian Charter of Rights and Freedoms' (1982) 14 Ottawa L Rev 366.
19 See Mandel, M, *The Charter of Rights and the Legalisation of Politics in Canada*, 2nd edn, 1994, Toronto: Thompson, pp 87–96.
20 For an alternative view, see Butler, AS, 'The Bill of Rights debate: why the New Zealand Bill of Rights Act 1990 is a bad model for Britain' (1997) 17 OJLS 323.

> Wherever an enactment can be given a meaning that is consistent with the rights and freedoms contained in the Bill of Rights, that meaning shall be preferred to any other meaning.

In other words, it provided a way of reading rights into existing legislation, not in defiance of its original meaning but creatively.

It was clear in advance of the White Paper that the Government would not favour the Canadian model. First, there is no codified constitution into which such legislation could be inserted and, therefore, it was always likely to be a simple Act of Parliament. The question was how effective a model would the Government present and what powers would it give the judges. In fact, and to the surprise of many, the Government came up with a unique and original approach to the problem – a 'British' model.

THE UK MODEL

The Human Rights Act gives effect to most of the rights contained in the Convention.[21] This, in itself, is an immense step. For the first time, people in the UK will be able to enforce their Convention rights in the domestic courts. Anyone living in the jurisdiction of the UK, whether British citizen or foreign national can claim these rights. They can go to any court or tribunal if they believe their rights are being violated. A complaint can be made against an Act of Parliament, subordinate legislation, the operation of the common law or the action of a public body or official.

All public authorities will have to comply with the provisions of the Convention. Even a failure to act can be construed as non-compliance. Not only are central and local government, the courts, police and immigration officials covered by the Act (as one would expect), but also any 'person' whose 'functions are of a public nature'.[22] This could include not only the public functions of privatised utilities, but also the Church of England in so far as it carries out a public function. When the scope of the Bill sunk in, many of those who had welcomed it unreservedly at first (such as the Bishops in the House of Lords) began to have doubts or to seek exemptions. Particular concerns have been raised by journalists who fear the effects of Art 8 of the Convention, which upholds the right to privacy, even though Art 10 guarantees a right to freedom of expression. The Government's response has been that there is no intention to introduce a privacy law, setting out the arguments in a detailed research paper.[23]

---

21 ECHR, Arts 1 and 13 are omitted.
22 Human Rights Act 1998, s 63(c).
23 Government Research Paper 98/25, 13 February 1998.

However, this part of the Act will vastly extend the scope of the courts to review the actions of public authorities. Previous powers of judicial review have been limited. A decision made by public authorities could only be challenged if it was such that no reasonable person could make it (or if it were illegal or procedurally improper). The actual decision, if taken properly, was, however, immune. This is no longer true. On the coming into force of the Act, any action thought to breach human rights can be challenged. Even the courts themselves are not immune. A judicial decision that breaches the Convention may also be challenged.

If a court finds that there has been a breach of human rights, they can grant 'such relief or remedy as it considers just and appropriate'.[24] If the courts hearing the case already have the power to award damages, they will be able to use this power in cases where the Convention is breached. The usual array of legal remedies will be available – issuing an injunction, requiring particular actions of the public body, quashing existing decisions. The new range of powers open to the courts is considerable.

However, the courts will not have the power to strike down primary legislation.[25] This issue is the single most contentious issue in modern human rights debate. There is a considerable body of public concern about the use of judicial discretion. The central role that Parliament plays in the political culture of Britain meant it was unlikely (at least in the first phase) that the courts would be given the power to overrule legislation held to be in breach of human rights. Nevertheless, the model advanced by the Government is far from being the 'weak' model its critics were proclaiming in advance.

The courts can interpret legislation as far as possible in a way that is compatible with the Convention. If the wording of an Act of Parliament can be understood to be consistent with the Convention, the courts will be entitled to that inference, although they must take into account the jurisprudence of the European Court. This will give the courts the power, if they wish to exercise it, to 'read' rights into existing legislation, even if they were absent from the wording and intentions of those who framed the legislation. Whether the courts will be creative with the opportunities offered is one of the most fascinating questions to be answered over the next years.

The Human Rights Act gives a role to the courts if they believe that an Act of Parliament is incompatible with the provisions of the Convention. In these circumstances, the courts can make a 'declaration of incompatibility' (s 4), in effect, the formal expression of an opinion that Parliament has got it wrong. In such circumstances, the Government can move quickly to find a remedy by

---

24 Human Rights Act 1998, s 8(1).

25 Although they will have the power to strike down legislation made in the devolved Assembly in Northern Ireland. Northern Ireland Office, *Rights, Safeguards and Equality of Opportunity*, agreement reached in the multi-party negotiations, Cmnd 3883, 1998, Belfast: Northern Ireland Office, para 2.

issuing a Statutory Instrument amending the particular legislation. This will have to be approved by both Houses of Parliament, thus ensuring there is the opportunity for parliamentary debate.

Francesca Klug, research fellow at Kings College in London, suggested this innovative and unique approach, an example of the Government's willingness to take external advice.[26] From the announcement that the Government intended to incorporate the Convention, in the Queen's speech in May 1997, it was clear that the Government would not give powers to the courts to strike down primary legislation. This can be interpreted cynically as an attempt to weaken the controls upon the use of government power. But, in fact, there is a good democratic case for this approach. The protection of human rights is not a simple task – balancing the right to privacy against the right to freedom of expression, for example, is a complex moral and political problem. In effect, where that balance is struck could determine just how freely the press is able to operate. Such a decision – with all the profound implications that follow – is surely best taken by Parliament in the full glare of publicity and where those with a view are able to vigorously lobby MPs, rather than by judges who are meant to be above the political fray.

Nor should the force of a formal declaration be overlooked. If the courts were to find an Act, or part of an Act, in breach of fundamental rights, then the moral and political pressure on the Government to act would be profound. Any decision not to act on the court's findings would need justifying and there is every prospect of a lively political debate. It is this aspect of the Government's proposals that is, in many ways, the most positive. If the powerful cultural effect of a Bill of Rights is to be felt, it needs fierce public discussion and debate, not to be buried in the dusty language of the courts.

The final innovative feature of the Act is the provision to ensure adequate scrutiny of legislation for its human rights implications. Every Bill coming before Parliament will include a human rights statement from the sponsoring minister stating whether the proposed legislation is compatible with the Convention. Clearly, any adverse statement will have to be carefully defended. For example, it might be that a Bill to ban tobacco advertising acknowledges a breach of the Convention right to freedom of expression, but defends it as being in the public interest.

The Government has also suggested creating a specialist human rights Parliamentary Committee as a joint committee of both Houses of Parliament. Charter 88 has suggested that such a Joint Committee, though rare, is the most appropriate model.[27] The powers of such a committee need to be wide ranging, including conducting of human rights audits of government departments and agencies, policy reviews and the monitoring of the use of

---

26   Klug, F, 'Models of incorporation' (1997) unpublished.
27   Byrne, I, *Parliamentary Protection of Human Rights: The Option*, 1998, London: Charter 88.

delegated powers to ensure that they comply with the provisions of the Convention.

FLAWS IN THE MODEL

Although innovative, the Government's approach to incorporating the Convention is far from perfect. Article 13 of the Convention states that there should be an effective remedy for breaches of the Convention. The Government has omitted to incorporate this clause, arguing that the act of incorporation itself represents the provision of a remedy for human rights abuses. This is in contrast to every other State, which has included Art 13 when incorporating the Convention into their domestic law. The absence of this clause leaves open the possibility that the courts may find a breach of human rights, but that the victim will still have to go to the European Court in Strasbourg for an effective remedy. A further problem is that, in the event of a declaration of incompatibility, the victim has no guaranteed redress. In the case of an asylum seeker, for example, he or she could be deported, even though the deportation procedure was found to be incompatible with the Convention. Clearly, this is a gap that needs to be filled.

The most glaring gap in the Government's proposals is the absence of a Human Rights Commission. The argument for such a Commission has been well set out by IPPR.[28] Incorporating the Convention is a radical step in the UK – there is no domestic experience of rights; indeed, the UK is a 'rights illiterate' society. A Human Rights Commission would have an invaluable role to play in promoting a better public understanding of human rights. It could advise people on possible cases and be an independent source of expertise to the Parliamentary Committee. It would help provide the teeth that are necessary if incorporation of the Convention is to be effective.

However, the Government has set its face firmly against creating such a commission. One problem is that it inevitably raised question marks over the future of the free standing commissions – the Commission for Racial Equality (CRE) and the Equal Opportunities Commission (EOC). While the CRE seemed relaxed about the creation of a Human Rights Commission, as long as there was no question of downgrading race discrimination issues, the EOC was less so. There appears to have been some lobbying in Whitehall to block the creation of a new body. It was not that Ministers needed a great deal of persuading. Pressure on the prisons budget meant that the Home Office was under acute financial strain – even the minimal cost of a Human Rights Commission was resisted. There may also have been a sense that, creating a further quango, which could be used to make life harder for other

---

28 IPPR, *A Human Rights Commission*, December 1997, London: IPPR.

government departments, was not worth fighting for politically. Whatever the reasons, there will be no commission, although campaigners will not let go of the issues. In the months to come, the Government will find itself under increasing pressure to create such a body. This pressure may be increased by the legislation implementing the Northern Ireland referendum. The Good Friday Agreement requires the setting up of a Human Rights Commission for Northern Ireland, and envisages the creation of a new Equality Commission to replace the existing Northern Ireland equality quangos.[29]

The Government has no plans to incorporate other human rights treaties into UK law. Labour Party policy has been to treat incorporating the ECHR as the first step towards creating a British Bill of Rights. This was reaffirmed at successive conferences. It did not, however, find its way into the manifesto for the 1997 election – the current Home Secretary has always made it clear that the Government wishes to incorporate the Convention and then take stock. There are a number of problems with this approach.

First, the Convention is an international treaty and was drafted as such. It was meant to be the backstop to a domestic Bill of Rights, the lowest common denominator below which no country should fall. To imagine it is satisfactory as a domestic instrument is to misunderstand its purpose. Secondly, it was drafted some time ago at the end of the Second World War. While imaginative and progressive in its day, it is not the last word in human rights thinking. If British industry were to develop new car, it would not start with the post-war Morris Minor, it would surely look for something more modern. Since it was drafted, a number of more comprehensive human rights treaties have been produced – for example, the United Nations Covenants on Civil and Political Rights and Economic, Cultural and Social Rights. There have also been specific conventions on race, women, children, torture, freedom of expression and others. Britain has signed up to all of these Conventions, albeit with reservations in some cases. There is no logical reason why they should not be incorporated into British law.

Of course, it could be argued that the result would be a hotchpotch of different instruments, and there is some logic to this argument. The sensible option would be for the Government to begin a widespread process of consultation about the human rights standards that should be incorporated into a British Bill of Rights, using the various conventions to which the Government is a signatory, as the starting point. Such a process took place in Canada prior to their implementing the Canadian Charter of Rights, and one of the effects of such a prolonged piece of public consultation – observers have argued – was the embedding of human rights values in Canadian society. Such a consultation would be best co-ordinated by a Human Rights

---

29 *Op cit*, Northern Ireland Office, fn 25, paras 5 and 6. The plan to amalgamate the equality bodies faced fierce opposition, but will go ahead.

Commission, and would be a way of popularising knowledge about human rights.

There is a more compelling political reason for moving beyond the Convention. The new political agreement reached in Northern Ireland accepts that a Bill of Rights is an essential building block of any settlement.[30] It is one of the few issues on which the majority of parties to the talks agree, although they do not agree on the basis for such a Bill.[31] What is clear, however, is the Convention on its own is not an adequate basis – any Bill of Rights for Northern Ireland would have to contain protections for language and culture not found in the Convention. This is accepted in the Agreement itself.[32] The dilemma for the Government would be to introduce a higher standard of human rights into Northern Ireland while seeking to ring fence these provisions from Britain. Such an attempt would almost certainly be doomed. Ironically, the conflict in Northern Ireland may well be the springboard for improving human rights overall in the UK.

CHANGING THE CULTURE

But, what effect will incorporating the ECHR have on the politics, law and culture of this country? Much will, no doubt, be written about its effect on the making of law. As with any Bill of Rights there is a danger that lawyers, to the exclusion of a wider audience, dominate the debate. It may be worth reflecting on the impact of the ECHR on culture, on the way people think and feel about issues. At the end of the day, all the laws in the world are useless unless people are prepared to respect and use them. Why should human rights standards take hold in the popular imagination?

For the first time in British history, there will be a clear set of human rights standards against which the conduct of public authorities can be judged. It will also assuage fears that 'human rights' claims are just a licence for selfish behaviour. The public debate about rights in Britain is uninformed, even among experienced political journalists. Furthermore, the influence of US style communitarianism on the New Labour leadership is strong. Its founder, Amitai Etzioni, while supporting a Bill of Rights, has argued for 'a moratorium on the minting of most, if not all, new rights'.[33] Etzioni has argued that a rights culture leads to the breakdown of society through the neglect of responsibilities. In his speech to the Labour Party conference in

---

30   *Op cit*, fn 25, Northern Ireland Office, paras 5(b), 5(c), 11, 26(a).
31   Irwin, C, *The Search for a Settlement: Report of a Survey Commissioned by Queens University Belfast/Rowntree Trust*, 1998, Belfast: Fortnight Educational Trust.
32   *Op cit*, fn 30, Northern Ireland Office.
33   Etzioni, A, *The Spirit of Community*, 1995, London: Fontana.

1997, Tony Blair talked of the language of duty rather than rights.[34] When in opposition, Jack Straw, the Home Secretary, talked of the need to 'break out of the language of dutiless rights'.[35]

While, in the context of the US, some of these anxieties might have foundation, they are somewhat bizarre in the context of the UK, where there have never been a set of enforceable rights in UK law. Nor is the language of duty alien to modern human rights thinking. Article 29 of the Universal Declaration of Human Rights says 'Everyone has duties to the community in which alone the free and full development of his [sic] personality is possible'.[36] The preambles to the two international Covenants that follow on from the Universal Declaration refer to 'the individual, having duties to other individuals and to the community ...'.

Modern human rights thinking is not another form of licence. Rights exist in balance with each other. The exercise of my rights has to co-exist with respect for the rights of others. We all have a mutual responsibility to each other. Both the courts and Parliament, when considering how to strike the balance, will have to weigh the rights and responsibilities involved in any decision. A Bill of Rights could provide a secular framework in which some of the more contentious moral issues of our time can be discussed.[37]

In this respect the Government's approach is particularly useful. The courts will have the power to issue declaratory judgements, which will inevitably have a powerful moral force. But, it will be for Parliament to make the final decision. One can imagine, for example, the courts deciding that a legislative ban on tobacco advertising is a breach of the tobacco companies' right to free speech. Parliament would then have to debate whether the right of the tobacco companies should override the public interest in promoting health. Should free speech be limited in such a way? Does the concept evolved by the court at Strasbourg that some limitations are 'necessary in a democratic society' apply in this instance? The opportunity for a more informed and public debate than we have managed so far is considerable. More informed and structured debate can only be good for democracy.

Incorporating the Convention into UK law could also have a dramatic effect on Parliament. Far too often, Parliament has been supine in the face of abuses of human rights by the executive. The doctrine of parliamentary sovereignty is the cornerstone of the unwritten constitution. In theory, it is highly democratic in that only elected representatives can make laws. But, in

---

34 Rt Hon Tony Blair MP, Prime Minister and Leader of the Labour Party, to the Labour Party Annual Conference, Brighton 1997.

35 Jack Straw MP to Charter 88 debate on 'Rights and Responsibilities', June 1996.

36 UN Doc E/CN 4/1996/7.

37 See Klug, F, *Reinventing Community – The Rights And Responsibilities Debate*, 1997, London: Charter 88.

practice, only that legislation which the government promotes (or tolerates in the case of the odd back bench Bill) has a reasonable chance of becoming law. Measures which threaten human rights – like the 1996 Asylum and Immigration Act – can be forced through, and measures which could protect rights, such as the private members Bill tackling discrimination against disabled people, can be lost. One of the real weaknesses of the unwritten constitution and the doctrine of parliamentary sovereignty is that there is no systematic method of protecting human rights.[38]

The Government's proposals could invigorate Parliament in a number of ways. Ministers and civil servants will have to identify the human rights implications of new legislation – allowing MPs to debate the issue in a more informed way. The creation of a specialist Parliamentary Committee will help develop real human rights expertise among a core group of MPs. Finally, the fast track procedure to consider declarations by the courts means that Parliament will have to think through all legislation in terms of human rights standards in a way that is not conceivable under the old system. Just as proper controls over public spending require both audit standards and a Public Accounts Committee, so the propagation of human rights values requires a set of standards and a means to scrutinise them.

Incorporating the Convention will, of course, set a new course in law. If the experience of other countries is at all relevant, we can expect to see early challenges from commercial companies if there are attempts to restrict their right to 'free speech'. Elsewhere, tobacco companies have used this kind of provision to challenge prohibitions on tobacco advertising. Of course, the manner of incorporation will leave the final say in the hands of Parliament rather than the courts – but this will test the mettle of MPs. Furthermore, notwithstanding the Government's assurances, it is almost certain that the Convention will produce a raft of challenges alleging breaches of the right to privacy. The most ironic effect of the Act may be that it will be used to strike down some of the law and order and immigration rules and regulations brought in by the this Government.

But, most important of all, the incorporation of the ECHR could help educate the wider public as to the real mean of human rights values. It is a document that can be taught in schools and colleges. Judgments made by the courts are likely to be the subject of public discussion and debate. The Convention will force all public authorities to examine their own obligations under the Convention. Its provisions will need to be incorporated into the training programmes of public officials. Human rights values will begin to permeate public life and it is in this – perhaps, more than any number of cases – where the true effect of this legislation will be most felt.

---

38   Klug, F, Starmer, K and Weir, S, *The Three Pillars of Liberty*, 1996, London: Routledge.

CHAPTER 19

HUMAN RIGHTS AND EASTERN EUROPE

Bill Bowring

INTRODUCTION

It is increasingly the case that textbooks and even more scholarly works analyse the European Convention on Human Rights (ECHR) as a body of doctrine to be treated by the same methods as topics of domestic law, in particular such methods as the dissection of judicial reasoning, for example. However, this mode of analysis must surely break down in the face of the complexities of Eastern Europe (and should perhaps be reviewed insofar as it is applied to domestic law). The events of 1989 (the fall of the Berlin wall) and 1991 (the collapse of the Soviet Union) have not signalled the apotheosis of Western liberal democracy and human rights. Indeed, Protocol 11 to the ECHR, which came into force in November 1998, abolishing the Commission and creating a new Court, may equally be the harbinger either of the devaluation and breakdown of the existing system, or of its triumphant consolidation across an unprecedentedly large territory.

First, it is necessary to say what is meant by 'Eastern Europe'. At one time, this phrase might have been used to describe those States east of the Iron Curtain, but not part of the Soviet Union. Russia's accession to the Council of Europe on 28 February 1996 completed a process which started two decades earlier at Helsinki (see below). This means that two of the most important European institutions concerned with the protection of human rights, the Council of Europe and the OSCE, have a territorial reach which extends to the Bering Straits. If 'Western Europe' accurately describes the States of the European Union, plus Norway and Switzerland, then 'Eastern Europe' by implication, includes everything to the east.

It is possible to identify three features common to this region, which in a number of cases, were in evidence even before 1989. The first, which is common to all, is that each State has, since 1989, adopted a new constitution (or, in the case of Latvia, restored the former 1922 Constitution), together with a variety of new arrangements, for example, constitutional courts and ombudsmen, to consolidate the rule of law and protect human rights. The second feature is that each State has ratified at least some of the major human rights instruments emanating from the United Nations and the Council of Europe, and many have accepted a degree of interference with internal affairs which would not have been contemplated during the Cold War, going further in this direction than many Western European States. The third feature, which may be considered problematic, is that the region is characterised, to varying extents, by a revival of ethnic, linguistic and national aspiration, signifying new problems of minority and group rights.[1] This is complicated by the existence, in many cases, of large settled minorities whose distinguishing characteristics are those of a majority in a neighbour – the extreme case being that of the 25 million strong ethnic Russian 'diaspora', many of whom settled in former Soviet Union territories.

THE COLD WAR

It would be wrong to suggest, as have some authors, that there was no law in either the former Soviet Union or its satellites in Central and Eastern Europe, nor was there concern at all for human rights. Nevertheless, the fact that the 1948 Universal Declaration of Human Rights was enshrined in binding treaties only nearly two decades later in 1966, and that civil and political rights were separated from social, economic and cultural rights, are symptomatic of a fierce ideological battle in relation to the protection of rights on a global scale. Moreover, the 'socialist' school of international law insisted, above all else, on State sovereignty and the right of non-interference in internal affairs. In Eastern Europe, therefore, the protection of fundamental rights was always in contention. These rights were, however, granted by the State, and, as Feldbrugge has put it, 'the citizen participated in them by being involved in the socialist system of production'.[2] The right to work was paramount, followed closely by rights to housing,[3] education, health care, and social security. The State, or the party system which all too frequently replaced it, sought to legitimise itself on the basis that it secured these rights, however unevenly and inefficiently. It is notable that, except in the cases of the German Democratic Republic and Romania, the old order self-destructed instead of being brought down by uprising or mass revolt.

---

1   See, most recently, Müllerson, R, 'Introduction', in Müllerson, R, Fitzmaurice, M and Andenas, M, *Constitutional Reform and International Law in Central and Eastern Europe*, 1998, The Hague: Kluwer, especially pp xvi–xxii; Pogany, I, 'International human rights standards and the new constitutions: minority rights in Central and Eastern Europe', p 155, in the same volume.

2   Feldbrugge, FJM, *Russian Law: The End of the Soviet System and the Role of Law*, 1993, Dordrecht: Martinus Nijhoff, p 217.

3   Van den Berg, G, 'The conflict of civil and administrative law in the USSR: right to housing and freedom of choice of residence in Soviet law and practice', in Ginsburg, S (ed), *Soviet Administrative Law: Theory and Practice*, 1989, Amsterdam: Kluwer.

RIGHTS AS IDEOLOGY

Nevertheless, prior to recent developments, there was no distinctive 'Eastern' model of human rights. The Council of Europe, as the 'sort of social and ideological counterpart'[4] to the military aspects of Western European co-operation represented by NATO, had a clear theoretical stance, based on liberal values. This, together with the existence of a hostile other in close proximity, provided the drive from which resulted the first effective system for the protection of (largely) civil and political rights, one to which its members' States were to cede substantial sovereignty. The Warsaw pact enjoyed no such ideological clarity. There is considerable irony in the fact that the consolidation of Stalin's power was crowned firstly by the USSR's accession to the League of Nations in September 1934 and, secondly, by his Constitution of 5 December 1936. This contained a model list of civil and political rights (listed after the main social and economic rights), entirely parasitic of Western models, primarily for window dressing purposes, one can be sure. Not much is to be found of Karl Marx's critique of civil and political rights, which poses questions for the nature and status of human rights which are as yet far from resolved:

None of the so called rights of man, therefore, go beyond egoistic man, beyond man as a member of civil society, that is, an individual withdrawn into himself ... and separated from the community. In the rights of man, he is far from being conceived as a species-being; on the contrary, species-life itself, society, appears as a framework external to the individuals, as a restriction of their original independence. The sole bond holding them together is natural necessity, need and private interest, the preservation of their property and their egoistic selves.[5]

There was effectively no attempt in Stalin's USSR to develop it a socialist conception of human rights. A Vyshinsky, the remarkable survivor and legal apologist for the Stalinist system, could say no more than: 'Proletarian declarations of rights frankly manifest their class essence, reflecting nothing of the desire of bourgeois declarations to shade off and mask the class character of the rights they proclaim.'[6] The same Vyshinsky was the USSR's permanent delegate to the United Nations at the session which adopted the Universal Declaration of Human Rights on 10 December 1948. The USSR abstained from voting for its adoption, but only on the grounds that there were insufficient mechanisms for guaranteeing rights; that it included no right to self-

---

4   Brownlie, I, *Basic Documents on Human Rights*, 3rd edn, 1992, Oxford: Clarendon, p 325.
5   Marx, K, 'On the Jewish question' (1843), in *Collected Works*, 1975, London: Lawrence & Wishart, Vol 3, p 164.
6   Vyshinsky, A, *The Law of the Soviet State*, 1948, New York: Macmillan, p 554.

determination; and that fascist speech might be permitted.[7] Nonetheless, the USSR ratified all the United Nations human rights instruments, such as the International Covenant on Civil and Political Rights (ICCPR) which it signed on 18 March 1968 and ratified on 16 October 1973. This compares favourably with the United States of America, for which the respective dates are 5 October 1977 and 8 June 1992!

THE END OF THE COLD WAR

The demise of the ideological foundations of the Soviet system should not, therefore, have come as too much of a surprise. 'Marxism-Leninism' rotted from within. Gorbachev announced, in his Report to the 19th All Union Conference of the Communist Party of the Soviet Union on 28 June 1988, that: '… in contemporary conditions human rights, and, above all, the right to life become the concern of the entire world community; they are internationalised, like many other aspects of social life.'[8] This set the seal on a general retreat from 'scientific communism' as the regime's legitimating ideology, to a new language of 'law-governed State' and 'common human values'. In the same report, Gorbachev announced the setting up of a truly revolutionary body (in Soviet terms), a Constitutional Review Committee, to verify the constitutionality of legislation and other legal instruments with 'sufficient powers to do it'.[9] The Committee started work in April 1990, and on 4 April 1991 requested the Supreme Soviet of the USSR to secure ratification of the Optional Protocol to the ICCPR. This enabled persons within the jurisdiction of the USSR to make individual complaints to the Human Rights Committee of the United Nations.[10] The request was complied with on 5 July 1991, placing the USSR ahead of the UK and US (as Russia remains to this date), in this respect.

THE CSCE/OSCE FROM 1975

The ideological transformation described above can be seen as the culmination of a process which began more than 10 years earlier. This was itself perceived in a particularly contradictory light at the time. The Final Act

7   See Bowring, B, 'Human rights in Russia: discourse of emancipation or only a mirage?', in Pogany, I (ed), *Human Rights in Eastern Europe*, 1995, Aldershot: Elgar, pp 87 and 98, and generally.
8   Gorbachev, M, *Report on Progress in Implementing the Decisions of the 27th CPSU Congress and the Tasks of Promoting Perestroika*, 1988, Moscow: Novosti, p 44.
9   *Ibid*, p 53.
10 VSND SSSR, 1991, No 17 item 502; *Sovietskaya Iustitsiya*, 23 December 1991, p 17.

of the Conference on Security and Co-operation in Europe (CSCE, now OSCE) was adopted in Helsinki on 1 August 1975, as the culmination of a process which had started on 3 July 1973. It was signed by 35 States including the US and the USSR. Under Section VII, entitled *Respect for Human Rights and Fundamental Freedoms, including the Freedom of Thought, Conscience, Religion and Belief*, the participating States recognised 'the universal significance of human rights and fundamental freedoms'. They also confirmed 'the right of the individual to know and act upon his rights and duties in this field'.[11]

At the time, the Helsinki Final Act was seen as a diplomatic triumph for Leonid Brezhnev, whose chief motivation was to secure the ratification of the status quo in Europe, especially the divided Germany.[12] The German Democratic Republic had been admitted to the United Nations (with the Federal Republic of Germany) on 18 September 1973, and the GDR's participation and adherence to the Helsinki Final Act gave its leader, Erich Honecker, a great deal of personal and political, pleasure and satisfaction.[13] Helsinki also contributed materially to the eventual demise of the regime and of the State itself – one of the few in history to have disappeared entirely, some 14 years later, in 1989.

However, during this period, nothing very much changed with regard to the USSR's internal policy towards human rights activism. The Soviet human rights movement had come into existence in 1967, led and inspired by the nuclear physicist Andrei Sakharov. In 1969, a group of some 14 activists, including Sergei Kovalyov, the future Russian human rights ombudsman, set up the Action Group for the Defence of Human Rights in the USSR.[14] They compiled the 'Chronicle of Current Events', the first *samizdat* (self-published) human rights bulletin. In September 1974, while the Helsinki negotiations were proceeding, Kovalyov became a member of the Moscow Group of Amnesty International. Within months, on 28 December 1974, he was arrested and charged with 'Anti-Soviet agitation and propaganda' under the notorious Art 70 of the then criminal code, and put on trial. Sakharov picketed the court on the day of the presentation of his Nobel Peace Prize[15] in 1975, and in respect of which he was refused permission to travel. Kovalyov was sentenced to seven years in a forced labour camp, followed by three years internal exile – in Magadan, in the Soviet Far East. Kovalyov was only permitted to return home to Moscow in 1987, after Gorbachev had come to power.

---

11 *Op cit*, Brownlie, fn 4, p 96.

12 See, eg, the pre-perestroika work by Kochan, L and Abraham, R, *The Making of Modern Russia*, 2nd edn, 1983, London: Penguin, p 453.

13 Childs, D, *The GDR: Moscow's German Ally*, 1983, London: Allen & Unwin, p 87.

14 Their 'Appeal to the UN' of 20 May 1969 is to be found in Saunders, G (ed), *Samizdat: Voices of the Soviet Opposition*, 1974, New York: Monad, p 365.

15 The citation called him 'the conscience of mankind' and said that he 'has fought not only against the abuse of power and violations of human dignity in all its forms, but has in equal vigour fought for the ideal of a state founded on the principles of justice for all'.

When, in December 1979, Sakharov denounced the Soviet military intervention in Afghanistan, the authorities had no doubt as to what to do. On 22 January 1980, Sakharov was banished to the 'closed' city of Gorky, and only brought back to Moscow by Gorbachev, to 'perform patriotic work', on 16 December 1986. He died on 14 December 1989 and has, since, achieved contemporary sainthood.

The Helsinki process nevertheless conferred vital legitimacy on human rights activists and on the ideology of universal human rights, and played a crucial role in helping the system to undermine itself in the USSR and in all its Eastern European satellites. Its important 'follow up' conference in Vienna in 1989,[16] and the Copenhagen meeting of the Conference on the Human Dimension of the CSCE in 1990,[17] provided an essential counterpoint to the revolutionary changes in the USSR. The Charter of Paris for a New Europe, adopted on 21 November 1990 by 34 States (following German reunification) contained the most solemn undertaking to abide by human rights and fundamental freedoms.[18] The next meeting of the Conference on the Human Dimension took place in Moscow, immediately prior to the final demise of the USSR in December 1991.

These changes have been reflected in adherence to United Nations instruments. The circumstances of the USSR's ratification of the ICCPR, and of its Optional Protocol, have been related above. All the States of Eastern Europe, and all but one of the former USSR, namely Kazakstan, had by early 1999 ratified this treaty.[19] Russia having acceded to the Optional Protocol, the first Russian cases have now been registered with the Human Rights Committee.[20] All of these States,[21] with the exception of Turkmenistan, have

---

16 For the concluding document, see *op cit*, Brownlie, fn 4, p 450.

17 For the document of the Copenhagen meeting, see *op cit*, Brownlie, fn 4, p 454.

18 *Op cit*, Brownlie, fn 4, p 474.

19 Albania, 4 October 1991; Armenia, 23 June 1993; Azerbaijan, 13 August 1992; Belarus, 12 November 1973; Bosnia and Herzegovina, 1 September 1993; Bulgaria, 21 September 1970; Croatia, 12 October 1992; Czech Republic, 22 February 1993; Estonia, 21 October 1991; Georgia, 3 May 1994; Hungary, 17 January 1974; Kyrgyzstan, 7 October 1994; Latvia, 14 April 1992; Lithuania, 20 November 1991; Macedonia, 18 January 1994; Moldova, 26 January 1993; Poland, 18 March 1997; Romania, 9 December 1974; Slovakia, 28 May 1993; Slovenia, 6 July 1992; Tajikistan, 4 January 1999; Turkmenistan, 1 May 1997; Ukraine, 12 November 1973; Uzbekistan, 28 September 1995; Serbia-Montenegro, 2 June 1971.

20 These cases have been presented by the very active Moscow Centre for the Protection of International Human Rights, led by the practising advocate Karina Moskalenko.

21 Albania, 11 May 1994; Armenia, 13 September 1993; Azerbaijan, 16 August 1996; Belarus, 13 March 1987; Bosnia-Herzegovina, 1 September 1993; Bulgaria, 16 December 1986; Croatia, 12 October 1992; Czech Republic, 22 February 1993; Estia, 21 October 1991; Georgia, 26 October 1994; Hungary, 15 April 1987; Kazakstan, 25 September 1998; Kyrgystan, 5 September 1997; Latvia, 14 April 1992; Lithuania, 1 February 1996; Poland, 26 July 1989; Macedia, 12 December 1994; Moldova, 28 November 1995; Romania, 18 December 1990; Russia 3 March 1987; Slovakia 28 May 1993; Slovenia, 16 July 1993; Tajikistan, 11 January 1995; Ukraine, 24 February 1987; Serbia and Montenegro, 10 September 1991.

ratified the United Nations 1984 Convention against Torture and Other Cruel, Inhuman and Degrading Treatment or Punishment.[22]

CONSTITUTION MAKING

Most Eastern European States moved quickly following the collapse of the USSR to establish themselves on a new constitutional footing.[23] Thus, a majority of Eastern European countries adopted wholly new constitutions.[24] In others, the former constitutions were substantially amended: the Hungarian constitution of 20 August 1949 was last amended by Act LIX in 1997, while Poland's 'Small constitution' of 17 October 1992 has finally been replaced by a new constitution of 2 April 1997, approved by referendum in October 1997. In these States, at least, the experience has been positive. Pogany concluded in 1993 that in Hungary:

> A genuine parliamentary democracy has been established in which respect for the law, fundamental rights, a social market economy, and the generally recognised rules of international law is guaranteed by the Constitution and assured by the Constitutional Court, even if considerable reliance was placed on the Court.[25]

Russia presents a different picture. It obtained a new constitution as a result of the referendum held on 12 December 1993, and only following the dissolution and shelling of the former Parliament, and the abrogation of the former, Brezhnev constitution of 1977. The process is now more or less complete, with the adoption of new constitutions by other States of the former USSR.[26] Ukraine, however, only adopted its new constitution on 28 June 1996.

In Pogany's view, 'the historical record suggests that there were relatively limited expressions of democracy and constitutionalism in most of the States of Eastern Europe prior to the sovietisation of the region'.[27] The dominant traditions were authoritarian, and in many cases moved toward a fascist

---

22 In force 26 June 1987; UNTS 1465, p 85. There are to date 104 parties to the Convention.

23 For an excellent analysis of the process, see Pogany, I, 'A New constitutional (dis)order for Eastern Europe?', in *op cit*, Pogany, fn 7, p 217.

24 These are: Bulgaria, 12 July 1991; Croatia, December 1990; the Czech Republic, 16 December 1992; Romania, 21 November 1991; Serbia and Montenegro, 27 April 1992; Slovenia, 23 December 1991; and the Slovak Republic, 1 September 1992.

25 Pogany, I, 'Constitutional reform in Central and Eastern Europe: Hungary's transition to democracy' (1993) 42 ICLQ 332, pp 354–55.

26 These are as follows: Armenia, 5 July 1995; Belarus, 1 March 1994; Estonia, 28 June 1992; Kazakhstan, 30 August 1995 (replacing an insufficiently – for President Nazarbayev – presidential constitution of 1993); Kyrgyzstan, 5 May 1993; Lithuania, 25 October 1992; Tajikistan, 6 November 1994; Turkmenistan, 18 May 1992; and Uzbekistan, 8 February 1992. Latvia has restored its Constitution of 15 December 1922.

27 *Op cit*, Pogany, fn 23, p 236; see, also, fnn 1 and 25.

regime. This pattern has been exacerbated by an upsurge in nationalism and the more or less uneasy coexistence of national groups. The prognosis is not optimistic: 'As in the inter-war period, fragile democratic and constitutional structures may collapse in the face of insoluble economic problems that threaten social stability and national cohesion.' This is especially the case for Russia and Ukraine.

CONSTITUTIONAL COURTS

Many of these constitutions provide for constitutional courts. This has been referred to as 'a major laboratory of constitutional works'.[28] In Poland, the creation of the Constitutional Tribunal (Trybunal Konstytucyjny) in 1985, and the granting of the power of judicial review to it in 1986, played an important role in Poland's transition to democracy.[29] Following the adoption of Poland's new constitution on 17 October 1992,[30] the Tribunal became still more activist. Bulgaria adopted the first new constitution on 12 July 1991,[31] with a Western European style of constitutional court, whose 12 judges were elected on the basis of one third each by the president, the National Assembly and a joint meeting of Supreme Court of Appeals justices and the Supreme Administrative Court. The Bulgarian judges have come into repeated conflict with the Socialist Party government, for example, over the issue of property ownership.[32]

Elsewhere in Eastern Europe, the development of constitutional review has followed Western models, by evolutionary development. Romania promulgated its new constitution on 8 December 1991, and established a constitutional court on 16 May 1992. This followed the French model of political rather than strictly judicial review, and is based on the Conseil Constitutionnel.[33] The Hungarian constitutional court, working within the

---

28 Ludwikowski, R, 'Constitution making in the countries of former Soviet dominance: current development' (1993) 23 Georgia J Int Comp L 155, p 158.

29 Brzezinski, M and Garlicki, L, 'Judicial review in post-communist Poland: the emergence of a Rechtsstaat?' (1995) 31 Stanford JIL 13.

30 This 'small constitution' replaced only seven chapters of the 1952 Polish constitution, dealing with the division of powers and local government; other provisions of the 1952 constitution remained in force.

31 See *op cit*, Ludwikowski, fn 28, pp 195, 204.

32 Krause, S, 'Bulgarian constitutional court rejects land law' (1995) OMRI Daily Digest, 20 June.

33 See *op cit*, Ludwikowski, fn 28, p 204.

new constitution adopted on 24 August 1990, has been called the strongest in the world.[34]

Such peaceful transformation has not been seen further east. The history of the Russian constitutional court has, to date, been exceptionally turbulent. Not only did it experience evolutionary problems, but it also enjoyed two quite distinct incarnations. Initially, it was born out of the dissolution of the Soviet Union at the end of 1991 and, in its first incarnation, had a political significance of prime importance, under the controversial leadership of its Chairman, Judge Valerii Zorkin. In 1992, it also spent a disproportionate amount of its time adjudicating upon what might have been the 'Russian Nuremburg', but which ended in a classic political compromise, the trial of the CPSU. Yuri Feofanov[35] argues that Russian society expected two mutually contradictory things from the court. The first expectation was of a Nuremburg style of trial in which decommunisation, like denazification, could take place,[36] and the second, an affirmation of the principles of democracy and law. Perhaps it obtained the latter. In any event, that first period of the court's existence ended in its suspension in September 1993, when the executive's tanks shelled the legislature. However, as Judge Ernest Ametistov points out, almost half the cases decided by the court during this phase of its existence concerned social and economic rights – rights to employment, housing, social security. These cases were all brought by individual citizens and, in every instance, the applicant won, judgments effecting consequent amendments in the law. Moreover, the court made regular use of a wide range of international instruments, including conventions and declarations of the International Labour Organisation.[37]

The new constitution of December 1993, although intended to represent an apotheosis of the rule of law and transition to democracy, remained without its 'third power' for a full 18 months, until March 1995. The court's only significant activity during its period of inactivity, apart from drafting its own new law, was the attempted suspension of two of its own members, including former Chairman Zorkin. Even following its rebirth, with a new chairman,

---

34 See Klingsberg, E, 'Judicial review and Hungary's transition from communism to democracy: the constitutional court, the continuity of law, and the redefinition of property rights' (1992) BYU L Rev 41; Sajo, A, 'Reading the invisible constitution: judicial review in Hungary' (1995) 15 OJLS 253.

35 Feofanov, Y, 'The establishment of the constitutional court in Russia and the communist party case' (1993) 19 Review of Central and Eastern European Law 623, pp 623–37. See, also, Sharlet, R, 'The Russian constitutional court: the first term' (1993) Post-Soviet Affairs 1.

36 See, also, Barry, D, 'The trial of the CPSU and the principles of Nuremburg' (1996) 22 Review of Central and Eastern European Law 255, pp 255–62.

37 Ametistov, E, 'Zashchita sotsialnikh prav cheloveka v Konstitutsionnom Sude Rossiiskoi Federatsii: perviye itogi i dalneishiye perspektivi' (The protection of social human rights in the constitutional court of the Russian Federation: first conclusions and further perspectives) (1995) 4 Vestnik Konstitutsionnovo Suda Rossiiskoi Federatsi (Bulletin of the Constitutional Court of the Russian Federation) 13.

Vladimir Tumanov, a Yeltsin supporter, the court could not escape political controversy, ruling in July 1995, that President Yeltsin's December 1994 decrees on 'disarming illegal armed formations in Chechnya' were 'fully consistent with the constitution'.[38] At the present time, the court is engaged in adjudicating upon a range of highly controversial issues, including the volatile relations between the Russian Federation and its subject republics and regions.[39]

Belarus is a case in point, which presents a rapid regression in the sphere of human rights, and which finally became a case of retrogression. The constitutional court, created by the new Constitution of 15 March 1994, came quickly into such sharp conflict with the controversial President Lukashenko, that on 4 December 1996, following his constitution amending referendum of 24 November, a number of judges resigned. On 4 March 1997, a new constitutional court of 11 judges was sworn in, six of whom are the president's appointees, and only four of whom had served on the previous court.

DOMESTIC SAFEGUARDS FOR HUMAN RIGHTS – THE ROLE OF THE OMBUDSMAN

It is in Russia that the introduction of the institution of the ombudsman has proved most controversial. According to Art 8 of the draft Constitutional Law of the Russian Federation on the Plenipotentiary of the Russian Federation for Human Rights,[40] which was not enacted during his term of office,[41] Sergei Kovalyov, as the first holder of such office in Russia's history was to have served in that capacity for a period of five years. In fact, his appointment as plenipotentiary, or ombudsman, lasted only from 17 January 1994 to 10 March 1995, when he was removed by the State Duma which had appointed him. His short term of office was marked by his passionate and controversial opposition to the war in Chechnya, and his fearless investigation of human rights abuses by the Yeltsin regime.[42] His time as chairman of the president's Commission on Human Rights, from 1 November 1993 until 23 January 1996,

---

38 Gaeta, P, 'The armed conflict in Chechnya before the Russian constitutional court' (1996) 7 EJIL 563.

39 Vitruk, N, 'The constitutional court of the Russian Federation and the protection of the (constitutional) fundamental rights and freedoms of citizens', in *The Protection of Fundamental Rights by the Constitutional Court, Proceedings of the UniDEm Seminar*, 1996, Brioni: Council of Europe.

40 'Konstitsutsionniy Zakon Rossiiskoi Federatsii ob Upolnomochennom Rossiiskoi Federatsii po Pravam Cheloveka', reprinted in (1994) Rossiiskii Biulleten po Paravam Cheloveka 4 (Russian Bulletin for Human Rights, Vypusk) 172, pp 172–78.

41 A law was finally enacted on 26 February 1997 and, by February 1998, no appointment had been made.

42 See, generally, Bowring, B, 'Sergei Kovalyov: the first Russian human rights ombudsman – and the last?', in *op cit*, Müllerson *et al*, fn 1, p 14.

proved equally turbulent.[43] His successor, appointed following a political compromise in May 1998, is Oleg Mironov, a Communist!

The Russian ombudsman is not the only such institution in Eastern Europe. The precedent had already been set in one former 'socialist' State, Poland, prior to 1989. On 15 April 1987, the Polish *Sejm* passed the Act creating the Polish ombudsman, known as the 'Commissioner for Civil Rights Protection'.[44] The first commissioner, appointed in November 1987, was Eva Letowska, Professor of Civil Law at the Polish Academy of Sciences. In the early years, prisons, labour law and property claims constituted the largest proportion of complaints referred to her.[45] Elcock concluded that she had 'a degree of independence and effectiveness similar to that which has developed in older democratic States',[46] but her remit did not extend to violations of human rights. Lithuania and Hungary[47] have also established ombudsmen and, in September 1995, the outgoing Latvia's Way government passed Regulations on the National Human Rights Office, establishing an ombudsman's office, which will hear individual complaints of human rights violations, as well as advising the government (*Saeima*) and the public.[48]

A recent attempt at the creation of such a body is the 'ombudsperson', who is part of the Commission of Human Rights (the other part is the Chamber of Human Rights) established by the Dayton Agreements of 14 December 1995.[49] Jessica Simor, who worked as legal adviser to Dr Gret Haller, the ombudsperson, concludes that if the ombudsperson used her powers to take an active role in investigating individuals' complaints against the authorities, her work would be of assistance not only to them, but to the other bodies working for democratisation. Simor is strongly opposed to attempts to treat human rights as 'something separate and independent from the other elements of a democracy'.[50]

---

43 See Henderson, J, 'The Russian ombudsman' (1998) 2 EPL 184.

44 Elcock, H, 'Making bricks without straw? The Polish ombudsman and the transition to democracy' [1992] Int J Soc L 173, pp 173–82.

45 Professor Letowska herself has written in English about her experiences. See Letowska, E, 'The Polish ombudsman (the commissioner for the protection of civil rights)' (1990) 39 ICLQ 206, pp 206–17; and 'The ombudsman and basic rights' (1995) 4(1) East European Constitutional Rev 63; see, also, Brzezinski, M, 'The emergence of judicial review in Eastern Europe: the case of Poland' (1993) 41 AJCL 153.

46 *Ibid*, Brzezinski, p 180.

47 But, it is the constitutional court which has played the most important and controversial role in Hungary – see Sajo, A, 'Reading the invisible constitution: judicial review in Hungary' (1995) 15 OJLS 253.

48 'Constitution watch: Latvia' (1995) 4(4) East European Constitutional Rev 17.

49 The General Framework Agreement for Peace in Bosnia and Herzegovina, signed in Paris. See Simor, J, 'Tackling human rights abuses in Bosnia and Herzegovina: the Convention is up to it, are its institutions?' (1997) 6 EHRLR 644.

50 *Ibid*, p 662.

THE COUNCIL OF EUROPE

Almost all the Eastern European States, and many of those of the former USSR, have joined the Council of Europe. It is instructive to note the 'waves' in which these States acceded. Hungary was in the lead, joining on 6 November 1990, closely followed by Poland on 26 November 1991. Bulgaria (7 May 1992), Slovenia (14 May 1993), Czech Republic (30 June 1993), Slovakia (30 June 1993) and Romania (7 October 1993) were able to satisfy the Council of Europe within the next two years. The Balkans posed greater problems, with Albania joining on 13 July 1995, Macedonia on 9 November 1995 and Croatia on 6 November 1996.

There has been a great increase in the number of Polish applicants. In 1992 just 240 provisional files were opened by the European Commission on Human Rights. In 1994, there were 979, and, in 1995, 1,113. Cases declared admissible included those on the answering of prisoners' mail, length of civil proceedings and length of detention on remand.[51]

There is a similar pattern with respect to the States of the former USSR. Those which have joined the Council of Europe were led by Estonia and Lithuania, both of which States acceded on 14 May 1993. Latvia, with its sensitive possession of a large ethnic Russian minority and consequent problems relating to citizenship, joined on 10 February 1995, followed by Moldova on 13 July 1995. Ukraine was permitted to accede to the Council on 9 November 1995, while Russia, despite very serious misgivings, and due to a possibly deliberate misunderstanding of the obligations involved, finally joined on 28 February 1996.[52] Both Russia and Ukraine have been, and continue to be, subjected to intense pressure from the Council of Europe's Parliamentary Assembly, to cease their use of the death penalty.

All these States have ratified the ECHR. Most recently, on 20 February 1998, the Russian State Duma voted by 294 votes to 11 to ratify the Convention. Despite the fact that Russia had not yet ratified it, the European Commission on Human Rights had received more than 800 complaints from Russian citizens following Russia's accession to the Council of Europe in 1996.[53]

Moreover, 14 of the new members of the Council of Europe[54] have ratified the 1987 European Convention for the Prevention of Torture and Inhuman or

---

51 Drzemczewski, A and Nowicki, M, 'The impact of the ECHR in Poland: a stock taking after three years' (1996) 3 EHRLR 261.
52 See Bowring, B, 'Russia's accession to the Council of Europe and Human rights: compliance or cross-purposes?' (1997) 6 EHRLR 628.
53 (1998) Novye Izvestiya, 6 February.
54 Albania, Bulgaria, Croatia, the Czech Republic, Estonia, Hungary, Moldova, Poland, Romania, Russia, Slovakia, Slovenia, Macedonia and Ukraine.

Degrading Treatment or Punishment (ECPT).[55] Each party to the ECPT is obliged to permit visits by the Committee established under it 'to any place within its jurisdiction where persons are deprived of their liberty by a public authority' (Art 2). This represents the most significant breach to date of the previously paramount principles of State sovereignty and non-interference. To the surprise of many observers, on 20 February 1998 the Russian State Duma voted, by 348 votes to 9, to ratify the Torture Convention – although the deputies voted not to ratify Protocol 6 to the European Convention, which prohibits capital punishment.

The Council of Europe's 1995 Framework Convention on the Protection of National Minorities[56] entered into force on 1 February 1998, following 12 ratifications. By 10 February 1998, it had been signed by 37 States, and ratified by 18.[57] The preamble to the Convention states that 'the upheavals of European history have shown that the protection of national minorities is essential to stability, democratic security and peace in this continent'. Yet, as Rein Müllerson points out, minority rights issues across the whole of Eastern Europe pose grave dangers, especially where Russian minorities are concerned, and nationalisms compete. 'Like the components of binary chemical weaponry they become especially poisonous and deadly when merging with each other.'[58] One leading Russian scholar recently stated that 'safeguarding the human rights of Russians in the territories of the former Soviet Union has become a matter of national survival for Russia'.[59] In these circumstances, the Convention, with its almost non-existent enforcement mechanisms, lack of a definition of its subject matter, and its discretionary character, may be of dubious effectiveness or legitimacy.

CONCLUSION – SYSTEMS BREAKDOWN OR NEW BEGINNINGS?

It is impressive and even unexpected that so many States of the former Soviet Union and Eastern Europe have joined so many international organisations, and ratified so many human rights conventions. It is already possible to say that the rule of law and effective protection of human rights have now been consolidated in States such as Poland, Hungary and the Czech Republic.

---

55 In force 1 February 1989. For the text, see *op cit*, Brownlie, fn 4, p 383.

56 Council of Europe ETS 157.

57 Ratifications: Croatia, 11 October 1997; Estonia, 6 January 1997; Moldova, 20 November 1996; Romania, 11 May 1995; Slovakia, 14 September 1995; Macedonia, 10 April 1997; Ukraine, 26 January 1998. Russia signed on 28 February 1996, on joining the Council of Europe. Armenia ratified on 20 July 1998.

58 *Op cit*, Müllerson, fn 1, p xix.

59 Cited *ibid*, fn 1, p xviii.

However, the political and economic context of Russia and other FSU states is not at all conducive to the creation of a human rights culture. In relation to Russia itself, it has been demonstrated by David Kotz that Russia's gross domestic product fell by 42% and industrial production fell by 46% between 1992 and 1995.[60] Unemployment had reached 9.6% by April 1997, and 6.4 million people out of the total workforce of 72 million were considered underemployed. For those in work, the average wage was US$152 per month.[61] Even then, there is no guarantee that wages will be paid. According to the International Confederation of Free Trade Unions, Russian workers were owed more than US$9 billion in back wages by September 1997. In December 1997, in a decision said to have been the result of government pressure, the Russian constitutional court decided that Art 855 of the new Civil Code, giving priority to the payment of wages over taxes, was unconstitutional. This was a blow to trade union attempts to secure payment of wage arrears through legal action.[62]

The collapse of the USSR, and the widespread internal conflicts which have obtained in newly independent States and their neighbours, have created economic, social and political problems which have resulted in forced migration and refugee problems. There were more than two million such migrants in 1993, according to government figures based on registration with the Federal Migration Service. This organisation also estimates that there are over 500, 000 illegal immigrants in Russia.[63]

Particularly grave violations of human rights are to be found in the prisons of Russia and other States of the former USSR. On 1 July 1997, according to official statistics, 273,367 persons were occupying detention facilities designed for 182,358, that is, 149.9% of the designed capacity. Of these, more than 80, 000 were estimated to be infected with tuberculosis.[64] On 24 December 1997, the State Duma approved the amnesty proposed by President Yeltsin on 20 August, with a view to releasing some 35,000 prisoners. This, however, may simply have the effect of increasing the rate of tuberculosis infection in the population at large.

Although President Yeltsin appears determined that Russia should comply with Council of Europe requirements, there are a number of respects

60 Kotz, D, 'Revolution from above; the demise of the Soviet System', in Weselovsky, T, *Russia: The Roots of Labor Malaise, Radio Free Europe*, 11 February 1998, Radio Liberty, website http://www.rferl.org/nca/features/1998/F.RU.980211152.html.

61 US Department of State, *Russia Country Report on Human Rights Practices for 1997*, released on 30 January 1998, website http://www.state.gov/www/global/human_rights/1997_hrp_report.

62 Borisov, V, Director of the Moscow Institute for Comparative Research into Industrial Relations, quoted in *op cit*, Weselovsky, fn 60.

63 Tessier, K, 'Immigration law in the Russian Federation', website http://www.law.indiana.edu/glsj/vol3/no1/tessrtr1.html.

64 See *op cit*, US Department of State, fn 61.

in which his policies appear to be moving in the opposite direction. One notorious example is the Law on Freedom of Conscience and Religious Organisations which became law on 26 September 1997, and which was welcomed by communists and nationalists alike.[65] In the view of many Russian and international observers, this law discriminates against many religious groups, and violates the Russian Constitution, as well as Russia's international human rights obligations. Another example is the response to organised crime, which is known to have penetrated the whole of Russian society.[66] Yeltsin's Decree No 1226 of 14 June 1994, which gave the police extensive powers, including the right to hold suspects for up to 30 days without charge, was not rescinded until June 1997, despite the fact that it violated fundamental human rights.[67]

There are now many excellent non-governmental organisations at work in Russia and across Eastern Europe, and, consequently, it is possible to say that a genuine civil society is developing.[68] The changes in the direction of consolidated democracy and effective protection of human rights are almost certainly irreversible. But a return to authoritarianism in this region cannot be ruled out, as is borne out by the example of Belarus. A flood of applications from Russia may yet pose insuperable logistical, political and other problems for the protection mechanisms of the Council of Europe.

65   Yuri Belov, a deputy of the KPRF fraction, said 'We, communists, atheists by conviction, are in favour of defending the Orthodox Church' – see Levinson, L, 'Neterpimost v Zakone' (Intolerance by law) (1997) *Express Chronicle*, 26 September.

66   See Lloyd, J, 'Mafia capitalism: the warning from Russia' (1998) 34 Prospect, January; Voronin, Y, 'The emerging criminal State: economic and political aspects of organised crime in Russia' (1996) 2 Transnational Organised Crime 53.

67   See *op cit*, Bowring, fn 52, p 642.

68   See Ruffin, M, McCarter, J and Upjohn, R, *The Post-Soviet Handbook. A Guide to Grassroots Organisations and Internet Resources in the Newly Independent States*, 1996, Center for Civil Society International, Seattle: Washington UP.

CHAPTER 20

ETHNIC DIMENSIONS OF INTERNATIONAL HUMAN RIGHTS

Patrick Thornberry

INTRODUCTION

The human rights response to ethnic[1] issues has fluctuated considerably since the founding of the United Nations and the emergence of the regional intergovernmental organisations. There are reasonably coherent phases in legal dealings with the ethnic question. Each stage of development is at once the product and the progenitor of other life forms. The phases are not hermetically sealed off from one another, but have led into each other in complex ways which this essay explores. The essay also links developments in minority rights with indigenous questions even though the trajectories of the two are not entirely congruent. Attempts are made to differentiate developments, analyses and projections for the two constituencies where appropriate.

As a beginning, it is as well to intimate some idea of what we mean by minorities and indigenous peoples. On the first term, the approach of United Nations special rapporteur, Capotorti, is typical of many efforts, describing a minority as:

> A group numerically inferior to the rest of the population of the State, in a non-dominant position, whose members – being nationals of the State – possess ethnic, religious or linguistic characteristics differing from those of the rest of the population and show, if only implicitly, a sense of solidarity, directed towards preserving their culture, traditions, religion or language.[2]

Article 1.1 of the ILO Convention on Indigenous and Tribal Peoples states that the instrument applies to:

(a) tribal peoples in independent countries whose social, cultural and economic conditions distinguish them from other sections of the national community, and whose status is regulated wholly or partially by their own customs or traditions or by special laws or regulations;

(b) peoples in independent countries who are regarded as indigenous on account of their descent from the populations which inhabited the country,

---

1   For general views from a variety of perspectives, see Hutchinson, J and Smith, AD, *Ethnicity*, 1996, Oxford: OUP.

2   Capotorti, F, *Study on the Rights of Persons belonging to Ethnic, Religious and Linguistic Minorities*, 1991, New York: UN, para 568.

or a geographical region to which the country belongs, at the time of conquest or colonisation or the establishment of present State boundaries and who, irrespective of their legal status, retain some or all of their own social, economic, cultural and political institutions.

Article 1.2 adds that 'Self-identification as indigenous or tribal shall be regarded as a fundamental criterion for determining the groups to which the provisions of this Convention apply'. It must be observed that general international law has not advanced to a canonical definition of terms – nor is there any consensus on what constitutes a 'national' minority. Capotorti's views have been challenged by the United Nations Human Rights Committee. There is a politics of definition circulating around the recognition of indigenous peoples in the United Nations draft Declaration on the Rights of Indigenous Peoples, with (some) governments pressing for definition and the indigenous resisting.[3] Some even refuse to use 'peoples' preferring 'populations' or just 'indigenous people'. There is and will continue to be an interpenetration between the legal regimes for such groups in international law. The two groups are not yet sealed into separate ethnic boxes.

The 50th anniversary of the Universal Declaration on Human Rights is highly appropriate for celebration. It should also be recalled that 1998 is also the anniversary of the Convention against Genocide, and that, in the words of Jacques Derrida:

> Never have violence, inequality, exclusion, famine, and – economic oppression affected as many human beings in the history of the earth and humanity – let us never neglect this macroscopic fact, made up of innumerable singular sites of suffering: no degree of progress allows one to ignore that never before, in absolute figures, have so many men, women and children been subjugated, starved or exterminated.[4]

Concentration on issues of minorities and indigenous peoples is not intended to obscure or neglect other sites of suffering. And it may be remarked that, in the repertoire of oppression, the sufferings of minorities and indigenous peoples have been extreme, resulting in great cultural losses to humanity.[5] Moving into the next millennium, we may be tempted to ask once again Kant's question about whether humanity has indeed made moral progress, though the temper of postmodernism is against posing questions in this absolute manner.[6]

---

3   Marantz, BD, 'Issues affecting the rights of indigenous peoples in international fora', in *People or Peoples; Equality, Autonomy and Self-Determination: The Issues at Stake of the International Decade of the World's Indigenous People*, 1996, Montreal: International Centre for Human Rights and Democratic Development, pp 9–77.

4   Derrida, J, *Spectres of Marx*, 1994, cited by Marks, S, 'The end of history? Reflections on some international legal theses' (1997) 3 EJIL 449, p 457.

5   On the indigenous side, see Independent Commission on International Humanitarian Issues, *Indigenous Peoples: A Global Quest for Justice*, 1987, New Jersey: Zed.

6   The issue is discussed by Bobbio, N, in *The Age of Rights*, 1996, Cambridge: Polity.

INDIVIDUAL RIGHTS, SELF-DETERMINATION,
STRAWS IN THE WIND

In this first United Nations phase, following the collapse of the League of Nations – 'dwindled into a ghost not fit to cope',[7] minority rights were not an explicit concern of policymakers and those who drafted the foundation documents of contemporary human rights law. The League had developed an extensive repertoire of instruments and procedures to deal with minority issues in a limited group of mostly Central and East European States.[8] The approach was humanitarian and pragmatic – the area of operation was regarded as a kind of 'fault-line' between civilisations: Catholic, Orthodox and Moslem. Rights of inhabitants, rights of nationals and of nationals belonging to minorities were specified, and the minority rights elements internationalised. The system was caught up in the strains of inter-war politics, and despite much good work on the minutiae of rights, was undermined from within and without.

There is no specific reference to minorities in either the United Nations Charter or the Universal Declaration of Human Rights. The ethnic issue was not neglected but was expected to make its way through the new principles of human rights on the basis of non-discrimination on grounds such as 'race, sex, language or religion'.[9] The omission of minorities from key instruments had significant effects in the latter half of the century. Human rights, the continuation and instantiation of the great meta-narrative of the Enlightenment, were set to characterise the UN age.

The approach was centred on the individual person (although society, community and family also figure in the Universal Declaration),[10] the concern was global, the promise was limitless. The great leveller of non-discrimination and the possibilities of equality of opportunity opened up by it, would make attention to the rights of particular groups supererogatory. Consequently, League ideas of protecting specific groups were elbowed aside. American style optimism was official – individual freedom, development and the market would guarantee the future. In the buccaneering age of rights, the desire to be attached like a limpet to local identities seemed regressive and anachronistic, a transient symptom of fear of the future, to be soothed and then phased out.[11]

---

7   Browning, R, 'Childe Roland to the Dark Tower Came' (1855).

8   Thornberry, P, *International Law and the Rights of Minorities*, 1992, Oxford: Clarendon, Chap 3.

9   UN Charter, Arts 1(3), 13, 55(c) and 76(c). The prohibited grounds of discrimination are amplified in Art 2 of the Universal Declaration.

10 Daes, EI, *Freedom of the Individual Under Law: An Analysis of Article 29 of the Universal Declaration of Human Rights*, 1990, New York: UN.

11 See examples of characterisation of the indigenous as doomed peoples in Tennant, C, 'Indigenous peoples, international institutions and the international legal literature from 1945–93' (1994) 16 HRQ 1.

The key was the development or consolidation of secure national identities, essentially monolithic, homogeneous, constrained and stable, through which citizens could look out on the world and face the future with confidence. It was appropriate, therefore, that the engineering of nations and State should proceed without much hindrance from international standards. The nation building momentum increased with the addition of a raft of new States to United Nations membership. Many of the States were conglomerates with vast territories and complex demographics. They would either stand whole or fall apart, hence the urge to 'construct' peoples from the arcane geometries of the colonial powers, whose boundaries would only be defensible as boundaries of new States if their populations were stamped with the stamp of unity through education and fear.[12]

In the United Nations Charter, the approach was sanctified by the principle of the sovereign equality of States, non-interference in the domestic affairs of States, and the principle of self-determination. This last principle fast became a right of the whole 'people' in a colonial territory to immediate independence, together with a guarantee of territorial integrity, at least against the machinations of colonial powers pursuing divide and rule policies.[13] Western States did not protest too much against the etiolation of local identities. After all, they had been through the same processes themselves, and were still going through them. Their liberalism squeezed out ethnic entities such as minorities and indigenous peoples which were located between State and individual, as if the entities were surplus terms lined up for excision with Occam's razor. The geopolitical elements filtered into lawmaking processes at international and domestic levels.

But, there were other straws in the wind, and drawing out the implications of a phase, legal or otherwise, may disguise real complexities. The protection of minorities was listed among the terms of reference of the United Nations Commission on Human Rights (the Commission)[14] which established a subordinate body – the Sub-commission on Prevention of Discrimination and Protection of Minorities (the Sub-commission), at its first session in 1947.[15] The use of the term 'minority' in the Sub-commission's title was important for the future. The Sub-commission undertook important work on the clarification of minority rights, and took the initial steps in drafting the crucial Art 27 of the International Covenant on Civil and Political Rights (ICCPR):

---

12 These issues are regularly discussed in works on the principle of self-determination. See, among many such, Tomuschat, C (ed), *Modern Law of Self-Determination*, 1993, Dordrecht/Boston: Kluwer; Cassese, A, *Self-Determination of Peoples: A Legal Reappraisal*, 1995, Cambridge: Grotius.

13 Expressed in, eg, para 6 of the 'Colonial declaration' – GA Res 1514 (XV) 1960.

14 The terms of reference of the Commission were approved by the Economic and Social Council in GA Res 5 (I) February 1946, amended by GA Res 9 (II) June 1946.

15 For UN history, see Capotorti, *op cit*, fn 2, paras 141–48.

In those States where ethnic, religious or linguistic minorities exist, persons belonging to such minorities shall not be denied the right, in community with the other members of their group, to enjoy their own culture, to profess and practise their own religion, or to use their own language.[16]

Inter alia, the difference between non-discrimination and minority rights was also elaborated by the Sub-commission:

(1) Prevention of discrimination is the prevention of any action which denies to individuals or groups of people equality of treatment which they may wish.

(2) Protection of minorities is the protection of non-dominant groups which, while wishing in general for equality of treatment with the majority, wish for a measure of differential treatment in order to preserve basic characteristics (differential treatment of such groups or individuals belonging to such groups is justified when it is exercise in the interest of their contentment and the welfare of the community as a whole.[17]

The Council of Europe incorporated the phrase 'association with a national minority' into the non-discrimination clause (Art 14) of the ECHR. The Council of Europe has been slow to address the implications of the term 'national minority', but eventually did so.[18] A small spread of bilateral treaties engaged locally with the minorities issue; the arrangements are still there, supplemented by an enormous explosion of 'minority rights bilateralism' in the 1990s.[19]

Even though the United Nations Charter and the Universal Declaration did not engage directly with minority rights, General Assembly resolution 217C(III), passed on the same day as the Universal Declaration, declared that the United Nations could not remain indifferent to the fate of minorities.[20] There was a curious crossover between the drafting of the Universal Declaration and the drafting of the Genocide Convention, both finalised in 1948. It seems fairly clear that the omission of a specific Article on cultural genocide from the Genocide Convention following extensive debates affected the Universal Declaration.[21] The prohibition of cultural genocide was unacceptable to those who drafted the Convention precisely because of implications it would have had for nation-building processes.[22] Its

16 *Op cit*, Capotorti, fn 2, paras 165–71.
17 E/CN 4/52, s V.
18 Notably, in the Framework Convention for the Protection of National Minorities, adopted in 1994.
19 See the 'agreements, arrangements and political declarations' incorporated in the Pact on Stability in Europe, March 1995, discussed in Benoit-Rohmer, F, *The Minority Question in Europe*, 1996, Strasbourg: Council of Europe.
20 *Op cit*, Thornberry, fn 8, Chap 13.
21 The author is indebted to Morsink, J, for extracts from an unpublished work on the Universal Declaration and minority rights.
22 *Op cit*, Thornberry, fn 8, Pt II .

unacceptability was promoted by arguments about the inability to define the elements of cultural genocide.[23]

Some States were clearer about the need to destroy before building – even if they did not employ such a threatening vocabulary. So genocide was understood as essentially physical and biological. The element in Art II(e) of 'forcibly transferring the children of the ["national, ethnical, racial, or religious"] group to another group' is all that remains of the concept of cultural genocide,[24] unless one extends the idea of 'mental harm' in Art II(b) to cultural damage. Nevertheless, the effect of the Convention on minority rights was equivocal – genocide was a crime of group destruction,[25] and that such a concept could exist was important for future reflections of the international community on culture and ethnicity and how to deal with such phenomena. Somewhere in all this, minority rights were locked into Cold War arguments.

The Soviet Union and Yugoslavia were sponsors of initiatives in the field of minority rights, as they sponsored the collective right of self-determination.[26] Both insisted that they had something to teach other States on the issue of minorities. Their view of minority rights cohered with their claims for the collective ethos and for economic and cultural rights. This had a double effect. The negative side of this was that Western States, notably the US, kept a distance from minority rights tainted with Bolshevism. In more positive terms, Soviet and Yugoslav ideas and drafts kept alive a certain scepticism about the claims of the individual rights model to solve all contemporary problems relating to ethnicity.

In this first phase, indigenous peoples were locked into policies associated with indigenism – integration, assimilation or civilisation of the Indians. Such policies were not dissimilar from assimilationist policies pursued against minorities. The themes emerged with some force in the work of the ILO which, with the co-operation of much of the United Nations system, produced ILO Convention No 107 of 1957 on the Protection and Integration of Indigenous and other Tribal and Semi-Tribal Populations in Independent Countries.[27] 'Integration' meant assimilation. In the eye of the Convention, the indigenous were vulnerable societies on the verge of disappearance. The

---

23 Robinson, N, *The Genocide Convention: A Commentary*, 1960, New York: Institute of Jewish Affairs.

24 For reflections on Australian experience in the matter of 'stolen children', see Pritchard, S, *The United Nations Draft Declaration on the Rights of Indigenous Peoples: An Analysis*, 1996, Aboriginal and Torres Strait Islander Commission, pp 75–82.

25 A denial of 'the right of existence of entire human groups' GA Res 96 (I), December 1946.

26 See the texts of early Yugoslav drafts of the UN Declaration on Minority Rights in Phillips, A and Rosas, A (eds), *Universal Minority Rights*, 1995, Abo and London: Abo Akademi and Minority Rights Group.

27 Discussed in Bennett, G, *Aboriginal Rights in International Law*, 1978, London: Royal Anthropological Institute of Great Britain and Ireland.

Convention would encourage States to help them on their way, but would smooth the transition. Their cultures and languages were not permanent, enduring features of the human landscape.[28] These 'populations' would integrate, learn the national language, be educated by State functionaries or missionaries with delegated powers, and be developed in ways that were good for them.

A resolution of the Fourth Conference of American States Members of the ILO in 1948 had stated explicitly that the problems of indigenous populations, and the action required to solve them, are essentially social and economic in character. The resolution described the populations as important manpower resources, the more effective utilisation of which would contribute to their own good and that of the national economy as a whole.[29] Convention 107 incorporates all these notions. Twenty seven States ratified it. Nevertheless, there is some equivocality here, as with the policies on minorities. The term 'populations' in the title of the Convention could be seen as a tilt towards the collective ethnic unit. The recognition of indigenous land rights in the Convention was also an introduction to a broader appreciation of some characteristics of sub-national units. In the 1950s in particular, the doctrine of self-determination was used to implicate indigenous peoples in the struggle of some Western powers to arrest processes of decolonisation. Belgium[30] warned the anti-colonial States about the presence of the indigenous on their territories, who would in turn claim self-determination. This was intended to stoke fears,thus militating against greater recognition of the sub-national. It is ironic that this same principle of self-determination is now asserted by the indigenous as their birthright.[31]

GLIMMERINGS OF AN AGENDA

From the late 1970s onwards, approaches to the ethnic question were changing. The minority rights international law programme was in *statu nascendi*, spurred by the publication of the Capotorti Report in 1977 with associated academic writings.[32] The International Covenants were in force. The tentative sounding Art 27 (above) was waiting to be explored – a process

---

28 See *op cit*, Tennant, fn 11.
29 Cited in Martinez-Cobo, J, special rapporteur, Study of Discrimination against Indigenous Populations, E/CN 4/Sub 2/1982/2/Add 1, paras 45–47.
30 In the so called 'Belgian thesis' – discussed in Thornberry, P, 'Self-determination, minorities, human rights: a review of international instruments (1989) 38 ICLQ 867.
31 Notably, in Art 3 of the UN Draft Declaration on the Rights of Indigenous Peoples. See, in general, Anaya, SJ, *Indigenous Peoples in International Law*, 1996, New York: OUP.
32 *Op cit*, Capotorti, fn 2.

which produced *Lovelace v Canada*[33] and other cases,[34] proving that Art 27 could, after all, have some uses.

For many years, the Article bore the main burden of expressing a general international treaty standard on minority rights. Other references, such as Art 5.1(c) of UNESCO's Convention against Discrimination in Education,[35] were locked into the non-discrimination paradigm, and even more grudging in their acceptance of minority rights.[36] Then, the international community witnessed the slow movement of a United Nations draft Declaration on Minority Rights, which, in one of history's small ironies, was submitted to the United Nations by Yugoslavia in 1978.[37] The highly assimilationist ILO Convention 107 on Indigenous and Tribal Populations gradually made way for the more participation oriented and less assimilationist Convention No 169 on Indigenous and Tribal Peoples, work on which began in the mid-1980s.[38] The United Nations Working Group on Indigenous Populations began its work in 1982. The CSCE/OSCE had made reference to national minorities in the Helsinki Final Act in 1975. There was enough in this to ground a steady elaboration of principle as the CSCE juggernaut rolled on through the succeeding decades.[39] The CSCE processes also struck at Central and Eastern Europe, the historic depository of minority rights in international law. Liberals were becoming more curious about minority rights, digressing on individual and collective rights and looking afresh at neglected aspects of political community.[40]

---

33   Communication No 24/1977, Views of the Human Rights Committee, A/36/40 (1981).

34   Spiliopoulou-Aokermark, A, *Justifications of Minority Protection in International Law*, 1997, Uppsala: Iustus Forlag, pp 157–74.

35   Discussed by the present author in Minority Rights Group (ed), *Education Rights and Minorities*, 1994, London: Minority Rights Group and UNICEF.

36   According to Art 2(b), it shall not constitute discrimination if separate educational systems or institutions are set up 'for religious or linguistic reasons', if participation is optional and the education conforms to standards for education at that level. Article 5.1(c) provides that it is 'essential to recognise the right of members of national minorities to carry on their own educational activities' which may include schools and own language teaching provided that 'this right is not exercised in a manner which prevents the members of these minorities from understanding the culture and language of the community as a whole and from participating in its activities, or which prejudices national sovereignty'; caveats are also inserted on the standard of education and the optional nature of the schools.

37   See *op cit*, Phillips and Rosas, fn 26.

38   Swepston, L, 'A new step in the international law on indigenous and tribal peoples: ILO Convention No 169 of 1989' (1990) 15 Oklahoma City UL Rev 677.

39   Amor Martin Eåstebanez, M, *International Organizations and Minority Protection in Europe*, 1996, Turku/Abo: Abo Akademi University; Bloed, A, Leicht, L, Nowak, M and Rosas, A (eds), *Monitoring Human Rights in Europe: Comparing International Procedures and Mechanisms*, 1993, Dordrecht: Martinus Nijhoff.

40   Developments are captured in Van Dyke, V, *Human Rights, Ethnicity and Discrimination*, 1985, London: Greenwood.

The universal rights/non-discrimination package was not in itself sufficient to meet the needs of all minority groups. Equality and non-discrimination could, while accepted as the vital first step in the protection of minorities, also function as part of a totalising project, complementing other aspects of the homogenisation of States. In the work of the Committee on the Elimination of Racial Discrimination, the Convention on that subject would eventually become more sensitive to cultural differences, and less obsessed with combating the apartheid type of segregation. The doctrine of apartheid exercised a pernicious influence on the understanding of minority rights. But State-imposed racial segregation, and group demands for a measure of separate recognition in cultural spheres in order to guarantee cultural existence and survival, are two different things.[41]

IDENTITY AND ANXIETY

The requisite boost in international legal terms for minority rights arrived at the end of the 1980s. By that time, the concern with political decolonisation in Africa and Asia had largely ebbed away and the focus shifted to economy and development. Self-determination as a concept had become linked with human rights. The International Covenants were crucial to this development in view of their common Art 1 on self-determination, although earlier instruments on self-determination had also incorporated (neglected) reflections on human rights.[42] Self-determination and human rights were now understood as reciprocally related.[43] If self-determination underpinned human rights, so human rights limited self-determination. Independence and State building were not excuses for rights violations, though such violations continued often on a massive scale in the name of forging or defending the nation. The unravelling of the Soviet Union and Yugoslavia revealed discrete peoples, with sharply differentiated identities, claiming self-determination as their turn, turning to violence to achieve it 'like knavish crows ... all impatient for their hour'.[44] Identity and culture emerged as key post-modern themes, overriding consciousness of class as the authentic mediator of social relations. The politics of ethnicity and nationalism were the surrogate bodies, the carriers of the new consciousness into social action. They unleashed

---

41 See the masterly exposition of the differences between the system of apartheid and minority rights by Judge Tanaka in South-West Africa Cases (Second Phase), 1966, International Court of Justice.

42 Including GA Res 1514 (XV) 1960.

43 See the essay by the present author on the democratic or internal aspect of self-determination in *op cit*, Tomuschat, fn 12.

44 William Shakespeare, *Henry V*, Act 4, Scene 2.

satisfaction, euphoria and violence in equal measure. Liberal theory woke up to a world of shattered communities and found that history had not ended.[45]

As new entities revealed themselves like a series of Russian dolls, international organisations moved to act in relation to minorities; the CSCE/OSCE and the United Nations were quick off the mark, the Council of Europe somewhat slower. The United Nations can always employ a range of instruments of hard and soft law, whereas the Council of Europe prefers to proceed by the cumbersome but steady treaty method and set up treaty bodies to ensure consistent implementation. Even the United Nations Convention on the Rights of the Child contained identity references, almost obligatory in 1990, and included the following adaptation of Art 27 of the ICCPR:

> In those States in which ethnic, religious or linguistic minorities or persons of indigenous origin exist, a child belonging to such a minority or who is indigenous shall not be denied the right, in community with other members of his or her group, to enjoy his or her own culture, to profess and practise his or her own religion, or to use his or her own language.[46]

Besides applying the ICCPR norm to children, the provision employs gender neutral language and yokes together minorities and indigenous peoples – in this case employing the language of individual rights. The new consciousness can also be measured by considering the drafting of the United Nations Declaration on Minority Rights. Modest drafts were presented to the United Nations in 1978 and 1979. By 1989, there was virtually no agreed text. By 1990, a full text had been given a first reading; the second reading was complete to all intents and purposes by December 1991, when a working group of the Human Rights Commission rounded up its work in a frenzy of drafting involving face to face informal drafting groups. The General Assembly adopted the Declaration in December 1992.[47] The interval between the first and second reading was, in United Nations terms, like the short life of a mayfly.

Two treaties on minorities have resulted from the work of the Council of Europe: the European Charter for Regional or Minority Languages 1992 (the Languages Charter) and the Framework Convention for the Protection of National Minorities (the Framework Convention), opened for signature in 1995.[48] The OSCE was perhaps better adapted than the Council of Europe for

---

45 An excellent spectrum of essays is presented in Kymlicka, W (ed), *The Rights of Minority Cultures*, 1995, Oxford: OUP.

46 ICCPR, Art 30. See, also, Arts 2, 8, 20, 23 and 29, for further aspects of culture and identity.

47 The chronology is detailed in Thornberry, P, 'The UN Declaration on the Rights of Persons belonging to National or Ethnic, Religious and Linguistic Minorities: background, analysis and an update', in *op cit*, Phillips and Rosas, fn 26, pp 13–76.

48 The Framework Convention entered into force on 1 February 1998.

'rapid reaction', a virtue of using non-treaty but 'politically binding agreements' which are at the core of the OSCE enterprise.[49] In terms of standards, the OSCE Copenhagen Document of the Human Dimension (the Copenhagen Document) still represents something of a high water mark in the recognition of minority rights. The OSCE also adopted a specific 'mechanism' for minorities – the High Commissioner on National Minorities, to date a highly personalised office occupied by the charismatic Mr Max van der Stoel.[50]

MINORITY RIGHTS ARE HUMAN RIGHTS

The integration of these relatively new instruments on minority and indigenous rights with international law presents its own difficulties. The rights are not a single issue enthusiasm.[51] Applying this in the context of indigenous rights, Brownlie rather caustically observes:

> Many writers – scholars, as the Americans like to say, are specialists in human rights, rather than general international law, and specialists in indigenous peoples rather than human rights. Some, at least, of these super specialists suffer from super tunnel vision. it does not seem to occur to them that their subject of special interest belongs to a much wider world of normative development ...[52]

The point is that minority and indigenous rights interface with the other principles of human rights and the norms and structures of international law. The Framework Convention puts it more gently:

> The protection of national minorities and of the rights and freedoms of persons belonging to those minorities forms an integral part of the international protection of human rights, and as such falls within the scope of international co-operation.[53]

This is not the League of Nations revisited. In that period, there was a blank space outside the minorities system; an absence of rights guaranteed to individuals by international law. In the new human rights system, it is difficult to say where minority rights begin and end. General human rights apply to members of minorities as they apply to everyone. Clauses in international instruments on the basic principles of non-discrimination and

---

49 Bloed, A (ed), *The Conference on Security and Cooperation in Europe: Analysis and Basic Documents*, 1993, The Hague: Martinus Nijhoff.

50 *The Role of the High Commissioner on National Minorities in OSCE Conflict Prevention*, 1997, The Hague: Foundation on Inter-Ethnic Relations.

51 Points made by Brownlie, I, in Brookfield, FM (ed), *Treaties and Indigenous Peoples*, 1992, Oxford: Clarendon.

52 *Ibid*, p 63.

53 Framework Convention, Art 1.

equality are also for general application and directly implicate minorities. Minorities can or should also participate in general self-determination processes, though they are not named as the holders of the right, which is the province of 'peoples'.[54] Indigenous peoples regard themselves as more than minorities and claim self-determination.[55] Nevertheless, they pushed forward the boundaries of minority rights, notably in the context of Art 27 of the ICCPR.[56] Most of the leading ICCPR cases on Art 27 concern indigenous peoples, starting with *Lovelace v Canada*.[57] The Articles or paragraphs on minority rights in the general texts, such as the ICCPR or the UNESCO Convention on Discrimination in Education ,must read coherently with all the rights contained therein.

The pre-existing format of human rights, and the minority rights superimposed on it, generate a host of questions. The new rights generate more controversy than most. They have as much force as other rights and, like all rights, exist in a state of (one hopes, creative) tension with the rest, including generalised principles such as non-discrimination.[58] The relationship between the various registers of principle will engage the international community for some time to come. For international law, it is not a question of moving from a norm of non-discrimination to one of minority rights. Both norms are simultaneously valid; mutually supportive interpretations are mandated systemically. The organs which instrumentalise norms of non-discrimination have gradually become more sensitive to cultural and identity issues. By way of example, take one of the general recommendations[59] of the Committee on the Elimination of Racial Discrimination (CERD), considers that discrimination against indigenous peoples is covered by the Convention on the Elimination of All Forms of Racial Discrimination (ICEARD). There is ample scope for this determination, despite the absence of the term 'indigenous' in the Convention, which covers discrimination on relevant grounds of 'race, colour, descent, or national or ethnic origin', CERD opts for a description of the specific discrimination as including 'that based on indigenous origin and identity'. It expresses the specific manner in which anti-indigenous discrimination is constituted by loss of 'land and resources to colonists, commercial companies and State enterprises', which has the effect that 'the preservation of their [the indigenous peoples'] culture and ... historical identity has been and still is

---

54 See Thornberry, in *op cit*, Tomuschat, fn 12.
55 UN draft Declaration on the Rights of Indigenous Peoples, Art 3.
56 *Op cit*, Spiliopoulou-Akermark, fn 34.
57 Communication No 24/1977, Views of the Human Rights Committee, A/36/40 (1981).
58 Consult Lerner, N, *Group Rights and Discrimination in International Law*, 1991, Dordrecht: Martinus Nijhoff.
59 CERD/C/51/Misc/3/Rev 4, 18 August 1997.

jeopardised'.[60] CERD also emphasises the role of States which are called upon '... to recognise and respect indigenous culture, history, language and way of life as an enrichment of the State's cultural identity and to promote its preservation'.[61]

It is clearly the view of the CERD that the ICEARD's provisions on special measures are not contradicted by attention to the promotion of indigenous identity through State policy. This point can be applied to other 'ethnic' issues without strain. Conceptualising the relationship between minority rights and general human rights offers safeguards against ethnocentric intolerance. The rights of one group or one person will not be allowed to override or subdue into insignificance the rights of others.

ISSUES AND PERPLEXITIES

Complex interpretive and philosophical issues pervade the canon of ethnic rights. If the non-discrimination legal formation is becoming more sensitive to issues of culture and identity, there are parallel struggles. One is the relationship between the individual and the collective. Human rights law insists that collective rights should not undermine individual rights; but the converse is also true. This leads, in *Lovelace*, *Kitok*[62] and other cases, to soft metaphors of 'balance' between the communal and individual 'rights'. Just as individuals may be destroyed by exclusion from community, so are communities destroyed by excessive exercises in self-identification by those claiming membership of particular communities. Can anyone leave or 'exit' the community? Can the community expel individuals who claim membership in it? And, where are the limits of communal self-expression or cultural authenticity? Are communities permitted to discriminate in terms of gender, or disability? Can they limit freedom of association, freedom to work, freedom of thought, conscience or religion, or freedom of expression? Who speaks for the 'community'?[63] The situation may easily arise where leaders claim the force of 'tradition' for their exclusive rights to voice the communal opinion, drowning any dissent within the community in a deep pool. All of these questions bring in reflections on rights which are recognised in one way or another in contemporary international law: the communal right to exist;[64]

---

60 CERD/C/51/Misc/3/Rev 4, 18 August 1997, para 3.

61 *Ibid*, para 4a.

62 Before the UN Human Rights Committee, *Kitok v Sweden*, Communication No 197/1985, Views of the Committee, A/43/40 (1988).

63 See the useful discussion in Perry, MJ, 'Are human rights universal? The relativist challenge and related matters' (1997) 19 HRQ 461.

64 See, eg, Art 1 of the UN Declaration on the Rights of Persons belonging to National or Ethnic, Religious and Linguistic Minorities, promulgated by GA Res 47/135, 18 December 1992.

the individual right to self-identify.[65] The texts also affirm that individuals may not be compelled to use minority rights, nor compelled by the State to renounce them.[66]

In the case of indigenous peoples in particular, the normative structure of individual human rights, while reinforcing aspects of personal security, may leave their communities vulnerable, hence their conversation with the international community, and their interrogation of the language of human rights to assess its security potential. Hence also, their support for 'radical' texts such as the draft United Nations Declaration on Indigenous Rights, suffused with collective rights, and their aspiration to engage the powers in the United Nations on the basis of a strengthened presence – not quite equal to States, but an integral part of the whole apparatus.[67]

THE RIGHTS: MINORITIES

So, which minority or indigenous rights have been brought to human rights and which have not? The language of minority rights in its many variants employs fundamental concepts such as group existence and identity. It also elaborates principles of participation in cultural, social, economic and public life. Development processes are also affected by the movement in minority rights.[68] The new law greatly concerns itself with questions of education and language. It values reciprocity of learning between minority and other communities in the State. The law implicates group participation in the design of national curricula related to minority interests. It seeks to amplify the scope of minority language teaching on schools and ensure access to all levels of

---

65 ILO Convention No 169 on Indigenous and Tribal Peoples in Independent Countries, Art 1.2, provides: 'Self-identification as indigenous or tribal shall be regarded as a fundamental criterion for determining the groups to which the provisions of this Convention apply.'

66 See, eg, UN Declaration on Minority Rights, Art 3.2 and Council of Europe's Framework Convention, Art 3.1, both of which relate to the exercise of rights by members of minorities as matters of choice by individuals. Copenhagen Document of the OSCE Human Dimension, para 32, bites deeper in providing that 'To belong to a national minority is a matter of a person's individual choice and no disadvantage may arise from the exercise of such choice'.

67 The implicit reference here is to the idea of a permanent forum in the UN for indigenous peoples, a proposal stemming from the Vienna Declaration of the World Conference on Human Rights in 1993. The idea continues to be supported by UN bodies, including the General Assembly and the Commission on Human Rights. In GA Res1998/20, the Commission decided to set up an ad hoc working group 'to elaborate and consider further proposals for the possible establishment of a permanent forum'.

68 These topoi emerge and re-emerge in the instruments on minority rights – the UN Declaration on Minority Rights carries most of them.

education.[69] International standards demand respect for traditions and customs unless specific practices within them contravene human rights principles,[70] a determination which is not to be made lightly. The United Nations Declaration on Minority Rights does not 'confront' cultures as if they were aberrations of nature, but will deconstruct them when the occasion demands to condemn unacceptable practices.[71] As the Human Rights Committee reminds us, culture manifests itself in many forms,[72] and multiple manifestations are accommodated in one way or another by the newly installed norms. The texts have also sought to revalue community, place and individual names.[73]

The rights also increasingly penetrate the public realm, in affirming, for example, the right to use a minority language before public authorities.[74] Such a right is not to be found in the general law of human rights nor under Art 27 of the ICCPR, but is found in tentative, qualified forms in the Council of Europe's Language Charter and Framework Convention. Minority rights do not incorporate the principle of self-determination, although contemporary readings of that principle respect their participation in self-determination processes: the democratic face of self-determination, the 'internal aspect' associated with human rights. Neither do minority rights appropriate the spaces of autonomy.[75] Autonomy is referred to in key texts such as the CSCE/OSCE Copenhagen Document, although its positive effects are only noted with interest. The term does not appear in the United Nations Declaration on Minority Rights, nor in the General Comment of the Human Rights Committee on Art 27 of the ICCPR. Autonomy is not mandated by international law as a solution to minority problems. In some areas of the world, such as Central Europe, the word 'autonomy' provokes disputes among neighbours,[76] though no one is quite clear what it means. Autonomy is

---

69 Thornberry, P and Gibbons, D, 'Education and minority rights: a short survey of international standards' (1996–97) 4 Int J Minority and Group Rights 2, p 115.

70 For some typical issues, see the follow up report on Traditional Practices affecting the Health of Women and Children, Mrs Halima Embarek Warzazi, special rapporteur, E/CN 4/Sub 2/1997/10.

71 United Nations Declaration on Minority Rights, Art 4.2.

72 General Comment No 23, 1994, of the Human Rights Committee on Art 27 of the International Covenant on Civil and Political Rights, A/49/40, Vol I, 107–110, para 7.

73 Notably, Framework Convention, Art 11.

74 *Ibid*, Art 10.

75 Hannum, H, *Autonomy, Sovereignty and Self-Determination – The Accommodation of Conflicting Rights*, 1990, Philadelphia: Pennsylvania UP. See, also, Suksi, M (ed), *Autonomy: Applications and Implications*, 1998, The Hague: Kluwer.

76 Hence, the famous '1201 question' – a reference to that recommendation of the Parliamentary Assembly of the Council of Europe, which contained, in Art 11, a guarded affirmation of a right to autonomy. Hungarian diplomacy in particular attempted to transcribe 1201 into its bilateral treaties with neighbouring States and convert it into binding domestic law. Various strategies were adopted in the ensuing row to downgrade the importance of the recommendation.

used to describe anything from self-administration of schools and cultural clubs to fundamental decentralisation of State activities linked to notions of regionalisation and subsidiarity. What governments tend to fear is the territorial variety.[77] After all, picking out an autonomy as a defined area on the map can lead to new forms of sub-State recognition and thus to claims of self-determination and secession. Accordingly, international law has been careful to escape such implications, refusing to translate the variety of local applications into a general mandate. In any case, much of what could be achieved through the employment of 'autonomy' language could be achieved by employing the 'ordinary' language of individual rights exercised 'in community with' others. The prognostications of commentators and activists of minority rights about the inevitability of the move to 'group rights' have not been borne out in any dramatic fashion as regards autonomy.[78] Collective rights elements have insinuated themselves in more subtle ways into the corpus of human rights.

THE RIGHTS: INDIGENOUS PEOPLES

There is a difference between the texts on minorities and those on indigenous peoples. Preoccupations about culture, identity, education, language, and participatory processes are mostly shared. The indigenous texts are less constrained on the collective/individual rights spectrum – inclining greatly to the former, with variable 'safeguards' in the name of general human rights. For many groups who are mainly, but not exclusively indigenous, land is an essential part of their culture.[79] But, whereas the texts of minority rights dabble in the currency of shared rights in the area of toponymy, language education, and freedom from gerrymandering, which would lower possibilities of exercising political and cultural rights, the texts on indigenous peoples are replete with land rights.

Many indigenous groups regard the text sections on land rights as the essence of their struggle for survival. Land rights are more than the name suggests – they are about resources, religious practices, and fundamental senses of community belonging. As the Human Rights Committee has recognised, some groups may have no existence outside a territory.[80] Denial

---

77 Thornberry, P, 'Images of autonomy and individual and collective rights in international instruments on the rights of minorities', in *op cit*, Suksi, fn 75, pp 97–124.

78 Lerner, N, 'The evolution of minority rights in international law', in Brolmann, C *et al* (eds), *Peoples and Minorities in International Law*, 1993, Dordrecht: Martinus Nijhoff, pp 77–101.

79 For an attempt to link minority and indigenous issues on the question of land rights, see Plant, R, *Land Rights and Minorities*, 1994, London: Minority Rights Group.

80 'There is no place outside the Tobique reserve where such a community exists', Human Rights Committee, in *Lovelace* Communication No 24/1977, Views of the Human Rights Committee, A/36/40 (1981), para 15.

of access to such a territory, dislocation, dam building, deforestation, logging, mining, fires and floods, may all destroy whole communities. The United Nations draft Declaration deploys the language of ethnocide and cultural genocide to catch the essence of such processes and phenomena in their effects on communities,[81] and whereas minority rights do not trespass on the territory of the international law principle of self-determination, the indigenous texts do.[82] As a collective movement, indigenous peoples have mounted a frontal challenge to the 'orthodoxy' of self-determination, by questioning and subverting that concept in the name of general human rights, despite the admonitions of some who suggest that they let it go.[83] After all, if 'all peoples' have the right to self-determination, why not indigenous peoples? They insist on the concept as the best vehicle for carrying their claims and aspirations.[84] They do not generally equate self-determination with secession. Indeed, views among them vary greatly. The expression of its basis by Australia in a United Nations drafting exercise on indigenous rights captures the spirit of their claims:

> Australia considers that self-determination encompasses the continuing right of peoples to decide how they should be governed, the right to participate fully in the political process and the right of distinct peoples within a State to participate in decisions on, and to administer, their own affairs ... sovereign independence is not feasible for every self-defined 'people' ... A concept of self-determination within existing State boundaries, involving the full observance of individual and group rights, holds out a better hope of ensuring stability, human development and human security ...[85]

Many indigenous groups might express this aspiration in more simple language. Witness the following conversation:

> 'What is self-determination?' asked the young Arakmbut man.

> 'Why do you ask?' I said.

> 'I have heard the word used by indigenous leaders in the town and have read it. My father and the old men do not know what it is and so I am asking you.'

> 'Self-determination is about the right of indigenous peoples to control their lives without unwanted outside interference.'

---

81 UN draft Declaration, Art 7.

82 According to Art 3 of the UN draft Declaration on the Rights of Indigenous Peoples: 'Indigenous peoples have the right of self-determination ...'

83 For a claim that this represents a misplaced strategy for the peoples, see Corntassel, JJ and Primeau, TH, 'Indigenous sovereignty and international law: revised strategies for pursuing "self-determination"' (1995) 17 HRQ 343, pp 343–65.

84 Art 3 of the UN draft Declaration on the Rights of Indigenous Peoples, E/CN 4/Sub 2/1994/2/Add 1.

85 Statement of the Australian delegation to the working group of the Commission on Human Rights charged with the elaboration of a declaration on indigenous rights, Geneva, 21 November 1995 (on file with author).

'Oh, so that's what it is.'[86]

It did not require further explanation.

WHAT NEXT?

Through the 1990s, the international community addressed the challenge of exploded ethnicity by depositing sheaves of documentation on the table. These new(ish) human rights standards respond actively to the developments and, are activist at the same time. They are meant to do something and are not meant simply to be admired. The connections between the ideal and the pragmatic are always fairly close in the case of international human rights, the instruments are not a collection of timeless truths but have a culture, a history and reflect configurations of power. They are, like other texts, 'situated'.

The link between the pragmatic and the Utopian appears particularly close in the case of minority rights.[87] Oppression of identifiable groups is visible and can engage their kinsfolk; oppression of individuals can be more like the silent operations of nature. The peculiar tension in the texts on minority rights is that they attempt to ameliorate the tensions but may also create them by rendering the groups even more visible. Hence the international law of minority rights places the rights in an overtly political setting. This explains why so many texts contain safeguards about territorial integrity;[88] why they avoid identifying territorial constituencies, or investing autonomies with 'rights'. It has ever been thus, from before the time of the League of Nations. Minority rights were always 'international' in their potential consequences, with a sharp political edge, spilling over State boundaries. The politics of indigenous rights are 'the same but different'. One of the chief characteristics of indigenous politics at the international level is self-organisation.[89] There is now in existence what may be called 'an' or 'the' international indigenous movement. Indigenous organisation was spurred on by the example of decolonisation of the Empires of the West, by the civil rights struggles of the 1960s, by the Cold War with the mutual probing between East and West of internal human rights issues, by problems with the concept of development and its neglect of indigenous factors,[90] by an occasional alliance with

---

86 Gray, A, *Indigenous Rights and Development: Self-Determination in an Amazonian Community*, 1997, Providence, Oxford: Berghahn, p 1.

87 Mullerson, R, *Human Rights Diplomacy*, 1997, London: Routledge.

88 See UN Declaration on Minority Rights, Art 8.

89 Wilmer, F, *The Indigenous Voice in World Politics*, 1993, London: Sage.

90 Hence the attention given by UNCED – the Rio Conference on Environment and Development – to indigenous issues.

environmentalists,[91] and the growth of international human rights law including its sharp focus on racism.[92]

The style and ethos of indigenous rights movements links in with transformations of political community at the sub-national level and has prompted them. The challenge to States is different from that posed by minorities in some respects. It is not (typically) about fears of secession (though it is also true that this appeals only to some minorities) but is about resources and territories. The indigenous challenge to international law is about securing survival on terms which appeal to the peoples – survival and flourishing on their terms, at least in part. They have learned the language of human rights, and they are in process of adapting it to their usages through sometimes painful struggle. Some States would even deny the rights of indigenous peoples to define themselves. Some attempt to capture agendas exercising 'soft power' which can harden up by shutting out indigenous voices. There are dilemmas. Indigenous peoples are empowered by rights but also transformed by them. Pristine innocence of this world seems to be an option open to very few groups.

MOVING ALONG THE PATH

The developments in minority and indigenous rights will take specific paths into the next millennium. For minorities and indigenous peoples, the Human Rights Committee and CERD, the Committee on the Rights of the Child, the Committee on the Elimination of Discrimination against Women, and other UN treaty bodies will to continue to develop the normative content of long established human rights. The United Nations Working Group on Minorities should gather momentum after a cautious start in its first three years. The Working Group can assist in the development of an international minority movement analogous to the international self-organisation of indigenous peoples, though it may be surmised that minorities are more diverse in characteristics and aspirations than the indigenous. All branches of the United Nations will continue the process of sensitisation to ethnic issues mandated by the United Nations Declaration on Minorities and the World Conference on Human Rights. Phenomena of racial and religious intolerance, xenophobia and racism will continue to occupy special rapporteurs and other

---

91 The two viewpoints are not always in harmony: Gray, A, *Between the Spice of Life and the Melting Pot: Biodiversity Conservation and its Impact on Indigenous Peoples*, 1991, Copenhagen: IWGIA.

92 The UN is now into its third decade to combat racism and racial discrimination. The first decade was proclaimed by GA Res 3057 (XXVIII), 2 November 1973. In addition, there have been two World Conferences to Combat Racism and Racial Discrimination, held at Geneva in 1978 and 1983.

'mechanisms'.[93] At the Council of Europe, the work of the Advisory Committee under the Framework Convention[94] should bring fresh impetus to understanding and applying minority rights in Europe (and, perhaps, outside since the Framework Convention is not confined to European States).[95]

The integration of these texts and others such as the Language Charter with general international law and human rights is the work of generations, and inappropriate for soundbites or snap judgments. The standards are in place, but they do not necessarily deal adequately with some of the pressing questions of minority rights. Hence, for example, the Foundation on Inter-Ethnic Relations based in The Hague has convened reflection groups of international lawyers and education and language specialists, to elaborate upon The Hague Recommendations on the Education Rights of National Minorities,[96] and the Oslo Recommendations on Linguistic Rights.[97] The Hague Recommendations are being processed by the United Nations for possible 'universalisation', beyond the limits of the OSCE.[98] The ethnic dimensions of migration, transboundary co-operation, local and regional self-government, and demographics will further reveal themselves in the work of the Council of Europe and other organisations.[99] Discrimination against the Roma will not disappear but it will attract increasing international opprobrium.[100]

For indigenous peoples, two great ambitions predominate: the adoption by the United Nations General Assembly of the draft Declaration on the Rights of Indigenous Peoples, and the incorporation of a Permanent Forum for Indigenous Peoples into United Nations structures. The former is a radical document which incorporates the claims of indigenous peoples to self-determination as well as multiple forms of autonomy and own institution control, an indigenous citizenship, extensive provisions on land and resources, and a reconsideration of the historic treaties by which domination over them was secured and protection guaranteed. States are fighting the draft tooth and nail, using some old tricks. They demand definition as the price of progress, and attempt to reduce self-determination to autonomy. They accuse the indigenous of selfish unconcern with the rights and fate of others.

---

93 See Report of the Secretary General, Racism, Racial Discrimination, Xenophobia and Related Intolerance, E/CN 4/1998/77.

94 Framework Convention, Art 26.

95 *Ibid*, Arts 27 and 29.

96 1997.

97 1998.

98 This 'universalisation' programme was initiated at the third session of the UN Working Group on Minorities in 1997.

99 Thornberry, P and Amor Martin Eåstebanez, M, *The Council of Europe and Minorities*, Doc COEMIN, 1994.

100 Liegeois, J-P and Gheorghe, N, *Roma/Gypsies: A European Minority*, 1995, London: Minority Rights Group.

Governments generally pretend that international law of self-determination and human rights is fixed and immutable, or sufficiently enough to disallow indigenous claims particularly in the realm of collective rights.[101] In the meantime, the less exciting process of implementing ILO Convention 169 is set to continue, producing positive results for indigenous peoples at a lower political temperature. The Americas should also see their own Declaration on Indigenous Rights under the aegis of the OAS come into play before too long, a long overdue recognition of the havoc wreaked on local cultures by the incomers of the last 500 years. Indigenous rights are written all over the international agenda at present, from the programmes of the World Bank to the development policies of European States – even the Netherlands has become a party to ILO Convention 169 despite the absence of indigenous and tribal peoples (in the ILO sense) on its territory.

The above are imminent developments, but what of the broader agenda? There clearly needs to be further reflection and activation of the standards, and improvement of mechanisms to guarantee respect for rights. The reference here is primarily to international mechanisms. In a sense, these are supplementary to national mechanisms where the rights will touch the lives of individuals. On the other hand, many peoples are blocked at home from finding justice and reach out to the international community for redress. And monitoring by and through international organizations needs to continue, despite perceived tendencies to 'nationalise' international law, and to drive justice and equity off the agenda.[102] There is also a need for education in tolerance and intercultural respect. Minority rights depend also on the development of a vibrant democracy and civil society, respecting the rule of law. In the age of rights, there has, it has been suggested, a turn away from individual responsibility.[103] There are difficulties in locating this in the structure of international law with its generally vertical approach to responsibility, only approaching the personal in the area of war crimes and genocide. In the case of minorities, the demand for responsibility has often degenerated into a demand for loyalty.[104] However laudable the objective of loyalty, it is not laudable to impose extra layers of responsibility on often fragile groups. Loyalty must be earned, not demanded, and certainly not demanded as a condition for the enjoyment of fundamental rights.

---

101 The issues are being played out at the sessions of the Drafting Group set up by the UN Commission on Human Rights to 'process' the draft Declaration on the Rights of Indigenous peoples. See Report of the Working Group Established in Accordance with Commission on Human Rights GA Res 1995/32, UN Doc E/CN4/1998/106.

102 Alston, P, 'The myopia of the handmaidens: international lawyers and globalisation' (1997) 3 EJIL 435, pp 435–48.

103 See, in general, Avineri, S and de-Shalit, A, *Communitarianism and Individualism*, 1992, Oxford: OUP.

104 *Op cit*, Thornberry, fn 8.

It has been widely observed that sovereignty is leaking out from the State in two directions – towards supranational organisations and to sub-State or sub-national groups.[105] Sovereignty is less concentrated than before and more amorphous. The international movement in human rights has played a critical part in these developments.[106] Human rights are a matter of international concern and dictators find it increasingly difficult to hide behind the barriers of domestic jurisdiction. The contemporary enhancement of minority and indigenous rights is not merely a consequence of the diffusion of sovereignty, it is also a proximate cause.[107] If sovereignty is modified by human rights, it is modified by ethnic group rights. If government legitimacy is linked to human rights, it is also linked to the treatment of ethnic groups.[108] Minority and indigenous rights lead to a de-centring of loyalty away from exclusive loyalty to the State. The individual, the family, the local community, the region, the 'imagined community'[109] of race, tribe or nation, the State and perhaps the cosmopolitan community, or just humanity at large, circle round the affections as competing foci of loyalty for many contemporary human beings.[110] And international law suggests that this confusion is legitimate; all have claims in various ways.

One effect of the internationalisation of minority rights with its attendant dispersion of loyalties, is greatly to complicate matters for governments. The standards assert that diversity is good for you; that homogenisation diminishes the personality. Heavy nation building projects are not in vogue; lightness[111] and self-expression are. Simple majoritarianism is not any longer regarded as the best expression of democracy. Locality and place are important as are roots and history. Authoritarianism is to give way to dialogic communities. Even sovereignty is recast less as authority and more as dialogue, taking care to include all groups whose interests are affected.[112] These are developments and trends. But there are also counter-intuitions.

Governments still largely call the shots in international organisations, however much plagued by civil society and bureaucratic pressure. Governments continue to resist the elaboration of collective rights. They still deny the existence of minorities and indigenous peoples on their territory

105 Simpson, GJ, 'The diffusion of sovereignty: self-determination in the post-colonial age' (1996) 32 Stanford JIL 23, pp 255–86.
106 Hsiung, JC, *Anarchy and Order: The Interplay of Politics and Law in International Relations*, 1997, Boulder: Lynne Rienner, Chap 6.
107 Linklater, A, *The Transformation of Political Community*, 1998, Cambridge: Polity.
108 *Op cit*, Marks, fn 4.
109 Anderson, B, *Imagined Communities: Reflections on the Spread of Nationalism*, 1983, London: Verso.
110 *Op cit*, Linklater, fn 107.
111 Calvino, I, *Six Memos for the Next Millennium*, 1996, London: Vintage, p 1.
112 Scott, C, *State Sovereignty: The Challenge of a Changing World*, 1993, Ottawa: CCIL.

without fear of repercussion.[113] Minorities and indigenous peoples can also be selfish, and become fundamentalist. It can appear selfish to claim rights and ignore duties. The subversive effects on the state of the new politics of minority recognition can in turn subvert ethnic groups. Ethnicity and cultural authenticity do not always sit easily with claims for recognition – within groups – of the rights of women, of dissenters.[114] Ethnicity can lead to the creation of ghettoes. Thus we write from as witness to some great battles for the soul of the age – an age like any other of incomplete tendencies, or to adopt another title from Calvino, 'a castle of crossed destinies'. It at least seems tolerably clear that human rights will continue as a favoured language to empower the disempowered and cross the ether between the localities of this world. But, it will change and outcomes are uncertain. Vigilance is required to guard the *acquis*.

The community element in minority and indigenous rights can lead to a growth of self-organisation which is also guarantees the defence of rights. The assertion of such rights will succeed best if it becomes clearer that all have an interest and will benefit from securing respect for rights, in some or other version of the common good. Whether the agenda of ethnic rights will emerge in a praxis of redemption, bringing peoples and cultures to salvation, who knows. Mired in our own time, we seem to be like Yeats' Caesar:

> Our master Caesar is in the tent
> Where the maps are spread,
> His eyes fixed upon nothing,
> A hand under his head.
> *Like a long-legged fly upon the stream*
> His mind moves upon silence.[115]

Nonetheless, law, politics and culture will engage with minority and indigenous rights for some time. There will be some gains and some losses. Despite the stresses endured by many groups and the certainty that cultures will disappear and not simply be 'transformed', despite intellectual pessimism regarding the ability of human rights to transfigure real lives, despite the dreary continuum of Derrida's 'innumerable singular sites of suffering', the changing configuration of international law should encourage us to remain optimistic. We may even discern a 'mounting tendency to impose what is just through what is unjust ... perhaps this is the germ of an immense metropolis'.[116]

---

113 Notably, France, which continues to deny the relevance of minority rights for the French nation, see comment in the present author's article in *op cit*, Phillips and Rosas, fn 26. Also, *Hopu and Bessert v France*, CCPR/C/60/D/549/1993, 30 September 1997.

114 *Op cit*, Perry, fn 63.

115 Yeats, WB, 'Long-legged fly' (1939).

116 *Op cit*, Calvino, fn 111, p 125.

CHAPTER 21

MIGRATION AND THE REFUGEE QUESTION

Paul Okojie

Refugees are of every race and religion and can be found in every part of the world. Forced to flee out of fear for their lives and liberty, they often give up everything – home, belongings, family and country – for an uncertain future in a strange land.[1]

THE COLOUR LINE

In Europe today, non-white migration continues to excite strong sentiments. This chapter attempts to discuss reasons why the word migrant has become synonymous with the word 'black' when this is palpably not the case and why EU governments are avoiding their obligations under the 1951 UN Convention on Refugees, by describing refugees as 'economic migrants'. It concludes by inviting the international community to broaden the definition of the refugee in order to take account of the reality of the position of the asylum seeker today.

REFUGEES – INVOLUNTARY MIGRATION

Migration of people from their homeland to other countries is a well established phenomenon, but their acceptance in the country of migration is often grudging, one possible exception being the Cold War years when refugees were frequently given sanctuary in order to score political points. According to Heisler, 'The Cold War made it easy to ignore the prospect of large scale emigration from the East ...'.[2]

---

1 UNHCR, *The State of the World's Refugees: A Humanitarian Agenda*, 1997, Oxford: OUP.
2 See Heisler, MO, 'Migration, international relations and the new Europe: theoretical perspectives from institutional political sociology', in Cohen, R (ed), *Theories of Migration*, 1996, Cheltenham: Elgar, p 461.

Migration occurs either voluntarily,[3] by compulsion[4] or through necessity.[5] States retain the ability to control the growth of voluntary migration and are not subject to any international treaty obligation with regard to their domestic immigration policies. A clear example of this is Japan, which, according to Sowell:

> ... with a population of 124 million people, ... permitted 1.2 million aliens to be legally registered in 1991, less than 1% of its population. Moreover, a significant fraction of these are people of Japanese ancestry from Brazil and other countries ... Few, if any, modern industrial nations have managed to remain as insulated from immigration and to retain as homogeneous a population.[6]

This policy is sustained because Japan insists on strong 'norms of mandating exclusion, even for third or fourth generation descendants of immigrants; and they stigmatise returning expatriates – even children taken abroad for a few years by businessmen on temporary assignment abroad.'[7] Australia, which used to pursue a 'whites only' immigration policy, abandoned it many years ago. There can be no doubt that the refugee who, either by compulsion or necessity, leaves his or her country deserves a different consideration from the voluntary migrant. However, for economic, cultural and political reasons, both the voluntary migrant and the refugee rarely find themselves readily accepted. The number of people seeking asylum is often cited as a reason for the reluctance to grant sanctuary to refugees. In a banner headline, a leading UK newspaper drew attention to the cost of refugees – '£2 billion a year', and stated that '60,000 are missing in the system'. It then stated that the Government is committed to the 'overhaul of "shambolic" asylum laws'. In its editorial, the paper questioned why 'Italy, the first port of call for anybody fleeing the Balkans, receives only 1,200 asylum seekers each year, against our 30,000'.[8]

The numbers seeking sanctuary may be an element, but are not the only the reason why refugees do not enjoy ready acceptance. In relation to Jewish migration, anti-semitism was a potent factor. Sowell recalls that:

> ... when shiploads of Jewish refugees from Nazi persecution in Europe tried to escape to the Western Hemisphere on the eve of World War II, many were turned away. The most famous of these ships ... was the liner, St Louis, which,

---

3 Eg, immigration, the Irish escaping famine in the 1840s, would, in today's world, be described as 'economic migrants'; 'nearly two fifths of all the people born in Ireland were living outside of Ireland by 1891', see Sowell, T, *Migrations and Cultures: A World View*, 1996, New York: Basic Books, p 35.

4 By expulsion, eg, the expulsion of Pakistanis and Indians from Uganda in the 1970s, or the mass exodus of the boat people from South East Asia.

5 Fear of persecution, eg, Palestinians escaping persecution in Israel or ethnic cleansing in the Balkans.

6 *Op cit*, fn 3, Sowell, p 44.

7 *Op cit*, fn 2, Heisler, p 463.

8 (1998) *The Daily Telegraph*, 23 November, p 21.

in 1939, was turned away from Cuba and the United States and was forced to return to Europe.[9]

THE MIGRANT IN HISTORY

The international refugee system which governs the granting of sanctuary to refugees and asylum seekers today grew out of particular world crises. Of most relevance was the experience of the Jews and Armenians following the collapse of the Ottoman and Austrian-Hungarian empires at the end of the First World War. Current refugee policies were thus shaped in the 1920s and became universal in the 1950s, following the human catastrophes arising out of the First and Second World Wars.

The discussion of the refugee question therefore requires an understanding of the position of the Jews in Central and Eastern Europe before the cataclysmic problems experienced in Germany in the 1930s. It is estimated that about 350,000 Jews lived in Poland and Lithuania at the end of the 17th century. In the same period 10,000 Jews lived in Hungary and about 50,000 Jews in Bohemia-Moravia. The Jewish population in Prague alone (11,000)[10] exceeded the number of Jews in Hungary. Russia's annexation of parts of Poland, in 1795, brought Russia's Jewish population to 800,000. Prior to this, Russia already had a policy of trying to assimilate its Jewry. The Jews were persecuted in various ways, for example, being forced to eat pork and to make the sign of the cross. There were other violations of Jewish tradition, such as being pressured to become Christian in religion and to adopt Russian culture. The long beards and long coats traditional among Jewish men were also forbidden and policemen carried scissors with which they were authorised to trim the beards of any Jews they encountered on the streets who were caught violating this law.[11]

Czar Nicholas pursued anti-Jewish policies until he was succeeded by his son, Alexander II, in 1855. The assassination of Alexander II, for which the Jews were blamed, sparked new waves of anti-Jewish policies under the reign of Alexander III in 1881. The pogrom against the Jews in 1880 caused millions of Jews to emigrate to the US and elsewhere from 1881–1914.[12] The persecution was not confined to the lower end of society. As Sowell has identified, 'Universities in Eastern Europe became centres of anti-Semitism and fascism in the inter-war period'.[13] Historically, countries are reluctant to

---

9   *Op cit*, fn 3, Sowell, p 286.
10 Rybar, C, *Jewish Prague*, 1991, Prague: TV Spektrum; *op cit*, fn 3, Sowell, p 262.
11 *Op cit*, fn 3, Sowell, p 263.
12 *Ibid*, p 264.
13 *Ibid*, p 266.

rush to assist people who are victims of other people's problems. Thus, the 'ships carrying Jewish refugees from Europe during the era of the Nazi persecutions were turned away from port to port'.[14]

Today countries are restricting further their policies on immigration and asylum.[15] Under the Austrian Presidency of the European Union, a proposal has been put forward which would lead to the abandonment of the 1951 UN Convention on Refugees.[16] In Belgium, it took the death of an African refugee in Brussels at the hands of Belgian officials[17] for the public to take notice of the harsh treatment of refugees there.

FORGING A REFUGEE POLICY

As stated above, the First World War, the demise of the Ottoman Empire and the Russian Revolution started the process of putting together an international policy on refugees.[18] One and a half million people were displaced during the First World War, their misery and lack of ready sanctuary exposing the absence of an effective scheme for resettling people on a massive scale.

In 1921, the League of Nations started building a structure which was to lead to the adoption of a universal approach in 1951. The 1921 scheme for assisting refugees was partial rather than comprehensive. The League had no mandate to compel countries to take them, therefore, much depended on the goodwill of member countries, as it still does today. In the early years, the League preferred to try to repatriate people, most of whom came from south eastern Europe and the USSR. However, it also organised massive relief operations to alleviate the suffering of refugees.

The problem of attempting to settle, in other countries, the refugees who could not or did not want to return to their country of origin proved intractable.[19] This problem continues for the United Nations High Commission for Refugees, the League's successor organisation, today.

The appointment in 1921 of the Norwegian, Fridtjof Nansen, the first High Commissioner for Refugees, was an attempt to find a solution to the growing

---

14 *Op cit*, fn 3, Sowell, p 45.
15 The UK Government has decided to appoint 'airline liaison officers [to] prevent passengers without the proper papers boarding places to Britain': (1998) *The Guardian*, 24 September, p 7. This runs contrary to the fact that, in certain circumstances, those facing persecution cannot obtain 'proper papers' from their persecutors.
16 (1998) State Watch, November 1998.
17 (1998) *The Observer*, 27 September. To their credit, many ordinary Belgians, black and white, came out to demonstrate their disapproval of the thuggish behaviour of the officials responsible for the refugee's death.
18 *Op cit*, fn 3, Sowell, p 6; UNHCR, *The State of the World's Refugees*, 1993, London: Penguin, p 11
19 Joly, D, *Refugees: Asylum in Europe*, 1992, London: Minority Rights Group.

refugee problem. At this time, the refugee question was seen as a European problem. Nansen understood well the reluctance of countries to provide open door support for refugees and continued with the repatriation policy which he knew was favoured by Member States. Member States had expected the repatriation of prisoners to bring the refugee problem to an end, but this approach was controversial, because of allegations of the mistreatment of those who were repatriated.

Nansen introduced new ideas in trying to ease the plight of the refugee by attempting to introduce identity papers which he hoped Member States would recognise as conferring refugee status on their holders. This came to be known as a 'Nansen passport'.[20] In 1922, there was no universal definition of what constituted a refugee. This status was determined by an individual's country of origin or territory, for example, 'Russian'[21] or 'Armenian'[22] refugee. This method of recognition posed its own problem. The countries concerned often denied any official persecution policy against the refugees and questioned the rationale for conferring such a status on the group affected.[23] The League's other principal problem was how to protect in-country refugees against expulsion. This proved equally difficult, although the problem was of the League's own making because of its insistence that only refugees outside their country could receive assistance. The plight of the internally displaced was ignored by their oppressors, as is shown by the Jewish experience.

After Nansen's death in 1930, his successor tried to grapple with the problem of the in-country refugee. In 1935, he resigned in protest against the failure of the international community to change the rules in order to help the Jews whom the Nazis had prevented from leaving Germany with their assets.[24]

His resignation was indicative of the serious misgivings being expressed generally about the handling of the refugee question at international level.

---

20 An arrangement with regard to the Issue of Certificates of Identity to Russian Refugees, 355 LNTS 238, 5 July 1922.

21 'Russian refugee:any person of Russian origin who does not enjoy the protection of the Government of the Union of Soviet Socialist Republics and who has not acquired any other nationality.'

22 'Armenian refugee: any person of Armenian origin, formerly a subject of the Ottoman Empire, who does not enjoy the protection of the Turkish Republic and who has not acquired any other nationality.'

   See Report by the Commissioner, League of Nations Doc 1926 (XIII.2), p 3, quoted in Hathaway, JC, 'The evolution of refugee status in international law: 1920–1950' (1984) 33 ICLQ 353.

23 *Op cit*, fn 18, UNHCR, p 11.

24 *Op cit*, fn 19, Joly.

In 1938, an Intergovernmental Committee on Refugees for the first time accepted that internally displaced persons could, under certain circumstances, be recognised as refugees.[25] Two types of refugees were covered:

(1) persons who have not already left their countries of origin (Germany, including Austria), but who must emigrate on account of their political opinions, religious beliefs and racial origin; and

(2) persons as defined in (1) who have already left their country of origin and who have not yet established themselves permanently elsewhere.[26]

The Committee considered the position of 'economic migrants' and drew a distinction between migrants who were the 'victims of economic sanctions or proscription', and therefore entitled to protection, and 'persons who had left Germany for economic reasons, but without being compelled to do so, or [who] had gone abroad in order to evade taxation'.[27]

The displaced, therefore, fell into different categories. According to Hathaway, Russian migrants consisted of:

... individuals, families and entire armies fleeing the destruction and suffering caused by the Russian Revolution. Some individuals left ... in order to avert material devastation and famine, others fled because they held political convictions fundamentally at odds with those of the Bolsheviks.[28]

Included in the above list are those who would today be regarded as economic migrants. The International Red Cross urged the League of Nations to adopt a broad approach and to accept that the duty to assist the Russian migrants as not only a 'humanitarian duty', but also 'an obligation in international justice'.[29] The concept of 'international justice' did not prevail, though the Office of the High Commissioner for Refugees was asked to take broad responsibility for dealing with the 'legal status, repatriation and the co-ordination of externally-financed relief operations'.[30] The emphasis was still on repatriation and there was still no universal definition of the status of the refugee.

In 1947, when the United Nations replaced the League of Nations, the International Refugee Organisation (IRO) was set up to take over the refugee functions previously discharged by the League of Nations. The IRO was responsible for refugees from the First and Second World Wars. There were over 20 million peopled displaced by the Second World War. The IRO followed its predecessor's approach of repatriating people to their countries of

---

25 *Op cit*, fn 22, Hathaway, p 371.

26 *Ibid*, see Resolution of the Intergovernmental Committee on Refugees ICR Doc 14 July 1938, cited at p 370.

27 *Ibid*, p 365.

28 *Ibid*, p 351.

29 *Ibid*.

30 *Ibid*.

origin instead of assisting them to settle in new ones. This policy was unrealistic, in that not all displaced persons wanted to return to their country of origin. The IRO was more willing than its predecessor to accommodate those with valid objections to returning home because of persecution or fear of persecution on grounds of race, religion, nationality or political opinion.

Following further reviews, the IRO was replaced by a stronger system, namely, the Office of the United Nations High Commissioner for Refugees (UNHCR) in 1951. The General Assembly defined the function of the UNHCR as 'providing international protection ... and ... seeking permanent solutions for the problems of refugees'.[31] This marked the beginning of a new era in the UN refugee system. It will be remembered that the original schemes under the League of Nation and the IRO were aimed at protecting European refugees. The old schemes were also premised on the assumption that the refugee problem would be solved once displaced people had been repatriated, on the basis that:

> When the UNHCR was set up in 1951, it had a projected life span of three years. It was assumed that the existing post-Second World War refugees would be integrated into the societies in which they had found refuge, and that the organisation could be disbanded.[32]

The 1951 Convention provided a partial universal definition of the refugee and replaced the 'Nansen passport' with the 'Convention Travel Document' for refugees.

THE CRUX OF THE MATTER

The pre-1951 rules for dealing with refugees rest on a humanitarian platform without enunciating a clearly stated legal right to refugee status. This legal framework left many issues unresolved. Although the Convention is a marked improvement, its major weakness is that its response to displaced people is still insufficient.

The international community expects sovereign nations to observe good standards of behaviour and to protect all their citizens by not subjecting them to arbitrary laws and abuses of human rights. According to the UNHCR, citizens are 'entitled to look to their own governments and State institutions to protect their rights and physical security, even if imperfectly'.[33] This is the concept known as 'national protection'. Because of the strength of this idea, there is no enforcement process which can be invoked against States who cause migrants to flee.

---

31 *Op cit*, fn 18, UNHCR, p 11.
32 *Ibid*, p 3.
33 *Ibid*, p 5.

What if certain groups are excluded from national protection? This occurs when, according to the UNHCR, people are compelled to leave their country of origin because they:

... know that they cannot rely, at home, on the protection of police, access to a fair trial, redress of grievances through the courts, nor expect the prosecution of those who violate their rights or get help from their country's consular services when abroad. These are among the legal and social protections that a properly functioning government is normally expected to extend to its nationals at home and abroad.[34]

A clear example of the denial of such protection is the decree passed by Nazi Germany to the effect that:

None but members of the nation may be citizens of the State. None but those of German blood, whatever their creed, may be members of the nation. No Jew, therefore, may be a member of the nation.[35]

Another example is provided by the 50,000 Asians who were permitted to take only £55 when expelled by Idi Amin in 1972.

In spite of international covenants,[36] many people are compelled to flee 'in terror of abuses perpetrated by the State. In other instances, they are escaping from oppression that the State is powerless to prevent because it has lost control of territory or otherwise ceased to function in an effective way'.[37]

The number of people forced to leave their homes or countries because of persecution or abuse of human rights has grown dramatically since the end of the Second World War. According to the UNHCR, the world population of displaced people in 1997 is a staggering 22 million, of which 13 million are refugees.[38] The nature of the refugee system has changed substantially since the 1900s. Many of today's refugee problems occur as a result of civil war or armed conflicts.[39] Examples are those in Afghanistan, Albania, Burundi, the Democratic Republic of the Congo, Liberia, Rwanda, Sierra Leone, Somali,

---

34 *Op cit*, UNHCR, fn 18, p 11.

35 Simpson, J, *Refugees: A Review of the Situation since September 1939*, 1993, Oxford: OUP, p 59.

36 The United Nations Charter; the Universal Declaration of Human Rights; the International Covenant on Civil and Political Rights (ICCPR); the International Covenant on Economic, Social and Cultural Rights; Convention on the Elimination of All Forms of Racial Discrimination; the Convention on Elimination of All Forms of Discrimination against Women; the Convention against Torture and Other Cruel, Inhuman or Degrading Treatment; Convention on the Rights of the Child; Declaration on the Right to Development.

Lindholt, L, *Questioning the Universality of Human Rights: The African Charter on Human and Peoples' Rights in Botswana, Malawi and Mozambique*, 1997, Aldershot: Ashgate.

37 *Op cit*, fn 18, UNHCR, p 5.

38 *Ibid*, pp x, 2.

39 *Ibid*, p 69.

Sudan and the former Yugoslavia. It should be noted that many more are displaced within their national boundaries. According to UNHCR statistics, about 30 million people are displaced in this way,[40] either due to natural disaster, political conflicts or both. The magnitude of the problem is better appreciated by taking account of the fact that from 1960 to 1969, the number of refugees never exceeded 1.5 million in any one year. In 1976, however, the number rose above 2.5 million and has grown inexorably since.

The total number of people of concern to UNHCR rose from 17 million in 1991 to a record 27 million in 1995. Although there is no typical refugee producing region as such, the UNHCR's reports show that most of the refugees are to be found in 'low and middle income regions of the world, particularly Africa, Asia and parts of the former Soviet Union.[41]

LEGAL PROTECTION TODAY

The refugee today enjoys far greater legal protection than previously enjoyed in the early part of this century. This does not overcome the fact that refugee status in international law still has a narrow definition. The 1949 Geneva Convention Relating to the Protection of Civilian Persons as amended by the Additional Protocols of 1977, expressly excludes conflicts such as riots or sporadic violence, even if these acts may be aimed at a given group over a period of time. This creates the absurdity that those experiencing 'ethnic cleansing' could, on one level, be seen as involved in an internal conflict and would then be denied refugee status. There are, therefore, many people living in a state of constant insecurity, without being able to claim refugee status.

If the 1949 Geneva Convention excludes victims of internal conflict, how far does the Convention Relating to the Status of Refugees 1951 (the Geneva Convention),[42] and the Protocol Relating to the Status of Refugees 1967, protect the modern refugee?

The essentials are of the Convention are as follows:

- protection against *refoulement* (Art 33) – an important prohibition against expelling or returning a refugee to the frontiers of countries or territories where his or her life or freedom would be threatened on account of the

---

40 *Op cit*, fn 18, UNHCR, p 5.

Deng, F, *Protecting the Internally Displaced: A Challenge for the United Nations*, Report by the Special Representative of the Secretary General on Internally Displaced Persons to the UN Commission on Human Rights, 1993. Brookings Institute.

41 *Op cit*, fn 18, UNHCR, p 5.

42 It was adopted by the United Nations Conference on the Status of Refugees and Stateless Persons held in Geneva, 2–25 July 1951 and it came into force nearly three years later: 27 April 1954.

refugee's race, religion, nationality, membership of a particular social group or political opinion. This is a rule which has been known to be ignored by some European countries, including the UK Government;

- Art 1 (as amended by Art 1(2) of the 1967 Protocol) states that a refugee is a person who:
  - owing to a well founded fear of being persecuted for reasons of race, religion, nationality, membership of particular social group or political opinion, is outside the country of his or her nationality and is unable to or, owing to such fear;
  - is unwilling to avail himself or herself of the protection of that country; or who, not having a nationality and being outside the country of his or her former habitual resident ..., is unable or, owing to such fear, is unwilling to return to it;
- a person who satisfies Art 1 is entitled to a number of specific rights:
  - residence, education, freedom of movement, employment, access to courts, naturalisation, subject, of course, to national laws.

As to the interpretation of the Convention, regard must be had to the Convention on the Law of Treaties (Vienna) 1969. Furthermore, in 1988, the UNHCR issued its *Handbook on Procedures and Criteria for Determining Refugee Status*.[43]

THE EUROPEAN UNION AND THE 1951 CONVENTION

By various arrangements such as the Schengen Agreement[44] and the Dublin Convention 1990, European Union countries have weakened the importance of the 1951 Convention. By way of example, the Dublin Convention, which came into effect in September 1997, makes provision for Member States to exchange information about refugees with the effect that an application to one EU Member State is treated as if it were an application to all EU Member States. Information is routinely collected on the number of asylum seekers, nature of the asylum claim, and mode of entry into the EU. A network of countries stretching from the EU to Australia and Canada are sharing information about the movement of refugees.[45] Under the Austrian Presidency of the EU, a proposal has been put before the Justice and Home Affairs Committee (K4 Committee – the 'Third Pillar'). The paper proposes

43 Obtainable from the UNHCR, 7 Westminster Palace Gardens, Artillery Row, London SW1P 1RR, UK.
44 Monar, J and Morgan, R (eds), *The Third Pillar of the European Union: Cooperation in the Field of Justice and Home Affairs*, 1994, Brussels: European Interuniversity Press.
45 (1997) 7(6) State Watch 4.

dividing Europe and the world into concentric zones. In the centre will be the Schengen Member States who will be protected by a 'concentric moat'. The countries that have applied for membership of the EU will be asked to bring their policies in line with those of the Schengen Group as a precondition to joining it.[46] This, of course, is not a particularly onerous obligation. 'Countries of emigration (Africa, the Middle East, Asia) are in the third circle and the primary task there is to eliminate the push factors'[47] and 'the extent of development aid granted can be assessed on [this] basis.'[48] The document recommends the abandonment of the 1951 UN Convention. Although the ideas have received less than favourable acceptance in K4 Committee, the Austrians have committed themselves to press ahead with their proposals in the December 1998 summit.[49] The Austrians claimed in the document that 'every immigrant in the first world is there illegally'[50] and, thus, casts doubt on the wisdom of the EU adopting a common visa policy, as 'most immigrants arrive illegally without a visa'.[51]

By contrast, the African Charter on Human and People's Rights 1981 – adopts a different approach to the 'refugee' question. Article 1(2) of the Charter extends the term refugee to any one who:

> ... owing to external aggression, occupation, foreign domination or events seriously disturbing public order in either part or the whole of his or her country of origin or nationality, is compelled to leave his or her place of habitual residence in order to seek refuge in another place outside his or her country of origin or nationality.

This definition avoids the 1951 UN Convention concept of the 'well founded fear of persecution' as a prerequisite to the granting of asylum. The American Convention on Human Rights – Pact of San Jose, Costa Rica 1969 – and the Cartagena Declaration on Refugees 1984 are modelled on this broad approach pioneered by the Organisation of African Unity.

The opposite approach has been amply demonstrated by the EU in the Convention Determining the State Responsible for Examining Applications for Asylum Lodged in One of the Member States of the European Communities 1990,[52] which favours a more restrictive approach, described as promoting the development of 'fortress Europe'.

---

46 (1997) 7(6) State Watch 4.
47 *Ibid.*
48 *Ibid.*
49 *Ibid.*
50 Reported in (1998) 187/98-10 Migration News Sheet, October, p 1.
51 *Ibid.*
52 The Dublin Convention – an inter-governmental arrangement and not strictly within the scope of EU laws.

WEAKNESSES IN THE UN CONVENTION

A major flaw in the system set up under the UN Convention is the failure to confer a right of asylum on refugees. Instead, it merely establishes guiding principles to be observed by signatories to the Convention. As already indicated, countries have always been reluctant to grant sanctuary to refugees and the West is rapidly enacting draconian measures to deter the entry of immigrants and refugees,[53] even though there has been a fall in the number of those seeking asylum in the EU.

According to the figures issued in January 1997, applications for political asylum in EU Member States continue to fall. In the first six months of 1996, they totalled 107,144, as against 121,651 for the same period in 1995, a fall of 12%, continuing the trend started in 1993.[54] The statistics show that Germany received over half of all applications: 57,489 in the first half of 1996. This was 3% down on the first half of 1995. The next three Member States in terms of total applications all recorded much more substantial falls: the UK down 25% to 14,860, the Netherlands down 30% to 10,025, and France down 32% to 7,846.

All 11 Member States with available data recorded decreases. Sweden was down 43% to 2,715 and Denmark 10% to 2,204. Belgium's decline was much smaller: 3.5% to 5,489. Italy's fall was 63% but from an already low figure of 833, to 305.

Over the same period, the US registered a 19% rise to 75,791. Applications to Switzerland were also up – by 5.5% to 8,216. Turkey constituted the second largest source of refugees in 1996, while it was the third largest source of asylum applications to European countries in the 10 years to 1995. According to EU data, the former Yugoslavia ranked first. Since 1994, Turkey has replaced Romania in second position.

According to the UNHCR, the number of people seeking asylum in 1998 has declined. This, should be put in perspective, however:

> In the last three years, the number dropped to 22.3 million as of 1 January 1998. Despite the overall fall, this figure still represents one out of every 264 people on earth. They include refugees, returnees and persons displaced within their own countries.[55]

From 1985 to 1995, well over half (200,000) of applications of Turkish origin were directed to Germany. See Table 1, below.

---

53 Home Office, *Fairer, Faster and Firmer – A Modern Approach to Immigration and Asylum*, Cm 4018, 1998, London: HMSO.

54 The data is in a report by Eurostat, the Statistical Office of the European Communities in Luxembourg, 1998, Eurobarometer.

55 UNHCR website http://www.unhcr.ch/.

Table 1: Number of asylum applications

	January–June 1995	January–June 1996	Percentage fall
Germany*	59,368	57,489	-3%
UK*	19,800	14,860	-25%
Netherlands	14,382	10,025	-30%
France**	11,575	7,846	-32%
Belgium	5,689	5,489	-3.5%
Austria	n/a	3,509	
Sweden	4,746	2,715	43%
Spain*	2,395	2,371	-1%
Denmark	2,443	2,204	-10%
Finland	420	331	-21%
Italy	833	305	-63%
EU	**121,651**	**107,144**	**-12%**

* Data does not include dependents.

** Data does not include minor dependents.

Data for Greece, Ireland, Luxembourg and Portugal are not available, but numbers of asylum applicants in these countries are very small.

Source: EUROSTAT, 'Asylum-seekers in Europe in the first six months of 1996', in Quarterly Bulletin, Population and Social Conditions, (1996) 2. Report published in Brussels 20 January 1997. The report is produced in collaboration with the Secretariat of the Intergovernmental Consultations on Asylum, Refugee and Migration Policies in Europe, North America and Australia (IGC).

THE UK POSITION

Both the proposal presented by the Austrian Presidency to the K4 Committee and the UK Government's document on the reform of domestic immigration and asylum laws do not tackle issues concerning the causes of oppression and the complicity of Western countries in causing the problems in the first place. The West, for example, supported the Talibans against the legitimate government of Afghanistan simply because that regime was Communist. The

Americans armed Svambi in Angola against the Neto government because of his government's socialist leanings.[56]

The catalogue of western collusion with oppressive regimes is endless. The UK Government's White Paper on immigration and asylum in essence questions the obligation which the 1951 Convention places on signatory countries. The White Papers sells the myth that no 'prosperous Western country is immune from being targeted' by those determined to undermine the tough immigration rules in the West.[57] The Government boasts of the fact that the UK was the first to 'ratify the Europol Convention and supported the decision to give Europol a role in combating illegal immigration and *has had* a significant part to play in developing:

> ... the Convention European Automated Fingerprint Recognition System (Eurodac) – an EU-wide computerised system for storing and accessing fingerprints of asylum applicants over 14 years of age. The Eurodac Convention was intended initially to apply only to asylum seekers to create a computerised central database of fingerprints of asylum seekers across the EU, now, it is being extended to illegal immigrants. We shall continue to strengthen co-operation of this kind.[58]

The UK's immigration and asylum policies have become indistinguishable and, as the above information suggests, officials have the encouragement to treat all non-white applicants as suspects. This is the background against which to comprehend the aforementioned killing of an African refugee by Belgian officials at the international airport in Brussels. It is reported that officials in Brussels routinely hold pillows to the mouths and noses of black refugees to make it easier for them to be removed from Belgium.[59]

The UK was for a long time regarded as a country friendly and sympathetic to genuine refugees. Recent policies cast doubt on this image, if it ever was a true one.

While the UK does little to assist refugees, it does most to denounce them. It is common knowledge that the situation in the former Yugoslavia created refugees from Bosnia and Herzegovina. While Germany took 345,000 refugees from both areas, the UK Government took 6,000, a few hundred more than a poorer country such as the Czech Republic, which took 5,884 refugees. The UK Government has constantly denounced many refugees as bogus and refused them sanctuary on this basis.

As the Austrian document on immigration and asylum demonstrates, European countries are convinced that all asylum seekers come to Europe.

---

56 See Stockwell, J, *In Search of Enemies: A CIA Story*, 1997, Somerville: Replica.
57 *Op cit*, Home Office, fn 53, p 14.
58 *Ibid*, p 14; (1998) 187/98-10 Migration News Sheet, October, pp 7–8.
59 (1998) *The Observer*, 27 September.

The information presented below tends to throw a different light on the role which poor countries play in supporting asylum seekers.

Table 2: Refugees from the Horn of Africa: principal countries of asylum

Country of asylum	Number of refugees
Djibouti	
Somalis	23,000
Ethiopians	2,000
Egypt	
Somalis	3,500
Sudanese	1,500
Eritrea	
Somalis	2,000
Ethiopia	
Somalis	288,000
Sudanese	76,000
Djiboutians	18,000
Kenya	
Somalis	171,000
Sudanese	33,000
Ethiopians	7,000
Sudan	
Eritreans	328,000
Ethiopians	51,000
Uganda	
Sudanese	224,000
Yemen	
Somalis	44,000
Eritreans	2,500
Ethiopians	1,000
Zaire	
Sudanese	97,000
Total	**1,372,500**

Source: UNHCR, *The State of the World's Refugees: A Humanitarian Agenda*, 1997, p 75.

Set against these figures, the UK Government's complaint that there will be 38,000[60] people in 1998–99 seeking asylum pales into insignificance. While the UK Government is bemoaning the number of potential, as opposed to actual applicants in 1998–99, a country such as Uganda has provided haven for 224,000 Sudanese.

ACCEPTING REFUGEES

Should other countries be expected to provide the protection which the refugee's home country is unwilling to provide? Many European countries are increasingly questioning the assumption underpinning the 1951 Convention that they should. That some countries have deliberately organised or orchestrated the mass expulsion of some of their citizens cannot be denied. According to Cohen and Joly, this issue has been 'politicised and internationalised' especially this century.[61] Supporting this view, Castles and Miller predict that the last decade of this century and the first of the 21st will be *the* age of migration.[62] What is to be done as more people are displaced? How far can people continue to rely on a Convention to which European countries have seemingly conspired to undermine?

REFUGEES AND PUBLIC OPINION

In spite of the international legal framework for the treatment of refugees, the decisive factor as to whether or not sanctuary should be given is public opinion. In the Cold War period, a refugee or defector from the old Eastern Bloc may have enjoyed popular acceptance. Others often received hysterical and hostile treatment in the media. They were never considered to be 'proper' refugees, regardless of evidence to the contrary. In Europe, refugees are not just refugees, they are either 'economic migrants' or just plain 'bogus'. The refugee's motive for fleeing his or her country is seen as a calculated desire to gain economic opportunities in the West. It is not uncommon for those who flee persecution in their own country to meet with persecution in Europe. An example is the detention of an Algerian writer in a British prison. According to Amnesty International:

> The writer [spent] six months in Wormwood Scrubs (a prison) before being released and granted asylum. But his 10 months' incarceration was not due to

---

60 *Op cit*, Home Office, fn 53, p 12.

61 Cohen, R and Joly, D, 'Introduction: the new refugees of Europe', in Joly, D and Cohen, R (eds), *Reluctant Hosts: Europe and Its Refugees*, 1989, Aldershot: Avebury.

62 Castles, S and Miller, MJ, *The Age of Migration: International Population Movements in the Modern World*, 1993, London: Macmillan, p 3.

any conviction by a court. No British court ever considered his position. In common with hundreds of men and women whose only crime is to have sought asylum, the writer was incarcerated on the mere say so of low ranking immigration officials, acting without reference or effective accountability to any court or independent review body.[63]

This is done in the name of controlling the 'influx of aliens'! Note that word: 'influx'.

The Amnesty Report went on to observe that:

Over the past decade, the British Government has implemented a seemingly endless stream of new and ever more oppressive measures against asylum seekers, all intended to prevent or deter new arrivals. Not least among these deterrent measures has been the arbitrary and prolonged detention of many asylum seekers, in purpose built detention centres and criminal prisons, while their claims are examined. Driven from their homes by repression and state of terror, these vulnerable individuals have made long and dangerous journeys to reach what they hope will be a safe haven only to find themselves incarcerated, often for many months, in the United Kingdom.[64]

Refugees are perceived as scheming at every opportunity to board the first available flight to Europe! The UNHCR report above indicates clearly that many poor countries carry a disproportionate burden of the refugee problem. This fact is never reported in the West. Why the paranoia that all Africans are on their way to Europe to seek asylum? According to the UNHCR, refugees of every race and religion and can be found in every part of the world. Forced to flee out of fear for their lives and liberty, they often give up everything – home, belongings, family and country – for an uncertain future in a strange land. The human misery and suffering which refugees experience are often forgotten in official and media circles within Europe.

WHO IS AN ECONOMIC REFUGEE?

Anyone forced to leave his or her home and country under conditions of torture or oppression is both a refugee and in need of new economic opportunities. The two are interlinked, it is not possible to be the one and not the other. Nonetheless, the political battle over this issue is rapidly undermining the logic of developing a meaningful way of protecting refugees.

International law obliges all countries who are signatories to the conventions protecting social and political rights to take steps to respect the social, economic and cultural rights of those in their territory without discrimination of any kind. Such obligations are violated each time a

---

63 Amnesty International, *Cell Culture: Asylum Seekers in the UK*, 1997, London: AIUK.
64 *Ibid.*

displaced person is turned away on account of being an 'economic refugee'. Admittedly, the obligation 'to take steps' does not confer a justiciable right on the part of the refugee, but States who do not consider taking them could be said to be failing to honour their treaty obligations. A person who is considered to be an 'economic refugee' is consequently doomed in the light of present day conditions and stands little or no chance of gaining asylum. But this narrow and restrictive notion of the economic refugee needs to be challenged. A person should not be deemed to be outside the protection of the various international conventions on this ground alone. Economic persecution can of itself be a source of discrimination against a social group. It is, therefore, helpful to draw attention to the judgment of the Canadian Immigration Appeal Board in *Guillermo Lautaro Diaz Fuentes*[65] which called on judicial and quasi-judicial authorities to pay careful attention to the context in which economic circumstances are raised:

> ... what we must find out is whether behind the apparent personal and economic motives, there exists a fear of persecution ... The distinction between an economic migrant and a refugee is not always easy to establish, but what is important to keep in mind is that, if a person is a refugee, the fact that he also is or may be an economic migrant does not deprive him of his status as a refugee.

This view was not only upheld, in the case of *Abeba Teklehaimanot v Immigration Appeal Board*,[66] but the Canadian Federal Court of Appeal stated that there was no contradiction between being a refugee and seeking to better or improve oneself. This proactive attitude is not the view favoured within the European Union, where the prevailing attitude appears to be that any desire to improve oneself taints one's refugee status. Even on the core value of persecution – the *raison d'être* of the convention on refugees – courts in some European Union countries fail protect refugees against administrative decisions made against their rights and interests. Few heed the judgment in the Canadian case of *Charles Kwado Amoah*,[67] in which the court stated that 'it is not necessary for an individual to be beaten or tortured for him to have a feeling of persecution. It is sufficient if his fundamental freedom, his feelings of membership in a particular social group or the expression of his opinions are threatened for a well founded fear to arise'.

The third country and carrier liability rules in most European Union countries are conscious policy measures aimed against refugees and asylum seekers. These retrograde steps are further worsened by the absence of adequate and effective independent appeal mechanisms.

---

65 (1974) 9-IADC 323; affirmed 52 DLR (3d) 463 (FDCA).
66 (1980) FCAD, A-730-79, September 8.
67 (1987) IABD 100X, November 2.

TURNING THE SCREW

The growth in refugee numbers, as already stated, has been phenomenal. This, however, is no justification for providing less support. The growth represents a real increase in the conditions and circumstances which lead to the displacement of people. In Africa, for example, conditions in Burundi, Rwanda, Liberia, Sudan, Somalia, Nigeria (Ogoni) and Sierra Leone, to name a few, have added, in a short space of time, to a dramatic increase in the number of people forced to leave their homes and countries.

As far as Europe is concerned, people are made to think that all asylum problems end up on Europe's doorsteps. This belief only serves to fuel a pre-existing anti-immigrant feeling. The release and use of statistics in this field can have misleading as well as negative social consequences. An example of this is the release of official asylum statistics by the Home Office in the UK to show that bogus asylum seekers are undermining Britain's fair asylum system. As shown above, Britain's record of offering asylum to applicants is poor at best.

Table 3: Asylum applications 1994

Europe	5,270
North America	980
Africa	16,960
Middle East	1,985
Asia	7,515
Others	125
Total	**32,830**

Source: Home Office, *Immigration Statistics*, 1994.

As the statistics indicate, the total rose by 10,000 on the 1993 figures. The Home Office boasted that only 825 people were granted refugee status in 1994, as opposed to 1,590 in 1993. This type of statistic is overtly political and aimed at proving that the Government is pursuing a relentless policy to prevent 'bogus' refugees from obtaining asylum.

This negative attitude to refugees is prevalent and dominant. Governments fail to take pride in helping those in need – that would mean highlighting the right reasons; they prefer to show that they are 'tough' on the number of foreigners seeking settlement, whether temporary or permanent. The standard belief in the UK and in other European Union countries too is that 'there are too many foreigners' a euphemism for non-Caucasians.

According to the Home Secretary in the last Conservative administration, his mission was to convince his political audience that his tough policy would ensure that 'there will not be too many foreigners in this country'.[68]

This suggests that countries such as Britain are not looking at the refugee problem in round terms, but are more concerned about 'the number of foreigners' entering the UK.

A British Home Secretary gloated at the fact that of the over 32,000 asylum applications he received in 1993, he successfully reduced the applications granted from 1,590 in 1993 to 825 in 1994! Are the rest bogus? This is what we are asked to assume. His audience may be impressed, but this statement bears no relationship to the human tragedy behind the statistics.

The way the statistics were published is a touch more cynical and less subtle. By publishing the refugee's country of origin, the statistics lend support to the preordained view that the majority of refugees fleeing poor countries should be seen as economic migrants who do not deserve the protection they seek under the Geneva Convention.

The obligations of signatory countries to the Geneva Convention are clear. The figures shown above do not support the popular view that the number of people seeking asylum in the UK is greater than those seeking asylum elsewhere. On the contrary, the UK Government does its utmost to avoid taking refugees. Although there has been a significant drop in the number of people seeking asylum in Western European countries, the hysteria about 'bogus' asylum applications continues to affect the way in which refugees are treated in Europe.

REFUGEES OUTSIDE EUROPE

Contrary to popular opinion, the number of refugees who seek asylum in Europe is small. A fact which is less well known is that developing countries do a great deal more under very strained circumstances in allowing displaced people and refugees into their countries.

The evidence presents a different picture about the refugee question. While the West often complain about the refugee burden and the pressure on them to grant asylum to an increasing number of asylum seekers, the UNHCR statistics show that in 1992, none of the European Union countries, with the exception of Germany was in the top 50 countries ranked according to the ratio of refugee population to gross national product *per capita*. The top five

---

68   As cited in the Home Office Immigration Statistics (1994) 17(94) Home Office Statistical Bulletin.

countries are from the developing countries: Malawi, Pakistan, Ethiopia, United Republic of Tanzania and Sudan.

AMELIORATING THE SITUATION

The first step in improving the lot of the refugee is to re-examine the legal definition of the term. As currently defined, it encourages the avoidance of obligations by the international community. Countries will be less able to avoid their obligations if the 1951 United Nations Convention definition is abandoned. The definitions adopted by the African and Latin American countries would appear to more than broadly reflect the reality of refugees' situations in the modern world. The 1951 definition is tainted by the fallout of the Second World War.

The causes of conflict are numerous and solutions to them still elude the international community because of the vested economic interests of the countries most able to solve the problems. The next century will see a growth in the number of people displaced from their home and forced into exile because of the failure of the international community to develop adequate or effective measures for the resolution of conflicts.

The UNHCR's ability to act in the broad interest of refugees is circumscribed by the attitude of the principal Member States of the Security Council. The European Union States have effectively re-drawn their asylum laws,[69] despite of paying lip service to the 1951 United Nations Convention. What, then, are the chances of the international community adopting a new and more realistic definition of the refugee? It is the influence of the Western countries that will prevail in the adoption of a new definition and this, regrettably, is out of proportion to the number of refugees they allow into their countries. The intention here is not to engage in the ritual denunciation of the West. Many refugees are helped and have been helped in the West. However, the law relating to refugees needs to be broadened in order to ensure a more equitable sharing of the refugee burden and to remove the anomalies which allow a poor country such as Malawi to bear the highest refugee burden in modern history.

The European Union countries need now to change their hitherto negative attitude to refugees. A pro-active approach is required to improve public support for measures designed to alleviate sufferings which refugees encounter both at the point of displacement and when they arrive in Europe. The first important step is to end the situation where those fleeing persecution from their own countries are subjected to further persecution and degrading

---

69 The Schengen Agreement; the Dublin Convention and the Aznar Protocol (the Protocol on Asylum for Citizens of the European Union – this protocol has been criticised by both Amnesty International and the UNHCR).

treatment in Europe. International action should be taken to reduce or remove the conditions which cause people to flee their homes and the West should disavow States who repress their citizens.

BIBLIOGRAPHY

African Rights, *Rwanda: Death, Despair and Defiance*, 1995, London: African Rights

Agreement Reached in the Multi-Party Negotiations, Cmnd 3883, 1998, Belfast: Northern Ireland Office, 10 April 1998

Alderson, J, Gostin, L, Martin, I, McCabe, S, Mason, C and Wallington, P, *Civil Liberties and the Miners Dispute*, 1984, London: NCCL

Alkema, EA, 'The third party applicability or "Drittwirkung" of the European Convention on Human Rights', in Matscher, F and Petzold, H, *Protecting Human Rights: The European Dimension. Essays in Honour of Gérard J Wiarda*, 1988, Cologne: Carl Heymanns

Allen, R, *But For The Grace: The True Story of a Dual Existence*, 1954, London: Allen

Alston, P (ed), *The Best Interests of the Child*, 1994, Oxford: OUP

Alston, P (ed), *The United Nations and Human Rights: A Critical Appraisal*, 1992, Oxford, OUP

Alston, P, 'Conjuring up new human rights: a proposal for quality control' (1984) 78 AJIL 607

Alston, P, 'Out of the abyss' (1987) 9 HRQ 332

Alston, P, 'Revitalising United Nations work on human rights and development' (1991) 18 Melb UL Rev 216

Alston, P, 'The myopia of the handmaidens: international lawyers and globalisation' (1997) 3 EJIL 435

Alston, P, 'The right to peace, colloquium on the new human rights: the rights of solidarity', Mexico 1980 UNESCO DOC SS – 80/CONF 806/7

Alston, P, 'The unborn child and abortion under the draft Convention on the Rights of the Child' (1990) 12 HRQ 157

Alston, P (ed), *The United Nations and Human Rights: A Critical Appraisal*, 1992, Oxford: Clarendon

Alston, P, Parker, S and Seymour, J (eds), *Children, Rights and the Law*, 1992, Oxford: Clarendon

Ametistov, E, 'Zashchita sotsialnikh prav cheloveka v Konstitutsionnom Sude Rossiiskoi Federatsii: perviye itogi i dalneishiye perspektivi' (The protection of social human rights in the constitutional court of the Russian Federation: first conclusions and further perspectives) (1995) 4 Vestnik Konstitutsionnovo Suda Rossiiskoi Federatsi (Bulletin of the Constitutional Court of the Russian Federation) 13

Amnesty International, *A Policy of Denial*, February 1995, London: AIUK

Amnesty International, *Amnesty International Annual Report*, 1996, London: AIUK

Amnesty International, *Amnesty International News*, January 1998 (AI Index: NWS 21/01/98), London: AIUK

Amnesty International, *Amnesty International Annual Report*, 1997, London: AIUK

Amnesty International, *Amnesty International Annual Report*, 1992, London: AIUK

Amnesty International, *Cell Culture: Asylum Seekers in the UK*, 1997, London: AIUK

Amnesty International, *International Issues 1995–96*, December 1996, London: AIUK

Amnesty International, *International Issues 1997–98*, April 1998, London: AIUK

Amnesty International, *Mexico 'Disappearances': A Black Hole in the Protection of Human Rights* (AMR 41/05/98), 1998, London: AIUK

Amnesty International, *No Security without Human Rights*, October 1996, London: AIUK

Amnesty International, *Rape and Sexual Abuse: Torture and Ill Treatment of Women in Detention*, 1991 (Act 77/11/91), London: AIUK

Amnesty International, *Report on the State of the Amnesty International Movement*, November 1997 (AI Index: ORG 53/05/97), London: AIUK

Amnesty International, *Review of Amnesty International's Research*, June 1992 (AI Index: POL 40/01/92), London: AIUK

Amor Martin Eåstebanez, M, *International Organizations and Minority Protection in Europe*, 1996, Turku/Abo: Abo Akademi University

An-na'im, A, 'Cultural transformation and normative consensus on the best interests of the child', in Alston, P (ed), *The Best Interests of the Child*, 1994, Oxford: OUP

Anaya, SJ, *Indigenous Peoples in International Law*, 1996, New York: OUP

Anderson, B, *Imagined Communities: Reflections on the Spread of Nationalism*, 1983, London: Verso

Annan, K, 'Strengthening United Nations action in the field of human rights: prospects and priorities' (1997) 19 Harv HRJ 1

Asia Watch, *Silencing All Critics: Human Rights Violations in Singapore*, 1989, New York: Asia Watch

Avineri, S and de-Shalit, A, *Communitarianism and Individualism*, 1992, Oxford: OUP

Banks, K, 'Social security – objective justification in the context of indirect discrimination' (1991) 20 ILJ 22

Barnard, C, *EC Employment Law*, 1997 (rev edn), Chichester: Wiley

Barry, D, 'The trial of the CPSU and the principles of Nuremburg' (1996) 22 Review of Central and Eastern European Law 255

Barsh, B, 'Right to development' (1991) 13 HRQ 321

Barsh, RL, 'Indigenous peoples: an emerging object of international law' (1986) 80 AJIL 369

Bartholet, E, *Family Bonds: Adoption and the Politics of Parenting*, 1993, Boston: Houghton Mifflin

Bayefsky, A, 'United Nations human rights treaties: facing the implementation crisis' (1996) 15 Windsor Yearbook of Access to Justice 189

Bean, D, *Law Reform for All*, 1996, London: Blackstone

Beavis, S and Brown, P, 'Shell has human rights rethink' (1996) *The Guardian*, 6 November

Beddard, R, *Human Rights and Europe*, 1993, Cambridge: Grotius

Behrman, SJ and Kistner, RW, 'A rational approach to the evaluation of infertility', in Newill, R, *Infertility in Marriage*, 1974, Harmondsworth: Penguin

Beirne, M, 'Observations about observing' (1996) *JustNews*, September, p 1

Beirne, M, *The Misrule of Law: A Report on the Policing of Events During the Summer of 1996 in Northern Ireland*, 1996, Belfast: CAJ

Bell, C, Hegarty, A and Livingstone, S, 'The enduring controversy: developments in affirmative action law in North America' (1996) 3 Int J Discrimination L 253

Bell, M and Waddington, L, 'The 1996 intergovernmental conference and the prospects of a non-discrimination Treaty article' (1996) 25 ILJ 320

Bell, M, *EU Anti-Discrimination Policy: From Equal Opportunities between Women and Men to Combating Racism*, LIBE 102 EN, 1998, Brussels: European Parliament

Bennett, G, *Aboriginal Rights in International Law*, 1978, London: Royal Anthropological Institute of Great Britain and Ireland

Benoit-Rohmer, F, *The Minority Question in Europe*, 1996, Strasbourg: Council of Europe

Bercusson, B, *European Labour Law*, 1996, London: Butterworths

Bertsch, K, *The MacBride Principles and US Companies in Northern Ireland*, 1991, Washington DC: Investor Responsibility Research Centre

Bew, P and Gillespie, G, *Northern Ireland: A Chronology of the Troubles 1968–93*, 1993, Dublin: Gill & Macmillan

Bieback, KJ, *Indirect Discrimination within the Meaning of Directive (CE) 79/7 in the Social Security Law of the EC Member States*, 1996, Brussels: European Commission

Bilder, R, 'The individual and the right to peace: the right to conscientious dissent' (1980) 11 Bulletin of Peace Proposals 387

Binion, G, 'Human rights: a feminist perspective' (1995) 17 HRQ 509

BIRW, *'Bloody Sunday': Submission to the United Nations Special Rapporteur on Summary and Arbitrary Executions: The Murder of 13 Civilians by Soldiers of the British Army on 'Bloody Sunday', 30 January 1972*, 1994, London: BIRW

BIRW, *British Irish Rights Watch 1992–97*, 1997, London: BIRW

Black, I and Fairhall, D, 'The profits of doom' (1997) *The Guardian*, 16 October

Black, M, *Children First: The Story of UNICEF, Past and Present*, 1996, Oxford: OUP

Blackburn, R, 'A Human Rights Committee for the UK Parliament – the options' [1998] EHRLR 534

Blackburn, R and Taylor, J (eds), *Human Rights for the 1990s*, 1994, Poole: Mansell

Bloed, A (ed), *The Conference on Security and Cooperation in Europe: Analysis and Basic Documents*, 1993, The Hague: Martinus Nijhoff

Bloed, A, Leicht, L, Nowak, M and Rosas, A (eds), *Monitoring Human Rights in Europe: Comparing International Procedures and Mechanisms*, 1993, Dordrecht: Martinus Nijhoff

Blom, J, Fitzpatrick, B, Gregory, J, Knegt, R and O'Hare, U, *The Utilisation of Sex Equality Litigation Procedures in the Member States of the European Community*, 1996, Brussels: European Commission

Boli, J and Thomas, GM, 'World culture in the world polity: a century of international non-governmental organisation' (1997) 62 Am Soc Rev 171

Bonner, D, 'Combating terrorism in the 1990s: the role of the Prevention of Terrorism (Temporary Provisions) Act 1989' [1989] PL 440

Bornstein, K, *Gender Outlaw: On Men, Women and the Rest of Us*, 1994, London: Routledge

Bowring, B, 'Human rights in Russia: discourse of emancipation or only a mirage?', in Pogany, I (ed), *Human Rights in Eastern Europe*, 1995, Aldershot: Elgar

Bowring, B, 'Russia's accession to the Council of Europe and human rights: compliance or cross-purposes?' (1997) 6 EHRLR 628

Boyle, A and Anderson, M (eds), *Human Rights Approaches to Environmental Protection*, 1996, Clarendon: OUP

Boyle, K, 'Human rights and political resolution in Northern Ireland' (1982) 9 Yale J World Pub Order 156

Boyle, K, Hadden, T and Hillyard, P, *Law and State: The Case of Northern Ireland*, 1975, London: Martin Robertson

Boyle, K, Hampson, F and Reidy A, 'Enforcing fundamental human rights: the European Court of Human Rights and Turkey' (1997) 15 Neth QHR 161

Brennan, WJ Jr, 'The quest to develop a jurisprudence of civil liberties in times of security crises' (1988) 18 Isr YB HR 11

Brett, A, 'Indirect discrimination in social security schemes' [1997] 4 Web JCLI

Brolmann, C *et al* (eds), *Peoples and Minorities in International Law*, 1993, Dordrecht: Martinus Nijhoff

Brookfield, FM (ed), *Treaties and Indigenous Peoples*, 1992, Oxford: Clarendon

Brookings Report, *see* Deng, F

Brown, LD, *Creating Social Capital: Non-governmental Developmental Organisations and Intersectional Problem Solving*, 1994, Boston: Institute for Development Research

Brownlie, I, 'Humanitarian intervention', in Moore, JN (ed), *Law and Civil War in the Modern World*, 1974, Baltimore, MD: John Hopkins UP

Brownlie, I, *Basic Documents on Human Rights*, 3rd edn, 1992, Oxford: Clarendon

Brysk, A, 'Social movements in Argentina' (1993) Comparative Political Studies 259

Brzezinski, M and Garlicki, L, 'Judicial review in post-communist Poland: the emergence of a Rechtsstaat?' (1995) 31 Stanford JIL 13

Brzezinski, M, 'The emergence of judicial review in Eastern Europe: the case of Poland' (1993) 41 AJCL 153

Buergenthal, T, 'The human rights revolution' (1991) St Mary's LJ 3

Buergenthal, T, 'The normative and institutional evolution of international human rights' (1997) 19 HRQ 722

Buergenthal, T, 'To respect and ensure: State obligations and permissible derogations', in Henkin, L (ed), *The International Bill of Rights: the Covenant on Civil and Political Rights*, 1981, New York: Columbia UP

Buergenthal, T, *International Human Rights*, 2nd edn, 1995, St Paul: West

Bullough, B, Bullough, V and Elias J, *Gender Blending*, 1997, New York: Prometheus

Bunch, C, 'Women's rights as human rights: towards a re-vision of human rights' (1990) 12 HRQ 486

Burrows, N and Mair, J, *European Social Law*, 1996, Chichester: Wiley

Butler, AS, 'The Bill of Rights debate: why the New Zealand Bill of Rights Act 1990 is a bad model for Britain' (1997) 17 OJLS 323

Byrne, I, *Parliamentary Protection of Human Rights: The Options*, 1998, London: Charter 88

Byrnes, A, 'The "other" human rights treaty body: the work of the Committee on the Elimination of Discrimination Against Women' (1989) 14 Yale J Int L 1

Byrnes, A, 'Women, feminism and international human rights law: methodological myopic, fundamental flaws or meaningful marginalisations?' [1992] AYIL 205

Calvino, I, *Six Memos for the Next Millennium*, 1996, London: Vintage

Campbell, C, *Emergency Law in Ireland, 1918–25*, 1994, New York: OUP

Campbell, T (ed), *Human Rights: From Rhetoric to Reality*, 1986, Oxford: Blackwells

Capotorti, F, *Study on the Rights of Persons belonging to Ethnic, Religious and Linguistic Minorities*, 1991, New York: UN

Cassel, D, 'Corporate initiatives: a second human rights revolution?' (1996) 19 Fordham ILJ 1963

Cassese, A, *International Law in a Divided World*, 1986, Oxford: Clarendon

Cassese, A, *Self-Determination of Peoples: A Legal Reappraisal*, 1995, Cambridge: Grotius

Castles, S and Miller, MJ, *The Age of Migration: International Population Movements in the Modern World*, 1993, London: Macmillan

Centre for European Legal Studies, 'The Human Rights Opinion of the ECJ and its constitutional implications', in *CELS Occasional Paper No 1*, 1996, Cambridge: CELSCU

Centre for European Legal Studies, *The Independent Commission on International Humanitarian issues, Indigenous Peoples: A Global Quest for Justice*, 1987, London: Zed

Centre for Women's Global Leadership, *Gender Violence and Women's Human Rights in Africa*, 1994, New Jersey: Plowshares

Chan, J, 'Hong Kong's Bill of Rights: its reception of, and contribution to, international and comparative jurisprudence' (1998) 47 ICLQ 306

Charlesworth, H, Chinkin, C and Wright, S, 'Feminist approaches to international law' (1991) 85 AJIL 613

Charter 88, 'The Charter' (1988) *The Guardian*, 30 November

Childs, D, *The GDR: Moscow's German Ally*, 1983, London: Allen & Unwin

Chowdhury, SR, *Rule of Law in a State of Emergency*, 1989, London: Pinter

Churchill, R and Young, J, 'Compliance with judgments of the European Court of Human Rights and decisions of the Committee of Ministers: the experience of the United Kingdom 1975–87' (1991) 62 BYIL 283

Clapham, A, 'The privatisation of human rights' (1996) 1 EHRLR 20

Clapham, A, *Human Rights in the Private Sphere*, 1993, Oxford: Clarendon

Clark, R and McMahon, J (eds), *Contemporary Issues in Irish Law and Politics, No 1*, Dublin: Round Hall/Sweet & Maxwell

Cohen, B and Staunton, M, 'In pursuit of a legal strategy: the National Council for Civil Liberties', in Cooper, J and Dhavan, R, *Public Interest Law*, 1986, Oxford: Blackwells

Cohen, R and Joly, D, 'Introduction: the new refugees of Europe', in Joly, D and Cohen, R (eds), *Reluctant Hosts: Europe and Its Refugees*, 1989, Aldershot: Avebury

Cohen, R (ed), *Theories of Migration*, 1996, Cheltenham: Elgar

Cohen, S, 'Conditioning US security assistance on human rights practices' (1982) 76 AJIL 246

Cohen, S, 'Government responses to human rights reports: claims, denials and counterclaims' (1996) 18 HRQ 518

Cohn, I, 'The Convention on the Rights of the Child: what it means for children in war' (1991) 3(1) International J of Refugee Law 100

Comeau, P, 'Women succeed in Vienna where others fail' (1993) 2(2) Human Rights Tribune 22

Committee against Torture, *Conclusions and Recommendations of UNCAT*, November 1995, Geneva: UN

Committee of Inquiry into Human Fertilisation and Embryology, *Report of the Committee of Inquiry into Human Fertilisation and Embryology*, Cmnd 9314, 1984, London: HMSO

Committee on the Administration of Justice, *CAJ Submission to the United Nations Committee on the Rights of the Child*, 1 August 1994, Belfast: CAJ

Committee on the Administration of Justice, *Making Rights Count*, 1990, Belfast: CAJ

Committee on the Administration of Justice, *Racism in Northern Ireland*, 1992, Belfast: CAJ

Committee on the Administration of Justice, 'Working with others', in *Annual Report*, 1995, Belfast: CAJ

Committee on the Administration of Justice, *No Emergency, No Emergency Law*, 1993, Belfast: CAJ

Compa, L and Diamond, S (eds), *Human Rights, Labor Rights and International Trade*, 1996, Philadelphia: Pennsylvania UP

Compa, L and Hinchcliffe-Darricarrere, T, 'Enforcing international labor rights through corporate codes of conduct' (1995) 33 Col J Trans'ntl L 637

Conaghan, J, 'Pregnancy, Equality and the European Court of Justice: interrogating *Gillespie*' (1998) 3 IJDL 115

'Conference – peace and human rights = human rights and peace: final document' (1979) 10 Bulletin of Peace Proposals 224

Connerton, P (ed), *Critical Sociology*, 1976, Harmondsworth: Penguin

Cook, R, 'International human rights law concerning women: case notes and comments' (1990) 23 Vand J Trans L 779

Cook, R, 'Reservations to the Convention on the elimination of all forms of discrimination against women' (1990) 30 Va J Int L 643

Cook, R, 'Women's international human rights law: the way forward' (1993) 15 HRQ 230

Cook, R, (ed), *Human Rights of Women: National and International Perspectives*, 1994, Philadelphia: Pennsylvania UP (Pennsylvania Studies in Human Rights)

Coomaraswamy, R (UN *Special Rapporteur* on Violence against Women), 'Reinventing international law: women's rights as human rights in the international community', 1997, Harvard Rights Program, Harvard Law School

Cooper, J and Dhavan, R, *Public Interest Law*, 1986, Oxford: Blackwells

Copelon, R, 'Recognising egregious in the everyday: domestic violence as torture' (1994) 25 Colum HR L Rev 291

Corntassel, JJ and Primeau, TH, 'Indigenous sovereignty and international law: revised strategies for pursuing "self-determination"' (1995) 17 HRQ 343

Cossey, C, *My Story*, 1991, London: Faber and Faber

Council of Europe, *Survey of Activities and Statistics*, 1997, Strasbourg: Council of Europe, website http://www.dhcommhr.coe.fr/eng/97tables.bil.html

Courtney, A, *Domestic Violence – A Political Issue*, May 1998, Northern Ireland Report, Belfast: Women's National Commission in association with women's organisations in Northern Ireland

Courtney, A, *Sharing Shifting Shaping – Women on the Move*, May 1998, Northern Ireland Report, Women's National Commission in association with women's organisations in Northern Ireland

Crawford, G, *Promoting Democracy, Human Rights and Good Governance through Development Aid: A Comparative Study of Four Northern Donors*, 1995, Leeds: University of Leeds Centre for Democratisation Studies (Working Paper)

Cremona, M, 'Human rights and democracy clauses in the EC's trade agreements', in Emiliou, N and O'Keefe, D (eds), *The European Union and World Trade Law*, 1996, Chichester: Wiley

Curtin, D, 'Scalping the Community legislator: occupational pensions and *Barber*' (1990) 27 CML Rev 475

Daes, EI, *Freedom of the Individual Under Law: An Analysis of Article 29 of the Universal Declaration of Human Rights*, 1990, New York: UN

Dallmeyer, D (ed), *Reconceiving Reality: Women and International Law*, 1993, Washington: American Society of International Law

Dankwa, EVO, 'Conference on regional protection systems of human rights protection in Africa, the Americas and Europe' (1992) 13(7–8) HRLJ 314

Davis, P (ed), *Human Rights*, 1988, London: Routledge

Davison, S, *Human Rights*, 1993, Buckingham: OU Press

Deakin, S, 'Part time employment, qualifying thresholds and economic justification' (1994) 23 ILJ 151

Deng, F, *Protecting the Internally Displaced: A Challenge for the United Nations*, Report by the Special Representative of the Secretary General on Internally Displaced Persons to the UN Commission on Human Rights, 1993, Geneva: Brookings Institute (Brookings Report)

Departmental Committee on Human Artificial Insemination, *Report of the Departmental Committee on Human Artificial Insemination*, Cmnd 1105, 1960, London: HMSO (Feversham Report)

Department of Health and Social Services and Northern Ireland Office, *Tackling Domestic Violence – A Policy For Northern Ireland*, 1995, Belfast: Department of Health and Social Services and Northern Ireland Office, HMSO

Derrida, J, *Spectres of Marx*, 1994, cited by Marks, S, 'The end of history? Reflections on some international legal theses' (1997) 3 EJIL 449

Dias, C, 'Five not 25 should be our post-Vienna motto' (1993) 2(2) Human Rights Tribune 31

Dicey, AV, *Introduction to the Study of the Law of the Constitution*, 10th edn, 1959, London: Macmillan

Dicker, R, 'Monitoring human rights in Africa' (1991) 29(3) J Mod African Studies 503

Dickson, B (ed), *Human Rights and the European Convention: The Effects of the Convention on the UK and Ireland*, 1997, London: Sweet & Maxwell

Dickson, B, 'Northern Ireland's emergency legislation – the wrong medicine?' [1992] PL 592

Dickson, B, 'Protecting human rights through a constitutional court: the case of South Africa' (1997) 66 Fordham L Rev 531

Dickson, B, *Introduction to French Law*, 1994, London: Pitman

Dinstein, Y, 'The reform of the protection of human rights during armed conflicts and periods of emergency and crisis', in International Colloquium on Human Rights (ed), *The Reform of International Institutions for the Protection of Human Rights: First International Colloquium on Human Rights*, 1993, Bruxelles: Bruylant

Docksey, C, 'The principle of equality between men and women as a fundamental right under Community law' (1991) 20 ILJ 258

Doerfal, J, 'Transsexuality and the European Convention on Human Rights' (1998) (unpublished essay)

Donnelly, P, 'Human rights at the UN 1955–85: the question of bias' (1988) 33 ISQ 275

Driedger, EA, 'The Canadian Charter of Rights and Freedoms' (1982) 14 Ottawa L Rev 366

Drinan, R and Kuo, T, 'The 1991 battle for human rights in China' (1992) 14 HRQ 21

Drzemczewski, A and Meyer-Ledwig, J, 'Principal characteristics of the new ECHR control mechanism, as established by Protocol 11, signed May 1994' (1994) 15(3) HRLJ 81

Drzemczewski, A and Nowicki, M, 'The Impact of the ECHR in Poland: a stock taking after three years' (1996) 3 EHRLR 261

Drzemczewski, A, 'The need for radical overhaul' (1993) 143 NLJ 126

Dyson, B, *Liberty in Britain: A Diamond Jubilee History of NCCL*, 1994, London: Civil Liberties Trust

ECHR websites http://www.dhcour.coe.fr/speeches.htm; http://194.250.50.201(02.06.98)

Edwards, M, 'Organisational learning in non-governmental organisations: what have we learned?' (1997) 17 Public Administration and Development 235

Ehrenberf, D, 'From intention to action: an ILO-GATT/WTO enforcement regime for international labor rights', in Compa, L and Diamond, S (eds), *Human Rights, Labor Rights and International Trade*, 1996, Philadelphia: Pennsylvania UP

Eide, A, Krause, K and Rosas, A (eds), *Economic, Social and Cultural Rights: A Textbook*, 1995, Dordrecht: Kluwer

Eilser, R, 'Human rights: toward an integrated theory for action' (1987) 9 HRQ 287

Ekins, R and King, D, *Blending Genders: Social Aspects of Cross-dressing and Sex-changing*, 1996, London: Routledge

Elcock, H, 'Making bricks without straw? The Polish ombudsman and the transition to democracy' (1992) Int J Soc L 173

Ellis, GB, *Infertility: Medical and Social Choices*, 1988, US Congress, Office of Technology Assessment: Biological Applications Program

Emiliou, N and O'Keefe, D (eds), *The European Union and World Trade Law*, 1996, Chichester: Wiley

Engle, K, 'After the collapse of the public/private distinction: strategising women's rights', in Dallmeyer, D (ed), *Reconceiving Reality: Women and International Law*, 1993, Washington: American Society of International Law

EOCNI Briefing, 'Northern Ireland Bill fails women', August 1998, Belfast: EOCNI

EOCNI, *Twenty-First Report*, March 1997, Belfast: EOCNI

EOCNI, *Where Do Women Figure?*, 1996, Belfast: EOCNI

Epstein, J and Straub, K (eds), *Body Guards: the Cultural Politics of Gender Ambiguity*, 1991, London: Routledge

Eriksson, J, *The International Response to Conflict and Genocide: Lessons from the Rwanda Experience*, Synthesis Report, 1996, Copenhagen: Steering Committee of the Joint Evaluation of Emergency Assistance to Rwanda

Ethical Trading Initiative website http://www.ethicaltrade.org

Etzioni, A, *The Spirit of Community*, 1995, London: Fontana

Eveleth, A, 'Too little, too late for NGOs' (1998) *South Africa Mail & Guardian*, 18 September

Ewing, KD and Gearty, CA, *Democracy or a Bill of Rights?*, 1991, London: Society of Labour Lawyers

Ewing, KD and Gearty, CA, *Freedom Under Thatcher: Civil Liberties in Modern Britain*, 1990, London: Clarendon

Eyal, J, 'Conspiracy of silence' (1996) *The Guardian*, 11 December

Farran, S, 'Facing contemporary challenges' (1997) 22 EL Rev 18, HRC 17–31

Fearon, K, *Power Politics and Positioning*, 1996, Belfast: Democratic Dialogue

Feldbrugge, FJM, *Russian Law: The End of the Soviet System and the Role of Law*, 1993, Dordrecht: Martinus Nijhoff

Fenwick, H, *Civil Liberties*, 2nd edn, 1998, London: Cavendish Publishing

Feofanov, Y, 'The establishment of the constitutional court in Russia and the communist party case' (1993) 19 Review of Central and Eastern European Law 623

Ferguson, C, 'Redressing global injustice – the role of law' (1980–81) 33 Rutgers L Rev 410

Feversham Report, *see* Departmental Committee on Human Artificial Insemination

Finn, JE, *Constitutions in Crisis – Political Violence and the Rule of Law*, 1991, New York: OUP

Fisher, D, 'Critics see nation switching roles with Soviets: own rights eroding, Britons say' (1989) *LA Times*, 6 April

Fitzpatrick, B, 'Equality in occupational pension schemes: still waiting for *Colorol*' (1994) 23 ILJ 155

Fitzpatrick, B, 'Summary of the conference', in *Beyond Equal Treatment: Social Security in a Changing Europe – Report of the Conference of the Irish Presidency of the European Union, Dublin, 10–12 October 1996*, Dublin: Department of Social Welfare

Fitzpatrick, B, Hegarty, A and Maxwell, P, 'A comparative review of the law on equality of opportunity', in Magill, D and Rose, S (eds), *Fair Employment Law in Northern Ireland: Debates and Issues*, 1996, Belfast: Standing Advisory Commission on Human Rights

Fitzpatrick, B, Hegarty, A and Maxwell, P, 'Trends in employment equality law: a comparative review', in Clark, R and McMahon, J (eds), *Contemporary Issues in Irish Law and Politics, No 1*, Dublin: Round Hall/Sweet & Maxwell

Fitzpatrick, J, *Human Rights in Crisis: the International System for Protecting Rights During States of Emergency*, 1994, Philadelphia: Pennsylvania UP

Fitzpatrick, P (ed), *Dangerous Supplements: Resistance and Renewal in Jurisprudence*, 1991, London: Pluto

Fonteyne, JP, 'The customary international law doctrine of humanitarian intervention' (1974) 4 California Western ILJ 203

Forde, M, 'Non-governmental interferences with human rights' (1985) 66 BYIL 253

Foster, N, *German Legal System and Laws*, 2nd edn, 1996, London: Blackstone

Foundation on Inter-Ethnic Relations, *The Role of the High Commissioner on National Minorities in OSCE Conflict Prevention*, 1997, The Hague: Foundation on Inter-Ethnic Relations

Franck, T, 'Is personal freedom a Western value?' (1997) 91 AJIL 593

Franck, T, 'Who killed Art 2(4)? Or: changing norms governing the use of force by States' (1970) 64 AJIL 809

Freeman, M and Veerman, P (eds), *The Ideologies of Children's Rights*, 1992, Dordrecht: Kluwer

Frey, B, 'The legal and ethical responsibilities of transnational corporations in the protection of international human rights' (1997) 6 Minn J Global Trade 153

Gaeta, P, 'The armed conflict in Chechnya before the Russian constitutional court' (1996) 7 EJIL 563

Galey, ME, 'Promoting non-discrimination against women: the UN Commission on the Status of Women' (1979) 23 ISQ 273

Gallagher, A, 'Ending the marginalisation: strategies for incorporating women into the United Nations human rights system' (1997) 19 HRQ 283

Gamble, A and Wells, C (eds), *Thatcher's Law*, 1989, Cardiff: Cardiff UP

Gearty, CA, 'The ECHR and the protection of civil liberties: an overview' [1993] CLJ 91

Gender Trust, *Gender Trust Handbook*, 1990, London : Gender Trust

Gibson, D, *The Law of the Charter: General Principles*, 1986, Toronto: Carswell

Ginsburg, S (ed), *Soviet Administrative Law: Theory and Practice*, 1989, Amsterdam: Kluwer

Good Friday Agreement, *Agreement Reached in the Multi-Party Negotiations,* Cmnd 3883, 1998, Belfast: Northern Ireland Office

Gorbachev, M, *Report on Progress in Implementing the Decisions of the 27th CPSU Congress and the Tasks of Promoting Perestroika*, 1988, Moscow: Novosti

Gordon, R and Wilmot, R (eds), *Human Rights in the UK*, 1996, London: OUP

Government of Ireland, *Challenges and Opportunities Abroad: The White Paper on Foreign Policy,* 1996, Dublin: Government of Ireland

Government of Ireland, *Bloody Sunday and the Report of the Widgery Tribunal: the Irish Government's Assessment of the New Material*, June 1997, Dublin: Government of Ireland

Graber, C and Teubner, G, 'Art and money: constitutional rights in the private sphere' (1998) 18 OJLS 61

Gray, A, *Between the Spice of Life and the Melting Pot: Biodiversity Conservation and its Impact on Indigenous Peoples*, 1991, Copenhagen: IWGIA

Gray, A, *Indigenous Rights and Development: Self-Determination in an Amazonian Community*, 1997, Providence, Oxford: Berghahn

Green, J and Wilchins, R, 'New men on the horizon' (1996) 33 FTM Newsletter, January, San Francisco: FTM International

Griffiths, J, *The Politics of the Judiciary*, 1985, London: Fontana

Gross, B, 'Towards a human rights century' (1991) 13 HRQ 387

Gross, O, '"Once more unto the breach" – the systemic failure of applying the European Convention on Human Rights to entrenched emergencies' (1998) 23 Yale LJ 437

Gross, O, *Theoretical Models of Emergency Powers*, 1997, Harvard: Harvard Law School (SJD dissertation)

Guest, I, *Behind the Disappearances: Argentina's Dirty War Against Human Rights and the United Nations,* 1990, Philadelphia: Pennsylvania UP

Gunning, S, 'Arrogant perception, world travelling and multicultural feminism: the case of female genital surgeries' (1991–92) 23 Colum HR L Rev 189

Gunter, MM, *The Kurds and the Future of Turkey*, 1997, New York: St Martin's Press

Hamilton, C and El-Haj, A, 'Armed conflict; the protection of children under international law' (1997) 5 IJCR 1

Hammarberg, T, 'Children', in Eide, A, Krause, K and Rosas, A (eds), *Economic, Social and Cultural Rights: A Textbook*, 1995, Dordrecht: Kluwer

Hannum, H, *Autonomy, Sovereignty and Self-Determination – The Accommodation of Conflicting Rights*, 1990, Philadelphia: Pennsylvania UP

Harris, D, *The European Social Charter*, 1984, Charlottesville, VA: Virginia UP

Harris, DJ, O'Boyle, M and Warbrick, C, *Law of the European Convention on Human Rights*, 1995, London: Butterworths

Hart, M, 'The WTO and the political economy of globalisation' (1997) 31 J World Trade 75

Hartman, JF, 'Derogation from human rights treaties in public emergencies' (1981) 22 Harv ILJ 1

Hartman, JF, 'Working paper for the committee of experts on the article derogation provision' (1985) 7 HRQ 89

Hathaway, JC, 'The evolution of refugee status in international law: 1920–1950' (1984) 33 ICLQ 353

Hausermann, J, 'Note on NGO participation in the UK delegation', in Sex and Race Equality Division, Department for Education and Employment, *Report of the UK Delegation on the UN Fourth World Conference on Women*, 1996, London: HMSO

Hegarty, A, 'Observing the rule of law: experiences from Northern Ireland' (1997) 66 Fordham L Rev 647

Heisler, MO, 'Migration, international relations and the new Europe: theoretical perspectives from institutional political sociology', in Cohen, R (ed), *Theories of Migration*, 1996, Cheltenham: Elgar

Henderson, J, 'The Russian ombudsman' (1998) 2 European Public Law 184

Henkin, L, *The Rights of Man Today*, 1979, London: Stevens

Henkin, L (ed), *The International Bill of Rights: the Covenant on Civil and Political Rights*, 1981, New York: Columbia UP

Hepple, B and Szyszczak, E (eds), *Discrimination: The Limits of Law*, 1993, London: Mansell

Hervey, T and O'Keefe, D (eds), *Sex Equality Law in the European Union*, 1996, Chichester: Wiley

Hervey, T, 'Legal issues of the *Barber* Protocol', in O'Keefe, D and Twomey, P (eds), *Legal Issues of the Maastricht Treaty*, 1995, Chichester: Wiley

Hervey, T and O'Keefe, D (eds), *Sex Equality Law in the European Union*, 1996, Chichester: Wiley

Heuston, RFV and Buckley, RA, *Salmond and Heuston on the Law of Torts*, 21st edn, 1996, London: Sweet & Maxwell

Higgins, R, 'Derogations under human rights treaties' (1976–77) 48 BYIL 281

Higgins, R, 'The United Nations: still a force for peace?' (1989) 52 MLR 1

Higgins, T, 'Anti-essentialism, relativism and human rights' (1996) Harv WLJ 89

Hillyard, P, *Suspect Community – People's Experience of the Prevention of Terrorism Acts in Britain*, 1993, London: Pluto

Himes, J (ed), *Implementing the Convention on the Rights of the Child, Resource Mobilization in Low-Income Countries*, 1995, Dordrecht: Kluwer

Bibliography

Hinds, B, Hope, A and Whitaker, R, *From The Margins To The Mainstream – Working Towards Equality, Development and Peace,* Northern Ireland/Beijing NGO Report, 1997, Belfast: Northern Ireland Women's European Platform

Hirst, P and Thompson, G, *Globalisation in Question,* 1996, Cambridge: Polity

Holmes, S and Tymstra,T, '*In vitro* fertilisation in the Netherlands: experience and opinions of Dutch women' (1987) 4 J In Vitro Fertilisation and Embryo Transfer 116

Home Office, *Fairer, Faster and Firmer – A Modern Approach to Immigration and Asylum,* Cm 4018, 1998, London: HMSO

Hooper, A (Sir), 'The impact of the Human Rights Act on judicial decision-making' [1998] EHRLR 676

Horgan, J, *Mary Robinson: An Independent Voice,* 1997, Dublin: O'Brien

Howard, R, 'Cultural absolutism and the nostalgia for community' (1993) 15 HRQ 315

Howe, RB and Andrade, MJ, 'The reputations of human rights commissions in Canada' (1994) 9 Canadian J Law Soc 1

Howe, RB, 'The evolution of human rights policy in Ontario' (1994) 24 Canadian J Pol Sci 787

Hsiung, JC, *Anarchy and Order: The Interplay of Politics and Law in International Relations,* 1997, Boulder: Lynne Rienner

Hudson, M, 'Integrity of international instruments' (1948) 42 AJIL 105

Human Development Report 1997, as cited in (1998) *New Internationalist,* January–February

Humphrey, JP, 'Human rights: the necessary conditions of peace' (1990) 10(2) International Relations 117

Humphrey, JP, 'The Magna Carta of mankind', in Davis, P (ed), *Human Rights,* 1988, London: Routledge

Hunt, M, 'The "horizontal" effect of the Human Rights Act' [1998] PL 433

Hunt, M, *Using Human Rights Law in English Courts,* 1997, Oxford: Hart

Hunt, P, *The European Convention on Human Rights,* NCCL Policy Paper 21/88, 1988, London: NCCL

Hutchinson, J and Smith, AD, *Ethnicity,* 1996, Oxford, New York : OUP

ICJ, *States of Emergency, Their Impact on Human Rights,* 1983, Geneva: ICJ

ICTLEP, *Proceedings from the Fourth International Conference on Transgender Law and Employment Policy,* 1995, Houston: ICTLEP

Independent Commission on International Humanitarian Issues, *Indigenous Peoples: A Global Quest for Justice,* 1987, New Jersey: Zed

Interfund website http://www.pcb.co.za/interfund/frames.htm

International Colloquium on Human Rights (ed), *The Reform of International Institutions for the Protection of Human Rights: First International Colloquium on Human Rights,* 1993, Bruxelles: Bruylant

International Federation of Human Rights, *About FIDH,* 1997, Paris: FIDH

International Law Association, *Second Interim Report of the Committee on the Enforcement of Human Rights Law*, 1988, Warsaw: International Law Association (Warsaw Report)

IPPR, *A Human Rights Commission*, December 1997, London: IPPR

IRRC, *Social Issues Service: 1997 Background Report J: International Labor Standards*, 1997, Washington: IRRC

Irvine (Lord), 'The legal system and law reform under Labour', in Bean, D, *Law Reform for All*, 1996, London: Blackstone

Irwin, C, *The Search for a Settlement: Report of a Survey Commissioned by Queen's University Belfast/Rowntree Trust*, 1998, Belfast: Fortnight Educational Trust

Jackson, JD and Doran, S, *Judge Without Jury: Diplock Trials in the Adversary System*, 1995, New York: OUP

Jacobs, FG and White, R, *The European Convention on Human Rights*, 2nd edn, 1996, Oxford: Clarendon

Janis, MW, Kay, RS and Bradley, AW, *European Human Rights Law*, 1995, Oxford: Clarendon

Jeffcott, B and Yanz, L, 'Code breaking' (1998) 302 New Internationalist 23

Joly, D, *Refugees: Asylum in Europe*, 1992, London: Minority Rights Group

Joly, D and Cohen, R (eds), *Reluctant Hosts: Europe and Its Refugees*, 1989, Aldershot: Avebury

Jones, JW, 'The "pure" theory of international law' (1935) 16 BYIL 5

Kamminga, MT, 'Is the European Convention on Human Rights sufficiently equipped to cope with gross and systematic violations?' (1994) 12(2) Neth HRQ 153

Kausikan, B, 'Asia's different standard' (1993) 92 Foreign Policy 24

Keane, F, *Season of Blood*, 1995, London: Penguin

Kelly, M, 'Preventing ill treatment: the work of the CPT' [1996] EHRLR 287

Kentridge, S, 'The incorporation of the European Convention on Human Rights', in Wade, W (Sir) (ed), *Constitutional Reform in the United Kingdom: Practice and Principles*, 1998, Oxford: Hart

Kinzer, S, 'Rights abuses stain Turkey's democratic image' (1997) *NY Times*, 13 July, p 3

Klingsberg, E, 'Judicial review and Hungary's transition from communism to democracy: the constitutional court, the continuity of law and the redefinition of property rights' (1992) BYU L Rev 41

Klug, F, 'Introduction', in *A People's Charter*, 1991, London: Civil Liberties Trust

Klug, F, 'Models of incorporation' (1997) (unpublished paper)

Klug, F, 'The role of a Bill of Rights in a democratic constitution' (1992) Liberty internal briefing, 3 July

Klug, F, *A Bill of Rights*, 1991, London: Liberty

Klug, F, *A People's Charter*, 1991, London: Civil Liberties Trust

Klug, F, *Reinventing Community – The Rights And Responsibilities Debate*, 1997, London: Charter 88

Klug, F, Starmer, K and Weir, S, *The Three Pillars of Liberty*, 1996, London: Democratic Audit/Routledge

Kochan, L and Abraham, R, *The Making of Modern Russia*, 2nd edn, 1983, London: Penguin

Kommers, D, *The Constitutional Jurisprudence of the Federal Republic of Germany*, 1989, North Carolina: Duke UP

Koskenniemi, M, 'National self-determination today – problems of legal theory and practice' (1994) 43 ICLQ 241

Koskenniemi, M, 'The future of Statehood' (1991) Harvard IL Rev 347

Kotz, D, 'Revolution from above: the demise of the Soviet System', in Weselovsky, T, *Russia: The Roots of Labor Malaise, Radio Free Europe*, 11 February 1998, Radio Liberty website http://www.rferl.org/nca/features/1998/F.RU.980211152.html

Krause, S, 'Bulgarian constitutional court rejects land law' (1995) OMRI Daily Digest, 20 June

Krüger, HC, 'Selecting judges for the new ECHR' (1996) 17(11–12) HRLJ 401

Kumado, K, 'Conditionality: an analysis of the policy of linking development aid to the implementation of human rights standards' (1993) 50 ICJ Rev 23

Kymlicka, W (ed), *The Rights of Minority Cultures*, 1995, Oxford: OUP

Lacey, M and Haakonssen, K (eds), *A Culture of Rights: the Bill of Rights in Philosophy, Politics and Law, 1791 and 1991*, 1991, London: CUP

Landay, B, 'Human rights, multinational business and international financial institutions' (1994) 88 Proc ASIL 271

Langley Simmons, D, *Dawn: A Charleston Legend*, 1995, Charleston: Wyrick

Lauritzen, P, *What Price Parenthood?*, March/April 1990, Hastings Center Report

Law Commission, *Aggravated, Exemplary and Restitutionary Damages*, Report No 247, 1997, London: HMSO

Laws, J (Sir), 'The limitations of human rights' [1998] PL 254

Lawyers Committee for Human Rights, *Linking Security Assistance and Human Rights*, 1989, New York: Lawyers Committee for Human Rights

Le Blanc, L, 'Reservations to the Convention on the Rights of the Child' (1996) 4 Int J Children's Rights 351

Ledogar, R, 'Implementing the Convention on the Rights of the Child through national programmes of action for children' (1993) 1 IJCR 371

Lee, HP, *Emergency Powers*, 1984, Sydney: Law Book Co

Leiblum, SR *et al*, 'Unsuccessful *in vitro* fertilisation: a follow-up study' (1987) 4 J In Vitro Fertilisation and Embryo Transfer 46

Lerner, N, 'The evolution of minority rights in international law', in Brolmann, C *et al* (eds), *Peoples and Minorities in International Law*, 1993, Dordrecht: Martinus Nijhoff

Lerner, N, *Group Rights and Discrimination in International Law*, 1991, Dordrecht: Martinus Nijhoff

Leshko, I, 'Determine, define, modify gender' (1996) website
http://planetq.com/pages/lfeinberglnt.html

Lester (Lord), 'The European Convention in the new architecture of Europe' [1996] PL 6

Letowska, E, 'The ombudsman and basic rights' (1995) 4(1) East European Constitutional Rev 63

Letowska, E, 'The Polish ombudsman (the commissioner for the protection of civil rights)' (1990) 39 ICLQ 206

Levinson, L, 'Neterpimost v Zakone (intolerance by law)' (1997) Express Chronicle, 26 September

Lewan, KM, 'The significance of constitutional rights for private law: theory and practice in West Germany' (1968) 17 ICLQ 571

Liberty, A Bill of Rights: Liberty's Proposals for Democratic Entrenchment, a Briefing for the Labour Party, 1992, London: Liberty

Liegeois, J-P and Gheorghe, N, Roma/Gypsies: A European Minority, 1995, London: Minority Rights Group

Lillich, R, 'Civil rights', in Meron, T (ed), Human Rights in International Law: Legal and Policy Issues, 1984, Oxford: Clarendon

Lillich, RB, 'Forcible self-help by States to protect human rights' (1967) 53 Iowa L Rev 325

Lindholt, L, Questioning the Universality of Human Rights: The African Charter on Human and Peoples' Rights in Botswana, Malawi and Mozambique, 1997, Aldershot: Ashgate

Linklater, A, The Transformation of Political Community, 1998, Cambridge: Polity

Liu, A, Artificial Reproduction and Reproductive Rights, 1991, Aldershot: Dartmouth

Llewellyn, K, The Bramble Bush: On Our Law and Its Study, 2nd edn, 1951, New York: Oceana

Lloyd, J, 'Mafia capitalism: the warning from Russia' (1998) 34 Prospect, January

Logue, M and Whitaker, R, 'The future of EU social policy: Report of the Northern Ireland Committee, des Sages Consultation Seminar', in Equal Opportunities: Creating an Anti-Discrimination Framework and Culture, 1997, Belfast: Northern Ireland Council for Voluntary Action

Loude, A, Sister Outsider, 1984, California: Crossing Press/Freedom

Lowe, AV, 'Reservations to treaties and human rights, Committee General Comment No 24 (52)' (1997) 46 ICLQ 391

Lowry (Lord), 'National security and the rule of law' (1992) 6 Isr L Rev 117

Lowry, DR, 'Internment: detention without trial in Northern Ireland' (1976) 5 HR 261

Ludwikowski, R, 'Constitution making in the countries of former Soviet dominance: current development' (1993) 23 Georgia J Int Comp L 155

Lugones, NJ, Leyes de Emergencia: Decretos de necesidad y urgencia, 1992, Buenos Aires: La Ley

Lustgarten, L and Leigh, I, In From the Cold – National Security and Parliamentary Democracy, 1994, Oxford: Clarendon

Luxembourg European Council website
http://europa.eu.int/council/off/conclu/dec97.htm

Lyons, FSL, *Culture and Anarchy in Ireland 1890–1939*, 1979, Oxford: Clarendon

Lyons, FSL, *Ireland Since the Famine*, 2nd edn, 1973, London: Fontana

Machel, G, *Report on the Impact of Armed Conflict on Children*, GA Doc A/51/306

MacKinnon, CA, 'Rape, genocide and women's human rights' [1994] HW L Rev 5

MacKinnon, CA, *Toward a Feminist Theory of the State*,1989, Cambridge, MA: Harvard UP

MacLean, MA, 'Regulating choice: a constitutional law response to Professor John A Robertson's children of choice' (1995) 52 Wash & Lee L Rev 133

Magill, D and Rose, S (eds), *Fair Employment Law in Northern Ireland: Debates and Issues*, 1996, Belfast: Standing Advisory Commission on Human Rights

Mahoney, P, 'Judicial activism and judicial self-restraint in the ECHR: two sides of the same coin' (1990) 11(2) HRLJ 80

Mandel, M, *The Charter of Rights and the Legalisation of Politics in Canada*, 2nd edn, 1994, Toronto: Thompson

Marantis, D, 'Human rights, democracy and development: the European Community model' (1994) 7 Harv HRJ 1

Marantz, BD, 'Issues affecting the rights of indigenous peoples in international fora', in *People or Peoples; Equality, Autonomy and Self-Determination: The Issues at Stake of the International Decade of the World's Indigenous People*, 1996, Montreal: International Centre for Human Rights and Democratic Development

Marcuse, H, 'Repressive tolerance', in Connerton, P (ed), *Critical Sociology*, 1976, Harmondsworth: Penguin

Marie, J, 'Relations between people's rights and human rights: semantic and methodological distinctions' (1986) 7(4) HRLJ 195

Markesinis, B, *The German Law of Torts*, 2nd edn, 1990, Oxford: Clarendon

Marks, S, 'Emerging human rights: a new generation for the 1980s?' 33 Rutgers LJ 435

Marks, S, 'Nightmare and noble dream: the world 1993 conference on human rights' (1994) 53 CLJ 54

Marks, S, 'The end of history? Reflections on some international legal theses' (1997) 3 EJIL 449

Marx, K, 'On the Jewish question' (1843), in *Collected Works*, 1975, London: Lawrence & Wishart, Vol 3

Marx, K, *Collected Works*, 1975, London: Lawrence & Wishart, Vol 3

Mather, I, 'Ankara faces the reality of exclusion' (1997) *The European*, 18 December, p 16

Matscher, F and Petzold, H (eds), *Protecting Human Rights: The European Dimension. Essays in Honour of Gérard J Wiarda*, 1988, Cologne: Carl Heymanns

McCrudden, C, 'Institutional discrimination' (1982) 2 OJLS 303

McCrudden, C, *Benchmarks for Change: Mainstreaming Fairness in the Governance of Northern Ireland – A Proposal*, 1998, Belfast: CAJ

MacDonald, RStJ (ed), *The European System for the Protection of Human Rights*, 1993, Dordrecht: Martinus Nijhof

McKittrick, D, 'UN damns Ulster police intimidation' (1998) *The Independent*, 31 March

McLean, S, 'The right to reproduce', in Campbell, T (ed), *Human Rights: From Rhetoric to Reality*, 1986, Oxford: Blackwells

McLeod, I, Hendry I and Hyatt, S, *The External Relations of the European Community*, 1996, Oxford: Clarendon

Meron, T (ed), *Human Rights in International Law, Legal and Policy Issues*, 1984, Oxford: Clarendon

Miller, AS, 'Crisis government becomes the norm' (1978) 39 Ohio St LJ 736

Miller, AS, 'Reason of State and the emergent constitution of control' (1980) 64 Minn L Rev 585

Minority Rights Group (ed), *Education Rights and Minorities*, 1994, London: Minority Rights Group and UNICEF

Minority Rights Group Report, *War: The Impact on Minority and Indigenous Children*, 1997, London: UNICEF

Minty, AS, 'The anti-apartheid movement and racism in South Africa', in Wiletts, P (ed), *Pressure Groups in the Global System*, 1982, London: Frances Pinter

Monar, J and Morgan, R (eds), *The Third Pillar of the European Union:Cooperation in the Field of Justice and Home Affairs*, 1994, Brussels: European Interuniversity

Moore, JN (ed), *Law and Civil War in the Modern World*, 1974, Baltimore, MD: John Hopkins UP

Moran, LJ, '*Laskey v UK* : learning the limits of privacy' (1998) 61 MLR 77

Morinsk, J, 'The philosophy of the Universal Declaration' (1984) 6 HRQ 309

Mowbray, A, 'A new ECHR' [1994] PL 540

Mowbray, A, 'Procedural developments and the ECHR' [1991] PL 353

Mowbray, A, 'The reform of the control system of the ECHR' [1993] PL 419

Mower, G, *The Convention on the Rights of the Child*, 1997, Westport, Connecticut: Greenwood

Mullan, D (ed), *Eyewitness Bloody Sunday*, 1996, Dublin: Wolfhound

Muller, N, 'The World Bank, human rights, democracy and governance' (1997) 15 Neth QHR 21

Müllerson, R, 'Introduction', in Müllerson, R, Fitzmaurice, M and Andenas, M (eds), *Constitutional Reform and International Law in Central and Eastern Europe*, 1998, The Hague: Kluwer

Müllerson, R, *Human Rights Diplomacy*, 1997, London: Routledge

Müllerson, R, Fitzmaurice, M and Andenas, M (eds), *Constitutional Reform and International Law in Central and Eastern Europe*, 1998, The Hague: Kluwer

Na'im, A, 'Human rights in the Muslim world' (1990) 3 Harv HRJ 13

Newill, R, *Infertility in Marriage*, 1974, Harmondsworth: Penguin

Ní Aoláin, F, 'The emergence of diversity: differences in human rights jurisprudence' (1995) 19 Fordham Int LJ 101

Ní Aoláin, F, 'Where hope and history rhyme – prospects for peace in Northern Ireland?' (1996) 50 J Int Aff 63

Ní Aoláin, F, *An Investigation of the Right to Life in Situations of Emergency with Particular Reference to Northern Ireland*, 1997, Belfast: Queen's University (PhD dissertation)

Nielsen, L, 'Legal consensus and divergence in Europe in the area of human embryology – room for harmonisation?', in *Conceiving the Embryo: Ethics, Law and Practice in Human Embryology*, 1996, The Hague: Martinus Nijhoff

North Commission, *The Report of the Independent Review of Parades and Marches*, 1997, London: HMSO

Northern Ireland Independent Commission for Police Complaints, *Annual Reports, 1990–95*, London: HMSO

Northern Ireland Office, *Report of the Central Appointments Unit*, 1996, Belfast: HMSO

Northern Ireland Women's Aid Federation Annual Report 1997–98: Recent Landmarks in Development of Northern Ireland Women's Aid Federation, 1998, Belfast: Women's Aid Federation

O'Boyle, M, 'Torture and emergency powers under the European Convention on Human Rights: *Ireland v the United Kingdom*' (1977) 71 AJIL 674

O'Connell, D, *International Law*, 2nd edn, 1970, London: Stevens, Vol 2

O'Donnell, D, 'States of exception' (1978) 21 ICJ Rev 52

O'Hare, U, 'Positive action before the European Court of Justice' [1996] 2 Web JCLI website http://webjcli.ncl.ac.uk

O'Keefe, D and Twomey, P (eds), *Legal Issues of the Maastricht Treaty*, 1995, Chichester: Wiley

O'Neill, A and Coppel, J, *EC Law for UK Lawyers*, 1994, London: Butterworths

Office for Official Publications of the European Communities, *Equal Opportunities for Women and Men in the European Union: 1997 Annual Report*, 1998, Luxembourg: Office for Official Publications of the European Communities

Oloka-Onyango, J and Tamale, S, '"The personal is political" or "Why women's rights are indeed human rights: an African perspective on international feminism"' (1995) 17 HRQ 691

Olsen, F, 'Children's rights: some feminist approaches to the United Nations Convention on the Rights of the Child', in Alston, P, Parker, S and Seymour, J (eds), *Children, Rights and the Law*, 1992, Oxford: Clarendon

Oppenheim, L, *International Law: A Treatise*, 2nd edn, 1912, London: Longmans, Green, Vol 1

Oraá, J, *Human Rights in States of Emergency in International Law*, 1992, New York: OUP

Ott, D, *Public International Law in the Modern World*, 1988, London: Pitman

Palley, C, 'The evolution, disintegration and possible reconstruction of the Northern Irish Constitution' (1972) 1 Anglo-Am L Rev 368

Parker, S, 'Resources and child rights: an economic perspective', in Himes, J (ed), *Implementing the Convention on the Rights of the Child, Resource Mobilization in Low-Income Countries*, 1995, Dordrecht: Kluwer

Parratt, L and Foley, C, 'The UK Government's 13th Periodic Report to the UN Committee for the Elimination of Racial Discrimination' [1996] EHRLR 4

Parratt, L and Foley, C, *Criminalising Diversity, Criminalising Dissent*, 1994, London: Liberty

Partsch, KJ, 'Discrimination', in MacDonald, RStJ (ed), *The European System for the Protection of Human Rights*, 1993, Dordrecht: Martinus Nijhof

Partsch, KJ, 'Recent developments in the field of people's rights in human rights' (1986) 7(4) HRLJ 177

Perry, MJ, 'Are human rights universal? The relativist challenge and related matters' (1997) 19 HRQ 461

Pincus, I, *Between Insight and Action – Gender Equality, Men and Ambivalence in Municipal Organisations*, 1996, Sweden: Statskunskapens

Plant, R, *Land Rights and Minorities*, 1994, London: Minority Rights Group

Pogany, I, 'A new constitutional (dis)order for Eastern Europe?', in *Human Rights in Eastern Europe*, 1995, Aldershot: Elgar

Pogany, I, 'Constitutional reform in Central and Eastern Europe: Hungary's transition to democracy' (1993) 42 ICLQ 332

Pogany, I, 'The evaluation of United Nations peacekeeping operations' (1986) 57 BYIL 357

Pogany, I, 'International human rights standards and the new constitutions: minority rights in Central and Eastern Europe', in Müllerson, R, Fitzmaurice, M and Andenas, M (eds), *Constitutional Reform and International Law in Central and Eastern Europe*, 1998, The Hague: Kluwer

Pogany, I (ed), *Human Rights in Eastern Europe*, 1995, Aldershot: Elgar

Posner, M, 'Human rights and non-governmental organisations; foreword' (1997) 66 Fordham L Rev 627

Power, J, *Amnesty International: The Human Rights Story*, 1981, London: Pergamon

Prechal, S, 'Note on *Kalanke*' (1996) 33 CML Rev 1245

Price-Cohen, C, 'The role of non-governmental organisations in the drafting of the Convention on the Rights of the Child' (1990) 12 HRQ 136

Pritchard, S, *The United Nations Draft Declaration on the Rights of Indigenous Peoples: An Analysis*, 1996, Aboriginal and Torres Strait Islander Commission

Questiaux Report, *see* UN Commission on Human Rights

Quint, P, 'Free speech and private law in German constitutional theory' (1988) 48 Maryland L Rev 252

Reanda, L, 'The commission on the status of women', in Alston, P (ed), *The United Nations and Human Rights: A Critical Appraisal*, 1992, Oxford: Clarendon

Rehnquist, WH, *The Supreme Court: How it is*, 1987, New York: Quill

Reidy, A *et al*, 'Gross violations of human rights: invoking the European Convention on Human Rights in the case of Turkey' (1997) 15(2) Neth Q HR 161

Rice, AE and Ritchie, C, 'Relationships between international non-governmental organisations and the United Nations' (1995) 47 Transnational Assoc 254

Rinehart, LA, 'Infertility: the market, the law and the impact' (1994) 35 Jurimetrics J 77

Roberts, A and Guelff, R, *Documents on the Laws of War*, 1982, Oxford: Clarendon

Robertson, AH and Merrills, JG, *Human Rights in the World*, 3rd edn, 1989, Manchester: Manchester UP

Robertson, JA, *Children of Choice, Freedom and the New Reproductive Technologies*, 1996, Princeton, NJ: Princeton UP

Robinson, N, *The Genocide Convention: A Commentary*, 1960, New York: Institute of Jewish Affairs

Rogge, K, 'The victim requirement in Art 25 of the ECHR', in Matscher, F and Petzold, H (eds), *Protecting Human Rights: The European Dimension. Studies in Honour of Gerard J Wiarda*, 1988, Cologne: Carl Heymanns

Romany, C, 'Women as *aliens*: a feminist critique of the public/private distinction in international human rights law' (1993) 6 Harv HRJ 87

Rosenthal, P, 'The new Emergencies Act: four times the War Measures Act' (1991) 20 Manitoba LJ 563

Rossiter, CL, *Constitutional Dictatorship – Crisis Government in the Modern Democracies*, 1948, Princeton, NJ: Princeton UP

Rowe, N and Schlette, V, 'The protection of human rights in Europe after Protocol 11 to the ECHR' (1998) 23 EL Rev; Checklist No 1 HR/3, HR/8

Ruffin, M, McCarter, J and Upjohn, R, *The Post-Soviet Handbook: A Guide to Grassroots Organisations and Internet Resources in the Newly Independent States*, 1996, Center for Civil Society International, Seattle: Washington UP

Russia Country Report on Human Rights Practices for 1997, US Department of State website http://www.state.gov/www/global/human_rights/1997_hrp_report

Ryan, A, 'The British, the American and rights', in Lacey, M and Haakonssen, K (eds), *A Culture of Rights: the Bill of Rights in Philosophy, Politics and Law, 1791 and 1991*, 1991, London: CUP

Ryan, S, 'Nationalism and ethnic conflict', in White, B, Little, R and Smith, M (eds), *Issues in World Politics*, 1997, Basingstoke: Macmillan

Rybar, C, *Jewish Prague*, 1991, Prague: TV Spektrum

Sadasivam, B, 'The impact of structural adjustment on women: a governance and human rights agenda' (1997) 19 HRQ 630

Sajo, A, 'Reading the invisible constitution: judicial review in Hungary' (1995) 15 OJLS 253

Sandel, M, 'Justice and the good', in Sandel, M (ed), *Liberalism and its Critics*, 1984, New York: New York UP

Sandel, M (ed), *Liberalism and its Critics*, 1984, New York: New York UP

Saunders, G (ed), *Samizdat: Voices of the Soviet Opposition*, 1974, New York: Monad

Schabas, W, 'Reservations to the Convention on the Rights of the Child' (1996) 18 HRQ 472

Schermers, H, 'The Eleventh Protocol to the ECHR' (1994) 19 EL Rev 369

Schermers, H, 'Factual merger of the European Court and Convention on Human Rights' (1986) 11 EL Rev 350

Schermers, H, 'Has the ECHR got bogged down ?' (1988) 9(2) HRLJ 175

Schiek, D, 'More positive action in Community law' (1998) 27 ILJ 155

Schiek, D, 'Positive action in Community law' (1996) 25 ILJ 239

Scott, C, *State Sovereignty: The Challenge of a Changing World*, 1993, Ottawa: CCIL

Sex and Race Equality Division, Department for Education and Employment, *Report of the UK Delegation on the UN Fourth World Conference on Women*, 1996, London: HMSO

Sharlet, R, 'The Russian constitutional court: the first term' (1993) Post-Soviet Affairs 1

Shaw, J, 'Positive action for women in Germany: the use of legally binding quotas', in Hepple, B and Szyszczak, E (eds), *Discrimination: The Limits of Law*, 1993, London: Mansell

Shestack, J, 'The jurisprudence of human rights', in Meron, T (ed), *Human Rights in International Law, Legal and Policy Issues*, 1984, Oxford: Clarendon

Shestack, J, 'The philosophic foundations of human rights' (1998) 20 HRQ 202

Shraga, D and Zacklin R, 'The international criminal tribunal for the former Yugoslavia' (1994) 5 EJIL 360

Sieghart, P, *The Lawful Rights of Mankind*, 1986, Oxford: OUP

Simor, J, 'Tackling human rights abuses in Bosnia and Herzegovina: the Convention is up to it, are its institutions?' (1997) 6 EHRLR 644

Simpson, GJ, 'The diffusion of sovereignty: self-determination in the post-colonial age' (1996) 32 Stanford JIL 23

Simpson, J, *Refugees: A Review of the Situation Since September 1939*, 1993, Oxford: OUP

Singh, M, 'The role of civil society in promoting democratic development: some aspects of the South African debate', in *The Role of Voluntary Organisations in Emerging Democracies: Experience and Strategies in Eastern and Central Europe and in South Africa*, 1993, Copenhagen: Danish Centre for Human Rights/Institute of International Education

Singh, R, *The Future of Human Rights in the United Kingdom*, 1997, Oxford: Hart

Skidmore, P, 'Sex, gender and comparators in employment discrimination' (1997) 26 ILJ 51

Smart, C, 'Feminist jurisprudence', in Fitzpatrick, P (ed), *Dangerous Supplements: Resistance and Renewal in Jurisprudence*, 1991, London: Pluto

Smart, C, *The Power of Law*, 1989, London: Routledge

Sowell, T, *Migrations and Cultures: A World View*, 1996, New York: Basic Books

Spencer, S and Bynoe, I, *A Human Rights Commission: The Options for Britain and Northern Ireland*, 1998, London: IPPR

Spiliopoulou-Aokermark, A, *Justifications of Minority Protection in International Law*, 1997, Uppsala: Iustus Forlag

Steiner, H and Alston, P, *International Human Rights in Context: Law, Politics and Morals*, 1996, Oxford: Clarendon

Stockwell, J, *In Search of Enemies: A CIA Story*, 1997, Somerville: Replica

Stone, S, 'The empire strikes back: a post transsexual manifesto', in Epstein, J and Straub, K (eds), *Body Guards: the Cultural Politics of Gender Ambiguity*, 1991, London: Routledge

Suksi, M (ed), *Autonomy: Applications and Implications*, 1998, The Hague: Kluwer

Sunga, L, 'The commission of experts on Rwanda and the creation of the International Criminal Tribunal for Rwanda' (1995) 16(4) HRLJ 121

Swepston, L, 'A new step in the international law on indigenous and tribal peoples: ILO Convention No 169 of 1989' (1990) 15 Oklahoma City UL Rev 677

Szabo, A, 'Historical foundations of human rights', in Vasak, K and Alston, P (eds), *The International Dimensions of Human Rights*, 1982, Westport, CT: Greenwood, Vol II

Tennant, C, 'Indigenous peoples, international institutions and the international legal literature from 1945–93' (1994) 16 HRQ 1

Tenofsky, E, 'The War Measures and Emergency Acts: implications for Canadian civil rights and liberties' (1989) 19 Am Rev Can Stud 293

Teson, F, 'International human rights and cultural relativism' (1985) 25 Virginia JIL 869

Tessier, K, 'Immigration law in the Russian Federation' website
http://www.law.indiana.edu/glsj/vol3/no1/tessrtr1.html

Tettenborn, A, *Law of Restitution in England and Ireland*, 2nd edn, 1996, London: Cavendish Publishing

Thalif, D, 'Right wingers block UN children's treaty' (1995) International Press Service, 15 February

Thalif, D, 'United Nations cracks down on the use of child soldiers' (1997) International Press Service, 12 October

Thatcher, M, *The Downing Street Years*, 1993, London: HarperCollins, Vol 1

The United Nations and the Advancement of Women: 1945–95, 1995, UN Blue Books Series, New York: Department of Public Information, United Nations, Vol VI

Thornberry, P and Gibbons, D, 'Education and minority rights: a short survey of international standards' (1996–97) 4 Int J Minority and Group Rights 2

Thornberry, P, 'Images of autonomy and individual and collective rights in international instruments on the rights of minorities', in Suksi, M (ed), *Autonomy: Applications and Implications*, 1998, The Hague: Kluwer

Thornberry, P, 'Is there a phoenix in the ashes? International law and minority rights' (1980) 15 Texas ILJ 433

Thornberry, P, 'Self-determination, minorities, human rights: a review of international instruments' (1989) 38 ICLQ 867

Thornberry, P, *International Law and the Rights of Minorities*, 1992, Oxford: Clarendon

Thornton, P, *Decade of Decline: Civil Liberties in the Thatcher Years*, 1989, London: NCCL

Tomuschat, C (ed), *Modern law of Self-Determination*, 1993, Dordrecht: Kluwer

Tomuschat, C, '"Quo vadis argentoratum ?", the success story of the ECHR – and a few dark stains' (1992) 13(11–12) HRLJ 402

Tomuschat, C, *'Quo Vadis, Argentoratum*? The success story of the European Convention on Human Rights and a few dark stains' (1992) 13(11–12) HRLJ 401

Toth, AG, 'The European Union and human rights: the way forward' [1997] 34 CMLR 491

Townshend, C, *Political Violence in Ireland: Government and Resistance Since 1848*, 1983, New York: OUP

UN Commission on Human Rights, 'Study on the implications for human rights of recent developments concerning situations known as states of siege or emergency', 35th session, agenda item 10, UN Doc E/CN 4/Sub 2/15 (1982) (Questiaux Report)

UN, *World Investment Report 1993: Transnational Corporations and Integrated International Production*, 1993, New York: UN

UNHCR, *The State of the World's Refugees: A Humanitarian Agenda*, 1997, Oxford: OUP

UNICEF and Minority Rights Group Report, *War: The Impact on Minority and Indigenous Children*, 1997, London: UNICEF

UNICEF, *The Progress of Nations 1996,* New York: UNICEF

UNICEF, *The State of the World's Children*, 1995, Oxford: OUP

UNOCHA Lessons Learned Unit, 'Afghanization: the promotion and registration of Afghan NGOs', in, *Afghanistan Report: Co-ordination in a Fragmented State*, 1998, OCHA Online, Afghanistan website http://www.reliefwebint./dha_ol/programs/United nationsocha/afgrpt/lessons.html

US Department of State, 'Country reports on human rights practices for 1997 – Turkey' website http://www.state.gov/www/global/human_rights/ 1997_hrp_report/

Valdés, D, *La Dictadura Constitucional en América Latina*, 1974, Mexico: Instituto de Investigaciones Juridicas;

Van Bueren, G, 'Protecting children's rights in Europe' (1996) 2 EHRLR 171

Van Bueren, G, 'The international legal protection of children in armed conflicts' (1994) 43 ICLQ 809

Van Bueren, G, 'The struggle for empowerment: the emerging civil and political rights of children', in *Selected Essays on International Children's Rights*, 1993, Geneva: Defence for Children International, Vol 1

Van Bueren, G, *International Documents on Children*, 1993, Dordrecht: Kluwer

Van Bueren, G, *The International Law on the Rights of the Child*, 1995, Dordrecht: Kluwer

Van den Berg, G, 'The conflict of civil and administrative law in the USSR: right to housing and freedom of choice of residence in Soviet law and practice', in Ginsburg, S (ed), *Soviet Administrative Law: Theory and Practice*, 1989, Amsterdam: Kluwer

van Dijk, P and van Hoof, GJH, *Theory and Practice of the European Convention on Human Rights*, 3rd edn, 1998, The Hague: Kluwer

van Dijk, P and van Hoof, GJH, *Theory and Practice of the European Convention on Human Rights*, 2nd edn, 1990, Deventer: Kluwer

Van Dyke, V, *Human Rights, Ethnicity and Discrimination*, 1985, London: Greenwood

Vasak, K and Alston, P (eds), *The International Dimensions of Human Rights*, 1982, Westport, CT: Greenwood, Vol II

Voronin, Y, 'The emerging criminal State: economic and political aspects of organised crime in Russia' (1996) 2 Transnational Organised Crime 53

Vyshinsky, A, *The Law of the Soviet State*, 1948, New York: Macmillan

Waddington, S, *Women and Europe: A Statistical Portrait*, 1997, Leicester: Rural

Wade, ECS and Bradley, AW, *Constitutional and Administrative Law*, 11th edn, 1993, Harlow: Longman

Wade, W (Sir) (ed), *Constitutional Reform in the United Kingdom: Practice and Principles*, 1998, Oxford: Hart

Wade, W (Sir), 'Human rights and the judiciary' [1998] EHRLR 520

Wade, W (Sir), 'The United Kingdom's Bill of Rights', in *Constitutional Reform in the United Kingdom: Practice and Principles*, 1998, Oxford: Hart

Wadham, J, 'Why incorporation of the European Convention on Human Rights is not enough', in Gordon, R and Wilmot, R (eds), *Human Rights in the UK*, 1996, London: OUP

Walker, C, *The Prevention of Terrorism in British Law*, 2nd edn, 1992, Manchester: Manchester UP

Walsh, D, *The Bloody Sunday Tribunal of Inquiry: A Resounding Defeat for Truth, Justice and the Rule of Law*, 1996, Derry: Bloody Sunday Trust

Walsh, DPJ, *The Use and Abuse of Emergency Legislation in Northern Ireland*, 1983, London: Cobden Trust

Warbrick, C, ' Rights, the ECHR and English law' (1994) 19 EL Rev 34

Warsaw Report, *see* International Law Association

Weatherill, S and Beaumont, P, *EC Law*, 2nd edn, 1995, London: Penguin

Weiss, TG and Gordenker, L (eds), *NGOs, the United Nations and Global Governance*, 1996, Colorado: Reinner

Weissbrodt, D and McCarthy, J, 'Fact finding by international non-governmental human rights organisations' (1981) 22 Virginia J Int L 1

Weissbrodt, D and Parker, P, *Orientation Manual: The UN Commission on Human Rights, its Sub-Commission and Related Procedures*, 1992, Minneapolis: Minnesota Advocates for Human Rights and the International Service for Human Rights

Weissbrodt, D, 'Human rights: an historical perspective', in Davis, P (ed), *Human Rights*, 1988, London: Routledge

Weissbrodt, D, 'The contribution of international non-governmental organisations to the protection of human rights', in Meron, T (ed*), Human Rights in International Law: Legal and Policy Issues,* 1989, Oxford: Clarendon

Weissbrodt, D, 'The three "theme" special rapporteurs of the UN Commission on Human Rights' (1986) 80 AJIL 685

Welch, CE, 'Human rights and African women: a comparison of protection under two major treaties' (1993) 15 HRQ 549

Welch, CE, *Protecting Human Rights in Africa: Roles and Strategies of Non-Governmental Organisations,* 1995, Philadelphia: Pennsylvania UP

Welch, CE, *Protecting Human Rights in Africa: Roles and Strategies of Non-Governmental Organisations,* 1995, Philadelphia: Pennsylvania UP

Weselovsky, T, *Russia: The Roots of Labor Malaise, Radio Free Europe,* 11 February 1998, Radio Liberty website http://www.rferl.org/nca/features/1998/F.RU.980211152.html

Whelan, L, 'The challenge of lobbying for civil rights in Northern Ireland: the Committee on the Administration of Justice' (1992) 14 HRQ 149

White, B, Little, R and Smith, M (eds), *Issues in World Politics,* 1997, Basingstoke: Macmillan

White, RCA, 'State of ratification of human rights instruments' (1998) 23 EL Rev Checklist No 1 HR

Whiteford, E, 'Occupational pensions and European law: clarity at last?', in Hervey, T and O'Keefe, D (eds), *Sex Equality Law in the European Union,* 1996, Chichester: Wiley

Whiteford, E, *Adapting to Change: Occupational Pension Schemes, Women and Migrant Workers,* 1996, The Hague: Kluwer

Whittle, S, 'Legislating for transsexual rights: a prescriptive form', in Bullough, B, Bullough, V and Elias J, *Gender Blending,* 1997, New York: Prometheus

Widgery Report, *Report of the Tribunal Appointed to Inquire into Events on Sunday 30 January 1972,* 18 April 1972.

Wilchins, R, *Read My Lips: Sexual Subversion and the End of Gender,* 1997, New York: Firebrand

Willan, P, 'War crimes court vote goes against Washington' (1998) *Irish Times,* July 18

Wiletts, P (ed), *Pressure Groups in the Global System,* 1982, London: Frances Pinter

Wilmer, F, *The Indigenous Voice in World Politics,* 1993, London, New Delhi: Sage

Winter, J, *Conditions in Detention in Castlereagh,* 1995, London: BIRW

Winter, J, *Human Rights Human Wrongs: A Guide to the Human Rights Machinery of the United Nations,* 1996, London: BIRW

Wiseberg, L, 'NGO self-examination is the missing link in ECOSOC Review' (1994) 2(3) Human Rights Tribunal 11

Wiseberg, L, 'Protecting human rights activists and NGOs' (1991) 13 HRQ 525

Wolfson, C, 'Children's rights: theoretical underpinning of the best interests of the child', in Freeman, M and Veerman, P (eds), *The Ideologies of Children's Rights*, 1992, Dordrecht: Kluwer

Women's National Commission, 'In pursuit of equality – a national agenda for action', Policy Paper 2, UK: COI for the Women's National Commission

World Bank, *Governance: The World Bank's Experience*, 1994, Washington DC: World Bank

World Federalist Association, *A New World Order: Can it Bring Security to the World's People? Essays on Restructuring the United Nations*, 1991

Wright, Q, 'National courts and human rights – the *Fujii* case' (1951) 45 AJIL 73

WTO, *International Trade Trends and Statistics*, 1996, Geneva: WTO

Zander, M, *A Bill of Rights?*, 4th edn, 1997, London: Sweet & Maxwell

Zearfoss, S, 'Note, the Convention for the elimination of all forms of discrimination against women: radical, reasonable, or reactionary?' (1991) 12 Mich J Int L 903

Zwaak, L, 'The European Court of Human Rights has the Turkish security forces held responsible for violations of human rights: the case of Akdivar and others' (1997) 10 Leiden JIL 99

INDEX